OVERLAPPING GENERATIONS

INTERNATIONAL SYMPOSIA IN ECONOMIC THEORY AND ECONOMETRICS

Series Editor: William A. Barnett

Recent Volumes:

Volume 17:	*Topics in Analytical Political Economy* Edited by Melvin Hinich & William A. Barnett
Volume 18:	*Functional Structure Inference* Edited by William A. Barnett & Apostolos Serletis
Volume 19:	*Challenges of the Muslim World: Present, Future and Past* Edited by William W. Cooper & Piyu Yue
Volume 20:	*Nonlinear Modeling of Economic and Financial Time-Series* Edited by Fredj Jawadi & William A. Barnett
Volume 21:	*The Collected Scientific Works of David Cass – Parts A–C* Edited by Stephen Spear
Volume 22:	*Recent Developments in Alternative Finance: Empirical Assessments and Economic Implications* Edited by William A. Barnett and Fredj Jawadi
Volume 23:	*Macroeconomic Analysis and International Finance* Edited by Georgios P. Kouretas and Athanasios P. Papadopoulos
Volume 24:	*Monetary Policy in the Context of the Financial Crisis: New Challenges and Lessons* Edited by William A. Barnett and Fredj Jawadi
Volume 25:	*Banking and Finance Issues in Emerging Markets* Edited by William A. Barnett and Bruno S. Sergi
Volume 26:	*Asia-Pacific Contemporary Finance and Development* Edited by William A. Barnett and Bruno S. Sergi
Volume 27:	*Advanced Issues in the Economics of Emerging Markets* Edited by William A. Barnett and Bruno S. Sergi
Volume 28:	*Recent Developments in Asian Economics* Edited by William A. Barnett and Bruno S. Sergi
Volume 29A:	*Environmental, Social, and Governance Perspectives on Economic Development in Asia* Edited by William A. Barnett and Bruno S. Sergi
Volume 29B:	*Environmental, Social, and Governance Perspectives on Economic Development in Asia* Edited by William A. Barnett and Bruno S. Sergi
Volume 30:	*Quantitative Analysis of Social and Financial Market Development* Edited by William A. Barnett and Bruno S. Sergi
Volume 31:	*Comparative Analysis of Trade and Finance in Emerging Economies* Edited by William A. Barnett and Bruno S. Sergi

INTERNATIONAL SYMPOSIA IN ECONOMIC THEORY AND ECONOMETRICS VOLUME 32

OVERLAPPING GENERATIONS: METHODS, MODELS AND MORPHOLOGY

BY

STEPHEN E. SPEAR
Carnegie Mellon University, USA

and

WARREN YOUNG
Bar Ilan University, Israel

emerald
PUBLISHING

United Kingdom – North America – Japan
India – Malaysia – China

Emerald Publishing Limited
Howard House, Wagon Lane, Bingley BD16 1WA, UK

First edition 2023

British Library Cataloguing in Publication Data
A catalogue record for this book is available from the British Library

ISBN: 978-1-83753-053-3 (Print)
ISBN: 978-1-83753-052-6 (Online)
ISBN: 978-1-83753-054-0 (Epub)

ISSN: 1571-0386 (Series)

To our wives, Ann and Sara
Who put up with all the time that went into this work.

CONTENTS

LIST OF FIGURES AND TABLES

Figures

Note: *The colored versions of the graphics can be found online, either in the ebook version or on the last preprint in the Carnegie Mellon institutional archives.*

Table

ACKNOWLEDGMENTS

We are grateful to all of the living protagonists in the OLG story we tell in this book, who took the time to converse with us by email in response to our various inquiries.

We are particularly indebted to Alan Auerbach and Larry Kotlikoff, who sat down with us for a Zoom meeting at the height of the Covid-19 pandemic for an interview, and to Phillippe Weil who did the same. Alan and Larry helped structure our thinking about how OLG theory met practice. Phillippe's advice helped guided our treatment of the perpetual youth versions of the OLG model.

Finally, Karl Shell has been a mentor to us on this project from the very start. His knowledge of the OLG model – based on his own seminal research on it and from his contact with a great many of the formative papers on the model in his years as the (founding) editor of the *Journal of Economic Theory* – helped keep the project focused on the key elements of a research program in which there are many interesting, but tangential, threads.

INTRODUCTION

In the early days of personal computing, there were two competing computer operating systems vying for consumers' dollars. One was Microsoft's MS-DOS system, and the other was Apple's MacIntosh system.

Microsoft's system was a clunky command line system, based on the original IBM disk operating system. Apple's system used a windowed graphical user interface based on Xerox's original X-windows interface for Unix. Of these two systems, the MacIntosh was by far the easier to use. Switching between applications was as simple as mousing the pointer from one window to another and clicking. On a Microsoft machine, switching involved quitting out one application, entering commands to start a new application, and then settling down to work in the new application, hopefully without needing to go back to the first one!

It is well-known by now that of these two competing computer operating systems, Microsoft became dominant, despite its obvious inferiority to the MacIntosh. The reason for this is the stuff of an Industrial Organization course case study, but the factors leading to Microsoft's dominance include the state of technology, political and economic differences of opinion, and the lock-in effects generated by the network of applications that ran on the two different platforms. That the MacIntosh was the better technology, though, is clearly apparent from the fact that MS-DOS steadily evolved from its initial command line structure into a system centered on Xerox's windowed graphical user interface, which Microsoft now calls Windows.

This particular example of what we call the standardization trap is not new. A careful study of the history of the automobile clearly shows that electric cars developed alongside steam- and gasoline-powered cars, with electric vehicles being the better technology in the early phases of development. The market for automobiles tipped to internal combustion only after Henry Ford's improvement on Ransom Olds' patented assembly line process allowed him to mass produce cheap Model T's that ran on gasoline. The superiority of electric vehicles is only now becoming apparent, with the advent of serious repercussions due to global warming, and with the development of high-capacity batteries that allow electric cars to travel long distances. But even before these recent developments, diesel-electric hybrid technology replaced steam as the optimal power source for heavy

Overlapping Generations: Methods, Models and Morphology
International Symposia in Economic Theory and Econometrics, Volume 32, 1–9

Published under exclusive licence by Emerald Publishing Limited
ISSN: 1571-0386/doi:10.1108/S1571-038620230000032002

freight trains, and this technology has recently found its way into automobiles as well.

In the history of electrification, competing systems developed by Thomas Edison – direct current – and Nicola Tesla – alternating current – existed side-by-side, with alternating current finally winning out for the almost trivial reason that it is easier to change voltages with AC. Today, DC adapters routinely make voltage adjustments, and, as a result, all modern electronics run on DC. As locally generated electricity from renewable sources starts to come online, the electricity market might well tip back to Edison's favored DC technology.

Standardization traps aren't limited to new technological innovations. They occur in the realm of ideas as well. In fact, the scientific method operates by allowing competing hypotheses to be tested against empirical facts, with the hypothesis best able to explain the data enjoying at least temporary status as king of the hill. How long different hypotheses can stay on top depends on the quality of the empirical data available for testing, and on the sharpness of predictions, the reigning hypothesis generates.

Science characterizes reigning hypotheses as paradigms, although one should note that the original meaning of the word paradigm from Greek was one of side-by-side comparison. Thomas Kuhn originated the notion of a paradigm shift for the replacement or selection of one theory or hypothesis over others as the premier object of study.

In contemporary physics, we see this process at work in the parallel development of different theories for unifying general relativity's characterization of gravity with the underlying structure of quantum mechanics. As yet, there has been no compelling reason for one approach to supplant others, so no standardization trap or paradigm shift has occurred.

Historically, the debate over whether the universe was static or dynamic allowed both perspectives equal validity, to the point that Einstein made his famous blunder in setting the cosmological constant in the field equations of general relativity so that expansive and contractive forces would balance out, leaving the universe static. Despite the fact that in 1922, Alexander Friedmann had shown that the general relativity equations could accommodate different cosmological shapes and dynamics. Only in 1929, after Edwin Hubble discovered the uniform red shift of galaxies in all directions (with the implication that space was itself expanding), did Einstein correct his blunder. With this correction, a paradigm shift occurred, and the Big Bang became the standardized theory of cosmology. Whether a new theory will ultimately replace the Big Bang (and hence whether this was a trap) remains to be seen.

In the social sciences, a much slower research cycle, a relative paucity of empirical data, and limited possibilities for conducting experiments that generate new data lead to the possibility of much longer coexistence between competing theories, and greater opportunities for incomplete or incorrect theories to get locked in as the dominant paradigm, with all the attendant problems this raises for correcting the science when resources flow elsewhere.

We will argue here in this book that this is precisely the situation that macroeconomics and general equilibrium theory currently face. The problem arises out of the fact that two competing dynamic, stochastic, general equilibrium (DSGE) models have evolved as workhorse models for macroeconomic analysis, which we define broadly to include monetary economics, business cycle theory, economic growth, public finance/optimal taxation, and fiscal policy analysis.

To indicate the conundrum macro faces with these models, let us start with the crudest possible characterization of them.

The first model consists of a single, so-called "representative" agent who lives forever. Time enters the model as a sequence of discrete periods. The agent has access to technology for producing goods and services. The agent values these goods and services according to a utility function defined over consumption in each period, and the agent discounts utility in each period using a constant discount factor $0 < \beta < 1$. With these features in place, the agent's economic problem is to choose a series of investments in capital (or technology more generally) to maximize intertemporal utility subject to the constraint that invested resources can't be consumed.

The second model consists of a sequence of agents born at different times (with time also entering discretely) who overlap with and can trade with agents born earlier. Agents in this model live finite lifetimes. As with the first model, agents have access to technology for producing goods and services, and value consumption of goods and services via a utility function defined over consumption in each period of life. Agents in this model may or may not discount future utility. With these features in place, agents in this second model choose lifetime consumption and saving to maximize lifetime intertemporal utility, with savings becoming available for investment in technology.

By way of simplifying nomenclature, we will follow the conventional economic practice of referring to the first model as the infinite-lived agent (ILA) model and the second model as the overlapping generations (OLG) model.

The ILA model was originally developed by Frank Ramsey in 1928 as a way of modeling economic growth. Ramsey viewed the optimization problem posited in the model as the goal of a central planner, with the objective function of the problem (the representative agent's intertemporal utility) viewed as a social welfare function that put specified welfare weights on future generations' utility. The model was adopted and elaborated on by John Von Neumann (1937) and saw parallel development in the 1940s and 1950s by Maurice Allais (1947), Edmond Malinvaud (1953), and Robert Solow and Paul Samuelson (1956).

Work by David Cass in the mid-1960s showed how to completely characterize the optimal trajectories in this infinite-horizon general equilibrium model. Since Cass' work coincided with work by the then more senior and better-known Tjalling Koopmans, the resulting model is now universally known within the economics profession as the Ramsey–Cass–Koopmans (RCK) model, though it is sometimes also referred to as the neoclassical growth model. For details on these developments, see Spear and Young (2014).

The OLG model first appeared in 1947 in the Technical Appendix of Maurice Allais' book *Economie et Interet*. Because the model appeared only in the Appendix and the work in which it appeared was published in French, Allais' application of the model received very little attention in the English-speaking sector of the economics profession.

The OLG model was reinvented (or rediscovered) a decade later by Paul Samuelson (1958). Samuelson's model generated intense interest among general equilibrium theorists and monetary economists. General equilibrium theorists were interested in the fact that Samuelson's model could admit competitive equilibria which were not Pareto optimal, a contradiction of the First Welfare theorem for static general equilibrium models. Monetary economists focused on the fact that a role for money appeared naturally in Samuelson's model as a means of saving for retirement. A few years later, Peter Diamond (1965) reworked the OLG approach by introducing production into the model. This made possible a more realistic way of dealing with government debt and extended OLG into the areas of public finance, fiscal policy, and social security.

At roughly the same time that Samuelson was working on his early version of the OLG model, Gerard Debreu (1954) published work showing that Ramseyan-type models satisfied the second welfare theorem, allowing him to explicitly find prices that would support the Pareto optimal allocations obtained by the central planner as competitive equilibrium allocations for a large number of identical agents whose preferences were given by the central planner's social welfare function. This result was generalized by Takashi Negishi (1960) who showed how to extend Debreu's result to allow for any finite number of infinite lived agents. This appears to be the first instance in which the central planner was reinterpreted as an actual economic actor.

Now, on its face, a model in which actual economic agents live forever is problematic, and it isn't surprising that while there was some work being done on Samuelson's model in the 20 years after his seminal paper, there was no work (per a search of EconLit for "representative agent") being done on ILA models (as distinct from the planning version of the RCK model) during the comparable period.

It is also not surprising that perhaps the most important paper in modern macroeconomics, Robert Lucas' 1972 paper "Expectations and the Neutrality of Money," was based on a very sophisticated stochastic extension of the OLG model. The OLG framework allowed (as we noted above) the introduction of money, and individual agents (as opposed to a planner), together with random shocks to both the demand for goods and the supply of money, which then allowed Lucas to present a simple model of how a signal extraction problem could generate a short-run positive relationship between inflation and real output. He also introduced macroeconomists and general equilibrium theorists to the rational expectations paradigm along the way.

Shortly after Lucas published his path-breaking '72 paper, Robert Barro (1974) took Samuelson's OLG framework and showed how it could be transformed into the representative agent ILA model of Debreu and Negishi. Barro's insight was that if one interpreted the finite-lived agents of the OLG model as families, and families propagated lineally, and each parent family left positive bequests to their immediate offspring such that the resulting intergenerational allocation maximized the discounted infinite sum of utilities of all generations, then the OLG model with bequests was identical to the representative agent ILA model. As an added benefit, Barro's construction showed how forward dynamic programming techniques introduced in economics a decade earlier by Roy Radner (1967) could be applied to indicate the generational separation between agents in the ILA model and to solve the infinite-horizon optimization without transversality conditions.

Barro's reinterpretation of OLG came at roughly the same time that William Brock and Leonard Mirman were showing how to extend the RCK model to stochastic environments, a development that then fed directly into the work of Finn Kydland and Edward Prescott which launched real business cycle theory – based on the stochastic representative agent ILA model – in the mid-1980s. For details on this history, see Young (2014).

The chart below, based on a search of the American Economics Association's EconLit database, shows the growth of publications based on the OLG model from its introduction through the early 1990s.

Viewed in isolation, this seems like impressive growth in interest in and work on OLG models. However, when we do an EconLit comparison of the DSGE research (i.e., using the search term "dynamic stochastic general equilibrium") using models based on the OLG framework with those based on the ILA framework, the result is stunning. Prior to the early 1990s, there is no research of any type on DSGE. The topic then explodes for ILA-based models, with some growth in the early 2000s for OLG-based models, as illustrated in the chart below.

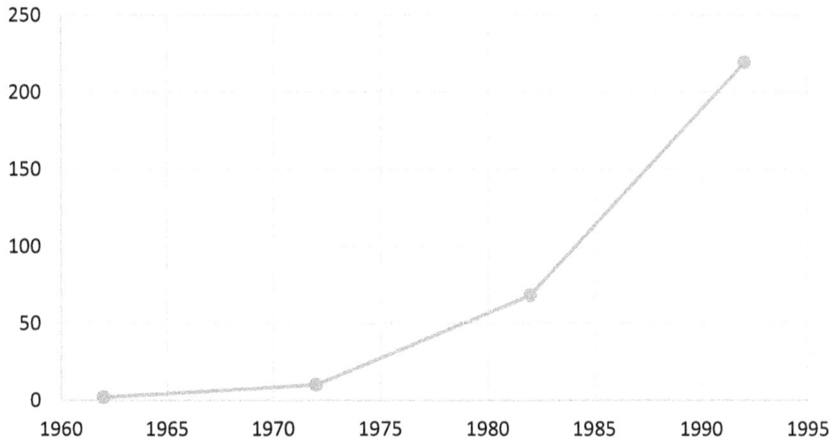

Early OLG Publications. *Source*: Compiled by authors from *Econlit* database, 1960–1995.

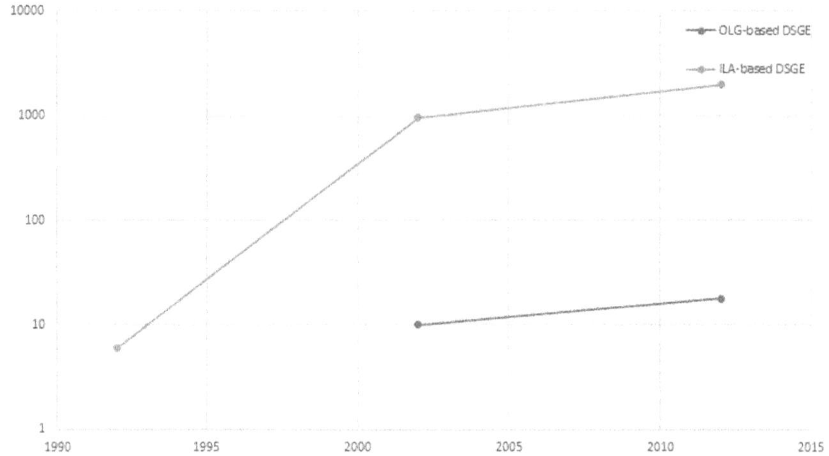

DSGE Research by Model Type. *Source*: Compiled by authors from the *Econlit* database, 1990–2015.

We use a log scale for this chart because the growth in ILA-based DSGE papers has been exponentially greater than that for OLG-based models.

While macroeconomists routinely describe OLG and ILA models as workhorses, it is clear that the ILA model is pulling a great deal more weight than OLG. At the same time, a search on "stochastic" and "overlapping generations"[1] generates the following:

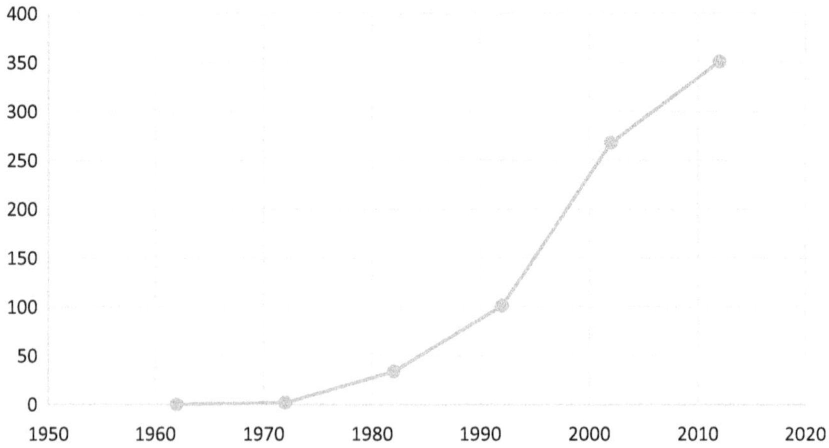

Stochastic OLG. *Source*: Compiled by authors from the *Econlit* database, 1950–2020.

So, work on stochastic OLG models did continue apace – much of it stimulated by the publication of Lucas's '72 paper – and in fact grew, but at nowhere near the rate at which applications of the ILA model in macro were growing. Indeed, as we will see, even Lucas, who pioneered the use of stochastic OLG models, changed workhorses in midstream.

An additional piece of data that supports this contention comes from a study by Kim et al. (2006). Based on a list of papers appearing in major economics journals over the period 1970–2005 with at least 500 citations in the ISI Web of Science/Social Science Citation Index, the authors concluded that there had been a significant shift in the emphasis placed on theory as against empirical work, and on the various subfields that attracted the attention of researchers in economics, with a shift from both micro and macroeconomics to growth and development during the 1990s.

What is relevant for our purpose is the placement of four watershed papers – three based upon the dynastic/infinite-lived agent model, as against a single paper based on the overlapping generations model – in their listing of articles receiving more than 500 citations over the period. The three ILA papers were those by Barro (1974), Kydland and Prescott (1982), and Lucas (1988). The OLG-based paper is Lucas (1972). The 1988 *Journal of Monetary Economics* paper by Lucas is listed at number 15, with 1,772 citations. The 1974 *Journal of Political Economy* paper by Barro is listed at number 29, with some 1,209 citations. The 1982 *Econometrica* paper by Kydland and Prescott had 814 citations, coming in at 61. The OLG paper by Lucas, published a decade earlier, in the *Journal of Economic Theory* in 1972, had 838 citations, and comes in only three places before Kydland and Prescott, at number 58. Although published a decade after Lucas's OLG-based paper, the ILA-based Kydland and Prescott paper had caught up in terms of citation impact with that of Lucas. Lucas' own 1988 paper "On the Mechanics of Economic Development," which uses the ILA methodology, had also clearly eclipsed his earlier OLG paper.

This illustrates the twilight of the old OLG-based approach as proxied by Lucas (1972) and the rise of the new ILA-based approach as proxied by Kydland and Prescott (1982) and Lucas' own adoption of the ILA framework as his basic research agenda, albeit retaining OLG as an analytical device to be applied in specific cases; see, for example, Lucas (1986).[2] But more is at stake here. The Kim et al. piece clearly shows the shift away from theory toward empiricism, and the high placement of Barro's 1974 paper likely reflects the way macro people often started by positing an OLG model, but then allowed bequests and invoked Barro to justify working with the more convenient, recursive methodology provided by the ILA framework.

This is exactly the process we are trying to describe. The key question is why did macroeconomists feel the need to do this? Computational efficacy? Mathematical tractability? Ideological predisposition? If so, it illustrates the process of a particular paradigm coming to "rule the roost." And the fact that – with the exception of the 1972 paper by Lucas – there was nothing on the Kim et. al. list that reflects OLG, shows exactly what occurred. ILA came to rule the roost, not perhaps

Total Dissertations Awarded.

	OLG	CL	RCK	RBC	Stochastic Growth
1960–1979	2	8			84
1980–1999	522	128	12	407	491
2000–2020	1,254	133	49	1,394	639
Totals	1,778	269	61	1,801	1,214
OLG Total	2,047				
ILA Total	3,076				

Source: Compiled by authors from ProQuest Dissertations Database.

because it was the "best" or most realistic model, but rather because it was the easiest to work with.

Our final data showing the relative ascendence of the ILA model over OLG comes from the ProQuest database of dissertations awarded between 1960 and 2020. When we search by various model-related keywords – "overlapping generations," "consumption loans," "Ramsey-Cass-Koopmans," "real business cycles," and "growth" – we get the numbers reported in the table above.

As with the data on publications based on each model, while there has been growth in the number of doctoral students trained in both models, ILA outpaces OLG significantly.

The ILA applications in macro were not without critics and substantive critiques. Among the early critiques was a paper by Kyle Bagwell and B. Douglas Bernheim which made the obvious point that families don't propagate lineally. Rather, given standard taboos against incest, families propagate as trees. Bernheim and Bagwell (1988) showed that if family structures were modeled realistically, and all families were interconnected via positive transfers (as in Barro's model), then everything was neutral. Markets played no role in the Bernheim–Bagwell model for the simple reason that internal transfer adjustments between families could restore the optimality of allocations without the need for market interventions following any perturbations to the original optimal equilibrium. A more recent study by Engineer and Welling (2004) argues persuasively that the overlapping generations structure and the economic consequences generated by age heterogeneity conform closely to anthropological structures delineated in Stewart (1977) known as graded age-group sets. As Engineer and Welling argue, their results

> establish that OLG models can accurately represent a large subset of actual age-group societies called graded age-set societies. Thus, an OLG model bears a close resemblance to reality. (Engineer & Welling, 2004, p. 454)

Together with data showing that most families do not leave substantial bequests to their children – investing instead in human capital bequests via K-12 education and beyond – it is hard not to come away from a study of these two workhorse models without the feeling that one of them is a PC and the other is a Mac.

Our purpose here, then, is to elucidate the technical and intellectual forces that have generated the current situation in which macroeconomics seems to be caught in a standardization trap based on a problematic choice of models.

NOTES

1. Strictly speaking we search on "generations" since early use of the model did not refer to overlapping generations at the time.

2. We could also add Lucas' other seminal 1978 paper, "Asset Prices in an Exchange Economy," to this list, since it had 772 citations and came in at number 70 in the Kim et al. paper.

CHAPTER 1

ORIGINS OF THE WORKHORSE MODELS

1.1 INFINITE-LIVED AGENTS AND THE NEOCLASSICAL GROWTH MODEL

Of the two workhorse models, ILA is somewhat older, having its origin in a remarkable paper by Frank Ramsey (1928). Ramsey's specification of the model was consistent with contemporary specifications, with the exception of his assumption that society eventually became satiated in consumption. Ramsey's objective function for society was a standard sum over time of instantaneous utility payoffs (possibly discounted), which he interpreted explicitly as the valuation of a utilitarian social planner. This explicit normative interpretation would persist until the mid-1970s. Ramsey needed the satiation assumption to force the dynamics of the model to converge over time to a steady-state at the social bliss point. This assumption was later dispensed with when the mathematics for analyzing the more general case of non-satiated utility became available.

Ramsey's model received scant attention during the 1930s and WWII years, although the model was adopted and elaborated on by John Von Neumann (1937). An additional citation to the paper comes from Paul Samuelson (1943). There, Samuelson terms Ramsey's approach as "brilliant" (p. 67), though he elided the section of his 1943 paper that contained his summary and citation of Ramsey from his *Foundations of Economic Analysis* (Samuelson, 1947).

During the immediate post-war period (1945–1955), Ramsey's paper is noted by the major growth theorists, including Koopmans, Malinvaud, Samuelson, and Tinbergen. As noted above, these authors followed Ramsey's lead in interpreting the social objective function as that of the central planner. Samuelson (1943) discussed this interpretation explicitly (p. 62):

> Let us assume, therefore, a condition of perfect certainty and an economy consisting of one or more individuals. We further assume, since otherwise the discussion can end before it starts, that there is no intrinsic rate of time preference. We need not speculate as to whether or not this

Overlapping Generations: Methods, Models and Morphology
International Symposia in Economic Theory and Econometrics, Volume 32, 11–17

ISSN: 1571-0386/doi:10.1108/S1571-038620230000032004

> implies infinite life expectations for the individual, for his family etc., since in any case we are not concerned here with the realism or the usefulness of the argument. For our purposes it is convenient to adopt the quite arbitrary assumption that utility is a given function of income in each period; more specifically, that it is the same function at each instant of time and that the individual acts so as to maximize the sum of utilities thus defined over all future time.

The culmination of what we might call the Ramsey project comes in the early 1960s with the work of Cass, Koopmans, and Malinvaud. These authors complete the correct mathematical characterization of the solution to the planner's problem without the assumption of satiated preferences. Malinvaud's key contribution is his demonstration of the importance of capital value minimization in preventing optimal overaccumulation of capital, which he characterized mathematically in what we now call a transversality condition. Cass' key contribution is the application of mathematical techniques from Pontryagin, Boltyanskii, and Revaz (1960) to derive the transversality condition, which insured convergence of any optimal trajectory to the optimal long-run steady-state (and which implies Malinvaud's capital value minimization condition). For a detailed history of these developments, see Spear and Young (2014) on the Cass–Malinvaud–Koopmans nexus.

The positivist development of growth starts after WWII with the work of John von Neumann and was then picked up and moved forward by Paul Samuelson, Robert Solow, and their coauthors. The positive approach is partial equilibrium in nature, focusing as it does on the role of production and capital accumulation as drivers of economic growth. Specifically, this literature takes a distinctly Keynesian view of the consumption side of the economy, using the empirical relationship between consumption and income to calibrate the savings rate in the various models. Even in treatments that do posit a central planner, most of the action in these models is driven by production, as noted explicitly by Malinvaud (1985):

> In the previous sections we have seen how theories of interest, capital and growth may prove interesting properties resulting only from the fact that most productive operations can be described as taking place within one period or several successive periods. For, apart from a reference to consumer preference in the last example, we have so far considered only production. (p. 307)

Among the important results developed in this literature are the delineation of turnpike properties of balanced growth, the remarkable no-arbitrage relationship between the value of capital as an output of production and its value as an input in subsequent periods, and the Solovian convergence results. All of these results arise from the optimality calculations for general multisector capital models of the type first considered by von Neumann.

At roughly the same time that the two distinct strands of the neoclassical growth literature were developing in the post-war period, Gerard Debreu put forward an abstract, theoretical analysis of the same model. Debreu (1954) extends the finite-dimensional Arrow–Debreu–McKenzie model to allow for infinitely-many commodities. He explicitly cites Malinvaud's work on the capital model as the justification for considering an infinite-dimensional commodity space. He then establishes that the model satisfies the two standard welfare theorems and shows how to decentralize the Pareto optimum found by the Ramseyan central planner as a competitive equilibrium. While Debreu does not concern himself with the question of whether the people who inhabit his model can live forever, he is explicit in interpreting the agents in the model as individuals or households.

Malinvaud (1985) noted the key problem with this abstract, but still rather a cavalier specification of the consumption side of the economy:

> We see immediately that analysis by periods is appropriate for such problems. We must certainly take account of the fact that an individual lives through several successive periods; but we must also note that no individual lives indefinitely. We should also recognise that generations are renewed from one period to another. (p. 308)

The question of how to interpret the infinite-lived representative agent – is it a planner or an actual participant in the underlying economy – remains much as Samuelson originally described in his 1943 paper: a convenient abstraction from reality. Ironically, it is Samuelson's development of the overlapping generations model in 1958, plus about a decade's worth of work on the model by others, that leads ultimately to the dynastic family interpretation of the ILA model at the hands of Robert Barro.

1.2. THE OVERLAPPING GENERATIONS MODEL: ORIGINS AND DISSEMINATION

The overlapping generations model is distinctly different from the infinite-lived representative agent or household in the Ramsey–Cass–Koopmans model. OLG agents live finite lifetimes, with new agents being born into the economy over time, so that the economy goes on forever with older and younger generations overlapping. Unlike the ILA model examined by Debreu (1954), the OLG model admits competitive equilibria which violate the welfare theorems, a fact that has led to a number of surprising discoveries and corresponding contentious issues in the ongoing debate over the appropriate role of government in the economy.

The genesis of the idea that the human lifecycle and the structure of human families ought to play an important role in economic activity is probably lost to history, since the idea is not particularly deep and certainly not radical. The first written consideration of these factors in economics, however, can be traced back to Irving Fisher (1907) and Fisher (1930). While Fisher has no formal overlapping generations-like model in his 1930 book *The Theory of Interest, as Determined by Impatience to Spend Income and Opportunity to Invest It*, he does make repeated references to intergenerational considerations as a determinant of interest rates. The key passage in his 1930 book is from Section 9.5:

> But whereas the shortness and uncertainty of life tend to increase impatience, their effect is greatly mitigated by the fifth circumstance, solicitude for the welfare of one's heirs. Probably the most powerful cause tending to reduce the rate of interest is the love of one's children and the desire to provide for their good. Wherever these sentiments decay, as they did at the time of the decline and fall of the Roman empire, and it becomes the fashion to exhaust wealth in self-indulgence and leave little or nothing to offspring, impatience and the rate of interest will tend to be high. At such times the motto, "after us the deluge," indicates the feverish desire to squander in the present, at whatever cost to the future.

> On the other hand, in a country like the United States, where parents regard their lives as continuing after death in the lives of their children, there exists a high appreciation of the needs of the future. This tends to produce a low degree of impatience. For persons with children, the prospect of loss of earnings through death only spurs them all the more to lay up for that rainy day in the family. For them the risk of loss of income through death is not very different from the risk of cessation of income from any ordinary investment; in such a case the risk of cessation of future income through death tends to lower their impatience for income. This act supplies the motive for life insurance. A man with a wife and children is willing to pay a high insurance premium in order that they may continue to enjoy an income after his death. This is partly responsible for the enormous extension of life insurance. At present in the United States the insurance on lives amounts to over $100,000,000,000. This represents, for the most part, an investment of the present generation for the next.
>
> An unmarried man, on the other hand, or a man who cares only for self-indulgence and does not care for posterity, man, in short, who wishes to "make the day and the journey alike," will not try thus to continue the income after his death. In such a case uncertainty of life is especially calculated to produce a high rate of time preference. Sailors, especially unmarried sailors, offer the classic example. They are natural spendthrifts, and when they have money use it lavishly. The risk of shipwreck is always before them, and their motto is, "a short life and a merry one." The same is even more true of the unmarried soldier. For such people the risk of cessation of life increases their impatience, since there is little future to be patient for.
>
> Not only does regard for one's offspring lower impatience, but the increase of offspring has in part the same effect. So far as it adds to future needs rather than to immediate needs, it operates, like a descending income stream, to diminish impatience. Parents with growing families often feel the importance of providing for future years far more than parents in similar circumstances but with small families. They try harder to save and to take out life insurance; in other words, they are less impatient. Consequently, an increase of the average size of family would, other things being equal, reduce the rate of interest.
>
> This proposition does not, of course, conflict with the converse proposition that the same prudent regard for the future which is created by the responsibilities of parenthood itself tends to diminish the number of offspring. Hence it is that the thrifty Frenchman and Dutchman have small families. (pp. 85–87)

The last two paragraphs could have come from Richard Easterlin's work on the demographic transition, and indicate clearly that Fisher viewed the internal dynamics of the family, and the resulting intergenerational dynamics of the economy, as important factors in determining intertemporal economic activity.

The first formal overlapping generations models were introduced to the economics profession in two waves. In the first, Maurice Allais wrote down a version of the model in an appendix to his book (published only in French) *Economie et Interet* (Allais, 1947). In the second wave, coming 11 years after the publication of Allais' book, Paul Samuelson published his 1958 article. This article introduced English speaking economists to the overlapping generations model, and, for many years, Samuelson's paper was cited as the original source for the model. Indeed, until Malinvaud published papers in 1986 and 1987 pointing up Allais' priority, the economics profession uniformly credited Samuelson with the introduction of model (see Grandmont, 1989 for a detailed explication of Allais' development of the OLG model). Even today, Allais' contribution is frequently overlooked. Weil (2008) started his paper celebrating the golden jubilee of the OLG model by writing: "Paul Samuelson's (1958) overlapping generations model has turned 50." It is only in a footnote two pages into the article that Weil notes that Maurice Allais derived the same model in 1947. While Weil is quite gracious in noting Allais' priority, the misassignment of priority to Samuelson for the OLG model is quite common. The answer to the question of why Allais' contribution was not noted until well after Samuelson's is likely a matter of (a) the work being published only in French; and (b) as Malinvaud (1987) noted: "The treatment in the appendix is analytically rather complex, leading to consideration of many cases and to introduction of long formulas" (p. 103).

Malinvaud (1953) used Allais' OLG structure, though as he himself notes in his 1987 *Journal of Economic Literature* communication (Malinvaud, 1987), the OLG structure did not play a major role there. Malinvaud used the OLG structure in a manner similar to that used 30 years later by Balasko and Shell in their well-known papers on the overlapping generations model. Specifically, he used the fact that with the OLG demographic structure, only finitely-many agents would be alive at a given time. This allowed him to write down individual allocation vectors as infinite-dimensional vectors (given the infinite horizon of the model), having only finitely-many non-zero entries. It also allowed him to add up allocations over the full economy with all aggregate entries being finite. Finally, he used a time truncation to produce a sequence of economies of increasingly longer (but finite) time horizons that he could apply the standard finite-dimension separating hyperplane theorem to, together with a nested set argument to show existence of support prices for characterizing the optimal accumulation sequence.

Samuelson's OLG development in his 1958 paper worked with a pure exchange economy and emphasized both positive and normative elements. On the positive side, he developed the initial model assuming that agents lived three period lives, so that there was no so-called "Samuelson-Gale" dichotomy in the original model. The three period life cycle allowed Samuelson to capture the essential empirical fact of the hump-shaped age-income relationship. By assuming that agents in their third period of life had very low endowments, Samuelson built in the need for retirement saving that was an obvious fact of the life cycle by the middle of the twentieth century. His assumption that goods were completely perishable, and the absence of a social credit system, captured the harsh reality of penury in old age that Samuelson had likely observed growing up during the depression, but which was also a historical fact of life throughout the ages when elderly parents had to count on the love of their children to keep them alive. Indeed, Shakespeare based one of his best-known plays, *King Lear*, on this theme. Finally, Samuelson showed how a social credit system – which he characterized as the "social contrivance of money" could alleviate this hardship and co-dependence within families by allowing for independent asset accumulation.

The normative elements of Samuelson's model included his demonstration of the existence of competitive equilibria which were not Pareto optimal, and his demonstration, via the introduction of a fiat money asset, of a role for government in improving the economic functions of society via management of the money supply or provision of Social Security. Finally, in looking at the optimal solution with money, Samuelson deduced that the equilibrium rate of interest would be precisely equal to the biological rate of growth of population in the economy. If we take the population growth rate to be zero, this yields an equilibrium interest rate of zero, since in equilibrium, whatever savers don't consume, dis-savers consume (given the compete perishability of goods). This result sparked a good deal of debate, with two formal criticisms of the model published in the *Journal of Political Economy* (*JPE*) by Abba Lerner and William Meckling, which we examine in detail below. But we should emphasize that Samuelson's only actual use of the two period lived agents version of his model was in the section where he tries to starkly illuminate the nature of the social welfare trade-off implicit in the model.

It is also of considerable interest that Samuelson had a strong interest in population dynamics in biology. This work is documented in Ronald Lee (2019), where Lee notes:

> Who now knows that Samuelson published two papers on the two-sex problem in demography? Or two papers on predator-prey models? A paper on the reversibility of time in population processes? Five papers generalizing and critiquing Fisher's concept of reproductive value, a concept that plays a key role in evolutionary theory? Analyses of evolutionary theories of altruism and kin selection? (p. 474)

For our purposes, the most interesting aspect of this work is that in the biological study of animal population dynamics, there are two approaches to looking at how animal populations evolve. One assumes a lineal process, typically based on looking at the females of a species, which then unfolds over time under the influence of environmental and genetic factors that bear on survival and reproduction. The second type of model assumes that generations of organisms overlap, with some resource consideration required of parent generations to ensure the survival of offspring. Given Samuelson's interest in and work on population dynamics, he would surely have been aware of the explicit use of the term "overlapping generations" from the biology literature, and yet in his own economic application of the core idea, he opted not to refer to overlapping generations.

This then raises the question of how the economics profession came to call the model not by Samuelson's "consumption loans" moniker, but by the OLG terminology that is now standard. A search of the EconLit database for the phrase "overlapping generations" restricted to the time period 1940–1970 returns no hits, because Samuelson routinely referred to his model as one of "consumption loans," and all of the early follow-on papers followed Samuelson's lead on this. A similar search on Google scholar returns a large number of hits, but all of this work is in biology, specifically population dynamics studies. As we noted above, it is ironic that Samuelson would have been so well-versed in this field, but not think to (or actively resist thinking to) call his model one of human overlapping generations. In any event, the first use we have found of the phrase – albeit in the context of a comment on Diamond (1965) – appears in Bierwag, Grove, and Khang (1969), while in the same year Phelps and Shell (1969) used the term "population overlap" in the context of their interpretation and extension of Samuelson's 1958 model. Barro (1974) also uses the term in reference Samuelson (1958). The next references found using the phrase are to be found in

Buchanan (1976) commenting on Barro's paper, in Shell (1977), and in Wallace (1977a, 1977b).

Since that time, the use of "consumption loans" has died out in favor of the standard overlapping generations terminology. So, going forward, we will refer to the model as overlapping generations or OLG rather than the earlier Samuelsonian terminology.

CHAPTER 2

OLG – THE NEXT GENERATIONS, 1960–1970

Samuelson's model generated significant interest among the upcoming young generation of both general equilibrium theorists and capital theorists. Demographers generally refer to the people born between 1921 and 1940, which includes this group, as the silent generation. As we will see, the economists among them were anything but silent. This group included David Cass, Peter Diamond, David Gale, Karl Shell, David Starrett, and Menahem Yaari. Their work in following up on the issues and conundrums raised by Samuelson's article set the research agenda on the OLG model for the next 30 years.

To understand how this group of theorists shaped this agenda, though, we need to first examine the economics profession's immediate response to the publication of Samuelson's paper. This was captured in a series of communications published in the *JPE* between Samuelson and Abba Lerner in 1959, and Samuelson and William H. Meckling in 1960. So, we turn first to these.

2.1 THE LERNER-SAMUELSON DEBATE

The first shot in the Lerner–Samuelson debate was fired by Lerner (1959). Lerner's objection to Samuelson's analysis turns on his definition of optimality, which he bases (as Samuelson notes in his reply) on a utilitarian social welfare function that weighs generations according to their sizes. Given this, he and Samuelson agree that the optimal gross interest rate should be one when the population is not growing. Lerner asserts, however, that in the case where the population is growing, the optimal interest rate should remain zero. In his reply to Lerner, Samuelson (1959) shows that this would be true if the social planner's optimization problem was based on the utilitarian objective function. Crucially, though, Samuelson noted that his analysis was not normative, but positive in asking what kind of equilibrium would be supported if there were some mechanism

Overlapping Generations: Methods, Models and Morphology
International Symposia in Economic Theory and Econometrics, Volume 32, 19–41

ISSN: 1571-0386/doi:10.1108/S1571-038620230000032006

for allowing intergenerational transfers to occur. This mechanism is Samuelson's "social contrivance of money," though in Lerner's telling it becomes the Social Security system and Lerner's chief objection is the governmental taking required for a pay-as-you-go system to operate.

Samuelson's reply to Lerner does make the point that for normative analyses, the choice of social welfare function is important, though this shouldn't detract from the use of positive economic models for analyzing social institutions such as money. The focus in this discussion on social welfare also echoes the earlier concerns with the question of how to weight different generations, going back to Ramsey (1928), the concerns of the capital theorists about how to handle growth models which didn't discount the future, the interest expressed by the Vatican in the subject – manifested in their hosting of a scientific conference on development and growth in 1963 – and continuing into contemporary debates over global warming.

A second important feature of Samuelson's reply to Lerner is that it works exclusively in the two-period lived agents setting, in contrast to his own use of the three-period model in the paper, and to Lerner's casting of his own (non-mathematical) arguments in the three-period setting. This setting highlights the various issues involving intergenerational transfers in a particularly stark fashion, and likely gave impetus to future work which focused solely on the two-period model. Samuelson closes his reply to Lerner with the droll statement:

> In defending the logic of my own exposition, I hope I shall not be construed as belittling Lerner's contribution. Who knows, if I read his paper a third time, I might become convinced of the errors of my way. (p. 522)

2.2 THE MECKLING-SAMUELSON DEBATE

In the aftermath of Samuelson's debate with Lerner, Meckling (1960) published a comment also taking exception to Samuelson's results, though using more formal mathematical reasoning, which forced Samuelson, in his reply, to clarify a number of points from the original paper in a way that now looks like a blueprint for the OLG research program that was subsequently carried out by the next generation.

Like Lerner, Meckling insists that Samuelson's zero-interest rate equilibrium can only arise if one takes the view of a central planner who equally weighs all generations currently living in any given time period. He adds that the biological interest rate also seems to fly in the face of Irving Fisher's observation that resources and preferences jointly determine interest rates, noting that in Samuelson's model, any preferences (not giving rise to corner solutions) give the same equilibrium interest rate.

Meckling goes on to insist, however, that in the absence of a benevolent planner, the arrangement of loans and their repayment must be a matter of bilateral negotiations. In the context of Samuelson's original three-period model, this means that only the young and middle-aged can borrow and lend to each other, with the old only capable of taking repayment of loans negotiated earlier in life. This leads him to conclude that the only possible equilibrium is one involving intergenerational autarky. Finally, Meckling also makes the interesting observation that the Samuelsonian equilibrium is likely to be unstable in the dynamics of the model around the zero-interest rate steady state and suggests that such instability makes observing such an equilibrium as a positive economic outcome unlikely.

Meckling concludes his critique by allowing for the possibility of the "social contrivance of money" or related social contracts as a way of supporting the Samuelsonian equilibrium, but in a footnote (fn. 9 on p. 75) to this section, he relates these mechanisms to what we have come to call Ponzi schemes.

Samuelson (1960) replying to Meckling is a *tour de force*.

His analysis of the equilibrium equations governing the model begins by noting that in looking at steady states, he is interested only in the roots of the equations given by the market-clearing condition for the model and the budget constraints (i.e., Walras' law). These equations are worth noting, and take the form

$$S_1(R,R)+S_2(R,R)+S_3(R,R)=0$$

$$S_1(R,R)+RS_2(R,R)+R^2S_3(R,R)=0.$$

Here, R is the gross interest rate, and $S_i(R,R)$ is the savings of young, middle-aged, and retired agents. Multiplying the first equation (market-clearing) by R and subtracting it from the second yields

$$(1-R)S_1(R,R)+(1-R)RS_3(R,R)=0.$$

If $R<1$, then the common term can be canceled, leaving Meckling's basic equilibrium equation (corresponding to intergenerational autarky). But, as Samuelson notes, if $R=1$, there are other equilibrium savings schemes (which implement the Samuelsonian outcome) that also satisfy the equilibrium equations. This feature shows up again later (in the work of Balasko and Shell, and of Kehoe and Levine for pure exchange models) in the guise of an equilibrium condition of the form

$$(1-R)m=0,$$

which states that either the equilibrium to the model involves no intergenerational resource transfers (in which case $R<1$) or the equilibrium will have agents holding valued quantities of money, $m>0$.

On the Fisher critique, Samuelson replies that in looking at the possible steady-state equilibria of the model (which he refers to as "statical" equilibria), it is the interaction of consumer demand (determined by budget constraints and preferences) together with the resource constraints that determine the equilibrium prices and allocations, just as in Fisher or any other general equilibrium model. While this is a relatively minor point in both Lerner's and Meckling's critiques, it foreshadows coming work showing how differences in the distribution of resources, or the introduction of productive assets would affect the equilibrium interest rates in the model.

On the dynamic properties of the model, Meckling observes correctly – and Samuelson gives him credit for this – that for a general three-period model, the perfect foresight equilibrium dynamic system would involve a third-order difference equation, and that the Samuelsonian equilibrium for this model would not be forward stable. Samuelson acknowledges this and points to the fact that he demonstrated the same result in a two-period model with log-linear preferences. He notes, though, that this was done in the context of showing that *laissez-faire* market forces would lead to a demonstrably suboptimal equilibrium.

For the general dynamic system, Samuelson then observes that it is in fact indeterminate, since it consists of a third-order difference equation but only two initial conditions. He notes that for it to be possible for the system to recursively determine a sequence of (non-stationary) equilibrium interest rates, a terminal condition would need to be appended to the model. In the absence of a central planner able to impose a condition such as Malinvaud's capital value minimization condition, there is no natural terminal condition for the OLG dynamic system. This observation also foreshadows a large body of work undertaken by subsequent generations of OLG theorists on the role of dynamics in determining the optimality properties of the model.

As a final note on the dynamic systems analysis in Samuelson's reply to Meckling, the issue of whether or not a steady state was stable would merge with Samuelson's indeterminacy observation in what became a long-running (indeed, continuing) debate over the determinacy of equilibrium in OLG economies. At issue here is the distinction between whether or not unstable behavior can ever be observed. Meckling argues (in his quaint parable of Martian vs. Terran economics) that the stable equilibrium is the only relevant one. Samuelson's response to this points out that stability depends on the boundary conditions imposed on the difference equation system, and that Meckling's example imposes a particular knife-edge condition which then gives rise to Meckling's stability result.

Curiously, Samuelson doesn't bring his knowledge of saddle-path stability in the capital model into the discussion, by way of suggesting that rational optimization can lead to otherwise unstable equilibria being determinate, in the modern sense. Indeed, in Samuelson and Solow (1956), the authors state that:

> Our economic problem is like the unconventional case of a point of maximum rather than minimum potential energy – as e.g., a stiff pendulum with its bob upright. Touch it with a molecule and it departs ever further from the unstable equilibrium point.
>
> For any point near the equilibrium there will be one special set of initial velocities such that [...] the resulting motion will asymptotically approach the equilibrium level. This special motion – and only it – will truly minimize the Hamilton-Lagrange integral over all time. Such a motion would be unstable with respect to any exogenous shocks or displacements, but if an intelligence bent on truly minimizing Hamilton's integral guided the pendulum, it could re-aim the pendulum so as to seek a true minimum. This re-aiming is, so to speak, what an optimizing society is constantly doing. (p. 548)

This process of "re-aiming" would be grist for the OLG theory mill for years to come.

On the question of whether the Samuelsonian equilibrium could be sustained, raised by both Lerner and Meckling, Samuelson makes the observation that while one can demonstrate the Pareto optimality of the competitive equilibrium for any finite truncation of the infinite OLG economy – which Balasko and Shell later dubbed Weak Pareto Optimality – determining full optimality for the infinite economy requires (as Samuelson puts it in footnote 6 of his reply to Meckling) a reformulation of the rules for optimality. Lerner and Meckling's argument against the rationality of the Samuelsonian equilibrium is that if exponential population growth were ever to halt, the last young generation to pay into the social Ponzi scheme would not receive full compensation because of the slowdown in growth. This argument has been manifested in other forms, such as the fact that each new young generation always has an incentive to undertake a currency reform that eliminates the existing old generation's claim to resources, while re-starting the Ponzi scheme in their own favor. Samuelson's reply is that:

> *Laissez faire* competitive pricing will, teleologically speaking, condemn a society to a negative interest-rate configuration that leaves, say, thousands of generations at a sub-Bentham optimum in order that the single terminal generation's property rights not be infringed. (p. 78)

This argument hardly settles the issue, as the contemporary debate over whether U.S. Social Security can survive the baby boomers' retirement shows. What the argument does do is show that later work by David Gale, David Starrett, and Peter Diamond tried to address questions already raised by the earlier Lerner–Meckling–Samuelson debate, albeit with a different focus, as will be seen below. This has not been noted until now. Moreover, the Lerner–Meckling–Samuelson debate can be seen to foreshadow later work on the core of an OLG economy.

We conclude our discussion of the Lerner–Meckling–Samuelson debate with a final quote from Samuelson's reply to Meckling, ostensibly made in the context of whether societies can adjust to changed economic conditions, but perhaps indicative of Samuelson's attitude toward the flak he was getting on the new model:

> Now, aside from the resulting interpersonal equity problem between the generations, there may well be the noteworthy problem of "cultural lag," in which the modes of behavior of one epoch are painfully clung to even after the time for them is past. (p. 77)

After the publication of Samuelson's seminal paper and the debate between Samuelson and the old guard about his new model's implications, it fell to a new generation of economic theorists to further the research agenda on overlapping generations models. These theorists – Peter Diamond (MIT), David Cass and Menahem Yaari (Yale), Karl Shell (MIT/Penn), David Starrett (Stanford) – were all trained in the then-new general equilibrium theory of Arrow and Debreu, and did their thesis work on applications of general equilibrium to growth. To this group, we add a member of the old guard, David Gale, whose training in mathematics and interest in economic models led him to address some of the early OLG conundrums. We consider the key works of each of these pioneers in the order of their publication.

But before this, we have to examine related work by Samuelson between 1968 and 1976. For example, in Samuelson (1975a), Samuelson wrote that in his earlier 1968 paper "The Two Part Golden Rule Deduced as the Asymptotic Turnpike of Catenary Motions" (Samuelson, 1968), both he and Diamond (1965) "combined the Solow model … with its pivotal role for capital, with the 1958 model of overlapping generations" (1975a, p. 533). In the same issue of *International Economic Review*, Samuelson published "Optimum Social Security in a Life-Cycle Growth Model" (Samuelson, 1975b), in which he introduced "An exact model of steady state, exponential-growth social security … into the life-cycle model of Modigliani [1954, 1974], Diamond [1965], Cass and Yaari [1967] and Samuelson [1958]" (1975b, p. 539). Using a combination of his two-generation 1958 approach and Solow's neoclassical model (1956), he dealt with the cases of no social security, as against the case where it exists, and then derived the characteristics of what he called "optimum social security" (1975b, pp. 541–543). He later acknowledged that this paper "was designed as a companion piece … and accordingly they were published back to back" (1976, p. 519).

However, it seems that Samuelson did not check the second-order conditions in his optimum growth rate for population paper, which lead to a somewhat overlooked critique by Deardorff (1976), and subsequent admission of error by Samuelson (1976). While tangential to the main thrust of this volume, the exchange revolved around Samuelson's extension of his 1958 model to include production and thus deserves a brief mention here. Deardorff wrote:

> In a recent contribution to this *Review*, Paul Samuelson … adapted his earlier consumption-loan model … to include production, and attempted to derive a rate of population growth that would maximize utility in steady state growth. His solution derived from necessary conditions for optimality, and he acknowledged the need for, but did not state or evaluate, the corresponding sufficiency conditions that would assure that his solution was actually optimal … Samuelson's solution is in fact *not* optimal in general. We concentrate primarily on the special case in which both utility and production functions are Cobb-Douglas. In that case we show that Samuelson's solution, for those parameter values for which it exists, provides a *global minimum* of steady state utility, not a maximum. [italics in original] (p. 310)

Samuelson's reply was "Mea culpa" (1976, p. 516), albeit he attempted to ease the severity of his oversight by posing further questions and tentatively pleading "nolo contendere?" (1976, p. 52).

2.3 THE DIAMOND MODEL

Diamond (1965) took the logical next step of introducing production into the model, extending Samuelson's pure exchange framework. One immediate and important effect this had was the demonstration that the introduction of productive assets would lead to equilibria in which interest rates were positive, as opposed to the case Samuelson highlighted when the population was not growing, where the optimal interest rate was zero. Diamond developed his model under the assumption that capital never depreciates, and we can illustrate the nature of his results in a very simple setting by introducing a durable productive asset like land or a Lucas tree.

To illustrate the features of this equilibrium, we work with a two-period model and make use of the standard offer curve diagram. In Fig. 1, we show the simplest case of no population growth (or other exogenously driven productivity growth), with only money available for transferring wealth between periods. We center the

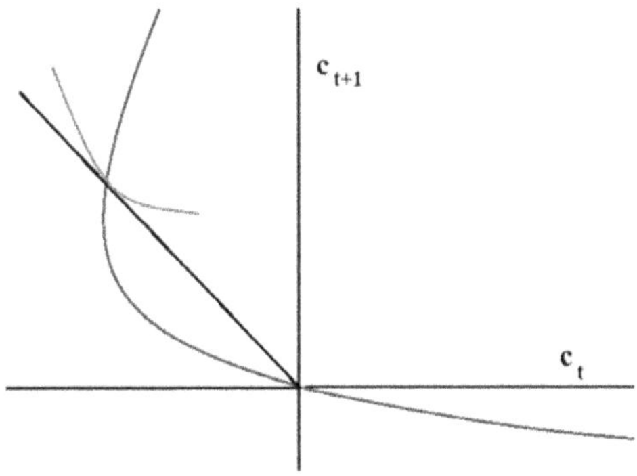

Fig. 1. Standard Offer Curve Diagram for Two-period OLG.
Note: Unless otherwise indicated, figures were produced by the authors. The colored versions of the graphics can be found online, either in the ebook version or on the last preprint in the Carnegie Mellon institutional archives.

offer curve on the (assumed stationary) endowment point for agents, under the assumption that young agents have more endowment than old, that is, the case Samuelson initially examined. The dark blue curve is the representative agent's offer curve between consumption at time t and $t + 1$. The 45-degree line in the negative quadrant shows the zero-interest budget constraint, which is also the economy's resource constraint, since all saving gets transferred from young to old one-for-one. Where the budget/resource constraint crosses the offer curve, we have a competitive equilibrium. The light blue indifference curve shows the representative agent's optimal choice for this case.

We can illustrate Samuelson's biological rate of interest result in the same diagram (reproduced as shown in Fig. 2) by introducing population growth, which makes more consumption available in period $t + 1$ because there are more young agents in the economy than there were in period t.

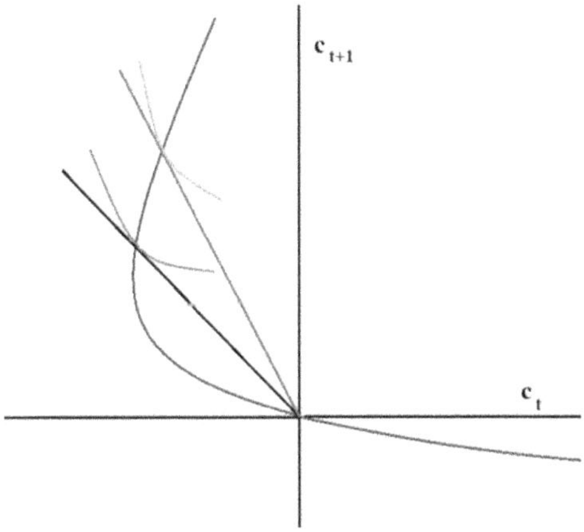

Fig. 2. Offer Curve With Population Growth.

In this diagram, the red line (having a slope equal to $1 + n$, where n is the rate of population growth) is the economy's resource/budget line, and where this intersects the offer curve determines the equilibrium. Again, we put in the pink indifference curve to illustrate the representative agent's optimal choice.

If we now introduce a productive asset, *a la* Diamond, this changes the total resources available in all periods in the model. Specifically, if we have a Lucas tree that drops a dividend in the amount of $D > 0$, this will shift the economy's resource constraint out along both the period t and $t + 1$ axes. We illustrate this in Fig. 3.

In this diagram, the offer curve is as before, while the purple line indicates the total resource constraint due to the productive dividend generated by the asset. The equilibrium for the economy is determined by the intersection of the resource constraint with the offer curve. The representative agent's budget constraint in this case, though, is different. It must pass through the origin (which, recall, represents the agent's endowment point) because the agent must use the sale of current endowments to finance the purchase of equity shares in the asset. The equilibrium price for the asset (in terms of consumption) is determined by the intersection of the agent's budget constraint with the offer curve at the point where the resource constraint crosses the offer curve. Since the slope of this line is greater than one in absolute value, the interest rate is positive. For reference, the dark line shows the old resource/budget constraint absent a productive asset. As before, we indicate in light blue the representative agent's indifference curve at the optimal consumption bundle.

We can also use this diagram to illustrate what we will call the quasi-inefficiency of the asset equilibrium generated by over saving. Specifically, with no growth, the golden rule for balanced growth (see, e.g., Phelps, 1965) requires the

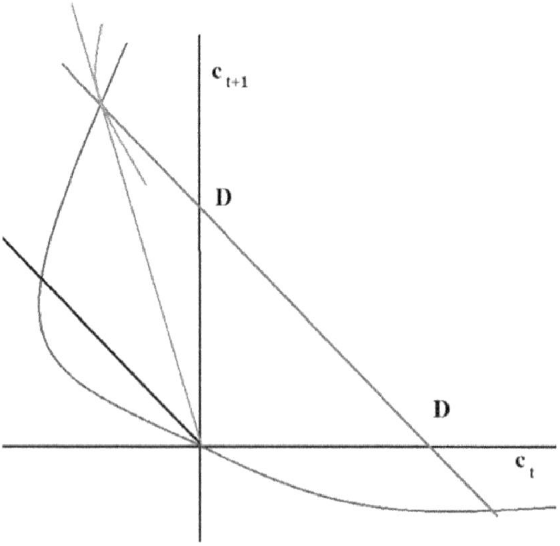

Fig. 3. Offer Curve With a Productive Asset.

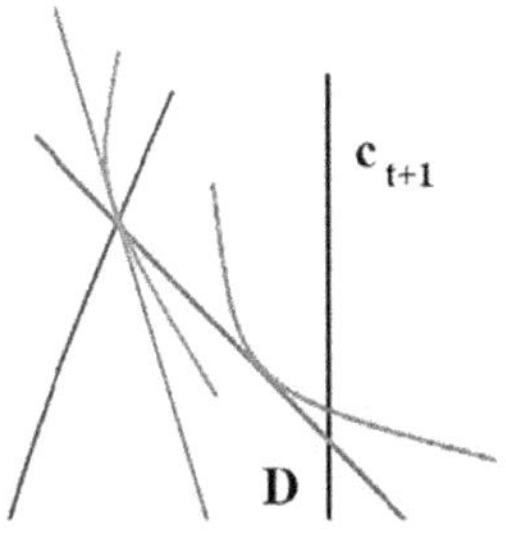

Fig. 4. Offer Curve Showing Competitive Equilibrium and Golden Rule.

interest rate to be zero. From Fig. 3, it is clear that with a productive asset, the interest rate must be positive. Fig. 4 shows a blow up of Fig. 3, indicating that optimal golden rule allocation, occurring where the representative agent's indifference curve is just tangent to the resource constraint:

We call this a quasi-inefficiency because, as should be clear from the diagram, to get to the golden rule allocation, a central planner would need to transfer resources from some initial group of old agents to the first group of young agents, and then maintain this transfer scheme in perpetuity. This redistribution makes every generation after the initial one better off, but it makes the initial old worse off, and hence, cannot be characterized as a Pareto improvement. We will see below that this point was first made formally by David Gale in 1972.

Returning to Diamond's model, we can use our diagrammatic set up to illustrate the inefficiency identified by Diamond and detailed in the example in Section 10 of the paper, using log-linear utility functions and Cobb-Douglas production. Fig. 5 shows the equilibrium for a productive economy (again using the Lucas tree set up), where the competitive equilibrium generates an allocation and associated interest rate which is below the rate of growth of the population. In the diagram, the purple line indicates the economy's resource constraint, the black line is the competitive equilibrium budget constraint for the representative young agent, and the light grey line is the budget constraint that would occur if the interest rate were equal to the rate of population growth. The same diagram can illustrate an efficient asset equilibrium by shifting the purple resource constraint out until it passes through or lies above the grey population growth line. The corresponding shift in the black budget constraint line will then show that the resulting equilibrium interest rate is greater than or equal to the population growth rate.

Diamond then looks at the effect of introducing different types of government debt and shows that if the economy was originally operating efficiently (i.e., where interest rates are greater than or equal to the population growth rate), debt reduces welfare. When the economy is operating in an inefficient region, debt may improve or decrease overall welfare.

We can also interpret the diagrams we've presented here for the case where productive capital must be accumulated (as in Diamond's one-sector setting), by interpreting the dividend in the Lucas tree case as the amount of output net

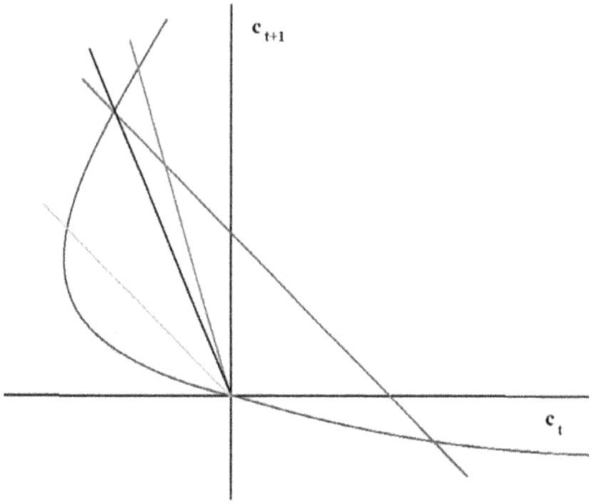

Fig. 5. Offer Curve for Inefficiency With Productive Asset.

of undepreciated capital plus new investment along the steady-state balanced growth path for the economy.

Before leaving Diamond's 1965 approach, we look at the development of his OLG approach over the period 1964–1973. After graduating from Yale as a mathematics major and a period as research assistant to Tjalling Koopmans at Cowles (see Koopmans, Diamond, & Williamson, 1962, 1964), he entered MIT as a graduate student in mathematics, but transferred to economics (KDW, 1964). His MIT Ph.D. thesis, supervised by Solow, consisted of three chapters. The first chapter – his job market paper – was based on his work with Koopmans on the infinite choice problem. After reading the thesis on growth of Srinivasan – his friend and colleague at Yale and Cowles – Diamond wrote a second thesis chapter extending Srinivasan's model (see Diamond, 2014). Then, following up on a suggestion by Solow, Diamond converted Salter's ideas about technical change, productivity, and cost reductions (Salter, 1960) into a growth model approach in a third thesis chapter entitled "Technical change and economic growth" (Diamond, 1963). What is interesting to note is that in the acknowledgments in his dissertation, Diamond thanked the members of his thesis committee, Samuelson and Fisher, and "the members of the intertemporal seminar – both in seminar meetings and outside."

Diamond left MIT and took up a position at Berkeley, which included teaching a class in public finance, and a lecture he gave turned into a 1964 Working Paper at University of California at Berkeley, which afterward became his classic 1965 *American Economic Review* (*AER*) paper. As he recalled (email November 6, 2018):

> In both 1963-4 and 1964-5, I taught a long year public finance course with a prerequisite in microeconomics, so it was for a small number of very good students. Having a whole year, I could go systematically through parts of the literature. When I was lecturing on topics where I did not follow an existing article closely, I prepared a handout. That lecture was the start of my use of OLG on the debt. I used OLG on taxation in two papers after I left Berkeley.

The 1964 working paper was issued by the Berkeley Institute of Business and Economic Research. The 1965 *AER* version contains additions in both text and footnotes, including discussion of the effects of external and internal debt, the absence of bequests, Walrasian versus Marshallian stability, and changes in wording, albeit there were more substantial differences, to which we now turn. After submission of his working paper to the *AER*, Diamond received referee's comments (provided as an attachment to the email communication) and based on them changed and corrected text and equations, and re-drew a diagram. For example, the referee suggested generalizing the utility function in the example of the Cobb-Douglas production and utility functions that appeared in the working paper, and Diamond did this accordingly. Finally, the referee called Diamond's attention to the fact that Modigliani did in fact deal "with the feedback effect of the national debt on the stock of capital via reduced income" (referee's report, paragraph 4). In his final footnote in the 1965 *AER* version, Diamond added this accordingly.

Regarding the 1964 working paper and 1965 *AER* paper, and his interaction with David Gale while at Berkeley, Diamond recalled (email November 5, 2018) that he had:

> [N]o memory of the exact version used at that time (1964), but I presented the model at the joint Berkeley-Stanford seminar at Stanford (as was the custom of those who presented) ... at the time, there was a good turnout at the joint seminars from both departments. I did note that Ken Arrow was there and seemed to find it interesting .... I did interact with David Gale while I was at Berkeley ... no memory of interacting with Gale on my paper – remember talking with him about his. My only memory of discussions with Gale is my suggesting to him that in a real model, which his was, it was wrong to interpret results as being about inflation.

Regarding his use of OLG in "two papers" after he left Berkeley, let us now turn to Diamond's 1970 *JET* and 1973 International Economics Association (IEA) Conference Proceedings papers. In an email dated November 6, 2018, Diamond recalled that he spent 1965-66 at Churchill College, Cambridge, where he wrote his paper "Incidence of an interest income tax" (Diamond, 1967, 1970, subsequently published in *JET* in 1970). After he had returned to MIT in September 1966, he said that he "talked economics a lot" with Karl Shell, who had since joined the department as an assistant professor. In the published version of the paper, Diamond wrote that he was indebted to Shell for "helpful discussion." Diamond used a "two-period" OLG model for analysis (1967, pp. 1–2, 1970, pp. 211–212).

The second of his two post-1965 OLG papers was his contribution to the 1970 IEA conference that appeared in the Conference Proceedings (Mirlees & Stern, 1973). In this paper, entitled "Taxation and public production in a growth setting," Diamond presented a welfare function as "a discounted sum of individual utilities where individuals are assumed to live for two periods" (1973, p. 215) and noted that "the presence of overlapping generations and the optimal growth model introduces two concepts of the intertemporal social marginal rate of substitution (1973, p. 216). He maintained that "in the first, one considers transferring the consumption of a single consumer over time; In the second, commodities are transferred between members of successive generations" (1973, p. 236). The advantage of this approach, according to Diamond, was that "the latter concept fitted with the discount rates that arise in standard optimal growth models, while the former is the concept which we can observe by watching individuals lend or borrow" (1973, comments by Diamond, pp. 236–237).

2.4 CASS AND YAARI

David Cass and Menahem Yaari also introduced a version of Samuelson's consumption loans model with production, done in a continuous time framework, in 1965, though this was after Diamond's paper was accepted for publication, since it is cited as forthcoming in the Cass–Yaari (1965) text. Like Diamond, they found that the competitive equilibrium generally did not correspond to the golden rule equilibrium. This paper was published in *Essays in the Theory of Optimal Economic Growth* (K. Shell, ed.), MIT, 1967.

Cass and Yaari published a second paper on Samuelson's model, Cass–Yaari (1966a) the following year focused on what Samuelson had called the "infinity paradox," the fact that the overlapping generations framework could give rise to inefficient competitive equilibria, and that these inefficiencies carried over to models with productive capital as well.

To quote from the Introduction to their paper:

> Professor Samuelson's article (1958) on an exact consumption-loan model of interest led to an interesting controversy. At issue were the determination and properties of interest rates in a dynamic economic system with no capital. One might have thought that these exchanges, between Samuelson (1959) and Lerner (1959) on the one hand, and between Samuelson (1960) and Meckling (1960) on the other, would result, if not in a complete resolution of the disagreements, at least in the emergence of a clear picture of what the issues are and how they might be treated. Unfortunately, such was not the case. The Samuelson-Lerner and the Samuelson-Meckling dialogues leave the reader rather perplexed, as though he had just watched a New Wave film – executed with brilliance, enjoyable while in progress, but not quite clear as to what is happening and never giving one a sense of resolution. (Cass & Yaari, 1966a, p. 353)

Working with the pure exchange, two-period model of Samuelson's paper, the Cass-Yaari analysis first notes that the only economic activity possible in such a setting is the distribution of total resources between members of the two overlapping generations. Their model assumes that young agents are endowed with one unit of the consumption good, while old agents have nothing. They then proceed to define the rate of interest for the economy as simply the return to consumption between an agent's two periods of life. Following their notation, we let c_t^a be the consumption of an agent born at time t in age $a = young, old$ (or, for simplicity, young = 1 and old = 2). The interest rate is then given by

$$1+r_t = \frac{c_{t-1}^2}{1-c_{t-1}^1}.$$

With the population growing at rate n, they then show that the economy's resource feasibility constraint is given by

$$c_t^1 + \frac{c_{t-1}^2}{1+n} = 1.$$

After some simple algebra, they are then able to show that as long as $c_t^a \neq 1$ then it has to be the case that $r_t = n$. What this construct shows is that the rate of interest is simply (and, as Cass–Yaari note) mechanically determined by the resource constraints, without any appeal to preferences or biology. Quoting from the paper:

> The main cause for suspicion seems to be the fact that a rate of interest has been determined without any reference to impatience and time preference or, more generally, to the utility function U. Somehow, the fact that *r* is a completely mechanistic construct, having no reference to markets, seems to have become blurred [in the Samuelson-Lerner and Samuelson-Meckling debates]. (Cass & Yaari, 1966a, p. 355)

The second important clarification that Cass and Yaari make to the understanding of the OLG inefficiency is the demonstration that technology, *per se*, doesn't make the potential inefficiency go away. Specifically, they drop the assumption that goods are completely perishable and introduce a simple storage technology that allows young agents to transfer resources one-for-one between youth and old age. The analysis then shows that young agents would optimally choose some positive level of storage (as long as preferences are such that consumption smoothing is desired) and make the point (see Fig. 2 in the paper) that this choice will lie strictly below the resource constraint generated by taking population growth into account.

One can also see from this analysis that even if the population were not growing, the storage equilibrium is not efficient, since it requires that a positive quantity of resources sit idle rather than being used for consumption. Cass and Yaari note that, as in Samuelson's paper, trade in this situation is not possible, since no young agent will be able to find someone willing to borrow from him now to receive the (population growth augmented) consumption when he is old. So, once again, there needs to be some form of intermediation between the generations for the economy to move away from the inefficient autarky allocation. They show, however, that in conventional accounting terms, no private intermediary would ever willingly undertake the job since their net worth would always be negative. Hence, this task is one that government (either directly or through the exercise of its monetary authority) would need to undertake.

The middle section of the paper examines a three-period model to show that there can be a role for competitive internal credit markets, though, in the absence of a social institution for promoting intergenerational trade, the competitive equilibrium would remain one of autarky.

The last part of the paper is, in many ways, the most interesting, since it begins to delve in detail into the question of what causes the OLG inefficiency. In the section titled "Efficiency and Infinity," Cass and Yaari begin by noting:

> The possible inefficiency (or non-optimality) of the competitive mechanism, as demonstrated by Samuelson and Diamond, has given rise to a certain amount of speculation, mostly on an

> informal basis. Many people (including Samuelson [for example, 1958, p. 474; 1959, p. 522] and Diamond [1965, p. 1134]) seem to feel that this phenomenon has something to do with infinity. What apparently leads one to point an accusing finger at "infinity" is the fact that for the standard general equilibrium model (which is finite) we have theorems which tell us that the competitive mechanism always leads to an optimum (and, a fortiori, to efficiency). Nevertheless, the role played by "infinity" in leading the competitive mechanism astray has remained, at best, rather vague. (Cass & Yaari, p. 364)

Cass and Yaari then set up a finite model that (in its steady state) looks like an OLG model by truncating time and identifying the last period with the first, so that the model becomes circular.[1] In this setting, the OLG structure is manifested in the fact that agents have preferences over goods they don't produce and must, therefore, seek out mutually beneficial trades. By setting up this model with more than two periods, Cass and Yaari are able to show that there can be no double coincidence of wants and that barter is therefore not tenable without further intermediation. In his later work with Balasko and Shell, Cass would refer to this friction as one of restricted participation in markets. In the OLG setting, the fact that agents live finite lives restricts participation in markets that are open when the agents aren't alive. In the circular model, this is captured via restrictions on preferences, via the observation that finite-lived agents can be viewed as infinite-lived agents who only care about consumption in finitely many periods. While the restricted participation argument is valid on its face, the circular structure Cass and Yaari impose on their example does permit the infinite shifting of resources among agents in the model, in the same way the normal OLG timeline does, so it can be argued that Cass–Yaari haven't really dispensed with infinity.

Cass and Yaari had a third OLG-related paper from 1966 (Cass & Yaari, 1966b) written after the "Re-examination" paper, though never published. In this paper, Cass and Yaari elaborated on the relationship between inefficient competitive equilibrium without money and the existence of monetary equilibrium. They show, in particular, that there can exist a valued fiat money equilibrium that is not Pareto optimal in a model where young agents have access to a storage technology (as in the "Re-examination" paper) if the price of money is low enough that agents wish to save via inventory. The paper also introduces the idea of commodity money, which enters the first-period utility function and shows by this example that non-monetary equilibrium (intermediated by commodity money) may be Pareto optimal. Interestingly, these results are a precursor to the results Cass later developed in his paper with Masahiro Okuno and Itzhak Zilcha, which we discuss below. It is also of note that Cass and Yaari anticipated Gale's results (also discussed below) in footnote 8 of this paper, where they note that if the representative agent's intertemporal marginal rate of substitution is bigger than one in absolute value, the associated allocation will be optimal.

Yaari (1965) was a solo-authored paper, which dealt not with overlapping generations, but with consumer decision-making when consumers faced uncertain lifetimes. In the paper, Yaari analyzed the effects of various considerations a consumer might face, including bequest motives, the need for life insurance, and the possibility of using annuities to finance retirement consumption. This work was later picked up by Blanchard (1985) who used Yaari's result to develop what is now referred to as a "perpetual youth" model (when not referred to simply as the Blanchard–Yaari model). In this model, young agents are born every period (or instance, in continuous time models), and have a fixed (age-independent) probability of dying. These agents purchase annuities (among other assets) which closes the model in the sense that when agents die, their terminal wealth accrues to the issuer of the annuity. This formulation generates a type of OLG model, though because of the assumption that the probability of dying doesn't vary with age, the model lacks much of the age-related heterogeneity found in the traditional OLG setting. We will discuss this model and the variants of it later.

2.5 SHELL

The next paper we consider is Shell (1971), "Notes on the Economics of Infinity." As the paper's title indicates, Shell is also tackling the question of what drives the OLG inefficiency result, and his analysis is somewhat at odds with that of Cass and Yaari. Shell attributes the inefficiency primarily to the doubly infinite structure of the OLG model – infinitely many agents and infinitely many commodities (consumption bundles in each time period) – relative to that of the neoclassical growth model, where the number of agents (or agent types) is restricted to be finite.

Shell's paper starts by demonstrating the inefficiency of competitive equilibrium in a particularly simple setting. He examines a two-period pure exchange model with one period overlap of generations, in which agents are endowed with and can consume a single good (which Shell calls chocolate). Preferences are linear, so that only the total amount of chocolate consumed over an agent's lifetime matters. Endowments are initially set so that each agent owns one unit of chocolate in each period of life. To close the model, there is an initial agent who lives through period one and only values chocolate consumed in that period and is endowed with one unit in that period.

With this set up, Shell then shows that there is a simple competitive equilibrium in which the price of chocolate in every period is one, and every agent consumes their endowment. (In general equilibrium terms, this would be a no-trade equilibrium.) Shell then shows that it is possible to Pareto improve on this equilibrium by having each young agent at time t give their endowment of chocolate to the old agent at time t. Given the linearity of preferences, no agent born after period 0 is made worse off, while the initial old agent in period 0 is made strictly better off.

This example can be generalized in a way that makes every agent better off. We start by defining transfers

$$\left(z_t^t, z_t^{t+1}\right) \in \mathbb{R}^2,$$

where the first transfer is taken from (or given to) the young agent born in period t in that period, and the second transfer is given to (or taken from) the same agent in their second period of life $t+1$.

Now, fix two numbers $\epsilon > 0$ and $0<r<1$ and define the transfers as follows:

$$z_t^t = -\epsilon \sum_{j=1}^{t-1} r^j$$

and

$$z_t^{t+1} = \epsilon \sum_{j=1}^{t} r^j .$$

Now, given any initial competitive equilibrium allocation $\left[x_t^t, x_t^{t+1}\right]_{t=1}^{t=+\infty}$, we define a new allocation $\left[\hat{x}_t^t, \hat{x}_t^{t+1}\right]_{t=1}^{t=+\infty}$ by

$$\hat{x}_t^t = x_t^t + z_t^t \textit{ and } \hat{x}_t^{t+1} = x_t^{t+1} + z_t^{t+1}.$$

Given the linear utility specification, since

$$z_t^t + z_t^{t+1} = -\epsilon \sum_{j=1}^{t-1} r^j + \epsilon \sum_{j=1}^{t} r^j = r^t > 0,$$

it follows that the hat allocation Pareto dominates the initial allocation. To show that the hat allocation is feasible, we note that

$$\hat{x}_t^t + \hat{x}_{t-1}^t = x_t^t + x_{t-1}^t - \epsilon \sum_{j=1}^{t-1} r^j + \epsilon \sum_{j=1}^{t-1} r^j = x_t^t + x_{t-1}^t.$$

So, since the initial allocation was feasible, the new allocation is also feasible. The last thing we need to do is make sure that we never have to violate the total resource constraint in making the transfers, that is, that $\left|z_t^t\right| \leq 1$ (the endowment of each young agent.) Given r, this can be shown to require that $\epsilon < \frac{1}{r} - 1$. The reader will, of course, recognize this as a standard Ponzi scheme. Shell later shows (in the 1980s), in a series of papers written with Yves Balasko, that a lower bound on the curvature of indifference hypersurfaces through an allocation will rule out these kinds of transfer schemes and guarantee that the allocation is Pareto optimal. Since it is the curvature of indifference surfaces that determines an agent's time preference, this example reintroduces Fisher's ideas about the role of impatience in the determination of interest rates.

From this initial example of competitive inefficiency, Shell then makes a series of observations. First, and perhaps most importantly, he notes that the aggregate value of the competitive allocation when the interest rate is zero is infinite, which immediately implies that the competitive equilibrium prices are not in the dual space to the commodity space, which is l_∞, in contrast to the results in Debreu's 1954 paper showing that with finitely many infinite-lived agents who discount the future appropriately, dual support prices always exist and, via the supporting hyperplane theorems, the corresponding allocations are Pareto optimal. While

Shell doesn't say this in the paper, the infinite valuation of the competitive equilibrium also makes it impossible to apply the standard general equilibrium argument for proving the first welfare theorem.

In the next section of the paper (Sec. 2.7), Shell then views the economy in the same way that Cass and Yaari did, from the general equilibrium perspective of a collection of infinite-lived individuals who only value consumption over two periods. Unlike Cass–Yaari, though, Shell views the inefficiency result as a matter of there being infinitely many agents, setting up a scenario akin to the so-called Hilbert hotel,[2] in which a hotel with infinitely many beds can always accommodate a new guest by having every existing guest move down one bed. In the economic case, Shell substitutes chocolates for beds, but the same idea is at work. This is also the reason that, in a finite truncation of the economy, the chain of improving transfers breaks down, and the original competitive allocation is then Pareto optimal.[3] Finally, Shell's observation on the infinite valuation of the zero-interest rate allocation is also relevant here, since truncation of the economy at a finite time renders the valuations finite, making the usual general equilibrium argument for the first welfare theorem operative. Both of these observations are formally codified in the Balasko-Shell papers.

To complete the discussion of Shell's implicit take on Cass–Yaari, he states, in discussing the potential fragility of Samuelson's social contrivance of money that the repudiation of intergenerational promises is not without empirical precedents:

> In the actual dynamic world, "monetary reform" merely leads to frustration of the $(k-1)$th generation's expectations. The most notable instance of such frustration is when the peasants' sons leave home for the city and fail to provide adequately for their parents' old-age. (Shell, 1971, p. 1007)

In Cass–Yaari, an analogous situation would arise from either their inefficient storage equilibrium or the efficient monetary equilibrium the first time a young agent invented a productive technology and offered to sell ownership shares in the new technology to his peers.

We also note that Shell's double infinity interpretation is not inconsistent with the Cass–Yaari reasoning that restricted participation is the source of the Samuelsonian inefficiency, since Cass–Yaari maintain the possibility of ongoing resource shifts by (in math terms) adding a point at infinity, which makes the time structure circular.

Shell concludes his paper by reconsidering the growth model's infinite-lived agent approach in the one-sector model and showing that a competitive inefficiency can arise there if agents don't discount the future. He shows this by converting the standard model into one equivalent to what Ramsey studied, with the long-run satiation point given by the golden rule steady-state equilibrium. He then notes that with competitive agents holding stocks of capital sufficient to maintain the golden rule allocation, the zero-interest rate at the golden rule equilibrium will lead these agents to liquidate all of their capital to increase consumption, leading to a deviation away from the optimal golden rule steady state.

2.6 STARRETT AND GALE

Working at roughly the same time that Shell was, Starrett (1972) clarified several issues relating to the interaction of production and distribution in OLG models and refined the notion of efficiency in the model.

Starrett sets up a general OLG model with population growth, but one of the first important things he establishes is that one need not limit the notion of growth to simply that of population. If there is exogenous growth in total factor productivity (as well as in population), then this will have the same effect in terms of distribution possibilities as simple population growth.

The second key observation that Starrett makes is that of distinguishing between models in which time is bi-infinite (running from $-\infty$ to $+\infty$) and those in which there is a beginning at $t = 1$, with an initial "generation" of agents consisting of everyone born prior to the first period. The beginning in such a model can be considered either an artificial truncation of the bi-infinite timeline serving the purpose of the analyst or as an actual beginning in terms of a new policy action or shock process impinging on the economy. Under either interpretation, Starrett shows that for the purposes of defining optimality, the two models are different.

For the bi-infinite model, the Samuelsonian or golden rule equilibrium is always optimal, since, as Starrett puts it

> [T]he type of transfers we have been discussing require that everyone participate, and this means everyone in the indefinite past as well as the indefinite future. If the economy starts planning at some base period (so that the indefinite past is irrelevant), these transfers are not the relevant ones. (Starrett, 1972, p. 281)

Starrett then notes that if the economy has a beginning, the pre-existing old generation will never willingly engage in intergenerational trades for the simple reason that they can never be compensated for doing so. Again, quoting Starrett

> Thus, in a model with beginning, there is a cost to consuming early; it is the cost of disenfranchising those alive at the beginning. Interest rates above the growth rate may be efficient after all, since they induce people to postpone consumption and hence help out the [initial] generations. (Starrett, 1972, p. 282)

This observation is then the basis for a key result extending the Diamond, Cass–Yaari, and Shell observations on efficiency showing that competitive equilibria in which interest rates exceed the economy's growth rate are efficient, while those with interest rates below the growth rate are inefficient.

The last paper we discuss in this chapter is Gale (1973). Gale was not part of the new crop of economists coming out of graduate school in the 1960s with their interest piqued by Samuelson's new model. Rather, he was part of the old guard (having earned his Princeton doctorate in 1949), but as a mathematician with interests in economic dynamics, his interest in the OLG model was natural. We include his paper because of the overlap of its findings with those of Starrett. The coincidence of the two papers is also an example of the universal phenomenon of ideas that are "in the air" leading to near-simultaneous publication, but where the senior author gets more recognition for the work than does the junior author. In this particular case, Google Scholar shows 67 citations of Starrett's paper (despite its publication in the top-tier *Journal of Political Economy*), while Gale's *JET* paper gets 690 cites.

Gale's approach to the OLG model was similar to Starrett's in that he first set up a general model that encompassed both the two- and three-period models considered by Samuelson and the later writers, though, like the others, Gale restricts his attention to the two-period setting for the explication of his results.

Gale identifies two distinct steady states for the general model, which he labels "balanced" and "golden rule" with corresponding equilibria which he calls (respectively) "classical" and "Samuelsonian." Gale's use of the term "balanced" refers to the accounting sense of a balance of payments, rather than the notion of a balanced growth path. He characterizes the classical case of a balanced steady-state equilibrium as one in which aggregate social savings (and hence debt) is zero. The Samuelsonian case has as its equilibrium the golden rule steady state.

Like Starrett, Gale defines optimality in terms of whether the transition from intergenerational autarky to the golden rule steady state is Pareto improving. In the context of the two-period model with only a single good, the autarky equilibrium is simply one of no trade. Gale's theorem 1 then states that a steady state must either be the golden rule or autarky, a result he characterizes as "amount[ing] to little more than a bookkeeping identity." This identity had already been derived by Samuelson in mathematical form, which we expressed earlier as the identify $(1-R)m=0$, with (again) R being the gross rate of interest, and m the valued quantity of money held by agents in the economy.

The next part of Gale's paper considers the stability properties of non-steady-state equilibria, notably using the kind of offer curve analysis that contemporary explications of the model rely on. Gale shows in this analysis that in the forward dynamics of the model, the optimal equilibria are always unstable. Specifically, he shows that in the classical case (no-trade, positive interest rates), any increase in saving will ultimately lead to an infeasible outcome, while any increase in debt will lead to movement away from autarky toward the golden rule steady state (though this must happen at the expense of the initial old generation). Since we cannot draw the graphic analysis of this situation any better than Gale did, we reproduce his diagrams in Figs. 6 and 7.

The first diagram represents the classical case, where endowments of the old are larger than those of the young. The curve labeled *PQ* is the offer curve, and, as the diagram indicates, the intersection of the offer curve with the downward sloping 45-degree line – which indicates the resource constraint that what one generation gives up, the other receives – at the point *e* is the optimal autarky equilibrium. The non-stationary equilibrium trajectories are indicated by the zigzagging lines between the offer curve and the resource constraint. One interesting thing to note from Gale's diagram (which he fleshed out later in the paper with an example, p. 27) is the possibility that the equilibrium dynamics could cycle. This anticipates later work by, among others, Jean Michel Grandmont a decade later, though Gale considers it simply "an amusing example of a 'business cycle'."

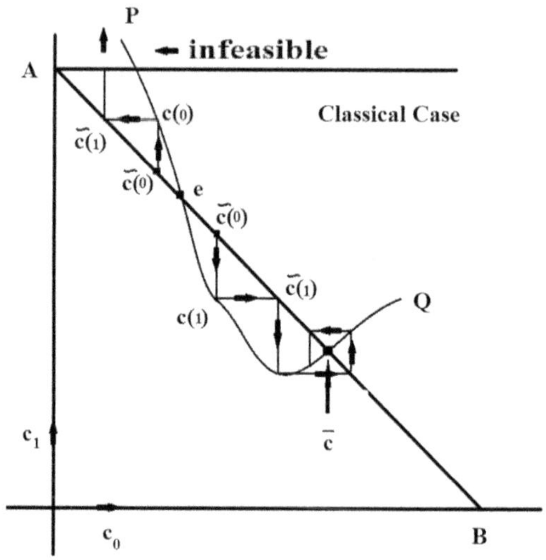

Fig. 6. Gale's Offer Curve Analysis of Classical Case.
Source: Adapted from Gale (1973).

The next diagram illustrates the Samuelsonian case, where the endowments of the young exceed those of the old.

In this diagram, *e* is the endowment point, and $\bar{c}$ is the equilibrium (optimal) consumption point. The curve again represents the representative agent's offer curve, and the zigzag lines between the offer curve and the 45-degree line indicate the dynamics of the model starting from a small perturbation away from the equilibrium point on the right.

We note that Gale's focus on stability was similar to that of Meckling in his critique of Samuelson's analysis. Gale interprets these stability results in the paper, saying

> I will conclude this discussion on a somewhat speculative note. The ultimate purpose of economic theory is presumably to explain economic phenomena. What, if anything, can be said about the present exercise in this connection? Again I would go back to the result [in the classical case]. Certainly, rapidly growing economies are objects of actual experience. Our findings suggest that the impetus to growth is given by starting conditions in which the [aggregate saving or debt] is negative. If [aggregate saving or debt] was initially zero it would take some kind of interference with the competitive mechanism to get things going (we discuss how this might be done in a later section) but the point is that such intervention would in our simplified world only be required once. Thereafter the invisible hand of prices could be allowed to take control and the economy would grow toward the golden rule optimum. It seems to me not inconceivable that things of this sort may be going on.
>
> In the same spirit, what can be said about the perversely nonoptimal behavior in the Samuelson case? Here I expect we will look in vain for real-life examples. While the Samuelson world is perfectly conceivable from a logical point of view it is probably not the one we live in – exactly because of the empirical facts adduced by Fisher relating to impatience and investment opportunities. (Gale, 1973, pp.17–18)

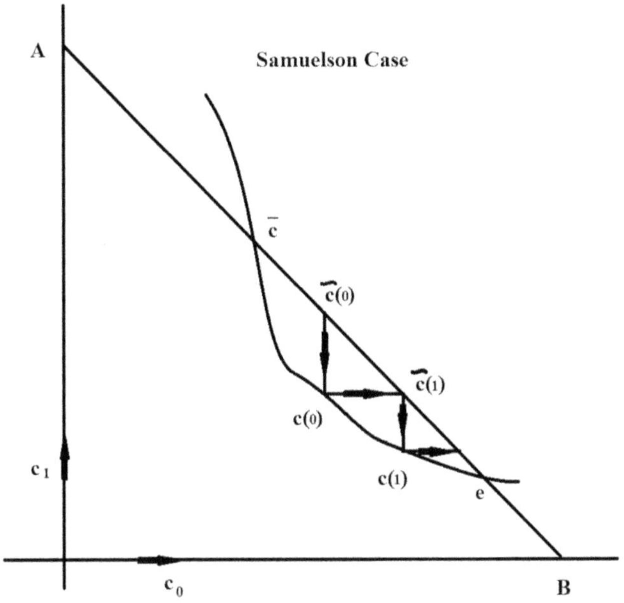

Fig. 7. Gale's Offer Curve Analysis for Samuelsonian Case.
Source: Adapted from Gale (1973).

In the later section, Gale discusses how a transition from the competitive outcomes to the golden rule might come about, noting that in the classical case, a small altruistic transfer from the initial old to the young would then start the market moving down toward the golden rule, as in Fig. 6.

For the Samuelsonian case, Gale introduces an intermediary (a la Cass–Yaari) which he calls a clearinghouse and suggests that the clearinghouse can issue some small initial credit to the existing old generation at the time (which he likens to Samuelson's social contrivance of money), allowing them to increase their second-period consumption by transferring the credit to the contemporaneous young agents. But Gale then notes that unless the clearinghouse can somehow coordinate the initial transfer to implement the golden rule equilibrium immediately, competition will drive the economy back to the inefficient autarky.

The odd thing about this discussion is its apparent unawareness of the determinacy issue initially raised by Samuelson in his response to Meckling, and particularly the possibility that rational forward-looking agents would find a way to make the jump to the appropriate equilibrium despite the simple forward-looking dynamics. What makes this even odder is that Gale was perfectly aware of dynamic models of growth where the steady-state equilibrium of the model is only saddle-path stable (see, e.g., Brock & Gale, 1969)

One additional aspect of Gale's paper merits attention. In the introduction, Gale states that

> Samuelson's paper may be thought of as analyzing two special examples of the Fisher model using the population point of view. Regarded in this way, however, it presents one striking and perhaps curious feature. As Samuelson himself observes, his examples have characteristics exactly opposite to those considered to be typical by Fisher and Bohm-Bawerk. Instead of impatient people whose income is delayed, he considers people who receive income in the early periods of their lives but none at the end. This leads him to situations involving negative rather than positive interest rates. Thus, in introducing his new approach to the interest rate problem Samuelson has at the same time chosen to analyze an economic world which is in a sense the reverse of that of the classical writers. (Gale, 1973, p. 14)

This statement would seem on its face to deny the reality of what Samuelson was trying to capture – that (at least in the modern world) people have to save for retirement. Samuelson was explicit about this in setting up the three-period model initially, where he notes that it is best able to capture the hump-shaped distribution of income by age. Much of the rest of Gale's paper then takes the two-period version of the model perhaps more seriously than it ought to as a way of explaining the empirical fact of positive interest rates by assuming that older people always have more money.

In this sense, the distinction between classical and Samuelsonian cases looks like an example of the old parable of the blind men and the elephant. Nevertheless, the distinction persists in the literature for the simple reason that even in general, multiperiod exchange models, the golden rule steady state can coexist with a classical steady state in which interest rates are greater than the population growth rate. But, as Diamond and Starrett showed, once we introduce production, interest rates will always be positive (as long as capital is productive), but competitive equilibrium may still be inefficient in a Samuelsonian sense, or efficient but not at the golden rule allocation.

The papers of Gale and Starrett, taken together, along with Samuelson's sections on the two-period model seemed to have had the effect of cementing the idea that two-period OLG models were somehow sufficient for general analytic purposes. While this would later be shown to be true by Balasko, Cass, and Shell (1980), the habit of working in the simplest possible framework seems to have started here.

What is interesting to recall here is that Gale's 1973 approach had appeared in an earlier University of California Berkeley Industrial Engineering and Operations Research Department Working Paper entitled "Price Equilibrium for Infinite Horizon Economic Models" (Gale, 1969). The research was supported by the Office of Naval Research and done while Gale held a Senior Postdoctoral Fellowship from the National Science Foundation at the University of Copenhagen, Denmark. According to Gale's abstract:

> The paper analyzes one-sector models of general equilibrium over an infinite time horizon in which there are an infinite number of agents, these being the members of successive generations. It is argued that such models are more realistic than the customary equilibrium models with finitely many agents. Three aspects of these models are then examined including: (1) non-optimalities in the form of productive inefficiency (as noted by Samuelson and others) and consumption non-optimality due to "inflationary" equilibria, (2) the role of "credit" and its effect on the equilibrium is discussed and (3) it is shown that for simple exchange models steady state equilibria are possible with a permanent imbalance of trade in which one country constantly exports to the other, a phenomenon which cannot occur in the classical model.

As we will see in the last chapter of the book when we examine the contemporary debate over the viability of the New Keynesian DSGE model, the issues Gale identifies here are precisely the ones that critics of contemporary macroeconomics feel should be addressed.

NOTES

1. In private communication with us, Yaari recollects that they ended up considering this version of the model after being asked about the possibility by Herb Scarf at a Cowles Foundation seminar presentation of the paper.
2. Shell attributes the example to George Gamov from his book *One, Two, Three … Infinity: Facts and Speculations of Science*. Gamov apparently neglected to cite Hilbert.
3. The same reasoning is at work in counter examples to the Brouwer fixed point theorem's applicability in infinite dimensional spaces; the ability to always shift over a dimension leads to a breakdown in the usual notions of compactness required by the Brouwer theorem.

CHAPTER 3

EXPECTATIONS AND THE NEUTRALITY OF MONEY C. 1972: FROM OLG TO STOCHASTIC OLG

While a purely logical approach to our topic would dictate looking next at the development of OLG models as models of money, the fact that history doesn't always proceed in neat logical steps dictates that we first deal with two important breaks in the logical flow. One, which will come in the following section, harkens back to the growth model and examines how the growth model's central planner became a dynastic family. The other, which we deal with here, is Robert Lucas' leapfrogging of the profession with his Nobel prize winning 1972 paper (Lucas, 1972).

When we say Lucas leapfrogged the profession, we mean that while OLG theorists such as Barro, Grandmont and Laroque and Shell, Starrett, and Wallace were working to address the criticisms raised by Lerner, Meckling, and others of OLG as a model of money, Lucas simply accepted that (in the words of his Nobel prize lecture, Lucas, 1996):

> [Samuelson's model] introduced a deceptively simple example of an economy in which money with no direct use in either consumption or production nonetheless plays an essential role in economic life. (p. 672)

He used the OLG framework to study the empirical puzzle in the relationship between money, prices, and real economic activity. The puzzle, which Lucas first encountered in David Hume's 1752 essays *Of Money and Interest*, stems from the fact that in the long run, money and prices are perfectly correlated, as one would be led to conclude from a simple reading of the quantity equation

$$MV = PY,$$

holding velocity V and real output Y constant at their long-run (detrended) average values. Lucas illustrates this with a graph taken from McCandless and Weber (1995), which we reproduce as shown in Fig. 8.

Overlapping Generations: Methods, Models and Morphology
International Symposia in Economic Theory and Econometrics, Volume 32, 43–51

Published under exclusive licence by Emerald Publishing Limited
ISSN: 1571-0386/doi:10.1108/S1571-038620230000032008

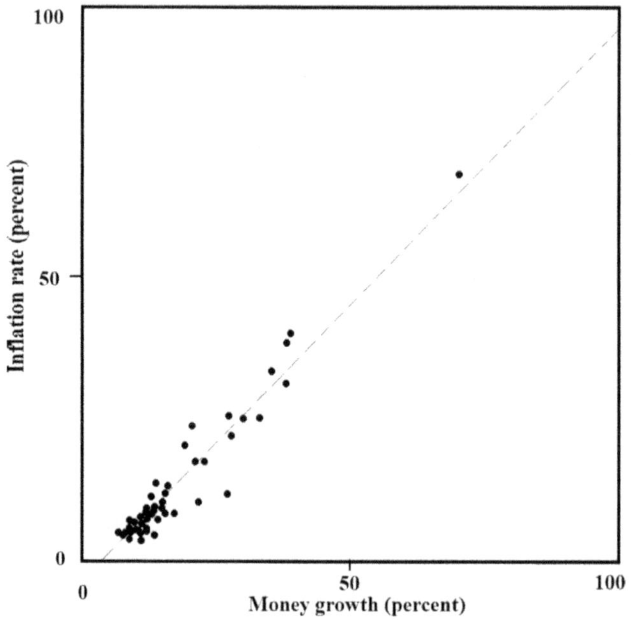

Fig. 8. Long-run Neutrality of Money.

This perfect correlation is generally characterized by saying that money is neutral: a 10% increase in the supply of money leads to a 10% increase in prices. From consumers' budget constraints or firms' profit functions, it is then easy to see that this implies that money will have no real long-run effects.

The monetary policy puzzle is that over short periods of time, changes in the money supply do have real effects. Lucas illustrates this with a series of graphs showing scatterplots of the unemployment and inflation rates for the United States over a number of different, relatively short periods of time. This data is taken from Stockman (1996). We reproduce these below as shown in Fig. 9.

The inverse relationship between these two measures seen in all of the graphs except the 1950–1959 one (and the last one, which covers the long-run period from 1950 to 1994) is known as the Phillips curve (after William Phillips, who first noted the statistical regularity). It was this short-run relationship, together with the fact that there is no long-run relationship that Lucas sought to explain theoretically using Samuelson's model.

In tackling this problem, Lucas made history. His training in macroeconomics, together with his rejection of the existing Keynesian approach of modeling aggregates directly, led him to think about how individual firms in the economy dealt with co-incident changes in both money and demand. This disaggregated approach was typical of the thinking of people Lucas was working with at the time at Carnegie Mellon University's Graduate School of Industrial Administration (GSIA). These people included Dave Cass, Marty Geisel, Leonard Rapping, and

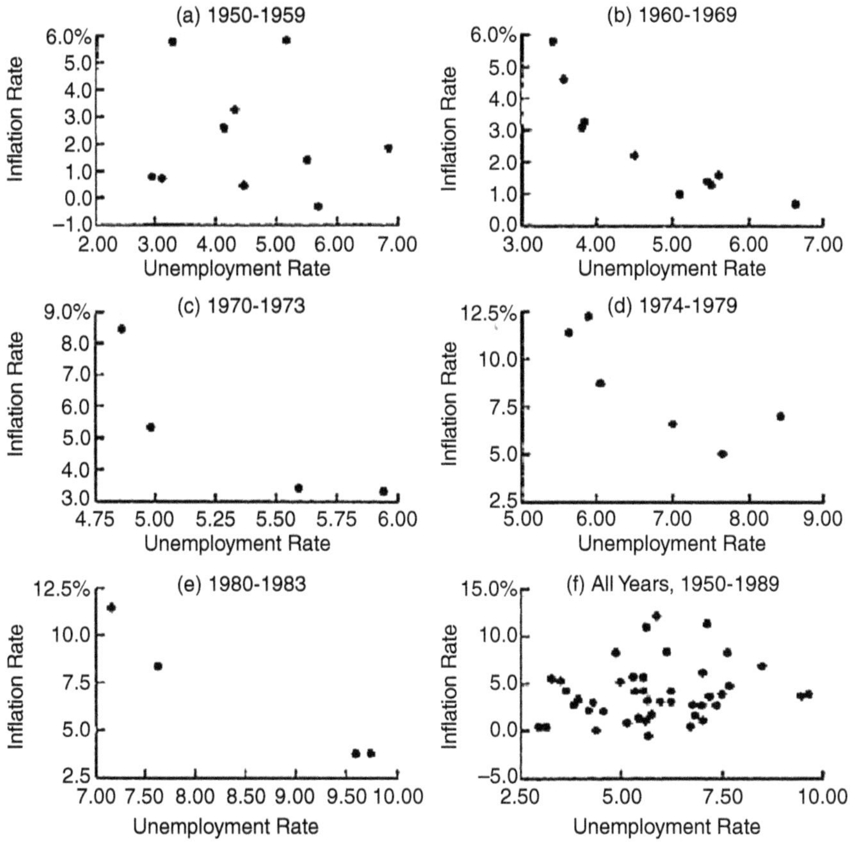

Fig. 9. Short-run Non-neutrality of Money.

Thomas Sargent (per Lucas' *Professional Memoir*, Lucas, 2001), all of whom approached macroeconomics as a general equilibrium phenomenon in which equilibrium is determined by the collective actions of forward-looking, optimizing agents who cannot be treated as if they were molecules in a balloon.

Lucas's early foray into understanding the Phillips curve relationship involved work with Rapping, in which they tried to explain the Phillips curve relationship in terms of agents' money illusion and adaptive expectations (see Lucas & Rapping, 1969). Lucas discusses this paper and its reception by the profession in detail in his memoir, concluding with the following:

> Before our paper was finished, Milton Friedman had used his Presidential Address to the American Economic Association to argue that in the long run, the unemployment rate would be independent of the inflation rate: There would be no Phillips-like trade-off between inflation and unemployment. Friedman's argument was theoretical, but his premises all seemed to Leonard and me to hold for our model. Yet our model did imply a long-run trade-off. Later, we came to see that this difference was due to our use of adaptive, rather than rational, expectations, but at the time we simply accepted it as an unresolved puzzle. (*Memoir*, p. 18)

The problem of adaptive expectations, of course, was that it generated a standing inconsistency between what agents in the economy were forecasting and what was actually happening. Earlier in his memoir, Lucas commented on this:

> Dick Schramm's GSIA thesis showed how to make a multiple capital good model operational econometrically. His model involved a lagged adjustment of price expectations to movements in actual prices. I remember a seminar presentation of Schramm's at which Jack Muth asked Dick why he had not assumed rational expectations. Of course, we all knew and admired Jack's paper "Rational Expectations and the Theory of Price Movements," but none of us knew how to exploit this idea econometrically. At that time, I thought of rational expectations as an elegant rationalization of the kind of lagged adjustment of expectations that Schramm assumed in his thesis, not as an alternate model. This was a half-truth that kept me from seeing the force of Jack's objections. (*Memoir*, p. 12)

In his Nobel lecture, Lucas elaborates on the consistency issue:

> As intertemporal elements and expectations came to play an increasingly explicit and important role, this modeling inconsistency became more and more glaring. John Muth's (1961) "Rational Expectations and the Theory of Price Movements" focused on this inconsistency and showed how it could be removed by taking into account the influences of prices, including future prices, on quantities and simultaneously the effects of quantities on equilibrium prices. The principle of rational expectations he proposed thus forces the modeler toward a market equilibrium point of view, although it took some time before a style of thinking that recognized this fact had a major effect on macroeconomic modeling. (*Nobel Lecture*, p. 671)

It was Lucas himself who forced the profession to confront the inconsistencies of the *ad hoc* modeling of expectation formation, and he did so by pulling together the tools of stochastic general equilibrium theory he'd been using in the early work with Rapping, Samuelson's model of overlapping generations, and a set of newly learned results from functional analysis in the 1972 *JET* paper. We note that Lucas' choice of Samuelson's model was a natural one not only because it admitted a role for money, but also because at the time Lucas was working, his choice of dynamic models would have been the RCK model or the OLG model. The RCK model back then, as we've argued, was viewed as a planning model. Lucas was interested in examining how actual firms would respond to changes in the money supply or real demand in an environment where price signals confounded the two effects. This interest itself dictated that he use a model populated by actual agents, rather than one in which individual actions were all squeezed into a planner's social welfare function. As we will see in the next chapter, Robert Barro's reinterpretation of the RBC framework as one of a finite number of dynastic families would end up nudging OLG aside as the model with the most realistic treatment of firms and families.

The model in the '72 *JET* paper is a two-period, stochastic overlapping generations model in which there are two sources of uncertainty. One source is the government's changes in the money supply, which Lucas models as a stochastic shock to the quantity of money. The other is a real, stochastic change in demand. The underlying idea behind this approach to explaining the short-run Phillips curve relation is that of *signal extraction*.

In the model, firms observe only the current price for their output, and this price can be affected by both the monetary and real shocks. Firms want to respond to the real shock, but not to the monetary shock. Under the assumption that firms form their expectations rationally, an individual firm's forecast of future prices will be the same as the economy's pricing function, which maps the stochastic state of the world (i.e., the monetary and real shocks combined) into a market-clearing equilibrium price. In Lucas' model, this mapping is monotone, so that firms, by observing the equilibrium price, can infer the underlying stochastic state of the world. This implies, for example, that if only one shock were operative, firms would know the state of demand or the money supply and make the optimal adjustment. In particular, if only the monetary shock is operative, firms will know this and take no action since nothing real has changed. In the opposite direction, if only the real shock is operative, firms will also infer the direction of change in demand from the price movements, and again respond optimally.

When both shocks are active simultaneously, firms must try to use their observation of price changes to extract the signal – real changes in demand – from the noise – changes in the money supply. Lucas shows in his model how the rational expectations assumption operationalizes this process and demonstrates that over the short-run, firms will make real adjustments after observed increases or decreases in the rate of inflation, but that over the long run, the persistence of the money supply shocks relative to the real shocks means that real output fluctuates around a long-run average, independent of the rate of inflation.

We turn next to the technical accomplishments of Lucas' paper, which had a more profound effect on macroeconomics than did Lucas' actual explanation of the Phillips curve puzzle.

To develop these ideas, we first present a simplified version of Lucas' model. We simplify the model by focusing on the pure exchange, and by imposing the simplest possible stochastic structure on the model: the endowments of the young fluctuate randomly with realizations being determined by the flip of a coin. Other than this, the model is the same. Agents live two periods, trade a single good, are risk-averse, and use fiat money to transfer wealth between youth and old age. As in Lucas' model, we assume that agents are in a Samuelsonian economy so that their endowment when young (in either state of nature) exceeds their endowment when old.

Following Lucas, we focus on the stochastic equivalent of a steady-state equilibrium. In this version of the model, the simplest such equivalent has the prices depending only on the exogenous endowment realizations, so we can write the prices as $p_t \in \left\{p^H, p^T\right\}$ (i.e., without any other time dependence). The rational expectations assumption in this case is captured by the assumption that agents know, conditional on the state of nature, that these prices will be the equilibrium prices.

With this specification, then, we can also write the lifetime allocation of the agent as $\left(x_1^s, x_2^{ss'}\right)$, with $(s,s') \in \{H,T\} \times \{H,T\} = \{H,T\}^2$. Note that in the OLG framework, young agents are born into a realized state of nature, so that the only uncertainty a typical young agent faces is generated by the stochastic fluctuations in the next period's price. The dependence of the second-period consumption on the first-period's state realization is through the fact that money holdings are determined in the first period of life and can, in principle, depend on that period's state realization. With this simplification, we can write a typical young agent's intertemporal optimization problem as

$$\max \pi^H\ u\left(x_1^s, x_2^{sH}\right) + \pi^L u\left(x_1^s, x_2^{sL}\right)$$

subject to

$$p^s\left(x_1^s - \omega_1^s\right) + m^s = 0$$
$$p^{s'}\left(x_2^{ss'} - \omega_2\right) - m^s = 0,$$

for all $(s,s') \in \{H,T\}^2$. We note that by adding the two budget constraints, we can convert the optimization problem into one with a single budget constraint. We write the constraints this way to emphasize the role that money plays in transferring wealth between periods.

Under standard assumptions on the utility function, the demand functions generated from this optimization will be differentiable everywhere. From the assumption that the economy is Samuelsonian, we know there will be a monetary equilibrium for the model.

To show the existence of an equilibrium for this model, write the excess demand functions of each agent as

$$z_1^s\left[p^H, p^T, \omega_1^s\right] = x_1^s\left[p^H, p^T, \omega_1^s\right] - \omega_1^s$$
$$z_2^{ss'}\left[p^H, p^T, \omega_1^s\right] = x_2^{ss'}\left[p^H, p^T, \omega_1^s\right] - \omega_2$$

for $(s,s') \in \{H,T\}^2$. The equilibrium conditions for the model are then given by

$$z_1^s\left[p^H, p^T, \omega_1^s\right] + z_2^{s's}\left[p^H, p^T, \omega_1^s\right] = 0$$

for $(s,s') \in \{H,T\}^2$.

Strictly speaking, this is a system of four equations in two unknowns. However, because of Walras' law, not all of the equations are independent. Note first that from the budget constraints, we have

$$p^s\left(z_1^s + z_2^{ss}\right) = 0,$$

which implies that $z_1^s + z_2^{ss} = 0$ as long as $p^s > 0$. This reduces the market-clearing conditions to

$$Z^H = z_1^H + z_2^{TH} = 0$$
$$Z^T = z_1^T + z_2^{HT} = 0.$$

We now show the following: $Z^H = 0 \Leftrightarrow Z^T = 0$. To prove this, note that

$$p^H Z^H + p^T Z^T = p^H z_1^H + p^H z_2^{TH} + P^T z_1^T + p^T z_2^{HT}$$
$$= \left(p^H z_1^H + p^T z_2^{HT}\right) + \left(P^T z_1^T + p^H z_2^{TH}\right) = 0,$$

since each of the expressions in parentheses is a budget constraint. The result then follows.

So, we are now left with a single equation in two variables. The two variables are not independent, however, since it is clear from the cross-state budget constraints that scaling both state prices by the same amount leaves the budget constraint unchanged. Hence, we normalize relative prices as $\rho = \frac{p^H}{p^T}.$ To complete the existence proof, we have the following:

Proposition: Z^H is an odd function (i.e., as $\rho \to 0$, $Z^H > 0$ and as $\rho \to \infty$, $Z^H < 0$).

Proof: Write the cross-state budget constraints as

$$\rho z_1^H + z_2^{HT} = 0$$
$$\frac{1}{\rho} z_1^T + z_2^{TH} = 0.$$

As $\rho \to 0$ non-satiation and the fact that endowments are positive imply that $z_1^H \to \infty$. Since $z_2^{ss'}$ is bounded below by $-\omega_2$, it follows that $Z^H = z_1^H + z_2^{TH} \to \infty$. Next, as $\rho \to \infty$, $z_1^T \to \infty$ by the same argument. From the second budget constraint above, then, for large ρ, $\frac{1}{\rho} z_1^T > 0$, so that $z_2^{HT} < 0$. From the first budget constraint, we can write

$$z_1^H + \frac{1}{\rho} z_2^{HT} = 0.$$

Again, by desirability, as $\rho \to \infty$, $z_2^{HT} \to \infty$ and for large ρ we have $z_2^{TH} > 0$ and hence $z_1^H < 0$. Combining the results, we have for large ρ that $Z^H < 0$. By continuity then, there must exist a $\hat{\rho}$ for which $Z^H = 0$, and hence, an equilibrium exists.

For general stochastic structures, this kind of argument generally isn't available. What makes the example here transparent is the fact that the finitely supported stochastic structure generates a model in which the endogenous prices are finite-dimensional vectors, and the resulting model can be solved using standard finite-dimensional techniques.

In models with continuous stochastic structures, such as Lucas', we can view the prices as infinite-dimensional vectors (or equivalently, as functions), but the problem of solving for the zeroes of the aggregate excess demand functions (of which we now have infinitely many) becomes (infinitely?) more complicated. In fact, since it is well-known that finding the zeros for systems of mappings is equivalent to solving a fixed-point problem, we can illustrate the complications that arise in general models via this kind of analysis.

So, suppose we have a continuous random state variable σ – for example, we can let the first-period endowment have a continuous rather than Bernoulli distribution. In order to solve their consumption optimization problems, young agents will need to forecast how they think the equilibrium price is going to depend on the stochastic state variable. Suppose the young agent in period t believes that $p_{t+1} = f_0(\sigma_{t+1})$.

If we take this forecast as fixed and solve for the market-clearing price given the forecast, we obtain what is known as the *temporary equilibrium*[1] price function $p_t = f_1(\sigma_t)$. Now, in general, the forecast and temporary equilibrium price functions will be different. At the rational expectations equilibrium, however, we will have $f_1(\sigma) = f_0(\sigma)$, which is to say the rational expectations equilibrium price function will be a fixed point of the mapping from forecasts to temporary equilibrium price functions. Lucas himself notes this in his memoir:

> Calculating a perfect foresight equilibrium for an industry, say, sounds as though it should involve solving a fixed point problem in a space of price paths: the actual path implies a forecast path, which in turn implies an actual path. (Memoir, 2001, p. 13)

Lucas solved this problem in the '72 paper via an application of the Banach contraction mapping theorem. While graduate students today learn this result in the context of forward dynamic programming applications in both micro and macro, at the time Lucas used the result, it was not well-known and would have been encountered only by practitioners working with the then-new tools of dynamic programming. Lucas discusses his introduction to these tools in his memoir:

> In my first years at GSIA I worked furiously to pick up the mathematics of optimization over time – calculus of variations, the maximum principle of Pontryagin, Bellman's dynamic programming – and of the differential equations systems these optimization problems produced. I worked on applications of these methods to problems in economics and operations research. Theoretically-minded economists of my cohort were doing the same thing all over in the world. I was studying the dynamics of investment at the firm and industry level, as were many others. Still others were studying optimal growth of an economy, optimal accumulation of human capital, optimal advertising and R and D investment, and so on. (Memoir, 2001, p. 14)

Lucas goes on to say that it was Ed Prescott who first introduced him to dynamic programming. When we asked Lucas where he first encountered the contraction mapping theorem, he replied:

> I was going over the CMU library copy of Bellman's book *Dynamic Programming*, and someone had written in pencil 'he means this is a contraction' at just the right place. I followed up this tip. I'm not sure Banach was mentioned there but somehow I got to Banach's book in French. I got a French Canadian student to help me to translate – which was easy because it was mostly math symbols! Later on Prescott told me about David Blackwell's great paper. (Lucas, personal communication, September 11, 2014)

In follow-up communication, Lucas added:

> My paper appeared in print in 1972 but was written in the late 60s. If had given the reference (as I should have!) that would send you to the right place, but I don't think I did. Anyway, this application was not to a Bellman equation, though the idea of a contraction is certainly there. This [forward dynamic programming] is all later than my early work with Prescott, who had introduced me to Blackwell's work.
>
> In terms of my education, the connection of this use of Banach is distinct, I think, from the "contraction" someone wrote in Bellman's book.
>
> The student would probably have been Marcel Boyer, who is now emeritus at Montreal. Marcel wrote an outstanding thesis that used the idea of a Banach space in a central way. Another possibility is Leon Courville, who went on to a successful career in banking. (Lucas, personal communication, September 11, 2014)

In addition to opening up a new research trajectory for him, Lucas' introduction to Bellman's and Blackwell's work also led to a new approach to teaching graduate macroeconomics. In the early 1980s, Lucas' lecture notes on dynamic programming had been typed up by someone unknown to us. These notes were later expanded on and published by Stokey and Lucas (1989), which is now one of the most widely used texts in graduate economics education.

We will return to discuss this book in more detail later, but we note here that the only material in the book on overlapping generations models is in Sec. 17.1 which essentially reproduces Lucas (1972).

NOTE

1. Temporary equilibrium models were introduced in the late 1970s by Jean Michel Grandmont. We examine his work in this area – which was based primarily on overlapping generations models – later in the book.

CHAPTER 4

INFINITE-LIVED AGENTS: DYNASTY, 1970–1980

As we indicated at the beginning of the previous chapter, we need to make a second digression in our story to examine how the other main workhorse model in dynamic economics – that of the infinite-lived representative agent – came to be understood as a model of finitely-many dynastic families. This interpretation is in marked contrast to the structure of the OLG model, which consists of infinitely-many unconnected individual families.

As we noted in Chapter 1, the original interpretation of the optimizing agent in the early development of the neoclassical growth model was that of a central planner. The planner's objective function could be simply aggregate consumption, an undiscounted social welfare defined over aggregate consumption, or a discounted social welfare function. The infinite "life" of the central planner was an approximation of the fact that planning institutions, or more generally, governments, typically outlive the individual people who populate the society over which the government reigns. Treating the government or planner as being infinitely lived (particularly when the objective function is discounted) is then simply a mathematical shortcut rather than any kind of profound statement about the organization of society.

This interpretation was not universal, as we noted above. Debreu's 1954 extension of the finite-dimensional Arrow–Debreu–McKenzie model to allow for infinite-dimensional commodity spaces simply assumes that there are finitely-many consumers whose preferences are defined over the commodity space. At this level of abstraction, there was no reason for Debreu to ponder the nature of his consumer household, so there was no corresponding discussion of planners versus families. Debreu's result, however, has been widely used in applications of the growth model, since it implies that one can always find a competitive equilibrium by solving for a Pareto optimum, that is, by solving the central planner's problem.

Overlapping Generations: Methods, Models and Morphology
International Symposia in Economic Theory and Econometrics, Volume 32, 53–59

Published under exclusive licence by Emerald Publishing Limited
ISSN: 1571-0386/doi:10.1108/S1571-038620230000032010

Cass (1965) foreshadowed the reinterpretation of the planner as a dynastic family by showing how to fully solve the growth model with the planner's objective function being the discounted utility of consumption. Cass himself never interpreted the growth model in anything but normative terms. While we don't have direct evidence of this in Cass' writing, his long-time friend and co-author Karl Shell shared his remembrance of Cass' view in an email:

> [Dave] was irritated by the application of "Ramsey-Cass-Koopmans" to non-planning problems. Dave and I agreed (possibly with somewhat different emphases) that optimal control problem is a central planning problem. (Shell, personal communication, August 21, 2021)

When the RCK model was translated into discrete time and solved using dynamic programming techniques, the interpretation of the objective function as belonging to a long-lived private-sector entity became natural.

The first explicit interpretation of the infinite-lived agent as a family appears in Arrow and Kurz (1969). Their analysis focuses explicitly on the optimization problem faced by a dynastic family which they define as consisting of a parent household that is concerned with "the welfare of all its present and future members" (p. 68). They also choose not to work with bequests, noting:

> The reason for our interest in this problem is the inadequacy of the common formulation of the problem as a consumer optimization over a finite horizon with a bequest motive. The point is that the bequest function itself is part of the problem; that is, the individual's bequest motive is founded on his concern with the welfare of future members of the family, and thus the infinite horizon formulation makes the bequest function part of the problem to be solved in connection with a continuous process of intergenerational transfers. The process of bequest itself is not as discontinuous as would be implied by the finite horizon formulation since the most important form of bequest is education. (p. 69)

This is in contrast to Yaari (1964) which considers a finite-lived family's optimization problem to give an exogenously specified bequest function. It is the arbitrariness of the bequest function in Yaari's paper that Arrow-Kurz objects to and eliminate from their analysis.

Arrow and Kurz go on to set up a model in which bequests are implicitly defined based on the solution to the control problem they solve to characterize the dynastic family's optimal allocation of consumption and wealth.

Gale also considered bequests in Gale (1973) (discussed above) by way of generalizing his key findings for the two-period model to a general multiperiod setting. Gale's treatment of bequests is not one of trying to define an optimal bequest, or (as in Yaari, 1964) to determine optimal or equilibrium consumptions in the presence of bequests. Rather, he allows the bequest process to be arbitrary and considers the aggregate bequests that are possible in the steady-state of the model. Following Gale, we let A denote aggregate assets (including bequests), ρ the equilibrium gross interest factor, and γ the gross rate of population growth. Gale's main finding (Theorem 5) is that

$$(\rho - \gamma) A = 0$$

which implies that either the economy is at the golden rule equilibrium steady-state or the asset accumulation is zero, meaning that there are no intergenerational transfers occurring. Gale does not link the possibility of bequests in the OLG setting with the neoclassical growth model, nor does he consider the question of family structure in this analysis.

The final step in completing the reinterpretation of the central planner as a dynastic family comes in Barro (1974). Barro starts with an overlapping generations model but adds the possibility that parents can leave bequests to their children. To simplify the model, Barro assumes a representative lineal family structure. He deals with the bequest function problem identified by Arrow and Kurz by assuming that the parent generation cares about the next generation's welfare (i.e., their utility), so that preferences in the model are non-paternalistically altruistic. Of course, this assumption ignores the caveat in Arrow and Kurz that for most families, the major bequest from parents to children is education, whether in the form of taxes paid to support public education or direct expenditures on private education. With this assumption on altruism, Barro observes that this gives rise to intertemporal preferences of the form:

$$V_i = U\left(c_{iy}, c_{io}, V_{i+1}\right),$$

where the function U is an aggregator over the consumptions of generation i and the future preferences of generations $i+1$. Barro then shows that given this specification of the family structure and preferences, the OLG model is equivalent to a model with infinite-lived agents, as long as the bequests between generations are strictly positive (or, in Barro's terminology, operative).

While Barro did not make use of the new tools of forward dynamic programming in his paper, the model he proposed meshes perfectly with the mathematical methods of forward dynamic programming, and we can use this framework to indicate the equivalence of Barro's model with the RCK model. We note first, though, that these techniques were formally introduced in the context of economic growth by Radner (1967), although there were indications throughout Bellman's writings about the applicability of dynamic programming to problems in economics.

To illustrate this applicability, let us consider a simple one-sector capital model with a single good that can be used either for consumption or as capital in production. Since this example is the one that Stokey et al. used to motivate the dynamic programming tools in their *Recursive Methods* text, our digression here will also show why the forward dynamic programming approach has come to dominate the optimal control methods previously used to analyze problems like these.

We assume that labor supply is fixed at one unit and inelastically supplied by households in each period. Production is given by a standard production function $f(k)$ which is strictly increasing, strictly concave, and satisfies $f'(0) = \infty$. The infinite-lived household in each period must allocate the current output $y_t = f(k_t)$ between current consumption and future capital (or future capital plus undepreciated current capital, which for simplicity we assume is zero). The household's preference over current consumption is given by a standard concave utility function $u(c)$ which is also strictly increasing and satisfies an Inada condition at $c = 0$.

With this specification, the reduced form period t utility of the household will be denoted

$$V(k_t, k_{t+1}) = u(f[k_t] - k_{t+1}).$$

As is standard in the capital theory literature, we refer to the function V as the *return function*. The household's intertemporal optimization problem is then one of choosing a sequence of capital stocks $\boldsymbol{k} = [k_0, k_1, \ldots, k_t, \ldots]$ to maximize intertemporal utility, which is given by

$$W(\boldsymbol{k}) = \sum_{t=0}^{\infty} \beta^t V(k_t, k_{t+1}),$$

where $0 < \beta < 1$ is the discount factor.

If we look at the one-sector optimization problem as we've defined it above, we note that since the return functions V are strictly concave (given the assumptions on utility and production functions), the household's objective function is concave. Hence, if standard concave programming theory holds for this class of problems, the first-order conditions should be necessary and sufficient to characterize the solution. The first-order conditions (also known as the Euler equations) for the problem here are

$$V_2(k_{t-1}, k_t) + \beta V_1(k_t, k_{t+1}) = 0, \ \textit{for} \ t = 1, 2, \ldots.$$

Here, the subscripts on the V function denote partial derivatives with respect to the first and second arguments. Since $V_{12}(k_t, k_{t+1}) = -u'(f[k_t] - k_{t+1}) \neq 0$, the implicit function theorem tells us that we can solve for k_{t+1} as a function of the other variables,

$$k_{t+1} = g[k_{t-1}, k_t],$$

which is a second-order difference equation. We will show that in fact, the correct optimal solution to the problem is given by a first-order difference equation $k_{t+1} = h(k_t)$. We will discuss why the current approach doesn't give a full solution after this.

For the dynamic programming approach to this problem, we define an arbitrarily given *continuation* or *value* function for the problem $W_0(k_{t+1})$, where the 0 subscript denotes an initial choice of value function (implying the possibility that the function can change over time), and we assume that the value function tells us the optimized value of our capital accumulation process from time $t + 1$ forward, given that we start with capital k_{t+1} at time $t + 1$. With this definition, we can define the actual value of the accumulation program at time t with a capital stock k_t by

$$W_1(k_t) = \max_{k_{t+1} \in T(k_t)} \{V(k_t, k_{t+1}) + \beta W_0(k_{t+1})\}.$$

Here, $T(k_t)$ is the constraint correspondence that restricts the choice of future capital to lie in the set $\{0 \le k_{t+1} \le f(k_t)\}$.

This functional equation – functional because it takes the function W_0 and produces a second function W_1 – defines an operator T on the space of functions in which the value function lives. If we can find a fixed point $\widehat{W} = T(\widehat{W})$, we would then have the value of the optimization program defined recursively in terms of itself. Let $\hat{k}(k)$ be the solution to the maximization above when $k_t = k$. By iterating the recursion at the fixed point, we get

$$\begin{aligned}\widehat{W}(k) &= V\left(k, \hat{k}[k]\right) + \beta \widehat{W}\left[\hat{k}(k)\right] \\ &= V\left(k, \hat{k}[k]\right) + \beta V\left(\hat{k}[k], \hat{k}^2[k]\right) + \beta^2 \widehat{W}\left[\hat{k}[k], \hat{k}^2[k]\right] \\ &\vdots \\ &= \sum_{t=0}^{\infty} \beta^t V\left(\hat{k}^t[k], \hat{k}^{t+1}[k]\right).\end{aligned}$$

Since we are maximizing the value of the return function at each period of time, we are clearly maximizing the intertemporal discounted sum of return functions, so this is the solution to the optimization. The functional equation at the fixed point is, of course, the Bellman equation

$$\widehat{W}(k_t) = \left\{V(k_t, k_{t+1}) + \beta \widehat{W}(k_{t+1})\right\}$$

and the key thing to note about this is that (assuming differentiability of $\widehat{W}$), the first-order condition for the maximization is

$$V_2(k_t, k_{t+1}) + \beta \widehat{W}'(k_{t+1}) = 0.$$

If the value function is twice-differentiable,[1] we will generally be able to solve (at least implicitly) for k_{t+1} as a function $k_{t+1} = h(k_t)$. This is clearly a first-order difference equation, as opposed to the second-order equation that arises from the Euler equations for the direct approach to solving the model.

The efficacy of the forward DP comes from the fact that it converts the infinite-dimensional direct optimization problem into a recursive finite-dimensional one. Instead of having to solve an infinite-dimensional optimization, we can solve a standard finite-dimensional one. As long as the various functions involved are concave – and it can be shown that as long as the return function V is concave, $\widehat{W}$ will be – then standard concave programming results apply, and the first-order conditions will be necessary and sufficient to characterize the solution. Of course, the algorithm does not (and cannot) banish the underlying infinite nature of the problem. Rather, it replaces one infinity – the discounted sum of utilities – with another – the value function, which is itself an infinite-dimensional object.

The potential difficulty of working with this new infinite-dimensional object should be clear from looking at the functional equation that gives rise to the Bellman equation. The operator T defined by the equation maps functions to functions. When we impose the typical assumption that the functions are continuous and bounded, we specify the domain of T as an infinite-dimensional normed linear vector space. It is well-known that finding fixed points of mappings on such spaces can be problematic. While the Brouwer theorem (for example) remains true, getting sets to be compact in these spaces involves significant restrictions on the subspaces one can consider, which limits the generality of the results obtained.

Fortunately for the dynamic programming framework, there is one fixed point theorem that applies very generally and works for the forward dynamic programming algorithm. This is none other than the contraction mapping theorem that Lucas saw penciled in the margin of Bellman's book. Contraction mappings don't require stringent assumptions on the underlying spaces they operate on, they have unique fixed points, and have the property that one can pick a starting value for the mapping and then iterate the map until it converges on the fixed point. This last property is particularly useful for computational applications.

In the discounted dynamic programming case, Bellman's student David Blackwell provided a pair of easily verified sufficient conditions for a mapping to be a contraction: that it be pointwise monotone and contracting on constant functions. These conditions have seen widespread application throughout dynamic economic analysis.

From this discussion, we can also see why the first-order conditions for the direct problem are only necessary. Since resources are bounded, the underlying commodity space that our infinite-lived agent operates in is l_∞. The return function and discounting map sequences in this space into a sequence of summable utility payouts, which lie in l_1. Since the resource inputs into the return function are bounded from below, we can (possibly with translation) view the sequence of discounted utility payouts as living in l_1^+, the space of summable sequences with non-negative elements. This, in turn, means that the intertemporal value function can be viewed as the sum of the discounted return function payouts, which will have its graph in the space $\mathbb{R} \times l_1^+$. Because l_1^+ has an empty interior, so will $\mathbb{R} \times l_1^+$. Hence, when we try to set up the supporting hyperplane argument used to show that the first-order conditions are also sufficient, the application of Minkowski's theorem fails, since this requires that at least one of the two convex sets being separated has a non-empty interior.[2]

For the direct problem, then, one needs to look at optimal control techniques for the necessary and sufficient conditions, and, as Cass showed in his 1965 paper using methods from Pontryagin's *Maximum Principle* text (Pontryagin et al., 1960), the additional required condition is the transversality condition.

The analysis here applies directly to Barro's model (based as it is on Diamond's OLG model with production) once one specifies a linear aggregator function U and assumes that parent households discount their offspring's utility.

The combination of Barro's results and the ease of application of the forward dynamic programming algorithm proved to be a heady mixture for macroeconomics, and it led to an explosion of work based on the neoclassical growth model with the optimizing agent interpreted as a dynastic family. Foremost among the new applications were the extension of the model to stochastic environments by

Brock and Mirman, and the application of this model to the study of business cycles by Kydland and Prescott.

This new interpretation of the growth model was not without its criticisms, and we will examine these later. But in the meantime, chronological time dictates that we first look at what was happening in the OLG world in terms of its role as a model of money, led primarily by Neil Wallace in the late 1970s, and the work of general equilibrium theorists in this period on understanding the dynamics of Samuelson's new model.

NOTES

1. Conditions under which this will obtain were established independently in Araujo (1991) and Santos (1991).
2. John Tukey published the first counterexample to the proposition that the interiority condition in Minkowski's theorem could be dropped. Interestingly, he published his paper "Some notes on the separation of convex sets" in the journal *Portugaliae Mathematica* in 1942 in order to ensure that the German mathematicians would be able to access the paper despite the wartime embargoes on trade in place at the time.

CHAPTER 5

OLG AND MONEY, 1970–1980

Lucas' 1972 "Expectations and the Neutrality of Money" paper opened the door for monetary theorists to explore the effects of money and monetary policy in the overlapping generations model, in spite of the objections raised by Lerner and Meckling in their commentary on Samuelson's paper about the lack of robustness of the monetary equilibrium.

5.1 NEIL WALLACE

The pioneer in applying Samuelson's new model to monetary economics was undoubtedly Neil Wallace. Wallace was a member of the 1960s cohort of graduate students whose training in macroeconomics was based on the Keynes–Samuelson notion that macroeconomics could be separated from individual optimizing behavior (what we now call the micro-foundations). From Wallace's *Macroeconomic Dynamics* interview (Altig & Nosal, 2017), we know he wasn't satisfied with the contemporary approach to macro and monetary economics:

> Tom Sargent and I were trying to build models which were elaborations of IS-LM. I won't speak for Tom, but I was stuck in a static mode. We had the view that things depend on people's expectations of inflation, and we wanted to endogenize the expectations. Our approach was to be clear about stocks and flows in IS-LM. But when you start thinking about that, you're naturally led to think about some kind of dynamics. At the time, I was also working with John Kareken and Tom Muench. Muench was a good operations researcher, so to him the idea that an equilibrium condition is a difference or differential equation didn't seem strange. But to me, that was just way out there. So although we were thinking about dynamics, it was in a very static way. Then I saw this paper by Lucas; I don't know why I read it, or tried to read it. In part, I did because Bob had been a classmate at Chicago and I had a high opinion of him. I picked up the paper, and it's talking about people, two-period lived people. What's that? There are no people in macroeconomics! I pretty much saw that the Phillip's curve ideas that Sargent and I had been working on were a dead end. That paper (Lucas '72) raised the standard, and there was no turning back. (Altig & Nosal, 2017, p. 1794)

Overlapping Generations: Methods, Models and Morphology
International Symposia in Economic Theory and Econometrics, Volume 32, 61–78

ISSN: 1571-0386/doi:10.1108/S1571-038620230000032013

Wallace's first paper using the OLG framework to study monetary policy issues was "On Simplifying the Theory of Fiat Money" (Wallace, 1977a). This paper was a largely non-technical piece arguing that monetary economics was about explaining patterns of exchange, and why fiat money has value, with the paper's focus on the second question. In the report, Wallace sets the stage by stating:

> My goal in this paper is to try to convince you to take seriously as models of fiat money various versions of the Samuelson/Cass-Yaari overlapping-generations consumption-loans model. (Wallace, 1977a, p. 1793)

Wallace's key argument is that the OLG demographic structure and the need for people to save for retirement creates a natural demand for assets. He then sets up two models, one as in Lucas '72 where production using only labor generates output, and the second including a durable asset (land) that may be productive. The two models generate differences in the demand for money in the sense that if the land is productive, holding equity shares in the land will dominate holding money as a means for transferring wealth between periods. Wallace then notes that while this poses a conundrum for a model purporting to explain why fiat money can have value, this conundrum is one that all models of money would share:

> The case is made by summarizing and interpreting what these models have to say about fiat money and by arguing that these properties are robust in the sense that they can be expected to hold in any model of fiat money. (Wallace, 1977a, p. 1792)

As Wallace states later in Kareken and Wallace (1981) on foreign exchange, "For a model of a fiat money economy to be acceptable, it must then be possible for the money (or if there are several, any one of them) to be dominated" and it is this feature that Wallace holds to be robust across any viable model of money. One implication of this requirement is that money does not appear as an argument in the utility or production functions of the model. Rather, its appearance is restricted to the budget constraints of the individual or firm. This edict was at odds with the view of money as a medium of exchange that cut through the inefficiencies associated with barter. We will discuss this controversy later in this chapter.

Wallace also addresses the tenuousness of the monetary equilibrium generated by the fact that every new generation has an incentive to repudiate the previous generation's money and reissue new money (also known as the seniorage problem). Wallace reiterates his contention here that any other form of money would also create this perverse incentive, and that only government restrictions can eliminate this possibility (Kareken & Wallace, 1981, p. 7). This observation raises an important feature of assets in the OLG setting. Wallace's discussion of the possibility of the rate of return dominance between assets implicitly assumes that it is possible for agents in the model to share ownership of the productive technology. In practice, this requires the original inventor/owner of the technology to create a system for sharing ownership rights in return for payment from new shareholders. This system takes the form of the stock market, and what is traded there are pieces of paper stating that ownership rights, in a given proportion, have been transferred to the holder of the piece of paper. But this paper can be just as easily repudiated as a given generation's money issuance. Absent some enforcement mechanisms, a firm could simply claim that stock certificates are fraudulent and refuse to honor requests for dividends. It is civil society and the rule of law behind these financial institutions that remove the tenuousness not only of fiat money but also of all paper assets. This argument also extends to real assets like land, which, absent a mechanism for enforcing ownership claims, can be seized as easily as any more portable asset.

Wallace (1977b) followed shortly on the heels of report no. 22 and provided the technical details that were missing in the first report. This report used a discrete-time version of the Cass–Yaari model, in the sense of providing a storage technology with the possibility for storage to yield strictly positive returns (e.g., wine) as well as an active, deterministic monetary policy. The key result of the paper is an affirmative technical demonstration of the assertions in the previous report, that when the real rate of return to storage exceeds that of money, there can be no monetary equilibrium in the model. The rate of return dominance question was one that ultimately led Wallace to reject the OLG framework as being the best model of money. From the interview:

> For a while there, I thought the overlapping-generations model was going to be the model of money. My attitude was to try to put that model to work in a number of applications. A classic problem in monetary economics, identified by Hicks back in 1935, is why money exists when there are higher return assets around. I had this idea that if we legally inhibit intermediation, then rate of return dominance would emerge. I wrote a couple of papers about that using an overlapping-generations model. In retrospect, I think the profession was right to reject that view of money. (Wallace, 1977b, p. 1795)

Despite the pessimism this result generated for Wallace, the paper itself made a key observation about the determinacy issue that Samuelson first raised. This observation was based on the possibility of unstable forward dynamics of non-stationary perfect foresight equilibria, and Wallace made the point that unless the economy was literally starting *de novo*, then the choice of an initial price in period 1 would be constrained by the expectations of the young in period -1 to satisfy the perfect foresight assumption.

A third OLG-related paper to come out of this period was the well-known Kareken and Wallace (1981) paper. This paper was highly influential in the debate over whether foreign exchange rates should be fixed or allowed to float freely. Kareken–Wallace uses an OLG model to show that under the *laissez-faire* free-floating exchange rate regime, the monetary equilibrium in the OLG model is indeterminate in the sense that the money demands for agents across the two countries can't be pinned down. This paper, together with the less well-known Kareken and Wallace (1977) paper established the OLG model as a workhorse for international trade.

5.2 THE 1978 MINNEAPOLIS FED CONFERENCE

In 1978, Kareken and Wallace organized a conference held at the Minneapolis Fed on "Models of Monetary Economies." As their introduction to the conference volume states:

> The Federal Reserve Bank of Minneapolis sponsored the "Models of Monetary Economies" conference precisely because some of its research staff were so doubtful about macroeconomic models, or about the monetary and fiscal policy implications of those models. The hope was that the Bank might, by financing the conference help in the development of more satisfactory models. (Kareken & Wallace, 1980, p. 1)

This conference attracted many of the major scholars working on OLG models and in monetary economics, and it generated a deep and impactful debate about how economists should think about money. The various papers presented, together with the comments of assigned discussants, and several written replies submitted after the conference, were put together in a conference volume edited by Kareken and Wallace, entitled "Models of Monetary Economies" issued by the Minneapolis Fed in 1980. Since many of the papers and commentary dealt with OLG models, it is worth reviewing this material.

The papers presented at the conference were:

1. "The Role of Money in Supporting the Pareto Optimality of Competitive Equilibrium in Consumption Loan Type Models" (David Cass, Masahiro Okuno, and Itzhak Zilcha).
2. "The Overlapping Generations Model of Fiat Money" (Neil Wallace):
   a. Discussion by James Tobin.
   b. Discussion by Jose Scheinkman.
3. "The Capital Stock Modified Competitive Equilibrium" (Martin Shubik).
4. "Equilibrium in a Pure Currency Economy" (Robert Lucas):
   a. Discussion by Leonid Hurwicz.
   b. Discussion by Milton Harris.
   c. Discussion by Frank Hahn.

Post-Conference contributions were:

5. "The Optimum Quantity of Money" (Truman Bewley).
6. "Some Remarks on Monetary Policy in an Overlapping Generations Model" (William Brock and Jose Scheinkman).
7. "Transaction Demand and Moral Hazard" (John Bryant).
8. "Money in Consumption Loan Type Models: An Addendum" (David Cass).
9. "In Defense of a Basic Approach" (David Cass and Karl Shell).
10. "General Equilibrium Approaches to the Study of Monetary Economies: Comments on Recent Developments" (Ross Starr).
11. "Models of Money with Spatially Separated Agents" (Rob Townsend).

The Cass–Okuno–Zilcha paper is something of a constructive contrarian exercise aimed at showing that two of the most commonly asserted features of the two-period lived OLG model don't hold. The paper characterizes these features in terms of two propositions about the existence and optimality of equilibrium. The existence proposition states that there is a monetary equilibrium if and only if there is no barter equilibrium which is Pareto optimal. The optimality proposition states that if there is a monetary equilibrium, then there is also a monetary equilibrium that is Pareto optimal. Via a series of counter-examples, the paper shows that:

1. There can be both monetary and non-monetary equilibria in the model, both of which are Pareto optimal.
2. There can be both monetary and non-monetary equilibria in the model, neither of which is Pareto optimal.

The notable thing about this paper was its early application of the community excess demand decomposition results of Debreu, Sonnenschein, Mantel, and others to construct the offer curves for a single good, two-period lived OLG economy with at least two agents.

We illustrate the constructive analysis of the paper using the diagrams from the paper itself in Fig. 10:

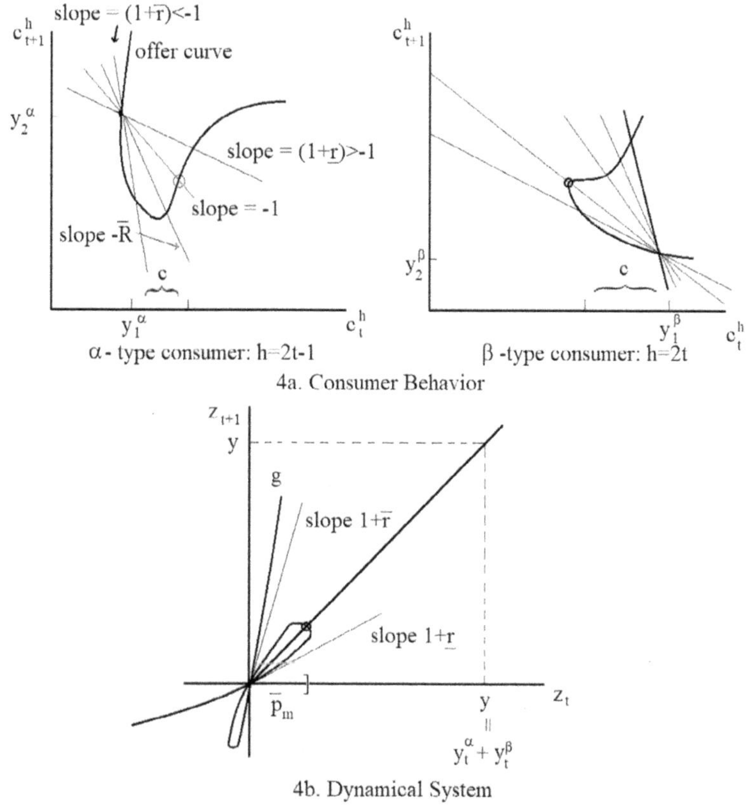

Fig. 10. Cass–Okuno–Zilcha Offer Curve Analysis. *Source*: Adapted from Cass et al. (1979).

The diagram shows two offer curves for two different consumers in the top two panels. The third panel shows the result of adding these two offer curves to get the aggregate offer curve, which has been recentered at the endowment point and reflected to show savings rather than consumption. Equilibria occur where the aggregate offer curve crosses the 45-degree line, and as is apparent from the diagram, there are two equilibria: one with strictly positive aggregate saving (the monetary equilibrium), and other at autarky but with a positive interest rate. This corresponds to example (1) above.

The paper provides a similar construction to show example (2). While these counter-examples do demonstrate the possible contradictions that can arise in the model, the authors note that the examples are, in fact, special, in the sense that:

> these specific examples embody somewhat extreme behavior, since (partly) vertical or horizontal offer curves implicitly require a region of inferiority for the good whose consumption is unchanged. (Kareken & Wallace, 1980, p. 56)

The key takeaway from the paper that the authors highlight is:

> [The] nonoptimality examples strongly suggest that – in general – something like continuous redistribution by means of creation (or destruction) of fiat money may be an indispensable lubricant for the efficient operation of an evolving market economy. (Kareken & Wallace, 1980, p. 44)

While it isn't clear whether these results had any influence on the standard conduct of monetary policy, the use of the excess demand decomposition theorems was picked up four years later and fruitfully applied by Kehoe and Levine, as we will see in the next chapter. As we will also see later, Cass himself provided a general proof, for the case where agents have standard preferences in which all goods are normal, that there always exists a steady-state equilibrium in which the interest rate is greater than or equal to zero.

Before proceeding, let us turn to the early development of the work of Okuno and Zilcha, before their collaboration with Cass. Okuno's 1974 Stanford Ph.D. was supervised by Kurz, with Shell, who was visiting Stanford, on his thesis committee. The thesis contained a chapter entitled "Equilibrium in an Infinite Horizon Model," which as Okuno recalled, while never published, was "a starting point of my joint research" with Zilcha (email April 4, 2020). Regarding how his collaboration with Zilcha come about, Okuno recalled (email April 4, 2020) that:

> In my second year at Illinois, Itzhak came as an assistant professor and his office was next to mine. Because he knew a lot about math (especially infinite space topology, etc., which I knew very little). So I proposed to do joint research on OLG models, which he happily accepted.

When asked how Cass became a co-author of the February 1979 *JET* paper – and Cal Tech WP December 1978 put out by Cass while visiting there – which was originally prepared for the Minneapolis Fed Conference, Okuno said:

> We (I and Itzhak) wrote a small paper and sent to either him or Karl, who invited us to their conference. Dave pointed out some mistake about the paper, and we started to find some example which was going to play a key role in our joint paper. Dave was excited about it and wrote the entire paper by himself with our example in it.

Then, when asked why he stopped publishing papers about problems of OLG and money, Okuno replied:

> My interest then was to find a sufficient condition for the existence of monetary equilibrium (price of fiat money being positive at the eq). I thought we had more or less solved this problem (approximate monetary eq., etc.) and also I started to think the issues of credit and trust are more important research topic than the fiat money. Moreover, when I came back to Illinois after a one year leave, those people I used to talk with (Itzhak, Andy Postlewaite, Rich Kihlstrom, David Schmeidler, etc.) were absent (most of them on leave), and I had to find a different research topic.

In an additional email dated April 5, 2020, Okuno wrote "I did not attend Minn conference and I don't recall participating in the work of writing the [Cal Tech] WP."

Regarding his work with Okuno and Cass, Zilcha, for his part, in an email dated April 4, 2020, recalled:

> First, we both were assistant professors at the Department of Economics, University of Illinois. (by the way, the theory group at this college of Business Administration included Len Mirman, Rich Khilstrom, Andy Postlewaite and Alvin Roth). I joined the department in 1975.
>
> We ... listened to a lecture by Neil Wallace in our seminar in which he claimed that in the Samuelson OLG model with fiat money there is a unique monetary competitive equilibrium (starting at date 0 and extending indefinitely). Okuno and I started working on this issue trying to contradict this claim. We had examples only, then we have written our *RES* paper which was published in July 1980 (see Okuno & Zilcha, 1980). This paper was submitted first to JET and rejected. Later in a conference David Cass told us that we did not write it well etc. but he was interested in the issue of existence of monetary equilibria and their Pareto optimality etc. We started collaborating with him and had nice results. In the meantime I moved to Cornell for one year and later to Tel Aviv University. I did not attend the Minnesota Fed conference.

Continuing with our discussion of the conference papers, Wallace's conference paper reprises the basic arguments in the two previous staff reports, though this paper puts more emphasis on the role of money as a store of value, and further amplifies the contention that money should never be an argument in an agent's utility function. On the store of value issue, he states:

> One claim seems to be that the overlapping-generations friction accounts for the "store-of-value" function of money only. As a consequence, it is argued, models built on it are quite misleading. In particular, the tenuousness of equilibria in which fiat money has value in models built on the overlapping-generations friction is due, according to this claim, to the fact that this friction does not account for the "medium of exchange" role of money. But this claim fails to recognize that tenuousness is an implication of the two defining properties of fiat money, inconvertibility and intrinsic uselessness, and not of the overlapping-generations friction. (Kareken & Wallace, 1980, p. 50)

In contrast to his defense of the store of value role created by the OLG setting in the two staff reports, Wallace downplays the role of legal restrictions, simply stating that "one can impose legal restrictions that give fiat money value" (Kareken & Wallace, 1980, p. 50). This reluctance to emphasize the role of government in the management of money leaves the door open for one of the discussants (Tobin) to claim that "there is no government commitment to the value of fiat money" (Kareken & Wallace, 1980, p. 85). It would remain for Cass and Shell, in their after-conference contribution, to argue that government debt – money or bonds – can serve no purpose if it doesn't serve first as a store of value.

Wallace's paper was followed by two discussions, one from James Tobin, and the other from Jose Sheinkman, so we turn next to these.

Scheinkman's discussion turns on the technical issue of the stability of the monetary equilibrium, which he describes as the source of tenuousness in the value of fiat money. Based on this, he develops a very clever model of infinite-lived agents who can trade on one of two markets. The first requires money for trade (implicitly imposing a Clower-type constraint), while the other market operates by barter. Trade in either market produces a desired composite good, and the trading mechanisms are such that neither market dominates the other. In this setup, then, Scheinkman shows that it is possible for a monetary equilibrium to become asymptotically demonetized, just as can occur in the OLG setting. He also identifies a condition on the agents' common utility function which precludes this asymptotic result and interprets this as making money essential – in its medium of exchange role – for the existence of long-run monetary equilibria. This condition also appears in models in which real balances enter the utility function, for the same reason: money is so essential for trade that even if the government runs a large inflation tax, people will continue to hold large amounts of money.

The last part of Scheinkman's discussion disputes Wallace's contention that the monetary equilibrium in a standard OLG economy cannot survive if there are assets available that pay strictly positive returns. Scheinkman argues that if agents live three periods and have an asset such as land or a tree available that can be purchased when young but only liquidated in their final period of life, then agents will wish to hold money to transfer wealth between their first and second periods of life.

We view this latter criticism of Wallace's contention as one of introducing a market incompleteness argument, since absent money, agents can only transfer wealth from period one to period three. In principle, this is no different from having a stochastic model with at least two states of nature, and one asset that generates positive returns. In this model, introducing a second asset – money, for example – will allow agents to improve risk-sharing and hence, money will have value.

While none of the conference papers or discussions address the stability issue in detail, we would note that, as in the earlier Samuelson–Meckling debate, questions about stability and determinacy are closely interrelated and depend strongly on whether or not rational agents' forecasts are subject to errors which can lead to the economy diverging from an optimal, monetary steady-state equilibrium.

Tobin's discussion is less technical and, possibly because of this, both more contentious about the focus of the conference, but also prescient in anticipating the direction of future research in monetary economics.

Tobin makes six objections to the contention that OLG should be the model for monetary economics:

1. The Cass–Okuno–Zilcha results show that money will have value only when the non-monetary equilibrium interest rates are below the growth rate of the population, but history shows us that money has always existed independently of interest rate conditions.
2. Historically, there have always been alternatives to money – land in particular – that serve as stores of value.
3. Again, citing the Cass–Okuno–Zilch paper, money will only have value if society exhibits the life-cycle pattern of saving followed by dissaving, which has not always been the case historically, but in these societies, there was still a role for money.
4. Via Barro's linkage of OLG and ILA, Tobin argues that even with such "constructive immortality" (which he acknowledges isn't realistic), he would expect that money would have some value.
5. If one accepts the two-period setup of the OLG models examined in the conference, it implies that people hold money for long periods of time, on the order of 25 years, which has no empirical foundation.
6. Fiat money should be dominated by a formal government transfer arrangement such as Social Security, where young generations paying into the PAYGO fund would be more likely to trust a formal agency than fiat money. In Tobin's words:

> The answer is that explicit promise carries more conviction than the decentralized market expectation; there is no governmental fiat commitment to the value of money. (Kareken & Wallace, 1980, p. 85)

These criticisms stimulated the Cass–Shell rebuttal, which we discuss in some detail below. The remaining two substantive sections of Tobin's discussion make several important points which seem to predict the evolution of monetary theory in the hands of search theorists like Kiyotaki and Wright, and many others. Among Tobin's observations in these sections are the following:

1. Money is a public good. Like language, it provides a way of communicating that will be understood universally within a society.
2. Money economizes on the information required to communicate relative prices, in the same way, that it economizes on the multiple coincidences of wants needed for effective barter-mediated exchange.
3. Although contracts can substitute for money in mediating exchange, the need to write down contingency clauses in contracting can become quite costly, another example of the importance of search costs in exchange. In this context, money functions as an insurance policy against the possibility that rare unanticipated contingencies lead to the breakdown of the trade itself.
4. When markets are incomplete, money can co-exist with other assets to facilitate risk-sharing.

Before we leave Tobin's discussion, we should note the irony in the fact that Tobin co-authored a paper in 1981 with Walter Dolde (Dolde & Tobin, 1981) which used simulations of a deterministic life-cycle model to evaluate the welfare costs and benefits of a pay-as-you-go Social Security system. In these simulations, agents live for six periods, which provides a significantly finer grid on which to examine agent behavior relative to the simple two-period lives of the models Tobin was criticizing at the Minneapolis conference. This simulation work was a direct precursor to later work by Summers, and by Auerbach and Kotlikoff using simulations of multiperiod deterministic OLG models to examine a variety of macroeconomic issues. The use of simulations for policy analysis was also a precursor to the practice now known as calibration. While we will discuss this work later in the book, a good overview of Tobin's OLG work can be found in Dimand (2022).

The Shubik and Lucas contributions to the conference volume, and the discussions of these papers deal with non-OLG models, so we omit detailed discussion of them here. Lucas' contribution is noteworthy, though, because taken together with Lucas (1978) it represents Lucas' switch away from OLG in favor of ILA models. We know this from Lucas' Introduction to his *Collected Papers on Monetary Theory* (Gillman, 2012) where he states that:

> When I moved from Carnegie-Mellon to Chicago in 1975, I began to teach in the first-year sequence in macroeconomics, a practice I maintained for more than twenty-five years. For the core (as we called it) I thought I needed a coherent approach to the basics of monetary theory, which I thought of as the quantity theory of money and the evidence that supported that theory. I wanted to do this in a way that made maximum use of modern general equilibrium theory. I'm sure I began with Samuelson's 1958 overlapping generations model and the developments of that theory due to David Cass, Menahem Yaari, and others, but I became dissatisfied with the abstractness of that framework and sought a view in which money is an asset that we hold to pay bills with, a factor in a *payments system*. (Gillman, 2012, p. xviii)

Examination of the "Pure Currency" paper from the Kareken-Wallace volume or the "Asset Prices" paper, makes clear that Lucas viewed the overall benefits of the infinite-lived representative agent approach – its amenability to forward dynamic programming tools, its adaptability to time-series data of any frequency, and its straightforward extendibility into stochastic regimes – as sufficient reason to prefer a model that, at best, describes the economic workings of the upper 5% of the income distribution.

As we will see going forward, Lucas was not the only macroeconomist to abandon the OLG framework in favor of the representative agent model, so, as we noted in the Introduction, a key question for us is why this happened. At the time Lucas was working on these two papers, his decision was, perhaps, understandable. If one compares the steady-state predictions of Diamond's OLG model with those of the standard RCK model, the two look quite similar. As we will see later, one of the key OLG projects of the 1980s was Rao Aiyagari's work looking at whether OLG and ILA models were observationally equivalent. To the extent that the outputs that distinct models deliver look the same, then, using the model which is simpler to analyze and more easily adapted to the data available seems like an easy call.

In fairness to Lucas (and others not named), he noted explicitly that Clower constraint models and OLG were two different ways of modeling financial frictions in Lucas (1984):

> The convention adopted in this paper that all traders alternate synchronously between centralized and decentralized markets is only one of many ways of utilizing the cash-in-advance constraint to study situations with incomplete markets. For example, Grossman and Weiss (1982) and Rotemberg (1982) examine models in which some agents are always engaged in securities trading but never all agents at the same time. Comparison of their results with those cited above makes it clear that the characteristics of the equilibrium depend critically on the nature of the assumed trading rules and timing conventions.
>
> The intergenerational models introduced by Samuelson (1958) provide another context for analyzing monetary issues within the general equilibrium framework used in the theory of finance. See Wallace (1980) for a useful description of recent developments.
>
> I do not see any way of judging which of these approaches will prove most useful for which questions that does not involve working out the implications of theories of both types. By pursuing the particular Clower-type approach used here. I do not mean to suggest that I view this question as closed at the present time. (Lucas, 1984, footnote 7, p. 21)

We turn next to the after-conference contributions. The first paper, Truman Bewley's "The Optimum Quantity of Money" works with the infinite-lived agents framework, so, as with the Shubik and Lucas contributions, we omit the discussion of the paper here.

The next OLG paper in the volume is the Brock–Scheinkman paper. This paper uses a simplified version of the Lucas model to study the effects of random variations in the money supply. The simplifications are along the same lines as the "easy Lucas" model sketched above. Specifically, in addition to the standard two-period lived agents assumption and the restriction to a single commodity, the Brock–Scheinkman model also focuses on pure exchange and discrete random shocks. As we noted above, these simplifications make analysis of the model considerably easier since the equilibrium objects in the model are now finite-dimensional Euclidean vectors rather than functions.

Brock and Scheinkman show the following results:

1. In a deterministic setting with perfect foresight, increasing the amount of money (i.e., generating inflation) leads to welfare losses (except for the initial generation).
2. With random money supply fluctuations, there is always a deterministic monetary policy that leads to the same welfare outcomes as the stochastic policy. In this case, however, because the relationship between the price level and the quantity of money is inverse (and hence, convex), increasing the variance of the random monetary policy can lead to welfare improvements.

John Bryant's conference paper would seem to have anticipated Tobin's criticisms since it focuses on the fact that in an OLG setting in which money can serve as a store of value, the moral hazard issues associated with contracting can lead to a medium of exchange role for money as well. The observation that contracts – which can serve as an alternative to money for mediating exchange (and indeed, does in the conventional Arrow–Debreu model) – can be costly to negotiate or enforce goes back to Brunner and Meltzer (1971). While these informational issues are not specific to the OLG environment, they do figure in the later development of models of money based on search.

The Cass addendum, "Money in Consumption-Loan Type Models: An Addendum," generalizes the Cass–Okuno–Zilcha example of the coexisting of non-optimal monetary and non-monetary equilibria to make the example robust to small perturbations of agents' preferences and endowments. The construction still requires that agents can become satiated in second-period consumption so that while the example is robust to perturbations, it remains special in the sense of requiring the relaxation of common non-satiation assumptions.

The Cass and Shell after-conference contribution, "In Defense of a Basic Approach," is a direct reaction to Tobin's critique of OLG as a model of money. The main thrust of the critique is their statement that:

> If money and bonds do not serve as a value store, then they cannot serve any other useful function. (Kareken & Wallace, 1980, p. 251)

Cass and Shell emphasize the point that money cannot have value in models with finite time horizons via the usual backward induction (aka "hot potato") argument, and they reject the argument that one can generate valued fiat money in a conventional Arrow–Debreu framework simply by including money in the utility function. Their rejection of money-in-the-utility function models is based on two observations. First, it doesn't explain why intrinsically useless fiat money might serve as a store of value. Second, the usual argument in favor of these models – that they capture the medium of the exchange value of money in cutting through Jevons' "double coincidence of wants" – ignores the fact that money is itself a technology the management of which can generate positive or negative impacts. As Cass and Shell note, "such reduced forms are at best poor proxies for their structural counterparts."

Fleshing out these ideas, Cass and Shell note that one can avoid the "hot potato" problem by working in an environment where the effective economic horizon is infinite, even though the individual economic actors themselves live finite lives and consume finite resources. They distinguish the OLG model from what they call the "received doctrine" by noting two key features of the model:

> First, it is genuinely dynamic. In this it significantly departs from the basically atemporal character of most received doctrine: There is explicit recognition of both the inherent mortality (as well as vitality) of the actors, together with the continual (as well as unceasing) evolution of their stage.
>
> Second, it is fundamentally disaggregative. In this it is founded in perhaps the oldest theoretical tradition in economics: There is a clear distinction between economic agents' objectives and constraints – and hence the mainsprings of their individual behavior – and the economic system's coherent resolution of their joint interaction. (Cass & Shell, 1983, p. 253)

They turn next to the question of whether there is any practical use in looking at the kinds of highly simplified and unrealistic models that were presented at the conference. The response to this question reads like a blueprint for the next 30 years of research on the OLG model.

They begin this discussion by noting that "the cardinal rule [is] that simple models can best be employed to produce counter examples," and then point to the first important counter-example, Samuelson's demonstration that the model can have competitive equilibria which violate the first welfare theorem. The next counter-examples they point to are the indeterminacy results first noted by Samuelson, based on the fact that the model can exhibit a continuum of non-stationary monetary equilibria (in the typical Samuelsonian setting), as well as cyclic equilibria which, as we saw above, were first noted by Gale.

Cass and Shell then venture into the new and less developed territory by raising questions about the usual assumptions economists make about what constitutes an appropriate set of state variables.[1] This leads to speculation about the possibility that purely extrinsic events – the occurrence or non-occurrence of sunspots, in their example – might have a self-fulfilling effect on economic equilibrium simply because agents in the model believed they would. As we'll see below, this speculation turned out to be correct, with papers by Cass and Shell, and by Costas Azariadis spawning a whole literature on extrinsic uncertainty and self-fulfilling prophecies in rational expectations equilibrium.

From this speculative discussion, Cass and Shell then note that:

> In fact, at this writing, there are virtually no well-established general theorems for the overlapping generations model available in the literature. The prime reason for this paucity of substantial results is clear: very little is known about the most basic properties of this model except in its rudest embodiments. (Cass & Shell, 1983, p. 255)

They then go on to provide a sketch of one possible generalization of the simplest two-period, one commodity, representative agent model that also happens to address Tobin's comment about how unrealistic it was to assume people would hold money for 25 years. The generalization Cass and Shell outline – which appears formally in Balasko, Cass, and Shell (1980) – involves allowing for (finitely) many agents who live arbitrary (but finite) lifetimes and consume any finite number of goods. They point out that by reinterpreting the length of the periods and appropriately adjusting the dimensions of the vectors of consumption and endowment commodities, the original model can be transformed into one where agents live for two periods with generations overlapping for one. As long as markets are complete, the two models are isomorphic.

The remainder of the paper enumerates a number of additional directions for research on OLG models. Cass and Shell note that whether one believes in OLG as a model of money *per se*, it is fundamentally a model in which agents need assets to finance consumption spending during their retirement years. As such, OLG provides a better micro-foundation for both capital theory and finance. Stochastic extensions of the model (following Lucas' pioneering paper) raise questions about the role of expectations (particularly given the later sunspot results conjectured here), socialization across demographic cohorts, and the need for models of economic learning.

The penultimate contribution to the conference volume is Ross Starr's "General Equilibrium Approaches to the Study of Monetary Economies: Comments on Recent Developments."

Starr makes two short points.

His first point notes that money can have value independently of its use as an asset for retirement saving if it is the only asset accepted by the government for the payment of taxes, or, even more simply, if agents in the model *expect* it to have value. The possibility that taxation gives money value is well-known (and was at the time of the conference), but Starr's comment on expectations reflected new developments in what became known as *temporary equilibrium* theory, pioneered by Jean-Michel Grandmont. We discuss this work in the next chapter.

Starr's second point is that standard sequence economies (whether with finite horizons or not) that don't have futures markets need an asset like money to implement equilibrium trades. This is akin to Arrow's results showing how to reduce the number of forward contingent claims markets required for an Arrow–Debreu equilibrium (with both time and uncertainty) by replacing the forward markets with assets that allow the transfer of wealth over time and across states of nature. What this argument lacks, however, is the motivation for saving, to begin with. There is an obvious sense in which the OLG model builds in what would otherwise have to be assumed – that is, that agents must save for retirement – but in the absence of individual human motivations for the creation of dynasties, this built-in retirement motive happens to be realistic.

The final contribution to the volume is Rob Townsend's "Models of Money with Spatially Separated Agents." Townsend looks at three distinct models.

1. The turnpike model, in which agents travel along an infinitely long road in one of two directions and are paired at each point of time with someone going the opposite direction. Under the assumption that the endowment distribution across agents is not Pareto optimal, Townsend shows that by introducing money that is passed back and forth across the road (chickens?), agents can engage in welfare- improving trades that are not possible without the monetary tokens, for reasons akin to those in the OLG model.
2. A modification of the turnpike model that allows agents to meet each other infinitely often, but still has the requisite mismatch of endowments between agents when they meet that makes Pareto-improving trades possible. In this setting, agents could resolve bilateral debts, but Townsend sets the model up so that when creditors meet their respective debtors, they never have the real resources available to redeem their debts. This, then, creates a role for money both as a store of value and as a medium of exchange.
3. Townsend's third model is a variant of the Cass–Yaari circular model combined with the friction Lucas introduced in his conference paper to create a transactions demand for money.

While none of these models is realistic – even in densely populated cities, creditors generally know where their counterparties live – they do explicate the kinds of frictions that contemporary search theoretic models of money have rationalized. For a detailed accounting of these developments, see the appropriately titled special *International Economic Review* issue *Models of Monetary Economies II: The Next Generation* (Wright, 2005). We will review the work combining OLG and search theory in Chapter 8.

5.3 THE TENUOUSNESS OF MONEY

The tenuousness of money issue and the possibility that every new generation could generate seniorage gains by repudiating old money in favor of new money found formal theoretical expression in the literature exploring core allocations in OLG models. For the Samuelsonian case, the core of the economy is empty, for the simple reason that at any time t, the current young will strictly prefer to issue new money, while all future agents are indifferent, so this coalition can block the implementation of the standard monetary equilibrium. The first paper to show this was by Hendricks, Judd, and Kovenock (1980).

While there were several papers looking at core-like issues in the OLG model – for example, Chae (1987) showed a short-run core equivalence result which is parallel to the concept of weak Pareto optimality – the core emptiness results for the full infinite horizon economy remains essentially a negative result. The original Hendricks, Judd, and Kovenock paper gets only 26 Google Scholar citations, and this tops the list of papers based on a search for "core" and "overlapping generations" on Google Scholar. But the result itself is indicative of the essential tenuousness of fiat money, and of the overall process of intergenerational resource transfers.

The final definitive words on the relationship between the optimality of the competitive equilibrium and the existence of a monetary equilibrium were produced in two papers, one by Cass and Larry Benveniste in 1986, and the second by Francois Duc and Christian Ghiglino in 1998.

Benveniste and Cass (1986) showed that when one removed the satiation assumptions that generated the Cass–Okuno–Zilcha counter-examples, as long as agents can trade zero net supply bonds, a fixed money supply will support a Pareto optimal stationary equilibrium for the Samuelsonian case with many goods and a single two-period lived representative consumer.

Curiously, the paper claims to provide an extension of the result to the case of many consumers, goods, and lifetimes under the condition that intergenerational trades from present to past generate Pareto improvements, in a follow-on unpublished working paper "On the Existence of Optimal Stationary Equilibria with a Fixed Supply of Fiat Money: II. The Case of Many Consumers with Arbitrary Lifetimes" (Cass, 1982). This paper does not seem to exist, and when we asked Benveniste about it, he replied (via private email correspondence dated May 29, 2022):

> The paper with Dave in *JPE* was done while I visited Penn in 1981. Dave walked into my office with the question. Do stationary monetary equilibrium exist. I solved proved it and that really is my history. I visited for two more years but Dave was focused on sunspots and I was pursuing other questions. The multi consumer version is a mystery to me. Dave talked a little about it but I don't remember seeing a finished version. So any reference is possible. Dave may have finished it himself.

Burke (1999) also cites the Cass paper, and he was able at our request to unearth a copy of the hand-written notes, which as they are don't constitute a full paper, but are extensive, running to 41 pages. We include these notes online at: https://doi.org/10.1184/R1/21926148.v1 by way of completing the historical record of this work.

Cass apparently decided not to write the work up as a formal paper or try to publish it, but he did pass the notes on to Francois Duc and Christian Ghiglino for them to use in the work they were pursuing on existence and optimality results for general OLG economies. The paper that came out of this was Duc and Ghiglino (1998), which cited the Benveniste–Cass work and provides a generalization of that work based on the theorem in Cass' extended notes that he provided Duc and Ghiglino. Ghiglino, in email correspondence (dated May 29, 2022) recalled that:

> Dave discussed with us his notes. These were his notes. I don't think there was ever a paper, only intentions and a non-polished (I think) [version] of the theorem. Dave was happy we used it and published it.

The theorem by Cass that Duc and Ghiglino use establishes the existence of steady-state equilibria for the general OLG model with interest rates greater than or equal to zero. When the interest rate is zero, the steady state is nominal. When the interest rate is greater than zero, there are no intergenerational transfers of resources, and the equilibrium is non-monetary. Duc and Ghiglino show that these equilibria (which can involve trade between agents of different ages as well as types) are Pareto optimal. Of course, when the model has only a single agent born per period and only one commodity, we are back in Gale's classical case world.

We complete our discussion of OLG as a model of money by noting that quite a few monetary economists agreed with Tobin's critique. Some of these additional critiques were aired at the 1983 Carnegie–Rochester Conference on Money, Monetary Policy, and Financial Institutions organized by Karl Brunner and Allan Meltzer. One particular paper, by Bennet McCallum (1983), is worth reviewing in some detail.

McCallum raises objections to the use of OLG as a model of money, based on the dynamic tenuousness argument, and on an argument that purports to show that money cannot serve as a medium of exchange in OLG economies. The tenuousness is the same as that posed by Tobin and others, which we have discussed above.

McCallum's argument that money cannot serve as a medium of exchange "builds upon the traditional presumption that an economy with a medium of exchange will be more productive than it would be if no such medium existed" (McCallum, 1983, p. 24). He then suggests that in an OLG model with capital, because the same leisure and consumption opportunities are available to agents whether or not money is available indicates that money in the OLG model cannot serve as a medium of exchange.

An immediate objection to this argument is its assumption that the model is one with capital. As Wallace noted repeatedly, capital is an asset that, if productive, dominates money as a store of value, in which case the price of money is zero. For a model with capital, it would seem that the more relevant direct question would be whether capital in the model is accepted as a medium of exchange. Given the abstract level at which the model is presented (both in McCallum's paper and in the others we have been examining), this question is impossible to answer. It could well be that agents in the model actually break off chunks of putty-like capital stock to trade (as long as it all ends up back at the factory in time for the next period's production run). Or it could be, as

McCallum suggests earlier in his paper, that the exchange process is unmodeled but exists in the background.

For a more relevant examination of the "traditional presumption," we would suggest looking at the Samuelsonian case in a pure exchange model, where money serves as a store of value. In this case, in the absence of money, the barter equilibrium cannot implement the intergenerational Pareto improving transfers that Samuelson first noted, so that the introduction of money does indeed make the economy more productive.

McCallum then examines the argument against money-in-the-utility function models. His development of these models takes the Cass–Shell criticism that these models are just reduced forms seriously, by positing a model in which the only arguments in an agent's utility function are consumption and leisure in each period of life. He then develops a sub-model based on Becker's home production paradigm which includes shopping time as an activity. This allows him to capture the inefficiency of barter relative to money as an explicit transaction cost that detracts from leisure. When this transaction technology is plugged back into the original utility function, the resulting indirect utility function looks like one in which money is an argument.

This particular approach, as we noted earlier, has been subsumed by more modern search theoretic models of money and transactions, but the basic idea of using an indirect utility representation remains a valid one.

To conclude this chapter on the early applications of OLG as a model of money, it seems fair to say that Wallace's ultimate rejection of OLG as THE model of money was correct. At the same time, though, there is a clear consensus in the papers and discussion that OLG creates a demand for assets – that is for a store of value – via the need for people to save for retirement, and the fact that storing commodities to meet this need is both unrealistic and inefficient. This demand-side consideration is absent in the alternative ILA-based models. This should be apparent from the fact that for money to have any value in these models, the use of money must be imposed exogenously via either cash-in-advance constraints, the condition that taxes must be paid in money, or the ad hoc inclusion of money as an argument in the utility function. We can also see this fact very simply by looking again at the simple one-sector capital model we examined in the section on dynastic models.

If we take the Lucas (1978) asset pricing model – where the technology is simply a Lucas tree that drops a given amount of output each period – and add the ability to store the output for one period, we can then ask whether our representative agent would ever avail herself of the storage option. The answer to this is simply no. As long as she discounts the future, there is no gain in saving any output in this case, since the tree will produce more output tomorrow. The only reason our infinite-lived representative agent would save, then, is if saving generated a positive return, that is, only if capital is productive. While most analyses of this kind of model focus on the fact that in the presence of productive capital, no agent will hold money because it is dominated in return, our point with this example is to show that the agent won't save – using any instrument – when the return to capital doesn't dominate other assets.

From this perspective, OLG generates a fundamental demand for assets of one kind or another, as a primitive of the model grounded in simple empirical observations of how people live. One might argue that the time-varying resource patterns that give rise to the demand for retirement saving could be built into ILA models, but for tractability, these would have to be cyclic, since it is difficult to see how retirement for eternity after working finitely many periods could be successfully financed. As Cass and Shell noted in the "Defense of a Basic Approach" post-conference contribution, it is the actual dynamism of new agents entering and old agents leaving that creates a world where finance isn't simply an afterthought of industry's need for machines.

NOTE

1. This is echoed in the Cass *Macroeconomic Dynamics* interview (Spear & Wright, 1998) when he talks about questioning Lucas about his assumptions that only the exogenous random shocks to money and population would affect the equilibrium prices in his '72 *JET* model.

CHAPTER 6

OLG AND THEORY, 1970–1980

While monetary economists were busy exploring the OLG model's store of value aspects, macroeconomists and general equilibrium theorists were also exploring the model, looking to establish the kinds of general theorems that Cass and Shell had suggested were needed in the "Basic Approach" paper. As we look at these developments, it will become apparent that the hub universities for theory work on the OLG model in the US were Harvard, Minnesota, MIT, and Penn, and work by scholars in France supported by CEPREMAP – which is an independent research agency under the aegis of the French Ministry of Research – and by the French Centre National de la Recherche Scientifique (CNRS). The French connection to OLG was channeled through Karl Shell, who spent a sabbatical year (1977–1978) at CEPREMAP (supported by the Gugenheim Foundation and CNRS), where he met Yves Balasko, Jean-Michel Grandmont, Roger Guesnerie, and Jean-Jacques Laffont. Shell, together with Dave Cass, had NSF grants that made it possible for them to invite these French scholars to spend time at Penn during this period.

6.1 TEMPORARY EQUILIBRIUM

Proceeding chronologically, we begin with Jean-Michel Grandmont and his work on temporary equilibrium models. Like Lucas, Grandmont was motivated by monetary issues in macroeconomics in his theoretical interests as a graduate student. Grandmont was also solidly in the micro-foundations camp, like many of his graduate contemporaries at the time. Summarizing from an extended email correspondence with us, over the period 1960-65, while studying engineering in Paris, Grandmont read a number of economic tomes including translations of Hicks' *Value and Capital*, and Samuelson's *Foundations*, which covered micro and general equilibrium theory on the one hand, and mathematical forms of Keynesian macro on the other, noticing the absence of linkage between macro and micro approaches.

Overlapping Generations: Methods, Models and Morphology
International Symposia in Economic Theory and Econometrics, Volume 32, 79–98

ISSN: 1571-0386/doi:10.1108/S1571-038620230000032015

The only glint of a connection he perceived was Hicks's temporary equilibrium formulation as manifest in *Value and Capital*, in which in a specific period rational decisions were made by agents given their expectations of the future environment, albeit in his view, there still existed a chasm between micro and macro.

Unlike Lucas, Grandmont was skeptical about the new rational expectations paradigm, believing instead that expectations should, of themselves, be taken as a psychological factor at work in economics (not unlike preferences), which was amenable to change through learning, but fundamentally more complex than the stochastic version of perfect foresight built into the rational expectations hypothesis. According to Grandmont, his publications that focused on temporary equilibrium were directed against the rational expectations and the Arrow-Debreu approaches, in as much as in his view they were both static and based on the rational expectations hypothesis that implied that all present and future decisions, including those of unborn agents, were taken at an initial point. In his view, Hicks's attempt to reconstruct dynamics in a realistic manner emanated from agents forecasting the future via a learning-based expectations function, dependent upon past information. This approach was advocated by theorists such as Arrow, Debreu and Hahn, allowing progress on temporary general equilibrium theory accordingly.

Grandmont's dive into temporary equilibrium theory started with a meeting with Debreu in his office at Berkeley, where he recalled that as a Ph.D. student he met Debreu and told him that he wanted to bring money into the general equilibrium framework. Debre replied that Grandmont first had to complete his PhD coursework, and besides that, as he [Debreu] had never addressed the topic, Grandmont would be on his own in dealing with the problem. Grandmont then said that luckily, one of the first courses he took in 1968 was an introductory Macro course given by Bent Hansen, based upon Patinkin's book, *Money, Interest, and Prices* which, at the time, was the leading monetary theory text. Grandmont then recalled that he came to understand the principle underlying the competitive nature of temporary equilibrium in the first term-paper he wrote, which consisted of reproducing Patinkin's approach with inside money in a two-period exchange economy with a single good. After a simple computation process taking a few minutes, he obtained two results. The first was that Patinkin's claim regarding temporary equilibrium with a positive price for money as existing via the real balance effect was actually not true in the case when expected inflation - fixed in the short run - was too large. The second was that existence could be reestablished in the case where the level of expected money price level was fixed; and this, by means of reintroducing intertemporal substitution. In other words, existence arguments based upon simplicity would illustrate the existence of monetary equilibria in a competitive sense, albeit in economies which were more sophisticated, that is with many agents and goods.

Grandmont completed his Berkeley Ph.D. thesis, one of the papers of which was the unpublished working paper Grandmont (1970), which gave rise to Grandmont (1973). This paper formally works with an infinite-lived agents setting, but agents' preferences are structured so that they only care about consumption between "this week" and "next week," which allows Grandmont to capture the short-run equilibrium effects generated by different specifications of the expectations function in the model.

Grandmont's first use of the OLG model came on his return to Paris in late 1970. After returning to work at CEPREMAP, Grandmont, along with Younes, attempted to construct a coherent micro-foundational based approach to money and macro using a methodology based on temporary equilibrium. The initial products of this project were two papers dealing with how money was integrated into models with infinite-lived agents who faced a cash-in-advance constraint. Grandmont - with Laroque - continued to work on the research program in the context of competitive OLG models initially with outside money. According to Grandmont, he and Laroque were the first to do this. They then continued to work with inside and outside money, and banking. According to Grandmont, these two frameworks, that is to say, the infinite horizon approach, with constraints based on cash in advance, and non-bequest OLG models, were characterized by financially based functions that could be analyzed by similar economic techniques. In further development of this work related to OLG-based on stochastic processes, Grandmont and Hildenbrand introduced stochastic shocks and a mathematical methodology that could be utilized irrespective of the length of agents' lives.

We can illustrate the basic setup of the OLG model in the temporary equilibrium framework using the simple two-period lived agents pure exchange model with a single commodity, as in the "easy Lucas" model outlined above.

The difference in the temporary equilibrium model is that agents are not assumed to have perfect foresight (in a deterministic setting) or rational expectations (in a stochastic setting). Instead, they must use currently available information (possibly including current prices in addition to lagged prices) to forecast the next period's price. Hence, a typical young agent will face the following sequential budget constraints:

$$p_t \cdot x_t + m_t = p_t \cdot \omega_t$$

$$\psi(p_t) \cdot x_{t+1} - m_t = \psi(p_t) \cdot \omega_{t+1},$$

where p_t is the price at the time t prevailing on the market, x_t is a period t consumption, m_t is money holdings, ω_t is the agent's endowment, and the function ψ is the agent's point forecast of the future price. As Grandmont notes in his paper with Younes, one can use standard backward dynamic programming procedures to determine the time $t+1$ utility-maximizing demand for the agent, given his period t consumption and money holdings. Going back to period t, one then maximizes utility with respect to consumption and money holdings taking the period $t+1$ demand and the forecast function as given. From here, having obtained the period t optimal demands relative to the given forecast, the temporary equilibrium is then simply the Arrow–Debreu equilibrium price for the static economy in period t. This equilibrium is referred to as "temporary" because, with different information, agents will change their forecasts, generating a possibly different Arrow–Debreu equilibrium.

One of the features that Grandmont highlighted in this work was the fact that because the standard Arrow–Debreu model admits multiple equilibria, it was possible for a dynamic model to do the same. This became an issue for Grandmont while he was studying Lucas' 1972 paper.

Grandmont stated that in 1981 he started to read Lucas' 1972 paper with the intention of destroying its premise but was blocked in this effort because of issues arising from the signal extraction problem in the Lucas model. As Grandmont put it, Lucas assumed that observation of the market price revealed an otherwise unobservable variable. Lucas then searched for an equilibrium where prices were functionally related to that variable, showed that this equilibrium existed, and claimed that it was unique. According to Grandmont, such a procedure was valid only in the case where the revealed variable that was hidden was uniquely associated with an equilibrium price. which may not be the situation. Grandmont agreed with Lucas on existence, but asserted that as there may be multiple equilibria, the economic argument in Lucas 1972 was invalid. Grandmont went on to say that he arrived at an understanding of what he saw as the basic error in Lucas 1972 via discussion with a colleague at CEPREMAP in 1981. Grandmont wrote to Lucas, with Lucas replying that there was indeed an error in the paper. Lucas wrote a corrigendum acknowledging the error but asserted that his argument was nonetheless still valid.

We will return to Grandmont's work in the next section, dealing with the theoretical work from the 1980s to 1990s, but there is a slight irony here in that Grandmont's paper with Hildenbrand on stochastic processes of temporary equilibria has an error: the asserted existence of an invariant measure for the equilibrium process was proven on the assumption that the temporary equilibrium of the model depended continuously on the lagged data. Martin Helwig (1980) pointed out that this amounted to assuming that the temporary equilibrium of the model was always unique.

Nonetheless, Grandmont's temporary equilibrium work was important because it showed that under weak assumptions about expectations, all the structural characteristics of the standard static Arrow–Debreu model would hold for the temporary equilibrium model. This allowed the importation into dynamic general equilibrium theory of all of the basic results of standard general equilibrium theory, and in particular, the smooth economies tools first developed by Debreu and later elaborated on in the work of Yves Balasko, who explored the manifold properties of the equilibrium set (see, e.g., Balasko, 2009).

These structural characterizations were later combined with measure theoretic techniques to extend the initial Grandmont–Hildenbrand characterization of temporary equilibrium stochastic processes to more general models (including the possibility of multiple equilibria) in fully rational expectations setting. We will discuss these results further in the chapter on stochastic OLG models.

6.2 OPTIMAL TAXATION AND PUBLIC FINANCE

There was a constellation of papers on optimal taxation that used the OLG framework written during this period, with contributions coming from a member of the not-so-silent silent generation, Ned Phelps, and several more from the early Boomer generation who were completing their graduate work at this time.

The first modern optimal taxation paper was written in 1971 by James Mirrlees, who generalized Frank Ramsey's 1927 analysis of the relationship between demand elasticities and tax revenues by adding heterogenous labor productivity (see Mirrlees, 1971). A natural extension of Mirrlees' work was to put the optimal tax problem into a dynamic context. This was important because taxes affect saving, which in turn affects capital accumulation and, in an OLG context, the ability of workers to finance their retirements.

Looking at this work chronologically (in terms of publication dates), Peter Diamond was one of the first to make such a dynamic extension, in Diamond (1973). Diamond's paper uses a two-period lived OLG model of growth to examine three possible ways a central planner would act to maximize a discounted sum of utilities over all generations. In the first scenario, the central planner can choose all quantities directly, and the solution to this is standard. In the second scenario, Diamond decentralizes the optimum obtained in the first scenario in the usual way, subject to the need for government debt to institute intergenerational transfers required of the optimum from the first scenario. (This need doesn't arise in the ILA setting because all intergenerational transfers in this model are internalized in the solution to the Pareto problem.) In the third scenario, Diamond considers the optimal taxation problem by letting his central planner choose prices, but not quantities, together with the assumption that there are now no lump sum transfers possible. For this analysis, Diamond defines two notions of the intertemporal marginal rate of substitution. The first is the usual individual MRS (relative to a numeraire good), while the second is the societal intertemporal MRS (or SMRS) which reflects the intergenerational terms of trade between periods. Diamond's analysis of the optimal tax problem shows that these two rates need not be aligned at the optimum, though if they are, they will be equal to the marginal rate of transformation (MRT) determined by the technology of the economy. If all of the rates are equal, that is, MRS = SMRS = MRT, then the allocation coincides with the fully optimal scenario one allocation. Diamond shows via an example of an economy with one consumption good plus a labor-leisure choice that the optimal tax equilibrium need not equal the full optimum.

A second early paper making the dynamic extension to the optimal taxation problem was Ordover and Phelps (1975). This paper works directly with the Mirrlees model – in particular with Mirrlees' assumption that workers have different productivities – but adds the structure of Diamond's version of the OLG model to look at the effects of capital accumulation, population growth, and retirement consumption to the optimization mix. The social welfare criterion that Ordover and Phelps adopt is not the usual utilitarian one, but rather a Rawlsian criterion based on maximizing the minimum utility obtainable across generations assuming the economy is evolving along a steady-state balanced growth path (driven by population growth). The justification given for this is

> The social welfare function we employ expresses the conception of economic justice championed by John Rawls: As a chain is no stronger than its weakest link, social welfare is only as great as the utility of the least well-off, the person or persons having minimum utility. Thus the redistributional optimum is "maximin." (Ordover & Phelps, 1975, p. 661)

The questions that the paper seeks to address are

> Should profits be taxed? Should they be taxed more heavily than wages? Might it be optimal to levy a proportionate wealth tax at a rate exceeding the average rate of profit on capital? (Ordover & Phelps, 1975, p. 661)

While these are interesting questions, to which the paper begins to provide (as the authors note) technical answers given the ethical choice of the maximin social welfare criterion, examining them fully is outside the focus of our study of the development of OLG models, so we leave it to the interested reader to pursue this in detail in the paper. We do note, however, that Phelps and Riley (1978) extended the analysis of Ordover and Phelps using the kinds of recursive dynamic programming techniques that later become popular via the Stokey et al. (1989) text, though in the context of Diamond's OLG model. This is possible because the central planner/government in the model is assumed to be an infinite lived institution, even though agents in the model are finite-lived. There is one quote, however, from the Phelps-Riley paper that is worth noting:

> [I]t must be a bit startling, on first encounter with the utilitarian doctrine, to see the saving by a multi-period household become an allegory of the proper accumulation by a multi-generation society. (Phelps & Riley, 1978, p. 103)

Their meaning here is quite clear: households are, for the most part, finite-lived families organized as overlapping generations. Utilitarian approaches that weight generations via discounting transform the "multi-generation society" into a simple (and unrealistic) "multi-period household," or, as Barro viewed it, a lineal dynastic family.

A second early application of the OLG model to public finance was Auerbach (1979), which used a version of the Diamond model to assess the effects of taxation on economic growth with capital heterogeneity. Auerbach also adopts the OLG dynamics, calling it "the neo-classical growth model introduced by Diamond." Auerbach was one of the first of the Boomer generation to adopt the OLG model in his work, and his non-chalance in simply referring to it as the neoclassical growth model, suggests a degree of acceptance of the naturalness of the OLG framework, given Diamond's work in showing how standard neoclassical production fit into Samuelson's model. That said, when we asked Auerbach why he settled on the OLG model for this work, he indicated that it likely had to do with his thesis advisor Marty Feldstein's earlier related work being set in a static two-period model, with OLG being the natural dynamic framework in which to extend Feldstein's analysis.

Other early applications of the OLG model to issues of taxation include work by Laurence Kotlikoff (who was a year ahead of Auerbach at Harvard) and Lawrence Summers.

Kotlikoff and Summers (1979) also extend the work by Feldstein on the topic of long-run versus short-run tax incidence using the two-period lived OLG framework of Diamond. Kotlikoff and Summers also include human capital accumulation in the model, although this is modeled as an individual agent's trading off leisure time versus training which leads to higher future income rather than as a parental investment in education.

As we noted above in our discussion of Tobin's use of multiperiod simulated OLG models, all three of these Harvard-trained scholars would make important use of the OLG model in their later work and were together pioneers in the use of realistically multiperiod OLG simulations for various types of policy analysis. We will return to discuss this work later in the book.

6.3 THE BALASKO–SHELL ANALYSIS

We turn next to the work of Yves Balasko and Karl Shell in their definitive papers on the OLG model, along with a paper co-authored by Balasko, Cass, and Shell during the same time period.

All four of these papers were influential in the development of the OLG model and were based on exploring the general equilibrium fundamentals of the model. These papers were:

1. "The Overlapping-generations Model I: The Case of Pure Exchange without money," *Journal of Economic Theory* 23.3, 1980, 281–306 (Balasko & Shell, 1980).
2. "Existence of Competitive Equilibrium in a General Overlapping-generations Model," *Journal of Economic Theory,* 23.3, 1980, 307–322 (Balasko, Cass, Shell, 1980).
3. "The Overlapping-generations Model II. The Case of Pure Exchange with Money," *Journal of Economic Theory* 24.1, 1981, 112–142 (Balasko & Shell, 1981a).
4. "The Overlapping-generations Model III. The Case of Log-linear Utility Functions," *Journal of Economic Theory,* 24.1, 1981, 143–152 (Balasko & Shell, 1981b).

As we noted above, Yves Balasko was a young scholar, who recently graduated from the Ecole Normale Superieur with a Ph.D. in Mathematics when Karl Shell met him in Paris and recruited him to work on the project of providing a full and detailed mathematical characterization of the OLG model.

All four of the papers look at deterministic, pure exchange versions of the OLG model. Of the four papers, the Balasko–Cass–Shell is the most general, although it focuses only on the question of the existence of competitive equilibrium in the model. This paper includes a formal demonstration of the claim made in the Cass and Shell "Basic Approach" contribution to the Kareken–Wallace (1980) volume that any OLG model can be converted into one in which agents live for two periods via a suitable reinterpretation of endowment and consumption vectors. The model examined here allows for heterogeneous agents within generations, general utility specifications – the only required properties of the utility function are continuity, non-satiation, and quasi-concavity – and the possibility that some endowments or consumptions are zero during some period(s) of an agent's life.

According to Shell in private communication, the three Balasko–Shell papers were written prior to the Balasko–Cass–Shell paper. Shell notes that after the equilibrium existence proof given in BS-I, they talked about how to weaken the assumptions used in that proof to provide a general proof of existence (see the bottom of p. 289 and top of p. 290). These arguments were formalized in the three-author paper.

The three Balasko–Shell papers make two important simplifying assumptions:

1. There is a representative consumer born in each period who lives two periods.
2. Preferences are smooth in the sense of the utility functions being continuously differentiable, with indifference curves bounded from below.

All three papers focus on pure exchange economies as well.

The BS-I paper looks at an economy in which there are forward markets on which agents can trade one period ahead to make or take delivery of commodities contracted over in the previous period. This assumption simplifies the basic analysis by ensuring that agents can freely transfer wealth between periods without the need for additional assets and asset markets. This leads, in particular, to a typical young agent facing a single budget constraint.

Since it will be useful going forward, we introduce some basic notation that Balasko and Shell use in their analysis of the model. With a single consumer born in each period and agents living in two periods, we follow Shell in referring to the young agent born in period t as Mr t.[1] Mr t's lifetime consumption vector is $x^t = \left[x_t^t, x_t^{t+1}\right]$, where x_t^s is the vector of goods Mr t consumes in period $s=t, t+1$. This notation – subscripts for birth dates, and superscripts for time periods – has become conventional in the general equilibrium analysis of OLG models. Endowments are denoted similarly, by $\omega^t = \left[\omega_t^t, \omega_t^{t+1}\right]$. Preferences are specified via a (possibly time-varying) utility function

$$u : \mathbb{R}_+^{2I} \to \mathbb{R},$$

which is assumed to be differentiable monotonic, strictly quasi-concave, with the closure of all indifference curves strictly contained in the positive orthant. Here, $I < \infty$ is the number of goods consumed. These assumptions are sufficient to guarantee that demand functions, and hence excess demand functions, are differentiable. With this notation, the budget constraint for a typical young agent born in period t is given by

$$p^t \cdot x_t^t + p^t \cdot x_t^{t+1} = p^t \cdot \omega_t^t + p^t \cdot \omega_t^{t+1}.$$

The analysis is undertaken assuming that there is an initial period, though this can be interpreted as simply the point at which the analyst "breaks into" an otherwise ongoing economy. For this, Balasko and Shell also define specific consumptions and preferences for the initial old generation, with their consumptions from youth taken as historically given.

Prices are introduced as infinite sequences $p = \left\{p^1, p^2, \ldots, p^t, \ldots\right\}$ with each $p^t \in \mathbb{R}^l_+$. Prices are normalized by taking the price of the first good in the first period, $p^1_1 = 1$. This specifies prices in present-value terms, with good one as the numeraire. Balasko and Shell denote the resulting price space by *S*.

As we noted above, Balasko and Shell use the same notational shortcut as in Malinvaud (1953), by letting Mr *t*'s consumption vector x^t also represent the infinite-dimensional vector

$$x^t = \left[0, \ldots, 0, x^t_t, x^{t+1}_t, 0, \ldots\right].$$

Via this shortcut, we can represent the consumption/endowment sets of each consumer as

$$X_t = \left(X^t_t, X^{t+1}_t\right) \subset \mathbb{R}^l_+ \times \mathbb{R}^l_+ \text{ or}$$

$$X_t = \left[0, \ldots, 0, X^t_t, X^{t+1}_t, 0, \ldots\right]$$

and the aggregate consumption/endowment set for the economy as

$$X = \left[X^1_0 + X^1_1, X^2_1 + X^2_2, \ldots, X^t_{t-1} + X^t_t, \ldots\right].$$

We make this point in somewhat more detail than do Balasko and Shell because it highlights the fact that any economically relevant functions defined on the economy's aggregate consumption space would only need to satisfy nice properties – continuity or differentiability – component-wise, so that the only topology one needs to consider for the model is the product topology.

Once the paper defines basic commodity spaces, preferences, consumer optimization problems, and allocations, it formally defines the set of *weakly Pareto optimal* allocations as those that cannot be Pareto dominated (in the usual sense) by any finite reallocation of resources among agents.

The most important contribution of this paper to the development of the OLG model is its proof of the existence of competitive equilibrium. The technique Balasko and Shell developed in this paper has been applied quite broadly in a variety of contexts to show the existence of equilibrium in OLG models. So, it is worth spending a little time examining their proof.

The proof proceeds in three main steps.

For the first step, let $f^s_t\left(p^t, p^{t+1}, p^t \cdot \omega^t_t + p^{t+1} \cdot \omega^{t+1}_t\right)$ be the demand function for Mr *t* in period *s*, when prices are $\left[p^t, p^{t+1}\right]$ and Mr *t*'s income or wealth is given by the value of his endowments $p^t \cdot \omega^t_t + p^{t+1} \cdot \omega^{t+1}_t$. Define Mr *t*'s excess demand in period *s* as

$$z_t^s = f_t^s - \omega_t^s$$

With this notation, Balasko and Shell define a *t-equilibrium* price sequence

$$p = \left[p^1, p^2, \ldots, p^t, p^{t+1}, \ldots\right] \in S$$

as any prices that solve the finite set of equations

$$z_0^1 + z_1^1 = 0$$

$$z_1^2 + z_2^2 = 0$$

$$\vdots$$

$$z_{t-1}^t + z_t^t = 0.$$

The next step in the proof shows that as long as resources in each period are bounded, one can find natural upper and lower bounds on the price vectors (see the paper for details on this). Imposing these bounds on the price vectors, one obtains a subspace of the price space $S^* \subset S$ such that each factor in S^* is compact. This then implies that S^* is itself compact in the product topology by Tychonoff's theorem.

The final step in the proof is to denote the set of t-equilibrium price sequences by $W(t)$, and to observe that by construction

$$W(t) \supset W(t+1) \text{ for all } t$$

Since the equations defining each t-equilibrium sequence are those one would obtain for a standard, static Arrow–Debreu economy, the usual tools used to show the existence of equilibrium in these economies shows that for all t, $W(t) \neq \varnothing$. Via the inclusion relationships, then, a generalized nested set theorem (Balasko and Shell refer the reader to a result in Bourbaki), the set

$$W(\infty) = \cap_{t=1}^{\infty} W(t) \neq \phi$$

The remainder of the paper is devoted to a welfare analysis of the competitive equilibrium.

The first result shown is that the competitive equilibrium is always weakly Pareto optimal. This is the closest analogy to the First Welfare theorem that one can obtain in the OLG model. The analog of the Second Welfare theorem is that every weakly Pareto optimal allocation can be supported as a competitive equilibrium after a suitable reallocation of endowments. These two results are established in *Proposition 4.4* of the paper. As we noted earlier, Samuelson was the first to observe that the First Welfare theorem would hold for any finite truncation of the model; the Balasko–Shell result generalizes this observation.

The analysis of when allocations are fully Pareto optimal proceeds by defining sequences of transfers between agents which are feasible (in the sense of adding up to zero), then showing that if there is a Pareto improving transfer between (say) Mr t and Mr $t-1$, then there must be non-zero transfers for all following agents as well. We can think of this in terms of the simple one-good model in which a transfer from any young agent to an old agent must be compensated in the following period by a transfer from the next period's young to the now old agent.

Balasko and Shell then show that under some technical assumptions on the boundedness of consumption sequences and supporting prices at any weakly Pareto optimal allocation, and given sufficient curvature of agents' indifference curves, then a version of the so-called Cass criterion

$$\sum_{t}^{\infty} \frac{1}{\| p^t \|} = \infty$$

is necessary and sufficient for the allocation to be Pareto optimal. In a one-good context, this result corresponds to having all interest rates being non-negative, or, equivalently, all intertemporal marginal rates of substitution being greater than or equal to one in absolute value. This result is established in *Proposition 5.6* of the paper.

The second Balasko–Shell paper builds on the results of the first paper by introducing fiat money. In terms of notation, this amounts to adding definitions for Mr t's period s money accumulation $x_t^{s,m}$, money transfers from the government m_t^s, and a (present-value) price for money $p^{t,m} \geq 0$. If the government pursues an active monetary policy so that the $m_t^s \neq 0$, the total (nominal) money supply is given by

$$M^t = \sum_{s=}^{t} \sum_{\tau=s-1}^{s} m_\tau^s.$$

Note that in this setting, Balasko and Shell allow the money transfers to be positive or negative so that at this level of abstraction, there is no real distinction between fiscal and monetary policy.

The key change from the BS-I paper is in the specification of the budget constraints. For a typical young agent, they now face two budget constraints

$$p^t x_t^t + p^{m,t} x_t^{m,t} = p^t \omega_t^t + p^{m,t} m_t^t$$

$$p^{t+1} x_t^{t+1} + p^{m,t+1} x_t^{m,t+1} = p^{t+1} \omega_t^{t+1} + p^{m,t+1} m_t^{t+1}.$$

These budget constraints can be combined into a single budget constraint by adding them, since markets will be complete as long as the price of money is strictly positive

$$\begin{aligned} p^t x_t^t + p^{t+1} x_t^{t+1} + p^{m,t} x_t^{m,t} + p^{m,t+1} x_t^{m,t+1} = \\ = p^t \omega_t^t + p^{t+1} \omega_t^{t+1} + p^{m,t} m_t^t + p^{m,t+1} m_t^{t+1} \end{aligned}$$

Competitive equilibrium in the model is then defined analogously to the definition in the non-monetary model, with the additional requirement that money markets clear, that is, the desired money holdings of all agents add up to the total money supply as long as the price of money is positive. If the price of money is zero, then any money holdings less than or equal to the total supply is an equilibrium.

With these preliminaries, Balasko and Shell show a key result: along any monetary equilibrium price sequence, the present-value price of money must be a non-negative constant. The proof is straightforward. Suppose $p^{m,t} \neq p^{m,t+1}$ for some periods t and $t+1$. Have the agent t set $x_t^{m,t} = -x_t^{m,t+1}$. From the budget constraints, we get

$$p^t x_t^t + p^{t+1} x_t^{t+1} + \left(p^{m,t} - p^{m,t+1}\right) x_t^{m,t} = \text{RHS},$$

where RHS denotes the agent's income. If the money price difference here is negative, then an arbitrarily large purchase of money in period t allows arbitrarily large lifetime consumption. If the price difference is positive, then an arbitrarily large sale of money (i.e., borrowing) again yields the possibility of arbitrarily large consumption. As long as agents' preferences are non-satiated, then, differences in the present value of money between periods lead to arbitrage opportunities that are inconsistent with equilibrium in the money market. Hence, in equilibrium, it must be that $p^{m,t} = p^m$ for all t. If $p^m = 0$, then we have a non-monetary equilibrium, while $p^m > 0$ gives a monetary equilibrium. As Balasko and Shell note, this condition is well-known from work on intertemporal capital accumulation, where it represents the no-arbitrage condition on durable capital.

Balasko and Shell use the monetary framework developed in the paper to develop a theoretical framework for analyzing monetary policies in the OLG model, though they note that at the level of abstraction in the paper, there isn't really a distinction between monetary and fiscal policy, since positive money transfers are also government spending (though without the imposition of a government budget constraint), while negative money transfers are taxes. To this end, the paper defines a *bonafide* monetary policy as a sequence of injections/withdrawals of fiat money that maintains a non-zero price of money.

Most of the middle part of the paper is devoted to examining the properties of *bonafide* policies. These include:

1. Long-run neutrality of money: if all money transfers are scaled up or down in the same non-zero proportion, the equilibrium allocations remain unchanged (*Proposition 4.7* of the paper).
2. If the allocation sequence is bounded above and $\| p^t \| \rightarrow 0$, so that interest rates are eventually positive, then $M^t = 0$. This is a general characterization of Gale's classical case (*Proposition 5.8* of the paper).
3. Equilibrium money prices are indeterminate; different price levels for the economy can be consistent with the monetary equilibrium associated with a given monetary policy (discussion after *Proposition 7.3* of the paper).

The last result is important because it implies that one cannot associate a unique equilibrium price of money with the set of equilibrium allocations and define this as the utility of having a store of value. This, in turn, means that any monetary theory based on money-in-the-utility function must ultimately be one of modeling the micro-foundations of transactions and representing the result as an indirect utility of money.

The third paper in the series examines a specific instance of the OLG model in which all agents' utility functions are log-linear. For a typical young agent, the utility function takes the form

$$u\left(x_t^{t+1}, x_t^t\right) = \sum\nolimits_{i=1}^{l} \alpha_t^{t,i} ln\ ln\ x_t^{t,i} + \sum\nolimits_{i=1}^{l} \alpha_t^{t+1,i} ln\ ln\ x_t^{t+1,i},$$

where the coefficients satisfy

$$\sum\nolimits_{i=1}^{l} \alpha_t^{t,i} + \sum\nolimits_{i=1}^{l} \alpha_t^{t+1,i} = 1.$$

With this specification, the paper then examines the monetary equilibria associated with different monetary policies and shows that the set of *bonafide* monetary policies is convex, and that, for a given specification of endowments and monetary policy injections, the set of equilibrium money prices is an interval.

We note that much of the analysis in BS-II and BS-III makes heavy use of the price-income equilibrium analysis developed by Balasko and detailed in Balasko (2016). While an explication of this approach to equilibrium analysis is beyond the scope of this text, Balasko and Shell's application of these techniques illustrates how the practice of micro-founding macroeconomic models makes possible the application of powerful tools from general equilibrium theory.

6.4 SUNSPOTS

The final topic we cover in this chapter is the development of so-called *sunspot* models, that is, models in which agents' beliefs are based on random events that are extrinsic to the economy, but which are self-fulfilling in the resulting stochastic rational expectations equilibrium. Before we embark on our examination of this work, we refer the reader to the very thorough the work of Cherrier and Saidi (2018) looking at the development and propagation of the sunspots idea in economics.

In looking at the genesis of the idea, there are three papers to consider. Chronologically, these are Shell (1977), Azariadis (1981), and Cass and Shell (1983).

According to Cass and Shell, the idea that there might be self-fulfilling rational expectations equilibria in an economy with no intrinsic uncertainty developed from conversations they began having after Cass moved from Carnegie Mellon to Penn in 1974. From the *Macroeconomic Dynamics* interview with Cass (Spear & Wright, 1998) (discussing the impact of Lucas' 1972 "Expectations and the Neutrality of Money" paper)

> I wasn't so interested in the macro, but what struck me, and this is related to some of my later work, was the assumption that Bob made to solve for equilibrium, that the state variables were obvious (that is actually the first time that I thought about the sunspot idea). Bob and I had some long discussions, and I would say, "Well Bob, why is this the actual state space in this model?" That question came up – and now I am jumping ahead – after I came to Penn. At

some point Karl and I started talking about that and we developed what we called the idea of sunspots. (p. 45)

Shell corroborates this in his *Macroeconomic Dynamics* interview (Spear & Wright, 2001):

I made a trial run on sunspots at the Penn theory workshop during the Spring of 1977. In May 1977, I gave the core of what became the Malinvaud lecture at the Dartmouth conference center on Squam Lake. It was at an MSSB [Mathematical Social Sciences Board] conference organized by Dave and me.

My lecture was in part a follow-up to my 1971 *JPE* OG *Notes [on the Economics of Infinity]*. Hence the focus was on the simple linear case. Immediately after the lecture, while still at the conference, Dave and I did an analysis of the nonlinear case, using Gale-like phase diagrams. (p. 721)

As Cass and Shell were working on fleshing out this new idea, the Economics Department at Penn hired Costas Azariadis as an Associate Professor. Azariadis did his graduate work at GSIA (Carnegie Mellon's business school, now called the Tepper School of Business), where Ed Prescott was his thesis advisor, though Azariadis counted Bob Lucas as a mentor there as well. Azariadis' early work from his thesis and time at Brown University as an Assistant Professor was in contract theory and applications of that to macroeconomics. He later became interested in dynamic macroeconomics and (presumably based on his knowledge of Lucas' work) decided that the OLG model was the way forward. From his *Macroeconomic Dynamics* interview (Durlauf, 2007):

The only problem was that few people, except Karl Shell and Dave Cass at Penn, cared much or knew much about OLG. When I suggested to Herschel Grossman that we had to bone up on that model if we wanted to do interesting work in macro, he asked how we should do that. To which I replied, only half in jest, that we had to move to Penn. And that is exactly what happened. I was offered a job at the Penn economics department in March 1977, moved to Philadelphia in August of the same year, and stayed there for the next 14 years. (p. 255)

During Azariadis' first few years at Penn, he and Shell became friends, and they talked a good bit about the sunspots idea. From the Shell interview:

Dave and I are the co-inventors of the sunspot equilibrium concept. Our original invention was explicitly based on OG dynamics. We later introduced sunspots into other general equilibrium models. I returned from Paris in June full of my OG work with Yves and my sunspots work with Dave. Dave picked us up at the Philadelphia airport, but was out of circulation for the rest of the summer. I gave Costas a copy of the Malinvaud lecture, and filled him in on what Dave and I had done beyond this. Costas was, for quite some time, resistant to the ideas, but we had a lot of time together and eventually he was persuaded. Costas did something that Dave and I did not do: He found *stationary* (Markovian) sunspot effects (in the Lucas model). (Shell interview. Op. cit. pp. 724–725)

Azariadis also recalls his skepticism about the sunspots idea in his interview:

[T]he issue of beliefs kept coming up in conversations between me and Karl Shell, mainly because he and I lived close to each other in West Philadelphia. We frequently walked home together from Penn, and used to debate about beliefs and other things. Karl had an early example of multiple equilibria in a 1977 French-language working paper. I found the idea interesting, but the example uncompelling. It was a static economy with flat indifference curves that became tangent to budget lines at many points. I told Karl his example was a fluke, something completely nongeneric. Rational expectations, I claimed, would surely rule out his "sunspots."

> I told Karl in 1979 that I was going to write down a robust example of an economy with indifference curves that were not flat. That, I hoped, would persuade him that "sunspots" could not exist. I had not counted on large income effects, which permit many equilibria in static economies, and many laws of motion in dynamic ones. When I finished my example, it turned out that I had made Karl's case better than he had done. He was right, and I was wrong, for a large family of OLG environments. (Op. cit., p. 256)

For the record, we note that Azariadis is incorrect in his recollection that Shell's "Monnai et Allocation" paper (Shell, 1977) was in French; it was not. The title page was in French, but the body of the paper was in English. We should also note that the model in Shell (1977) was not static, but in fact, use the OLG structure to construct sunspot equilibria around the deterministic steady state of the model.

The paper that resulted from this interaction was Azariadis' "Self-fulfilling Prophecies" (referenced above). From our perspective, this is a clear case of the kind of scientific discoveries based on intellectual cross-fertilization that have occurred in other cases in economics (see, e.g., Young, 1987, on the origins of IS-LM and Young (2014) on the origins of Real Business Cycle models).

However, at the time, Dave Cass didn't view things that way. From the Cass interview, it is clear he didn't share Shell's enthusiasm for Azariadis' paper:

> My view is that Karl explained the idea to Costas a number of times, and Costas finally picked up on it and he wrote a paper about it. He realized, not from a utility approach, but by having a first-order Markov system of probabilities, that one can get sunspot equilibria. Steve's thesis actually develops the general story, and he solved that problem long before, for example, Azariadis and Guesnerie did. But I have to credit Costas with something. When Costas produced a working paper or maybe even before that we realized that if we were going to develop the idea, we'd better get to it. (Cass interview. Op. cit. p. 50)

The reference here to "Steve's thesis" is to Spear (1984). That paper came about as a result of Cass' resentment directed at both Shell and Azariadis for what he perceived as the unauthorized use of the sunspot idea. From Spear's private recollection of the genesis of this paper:

> Dave called me into his office one morning while I was finishing up some work on my first thesis paper (which was all about temporary equilibrium), and sketched out the idea behind sunspot equilibria, and about how to characterize these in a simple OLG model where the extrinsic uncertainty is just a coin flip. I found the idea intriguing and went to work on it, finally coming up with a set of sufficient conditions for the existence of these equilibria. I have to admit that at one point I was stuck, and asked Costas for some help, which he gave gladly, though not without a bit of a funny look my way. It was quite a few years later that I learned that Dave had given me the problem to work on because of his anger at Azariadis.

According to private communication from Shell, this incident was the beginning of what he has called the "Cass–Shell divorce" though there were earlier indications of friction over Shell's openness to discussing ideas with colleagues and an apparent growing penchant toward secrecy on Cass' part.

Since Cass sadly is no longer alive and thus cannot answer questions regarding this incident, we can only speculate as to what might have generated this penchant.

As a general matter, secrecy in scientific work can serve one of two purposes. It can help ensure that priority for an idea is correctly established, or it can ensure that results, when finally released, are correct and properly understood.

Looking at Cass' career retrospectively, he never seems to have been particularly concerned about priority. In previous work (see Spear & Young, 2014), we have detailed the story of how a young Dave Cass, as a graduate student, worked out the solution to the constrained optimal control problem for the one-sector continuous-time growth model. A much more senior Tjalling Koopmans was also working on this problem, but his initial attempts to solve it were in error. After hearing from Edmond Malinvaud why his solution was wrong, Koopmans ended up getting help from Hirofumi Uzawa – who happened to be Dave Cass' thesis advisor – in the form of a preview of the thesis chapter in which Cass had solved the problem.

After the publication of both Cass' and Koopmans' papers, the economics profession's long-standing view of the work was that the two papers were developed independently and simultaneously, something we now know not to be true. Cass never let on that he knew this wasn't the case and went to his death insisting that the work had been independent and simultaneous.

From the Cass interview, commenting on this episode:

> Actually, Uzawa liked to one-up people. At some point he was talking to Tjalling about the problem, and Tjalling was describing what he was doing and Uzawa interrupted and said, "Well, I have a graduate student who did that problem." Then Tjalling got very nervous about it, he was always very nervous about …, oh, authorship and who was first and that sort of thing, and we had some correspondence. (Cass interview. Op. cit. p. 38)

On the rigor aspect of secrecy, Cass always emphasized accuracy and could well have viewed his work with Shell as preliminary enough to warrant keeping it under wraps. Despite this, Cass was not particularly secretive about collaborative work with colleagues. From Spear's private recollections:

> It was quite common to see Dave, Karl, and Costas sitting in the CARESS [Center for Analytic Research in Economics and the Social Sciences] lounge working through their ideas about sunspot equilibria on the board. Dave liked the lounge because, after the University had banned smoking in offices, he had had a large exhaust fan installed in the lounge to vent the cigarette smoke. Most of us in the graduate program would see them there when we went into the lounge to get coffee.

If we look carefully at the Cass–Shell "Do Sunspots Matter" paper in comparison with Azariadis' "Self-fulfilling Prophecies" paper, one clear distinction becomes apparent. Azariadis was focused on the macroeconomic implications of sunspot equilibria as a potential driver of business cycle fluctuations – akin to Keynes' notion of "animal spirits." Cass and Shell, on the other hand, were focused on understanding and explaining the general equilibrium frictions that could give rise to self-fulfilling prophecies. In Azariadis' paper, it is strong income effects that generate the possibility of sunspot equilibria. In the Cass–Shell paper, it is restrictions on trading opportunities and other frictions that lead to a failure of the welfare theorems that matter.

Since Cass and Shell had not yet worked these issues out in their research, it is entirely natural that Cass might have felt that Azariadis had been too cavalier with his results.

At the end of the day, we don't have definitive evidence of what led to Cass' resentment over the situation. It could be that the experience of being denied what should have been a clear priority for his work on the growth model in his thesis might have left Cass less open to the cross-communication of ideas during their early stages of development. This seems unlikely though, given that the neoclassical growth model is universally known today (and has been for many years) as the Ramsey–Cass–Koopmans model. It may be simply that Cass didn't feel that income effects were sufficient justification for putting forward the sunspot concept absent a deeper explanation of how the phenomenon arose.

But Cass' resentment did have repercussions. It led to the breakdown of a years-long productive research relationship between Cass and Shell, and ultimately to Shell's relocation to Cornell's Economics Department in 1986. It left Azariadis, then a still junior faculty member, alienated from the senior faculty who had been instrumental in recruiting him to Penn. When we asked Azariadis why he hadn't offered Cass and Shell co-authorships on the self-fulfilling prophecies paper, he replied:

> My, perhaps imprecise, recollection of the co-authorship issue you raise was that it never came up or was broached by anyone involved. One reason was that I started the prophecies paper in an attempt to show that Karl's 1977 example was a fluke. I thought that example could not be generic because rational expectations equilibria were locally unique in static models, as in the work of Radner, and saddles in dynamic models. It did not occur to me that Karl would co-author a paper that wanted to prove him wrong! (email May 28, 2022)

While it seems unlikely that Cass and Shell would have accepted a co-authorship had it been offered, given the direction that their own work took, the whole situation would have been considerably less problematic if Azariadis had presented Cass and Shell with a mini-seminar on his discovery, and worked through the issues of how to present the discovery and the allocation of credit before the publication of the paper. To his credit, Shell did not let his own concerns with this situation bias him in his position as Editor of the *Journal of Economic Theory*, which processed the Azariadis paper through to publication.

Since these two papers have been influential – Azariadis' paper has 1,143 citations on Google Scholar, and the Cass–Shell paper has 1,460, as of this writing – and because it will help to explicate the differences between the Cass–Shell and Azariadis' approaches to sunspots, it is worth spending some time looking at the results. We start with the Azariadis paper since it was published first.

The key insight that Azariadis had in looking at the sunspot question was in recognizing that a very simple stochastic process – a Markov chain on two-point support – was, in the limit, a cycle. Indeed, if one writes the transition probability matrix for this as

$$P = \begin{bmatrix} \pi_{11} & \pi_{12} \\ \pi_{21} & \pi_{22} \end{bmatrix},$$

where π_{ij} is the probability of starting in state $i = 1, 2$ and making a transition to state $j = 1, 2$. When $\pi_{ij} = 1, i \neq j$ then necessarily $\pi_{ii} = 0$ for i=1, 2, and the transition matrix degenerates to

$$P = \begin{bmatrix} 0 & 1 \\ 1 & 0 \end{bmatrix}.$$

But this implies that the process alternates deterministically between the two states, which is to say, the process is simply a cycle of period 2. What Azariadis did was to show that when the simple OLG model has a cyclic equilibrium, it will then also have a sunspot equilibrium (i.e., one which is genuinely stochastic) because the equations that define the equilibrium – the first-order conditions and market-clearing conditions – depend continuously on the probabilities associated with the transition matrix. We can illustrate this using the simple version of the Lucas model that we developed above. Specifically, the equilibrium equation

$$z_1^H + \frac{1}{\rho} z_2^{HT} = 0$$

is the same as in the stochastic model, except now, none of the endowments entering into the definition of the two excess demand functions is actually stochastic. In this case, given our assumption that we are dealing with a Samuelsonian economy in which the endowments of the young exceed those of the old, we know that one equilibrium value of the relative price ρ will be one.

We illustrate the possibilities graphically in Fig. 11.

The diagram shows the graphs of two different deterministic excess demand functions. The blue graph corresponds to an economy in which there is a unique (monetary) equilibrium with a relative price equal to 1. The red graph corresponds to an economy with three equilibria, two of which are different from the one with $\rho = 1$. For the red economy, it is possible for the equilibrium to cycle between the higher and lower equilibrium prices. This possibility, as we noted above, was foreseen by Gale, and is illustrated in Fig. 6, taken from Gale (1973). We replicate Gale's diagram in detail to show how the cyclic equilibrium can occur in Fig. 12.

In this diagram, the blue curve is the offer curve, and the red line is the resource constraint (downward sloping 45-degree line) which, if continued down to where it intersects the offer curve would indicate the endowment. The black square, where it intersects the offer curve shows the two cyclic equilibria that the economy

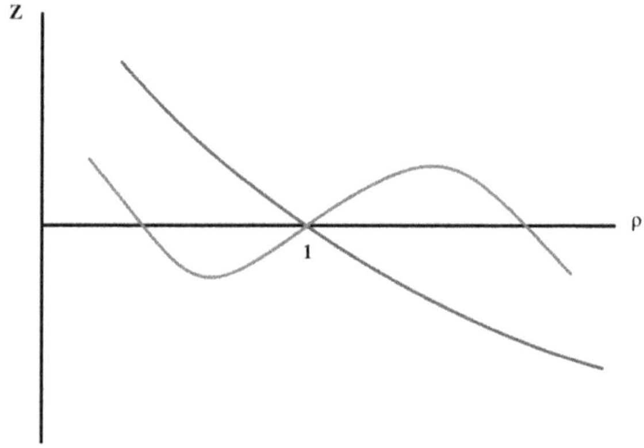

Fig. 11. Excess Demand Functions for Non-sunspot and Sunspot Equilibria.

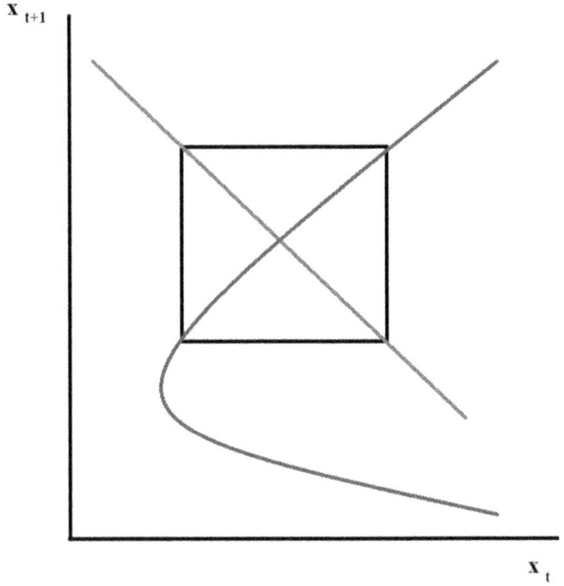

Fig. 12. Backward-bending Offer Curve and Cyclic Equilibrium.

oscillates between. Note that this requires the offer curve to bend back on itself, which occurs when the income effects are such that young agents will wish to save less when interest rates rise. In this Samuelsonian setting, interest rates would oscillate between being positive (at the upper equilibrium point) and negative at the lower point.

The Cass–Shell paper used a truncated version of the OLG model to simplify the analysis and focus on the general equilibrium aspects of the sunspot issue. As Cass and Shell note in a long footnote at the beginning of the paper:

> These examples [from Azariadis' paper], however, are based on very complicated dynamic models which do not permit us to separate the respective roles of generational overlap, the infinite time horizon, and government debt. In the present paper, we focus on the implications of generational overlap in a very simple equilibrium model. (Cass & Shell, 1983, p. 194)

The Cass–Shell paper focuses on the role of restricted participation in markets as the phenomenon that allows extrinsic uncertainty to matter, that is, to have a real effect on consumers' allocations and utility. The restriction on participation in their model is implemented by positing a generation of consumers who live two modeling periods and have access to securities markets for inside money (zero net supply bonds) and Arrow securities for insuring themselves against the perceived (but extrinsic) uncertainty. A second generation of consumers is born after the realization of the sunspot variable, lives out the second period only, and can trade only on current period spot markets for commodities.

This restriction on participation is similar to that examined by Cass and Yaari (1966), but the limitation to two periods simplifies the model considerably.

Cass and Shell show several important results. First, if markets are complete and participation is not restricted, then sunspots can never matter. Second, they show that with restricted market participation, if the underlying certainty economy has multiple equilibria, then one can obtain sunspot equilibria by randomizing over the multiple certainty equilibria. This is a quick and easy way to show that sunspots can matter. A second important point the paper makes (in *Proposition 7*) is that if the welfare theorems hold in a model, then there can be no sunspot equilibria. Cass and Shell tried to show in the Appendix to the paper that there could be non-trivial sunspot equilibria in a model for which the certainty equilibrium was unique. According to private communication from Shell (email dated September 5, 2022), two of Tom Muench's students had found a mistake in the Appendix which couldn't be fixed. In later work (see, e.g., Shell & Wright, 1993), Shell gave examples of models having unique certainty equilibrium and non-trivial sunspot equilibria.

While this third observation may seem trivial, its converse – that if the welfare theorems don't hold, the model can exhibit sunspot equilibria – raises a host of interesting possibilities for economic dynamics. Shell has dubbed this converse proposition the "Philadelphia Pholk" theorem because of the myriad results it has spawned as researchers looked into instances in which the welfare theorems failed to see if sunspots mattered.

The Philadelphia connection in Shell's quip is through Penn, via the number of economists who looked more deeply into the connection between market failures and sunspots. These economists include Cass, who spent much of the rest of his career studying incomplete markets, beginning with an example of how market incompleteness could give rise to sunspot equilibria (see, e.g., Cass, 1989). Shell and his student Jim Peck wrote several papers looking at the effects of imperfect competition as a source of sunspots, based on the Shapley–Shubik market game. They found an important connection between the notion of correlated equilibrium in game theory and sunspot equilibrium in the market game (see Peck & Shell, 1991). Spear showed, in the context of an otherwise conventional RBC model, that externalities in production could lead to the existence of sunspot equilibria (see Spear, 1991). A similar result was also shown by Kehoe, Levine, and Romer in the context of taxation (see Kehoe, Levine, & Romer, 1992).

In macroeconomics, the sunspots idea saw applications as the driver of aggregate shocks in real business cycle models, as well as interpretations of Keynesian "animal spirits" in models that linked the psychology of expectations formation with dynamic economics. We will examine these issues in more detail at the end of the book.

NOTE

1. Penn graduate students in the 70s and 80s who took Shell's OLG course always got a chuckle out of the fact that, at the time, Shell was apparently unaware of the other Mr T, a professional wrestler turned TV star.

CHAPTER 7

BOOMERS

As we noted in the Introduction, there was an explosion of new research done on the OLG model in the decade of the 1980s–1990s, much of it by baby boomers in or just finishing graduate school. As we noted at the beginning of the previous chapter, this work was concentrated predominantly at Minnesota, MIT, and Penn, for the simple reason that these researchers were trained by the previous academic generation who did the original work on the model.

In examining this work, we will proceed roughly chronologically, but also try to organize consideration by focusing first on developments with the deterministic OLG model, and then on stochastic extensions of it.

7.1 KEHOE AND LEVINE

We begin by looking at the work of Tim Kehoe and David Levine. We consider this to be coming from the MIT tradition, although Kehoe's Ph.D. was from Yale (working with Herb Scarf and Andreu Mas-Colell). While Kehoe's first job was at Wesleyan University (beginning in 1978), he moved to MIT in 1980. Levine's Ph.D. was from MIT in 1981, working with Peter Diamond and then-new assistant professor Tim Kehoe. The source of Levine's interest in OLG is obvious from the connection with Diamond. According to Levine, Kehoe's interest in OLG developed as they began looking at determinacy issues. From an email communication (dated July 14, 2022):

> Tim arrived at MIT my last year, September 1980, I finished in September 1981, and we were working on [the OLG project] by March 1982. I did a bunch of determinacy stuff in my dissertation but on game theory. I'm pretty sure we started with the finite players infinite horizon determinacy using the Negishi method which Tim was fond of and taught me. This was a natural extension of the work Tim was already doing on the finite economy case. I think we quickly wondered what happened in the OG model, and my best guess is we started talking about this sometime between March 1981 while I was a graduate student, and before February 1982 when I was at UCLA.

Overlapping Generations: Methods, Models and Morphology
International Symposia in Economic Theory and Econometrics, Volume 32, 99–157

ISSN: 1571-0386/doi:10.1108/S1571-038620230000032017

Most of the Kehoe–Levine (K&L) papers on OLG were produced during the early 1980s, while Kehoe was at MIT and Levine was a new assistant professor at UCLA. As Levine noted in an email to us dated June 12, 2022, "we worked via telephone calls and fax back then."

K&L approached the OLG model using the tools of general equilibrium theory, applied within the framework of dynamic systems analysis. Dynamic systems analysis was not new to economics, having been widely applied to the study of the neoclassical capital model in continuous time. Continuous-time formulations are generally easier to analyze since they are characterized by differential equations rather than difference equations, so it isn't particularly surprising that the early work of Ramsey, Malinvaud, Solow, Cass, and others was first formulated in continuous time. Discrete-time applications came about with the interpretation of economic time as planning time, where agents would formulate plans to be carried out over a discrete set of periods (e.g., weeks). Basic dynamic systems theory applies equally well to both treatments of time, though, as we noted above, continuous-time systems tend to be more tractable and amenable to analytic solutions. Thus, for example, in the stability analysis of the continuous-time capital model, the optimal steady state is usually saddle-path stable. As we will see later, discrete-time versions of the model can exhibit very different stability properties. The early 1970s was a period of rapid advancement in the understanding of discrete-time dynamic systems in mathematics, so it isn't surprising that economists interested in dynamic models would find a useful toolkit here. For details on these mathematical developments, see, e.g., Aubin & Dalmedico (2002).

As a preliminary matter, it will be useful to illustrate the basic structure of the discrete-time approach to dynamic systems analysis.

A dynamic system is a specification of state variables and a function or mapping which defines how the state variables evolve over time. If we denote our state vector by $z \in \mathbb{R}^n$, then we can represent the dynamic system as a *forward difference equation*

$$z_{t+1} = f(z_t).$$

A fixed point of the mapping $\hat{z} = f(\hat{z})$ is called a steady state, or a stationary point, or a rest point of the dynamic system. A fixed point $\hat{z}$ is locally stable if there exists a neighborhood $N(\hat{z})$ such that for any $z' \in N(\hat{z})$

$$\lim_{t \to \infty} f^t(z') = \hat{z},$$

where $f^t = f \circ f \circ \overbrace{\cdots}^{t \text{ times}} f$.

The *invariant manifolds* associated with a particular steady state are hypersurfaces $M \subset \mathbb{R}^n$ such that $\hat{z} \in M$, and if $z' \in M$, then $f(z') \in M$. Every steady state has associated with it two particular invariant manifolds, the so-called stable and unstable manifolds. Every element of the stable manifold converges to the steady state under forward iterations of the mapping *f*, while every element of the unstable manifold converges to the steady state under backward iterations of *f*.

We can get information about the stability of a dynamic system in the neighborhood of a steady state by examining the Jacobian matrix of the mapping *f* at the steady state, $Df(\hat{z})$. In particular, we will be interested in the eigenvalues of $Df(\hat{z})$. If all eigenvalues have modulus less than 1, then the steady state is stable. In general, some eigenvalues will be less than one while others are greater than one, in which case we call the steady state a saddle point. This is illustrated in Fig. 13.

A key result on dynamic systems is the *Grobman-Hartman Theorem*, which provides a characterization of local stability for so-called hyperbolic steady states of a dynamic system. A steady state $\hat{z}$ is hyperbolic if no eigenvalue of $Df(\hat{z})$ has modulus equal to one.

Theorem: If $\hat{z}$ *is a hyperbolic steady state of the dynamic system* $z_{t+1} = f(z_t)$,

then there exists a homeomorphic (generally non-linear) coordinate transformation of a neighborhood $N(\hat{z})$ *with itself which, when applied to the mapping f, yields the linear dynamic system*

$$w_{t+1} = \hat{z} + Df(\hat{z})[w_t - \hat{z}].$$

This result states that for hyperbolic dynamic systems, it is sufficient to study the stability properties of the linearization of the system around a fixed point. Note also that if we define new variables $x = w - \hat{z}$, then the dynamic system takes the simple form

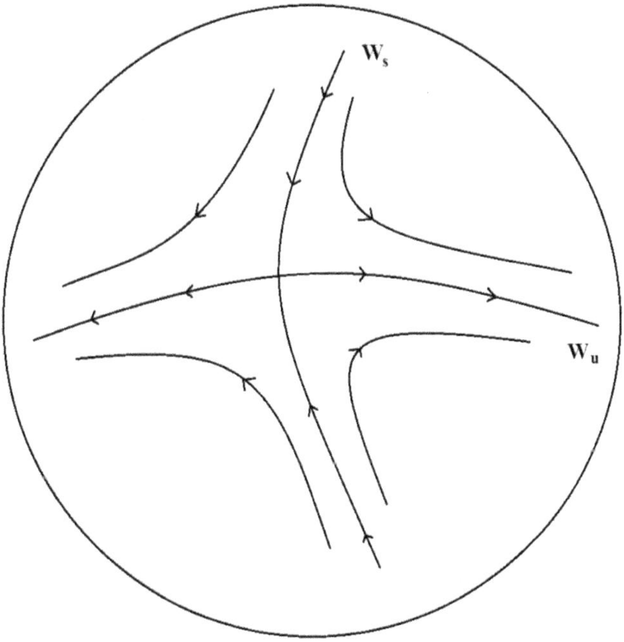

Fig. 13. Local Decomposition of Invariant Subspaces.

$$x_{t+1} = Df(\hat{z})x_t$$

and the steady state now occurs at the origin. If we also make a linear coordinate change to put the matrix $Df(\hat{z})$ in canonical form, we get

$$y_{t+1} = \Lambda y_{t.}$$

Now, if all of the eigenvalues of $Df(\hat{z})$ are distinct, then Λ will be a diagonal matrix with the eigenvalues of $Df(\hat{z})$ down the main diagonal. In this form, the action of the dynamic system is particularly transparent. Along the eigenspaces corresponding to eigenvalues that are less than one in modulus, the dynamic system behaves like a contraction mapping. Along the eigenspaces corresponding to eigenvalues having modulus greater than 1, the dynamic system is expanding. All trajectories not starting in one of the eigenspaces will be representable as linear combinations of the action of the system along various canonical subspaces.

The first K&L paper to explore the OLG model as a dynamic system was Kehoe–Levine (1984). This paper started life as "Indeterminacy of Relative Prices in Overlapping Generations Models" (1983 MIT working paper) which was focused (as the title suggests) on the issue of indeterminacy, with the regularity and dynamic systems analysis developed there as tools. The 1984 "Regularity in Overlapping Generations Exchange Economies" paper split off the dynamic systems analysis (and broadened it considerably), postponing the determinacy analysis to a later paper.

K&L simplified their analysis of the OLG environment by appealing to the same community excess demand results that Cass, Okuno, and Zilcha did in their 1980 paper. These results state that in a general equilibrium economy with n goods, any continuous function $f : \mathbb{R}^n_+ \to \mathbb{R}^n$ satisfying

1. f is homogeneous of degree zero (condition H)
2. f satisfies Walras Law: $p \cdot f(p) \equiv 0$ for all $p \in \mathbb{R}^n_+$ (condition W)
3. f is bounded from below (condition B)

will be the aggregate excess demand function for an economy consisting of at least n preference maximizing consumers. K&L add the condition that the aggregate excess demand functions they consider also be smooth (at least twice continuously differentiable), based on results from the study by Debreu (1974) and McFadden, Mas-Colell, Mantel, and Richter (1974).

For the two-period lived agents model, K&L denote the aggregate excess demand functions of the old living at time t by $z(p_{t-1}, p_t)$, and that of the young agents living at time t by $y(p_t, p_{t+1})$, where we follow their notation and use subscripts to denote time periods. The heterogeneity of agents across different ages necessitates this level of decomposition. With n goods traded in each period, K&L need at least n agents of each type in order to invoke the community excess demand theorems. In terms of the two aggregate excess demand functions, the market clearing condition is

$$z(p_{t-1}, p_t) + y(p_t, p_{t+1}) = 0.$$

Following the literature, K&L assumes the existence of a steady state equilibrium price p together with a scalar β such that

$$z(p,\beta p)+y(\beta p,\beta^2 p)=z(p,\beta p)+y(p,\beta p)=0,$$

where the second equality follows from the degree zero homogeneity assumption. The scalar β can be shown to be the intertemporal marginal rate of substitution for any individual consumer at the competitive equilibrium allocation. When $\beta=1$, the equilibrium is said to be nominal since it can be supported by having agents hold (fixed) money stocks in the amount $p\cdot z(p,p)=\mu>0$. From this definition, it then follows that $(1-\beta)\mu=0$ at any steady state, a condition we've seen before, that indicates that if money has value and is held in any positive quantity, then the intertemporal MRS of all agents in the economy must be equal to 1, and the equilibrium is a monetary one. When $\mu=0$, then β need not equal 1. When $\beta<1$, the associated competitive equilibrium will be inoptimal, while the opposite obtains if $\beta>1$.

This observation leads to K&L's first regularity condition: the systems of equations

$$z(p.p)+y(p,p)=0$$

$$-p\cdot y(p,p)=0$$

has no solution. This condition rules out the case where $\beta=1$ and $\mu=0$ simultaneously. The paper shows how to perturb the chosen aggregate excess demand functions so that they continue to satisfy conditions (*H*), (*W*), and (*B*) to get these equations to not hold if it happens that one's choice of excess demands has led to the equations being satisfied. Via the perturbation analysis, K&L shows that almost all excess demand functions satisfy this regularity condition, so that these economies (the regular economies) are generic.

With this assumption in place, K&L next go on to show that there will always be a steady-state equilibrium for the model with $\beta=1$, and a second steady state with $\beta\neq 1$. As we've seen before, if $\beta<1$, this steady state is the autarky equilibrium. When $\beta>1$, the equilibrium is Gale's classical case equilibrium. While K&L carry through their analysis for the case of both real and nominal steady states, we will simplify the analysis here by focusing only on the nominal case.

K&L let $q_t=[p_t,p_{t+1}]$, and write the equilibrium market clearing condition as

$$z(q_t)+y(q_{t+1})=0,$$

with $q=[p,p]$ denoting the steady-state equilibrium. They then linearize the equilibrium equations around the steady state in order to study the local dynamics on a neighborhood of the steady state. In order to do so, though, K&L need to invoke a second regularity condition, that

$$\left|D_{p_{t+1}}y(p_t,p_{t+1})\right|\neq 0,$$

in order to apply the implicit function theorem and infer the existence of a function $\hat{g}:\mathbb{R}^{2n}_{+}\rightarrow\mathbb{R}^{n}_{+}$ giving the equilibrium forward price p_{t+1} as a function of the prices at *t* and *t-1*. Since this formally defines a second-order difference equation system, applying standard dynamic systems theory to the model requires converting the second-order system into a first-order one, using the standard trick of writing

$$q_{t+1}=g(q_t)=\begin{bmatrix}\hat{g}(p_{t-1},p_t)\\ p_{t-1}\end{bmatrix}.$$

Linearizing this first-order difference equation system around the steady state then yields

$$\begin{bmatrix}p_t\\ p_{t+1}\end{bmatrix}=q_{t+1}=D_{q_t}g(q)q_t=\begin{bmatrix}\hat{g}_1 & \hat{g}_2\\ I & 0\end{bmatrix}\begin{bmatrix}p_{t-1}\\ p_t\end{bmatrix}=Gq_t.$$

Here, $\hat{g}_i$ is the matrix of partial derivatives of the mapping $\hat{g}$ taken with respect to the ith argument. These are determined in terms of the derivatives of the *z* and *y* functions using the standard implicit function theorem calculations. With these definitions, the paper then derives a set of restrictions on the derivatives of the excess demand functions implied by the economic conditions (*H*), (*W*), and (*B*). The boundedness condition doesn't restrict the derivatives, but homogeneity and Walras' Law imply, in turn, that β and *1* must be eigenvalues of the matrix *G*. Of course, at a nominal equilibrium, the only restriction is that *G* has a unit root. Other than these restrictions, the eigenvalues of *G* can be anything, subject to the restriction that, because *G* is a real-valued matrix, complex eigenvalues must occur in conjugate pairs.

As we noted earlier, applying the Grobman–Hartman theorem requires that the matrix $G=D_{q_t}g(q)$ has no eigenvalue with modulus equal to 1, which creates a problem. We can get around this problem, though, by restricting attention to the nominal case when the money supply $p_t\cdot z(p_{t-1},p_t)=\mu$ is constant. For this case, K&L consider the equilibrium dynamics of the model restricted to a *2n*-1 dimensional manifold which is invariant under the actions of the mapping $g_m=g\,|_{\mu=m}$ where *m* is the fixed money supply. In this case, the linearized local dynamics will be governed by the matrix $G_m=G\,|_{\mu=m}$. For this matrix, the eigenvector corresponding to the unit root in the original system will still be an eigenvector in the restricted system, but the corresponding eigenvalue is now zero, so that the restricted system will be hyperbolic. According to the Grobman–Hartman theorem, we know that there will be two linear subspaces E_s and E_u which are invariant under the actions of g_m and correspond to the stable and unstable invariant subspaces through the steady-state price vector *q*. Because G_m is now hyperbolic, the dimensions of these subspaces will be complementary, that is, $\dim E_s+\dim E_u=2n-1$.

K&L show how to analyze the case of a real steady state with $\beta\neq 1$ by noting that in this case, at the steady state, prices will be increasing or decreasing geometrically. By renormalizing prices by dividing them by a scalar function of p_t which is homogeneous of degree one, one obtains a stationary dynamic system similar to the one analyzed in the nominal case.

Kehoe and Levine (1984) is primarily methodological, though, as we noted above, it appears to have originated from a study of the question of determinacy of equilibrium in the OLG model. K&L return to this issue in Kehoe and Levine (1985). As we noted in our earlier discussion of Samuelson's original paper (and his debate with Meckling), Samuelson viewed the equilibrium trajectories in the OLG model as being pinned down only once there was a suitable terminal condition specified for the system of difference equations that determined the economy's trajectory. By Samuelson's definition of determinacy, then, the non-stationary equilibrium in the two-period lived agents model with one good, log preferences and a monetary steady-state equilibrium would be determinate, since given an initial condition close to, but not equal to the monetary equilibrium price, the resulting trajectory converged to autarky. In this example, the monetary equilibrium would have a terminal condition requiring that the equilibrium remains at the steady state, while in the non-stationary equilibrium, the terminal condition would be convergence to autarky. This notion of determinacy differed from the static general equilibrium notion which required that equilibrium prices were (at least local) isolated, so that comparative static analysis was possible based on perturbations of the underlying parameters of the economy.

In dynamic economic models where agents have perfect foresight (or rational expectations in stochastic settings), determinate terminal conditions can lead to non-isolated equilibrium trajectories which defy comparative static analysis. The simplest way to illustrate this is with the general K&L set-up outlined above, with an initial starting period. In this initial period $t=1$, we will have

$$z(a, p_1) + y(p_1, p_2) = 0.$$

Since agents have perfect foresight, they know how the equilibrium prices are determined, that is, they know

$$p_{t+1} = g(p_{t-1}, p_t).$$

Young agents forecasting the future prices using the economy's law of motion will then generate an equilibrium set of market clearing equations of the form

$$z(a, p_1) + y(p_1, g[a, p_1]) = 0,$$

but in this situation, because the function g is obtained from the equilibrium equations via the implicit function theorem, the equation above is identically zero. Hence, any period one price will be an equilibrium price. In the particular case where the law of motion converges to the steady state for any starting price, comparative static analysis based on underlying perturbations of the parameters defining the economy (in this case, the two excess demand functions) gives us no information on how the price in period one is determined. If the law of motion is divergent, then the only equilibrium that is viable is the steady state itself, which is locally unique.[1]

This result has important behavioral implications. In static (i.e., simple two-period) models, the equilibrium price will be generically determinate by standard general equilibrium arguments, and all agents need to forecast is the equilibrium price. A standard argument in models like these is that agents are rational and know the structure of the economy and can therefore calculate what the equilibrium price will be. In the dynamic OLG setting, the argument presented here shows that how agents forecast future prices is important, and that the assumption that agents know the economy won't necessarily make the equilibrium determinate.

This was the problem that K&L set out to study in Kehoe and Levine (1985). They approach the problem by comparing the determinacy results for a standard ILA model with finitely-many dynastic families and the two-period multi-good OLG model they analyzed in the "Regularity" paper.

For the ILA model, they use the Negishi (1960) approach together with techniques from differential topology pioneered by Debreu (1970) to show that the sequence of equilibrium prices for this economy is uniquely determined by the Negishi welfare weights corresponding to the given initial endowments. We can view this result from a dynamic systems perspective by going back to our development of the one-sector capital model using the discounted dynamic programming methods. The steady-state equilibrium for that economy is a saddle point. (This is a well-known result in capital theory.) The stable manifold associated with the steady state is simply the graph of the policy function that arises from the first-order difference equation delivered by the dynamic programming algorithm. The unstable manifold takes allocations asymptotically to zero or to the point where all resources are used to accumulate capital, leaving zero consumption. The optimal trajectory in this model is completely determinate, given the assumption that agents are rational and will know to follow the accumulation rule prescribed by the policy function. As K&L note, their determinacy result is a direct analog of the result developed by Debreu for static pure exchange economies.

For the OLG model, K&L note that the indeterminacy problem can be remedied if agents in the model use first-order forecasts, rather than the second-order forecast rule prescribed by the equilibrium law of motion for the economy. To show this, suppose agents forecast using the common forecast function $p_{t+1} = f(p_t)$. For this forecast function to be consistent with the equilibrium dynamics of the model requires that

$$\begin{bmatrix} f(p) \\ f^{\circ}f(p) \end{bmatrix} = \begin{bmatrix} f(p) \\ g(p, f[p]) \end{bmatrix},$$

for all admissible prices p. K&L show how to construct such a forecast function based on the linearization of the system given by the Grobman–Hartman homeomorphism, in which the consistency condition requires that

$$\begin{bmatrix} F \\ F^2 \end{bmatrix} = \begin{bmatrix} 0 & I \\ G_1 & G_2 \end{bmatrix} \begin{bmatrix} I \\ F \end{bmatrix}.$$

If we now let $H^{-1}\Lambda_f H = F$ be the canonical decomposition of the matrix F, we have

$$\begin{bmatrix} H^{-1}\Lambda_f H \\ H^{-1}\Lambda_f^2 H \end{bmatrix} = G \begin{bmatrix} H^{-1}H \\ H^{-1}\Lambda_f H \end{bmatrix}$$

or

$$\begin{bmatrix} H^{-1} \\ H^{-1}\Lambda_f \end{bmatrix} \Lambda_f = G \begin{bmatrix} H^{-1} \\ H^{-1}\Lambda_f \end{bmatrix}.$$

This implies that the matrix $\begin{bmatrix} H^{-1} \\ H^{-1}\Lambda_f \end{bmatrix}$ consists of eigenvectors of the matrix G, with Λ_f a Jordan matrix with the eigenvalues associated with the matrix F on the main diagonal.

To determine what the eigenvalues of F should be, K&L imposes the condition that the forecast prices lie in the stable manifold associated with the steady-state equilibrium, so that given an initial price, the resulting sequence of equilibrium prices will converge to the steady state. This pins down the terminal condition for the model. In addition to this property, K&L also require that the forecast function f be homogeneous of degree 1, since the equilibrium price function g is and that the function be smooth.

From the eigenvalue conditions above, one can construct the matrix F, and, by inverting the mapping between the linear and original non-linear systems, we find the desired forecast function f. Interested readers should consult the K&L papers for details. For our purposes, the key thing to note is that when equilibrium prices are restricted to the stable manifold of the steady-state prices, it provides a natural decomposition of the price dynamics akin to the saddle-path stability that occurs in the capital model. In particular, if the eigenvalues for the model "split" – for a monetary equilibrium, this means having $n - 1$ eigenvalues of G inside the unit circle, and $n - 1$ outside the unit circle. Given the K&L results on the (lack of) restrictions on the eigenvalues of G, we can characterize equilibria from different models depending on whether the associated matrix G has more stable roots than unstable roots, the same number, or more unstable roots. For the splitting case (equal numbers of roots), the equilibrium is determinate. For more stable roots than unstable, equilibria are indeterminate, and, as we will see later, sunspot equilibria can arise. The third case generates unstable equilibria which can only exist in steady state.

Kehoe and Levine (1985) invokes the Balasko–Cass–Shell result showing how to convert a multi-period model into a higher dimensional two-period model and given that they start out by working with aggregate excess demands and arbitrary (but finite) number of goods, their characterization results are quite general.

We will see later, though, that because the Balasko–Cass–Shell transformation doesn't work for stochastic models, there is a need for constructing lower-order forecast functions in multi-period models. The extension of the K&L procedure outlined here was provided by Kim and Spear (2021a).

We note that a similar set of restrictions on forecasting functions in the context of linear rational expectations models in macroeconomics were derived and published by Blanchard and Kahn (1980). This paper also characterizes various possible outcomes for this class of linear models in terms of the relationship between stable and unstable roots of the matrix that determines the equilibrium law of motion for the economy. Since this paper came before the K&L papers, these conditions are usually referred to as Blanchard–Kahn conditions.

7.2 CHAOS

While K&L were working out the local dynamics for general OLG models, Jean–Michel Grandmont was tackling a different question, that of characterizing the global dynamics of a very specific OLG model, the one commodity, two-period lived agents model of pure exchange. We have noted earlier that Grandmont's interest in temporary equilibrium models grew at least in part out of his disbelief in the rational expectations hypothesis. His initial interest in the possibility of complex dynamics occurring in the OLG model was also motivated by his frustration with the fact that, after the publication of Lucas (1972), rational expectations rapidly became the dominant paradigm in dynamic macroeconomics, particularly with the development of real business cycle models in the early 1980s (which we will discuss at some length in Chapter 9).

Despite Grandmont's determination to "kill off" rational expectations, the issue of multiplicity of equilibria which Grandmont focused on as a way of questioning the rational expectations hypothesis obviously didn't halt the widespread application of rational expectations in macroeconomics, though it did lead to serious questions about which equilibria might be selected, and how, when models gave rise to multiple equilibria. This issue was an important input in the then-developing literature on how agents might go about learning rational expectations. It was also an input into the development of measure theoretic techniques for characterizing rational expectations equilibrium in stochastic environments.

Grandmont's work did attract a lot of attention, though, for its demonstration that even very simple deterministic OLG models could generate equilibrium trajectories that were erratic, and which could be interpreted as business cycles. The paper which established this was Grandmont (1985).

Given its importance in our narrative so far, and the fact that, after Diamond and Samuelson, it is the most cited paper using the OLG approach, we present a brief history of the evolution of Grandmont's 1985 *Econometrica* article. The first version of the paper appeared in June 1983 as CEPREMAP working paper 8316, revised in September 1983 (Grandmont, 1983). The paper was "prepared for the IMSSS summer workshop at Stanford University" with support from the NSF, among other institutions. In October 1983, a version of the paper was presented at the University of Minnesota Institute of Mathematics and its applications workshop on price adjustment, quantity adjustment, and business cycles organized by Hugo Sonnenschein, and discussed by Goroff, Scheinkman, Sims, Wallace, and Woodford, whom Grandmont (1985) thanked for "their valuable comments and constructive criticisms" (p. 995, note 2).

In 1984, the paper appeared as Technical Report Number 438 of the Center for Research on Organizational Efficiency, IMSSS, Stanford (Grandmont, 1984). It was supported by an Office of Naval Research global grant covering IMSSS research at Stanford. What is interesting to note here is that the 1983 and 1984 versions of what was to become Grandmont's seminal 1985 *Econometrica* paper were much longer than the version eventually published. The reason for this is apparent from examining the earlier manuscripts: Grandmont included extensive development of his temporary equilibrium framework in section 2 of both the 1983 and 1984 working papers. In this development, he characterizes the periodic equilibria that can occur in the model as being subject to a learning process that eventually allows agents to correctly forecast future prices in these equilibria, a situation which he characterizes as one of the agents having "rational" expectations. From this material, it is clear that Grandmont was still trying to provide a workable alternative to the rational expectations hypothesis. That this material doesn't appear in the published version of the paper is likely due to significant pushback from referees and/or an Associate Editor/Editor at *Econometrica*, itself indicative of how entrenched the rational expectations assumption was in general equilibrium and macro theory by that time.

Grandmont's 1985 paper on this topic was not the first to be published, as he noted in the paper. That distinction belongs to Benhabib and Day (1982). The difference between the two papers in technical terms is marginal. In economic terms, though, the differences are significant. Benhabib and Day examined the dynamics around Gale's classical steady state, while Grandmont examined them around the Samuelsonian steady state. As we've noted earlier, the classical steady state in the one good, two-period lived model is Pareto optimal, so that in the Benhabib–Day model, the only way to get the erratic dynamics started is by transferring resources from the initial old to the young, which can't be done in a way that compensates the old for their loss. The Benhabib–Day model can be interpreted as one of an ongoing bi-infinite equilibrium, in which there is no beginning, though as we've noted previously in the context of determinacy of equilibrium, this just pushes the question of how this equilibrium was established back to minus infinity. A second drawback of the Benhabib–Day model is that it requires that there be an infinite-lived credit intermediary to enforce the repayment by the young of loans made by the previous generation's old agents, since they are no longer around to take repayment. Per private communication with us from Benhabib, they chose to work with the classical case because,

> [I]n the Samuelsonian case cycles and chaos dynamics were correspondences (or functions in backward dynamics), while in the classical case you got chaos with forward dynamics with a well-defined function. (Email from Jess Benhabib dated June 20, 2022)

Grandmont's model only requires Samuelson's "social contrivance of money" to facilitate the intergenerational trade required in the monetary equilibrium. In addition, as we've seen, in this case, the monetary equilibrium is fully Pareto optimal. The drawback to working with the Samuelsonian case, as Benhabib noted is that the forward dynamics, under parameterizations that give rise to erratic dynamics, are not given by a function, but by a correspondence. In Grandmont's paper, he focuses, therefore, on the backward dynamics, where consumption at time t is a function of consumption at time $t+1$. We note, however, that for both approaches, all of the equilibria obtained are stationary in the sense that their regular properties are invariant under shifts in the time parameter. Hence, a cycle of period n is the same going forward or backward and will be a stationary equilibrium in the bi-infinite interpretation of the model. The differences in the two models then come down to whether the stationary equilibrium is stable going forward or backward, and the issue of how to interpret the initial starting period.

Both models generate their erratic dynamics results by exploiting the then newly developed mathematics of chaos theory, a subarea of dynamic systems analysis focused on non-linear systems whose stationary equilibria can undergo bifurcations from simple steady states to cycles to chaos. This mathematics was developed primarily during the 1960s and 1970s by mathematicians like Feigenbaum, Hayashi, Lorenz, Li, Malgrange, Mandelbrot, May, Rulle, Shaw, Smale, and Yorke. It was also helped immensely by the simultaneous development of high-speed digital computers during this period.

While a full exposition of this math is obviously beyond the scope of this text, we can illustrate the fundamental ideas with a simple example, the well-known quadratic logistic map

$$x_{t+1} = ax_t(1 - x_t).$$

For $x_t \in [0,1]$ and $0 \le a \le 4$. The graph of the function that determines x_{t+1} given x_t is hump-shaped, and is illustrated in Fig. 14.

For different values of the parameter a, the time-series generated by iterating the logistic function will display different behaviors. For $a=2$, for example, it is easily verified that the fixed point of the simple dynamic system is $x=0.5$, and the derivative of the function at the fixed point is zero. This implies that the steady state at the fixed point is stable, and a simple computer analysis of the dynamics

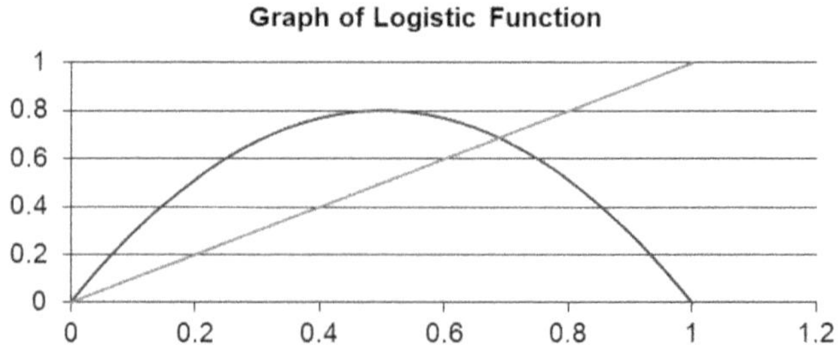

Fig. 14. Graph of the Quadratic Logistic Map.

for this case shows that, in fact, the mapping is globally convergent to the steady state.

For a=3.2, it is easy to verify that the derivative at the fixed point (which a simple calculation will show is equal to $\hat{x} = a - 1/a$) is negative, so that the graph of the function looks like that in Fig. 14. Since the derivative of the function is given for general a by

$$f'(x) = a - 2ax,$$

evaluating this at the fixed point gives us

$$f'(\hat{x}) = 2 - a.$$

It then follows that the derivative at the steady state for the case of a=3.2 is negative and bigger than one in absolute value, so that the steady-state equilibrium is no longer stable.

Instead, in this case, we get a two-period limit cycle in the long run, illustrated in Fig. 15 from an easy computer simulation.

As the value of a gets larger, the two-period cycles will become unstable, bifurcating to a four-period cycle, then an eight-period cycle, and so on with periods doubling at each bifurcation, until we obtain a cycle of "period" infinity, which Yorke dubbed "chaos." We illustrate this in Fig. 16 for the case of a=3.8.

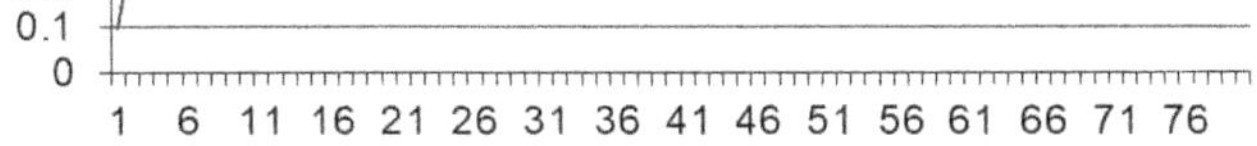

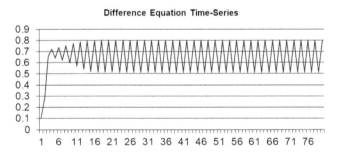

Fig. 15. Time-series Simulation for Cyclic Equilibrium.

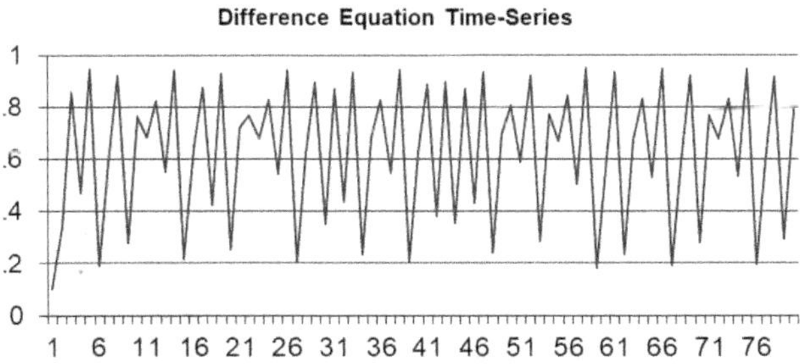

Fig. 16. Time-series Simulation for Chaotic Equilibrium.

The critical factor in getting a simple map like this to exhibit chaotic behavior is the hump-shape of the function, which needs to be steep on the end points, and flat through the middle and top. Iterating such a map will expand small neighborhoods near the extremes of the domain of the map, while contracting neighborhoods in the middle of the domain. This acts, in effect, the same way that a baker kneading bread dough does, constantly stretching and then folding the dough back in on itself. In fact, if the baker puts a drop of food coloring on the dough at the beginning of the process, the color will be smeared chaotically through the loaf by the time it is ready for baking. This is also the process by which soft plastics are colored, as many fascinating YouTube videos have demonstrated.

Since the non-linearity of the difference equation is the key to getting erratic dynamics, both Benhabib–Day and Grandmont need the OLG model to exhibit a hump-shaped offer curve, which imposes conditions on the curvature of the indifference curves of the young and/or old agents in the model. We can illustrate the workings of the two versions of the model using the offer curve diagrams introduced earlier. For the Benhabib–Day version of the model, the hump-shaped offer curve is illustrated in Fig. 17.

The corresponding diagram for the Samuelsonian case considered by Grandmont is illustrated in Fig. 18.

The function versus correspondence issue highlighted by Benhabib and Day is clearly illustrated in the two diagrams. In the second diagram, in particular, one can see that starting from any amount of saving by the young – that is, a movement along the x-axis to the left from the endowment point at the origin – gives rise to two possible consistent equilibrium trades.

These two pioneering papers started something of a fad in macro and general equilibrium theory, since they raised an obvious question: was it possible to get complicated dynamics in the other workhorse model? The answer to this question was yes, at least for multi-sector growth models, and was demonstrated forcefully in the *Journal of Economic Theory* symposium volume Grandmont and Malgrange (1986).

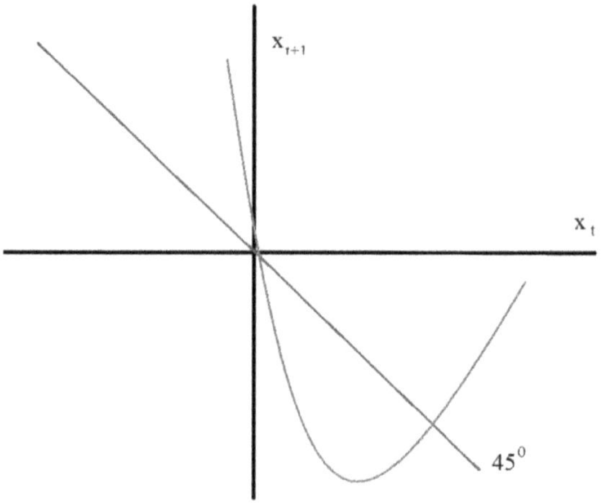

Fig. 17. Benhabib–Day Analysis.

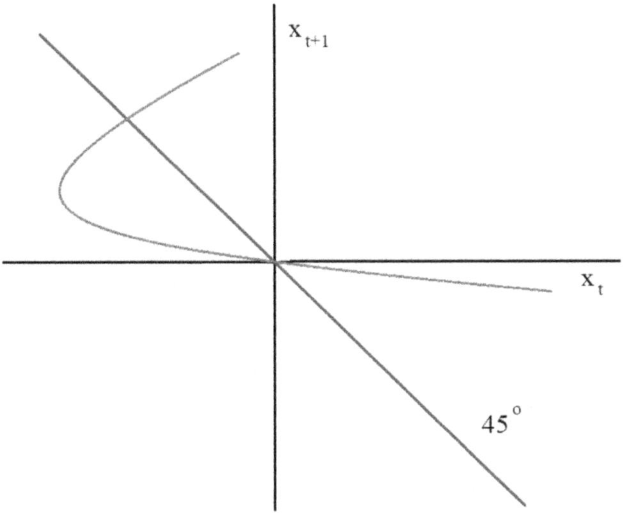

Fig. 18. Grandmont Analysis.

For the ILA models considered in the volume, there were two distinct approaches. One involved working directly with some version of the RCK model and showing conditions under which the policy function resulting from the representative agent's intertemporal optimization problem would be sufficiently hump-shaped. The second approach involved imposing liquidity requirements or cash-in-advance constraints on the model to get it to perform more like an OLG model.

As Grandmont and Malgrange note in their introduction to the volume:

> These studies show by way of examples that complex deterministic dynamics may arise in models where agents optimize over an infinite horizon, and are not confined to, say, overlapping generations models with "short-lived" traders as in Benhabib and Day [6] and Grandmont [24]. The same point is made by Woodford in his contribution to this volume, as we shall see. These works suggest accordingly that endogenous fluctuations of the sort that is considered in this issue, may occur at frequencies that have nothing to do with human life, contrary to what some critics had argued previously. (Grandmont & Malgrange, 1986, p. 5).

While a full accounting of the many important papers in this volume would take us too far afield of our current topic, we include this discussion because it clearly illustrates the concern that macroeconomists brought to the table over the need to be able to match time-series data of different frequencies to underlying theoretical models. We have touched previously on this issue with respect to Tobin's and others' use of computational multi-period OLG models and will return to discuss newer work in this vein later. But for now, we conclude our discussion of the chaos work by noting that all of this work has been criticized on the grounds of the unrealistic parameter value assumptions required to get the models to exhibit complex dynamics. For the OLG approaches of Benhabib–Day and Grandmont, the degree of risk aversion required of one group of agents or the other is unrealistically high. Grandmont's approach, for example, requires relative risk aversions for the old on the order of 9, while Benhabib–Day requires those of the young to be around 5. Empirical estimates of these coefficients are routinely less than 2. These parameterizations generate the backward-bending offer curve, which in turn implies that around the steady state of the model, increases in interest rates lead young agents to reduce their saving. Many macroeconomists view this requirement as unrealistic and harbor doubts that real-world economies generate the kinds of income effects necessary for this result to hold.

For the ILA models of chaos, the key condition for generating the appropriate curvature in the policy function is an unreasonably low discount factor (or correspondingly high rate of time preference). Boldrin and Montrucchio's examples from the *JET* symposium required discount factors on the order of 0.02 before chaotic trajectories occurred.

This volume also included two additional important OLG papers, those of Reichlin (1986) and Farmer (1986). Reichlin's paper extended Grandmont's model to allow for more realistic production processes and showed that cyclic equilibria could exist under conditions where the savings elasticity with respect to interest rates is positive. Farmer's paper also shows the existence of cyclic equilibria in a model with production using techniques based on Hopf bifurcations similar to those used by Reichlin. In Farmer's model, government debt policies that lead to the existence of equilibrium at the golden rule steady state also make possible the Hopf bifurcations in the presence of production. Farmer's results include two examples, one with CES production, and the second with Leontief production. More recent work by Bosi and Seegmuller (2005) has shown a basic equivalence between Reichlin's results and those of Woodford (1986a, 1986b). For a modern treatment of these results, see the study by Benhabib (2021).

7.3 OBSERVATIONAL EQUIVALENCE

Working at roughly the same time as Benhabib, Day, Grandmont, Kehoe, and Levine, S. Rao Aiyagari began looking at the question of what distinguished the OLG and ILA models, below the surface of their obvious differences. Aiyagari was a graduate of the University of Minnesota's economics Ph.D. program, having worked under Neil Wallace's supervision there. After graduating from Minnesota, he took a job at the University of Wisconsin's Madison economics department, though he also spent time as a visiting professor at New York University and Carnegie Mellon's Graduate School of Industrial Administration.

Aiyagari's observational equivalence (OE) research program was based on the observation that the Pareto optimal steady-state equilibria, and much of the associated non-stationary dynamics around the steady state in versions of the Diamond model look the same statistically as those coming out of the RCK model using the same specifications of preferences, endowments, and technology. From an econometric perspective, OE occurs when structural aspects of two different models can't be identified in the data. Aiyagari's analysis used functional analytic techniques to show how a given specification of either the OLG or RCK model could be mapped into the other model such that simulations of the two models would produce identical time-series data.

Aiyagari published three main papers on this topic. The first, Aiyagari (1985), looked at the simplest version of the Diamond model, with agents living in two periods, discounting future consumption. Aiyagari shows that under the assumption that preferences and technology are such that the steady state of the OLG model yields interest rates in excess of the population growth rate, one can construct an ILA economy in which the representative infinite-lived agent has the same preferences and technology as the OLG agents, which then gives rise to the same policy functions as in the OLG model. Hence, the two models are observationally equivalent. In the conclusion of the paper, Aiyagari notes that:

> It has been necessary to impose rather strong assumptions on the OLG model, assumptions which deliver a unique equilibrium, a unique and globally stable steady state, monotonicity, and differentiability of the function describing the evolution of the capital/labor ratio and more. With weaker assumptions, the range of dynamics that could be exhibited by OLG models is much larger, for instance, than that exhibited by [Discounted Dynamic Programming] models and observational equivalence cannot possibly hold. (Aiyagari, 1985, p. 220.)

This observation, together with the fact that the two-period lived agents assumption remained problematic in terms of how to fit data of different frequencies to the OLG model, led Aiyagari in his second OE paper to consider OLG environments with long-lived agents. Aiyagari (1988) looks at a sequence of OLG models in which agents live T period lifespans and examines the steady-state equilibria of the sequence as T gets large. Unlike the previous paper, this paper doesn't undertake trying to show the exact equivalence of the OLG and ILA models. Rather, Aiyagari made assumptions on the endowments of agents which guaranteed that the steady-state equilibria along the sequence were classical, in Gale's sense. The paper then showed that as T gets large, the steady-state equilibrium interest rate converges to the (common) rate of time preference, the equilibrium steady state is Pareto optimal, and all agents' consumption profiles converge to the corresponding permanent income profile for the given discount rate. What this analysis suggests is that in multi-period OLG models which generate positive equilibrium interest rates, the qualitative properties of the equilibrium steady state and nearby non-stationary trajectories are the same as those generated by a comparable RCK model.

There is one additional important result presented in the paper, though it is buried in a short discussion section at the end of the paper. We reproduce Aiyagari's statement of this result here:

> It is also possible to extend the results obtained here to include production and capital accumulation. The results parallel those in the classic one-sector growth model with a representative infinitely lived agent. A more difficult extension, attempted in Aiyagari [11], is to environments with uncertainty. For the special case of a logarithmic one-period utility function and random endowments, we were able to show that the one period ahead contingent claims prices converge (as T gets large) to the prices that would prevail in the analogous infinitely lived agent model. This was not possible for other utility functions because it turns out that so long as agents live three or more periods, consumption allocations and contingent claims prices depend

> on the entire infinite history of endowment realizations. This is essentially the same problem that arises in Spear [14] even though the intertemporal preferences here are time separable. (Aiyagari, 1988, pp. 114–115)

The reference here to Aiyagari (1988) is to an unpublished (and apparently lost) working paper version of this paper. The reference to Spear (1985) is to the paper "Rational Expectations in the Overlapping Generations Model," which we will discuss below.

The third paper in the OE project is Aiyagari (1987). This paper is an extension of the previous paper in that it allows for population growth and shows that the old question of whether monetary equilibria exist turns only on the relationship between agents' commonly held discount factors and the rate of growth of the economy as long as lifetimes T are long enough.

There was related follow-on work on OE done by Blackorby and Russell (1992). Blackorby and Russell study the OE question from the perspective of aggregation, asking whether a given OLG model with multiple agents can be aggregated across agents alive contemporaneously to obtain a model that looks like an infinite lived representative agent model. Because a complete aggregation result *a la* Gorman (for static economies) is impossible in this context, Blackorby and Russell use Aiyagari's OE approach but generalize it to allow for robustness to perturbations in the technology available to agents, as long as there is latitude for reallocating endowments.

Aiyagari's OE work and that of Blackorby and Russell were re-examined by Jones and Manuelli (1992). This paper showed that it is possible to get endogenous growth without increasing returns to scale in production in the OLG setting, as long as production exhibited constant returns to scale, and young agents were given sufficient income to drive the demand for growth. One of the consequences of this result, however, is that it contradicts the fact that in an infinite-lived agents setting with the same preferences and technology, there can be no endogenous growth. While the Blackorby and Russell extension of Aiyagari's results did not require the ILA model to have a steady state (and hence it was amenable to growth), their need for endowment reallocation in order to obtain their OE result precludes the possibility of endogenous growth.

The fact that the Blackorby and Russell work went unpublished is notable, since it speaks to the observed impact that this research program had on macroeconomics. From private communication with us, Russell comments on the struggle he and Blackorby went through trying to publish this paper:

> [A]fter rejections by (as I recall) *Econometrica, QJE, and ReStud* (with very long periods of review at each journal), we killed the paper rather than go down market with a paper that we thought belonged in one of the premier theory journals. The negative referee reports found no errors but rejected the paper essentially on the grounds that growth and macro theorists had no interest in the question posed by the paper.
>
> A few things to note: (1)[T]wo years after the rejection by *R.E.Stud,* we apparently had a change of heart about trying again and did submit the paper, without revision, to *Economic Theory* and then *J. Econ. Dev. Cultural Change,* with even more discouraging results. (2) It's interesting that the paper was taken most seriously by *Econometrica*, with a four-year review entailing two revise-and-resubmits. (3) By the time we got to the last two journal submissions, it seems that any initial interest had waned.

A second related paper in the OE literature was Huffman (1986) which focused on the asset pricing properties of SILA versus two-period stochastic OLG (SOLG) models and found that under some parameter restrictions, the two models were in fact observationally equivalent.

Looking back at Aiyagari's paper, the Google cites for the three papers were 36, 26, and 17, respectively, which would seem to indicate the same lack of impact that Blackorby and Russell got from the macroprofession for their work. At the same time, it is hard to argue with Russell's contention that these results were important enough at the time to merit publication in major outlets. Certainly, Aiyagari's work was visible, given *JET*'s visibility in the theory world. So why the low number of citations?

There seem to be two threads that one needs to follow to explain this. One is based on Aiyagari's ultimate findings (in the *JET*' 88 paper) that stochastic RCK and OLG models were not observationally equivalent. We postpone this discussion until we complete our coverage of the development of the SOLG framework. The second thread is the inherent negativity of the OE results for deterministic models. By "negativity" we mean the fact that if the two models were indeed equivalent, there would be no further reason for studying one or the other. We conjecture that as Aiyagari's results became well-known in macro, they helped to ultimately tip the market away from OLG toward ILA, and once this tipping occurred, there would be no further need to justify the use of the ILA framework by appealing to Aiyagari's equivalence results, leading in turn to the paucity of citations. The difficulty Blackorby and Russell had trying to publish their work, even shortly after the Aiyagari papers had appeared suggests that the tipping process was well underway by the early 1990s.

This observation leads naturally to the question of why the market would tip toward ILA and not OLG. We have already suggested that the development of relatively easy-to-use recursive dynamic programming methods played a key role here. To quote from Sargent (1996):

> The recursive methods used by Lucas's JET paper, and also by Lucas and Prescott (1971) and Brock and Mirman (1972), have come to dominate macroeconomics. Virtually every macroeconomist today reads, writes, and thinks [in] terms of dynamic programming. Recursive reasoning unearthed the 'time-consistency' problem, and led to characterizing the types of government policies that could be implemented sequentially. (pp. 542–543)

A second reason for the market to tip toward ILA was the subsequent development of models based on the recursive ILA methodology which incorporated frictions that allowed the resulting model to mimic behavior generated in the messier to analyze OLG setting, and it is to these models that we turn next.

7.4 INCOMPLETE MARKETS AND FINANCIAL FRICTIONS

When Aiyagari realized that his OE program had reached a dead end, he restructured his research to focus, for the most part, on ILA models with frictions that delivered equilibria resembling those that could arise in OLG environments.

Indeed, a Google Scholar search for Aiygari's work including the phrase "overlapping generations" returns 18 single- or co-authored papers listed in the search results. Without the "overlapping generations" phrase included the search returns 120 papers. (Aiyagari was a prolific scholar and would undoubtedly have produced many more top-quality papers if his life hadn't been cut short.)

Foremost among the new models that Aiyagari examined was an ILA model in which markets are incomplete. His most highly cited paper in this research program is Aiyagari (1994), with 3,798 Google Scholar cites. This paper took an otherwise standard one-sector RCK model and modified it by assuming that agents in the model face idiosyncratic shocks to their own labor productivity and face a borrowing constraint. The need for the borrowing constraint arises from the possibility that equilibrium interest rates could be negative, in which case disequilibrium Ponzi schemes become possible in the absence of some limit on borrowing. The borrowing constraint also arises naturally for the case where interest rates are positive given that consumption must be non-negative. The market incompleteness arises because agents cannot insure themselves against the idiosyncratic labor shocks.

Aiyagari's work built on the theoretical contributions of Truman Bewley in two papers (Bewley, 1977, 1986). For this reason, these models are generally referred to as Aiyagari–Bewley models, and later Aiyagari–Bewley–Huggett models in recognition of Mark Huggett's 1993 incomplete markets paper (Huggett, 1993). The market incompleteness generated by the idiosyncratic shocks leads agents to self-insure, that is, to save for the proverbial "rainy day." The precautionary savings so generated are what give these models their OLG flavor, while the assumption that shocks are idiosyncratic means that there are no aggregate shocks to complicate the analysis. This "trick" of restricting uncertainty to be idiosyncratic has been widely applied, not only in conventional Aiyagari–Bewley models but also in OLG models (see, e.g., Storesletten, Telmer, & Yaron, 2007). The usefulness of the trick is that because there are no aggregate shocks, one can ignore the wealth effects generated by changes in the wealth distribution in the model because they get washed out by the law of large numbers.

The second class of ILA-based models that generated OLG-like dynamics is the cash-in-advance models first introduced by Clower (1967) and featured prominently in Grandmont's and Malgrange's special issue of *JET* discussed above. The seminal papers in this literature were by Lucas and Stokey (1987) and Woodford (1986a). Woodford's paper is significant for a couple of reasons that are relevant to our examination of the OLG model.

First, according to Grandmont (in his communication with us), in Woodford's contribution, workers with infinite horizons are faced with constraints on their ability to borrow, with the result that they also solve problems emanating from a sequence of two-period overlapping maximization, such that when they are young they work and save money, which is spent on consumption when old, that is, one period later, similar to two-period models based on OLG, albeit with a resultant period length that is small.

Second, Woodford uses the fact that indeterminacy of equilibrium in the model is necessary and sufficient for the existence of sunspot equilibria in the two-period one good model – which was originally shown by Azariadis and Guesnerie (1986) –

to introduce an old econometric modeling trick, known as "bootstrapping," into macroeconomics. Bootstrapping involves setting up the first-order conditions (FOCs) for a dynamic optimization, but instead of setting the equations equal to zero, one sets them equal to a random variable whose mean is zero. Assuming that the FOCs can be solved for the forward endogenous state variable as a function of the lagged state variables and the bootstrap shock, one can show that this is in fact a rational expectations equilibrium, as long as the shocks are sufficiently small, and the steady-state equilibrium is locally forward stable.

We illustrate this process in a simple two-period, one good pure exchange OLG model. Let a typical young agent's stationary utility function $u(x_t, x_{t+1})$ over consumption in period t and $t+1$ satisfy the usual properties – at least twice continuously differentiable, strictly concave, differentiably monotonic, and satisfying an Inada condition as consumption in either period goes to 0. Also, assume endowments (ω_z, ω_2) are also stationary and such that the steady-state equilibrium is monetary with a fixed money supply $\overline{m} > 0$. The young agent's budget constraints take the form

$$p_t x_t + m = p_t \omega_1$$

$$p_{t+1} x_{t+1} = p_{t+1} \omega_2 + m.$$

From these, we can solve for consumptions in each period in terms of prices and money holdings (together with the fixed endowments) and reduce the agent's budget-constrained utility maximization problem to

$$\max_m u\left[\omega_1 - \frac{m}{p_t}, \omega_2 + \frac{m}{p_{t+1}}\right].$$

The FOCs for this problem are

$$-\frac{m}{p_t} u_1 + \frac{m}{p_{t+1}} u_2 = 0,$$

where u_i is the partial derivative of u with respect to the ith argument. We assume that the utility function is such that this equation can be solved (implicitly) for p_{t+1} as a function of p_t. To construct the bootstrap sunspot equilibrium, let $\{\alpha_t\}$ be a sequence of i.i.d. random variables with mean zero and variance σ^2. Set the FOCs above equal not to zero but to α_{t+1},

$$-\frac{\overline{m}}{p_t} u_1 + \frac{\overline{m}}{p_{t+1}} u_2 = \alpha_{t+1}$$

and evaluate the FOC at the fixed money supply $\overline{m}$. Solving this for the forward price gives us a first-order stochastic difference equation for the equilibrium (via the implicit function theorem)

$$p_{t+1} = g[p_t, \alpha_{t+1}].$$

If agents in the model now use this difference equation to forecast future prices, we will have

$$-\frac{\overline{m}}{p_t}u_1 + \frac{\overline{m}}{g[p_t, \alpha_{t+1}]}u_2 \equiv \alpha_{t+1},$$

since the function g was obtained from the implicit function theorem. If we now integrate on both sides with respect to the given density (or measure) for the α random variables, we get

$$\int \left\{ \frac{\overline{m}}{p_t}u_1 + \frac{\overline{m}}{g[p_t, \alpha_{t+1}]}u_2 \right\} d\mu(\alpha_{t+1}) \equiv 0.$$

But this is the first-order condition for a stochastic optimization problem. If the equilibrium stochastic process on prices remains in a sufficiently small neighborhood of the steady-state equilibrium price for the model, the equilibrium process will then be ergodic. In this case, we have a *bona fide* rational expectations equilibrium for the model, since $p_t = g[p_{t-1}, \alpha_t]$ is a solution to the equilibrium law of motion above. To guarantee that the equilibrium stochastic process doesn't wander away from a neighborhood of the steady state, it is sufficient that the steady-state equilibrium be forward stable, and that the variance σ of the sunspot process $\{\alpha_t\}$ be sufficiently small that no shock realization moves the REE price outside of the basin of attraction for the steady state.

We note that Woodford's paper develops the stochastic side of the model as one of a stationary infinite sequence of shocks and then derives equilibrium prices as functions of these abstract shock variables plus lagged prices. The analysis we present here is based on the more general results contained in an unpublished 1986 working paper by Woodford (1986b). As we will see later, this paper continues to be important.

This is the appropriate place to note, however, that Woodford's development of the infinite shock formulation of the OLG and CIA models owed its impetus to a debate he conducted at the time with Grandmont. According to notes that Woodford sent to Spear and Sanjay Srivastava while they were discussing what to do with their Spear, Srivastava, and Woodford (1990) paper, Grandmont had objected to Woodford's use of the bootstrapping technique in his contribution to the *JET* Symposium volume, on the grounds that the resulting equilibrium could not be "decentralized" because an "auctioneer" would have to select one of an arbitrary number of possible equilibrium forecasts for the model. This criticism was based on the fact that because the equilibrium law of motion is used as the forecast function, any initial time t price (or function of previous prices and exogenous variables) will generate an equilibrium. This criticism is difficult to follow because if one used an arbitrary (temporary equilibrium) forecast function to specify $p_t = h(p_{t-1}, \alpha_{t+1})$, we would get market clearing, but the agent's forecast would be wrong. The equilibrium becomes rational only if the agent uses the actual law of motion for the economy as his forecast.

Woodford made this argument to Grandmont, but to no avail, so he then undertook to reformulate the model using the infinite history of exogenous (sunspot) shocks as the state variables. Using functional versions of the implicit function theorem together with results from the K&L regularity paper, he showed that for the given sunspot stochastic process, the resulting equilibrium was in fact determinate. Grandmont apparently accepted this argument because Woodford's paper was accepted for the symposium volume (and, as we've seen, praised by Grandmont), even though Woodford notes that he never received a formal reply to his letter to Grandmont explaining the new approach.

If one compares the equilibrium derived here with the one we found for the easy Lucas model in Chapter 3, the equilibrium stochastic process for that model was of the form $p_t = f(\alpha_t)$, that is, there was no dependence of the equilibrium stochastic process on lagged endogenous state variables. This observation led a number of macroeconomists, Bennet McCallum notable among them, to propose the so-called "minimum state variable approach" to specifying equilibrium. McCallum (1999) justifies this approach by noting that it corresponds to the "bubble-free" solution of the model, reflecting only economic fundamentals. McCallum does acknowledge that alternative selection criteria based on learning are also useful, though he omits any mention of Woodford (1990) which shows how sunspot equilibria can be learned from empirical observation. We mention these controversies because they again illustrate the disagreements over what the right set of state variables is for OLG-type models.

The original Lucas–Stokey cash-in-advance paper gets 1,173 Google Scholar cites, while the Woodford paper gets 470. All of the work on these types of OLG-like models is summarized in the study by Benhabib-Farmer (1999) *Handbook of Macroeconomics* chapter, which itself gets 681 citations. So, clearly, these two substitutions of the basic ILA framework for an original OLG foundation have had an impact on macroeconomics, reinforcing our contention from the previous section that the relative ease of the recursive techniques available in the ILA model, and the apparent OE of the original OLG setting with the ILA plus friction convinced many a young macroeconomist that these were the models to work with. The large number of citations that these papers get also explains the low numbers accruing to Aiyagari's original OE work: with positive new models to reference, practitioners didn't need to reference the OE results (right or wrong) in Aiyagari's effort to conjoin the two models.

7.5 PUSHBACK

Over the same period that Aiyagari was looking at OE and Grandmont, Lucas-Stokey, Woodford, and others were looking at ways to generate OLG-like results in ILA environments, another group of young scholars was pushing back against the way ILA models were coming to dominate macroeconomics with the popularity of real business cycle models (see Young, 2014, for this history) and the emergence of the New Neoclassical Synthesis of RBC and New Keynesian models.[2] To analyze this pushback, we focus on several papers by Alan Auerbach, Douglas Bernheim (and co-author Kyle Bagwell), Laurence Kotlikoff, and Lawrence Summers.

We begin by looking at Bernheim–Bagwell (1988). This paper pushed back against Barro's contention that ILA and OLG models were essentially the same as long as families in the OLG model left active (i.e., positive) bequests to their offspring. The Bernheim-Bagwell criticism focused on Barro's assumption that dynastic families are lineal, pointing out that real family structures form trees, given that it takes two people to procreate and the standard taboos against incest.[3]

The Bernheim–Bagwell analysis starts by taking the tree structure as the given family structure and invokes a result due to Erdos and Reny (1959)[4] to justify the assumption that all of the nodes in the family tree are connected in the sense of allowing for positive transfers of wealth between families. Given this assumption, the analysis of the paper looks at the transfer game across the network of families and demonstrates, in an example, that government policy actions – for the specific example this is a tax on wages – have no effect because adjustments in transfers between families undo the distortion introduced by the taxes. The main analysis of the paper generalizes this and demonstrates that there can be no role for markets in such an economy: all economic interactions exhibit Ricardian neutrality.

These results obviously suggest that the likelihood that real economies are populated by large, interconnected dynastic families is quite low, which leads us back to the question of why macroeconomics became so dependent on such an unrealistic model. In an opening footnote to their paper, Bernheim and Bagwell address this issue:

> No doubt its popularity in part reflects considerations of analytic convenience. Overlapping-generations models not only are generally less tractable but also often give rise to equilibria with undesirable properties. Specifically, equilibria in overlapping-generations models may fail to be either efficient or locally unique (see Balasko Shell, 1980; Kehoe & Levine, 1985). Failure of local uniqueness is particularly troubling in any exercise involving comparative statics or dynamics. Thus Judd (1985) unabashedly attributes his adoption of the dynastic framework to analytic convenience. Unfortunately, this advantage may be illusory. In a recent paper, Gale (1985) has pointed out that, while Barro's dynastic solution is an equilibrium for the model he considers, this model also generally gives rise to a continuum of subgame-perfect intergenerational equilibria (see Selten, 1965, 1975), many of which are inefficient. By adopting dynastic assumptions, one therefore does not necessarily succeed in avoiding the problems that arise in the standard overlapping-generations framework. (Bernheim & Bagwell, 1988, p. 309)

As we saw earlier in looking at the Arrow-Kurz analysis of optimal bequests, the issue of how important intergenerational transfers are to economic activities has been a matter of close study. This study has continued with the work of Bernheim and a large group of other authors looking at the types of altruistic behavior at work in the real world. From this analysis, it seems clear that one cannot fully explain the shape of the wealth distribution without some form of dynastic intergenerational wealth transfers. But the key question here is how this shapes the operation of the macroeconomy. In private communication with us (email December 8, 2021), Bernheim addresses his own conclusions on the issue by stating that

> Despite that paper ["Fiscal Policy with Impure Intergenerational Altruism," *Econometrica* 2001, with Andy Abel], my eventual conclusion was that non-paternalistic altruism, which is essential for the dynastic representation, just isn't a plausible model of intergenerational transfers. Sure, I wrote some papers showing that bequest motives can be important, and I believe that too. I just don't think the non-paternalistic altruism framework is the right one (or even close). Some of that traces back to Bernheim–Shleifer–Summers, but I also think there are factors like warm-glow giving (Andreoni), as well as various kinds of intrafamily signaling issues (Bernheim & Severinov, JPE 2003, and Severinov's separate paper applying the idea to Ricardian equivalence). With these alternative models, there are certainly connections between generations, but they behave more like the bequest is a type of consumption, so the properties are more OLG-like. (At least, more like OLG models with uncertain horizons where people accidentally leave bequests.)

Bernheim (1989) is a follow-on paper, which looks at the Barro OLG formulation of the dynastic family model and demonstrates that the dynastic equilibrium could never arise as the solution to a standard social welfare optimization unless the social planner only cares about the current generation. In the usual case where we assume the planner (or government) puts positive welfare weight on all generations, Bernheim shows that the solution is one in which no parent family leaves bequests to their offspring. The intuitive reason for this is straightforward. At any time *t*, if bequests are strictly positive, the parent generation at *t*–1 must be indifferent between its own consumption and that of generation *t* (as must all prior generations). But, because of the OLG demographic structure, the young in generation *t* will prefer to get a larger bequest (and future generations will be indifferent). Hence, as long as the planner puts positive weight on generation *t*, he will wish to increase the bequests of all generations, which is clearly infeasible. Thus, the dynastic allocation cannot be a welfare optimum, and any such welfare optimum must have all bequests set to zero. While the dynastic equilibrium will be optimal if the planner only cares about the current generation, the OLG demographics of the real world give democratic governments incentives to value members of all currently living generations, even if concern for the far future is minimal. In this case, the inoptimality argument Bernheim presents holds. Finally, as Bernheim notes, this argument also appears in earlier papers looking at gift-giving equilibria (see, e.g., Bernheim, Shleifer, & Summers, 1986; Roberts, 1984).

There is a secondary macroeconomic issue worth mentioning in this context, which has a political dimension to it. The Barro (1974) paper implies that Ricardian equivalence holds in the ILA setting. Ricardian equivalence is the contention that rational agents will correctly anticipate that government spending must be paid for and will, therefore, increase saving if the government runs a deficit, anticipating future taxes. Similarly, they will reduce saving (and increase consumption) if taxes are levied contemporaneously since their future beneficiaries will benefit from the public goods (or transfers) they are paying for today. This question has been the focus of a great deal of study, with the modern consensus view being that the equivalence does not hold. (See, e.g., the Wikipedia article on this, https://en.wikipedia.org/wiki/Ricardian_equivalence, for a summary of the empirical results and references to the major papers on the topic.)

The political economy dimension to this debate is obvious: opponents of government social spending use the Ricardian equivalence results to argue that such spending is ineffective because it gets undone by the actions of the private sector. On this dimension, one of the implications of the Bernheim–Bagwell result is that unless one believes that markets are unnecessary (because like government, they too are ineffective), Ricardian equivalence cannot hold.

More detailed studies of the motives for bequests have also bolstered the Arrow–Kurz contention that most intergenerational transfers take the form of human capital investment in children, with the promise of future payoffs from these "bequests" giving children the incentive to incur the disutility that can be associated with schooling.

Kotlikoff and Summers (1981) used data from the Census, the national income accounts, the IRS and the Social Security administration to estimate how much of US annual savings for 1974 could be attributed to life-cycle retirement saving. From their calculations, they estimated that upwards of 80% of observed saving could not be explained by retirement motives. This estimate is in rough agreement with earlier studies cited by Kotlikoff and Summers, and in marked contrast to estimates obtained by Modigliani (1988), who estimated that only about 15% of observed saving was due to non-retirement motivated transfers. Modigliani also cites a number of other survey-based studies which agree with his estimates.

This raises the obvious question as to the motives for the excess saving (over retirement needs) observed by Kotlikoff-Summers and others. Is it for active bequest purposes (in the Barro sense) or precautionary, based on the uncertainties of health care costs combined with mortality risk? There were a number of follow-on papers stimulated by the Kotlikoff-Summers findings that strongly suggest that the answer to this question is that the saving is precautionary.

Kurz (1984) uses data from the 1979 President's Commission on Pension Policy to test two hypotheses about savings motives, based on the fact that in US society, giving and receiving transfers are generally viewed differently. As Kurz notes, outside of inheritances, there can be a stigma associated with receiving transfers given the typical American attitudes toward self-reliance. Giving transfers, on the other hand, is viewed positively as indicating compassion toward the needy. Kurz further posits that if the purpose of observed transfers was predominantly to support intrafamily optimal wealth management, then estimates of the effects of positive or negative transfers in censored equations would be the same, since no direct utility effects would be generated. Based on this, he conducts two econometric tests. One looks at the effects of increases in Social Security transfers on private transfers both received and given. The second looks at the coefficients on the receiving versus giving regression equations and asks whether they are the same.

Kurz's first test finds that based on the receiving equation estimates, there is a significant dollar-for-dollar reduction in private transfers received for each dollar increase in Social Security support. On the giving side, however, he finds no relationship. This result weakly supports the Ricardian neutrality prediction of the dynastic family interpretation of the OLG model, though the lack of effect on giving suggests that what's actually happening is that children are reducing transfers to their relatively poorer parents as the government picks up the slack.

Kurz's econometric test of the second hypothesis – that the coefficients on the giving and receiving equations should be the same – forcefully rejects this hypothesis. So, both of Kurz's test suggest that the dynastic bequest motive cannot explain the observed oversaving relative to retirement needs.

While there is a whole literature on the question of whether the observed saving is driven by bequest motives or precautionary motives (indeed, more than we can possibly survey here), the fundamental issue in answering the question is one of econometric identification, since in data terms, both motives result in the same outcome. To date, the problem still hasn't been completely resolved, though Ameriks, Caplin, Laufer, and Van Nieuwerburgh (2011) have made some significant headway by including survey questions in their econometric analysis. Their findings indicate that the precautionary motive for saving is quite strong, though they also find significant support for bequest motives among upper-income families with children. These findings support the contention – based on the fat tails of the distribution of inheritances in the US – that realistic macroeconomic models should be based on a hybrid of the OLG and dynastic family frameworks of the kind originally examined by Wilson (1980), Muller and Woodford (1988), and Wright (2005). That said, the jury is still out on this overall question. Benhabib and Bisin (2018) stress the importance of bequests in generating the observed skewness of the US wealth distribution, but highlight a number of different models that can generate such bequests. Among these is the conventional Barro interpretation of the OLG/ILA model, but there are other non-dynastic ways in which the required bequests can arise. Gokhale, Kotlikoff, Sefton, and Weale (2001), for example, use the Auerbach–Kotlikoff simulation model (which we discuss in detail below) with mortality risk, assortative mating, and differences in skills and time preference to show that purely accidental bequests due to imperfect annuitization can give rise to wealth distributions that match the observed data under realistic parameterizations of the model. Benhabib and Bisin also note that while fiscal policy has an obvious effect on the distribution of income and wealth, the converse is also true, so that for a model to fully capture the forces at work in determining how wealth is allocated, we need to model political economy interactions as well. Finally, there are empirical studies of intergenerational wealth dynamics that indicate that wealth is mean reverting. This occurs because families grow, and in the process, dissipate the wealth that earlier generations have accumulated, though the overall process is slow. For more details on this, see Wahl (2003).

The publication of Barro's 1974 paper also stimulated critical comment from Martin Feldstein and James Buchanan, published in the *JPE* in April of 1976. Both Feldstein and Buchanan based their criticisms not on the realism of the bequest mechanism at the heart of Barro's model, but on their contentions that Barro had overlooked (in Feldstein's comment) the possibility of economic growth, and (in Buchanan's comment) the real-world ways in which governments in a democracy decided on taxation or debt.

Feldstein's criticism looked back at the early development of the OLG model when a key concern was the growth of population (later amended to allow for endogenous growth), and the possibility that real interest rates might be below the growth rate of the economy as a whole. In this case, Feldstein pointed out that the government could maintain a level of debt in perpetuity, using growth in tax revenues to pay the interest on the debt, with the initial debt accumulation used for the benefit of the generation(s) alive at the time the debt is incurred.

Barro's reply to this concedes that in this situation, debt would increase net wealth, but argues that the stimulus afforded by the debt issue would have the effect of raising interest rates to the point that, in steady state, $r=g$. At the time of this debate, the US economy had not been through any protracted periods where real interest rates were lower than the economy's growth rate, though that changed in the decade following the financial crisis of 2008, prompting some economists to revisit the issue.

Buchanan's criticism, coming from a political economy perspective, was that most government provision of public goods or services was in fact financed by contemporaneous taxation, though he did hold up the Social Security system as an example where the means of payment of future benefits was not secured at the time the obligation to pay benefits was taken on. He cites Feldstein's work on the effects of Social Security on saving to bolster his point. Barro's response is basically one of disputing the validity of Feldstein's results.

Barro also directly addressed the Bernheim–Bagwell criticism in Barro (1989). Barro argues that if all of the members of a large economically interconnected family were all making the kinds of operative (i.e., positive) bequests that generate the excess neutrality results in Bernheim–Bagwell, then there would be incentives for members of the network to free ride on the contributions of others.

We find this argument suspect. In a conventional public goods model, agents care about their own consumption of the public good but would prefer not to pay for it if they think others will. Barro is interpreting a parent's altruistic care for their child as the public good, so that if that agent thinks her kid's spouse's parents will foot the bill for the down payment on their first house, they can free ride on that. While this likely happens sometimes in the real world, if the agents also care altruistically for their kid's spouse, and the altruistic preference relation between members of society is transitive, agents will care for their kid's spouse's parents as well and not want them to foot the whole bill. One could set-up a model with differing degrees of altruism, depending on some measure of relationship distance, and then examine how neutral things are relative to connection strength, but as far as we are aware, no one has done this yet. Given the empirical evidence against Ricardian neutrality (and presumably against everything neutrality), Barro's argument seems moot, at best. It is curious, however, that Barro chose this forum (i.e., his own book) to reply to the Bernheim–Bagwell critique rather than through the kind of communication in the *JPE* that Buchanan and Feldstein pursued after the publication of Barro's 1974 paper.

We note finally that an early version of Bernheim–Bagwell was cited by Barro and Becker (1986). This paper uses the Barro dynastic family formulation to study the effects of incentives, costs of childcare, and human capital investment costs on family fertility decisions. They cite Bernheim–Bagwell by way of acknowledging very briefly the problems associated with more realistic treatments of family formation but proceed to analyze a key component of what families do – procreation – using the tractable but unrealistic dynastic family framework. Barro and Becker wrote two additional papers, Barro and Becker (1988, 1989) examining family fertility decisions and the economic demand for children in the three years following their "Altruism and the Economic Theory of Fertility" paper. The second paper in the *QJE* cites Bernheim–Bagwell in the same throw-away manner as the "Altruism" paper. By the time the 1989 *Econometrica* paper is published, all mention of the Bernheim–Bagwell results is gone.

In 2018, we posed a series of questions to Robert Barro regarding his 1974 *JPE* paper. These related to (i) origins; (ii) early reception; (iii) terminology; (iv) citations in the paper, and (v) the Feldstein and Buchanan comments on it. The first question (personal communication October 12, 2018) asked: "Can you tell us how you came to refer to the model in your 1974 paper specifically as an 'overlapping generations model' as against using the term 'consumption-loans' model, which, following Samuelson 1958, seems to have been the more frequent usage?" He replied (October 12, 2018):

> I am surprised to see that the term overlapping-generations model is not in Samuelson 1958 or Diamond 1965. I used the term in my 1974 paper to describe what I thought was in Samuelson and Diamond. Malinvaud, 1987 JEL, argues that the idea of an overlapping-generations model is in Allais's 1947 book. However, I do not know whether the term overlapping generations was used in that book. And Allais's 1947 work seems to have had no influence on Samuelson 1958 or Diamond 1965 or surely on my 1974 paper (since I knew nothing of Allais's work). So, I really cannot say where I got the term overlapping-generations model for my 1974 paper.

We then asked about the following (October 13, 2018):

In your acknowledgements in JPE 1974, you wrote: "I have benefited from comments on earlier drafts by Gary Becker, Benjamin Eden, Milton Friedman, Merton Miller, Jose Scheinkman, Jeremy Siegel, and Charles Upton. The National Science Foundation has supported this research."

1. Regarding the early drafts of the paper. Were any of the drafts given at seminars or meetings, and if so, can you recall where and when, and what were the reactions to the paper?
2. Regarding the comments of those mentioned above. Do you recall what the comments were?

Barro replied (October 13, 2018):

> With respect to seminars, I remember it exactly. I presented the paper only twice, once in the money & banking workshop in Chicago Econ Dept. and once at a seminar in Chicago B. School. In the first, it is the only time I remember Friedman, Stigler, and Becker present together at a seminar. I recall an argument I had with Becker concerning the effects of inheritance taxes. I argued that these taxes made it less likely that an interior solution would apply for voluntary intergenerational transfers, but if the solution were still interior then the offsetting intergenerational transfers that produce Ricardian Equivalence would hold exactly. I remember Milton deep in thought on the matter for a couple minutes while no one said anything. Then he announced (apparently with great surprise) that Gary was wrong and I was right. I was also surprised in retrospect that Stigler never said anything about the term Ricardian Equivalence. That expression, not contained in my paper, became widespread only after James Buchanan's comment in the 1976 JPE.

In the B. School seminar, the only thing I remember is an interaction with Gene Fama. He kept complaining that a debt-tax swap should have no real effects. Then when I explained that his conjecture was consistent with my results, he decided that the results were interesting.

I also recall a lunch discussion that I had with Fischer Black. I took about 15 minutes to go through the argument for what is now called Ricardian Equivalence (based on offsetting intergenerational transfers). Fischer just listened carefully and said nothing. Then he finally said, "Sounds right to me."

I don't recall what the acknowledgments in my paper to other people were for.

Regarding the comments by Feldstein and Buchanan, we asked Barro (October 30, 2018):

Another minor puzzle, this time regarding your citations in your reply to Buchanan and Feldstein in *JPE 1976*. In their comments, they both used the term overlapping generations, and cited Samuelson as the original model. In your reply, *JPE 1976*, you cited Diamond and Cass-Yaari as OLG models, but didn't cite Samuelson at all … Do you recall why?

Barro answered (October 30, 2018):

As I recall, I thought Samuelson's framework was not so interesting because it neglected capital and, hence, capital accumulation. So, one could not really think about the possibility of over- or under-accumulation of capital.

We note that this issue was addressed quite explicitly in Diamond's OLG model with production and growth.

The second form of pushback against the dynastic family model came in the form of "bucking the trend" of using variations on the RCK model for policy analysis. This work involved applications of long-lived deterministic OLG models to study major public policy issues, continuing the work started by Tobin, as we've outlined previously. To examine these models, we focus on the contributions of Alan Auerbach, Laurence Kotlikoff, James Poterba, and Lawrence Summers.

Alan Auerbach and Larry Kotlikoff were graduate students together at Harvard (Kotlikoff graduated in 1977, Auerbach the next year), both of them are students of Marty Feldstein. Since Feldstein's work on taxation and social security was largely grounded in OLG, it is not surprising that Auerbach and Kotlikoff inherited his appreciation of the model. According to Auerbach, when we asked how he and Kotlikoff started working together on their OLG projects

I don't recall our discussing this while we were both in graduate school. We may have started when I was on the job market. Larry was in his first year of a three-year post-doc at UCLA and I stayed with him for a couple of days while I was interviewing there. We definitely did the initial research while he was still doing his post-doc, as our first RAs on the project were then UCLA graduate students (Maxim Engers & Jon Skinner). (private email correspondence of July 5, 2022)

Their initial collaborations quickly produced two papers, Auerbach and Kotlikoff (1983a) and (1983b). Both these papers use what has become known as the Auerbach–Kotlikoff simulation model, which is a 55-period deterministic Diamond version of the OLG model. This model is now generally referred to as the AK model[5]. These simulations typically incorporated additively separable CES utility functions for households and Cobb-Douglas production functions along with realistic specifications of the government's policy instruments for taxation and transfers. As we noted earlier, this work was a precursor to Kydland and Prescott's (1982) introduction of calibrated simulation of general equilibrium models into macroeconomics. We characterize the work as a precursor because in addition to the calibrated simulations of their model, Kydland and Prescott also undertook a detailed decomposition of important macroeconomic time-series via the development and application of the Hodrick-Prescott filter. The results of this detrending of the data generated a set of statistical regularities that Kydland–Prescott and others then tried to match with their models. We also note that in this work, Kydland and Prescott were working with the stochastic growth model, so their analysis was more general than that of Auerbach and Kotlikoff. We will examine the problems associated with simulating SOLG models with long-lived agents in the next section, but, in terms of the basic idea of replacing bound-to-be-rejected econometric estimation with realistically calibrated simulations, the Auerbach–Kotlikoff model is every bit as innovative as the Kydland–Prescott model.

The first of the two AK papers cited above lays out the simulation model in detail and then applies it to examine four examples of policy issues that the model can address. These are (from the text of the paper):

1. The excess burden associated with the taxation of capital income provides some limited scope for improving the welfare of all current and future cohorts when lump-sum taxes and transfers are available. However, given that lump-sum taxes and transfers are not available policy tools, "tax reform" proposals are likely to significantly reduce the welfare of some cohorts and significantly raise the welfare of others unless annual tax rates and their associated deficit levels are chosen with extreme care.
2. The inter-cohort allocation of the tax burden of government expenditure is a significantly more important determinant of national savings than the structure of taxation.
3. The long-run effect on the capital–output ratio of switching from a progressive to a proportional income tax with no change in the stock of government debt is roughly 13%.
4. Short-run crowding out of private investment by balanced budget increases in government expenditure is on the order of 50 cents per dollar, while long-run crowding out is 20 cents per dollar of government expenditure (Auerbach & Kotlikoff, 1983a p. 460).

The second paper examines the effects of providing government incentives for saving versus investment via the tax structure. The starting point for this analysis is the observation that in conventional static public finance models, the impact of tax incentives for saving (the supply side) or investment (the demand side) don't depend on who pays or receives the nominal tax or subsidy, just as with the conventional tax incidence analysis. In a dynamic, lifecycle context, though, the distinction affects different cohorts differently. Auerbach and Kotlikoff illustrate this using a simple two-period OLG model, showing that a subsidy to saving (new saving from income plus existing asset holdings) makes the old agents in the model better off by raising the value of their assets in the market. A subsidy to investment, however, makes the old worse off since by encouraging new saving, it effectively acts as a tax on consumption, which hurts the old. One consequence of this is its implication that conventional approaches to providing investment incentives – reduction in corporate profit taxes or other property income – if financed by government debt, create long-run incentives for increased consumption and hence reduced saving and reduced long-run equilibrium capital formation. Conversely, the paper shows that there is a range of subsidies to investment that, by crowding out consumption by richer, older agents, crowds in capital formation and can, if rates are chosen correctly, make the subsidy self-financing.

These qualitative policy implications are confirmed by the quantitative analysis Auerbach and Kotlikoff do with their calibrated 55-period OLG model. This paper is also one of the earliest to adopt the structure of sketching qualitative results using "toy" models, and then confirming and sharpening these results using richer, more realistic quantitative models, a practice that has become the norm in contemporary macroeconomic analysis.

The work in these two papers was followed by an unpublished paper Auerbach–Kotlikoff (1985), and an *AER* paper Auerbach–Kotlikoff (1987). The unpublished Social Security paper makes the point that because of the opacity of the benefits formulas the Social Security Administration uses, workers are unable to see the linkage between their marginal tax payments and the benefits it provides them on retirement. This absence of linkage can generate sizeable efficiency losses. The paper reports on the results of simulations using the AK model on efficiency gains that can result from tighter linkage of marginal taxes and benefits. Specifically, gains on the order of 1% of GDP are possible, according to the model, suggesting that even simple actions like providing workers with information about how their tax payments affect their benefits would be beneficial.

The *AER* paper looks at three major policy issues – consumption versus income taxation, investment incentives, and the crowding out (or in) effects of deficit spending – and indicates the results of the simulation model's output in each of these policy experiments. While these results were all reported in earlier work, the publication of this paper in the *AER* (widely considered one of the premier general interest publication outlets in economics) was a strong signal to the profession of the value of large-scale simulations, and a strong endorsement of the core value of the overlapping generations model.

From the theory side of macro, some of the most adamant pushback against the conventional ILA approach to macro has come from Roger Farmer. Farmer received his Ph.D. from the University of Western Ontario in 1982. His main thesis paper, "A New Theory of Aggregate Supply" (Farmer, 1984) used the OLG structure in conjunction with information asymmetry – specifically the moral hazard problem that occurs if workers are completely insured against productivity shocks – to come up with a model of aggregate supply with implicit contracts and the possibility of firm bankruptcy. As Farmer notes in the introduction to the paper

> In sharp contrast to either the new classical or the sticky price contract explanations of business cycle fluctuations, this theory is not a natural rate theory even in the long run. It predicts that the steady state employment level is an endogenous variable which varies systematically with fiscal policy. (Farmer, 1984, p. 920)

With a paper covering both OLG and implicit contracts – and one that would ultimately see publication in the *AER* – it isn't surprising that Farmer drew attention from the Penn faculty working in these areas and was recruited there as an assistant professor in 1983 (staying on until 1989 when he moved to UCLA, where he spent the rest of his career until retiring from there to move to the UK at the University of Warwick). Farmer's tenure at Penn included a year Mike Woodford spent there as a visiting assistant professor right after he graduated from MIT. The coincidence of Farmer and Woodford's interests led them to produce Farmer and Woodford (1984). As the reference to the paper notes, this paper remained unpublished even as the original working paper version garnered over 100 Google Scholar citations. The paper was eventually published as a legacy paper in *Macroeconomic Dynamics*. The paper uses a simple linear-quadratic two-period version of the Lucas '72 paper's OLG model, together with the bootstrapping procedure outlined above to examine how sunspot models could generate a number of macroeconomic results consistent with the empirical stylized facts. These included the pattern of interest payments on government spending and debt, the Phillips curve relationship, and the possibility of nominal wages being sticky even as real wages remain flexible. One innovation in this paper was the introduction of a fixed level of government spending financed by public debt. The effect of the government spending in the model is to then create two steady-state monetary equilibria, one of which is forward unstable (and corresponds to the Samuelsonian monetary equilibrium when government spending and debt are zero) and the other forward stable. The bootstrapping technique then generates sunspot equilibria on a neighborhood of the stable steady state.

A second key paper from Farmer's Penn tenure is Farmer (1986). This paper studies a version of the Diamond model in which the government, at some point in the past, has incurred debt (positive or negative) but then reverts to a policy of balanced budget spending (so that the deficit going forward is zero). Under these conditions, Farmer derives conditions on the asset demands and wages as functions of the interest rate that lead to a Hopf bifurcation in the equilibrium second-order difference equation, determined by the government's debt position. The paper shows that this dynamic system has two possible steady states, one where the debt is zero (Gale's balanced equilibrium) and one where the (gross) interest rate is one (the golden rule steady state). From here, a straightforward application of the implicit function theorem and related results from the Hopf bifurcation theorem allow Farmer to find conditions on the equilibrium difference equation such that the roots of the characteristic equation for the dynamic system are complex. When these roots are inside the unit circle, the limit behavior of the dynamic system is that of a continuous cycle. Farmer illustrates this with examples (both stable and unstable) based on plausible preferences and technologies.

We note that this paper was one of those included in the Grandmont-Malgrange *JET* symposium volume on complex dynamics. This established Farmer as one of the new generation of macro theorists following in the footsteps of Benhabib and Grandmont in exploring the implications of the OLG dynamic system. Much of Farmer's later work focused on the issue of indeterminacy more generally, in settings beyond the pure OLG model – in ILA settings, in the Blanchard–Yaari model (discussed below), and in dynamic games – and in this work he became one of the foremost young proponents of Shell's Philadelphia Pholk theorem. In pursuing this research, he has also become an important proponent of the need for macroeconomics to move beyond the New Neoclassical Synthesis and take seriously the theoretical results on complex dynamics, the role of expectations, and the possibility of indeterminacy in macroeconomic modeling.

Before we leave the subject of pushback against the ascendence of the ILA model, we should mention the development of what can be considered hybrid models, which combined features of the ILA and OLG model. There are four notable papers here. The first was Wilson (1980), the second was Blanchard (1985), the third was Muller and Woodford (1988), and the fourth was Wright (1988).

Wilson's paper provides an abstract formulation of general equilibrium in infinite horizon dynamic exchange economies. The abstractness of his formulation allows him to nest OLG models (infinitely-many finite-lived agents) and ILA models (finitely-many infinite-lived agents) along with the possibility of models with infinitely-many infinite-lived agents. Wilson has two key results. First, if there are only finitely-many infinite-lived agents, or almost all of the wealth in the economy is held by a finite number of infinitely lived agents, then a competitive equilibrium exists. The second result establishes versions of the two welfare theorems when the economy consists of a finite number of infinite-lived agents, or (as in the existence proof) a finite number of infinite-lived agents plus a negligible set of other agents. So, the positive results here pertain to the ILA model, though the paper does highlight what can go wrong (in terms of existence or optimality results) for OLG versions of the general model.

Blanchard's paper developed a continuous-time model in which agents face a constant probability of death once they are born. Large groups of new agents are also born in each instant of time, so that the model has an overlapping generations structure. The fact that agents die stochastically presents a potential problem in the sense that if they are holding positive amounts of wealth, this needs to be bequeathed to descendants in some way. Blanchard solves this problem by using a result due to Yaari, introducing annuities in the model that, in a competitive environment in which the law of large numbers holds, returns all unconsumed wealth to the insurance company issuing the annuities as part of the optimal contract. The paper itself uses this framework to examine how lifecycle income (and associated finite horizons) and government fiscal policies interact to determine steady-state equilibrium interest rates.

This paper stimulated a large literature exploring this new version of the OLG model, which we will examine later in the book. One aspect of the model which has been criticized for its lack of realism is the assumption that the probability of death is independent of agents' ages. This particular feature of the model makes working with it quite tractable, since it generates the kind of self-similar recursive structure found in the dynamic programming approach to the RCK model. The assumption isn't particularly realistic, since as people get older, their survival probabilities fall, but the tradeoff between tractability and realism isn't unreasonable.

In footnote 1 of the paper, Blanchard notes that Barro had suggested an alternative interpretation of the mortality probability, viewing it not as the probability of an individual agent dying, but rather as that of a family dying out, that is, a family dies without producing offspring. The note states that this interpretation is a better justification for the assumption that the probability of dying is constant. But, somewhat confusingly, Blanchard points to Gomperty's law to illustrate the kinds of probabilities arising empirically. The confusion (at least to our minds) stems from the fact that Gomperty's law reflects individual mortality risk, not family risk. The relevant empirical framework for examining family mortality risk is the Galton–Watson process, which looks, variously, at the likelihood of a given family name disappearing, the probability that a maternal mitochondrial lineage disappears, or, more generally, at the extinction probabilities for two-couple families via the bisexual Galton-Watson process. Although the most realistic process – the bisexual GW process – is also the most difficult to analyze, there is a general result due to Thomas Bruss[6] stating that as long as the mean reproductive rate per couple is bounded, and below one for sufficiently large populations, then the limiting family extinction probability is one. Based on the numbers from the GW process for name extinction, though, the probability that any given family name survives over five generations is in the 20–40% range. These numbers would seem to bolster the OLG interpretation of Blanchard's model, rather than Barro's interpretation of it as a realistic approximation of a model of dynastic families.

An early extension of Blanchard's model appears in Weil (1989). Weil modifies the Blanchard–Yaari model by allowing new generations of infinitely-lived agents to be born at each point of time. This structure mimics the overlapping generations structure in the influx of new young agents but dispenses with the terminal condition of finite death dates in Blanchard's model. Weil shows that in this setting, most of the characteristics of conventional OLG models obtain. There are inefficient competitive equilibria, asset bubbles (or sunspot equilibria) can exist, and the Ricardian neutrality of the conventional representative agent ILA model doesn't hold. As Weil notes, these results show that infinite lives and representative agents need not be the same. As we will note later in our discussion of efficiency notions, Weil's results also suggest that the resource flexibility generated by having new generations entering without pre-existing constraints on their behavior imposed by their predecessor generations is what drives the differences between OLG and representative agent economies. While we also recognize Weil's key point that infinite lifetimes don't rule out OLG phenomena, it will be convenient for our purposes to continue referring to the dynastic family model as ILA.

The Muller–Woodford paper took the straightforward approach to deal with the fact that while most parents don't leave large death bequests to their children, there are in fact families where large amounts of wealth are passed down through the generations. Their model assumes that finite-lived OLG agents (who don't leave bequests) coexist with infinite-lived agents, interpreted as a finite number of (types of) dynastic families. Muller and Woodford first point out that the introduction of even a single dynastic family in an otherwise uniformly OLG environment can have a dramatic effect, since prices must be summable in this case to prevent the dynastic family's wealth from becoming infinite. This result, in turn, rules out the possibility of inefficient equilibria which could exist in the model in the absence of the dynastic family. There are, however, other OLG-specific equilibrium properties that persist in the model, specifically, the possibility that equilibrium can be indeterminate. The main result of the paper is its demonstration that "Indeterminacy continues to be possible even when Barro 'dynasties' own a large fraction of total wealth, as long as their consumption is not too great a part of total consumption" (Muller & Woodford, 1988, p. 257). These results have also been the basis for a great deal of follow-on work examining these hybrid models which we will be examining further later in the book.

The study by Wright (1988) also uses the hybrid OLG-ILA model (citing both Wilson's and Muller-Woodford's contributions) in order to analyze how the institution of contracting affects the observed data collected by government agencies and other entities if the underlying equilibrium is, in fact, at an Arrow–Debreu Pareto optimum. In Wright's paper, workers are OLG-type agents who live $N \geq 2$ periods. This allows the introduction of age-related heterogeneity – in terms of discounting, risk aversion, and retirement horizon effects – that contribute to the observed differences in hours worked by age. Wright assumes that the employer in the model is an infinite-lived household who owns an asset such as land or entrepreneurial skill that allows it to produce output by combining labor hired externally with the household's unique asset.[7] As in Wilson or Muller-Woodford, the presence of the infinite-lived agent forces prices to be summable in order to guarantee that the aggregate value of the output stream is finite. Also, as in Wilson or Muller-Woodford, the resulting competitive equilibrium is Pareto optimal. Wright then introduces take-it-or-leave-it contracts in a way that has the resulting equilibrium allocation being equivalent to the Arrow–Debreu allocation. This allows him to compare the observed wages based on the data generated by the contracting equilibrium, and compare it with the actual wages determined in the Arrow–Debreu equilibrium. The observed individual wage based on contracting exhibits a bias which depends on the workers' interactions on the asset markets in the model, that is, on workers retirement and precautionary saving. Wright shows that this bias does not average out over workers of different ages. The bias arises because the contracting outcome replaces both labor market and securities market interactions with the contingent outcomes specified in the contract.[8] This paper, in a very real sense, takes Einstein's famous dictum that theory determines what we observe to heart. As Wright notes, he was not the first to make this observation – he credits Rosen (1985) with this – nor was he the last, since the paper is cited. But, the fact that the paper only gets 22 Google cites suggests that the profession was not (and is not currently) ready to confront the measurement distortions the paper delineates.

7.6 STOCHASTIC OLG

Lucas (1972) together with the demonstration of sunspot rational expectations equilibria by Azariadis, and Cass and Shell, made the study of SOLG models germane, particularly since they were not amenable to the kinds of recursive dynamic programming techniques codified in the Stokey and Lucas text.

A critical paper in this developing literature was Spear (1985) (from his University of Pennsylvania thesis, dated 1982). This paper looked at the existence of equilibrium question in a general, multi-good two-period lived SOLG model, under the same assumption on the appropriate state variables that Lucas used in his '72 paper, that is, that endogenous variables – price and allocations – depended only on the exogenous shocks to (in this case) endowments. Up to this point, all SOLG models (that we are aware of) worked with the assumption that only one good was traded, and agents lived two-period lives. Spear's paper, together with an unpublished thesis paper by Rao Aiyagari appear to be the only papers from this period to consider more general models. Spear's results showed that generically in preferences, it was impossible to find a rational expectations equilibrium in the more general model where the prices and allocations depended only on the exogenous shocks, or even finitely-many lags of the shocks.

From Spear's recollections of what got him started looking at this problem:

> After I finished the work on the sunspot model that lead to the "Sufficient Conditions for the Existence of sunspot Equilibrium" paper that Cass had gotten me started on, it seemed natural, given the Balasko, Cass and Shell results showing that any OLG model could be transformed into a two period lived agents model as long as one allowed for multiple commodities and general preferences, to take a look at showing existence of the stochastic steady state equilibrium in a general multi-good model.

We can illustrate this result using the machinery developed earlier to look at the simple Lucas model. Recall for that model that we had two exogenous shocks, *H* and *T*, that affected the endowment of the young. The stochastic steady-state market clearing condition for the model with one good was simply that the aggregate excess demand in each state was zero. For the multi-good model, the market clearing condition is the same

$$z_1^H + z_2^{HH} = 0$$

$$z_1^H + z_2^{TH} = 0$$

$$z_1^T + z_2^{HT} = 0$$

$$z_1^T + z_2^{TT} = 0,$$

where, as in the easy Lucas model, the excess demands are functions of the commodity prices p^H and p^T, though these are now vectors and the excess demand functions above are also vector-valued. Also as in the easy Lucas model, Walras' law restricts the equation system, since

$$p^s \cdot \left[z_1^s + z_2^{ss}\right] \equiv 0$$

for $s{=}H$ or T, and

$$p^s \cdot z_1^s + p^{s'} \cdot z_2^{ss'} \equiv 0$$

for $s \neq s'$, since these are budget constraints.

From the budget constraints, we also have two price normalizations available, since the first two constraints imply that we can normalize prices such that $\iota \cdot p^s = 1$ for s=H,T, where ι is a sum vector (i.e., a vector of 1's). With these preliminaries, we count equations and variables. The market clearing conditions constitute a system of 4ℓ equations, but because of the budget constraints (of which there are 4), we only have at most $4\ell - 4$ independent equations. Since prices are normalized, we have $2\ell - 2$ independent variables. In order to have at least as many variables as we have equations, then, we require that

$$4\ell - 4 \leq 2\ell - 2,$$

which can easily be seen to imply that $\ell \leq 1$, that is, we can only guarantee as many variables as independent equations in the one good model.

It is well-known that in linear equation systems, having at least as many variables as independent equations is a necessary condition for finding a solution to the equation system. This need not be true for non-linear equation systems, which complicates the analysis for showing whether or not the simple equilibrium exists.

Spear's approach to showing that in fact there will not be a solution generally was based on differential topology methods, in particular a version of Rene Thom's transversality theorem, which states that for almost all mappings from one manifold to another, the image of the mapping in its range will intersect any submanifold in the range transversely (i.e., the tangent spaces of the image and the submanifold will intersect in general position). We illustrate this in Fig. 19.

The pink and grey surfaces intersect along the blue line, and the intersection is such that small perturbations of either surface leaves the intersection qualitatively unchanged. This is the basic definition of transversal intersections. Non-transversal intersections are those involving tangencies. These are not in general position because a small perturbation of either surface leads to either non-intersection or transversal intersections. We illustrate this in Fig. 20 for one-dimensional surfaces (i.e., curves).

In Fig. 20, the red and blue curves are tangent. A perturbation upward or downward of the blue curve destroys the tangency, resulting in either two transversal intersections or no intersection. From the definition of transversal

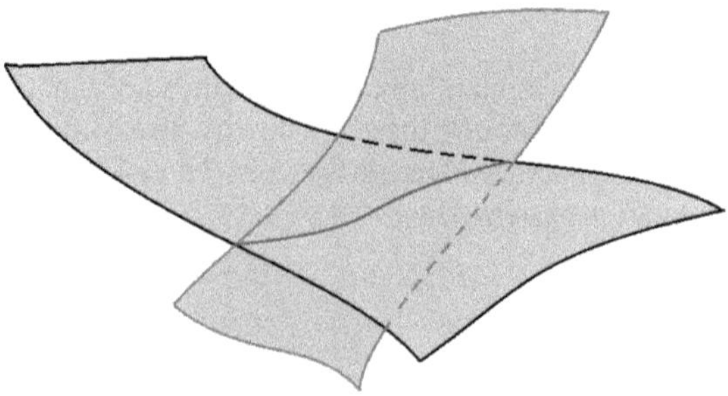

Fig. 19. Transversal Intersection.

Fig. 20. Non-transversal Intersection.

intersection in terms of the general position notion, it should also be clear that non-intersections are transversal (vacuously).

Thom's theorem applies more generally to what are known as the *jets* of a mapping, which consists of the Cartesian product of the graph of the mapping with the associated first, second, etc. derivatives of the mapping. Spear's proof of the general non-existence of simple equilibrium result involved taking the first-order conditions for agent's expected utility maximizations, together with the market clearing conditions, then using a subset of the first-order conditions to replace prices with utility gradient vectors. This then left a mapping defined by the system of equations depending only on the utility functions and their derivatives. Since this constitutes a system of linear equations, applying Thom's theorem boils down to counting equations and variables.

There were a couple of additional complications here. First, if the preferences in the model are additively separable over time, the simple equilibrium can be shown to exist.[9] This is what necessitated looking for genericity results in the space of utility functions rather than simply with respect to endowments. Second, because preferences over uncertain outcomes are in expected utility form, a direct application of Thom's theorem to the space of utilities over random allocations was not possible, requiring instead consideration of the Mather's (1970) multijet extension of Thom's theorem. This result was extended by Alex Citanna and Paolo Siconolfi to models with multiple heterogeneous agents in Citanna–Siconolfi (2007) using direct perturbation methods.

The significance of these results is simply that they imply that general stochastic overlapping generations models will have history-dependent equilibria, that is, equilibria which depend on the entire (infinite) history of shocks. This made working with general SOLG models difficult, since the state variable would be (generically) infinite dimensional.

We turn next to Aiyagari (1981) from his thesis. Chapter 3 of the thesis examines a two-sector model, which necessarily involves agents trading more than one good, so that Spear's result applies. From the thesis

> We are here interested in showing the possibility of a stochastic steady state where average q may be less than one while aggregate investment is positive in the context of an overlapping generations model. It appears to be difficult to do the above with rather general specifications of technology and preferences. One alternative is to select specific functional forms and numerical values for the parameters of the model and to compute numerically the equilibrium steady state distributions for average q and aggregate investment. (Aiyagari, 1981, p. 37)

The functional form for the young agent's utility function over the two goods ends up being equivalent to an additively separable specification, so that for the example, at least, the stochastic steady-state rational expectations equilibrium does exist. From this, it seems clear that Aiyagari was in fact aware that there could be problems with finding simple REE for general SOLG models. This fact is relevant for the next part of our story on the development of the stochastic model.

Aiyagari spent the 1987 academic year visiting at GSIA. He had overlapped in Minnesota's Ph.D. program with Dan Peled, who was then an assistant professor of economics at GSIA and who arranged for Aiyagari to visit. While Aiyagari was at GSIA, he and Spear began talking about Spear's thesis results. From Spear's recollections:

> Rao and I were both avid tennis players, and once we found out we had this mutual interest, we started playing once a week, usually in the late morning before lunch. It was natural, then, that we would spend time talking about research. Rao was quite interested in the result from my '85 *JET* paper.
>
> One day, after we'd been talking about this, and I'd explained how I got the result, Rao disappeared for a week. When he came back he stopped by my office and said that he'd been looking at a three period stochastic model with additively separable preferences and a single good, and the same problem of more independent equations than variables arose in that model. As we talked about, we realized that what was happening was that the portfolio rebalancing actions the middle-aged agents took in response to the resolution of uncertainty in their second period of life made the equilibrium history dependent in the same way that the time non-separability of preferences did in the two-period multi-good model. I encouraged Rao to write the result up as part of a paper he was working on at the time.

Aiyagari did in fact write this up as part of what became his 1988 *JET* paper, discussed previously. When the paper came out, Spear noticed that the only aspect of Aiyagari's discovery that was in the published paper was the brief paragraph at the end indicating that because of the history dependence issue, SOLG and stochastic ILA models couldn't be observationally equivalent. Again, from Spear's recollections:

> When I next ran into Rao – probably at a conference somewhere – I asked him what had happened to his write-up of the history dependence result, and he told me that he'd been asked by either a referee or *JET* Associate Editor (I don't remember exactly which) to "get rid of the negative results."

Unfortunately, the working paper versions of this paper appear to have been lost. Aiyagari's paper cites a University of Wisconsin working paper version from 1986, and via Spear's recollection, he issued a GSIA working paper version with the history dependence results included in 1987. The GSIA working paper collection was disposed of in the early 1990s when the school expanded into a new wing of its building, and a search by staff at Wisconsin's economics department was unable to find a copy of the 1986 version.

Via Karl Shell, we were informed that the *JET* editorial office records from then were lost when the editorial office moved from Cornell to NYU. We also contacted the living members of the *JET* editorial board from that period to ask if any of them recalled handling the paper for the journal but got only negative replies from the 19 of the 26 board members who responded.

So, we have an example here of a key result that has no formal documentation of how the result was obtained or proved. Henriksen and Spear (2012) provide a formal proof of the non-existence of short-memory rational expectations equilibrium for the three-period model with one good and additively time separable preferences (the same model Aiyagari worked with), and Citanna-Siconolfi (2007) indicate how their results can be extended to accommodate longer lifetimes, but by this time, there had been many studies done using this framework – we discuss these below – with the understanding that the equilibria would necessarily be history dependent.

One of the earliest papers to work in the history-dependent SOLG framework was Woodford (1986a, 1986b) which we discussed above. In this paper, Woodford looks at a general, multi-good two-period OLG economy and finds conditions under which a sunspot equilibrium will exist. The sunspot variables in the model are infinite sequences of realizations of draws from a general stationary distribution, and it is the fact that the equilibrium Woodford derives depends on the full infinite history of shocks which makes the result compatible with Spear's result. Woodford's technique in the paper involves a careful application of the implicit function theorem on Banach spaces, together with generalizations of the K&L results discussed above. One key result of this paper given its extension of the results presented in Woodford (1986a) to the multi-good environment is that it establishes that any degree of indeterminacy is necessary and sufficient for the existence of sunspot equilibrium. While we don't go into detail about the paper here, we do note that the result applies, with slight modifications, to a model in which endowments or other fundamentals are random.

Spear and Srivastava were the first to attempt to "tame" the history-dependent nature of the REE in the SOLG model by observing that at the time agent's formed expectations of future prices and chose optimal consumption demands based on these expectations, the observables in the economy were in fact finite. They showed, in Spear and Srivastava (1986), that there were lagged endogenous variables – prices, consumptions, Lagrange multipliers, etc. – that were sufficient statistics for the infinite history of shocks up to that point in time. By including these as state variables, they showed how to demonstrate existence of equilibrium working in terms not of direct functions but of probability measures. This approach avoided the limitations of the approach used by Grandmont and Hildenbrand, also discussed earlier. It also reinvented a wheel originally introduced to the economics profession by Blume (1982).

While the Spear–Srivastava paper developed its results primarily in terms of marginal probability measures (and they called the resulting equilibrium a Fulfilled Expectations Equilibrium), the Appendix to the paper showed how to extend the results to allow for conditional measures and a fully rational expectations equilibrium.

We note that this paper was focused solely on the SOLG model. A significant broadening of these results was developed in Duffie Geanakoplos, Mas-Colell, and McLennan (1994) (also using Blume's techniques), which we will discuss in more detail below.

Peck (1988) showed how to use the non-stationary deterministic equilibrium dynamics of the model to generate sunspot equilibria using the "bootstrapping" technique which we examined above in the context of Woodford's work. Unlike Woodford's approach, which focused on stationary sunspot equilibria, Peck's work looked at the possibility of non-stationary sunspot equilibria based on the local non-stationary dynamics around the steady-state equilibrium of the model. One reason for this, as Peck notes, was:

> Equilibria that appear to be nonstationary could in fact be stationary in a larger state space. In an economy with two or more commodities per period and random endowments, Spear shows that generically there do not exist (stationary) equilibria where the price is function of the current endowment. When the state space is expanded to include the current endowment and the previous price, Spear and Srivastava show that an equilibrium probability measure exists. (Peck, 1988, p. 21)

The connection between the non-stationary dynamics and the possibility of stationary sunspot processes was implicit in Woodford's 1986 paper, though the interpretation was complicated by the infinite-dimensional state space. The connection would reappear later in Spear (1988), and then again in work by Victor Rios-Rull, and the Duffie et al. paper referenced earlier.

Since Peck's use of the technique appears in his 1985 thesis (see reference in the 1988 paper cited above), his development of the technique was contemporaneous with Woodford's. Woodford has indicated (in an email dated July 10, 2022) that he was a visiting assistant professor at Penn in 1984, while Peck was a student there, and taught some classes on this topic. Per our email conversation with Woodford, "the similarity in our work may not be entirely coincidental."

When we asked Peck about his recollections, he told us (email correspondence dated July 11, 2022)

> I am sure that we had conversations about sunspots, but I am not sure that there was any direct cross-fertilization. I always thought of my contribution as showing that sunspot equilibria existed quite generally, without strong assumptions like backward-bending offer curves. The technique was about supporting period t behavior with two outcomes for period $t+1$ rather than one outcome, and seeing that each of the period $t+1$ outcomes could be supported by continuing along the offer curve or branching into two outcomes again, and so on. The technique itself just seemed like a way of solving the problem and not necessarily something to take credit for beyond the task at hand. I first saw Mike's paper with Roger after I was well underway with my job market paper and never had the sense that they borrowed my technique or anything like that. So to the extent that we did something similar, I guess you could say it was simultaneous discovery or that it was just a natural way to solve a problem.

When we asked Woodford where he first encountered the bootstrapping technique, he pointed to Shiller (1978), which shows how to construct these kinds of equilibria in the context of linear rational expectations models. Peck advised us in a follow-up email that he first heard the term "bootstrapping" used by Karl

Shell, though given the constellation of people around the Penn department at the time – Azariadis, Cass, Grandmont, Farmer and Woodford – the term was likely something in the air.

The next significant paper on SOLG chronologically was Spear (1988). Unlike the Spear and Srivastava paper, this paper imposes assumptions on the underlying model to guarantee that the rational expectations equilibrium prices are functions of state variables, rather than allowing for possible correspondences (due to multiple temporary equilibria). Furthermore, the paper shows that for an N agent, multi-good, two-period lived economy, the lagged price is a sufficient statistic for the infinite history of shocks, as long as the shocks are sufficiently small. The basic methodology of the paper is similar to Woodford's unpublished 1986 paper in using functional forms of the implicit function theorem together with the K&L results to show that as long as the non-stochastic competitive equilibrium is determinate, the rational expectations equilibrium will be given by a stochastic difference equation of the form

$$p_{t+1} = f\left(p_t, \omega_t, \omega_{t+1}\right).$$

This paper provided the theoretical foundation for the follow-on paper Spear, Srivastava and Woodford (1990), which used the bootstrap approach to show the existence of sunspot equilibrium in a general multi-agent, multi-good two-period SOLG model.

Again proceeding chronologically, the next big step in understanding the workings of general SOLG models was the Duffie et al. (1994) paper. This paper provided a general solution to showing how to obtain a Markovian equilibrium for general history-dependent models with very general stochastic shocks, and provided examples of the construction of such equilibria for SOLG models, for ILA models with finitely-many heterogeneous agents and incomplete markets, and for stochastic games. This paper had an interesting history. The working paper version circulated, and was cited, for a number of years before the paper was finally published in 1994. Via a search of Google Scholar, the earliest citations of the paper (as a working paper) relate to the 1988 Stanford GSB Working Paper (Duffie, Geanakoplos, Mas-Colell, & McLennan, "Stationary Markov Equilibria," working paper, Graduate School of Business, Stanford University).

There was some definite cross-fertilization between the work of Spear and Srivastava, and Spear, Srivastava and Woodford in the development of these results. Spear and Srivastava presented an early set of their results at the 1984 Summer meetings of the Econometric Society held at Stanford University in a session on Multiple Agent Models of Aggregates. The papers in the session were:

1. "Reconciling Individual and Aggregate Differences in Labor Markets: An Adverse Selection Approach," Bruce Smith, Federal Reserve Bank of Minneapolis.
2. "Liquidity Preference, Stabilization and Welfare," Scott Freeman, Boston College.

3. "Equilibrium Dynamics in a Stochastic Overlapping Generations Model," Stephen Spear and Sanjay Srivastava, Carnegie-Mellon University.
4. "A Rational Expectations Complete Contingent Claims Model: Estimation Using Post War U.S. Data," Timothy J. Kehoe, M.I.T., and David K. Levine, U.C.L.A.

DISCUSSANTS: Martin Eichenbaum, David Levine, Ed Prescott, Robert Townsend

CHAIRPERSON: Charles Whiteman. (From the Program of the 1984 North American Summer Meeting of the Econometric Society, *Econometrica*, Vol. 52, No. 6, November, 1984, pp. 1562–1570.)

John Geanakoplos and Andreu Mas-Colell were both in attendance at this conference.

The Spear, Srivastava, and Woodford paper was presented at both the 1986 Winter Meetings of the Econometric Society in New Orleans, in a session on General Equilibrium Theory, and a Mathematical Sciences Research Institute conference in March of 1986, with many of the same people in attendance. The papers included in the New Orleans session were:

1. "Determinacy in Large Square Economies," Timothy J. Kehoe, Cambridge University; David K. Levine, University of California-Los Angeles; Andreu Mas-Colell, Harvard University; and William R. Zame, SUNY-Buffalo.
2. "On the Finiteness of the Equilibrium Price Set," Beth Allen, University of Pennsylvania.
3. "On the Existence of Implementable Rational Expectations Equilibria," Mark Feldman and Christian Gilles, University of California-Santa Barbara.
4. "On the Structure of Equilibrium in Stochastic Overlapping Generations Models," Stephen E. Spear and Sanjay Srivastava, Carnegie-Mellon University; and Michael Woodford, University of Chicago.

DISCUSSANTS: Darrell Duffie, Stanford University; V. V. Chari, Federal Reserve Bank of Minneapolis.

CHAIRPERSON: Larry Jones, Northwestern University. (From the Program of the 1986 North American Winter Meetings of the Econometric Society, *Econometrica*, May 1987, Vol. 55, No. 3, pp. 733-748.)

As was standard at such conferences, there was a lot of conversation outside of the presentations on ongoing projects. Quoting from an email from Srivastava (dated July 14, 2022):

> If I recall, they [Duffie, Geanakoplos, Mas-Colell, and McLennan] were already working on the same problem … but it is interesting that several sets of people were working on the same double-infinity existence problem at the same time, not just in OLG models but other areas as well. In fact, around then, there was a lot of work going on with existence results with infinite numbers of agents and/or commodities, in competitive equilibrium models as well as others.

The main result of the Duffie et al. paper is the demonstration of the existence of what the authors call a "self-justifying set" of exogenous and endogenous state variables. The self-justifying aspect of this set is that if one starts from an element in the set and then determines the endogenous equilibrium values associated with this starting value, these will also be in the set. The method used to show the existence of this set is essentially the same one that Balasko and Shell used in the equilibrium existence proof for the non-stochastic model. One truncates the economy at a finite point of time $T<\infty$ and uses standard general equilibrium techniques to determine the possible equilibria. The basic existence results for the finite-horizon economies then generates a sequence of T-equilibrium sets which have the same kind of nesting property as in the Balasko–Shell model. The intersection of these sets then determines the self-justifying set, and the support for the equilibrium ergodic measure.

A second innovation in the paper is that of working with an *expectations correspondence*, which determines probability measures consistent with the temporary equilibrium determined for a given conditional probability measures that agents use to forecast future states. The need for using a correspondence here, rather than a function, arises from the possibility that there may be multiple temporary equilibria. This, of course, was the limitation in the Grandmont–Hildenbrand result on existence of REE, as well as a built-in limitation in Spear (1988). When this correspondence is restricted to the self-justifying sets, it generates a *time homogeneous Markov equilibrium* for the model. Any fixed point of the correspondence so defined determines an invariant distribution for the Markov equilibrium process (using Blume's terminology here).

While we don't go into detail here on these results, one notable fact is that while the paper shows existence of Markovian equilibria for models with endogenous state variables, it doesn't identify which state variables should be included. The question of which endogenous state variables to include became a central concern with the work of the next paper in this sequence of work on the SOLG model, Rios-Rull (1996).

Rios-Rull's paper extended the modeling strategy of Auerbach and Kotlikoff to stochastic environments with aggregate shocks. Following Aurbach-Kotlikoff, the model in the paper has agents who live 55 periods, with multiplicative aggregate random shocks to production (as in conventional RBC models). In looking at the stationary equilibrium for the model, Rios-Rull assumes that the relevant endogenous state variables should be the wealth distribution, in the form of the asset holdings of each type of agent in the economy. Based on this assumption, Rios-Rull defines a *recursive equilibrium* as a mapping from the cross-product space of individual asset holdings and exogenous states to equilibrium good and asset prices which satisfy individual agent's optimization problems, the representative firm's profit maximization problem, and market clearing conditions. The term "recursive" here reflects the fact that in characterizing agents' individual optimizations, Rios-Rull uses a value function specification of the dynamic programming problem. This forward recursion is equivalent to the backward dynamic programming solution to the finite lived agents' optimizations, although unlike in the ILA model, the value functions are generally time dependent. Nevertheless, the formulation gives a well-defined equilibrium concept, even if the terminology makes it easy to confuse with the equilibria that arise in ILA models via forward dynamic programming. Despite this confusion, the terminology has stuck.

Rios-Rull's choice of asset holdings as the relevant state variables is intuitive, since it is the portfolio rebalancing decisions of agents in the model that generate the history-dependence of the equilibrium. Assuming that the asset holdings (or wealth distribution) will be a sufficient statistic for the infinite history of shocks in the steady state is natural, although not formally justified based on the results of the Duffie et al. paper. When we asked Rios-Rull whether he was aware of the Duffie et al. paper, he replied (email dated July 15, 2022)

> It is hard to remember clearly, but probably I was aware of this paper from way before, although to be fair it was quite incomprehensible (measures on measures), at least for me.
>
> That the state was the wealth distribution was sort of obvious. Even though aggregate wealth is sufficient for prices today when labor is not a choice, it is clear that when it is it depends on the wealth at each age. Moreover savings depend on who owns the wealth.

However, it turns out that this need not always be true, as a number of papers demonstrated in the early 2000s (see, e.g., Krebs, 2004, and references there). A partial answer to this conundrum was provided 14 years later by Citanna and Siconolfi (2010) where they showed that set of OLG economies having recursive equilibria was dense in the space of all SOLG economies. In an echo of the earlier debates between Lucas, Cass and Shell over what constitutes the right set of state variables, this debate continues to this day. Spear's 1988 functional REE results have been applied by a number of authors working with general multi-period SOLG models, notably including Storesletten, Telmer, and Yaron (2007), where the lagged bond prices serve as sufficient statistics for the shock history. One possible explanation for why both approaches to summarizing the shock history work could be the fact that the equilibrium policy functions take the form of iterated function systems, which map the space of shock histories into the equilibrium realizations of the endogenous state variables. While the images of these mappings are generally quite complex, in simple cases where the aggregate shocks are finitely supported, they take the form of Cantor-like sets. Since every compact metric space is the image of the Cantor set under a continuous function (see, e.g., Aliprantis & Border, 2006), it may well be that there are homeomorphic mappings between the various possible state spaces that give rise to equivalent sufficient statistics for these models. We are at this time unaware of any formal results to this effect, however.

In addition to directly extending the Auerbach–Kotlikoff approach to SOLG models with aggregate shocks, Rios-Rull also allowed for the possibility that agents in the model could die before reaching the maximum possible (finite) lifespan, by introducing age-specific mortality risk. His model thus nests and extends the Blanchard–Yaari model as well. As in the Blanchard–Yaari model, Rios-Rull assumes the existence of perfect annuities markets that allow agents to insure against the mortality risk.

Rios-Rull's simulation results are quite interesting. First, he shows that the time-series generated by the simulations are quite close to the same series generated by the conventional ILA models, on the production side. Second, the volatilities in aggregate consumption and investment in the calibrated model are in line with what is found in ILA models. Third, unlike ILA models, the SOLG model generates time-series of hours worked that match actual data fairly closely (though it underpredicts the observed working patterns for the 22- to 44-year-old age group). Where the SOLG model differs significantly from the findings in conventional RBC models is in agents' deviations from the standard life-cycle hypothesis of perfect consumption smoothing. Rather, the observed age-consumption profile in the simulations is hump-shaped, in agreement with actual data. Subsequent studies have found that to fully match the observed age-consumption profiles in the data, however, one generally needs to include a borrowing constraint on the young. This requirement obviously suggests that asymmetric information about future prospects early in life is an important macroeconomic phenomenon. The fact that even without credit constraints the SOLG generates significant deviations from the predictions of the permanent income hypothesis has important welfare implications in its own right. In an earlier paper (Rios-Rull, 1994) based on the same simulations, Rios-Rull also showed that quantitatively, the allocations coming out of a model with sequentially complete markets relative to one with incomplete markets were negligible. Based on this, he concluded that it didn't matter for macroeconomic issues whether one worked with a model with a rich or sparse asset structure. This is something we will explore in more detail below.

Despite this important deviation on the distribution side from the predictions of RBC and related models, the macroprofession's take away from Rios-Rull's work was that it was demonstrating some kind of OE between SOLG and SILA models, since it matched up well on the production side. As a result, the paper has not been widely cited (getting 425 Google Scholar cites as of this writing), even though this paper was arguably ahead of its time in terms of where macroeconomics ought to be going. Indeed, we consider the lack of attention to this paper one of the key indicators that the macromarket was tipping away from OLG to ILA formulations. And again, the reason for this would seem to be that working with SOLG models was (despite Rios-Rull's choice of terminology) not recursive, borderline intractable, and irrelevant given the perceived OE of the two classes of models.

By way of documenting our claim that Rios-Rull's work has been widely ignored, we went through the first 26 pages of Google Scholar papers that cite Rios-Rull's 1996 paper (or earlier versions of it going back to 1990) and examined the papers to determine the reason for the citation to Rios-Rull. We stopped after 26 pages because although Google Scholar's ranking algorithm is not public, empirical studies of the results it returns – see, for example, Beel and Gipp (2009) – indicate that the number of citations a paper gets generally moves it higher in the rankings and closer to the front of the displayed results. Based on this, we are looking at a sample of the most influential papers that cite Rios-Rull's 1996 paper.

We classified these reasons according to whether the work in the paper was genuine follow-on work (which we call "relevant"); work in other modeling frameworks or purely econometric which cited Rios-Rull as justification or contrast to the work presented (which we call "in passing" citations); summary citations (pedagogic, laudatory, or handbook material); tangential citations where the underlying model was the same or similar to Rios-Rull's but without aggregate shocks; and vacuous citations (a cite in the paper's references but no discussion in the text or no actual citation). This sample of hits from Google Scholar constituted 218 papers. Table 1 summarizes the numbers in each category.

The "Top 5" heading indicates the number of papers in the "Relevant" and "Tangential" category published in one of the top five economics (or finance) journals. In the "Relevant" category, six of the papers (including one by Citanna and Siconolfi in *Econometrica*) are theoretical; of these five are by Citanna and Siconolfi in their series of papers examining the genericity of the recursive equilibrium, and one is by Kim and Spear characterizing the stochastic dynamic structure of recursive equilibrium in general SOLG models. The other top five publication in the "Relevant" category is Glover, Heathcote, Krueger, and Rios-Rull (2020) which examines the intergenerational redistributions generated by the 2007–2008 financial crisis and resulting recession.

Interestingly, in the "Tangential" category, 36 of the 51 papers (71%) deal with OLG models in which uncertainty is idiosyncratic, generally mortality risk or lifecycle income risk with variations on each of these. Of these papers, only one (Castaneda, Diaz-Gimenez, & Rios-Rull, 2003) was published in a top 5 journal. Of the remaining papers on idiosyncratic risk, 14 were unpublished (39%) and the rest (58%) were published in top to middle tier field journals.

In the "Relevant" group, many of the papers make important points about the difference between SOLG and SILA models. For example, Gomme, Rogerson, Rupert, and Wright (2004) replicates Rios-Rull's findings on hours worked by different cohorts, and notes that while the basic model can account for about 60% of observed variation, the model fits the data much more closely if one restricts attention to the middle-aged to retired cohorts. The model's fit breaks down with younger cohorts. The paper draws a couple of important conclusions from this. First, the effect appears to arise from the differences in planning horizons between younger and older agents. This is consistent with the view that finite horizons matter, and that it is the double infinity of agents and periods that makes the OLG and ILA models different. Secondly, for young agents facing long time horizons for whom the aggregate shocks appear temporary, search frictions are likely to matter in determining both contemporaneous hours worked and future ability to weather shocks that now seem more permanent. In a solo authored paper, Gomme (2008) compares the optimal inflation rates in comparably calibrated stochastic representative agent and OLG models and finds marked differences.

Table 1. Rios-Rull Citation Summary.

Category		%	Top 5
Relevant	31	14.22%	2 (6.5%)
In passing	63	28.90%	
Summary	42	19.27%	
Tangential	51	23.39%	10 (20%)
Vacuous	31	14.22%	
Total	**218**		

In the ILA framework, Friedman's rule of deflating at the real rate of interest is optimal. Gomme finds in large-scale SOLG models that significant inflation generated by lump-sum money injections can generate Pareto improvements by transferring wealth from older, richer agents to poor, younger ones. Heer and Maussner (2012) work with an extension of Rios-Rull's model in which agents live for 240 periods (to allow for calibration to quarterly data) to examine the effects of unanticipated inflation. Unlike Rios-Rull, their model is too complex to allow for computational simulations, but they are able to use Auerbach and Kotlikoff's techniques to solve for the model's steady-state equilibrium and then use simulations to calculate impulse-response functions. Their findings in this paper supports the findings in Gomme (2008) in the sense that wealth inequality is reduced by the inflation shock via transfers from older agents to younger.

Rios-Rull (1994) makes an important follow-up contribution to his own work (follow-up despite the fact that the paper was published before the 1996 *REStud* paper; working paper versions of this work had been circulating since 1990). As we noted above, in this paper, he uses calibrated simulations of long-lived SOLG models with aggregate shocks to compare the outcomes under different degrees of sequential market completeness (i.e., by giving agents different numbers of assets with which to hedge the aggregate risk). He finds that the degree of market incompleteness across different asset regimes makes very little difference in the welfare outcomes of agents. This result is consistent with results derived later by Henriksen and Spear (2012) which we discuss below. Intuitively, though, when one includes the wealth distribution as part of the description of the economy's state – which is to say the lagged asset holdings of agents are included as state variables – then in the presence of aggregate exogenous shocks, one can never have as many assets as there are states, so, in this sense, markets are always incomplete.

The Glover et al. paper (on which Rios-Rull is a coauthor, and the only non-theory paper in our "Relevant" category to make it into a top five journal) directly applies Rios-Rull's simulation framework to examine the effects of the recession following the 2007–2008 financial crises (the Great Recession) across households of different ages. Their review of the empirical data clearly indicates that this recession differentially affected different age groups, so the choice of the SOLG framework is clearly justified. Their findings show that while younger households were hurt by declining real wages during the recession, older agents were also hurt by declines in asset prices. These asset price declines actually benefited younger households since they were able to fund retirement asset purchases more cheaply.

In addition to these papers, there were a number of important papers (not all of which cite Rios-Rull, 1996) which applied the multi-period SOLG model to examine the effects of unfunded (pay-as-you-go or PAYGO) social security systems. We will discuss these papers in detail in the next chapter.

We are persuaded by the overall statistical analysis presented here together with the sample of follow-on results generated by Rios-Rull's model that this was indeed pioneering work that showed not only how the more realistic multi-period SOLG model could be used in macroeconomic analysis, but why it ought to be used in preference to the dynastic family alternative. We include our full bibliography of papers that cite Rios-Rull (1996) in Appendix 2 of the book for anyone interested in doing their own follow-up research.

7.7 WELFARE ISSUES

While we have looked in some detail at the welfare issues associated with the deterministic OLG model, there are additional welfare issues that are specific to the SOLG environment, so we examine these here. To do so, however, we need to first examine a couple of technical contributions that showed formally how the double infinity of the OLG environment differentiated the model from the ILA setting.

For deterministic models, we have two competing claims for why the first welfare theorem can fail in the OLG model, the Cass–Yaari restricted participation friction, and the Shell double-infinity friction. While the restricted participation friction has been important in explaining the role of money as a medium of exchange (and in the development of search models of money), money in these environments allows for Pareto improvements by effectively removing the restrictions on market participation. This is true in the circular model that Cass and Yaari originally considered, and it remains true in the turnpike (and other) models introduced by Townsend. Because these models are essentially static, one can't obtain the kind of inoptimality that occurs in OLG models where, for example, the monetary equilibrium has the value of money going asymptotically to zero.

This argument suggests that Shell's contention that it is the double infinity of agents and time periods that leads to the possibility of inoptimal competitive equilibrium. The mechanism Shell pointed to was the intergenerational transfer of resources analogous to the shuffling of guests in the Hilbert hotel. This mechanism was put on a sound mathematical foundation in Geanakoplos and Brown (1982). While this paper was never published, the basic arguments of the paper are outlined in the study by Geanakoplos (1989).

Geanakoplos and Brown use non-standard analysis to analyze the behavior of deterministic OLG economies "at infinity" by showing that all the basic properties of the model that hold at finite times T will hold when T is an infinite integer (see Robinson, 2016, or Anderson, 1991, for details on this mathematics). As Geanakoplos points out in his Palgrave chapter, in the standard Balasko–Shell proof of existence of equilibrium, in the finite truncated economy, one conventionally sets the excess demand of the last cohort of young agents *when they are old* to zero. Via the Balasko–Shell argument, then, this yields a particular competitive equilibrium. Geanakoplos–Brown show that by loosening this particular restriction "at infinity," we obtain all the possible equilibria for the model because of the slack in the markets at infinity. The significance of the slack being at infinity is based on the fact that it is society, not the individuals who make up the society, that has the resource slack available. This becomes particularly clear in the Geanakoplos–Brown analysis of what happens when money is introduced. In the monetary model, the initial old are endowed with some positive amount of money, which they can use to purchase actual goods from the young in period 1.

What gives money value, in the formal non-standard analysis, is the fact that money is backed by the addition of an endowment of goods in (transfinite) period $T+1$. What this result formalizes is the fact that money will have value as long as there is a social commitment or contract collateralizing the stock of money. In our previous discussion of the tenuousness of money, it was the possibility that the social contract might be breached that led to this tenuousness. The bottom line of the Geanakoplos–Brown analysis can be summarized by saying that when the future is flexible, many things can happen.

We can contrast the environment analyzed by Geanakoplos–Brown with the conventional ILA environment of the dynastic family. In these models, individuals (or families) themselves have the ability to transfer resources back and forth through time (including infinite time), so that the social slack at infinity in these models is internalized. Indeed, it is this property that gives rise to Ricardian equivalence in Barro's framework, or to the neutrality of everything in the Bernheim–Bagwell model. This internal versus external distinction between the two models is important in explaining the history dependence (and related Pareto optimality) issues in the SOLG setting.

The second result we wish to look at is Labadie (1986). Labadie studies a conventional two-period lived SOLG model in which the endogenous variables are functions of the exogenous stochastic process on a non-labor factor of production and shows in her main results that changes in the risk aversion of agents in the model have ambiguous effects on the endogenous variables. The reason for this is straightforward. In the two-period OLG environment, an increase (for example) in second period income will have an ambiguous effect on the intertemporal marginal rate of substitution because this depends on how rich or poor the agent is in their first period of life relative to their second. In a stochastic model, how rich an agent is when they are young is largely an accident of birth. How much real wealth they have in old age depends on the randomness of the prices of the assets they accumulate, and this accumulation is affected by the income effects generated by price changes from one period to the next. Because income and substitution effects for finite lived agents can move in different directions, the response of the intertemporal MRS is ambiguous.

In the ILA environment – in Labadie's case a version of the 1978 Lucas asset pricing model – an increase in next period's income always generates a negative response in the intertemporal marginal rate of substitution. Furthermore, any income effects get channeled through the equilibrium prices and payments to the non-labor factor of production in such a way that the return weighted expected intertemporal marginal rate of substitution is the same in every period. This result is possible in the ILA model because of the internalization of wealth flows between periods. In the presence of complete markets, this is also the reason that the resulting allocation of consumption is Pareto optimal.

We introduce this section with these results because this is what distinguishes the SOLG from its ILA counterpart. While the distinction can be difficult to see in deterministic settings, it manifests starkly in stochastic environments. We see this most clearly in the setting Aiyagari used, where OLG and ILA agents have the same additively time separable utility functions, trade a single good, and have the same random endowments (or produce with the same random technology). In both models, the portfolio rebalancing that agents undertake in each period generates pecuniary externalities that feed forward to subsequent consumption and savings decisions. In the OLG model, the effects of these externalities eventually come due at the end life, and, since some agents die every period, the changes in the wealth distribution generated by these externalities affect the equilibrium and generate the observed history dependence. In the ILA model, by contrast, the effects of the externalities are pushed forward "to infinity." As long as the shock process is stationary, infinite-lived individuals (or institutions) can offset the external effects by rebalancing the internal transfers at work between generations, *a la* Barro's bequest mechanism. This internalization of the pecuniary externalities eliminates any history dependence not built into the shocks and allows for the correspondingly simpler characterization of equilibrium relative to that of the OLG model.

With these preliminaries, we can extend the analysis of optimality from the deterministic model to the stochastic one.

The earliest results characterizing optimality in SOLG models that we have found are detailed in the study by Peled (1984). This paper examines the optimality of a stochastic steady-state equilibrium in a two-period, one good SOLG model (with finitely supported exogenous shocks) under the assumption that endowments are such that agents always wish to hold positive stocks of money. Aiyagari and Peled (1991) extended these results for general endowment distributions. Since these two papers use similar techniques, we illustrate them in the context of the 1984 Peled paper. The two-period lives and single good assumptions mean that the stochastic steady-state equilibrium of the model will have all endogenously determined variables given as functions of the aggregate shocks only. Peled also imposed the assumption that markets are complete, that is, agents can freely transfer wealth between periods and across states of nature. The optimality concept is that of conditional optimality (first introduced by Muench, 1977). Conditional optimality requires that the central planner work under the same constraints as the agents in the model. Specifically, this requires considering young agents born into different states of the world as different agents who then face uncertainty only over what will happen to them when they are old. In particular, this perspective rules out a fully *ex ante* consideration of intergenerational welfare. It does, however, correspond to the same constraints that the markets operate under, and as such, it gives us a framework for comparing market outcomes to optimal outcomes for the stochastic steady state.

Following Peled, we work in a pure exchange environment where the endowments are random. For simplicity, we also assume that preferences are represented by additively time separable C^2 utility function. So, for this simple model, we have exogenous aggregate shocks $s \in S = \{1, 2, \dots, N\}$ with $N < \infty$. We assume that shocks are generated by randomness of endowments and assume that the stochastic process on the shocks follow a first-order Markov process with the probability of state s' conditional on being in state s given by $\pi^{ss'} > 0$. Taking prices p^s to be prices of money in terms of consumption, we can use the budget constraints to write, for states $(s, s') \in S^2$

$$x_1^s = \omega_1^s - p^s x_1^{m,s}$$

$$x_2^{ss'} = \omega_2^{s'} + p^{s'} x_1^{m,s}.$$

Here, $x_1^{m,s}$ is the young agent's demand for money. Note that we allow second period consumption to depend on the shock from the first period because the money demand will generally depend on the young agent's birth state shock. As was the case with the easy version of the Lucas 1972 model, this will turn out not to matter in equilibrium, given a fixed initial injection of fiat money into the economy.

For a young agent born in state s, her optimization problem is

$$\max_{x_1^{m,s}} u\left(\omega_1^s - p^s x_1^{m,s}\right) + \sum_{s' \in S} \pi^{s'} u\left(\omega_2^{s'} + p^{s'} x_1^{m,s}\right).$$

The first-order conditions for this problem are

$$-p^s u'\left(x_1^s\right) + \sum_{s' \in S} \pi^{ss'} u'\left(x_2^{ss'}\right) p^{s'} = 0.$$

Since the marginal utility $u'\left(x_1^s\right) > 0$, we can rewrite this as

$$\sum_{s' \in S} \pi^{ss'} \frac{u'\left(x_2^{ss'}\right)}{u'\left(x_1^s\right)} p^{s'} = p^s.$$

Now, let $M = \left[m^{ss'}\right]$ be the $N \times N$ matrix with elements $m^{ss'} = \pi^{ss'} \frac{u'\left(x_2^{ss'}\right)}{u'\left(x_1^s\right)}$. In finance, M is called the pricing kernel or stochastic discount factor. Next, let $p = \left[p^s\right]$ be a vector of state-contingent money prices. We can then write the first-order condition as

$$Mp = p.$$

Evaluating the money holdings at the fixed money supply m, we then get the statement that at the monetary competitive equilibrium, the vector of state-contingent money prices must be an eigenvector of the matrix M with eigenvalue equal to one. Using the fact that in equilibrium, the second period consumption won't depend on the birth state, we can decompose the matrix M as

$$M = \hat{B}^{-1} \Pi \hat{C},$$

where

$$\hat{B} = \text{diag}_s \; u'\left(x_1^s\right)$$

$$\hat{C} = \text{diag}_{s'}\ u'\left(x_2^{s'}\right)$$

$$\Pi = \left[\pi^{ss'}\right] = \text{transition matrix.}$$

Since $\hat{B}$ and $\hat{C}$ are both real and diagonal, while the transition matrix is symmetric, the decomposition shows that M is real and symmetric. It then follows that all of the eigenvalues of M will be real, and that the eigenvectors of M will be orthogonal. Finally, by the Perron–Frobenius theorem, M will have one strictly positive root with an associated positive eigenvector. Since the eigenvector p is strictly positive (and orthogonality of the basis of eigenvectors implies that all other eigenvectors must have some negative components) it follows that 1 is the Perron–Frobenius root.

To check optimality of the equilibrium, let

$$M_0 = \left[\pi^{ss'} \frac{u'\left(\omega_2^{s'}\right)}{u'\left(\omega_1^{s}\right)}\right]$$

be the matrix with the elements as indicated. Since M_0 is also a positive matrix, the Perron–Frobenius theorem applies, so let $\lambda_f\left(M_0\right)$ denote the dominant root of M_0. We will show that if this root is strictly bigger than one, then the endowment allocation is not Pareto optimal. To do this, note that via the Perron–Frobenius theorem, there must exist a strictly positive vector $dx = \left[dx^s\right]$ associated with the Perron–Frobenius root, so that under the assumption that $\lambda_f\left(M_0\right) > 1$

$$M_0 dx = \lambda_f\left(M_0\right) dx \gg dx.$$

From the definition of M_0, this implies that

$$\sum_{s' \in S} \pi^{ss'} u'\left(\omega_2^{s'}\right) dx^{s'} > u'\left(\omega_1^{s}\right) dx^{s} \quad \text{for all } s \in S.$$

But this immediately implies that for each state s, we can find a positive state-contingent transfer from the young to the old that makes everyone better off. The main result of the Aiyagari–Peled paper in their Theorem 1 is that an interior competitive equilibrium allocation is Pareto optimal if and only if the dominant root of the pricing kernel is less than or equal to one.

In the Ayaigari and Peled paper, they note (p. 71) that Rodolfo Manuelli also provided a characterization of optimality for two-period lived single good SOLG exchange economies under the assumption that there is a single type of agent born each period, for more general stochastic processes of shocks. For details, see Manuelli (1990).

On the macroeconomic side, Able, Mankiw, Summers, and Zeckhauser (1989) used the Diamond model as the basis for examining dynamic efficiency when the economy is subject to aggregate shocks. As we noted earlier, in the deterministic Diamond model, the steady-state equilibrium is efficient if the interest rate is greater than or equal to the economy's growth rate. In stochastic environments, particularly those with multiple assets subject to different degrees of risk, deciding which interest rate to use for comparison becomes difficult. Because the standard Diamond model has two-period lived agents, complete markets, and the assumption of a single good, the stochastic steady-state equilibrium that Abel et al. analyzed is not history dependent, so their analysis is not complicated by needing to determine the endogenous distribution of asset holdings in the economy. The welfare criterion they use is that of *ex ante* expected social welfare based on a weighted sum of utilities for all generations. They justify the *ex ante* focus by noting that their interest is in the question of whether capital is being over-accumulated rather than on issues of intergenerational risk sharing.

Using this set-up, the paper ends up highlighting the ratio of a social dividend defined as aggregate profit net of new investment, and the value of the market portfolio. The key result of the paper is if this ratio is strictly positive for all time, then the economy is dynamically efficient. Conversely, if the ratio is strictly negative for all time, then the economy is inefficient. Intuitively, a positive ratio means that the economy is generating wealth in excess of that needed to maintain the capital stock, and this wealth is available for consumption, so the economy is not over accumulating capital. Based on this criterion, and accepting that we do not have the full data stream required to apply the criterion to actual economies, the paper uses the reasonably long data series on U.S. GNP (1929–1985) to estimate the dividend to market value ratios, and shows that these have been consistently positive (on the order of 2.4–4.2) for the US economy over the post-WWII period. Based on this data, Abel et al. concluded that the US economy has not been over accumulating capital.

The welfare criterion Abel et al. derived can also be expressed in terms of rates of return to assets relative to the economy's growth rate, where the standard Diamond criterion obtains in the sense that if the rate of return exceeds the growth rate for all time, the economy is efficient, while if the rate of return is below the growth rate for all time, the economy is inefficient. For this comparison, working with the rate of return on safe assets is, in principle, sufficient for making the efficiency determination. However, Abel et al. noted that

> Neither implication is very helpful in judging the dynamic efficiency of actual economies, where capital gains and losses cause the growth rate of the market value of the capital stock sometimes to exceed and other times to fall short of the safe interest rate. The result here is illuminating primarily in suggesting that comparisons of the safe interest rate with the average growth rate generally are not sufficient to resolve the issue of dynamic efficiency. (Abel et al., 1989, p. 12)

We note that the kinds of capital gains and losses the authors discuss here are precisely the results of portfolio rebalancing that drive the history dependence of equilibrium in more general SOLG models. Since these effects will also change the equilibrium values of assets in the economy, it isn't clear whether the original welfare criterion will hold up in a more realistic SOLG setting.

The next major paper to examine optimality in general SOLG models was by Chattopadhyay and Gottardi (1999). This paper uses an extension of the Balasko–Shell characterization of optimality in deterministic models based on the curvature of agents' indifference surfaces to derive necessary and sufficient conditions for *inoptimality*, based on an extension of the Cass criterion. Their main results provide a characterization for potentially non-stationary equilibria in the presence of sequentially complete markets (complete markets in the stationary model examined by Aiyagari and Peled). For stationary environments, they impose the assumption that there is only a single good being traded (to avoid the history dependence problem) and show that their optimality criterion is the same as that obtained by Aiyagari and Peled. Finally, they also provide a characterization of *ex post Pareto optimality* for economies with sequentially incomplete markets. *Ex post* optimality involves looking only at the realized allocations – as opposed to the *ex ante* allocations of the conditional optimality criterion – obtained in competitive equilibrium. As in the sequentially complete markets case, allocations here are allowed to be non-stationary, and the authors develop a criterion for inoptimality similar to the Cass criterion developed for the general complete markets case.

The Chattopadhyay–Gottardi results were extended by Gabrielle Demange to OLG economies in which agents live arbitrary long but finite lives, in Demange (2002). This paper works with explicitly history-dependent, possibly non-stationary, competitive equilibria, and examines both interim and full *ex ante* optimality, under the assumption that the stochastic process of aggregate shocks is finitely supported. Interim optimality conditions on history up to some point (and is obviously related to the conditional optimality concept used by Aiyagari and Peled), while full optimality is independent of history. Demange defines a sequence of state-contingent support prices for the model, and uses these *valuation processes* to examine the different optimality criteria. Demange's analysis first establishes (in parallel with the Balasko–Shell results) that for economies obtained by truncating at some finite-time period t, allocations are Pareto optimal if and only if they are supported by some valuation process. For the full infinite economy, Demange obtains a sufficient condition for interim/full optimality in terms of the summability of the expected prices. This is, of course, closely related to the Cass criterion results obtained by Chattopadhyay and Gottardi.

Like Chattopadhyay and Gottardi, Demange also deals with stationary economies and stochastic steady-state equilibria and shows that her results also imply the dominant root characterization results of Peled, and Peled and Aiyagari. But notably, neither Demange nor Chattopadhyay–Gottardi made any attempt to address the optimality question in the context of models with endogenous state variables.

The only paper we are aware of that attempts this is by Henriksen and Spear (2012). The Henriksen–Spear paper looks at a three-period lived, one good SOLG economy with a Lucas tree asset that pays a stochastic dividend. As we noted earlier, this paper formally demonstrates the generic non-existence of short-memory REE (generic because of the possibility that endowments may already be Pareto optimal). Because of this non-existence result, the paper examines the recursive competitive equilibrium, following Rios-Rull, in which equilibrium prices depend on the exogenous state of nature and on the lagged asset holdings of the young and middle-aged agents in the economy. The equilibrium for the model is then given by a pair of stochastic difference equations

$$a_{t+1} = A(a_t, s_{t+1})$$

$$p_{t+1} = P(a_t, s_{t+1}),$$

where a denotes the vector of asset holdings of the young – market clearing conditions can be used to eliminate the asset holdings of the middle-aged – and p is a vector of prices. The assets in the economy consist of zero net supply bonds and equity shares in the Lucas tree, so that the prices are those of the bond and equity, with consumption being the numeraire.

Under the assumption that the aggregate shock can take one of two values, the markets in this model are sequentially complete. The corrigendum to the paper shows that this implies the conditional optimality of competitive equilibrium, since young and middle-aged agents in the model are sharing risk optimally. But, under optimality criteria that take explicit account of the lagged endogenous state variables, there is a significant problem. As long as agents in the model are risk-averse – and this is a standard assumption in this setting – no benevolent central planner would ever introduce additional risk beyond that imposed by nature. So, as long as the central planner is allowed to make allocations dependent on all possible state variables – as opposed to being constrained to take the lagged state variables as given – she will choose not to make allocations dependent on the endogenous states. This result is intuitive, though Henriksen–Spear provide a formal derivation. The key result, then, is that any Pareto optimal allocation must be strongly stationary, in the sense of depending only on the exogenous states of nature.

We note that there is some confusion introduced by this paper's argument that markets are endogenously incomplete. As we noted earlier, markets are sequentially complete as long as there are as many assets as exogenous states of nature. But markets are incomplete more generally in the sense that there are always more states (both exogenous and endogenous) than assets. Indeed, as long as asset holdings are included as state variables, markets can never be complete in this sense.

The Henriksen–Spear paper also demonstrates explicitly that it is the income effects associated with portfolio rebalancing that generates the history-dependent equilibrium. The paper does this by considering a different version of the model in which there is no ownership of the tree asset. Rather, the dividend in each period is arbitrarily shared (in fixed proportions) between the living agents in each period. The asset market is restructured so that agents can buy or sell one-period zero net supply bonds, and Arrow securities that are required to be self-financing in the sense that they transfer wealth only across states of nature and not between periods. In static general equilibrium models, this asset structure is equivalent to any other structure as long as markets are complete, so that it serves only to illustrate the possibility of separating insurance activities from intertemporal wealth transfers. In the SOLG environment, however, the separation is important because, as Henriksen–Spear show, the resulting competitive equilibrium depends only on the exogenous shocks, and the risk sharing between agents is fully optimal.[10]

These results all extend to a model with production, though as with the tree asset, separating credit and insurance activities would require redistribution of the returns to capital. Since this separation also removes an important source of investment funds (the market for equities), actually implementing this kind of Pareto improvement seems problematic, to say the least. Nevertheless, the inefficient risk sharing in the model is significant. Fig. 21 reproduces the simulated consumption time-series from Henriksen–Spear, and the variance associated with the consumption of old agents is almost an order of magnitude higher than that of the middle-aged or young.

In this diagram, if agents were sharing risk optimally, then in the case where agents didn't discount future utility, all three time-series lines would coincide, in keeping with the permanent income hypothesis. As we have noted previously, this inefficiency also shows up in Rios-Rull's simulations, where the age-consumption profile is hump-shaped (see Table 5, p. 483 of his paper).

These results also raise questions about the applicability of the Abel et al. results. On the one hand, the simulations in multi-period SOLG models do

	c_y	c_m	c_r
Low State	0.19719	0.30268	0.45013
(SD)	0.00018	0.00099	0.00117
High State	0.2138	0.3249	0.51122
(SD)	0.0002	0.00112	0.00131

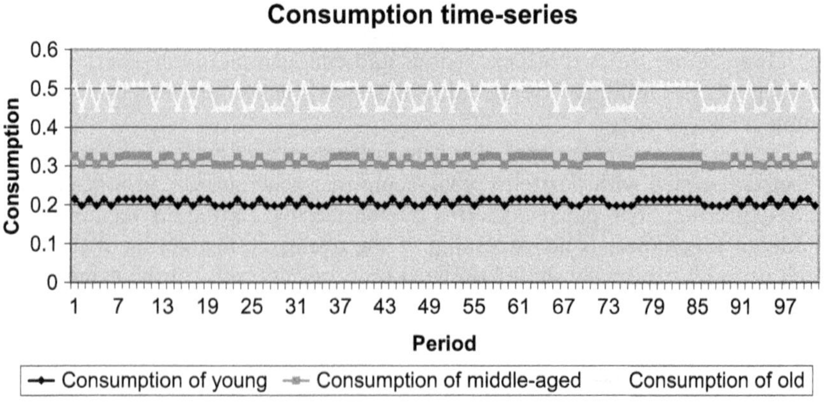

Fig. 21. Simulations From Henriksen–Spear (2012).

suggest that the history dependence of the equilibrium increases asset return volatility even though output moves only with aggregate shocks. Since, as Abel et al. have noted, real-world GDP looks significantly smoother than the asset markets, it may well be that the history dependence in these more realistic SOLG models isn't that important for the actual performance of the economy. On the other hand, the fact that financial crises historically have had severe impacts on the real economy suggests that asset and product markets are inextricably linked. And the fact that the last financial crisis occurred in 2008 suggests that we aren't done with them yet. Finally, the failure of risk sharing in the history-dependent equilibria of these models suggests that there is a potentially important role for government in the provision of social insurance. This issue, in the form of questions about Social Security, has been studied in a sequence of increasingly more realistic SOLG models in the past decade, and we will examine these studies in more detail in the next chapter.

NOTES

1. One can argue that if the initial period is simply the point where an observer breaks into the bi-infinite timeline, then the only appropriate perfect foresight price in period one is the one the old in that period were expecting in the previous period. But this simply pushes the determinacy question back to $-\infty$. In the presence of an unanticipated policy shock, or (as we will see later) of an expectational shock, the indeterminacy argument is completely valid.
2. If one accepts the contention laid out by Chatelain and Ralf (2018) that the New Neoclassical Synthesis will go the way of the old Neoclassical Synthesis because of its failure to explain involuntary unemployment and to identify the source of aggregate shocks, we should perhaps be referring to the Latest Neoclassical Synthesis here.
3. Kotlikoff (1983) produced a similar analysis which was never published. In his *Journal of Economic Perspectives* paper (Kotlikoff, 1988) he reports results akin to those obtained by Bagwell–Bernheim.
4. We note in passing that this is one of the earliest applications of network theory in economics to model local game theoretic interactions between players.
5. This is not to be confused with the Ak model of endogenous growth theory.
6. See Bruss (1984).
7. Strictly speaking, this should be a large number of small households who collectively own the means of the production, since the equilibrium concept used in the model is competitive.
8. This paper was written at a time when defined-benefit retirement contracts were giving way to defined-contribution contracts, so it would be interesting to see whether these changes in the contracting environment had an actual impact on the accuracy of the wage data collected.
9. According to Spear's recollections, Russell Cooper pointed this out during a Penn workshop on graduate student research. Spear and Cooper were classmates in Penn's Ph.D. program.
10. Kollmann (2020) has proposed incorporating private transfers from older agents to young that implement perfect risk-sharing as a way of making multi-period SOLG models tractable. The paper shows that under this assumption, aggregation across ages is possible and the resulting equilibrium looks like that of a conventional representative agent model. Of course, given the Henriksen–Spear results, the assumption amounts to substituting markets for risk-sharing with the kinds of interfamily transfers examined by Bernheim–Bagwell (1988).

CHAPTER 8

GEN X AND BEYOND: 1995–2015

In this chapter, we focus on the research on OLG models produced in the period from 1995–2015. While much of this work was done by the now old-guard Boomer scholars, the younger Gen X scholars coming out of graduate school during this period also made important contributions. If one searches in Google Scholar for the phrase "overlapping generations model" in the time period we are looking at here, it returns almost 20,000 hits. A similar query of the EconLit database for the same phrase and time period returns 1,250 hits. So, as we noted in the introduction, there was plenty of interest among economists in OLG, though it was dwarfed by the work being done using the ILA models of the new neoclassical synthesis. For our purposes, the plethora of OLG research forces us to narrow our focus and considered the work being done on stochastic overlapping generations models, since these offer the same tools for macroeconomic analysis of business cycles and government policy interventions as the dominant ILA models, though in a decidedly non-equivalent form.

We also note that among the Google Scholar hits for the SOLG search during this period were many policy applications based on stochastic two-period one good OLG models, despite the fact that it was well understood by this time that the results coming out of these models could differ significantly from those coming from more realistic models.[1] We note this not by way of suggesting this work was without value, but rather to note just how difficult working with the more realistic model actually was. Subject to the caveat that the two-period model might be unrealistic, economists working on issues where both lifecycle heterogeneity and uncertainty were important made what progress they could in the two-period framework.

We will begin by examining the theoretical breakthroughs made during this period on the characterization of stochastic steady-state equilibria, the efficiency properties of these equilibria, extensions of the model based on the Blanchard–Yaari perpetual youth model, and the detailed exploration of issues of indeterminacy that occurred during this time frame. We will then turn to look at a specific issue – Social Security – which received a great deal of attention during

Overlapping Generations: Methods, Models and Morphology
International Symposia in Economic Theory and Econometrics, Volume 32, 159–182

Published under exclusive licence by Emerald Publishing Limited
ISSN: 1571-0386/doi:10.1108/S1571-038620230000032019

this period using long-lived SOLG models. We complete the chapter by looking at developments in computation technologies and algorithms for simulating complex SOLG models.

8.1 THEORY

The initial subject of our theory focus here is the work mentioned earlier by Alessandro Citanna and Paolo Siconolfi. Citanna and Siconolfi both did their Ph.D.'s at Penn under the supervision of Dave Cass, with Siconolfi graduating in 1987 (putting him right on the cusp of Gen X), and Citanna graduating in 1995. By the time Citanna and Siconolfi were in graduate school, Cass had moved on from his OLG work to focus on models of market incompleteness. When we queried both Citanna and Siconolfi as to where they learned the OLG model, they both commented that the courses Cass taught were focused on his incomplete markets research, with their exposure to the OLG model coming from courses taught by Azariadis or Shell. Both Citanna and Siconolfi did their thesis work on incomplete markets, picking up OLG later in their careers.

Citanna and Siconolfi's first major SOLG paper was Citanna and Siconolfi (2007). This paper is an extension of Spear (1985) allowing for multiple types of agents in each generation, and in principle, for longer than two-period lifetimes. The paper defines short-memory equilibria as those in which endogenous variables depend only on finitely-many lags of the exogenous random shocks.[2] The proof that such equilibria do not exist generically is based on the same density of transversal intersections as in Spear's invocation of the multi-jet transversality theorems, but Citanna–Siconolfi uses a clever trick to avoid assumptions on preferences needed to apply the multi-jet results. Specifically, the multi-jet results require that at each solution point to the system of equations under consideration, it must be possible to independently perturb the underlying parameters of the system. For the SOLG application, the parameters would be the endowments and utility functions. Spear (1985) assumed that all goods were normal and showed that this would guarantee the applicability of the multi-jet theorem. Citanna–Siconolfi shows how to delete equations and variables corresponding to instances where two equations are satisfied at the same point in the domain, and the fact that there will be at most finitely many of these cases, to then argue via the transversal density results that the set of economies for which short-memory equilibria exist must be nowhere dense.

Citanna and Siconolfi (2008) used the perturbation techniques developed in their 2007 paper to show the generic existence of recursive equilibria (in the Rios–Rull sense) in the same class of models for which the various non-existence of equilibrium results are developed. The papers with these non-existence results are (in addition to Krebs, 2004) Kubler and Polemarchakis (2004) and Kubler and Schmedders (2005).

Citanna and Siconolfi (2010) showed the culmination of the techniques developed in the two previous papers, and its publication in *Econometrica* was well-deserved. The paper provides alternate proof of the existence of what Citanna and Siconolfi call simple Markov equilibria, which are equivalent to what Duffie et al. (1994) called stationary Markov equilibria. The existence proof starts with the history-dependent equilibrium that can be shown to exist using the same truncation method used by Balasko and Shell. From here, Citanna–Siconolfi show how to recursively build up equilibria in which histories are replaced by one-period lagged collections of exogenous shocks, individual wealth holdings, prices, and individual Lagrange multipliers as the state variables. The sufficiency of these variables for describing the competitive equilibrium follows from the first-order conditions for individual agents and the market-clearing conditions. Using a process they call "grafting," Citanna–Siconolfi show how to remove finite time sequences in which any initial Markov state returns to a previous state, and generate a consistent Markovian sequence of competitive equilibria.

Once the existence of the simple Markovian equilibria is established, Citanna–Siconolfi use the perturbation methods developed in their previous two papers to show that as long as there are sufficiently many households, the simple Markovian equilibrium can be obtained as a recursive equilibrium in which the state variables are the exogenous shocks and the wealth holdings of the agents. The need for heterogeneity across agents is to ensure that the relevant utility perturbations introduced in the previous papers can be applied.

In addition to the accomplishment of showing that for practical purposes one can work with the recursive equilibrium concept – and justifying Rios-Rull's intuition along the way – this result also provides a resolution to the question originally raised by the Lucas (1972) paper's assumption that the exogenous shocks alone were the right set of state variables. Citanna and Siconolfi (2010) show that the exogenous shocks and wealth distribution are the right variables if the equilibrium is determinate. If the equilibria of the model are indeterminate, then one can construct stochastic processes of sunspot equilibria associated with the stable manifold via the bootstrap process examined previously. The applicability of this construction is implied by the results in Woodford (1986b) but results on how to actually construct such equilibria in a Markovian form were first presented during this period in Bloise (2001, 2004). These results leave open the possibility for psychological phenomena – Keynes' animal spirits, contemporary notions of sentiments (Angeletos & La'O, 2013; Benhabib, Wang, & Wen, 2015; Spear, 1989), independent belief formation (Farmer, 2010), or behavioral processes like mental accounting (Goenka, 2003) or hyperbolic discounting (Kim & Li, 2020) – to have real economic effects. We discuss these developments below.

We also note that this theoretical work is in contrast to that of Krusell and Smith (1998) who looked at the effects of changes in the wealth distribution on the equilibrium in an Aiyagari–Bewley incomplete markets representative agent model. The Krusell–Smith paper took the approach of including various moments of the wealth distribution as state variables and found that for the version of the Aiyagari–Bewley model they examined, the mean of the distribution alone was sufficient to summarize the history, at least to a very close approximation. The theoretical foundation for this approach is from Duffie et al. (1994), together with Rios-Rull's assumption that wealth distribution was the correct endogenous state variable. In principle, if one knows all the moments (or better, the characteristic function of the wealth distribution, from which all the moments can be obtained), then one knows the distribution itself, and the recursive equilibrium can be computed. What is less clear is the robustness of their findings that only low-order moments are important. Storesletten, Telmer, and Yaron (2007) note in their computational appendix (Storesletten et al., p. 545) that their attempts to use finite collections of moments from the wealth distribution in their simulations did not give good results. Because of this, they instead adopted asset prices as the lagged endogenous state variable, which did work. It would seem from this observation that having a fully sufficient statistic for the shock history is important in general SOLG models in a way that isn't important in ILA models, even with market incompleteness. That said, however, Heer and Maussner (2009) claim to get good results using the Krusell–Smith algorithm for long-lived SOLG models, which is based on simulating the wealth distribution at each step of the algorithm. As they note, though, the procedure is quite a time-consuming. We will examine computation issues in more detail at the end of this chapter.

A second area of theoretical results from this period looked at issues of efficiency of equilibrium, extending the earlier work of Chattopadhyay–Gottardi and Demange. The key paper here is Bloise and Calciano (2008) which provides a general characterization of inefficiency in SOLG models.

The Bloise–Calciano approach uses the notion of *robust inefficiency* based on ideas introduced by Debreu (1951). Specifically, an allocation is robustly inefficient if it is Pareto dominated by some other allocation even after some resources in the dominating allocation are destroyed. Working in the same context of history-dependent equilibrium as Chattopadhyay–Gottardi and Demange and under the same assumption of sequential market completeness, Boise–Calciano show that inefficient allocations can be characterized in terms of their supporting present-value state contingent prices by defining an operator on the space of potential transfers by

$$T(e)_t = \frac{1}{p_t} E_t p_{t+1} e_{t+1}.$$

Their condition for robust inefficiency is that there exists a contingent transfer sequence e such that $\rho T(e)_t \geq e_t$ for $0 < \rho < 1$. By iterating on this recursive relationship, one obtains Bloise–Calciano's modified Cass criterion on the convergence of the infinite sum of inverses of the prices. Bloise and Calciano also show that this criterion is independent of the number of periods agents in the model are assumed to live, by converting the model into one in which agents formally live only two periods, based on the original reduction to two periods given by Balasko, Cass, and Shell (1980). Given this transformation, they show that if the allocation in the original economy was inefficient, it will also be inefficient in the transformed economy. One should note, however, that the transformation to two-period lives does not produce an economy equivalent to the original one, since the young agents in the transformed economy are born into given states of the world that were as-yet unrealized in the original model. This means that where they were able to make contingent trades in the original model, given the assumption of sequential market completeness, these would not be available in the transformed model so that sequential market completeness is lost. This doesn't matter for the efficiency characterization since it is the efficiency or inefficiency of the original allocation that is being examined, but it does show that once one recognizes that any improving sequence of transfers must continue forever, pairwise comparison of one period's prices with the expected values of future prices suffices to characterize efficiency. Finally, if one examines the proofs in the Appendix of the paper, it is also apparent (as the authors note in their Remark 4) that the assumptions of a single good or a single agent per generation are easily extended to more general economies. One of the most interesting aspects of this characterization of robust inefficiency is the fact that it can be made in terms of the eigenvalues of the operator T. Specifically, T must have an eigenvalue bigger than one corresponding to a sequence of Pareto improving transfers between agents. This is a direct extension of the Peled and Aiyagari-Peled results for the simpler two-period one-good model.

Much of the additional theory work during this period was based on Shell's Philadelphia Pholk theorem. Some of this work is relevant to the OLG story, and some of it is tangential. We include a discussion of this work here for completeness.

As we noted earlier, Peck and Shell did their pioneering work on imperfect competition, the existence of sunspot equilibria, and the relationship between sunspots and correlated equilibria, during this period. Cass, Geanakoplos and Mas-Colell, and Wilson started a research program looking at incomplete markets in the late 1980s, which spawned literature over the next two decades aimed at fully characterizing the equilibrium and welfare properties of models with incomplete markets. While Cass' original incomplete markets paper was motivated by his intention to show the existence of sunspot equilibria when markets are incomplete, most of this work is tangential to our subject, so we refer the reader to the surveys in Magill and Shafer (1991) and Staum (2007) for details.

A second strand in the Pholk theorem thread was work done in the ILA setting with externalities. Externalities play an important role in the growth model when one introduces taxes, which are required for most public policy applications, and human capital accumulation, which operates through spillover effects and shared research impacts to generate external increases in the productivity of other inputs to production. The first papers in this program were Spear (1991) and Kehoe et al. (1992) mentioned earlier. These papers established indeterminacy results by showing that in the presence of externalities, the saddle path dynamics of the conventional RCK model would bifurcate to make the stable manifold around the steady-state equilibrium higher in dimension than the number of predetermined variables. These results, in turn, imply the existence of sunspot equilibria via Woodford's results. Benhabib and Farmer (1998) examine related models in which production exhibits increasing returns to scale in economic environments which allow for competitive equilibrium. One of their models treats the factor that generates increasing returns (e.g., average human capital investment) as external to the firms' profit maximization decisions, and hence they can apply the Spear or Kehoe–Levine–Romer results directly. The second model looks at monopolistic competition using the well-known Dixit–Stiglitz model, which generates external increasing returns through the provision of intermediate goods. Benhabib and Farmer then shows directly for this model that the steady-state equilibrium of the model is indeterminate.

Farmer and Guo (1994) use these results to construct two calibrated RBC-type models, one with monopolistic competition, and the second with external increasing returns to scale, in which fluctuations are generated by sunspots, or, in Keynes' terminology, animal spirits. They examine simulations of their models together with those of a standard RBC model (taken from Hansen, 1985). The simulations generated by the external IRS model with sunspot shocks generate time series that match US post-war data as well or better than the standard RBC model, and the sunspot model does a better job of matching impulse-response data than the RBC model. These results present serious reasons for macroeconomists to consider models where demand-side shocks based on consumer sentiment, together with indeterminacies generated by OLG-type frictions, drive business cycle fluctuations, rather than the conventional modeling assumption that aggregate shocks are due primarily to random changes in productivity. Coupled with the empirical evidence on the scarcity of aggregate productivity shocks, this paper should have received more attention than it has. We make this statement based on the 754 Google Scholar cites to Farmer–Guo versus 3,319 cites to the Hansen (1985) paper.

The notion that sunspots – now redubbed animal spirits or consumer sentiment – might drive economic fluctuations experienced something of a revival during this period, independently of the work by Farmer and others on indeterminacy. The first of the new papers was by Angeletos and La'O (2013) and Benhabib et al. (2015). These papers generalize the earlier sunspot equilibrium results by allowing for heterogeneity in the sunspot variable, heterogeneity in the product markets, and internalization of sunspot signals. Angeletos and La'O use a model of different islands that are paired bilaterally for trade in each period, while Benhabib–Wang–Wen uses the Dixit–Stiglitz model of monopolistic competition, to generate the friction that lets sentiments matter. We note that the idea of internalizing the sunspot signal was not new to these papers. Spear (1989) used a model of two islands operating in separate "time zones" to show how each island's equilibrium price could serve as the other island's sunspot variable. Manuelli and Peck (1992) showed that the possible existence of sunspot equilibria in a model could serve to "amplify" the variation in equilibrium prices associated with small fluctuations in random fundamentals. Their model allowed for very small variance fluctuations in endowments in a model known to have a two-cyclic sunspot equilibrium (as in Azariadis, 1981). They showed that in addition to a stochastic steady-state with very small variance, there would be a second equilibrium with a larger variance close to the sunspot equilibrium, so that the fundamentals of the model served, in effect, as the sunspot signals.[3]

The papers on sentiments went significantly beyond the earlier general equilibrium demonstrations that fluctuations in beliefs could affect real economic activity, even in a rational expectations equilibrium, by embedding the sunspot mechanism in conventional and accepted macroeconomic frameworks. This represented a significant step away from the basic idea that shocks to production were responsible for business cycle fluctuations toward the more empirically plausible contention that demand fluctuations and indeterminacy of equilibrium were more likely to be the source of aggregate fluctuations.

In work related to sentiments but based on ideas coming out of behavioral economics, Goenka (2017) shows that a simple model of mental accounting (see Thaler, 1999) can give rise to sunspot equilibria. In Goenka's model, some consumers are boundedly rational and assign fixed expenditure shares to different subsets of commodities. These fixed shares associated with the mental accounting assumption manifest themselves in general equilibrium as if the boundedly rational consumers were credit constrained, and this friction then leads to the existence of the sunspot equilibrium.

These notions about demand-side variability were key drivers in much of the subsequent work on indeterminacy. Over the period 1991–2020, Roger Farmer wrote several articles denying the validity of two major elements in the New Classical Macroeconomic analytical toolkit: the Lucas Critique, and the Natural Rate Hypothesis (NRH). In Farmer (1991), he attacked the arguments and restrictions underlying the Lucas Critique argument as not only insufficient, but also presented a counter-example to the argument, and an alternative model selection criterion. Moreover, he identified general versions of OLG as being able to provide what he called a "Lucas-proof forecast rule" (Farmer, 1991, p. 331). A decade later, Farmer (2002) focused on the Favero and Hendry (1992) test of the Lucas Critique and found that the Lucas Critique, as he put it, "really does fail in practice" (Farmer, 2002, p. 112). A decade after this, Farmer (2013) presented an alternative to the NRH using a DSGE approach based on "beliefs" as a psychological parallel to "preferences" (Farmer, 2013, p. 244). Most recently, Farmer (2020) reviews the most recent advances in what he calls "the indeterminacy agenda" following on from Farmer (1993) and Benhabib and Farmer (1999).

Another related literature in this strand of ideas stems from William A. Barnett's work on bifurcations in economic models. This work is summarized in Barnett and Chen (2015), although the best characterization of the importance of this work is found (in our opinion) in Barnett and Eriylmaz (2022) in their introduction:

> Determinacy concerns the existence of a unique equilibrium path of a dynamic system. Equilibrium of a macroeconomic model is called determinate, as defined by McCallum (2009b), if it is locally unique and dynamically stable under relevant specifications of policy tools. Studying the determinacy issues in a wide range of models has been an important subject among macroeconomists. One of the reasons for high focus on the subject is the fact that uniqueness of the solution path plays an important role for policy makers and researchers. Determinacy is important to the monetary authority in determining policy to manage inflationary expectations and preventing self-fulfilling economic fluctuations. Indeterminacy permits existence of multiple solutions, which could be fundamental equilibria or nonfundamental sunspot equilibria, as suggested by McCallum (2003) and Bullard (2006), among other authors.
>
> McCallum (2003) further divides the indeterminacy cases into two categories: failure of the model to determine the values of nominal variables (nominal indeterminacy) or of real variables (real indeterminacy). But Woodford (2003b) finds the distinction to be insignificant. He argues that both types of indeterminacy are quantitatively indifferent. Models with indeterminate solutions, as stressed by Bullard and Mitra (2002), are considered undesirable for

> macroeconomic analysis and policy design. In the presence of indeterminacy, as pointed out by McCallum (2003), Gauthier and Guesnerie (2005), Beyer and Farmer (2007) and others, non-fundamental shocks trigger extra variance and fluctuations in the economy. Then decision makers, unable to acquire full information, encounter unforeseen problems in monetary policy design. (Barnett & Eriylmaz, 2022, p. 2)

Much of Barnett's work on indeterminacy has focused on the possibility that models used in policy analysis might exhibit bifurcations. Bifurcations are important because their possibility generally defines boundaries in the spaces of parameters that determine a model's dynamics which, when crossed, cause discontinuous changes in the dynamics around the model's steady-state equilibrium. To the extent that calibrated simulations of a model are used to study the impact of a particular policy, the uncertainties associated with the estimation of parameters need to be evaluated for whether the confidence regions contain bifurcation boundaries. Barnett and Chen (2015) have examples of policy-relevant models in which estimated parameter values are in fact close to bifurcation boundaries.

We close this discussion by noting that even in the absence of indeterminacy, general SOLG models generate the same kinds of "extra fluctuations" in the economy as Barnett noted above, due to the dependence of equilibrium on the distribution of wealth. The implications of such dependence were expressed nicely in Naryana Kocherlakota's Minneapolis Fed article (Kocherlakota, 2010):

> M]any modern macro models incorporate financial market frictions. However, these models generally allow households and firms to trade one or two financial assets in a single market. They do not capture an intermediate messy reality in which market participants can trade multiple assets in a wide array of somewhat segmented markets. As a consequence, the models do not reveal much about the benefits of the massive amount of daily or quarterly reallocations of wealth within financial markets. The models also say nothing about the relevant costs and benefits of resulting fluctuations in financial structure (across bank loans, corporate debt, and equity).

The extra fluctuations in general, multi-period SOLG models arise precisely from the portfolio rebalancing that occurs as agents realize trades and shocks and adjust their consumption and saving accordingly. Working with such models is, of course, difficult, as Victor Rios-Rull's work showed, but again quoting Kocherlakota from his Fed article:

> Over the past 25 years, a great deal of work has used models that incorporate financial market frictions. Most of these models cannot be solved reliably using graphical techniques or pencil and paper. As a consequence, progress is closely tied to advances in computational speed.

Again, we see the importance of computation and will address this in more detail below. There is an important postscript to this section, however. As we noted above, Roger Farmer's questioning of the empirical validity of the rational expectations hypothesis and the natural rate of unemployment hypothesis led him to a reconsideration of how markets (and labor markets in particular) come into equilibrium. It is well-known in economics that the standard assumption that prices move in opposition to excess demand is not generally valid (see Scarf, 1960). Since this mechanism for bringing markets into equilibrium can fail, and since wage rigidity is a well-known empirical fact in labor markets, Farmer opted to replace the usual wage equilibration mechanism with a search theoretic one where firms set supply to match demand in the product market, and then search for new employees if these are needed to meet this production target. Farmer (2010) lays out this model and shows that in the absence of a price mechanism for bringing labor markets into equilibrium, firms' beliefs about future demand are what determine equilibrium wages and prices. Farmer then introduces a "belief function," considered as a fundamental psychological object in the same way that economists consider preferences as psychologically given, to close the model. This new formulation of equilibrium introduces a new kind of long-run indeterminacy in which it is possible for unemployment to persist for long periods of time. These ideas were the impetus for the recent declaration in Vine and Wills (2020) on the project to rebuild macroeconomics, in support of the indeterminacy agenda for macroeconomics. While the jury is obviously still out on whether this approach will be more successful than RBC or NK macro, it is interesting that the treatment of beliefs as a fundamental vindicates Grandmont's views on rational expectations versus temporary equilibrium expectations that we discussed above. It is also completely consistent with the large literature on learning rational expectations in economics and suggests that work on learning in search-moderated equilibrium frameworks will be an important agenda item for macroeconomists going forward.

Beyond the direct application of indeterminacy results in the analysis of business cycle phenomena, there were also direct applications of the sunspots idea in the analysis of banking and bank runs. The early modern work on banking theory is reflected in Diamond and Dybvig (1983),[4] which developed a simple model of the intermediation activities of banks in uncertain circumstances where depositors can withdraw their funds prior to the maturation of projects the bank has invested in. The uncertainty associated with liquidity needs generates a coordination problem for the bank. If all depositors expect that most other depositors will leave their money in the bank until the investments mature and payoff, then the bank can in fact invest most of the funds deposited and generate a return for patient customers and a profit for the bank's owners. But, if depositors come to believe that their money isn't safe and choose to withdraw it independently of their liquidity needs, these expectations can cause a run on the bank. Absent some form of insurance against the run, the bank's failure becomes a self-fulfilling prophecy. Diamond and Dybvig themselves note that some form of sunspot dynamics could be used to provide a dynamic model of bank runs.

This possibility was shown to in fact hold in Peck and Shell (2003), where they construct a fully dynamic version of the Diamond–Dybvig model with a sunspot variable that coordinates agents' collective actions in the post-deposit game. Via this coordination mechanism, bank runs occur with positive probability in the model.

A second notable follow-on contribution to this banking literature was made by Benhabib, Miao, and Wang (2016), who embed a simple model of banking akin to the Diamond–Dybvig model in a representative agent setting. As in the static Diamond–Dybvig or Peck–Shell models, self-fulfilling prophecies that manifest themselves as bank runs can arise, but because of the dynamic setting of the Benhabib–Miao–Wang model, the information asymmetries that drive self-fulfilling bank runs in Diamond–Dybvig generate a much richer set of possibilities. Because bankers in the dynamic model care about their reputation, and because depositors understand the moral hazard problem that arises because of the banker's superior information about investment opportunities, the Benhabib–Miao–Wang model has additional constraints (specifically the incentive compatibility constraints) relative to the Diamond–Dybvig or Peck–Shell models, and this generates non-linearities in the model that make complex dynamic outcomes possible. Under the assumptions of limited liability and enforcement of banking contracts, the paper shows the existence of multiple equilibria, including deterministic chaos, which can lead to coordination failures in the model, and hence bank runs, defaults, and credit crises. The results suggest that banking regulations which include limits on leverage, central bank credit policies, and restrictions on bank size can be effective in stabilizing the banking equilibrium and preventing self-fulfilling crises.

8.2 SOCIAL SECURITY

The period between 1995 and 2015 also saw a resurgence of interest in Social Security. As we saw earlier, this was a topic of debate between Samuelson, Lerner, and Meckling based on Samuelson's deterministic two- and three-period OLG models. By the late-1970s and early-1980s, the large size of the Baby Boom generation, coupled with the relatively smaller size of Gen X began to generate policy concerns over where the retirement funds paid to Boomers would come from. This concern led to the creation of the Greenspan Commission to study the problem and to the eventual passage of the 1983 Social Security Reform Act which raised the Social Security and Medicare taxes on working members of the Boomer generation, with the provision that the Social Security Administration invest the resulting surplus in US government bonds.

Three notable early papers which attempted to study the effects of this tax change and other policy perturbations on Social Security were Huang et al. (1997) and De Nardi et al. (1999, 2001). All three of these papers studied large-scaled OLG models with some form of idiosyncratic risk and used numerical simulations to examine the welfare effects of various policy proposals, ranging from pure privatization, to privatization with buyouts of existing claimants to retirement benefits, to continuation of the PAYGO system while allowing surpluses to be invested in non-governmental assets. The models used were extensions of the Auerbach–Kotlikoff modeling technique, with the addition of idiosyncratic risks to mortality or income. As we noted earlier in our discussion of the aftermath of Rios-Rull's 1996 paper, the incorporation of idiosyncratic shocks became popular during this period, particularly given that, thanks to the law of large numbers, they could be handled using the same computational tools available for deterministic models. In this setting without aggregate retirement risk, the main findings of these three papers were that the various reforms increased the welfare of future generations by increasing the size of the capital stock, but did so at the expense of current generations.

Much of the resurgence of interest in Social Security after 2000 was generated by policy proposals put forth by US President George W. Bush's campaign in 2004 to allow working-age people to direct some of their Social Security payments to private investment accounts. During this debate, the Republicans stressed the fact that Social Security funds invested in US Treasury bonds earned very little interest compared to what was available on the stock market. The Democratic side (under the direction of Senator John Kerry's presidential campaign) stressed the fact that the stock market exposed elderly investors to substantial risk, pointing back to the way many retirees in the 1930s lost their life savings in the stock market crash of 1929.

Many of the papers on the subject of Social Security written during this period were based on two-period lived SOLG models. Since the non-equivalence of the two-period and multi-period SOLG model was well-known by this time, the two-period assumption in this work was clearly made for tractability reasons and offered as an approximation of what more realistic models would produce.

One particular paper which avoided the two-period assumption was Conesa and Krueger (1999). This paper avoided the problems of history dependence in SOLG equilibria by working with a model of idiosyncratic shocks similar to the Storesletten–Telmer–Yaron papers. The question addressed in the paper was whether political economy considerations would impose an impediment to moving an economy running an unfunded pay-as-you-go (PAYGO) social security system to a fully funded system in which individual contributions would earn higher returns than those generated by the unfunded system. The voting friction introduced in the model has the effect of creating a bias in favor of the status quo since agents already invested in the unfunded system would effectively lose their contributions during the transition to the fully funded system. Conesa and Krueger's quantitative analysis further shows that the bias in favor of the unfunded status quo is stronger when the idiosyncratic shocks to income lead to significant wealth heterogeneity across agents of the same age.

A second response to the inadequacies of the two-period approach was the adoption of full-blown computational analyses of multi-period SOLG models to analyze the effects of social insurance, following in the footsteps of Riso-Rull's pioneering computational analysis. An early important contribution to this literature was Krueger and Kubler (2002). In this paper, Krueger and Kubler work with a three-period lived SOLG model and show that PAYGO social security programs can be viable only when asset markets are incomplete, as long as there is an asset that pays a positive dividend in every state of nature (e.g., such as land or a Lucas tree). The reason for this is straightforward. With sequentially complete markets and a positive asset, returns to saving are always positive, so that private saving always dominates the pure transfers associated with unfunded social security systems. Krueger and Kubler work in a pure exchange environment subject to aggregate shocks and show that when the asset markets are incomplete, the introduction of a social security transfer system generates a Pareto improvement.

Krueger and Kubler (2006) follow up on their 2002 paper by adding production and capital accumulation to the model and increasing the number of generations from three to nine. We note that during the four years between the publication of these papers on social security, Kruger and Kubler also wrote an important paper on how to use projection methods to compute SOLG models, which made dealing with the computational complexity of the nine-period model workable. We discuss this paper in the section below on computation. In the 2006 paper, markets are again incomplete, for the same reasons as before, but now, the introduction of the social security program doesn't just reallocate savings as it did in the pure exchange model. It also has the effect of crowding out capital since the saving diverted to social security is no longer being used to fund firms' capital accumulation or replacement activities. Kruger and Kubler show that when only the risk-sharing aspects of the social security transfer are considered, the program generates a Pareto improvement. But when the crowding out effect of capital is factored back in, the overall effect of the program is to reduce welfare. In their quantitative model, the effect of introducing social security is a 6% reduction in the capital stock, leading ultimately to a 2% reduction in average output.

While the Krueger–Kubler paper made significant strides in using the general SOLG framework, its need to limit the number of periods considered to nine for computational tractability reasons left open the question of whether their results would change if agents lived longer lifespans. The first paper to tackle this question was by Hasanhodzic and Kotlikoff (2013). Agents in this model live 80 periods, working for 45 of them. Production in the model is subject to standard AR(1) shocks to total factor productivity, as well as shocks to depreciation. Agents in the model are borrowing constrained, to match the age-consumption profile generated by the model with the empirical profile.

Unlike Krueger–Kubler, Hasanhodzic–Kotlikoff focuses on assessing the degree of intergenerational risk generated by the model and assessing the extent to which markets or social insurance policies can mitigate this risk. Hence, while they find similar crowding out effects generated by the introduction of social security as in Krueger–Kubler, they control for these in examining the effects of social security on intergenerational risk. In terms of their results, they find for an initial calibration in which the shocks are set to match the variability of aggregate US wealth that the model generates little to no intergenerational risk. When they modify the calibration by increasing the size of the shocks to depreciation to match the variability of the equity returns (following Krueger–Kubler on this), they find that the model generates significant intergenerational risk. This suggests that the conventional wisdom of looking at the risk the stock market imposes on retirees does have some validity. Finally, under both calibrations, Hasanhodzic and Kotlikoff find that conventional asset markets or unfunded social security systems can effectively mitigate intergenerational risk.

We note that earlier considerations of social security costs and benefits led Auerbach and Kotlikoff (with some additional coauthors) to propose the concept of "generational accounting" as an alternative way of measuring the burden of government debt on future generations. Conventional measures of debt accumulation or decumulation look at a contemporaneous flow of funds away from or to consumers but don't take into account how the funds will be used – for the provision of public goods, public capital goods (infrastructure), or simply as transfers – with attendant costs and benefits that both accrue over time and confer differential benefits across agents of different ages. Generational accounting is a mechanism that attempts to break down the government's receipts and expenditures precisely in terms of cross-generation costs and benefits in a way that makes transparent the relationship between what a given cohort will pay in taxes over their lifetimes relative to what they will receive in benefits. This kind of accounting makes it possible to identify gainers and losers from given policy proposals, allowing a more straightforward application of the benefit principle to the intergenerational transfers such policies typically require.

While this accounting arrangement has been criticized on various grounds – see Cutler (1993) for a review of Kotlikoff (1993) – the concept does provide a way of thinking about the national income and product accounts in a dynamic context, organized around the graded age-set structure of the OLG model. Kotlikoff himself acknowledges the need (in Fehr and Kotlikoff, 1995) to consider dynamic accounting systems like the generational one in the context of fully dynamic general equilibrium models, and to a large degree, this idea comes to fruition in the Hasanhodzic–Kotlikoff paper.

The next paper in the series of works on social security systems in this period is by Harenberg and Ludwig (2015). The quantitative model Harenberg–Ludwig use has agents active for 58 periods (implying a life expectancy of 78 years assuming agents enter the market at age 21), and agents face both aggregate and idiosyncratic shocks. The assumption that the aggregate TFP shocks follow a four-state Markov process implies that the markets are not sequentially complete so that the Krueger–Kubler necessary condition is satisfied. In its overall structure, then the Harenberg–Ludwig model is quite similar to that of Storesletten, Telmer, and Yaron (2007), but the focus here is on the question of whether social security generates welfare improvement. The answer to this question is yes. Like Krueger and Kubler, the introduction of a PAYGO social security system in the Harenberg–Ludwig models generates a significant degree of crowding out, on the order of a 12% reduction in the capital stock. Unlike the Krueger–Kubler results, however, Harenberg–Ludwig find that the combined effect of aggregate and idiosyncratic shocks is super-additive, with the overall risk effects being significantly larger than the individual risk effects combined. In this setting, then, the social security system generates a significant improvement in intergenerational risk-sharing which more than offsets the losses due to crowding out.

The final paper we consider in this strand of literature on social security falls a little outside the time window we have set ourselves here, but we included it because of its close relationship to the other papers we've been considering. This paper is chapter 1 of Eungsik Kim's thesis (Kim, 2019), which considers a SOLG model with long-lived agents, calibrated along the same lines as in Hasanhodzic–Kotlikoff or Harenberg–Ludwig, but with the additional assumption of heterogeneity among agents within each age group. The heterogeneity is one of the income differences, which Kim characterizes as arising from differences in education. He posits three income classes, denoted as college-educated, high-school-educated, and drop-outs. The source of the income heterogeneity in Kim's model is increased productivity associated with greater education. Kim's calibration induces the required sequential market incompleteness per Krueger–Kubler, and he finds in his quantitative model that the introduction of a social security system has the same order of crowding out found by Kruger–Kubler or Haranberg–Ludwig (a 15% reduction in the capital stock and an associated 5% reduction in output). Unlike Haranberg–Ludwig, though, the introduction of social security affects different income classes differently.

First, because of the general equilibrium effects associated with crowding out, the introduction of social security in Kim's model raises the prices of the assets owned predominantly by the college-educated types, making them better off even though they are paying taxes that support the PAYGO transfer system. The dropouts in Kim's model also benefit because they end up receiving more in transfers than they lose in taxes. But the middle group of high-school graduates in Kim's model do not benefit, since they are rich enough to pay significant taxes toward the transfer system, but don't hold significant asset positions and hence miss out on the price improvements caused by crowding out. Kim's model demonstrates that in the face of heterogeneity across agents in the same cohort, some kind of political economy consideration is needed to determine whether or not a given society will wish to implement an unfunded social security system or not. In this sense, the paper is reminiscent of Conesa and Krueger (1999).

To complete our discussion of the social insurance applications of the SOLG model in recent years, we note that because most social security systems operate to transfer purchasing power from young agents to retirees, this mechanism misses the second inefficiency identified by Henriksen and Spear whereby young agents under consume to self-insure against asset market risk when retired. This is also apparent in the empirical studies of precautionary over saving. As we noted earlier, there are several substantial US government tax and spending provisions aimed at making life easier for the young, including the home mortgage interest deduction, deductibility of childcare and education expenses, public provision of K-12 education, public higher education institutions, and so on. These expenditures are on the same order of magnitude as those for social security, but there have been few attempts to study this aspect of intergenerational transfer in detail. Gale and Scholz (1994) provide a good overview of the importance of the issue. For a more recent study, see Yoo (2013), who shows using an applied three-period SOLG model with idiosyncratic income shocks that a reduction in the gift tax for *inter vivos* transfers generates a welfare improvement.

One strand of literature which deals with the nature of transfers between generations in a historical context, and which also arose during the period we are considering, was work on the so-called demographic transition. This is an empirical phenomenon associated with the onset of industrialization in which both mortality and fertility rates in the population fall in response to the increased standard of living afforded by industrial development. We examine this work in more detail in the next section.

8.3 DEMOGRAPHY AND WEALTH

Lifecycle models have long been used to examine the economic effects of demographic changes. One of the more profound demographic shifts that have ever occurred in human society is the observed demographic transition that occurs after the onset of industrial development. This transition was observed historically in developed Western nations following the industrial revolution which began in the late 1800s. The economic transition associated with industrialization is one of transforming the economy from an agrarian foundation to one based on manufacturing. The demographic transition associated with this economic shift is one in which families which were previously large and oriented toward farming become smaller and oriented toward factory work involving interactions with advanced technologies. Because these interactions require numeracy and literacy skills beyond those required of farmers, the transition sees parents investing in human capital across smaller cohorts of children, rather than in the large numbers of children that are useful in agrarian operations. The benefits of technology and scientific understanding of things like disease also lead to reductions in mortality, particularly among children, which also reduces the *ex ante* need for large families based on the expectation that some number of children would not survive.

While the literature on this topic is large, we will focus on the two most highly cited papers on this topic, Galor and Weil (2000) and Hansen and Prescott (2002). The Hansen–Prescott approach was based almost entirely on the changes in production that occurred over the course of the early industrial revolution, and, as they note:

> Although we found it convenient to study an overlapping-generations model in this paper, our results should carry over to an infinite-horizon context like that used in much of the growth literature. (footnote 11, p. 1209)

The essential changes that took place during the industrial revolution were the mechanization of previously labor-intensive manufacturing activities, enhanced by the use of, first, wood-fired steam engines and later coal-fired engines. This process made labor more productive in the factories than on the farms and the consequent increases in wages drew workers away from the land to the factories. Hansen–Prescott model this process by postulating two distinct technologies, one based on agricultural production, and the other based on mechanized manufacturing. The agricultural technology uses fixed land together with capital and labor to produce output. Hansen–Prescott refers to this as the "Malthusian" technology. The other technology, which Hansen–Prescott calls "Solovian" technology, uses only capital and labor. The modern technology's dispensation of the need for restrictive fixed land inputs captured the primary benefit of science in production by allowing for large amounts of output to be produced on small, compact parcels of land (the factory footprint) by multiplying labor productivity with steam-powered machinery. In addition to this specification of technologies, Hansen–Prescott posit an exogenous Malthusian mechanism whereby the population growth rate depends on the overall per capita output of the economy. They also assume that scientific contributions to the economy are exogenous and generate growth in total factor productivity at a constant rate (though they note in their calibration exercises that this need not be the case). The basis for the TFP growth assumption is Solow's empirical finding that most of the observed growth in TFP over the twentieth century cannot be explained by increases in labor or capital.

With these specifications of the model in place, Hansen–Prescott shows analytically and via calibrated simulations that the Solow sector of their model, starting from initial values that held in England before 1800, eventually becomes dominant in production, with the agrarian Malthusian sector going to zero asymptotically. Via calibration of the population growth function that captures the demographic transition, they are then able to replicate the observed patterns of the transition on investment in manufacturing relative to agriculture, the explosion in per capita income, and the decline in the value of land relative to output.

The one major criticism that can be leveled against the Hansen–Prescott approach is its inability to actually explain what was happening to households in terms of fertility and human capital investment decisions during the transition to industrialization.

The Galor–Weil paper takes the endogeneity of these decisions into account. They work with a three-period deterministic OLG model in which parents can trade-off the number of children produced with the amount of human capital invested in each child. Households face a minimum consumption requirement, reflecting the Malthusian survival imperative. Unlike the production process in Hansen–Prescott, Galor–Weil posit that production of output is generated by an increasing returns-to-scale technology in which labor productivity is enhanced by human capital investment, which in turn affects the rate of technological progress (the TFP effect observed by Solow). Because the human capital investment decisions are made by households rather than firms, firms in the model take the human capital of workers as given in their production decisions and hence operate in a perfectly competitive environment. We do note, however, that like Hansen–Prescott, Galor–Weil also take the fundamental scientific progress that drives the growth in TFP as exogenous. The primary reason both papers make this assumption stems from the discoveries in Shell (1966) and Romer (1990) that full endogenization of TFP growth would require explicitly identifying how inventive activity (in Shell's parlance) or technological change (in Romer's) was organized and paid for. In Shell's models, research was either a public good or one organized by a monopolist. In Romer's model, monopolistically competitive intermediate firms generated endogenous increasing returns-to-scale which, in turn, drove growth. Hansen–Prescott and Galor–Weil clearly recognized that the complexity of trying to introduce these features into their models would take the analysis too far afield from what they were trying to explain.

Given the dependence of scientific progress on human capital investments in the Galor–Weil model, together with simplifying assumptions on the nature of parental altruism that drives the quantity versus quality trade-off in household fertility decision-making, Galor–Weil show three key results. First, if parental household income is such that the minimal consumption constraint is binding, then increases in parental income always lead households to produce more children. Second, once parental income is such that the consumption constraint is no longer binding, then increases in parental income lead to no changes in either the number or quality of children produced. Finally, if parents expect that technological progress will occur between their children's second and third periods of life, they will substitute away from numbers in favor of investing in quality.

Galor–Weil then show how the dynamic system generated by the model can explain the demographic transition observed to take place both historically after the industrial revolution in the UK, the USA, and the Europe in the late 1800s, and in developing economies during the latter part of the twentieth century. The basic mechanism is the interaction between the way technological progress increases family income and investment in human capital, and the way that human capital investment then drives more technological progress. This identification of education as an important driver of growth in per capita income and standard of living had a lasting effect on the economics profession. Education now plays an important explanatory role not only as a driver of growth but in studies of income inequality, wealth inequality, discrimination, and political leanings. It is hard not to wonder, though, whether the neglect of the issues raised by Shell and Romer – the fact that increasing returns technologies breed monopolies – might not play an equally important, though neglected, role in understanding these issues. That, however, is the topic of a different book.

Another important application of large-scale SOLG models during this period was the study of the effects of demographic variation on economic activity. A number of studies from the early 1990s (see, e.g., Mankiw & Weil, 1989, or Poterba, Weil, & Shiller, 1990) found that housing values didn't seem to follow the kinds of forward-looking pricing that other, more conventional assets did, but rather, were strongly (though not exclusively) affected by demographic variations. This observation led Geanakoplos, Magill, and Quinzii (2004) (GMQ) to ask whether population movements might not affect the prices of assets that individuals accumulated and decumulated for retirement purposes. To analyze this, GMQ note that for the US economy, live births over the course of the twentieth century appear to follow a cyclic pattern, with a relatively large cohort born in the early 1900s, a much smaller cohort born during the depression years of the 1930s, followed by the baby boom cohort born in the years after WWII, followed by the relatively smaller Gen X cohort, and then the children of the baby boomers. We reproduce the graph from GMQ in Fig. 22. From this pattern, GMQ decided to model the demographic fluctuation as if it were a simple two-cycle, adopting a three-period OLG model as the simplest that would permit the existence of such demographic cycles. From this simplification, they then defined what they called the MY ratio, which was the ratio of the number of middle-aged agents living in a given period to the number of young agents. By comparing this ratio with the movement of the price-equity ratio for the Standard and Poor's index of stock prices (taken as a normalized measure of firms' value), they found a key piece of empirical evidence supporting the contention that demography influences asset values. We reproduce the diagram from GMQ below as Fig. 23.

To capture some of the randomness apparent in the asset prices, GMQ considered a stochastic version of the three-period OLG model having four possible aggregate shock states. The main findings of the paper are that the asset price variations in the model due to the endowment shocks are dwarfed by the fluctuations in generation size, to the point that asset prices become completely predictable in terms of population size. One of the predictions this model makes, then, is that the United States should expect to see a sustained bear market for stocks

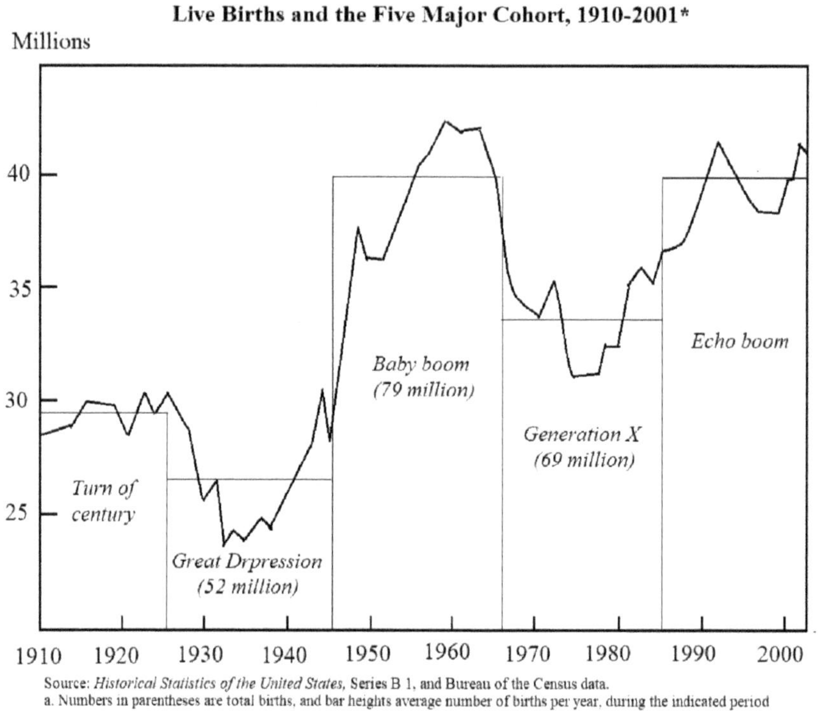

Fig. 22. Twentieth Century Birth Cohorts. *Source*: Adapted from Geanakoplos et al. (2004).

over the second and third decades of the twenty-first century as the Baby Boom generation retires and begins selling off assets to fund retirement. This prediction will also be something of a test of the older proposition about the importance of intergenerational transfers as a source of wealth relative to retirement accumulations if wealthier Boomer generation parents don't consume their accumulated wealth but rather pass it on to their children. For a different view of this hypothesis, see Poterba (2004).

In addition to their main findings, GMQ also identifies what they call a "favored cohort" effect generated by the model. Specifically, smaller generations are strictly better off relative to larger ones. In the GMQ model, the favored cohort effect occurs because of competition between agents in a large generation for retirement assets. The collective bidding up of asset prices, coupled with increases in the real rate of interest to preclude arbitrage between the bond and equity markets, leads to reduced consumption and lower lifetime expected utility. Since the GMQ model does not include production, there is no wage channel for welfare improvements based on the number of workers in the labor market, but even in this setting, we would expect that increased competition for jobs would lead wages to move adversely against the larger generation.

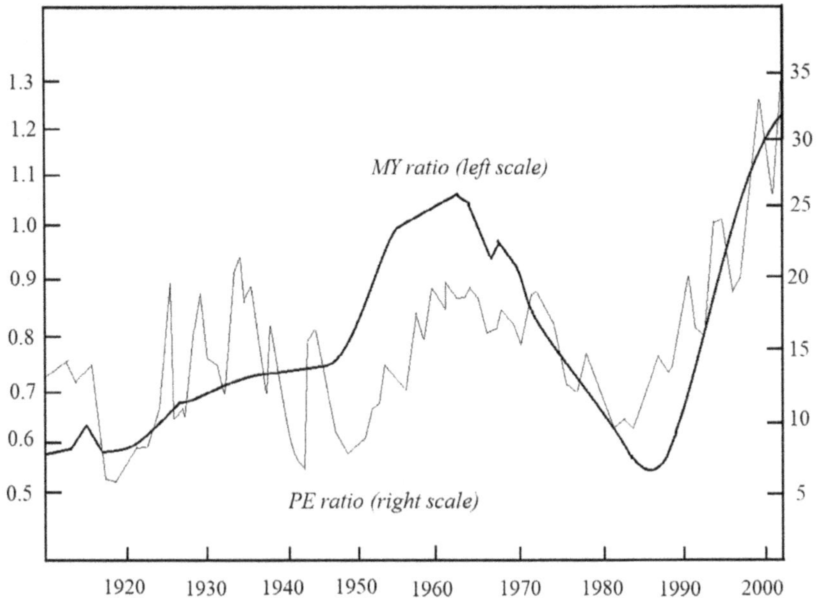

Fig. 23. MY Ratio and Stock Price Correlation. *Source*: Adapted from Geanakoplos et al. (2004).

8.4 SEARCH

As we noted in Chapter 5, the fact that the OLG model embodied a natural motive for retirement saving which could give otherwise intrinsically useless asset (fiat money) value didn't resolve the debate over whether the store of value function alone was a sufficient reason for the existence of money, or whether monetary theory would also need to include a medium of exchange role for money as well. The answer to this question came with the development of search models of money, the pioneering work in this area being Kiyotaki and Wright (1989). The Kiyotaki and Wright (KW) paper develops a simple model based on having heterogeneous infinite-lived agents who produce goods they do not wish to consume. The infinite-lived agents assumption here does not involve the controversial interpretation of family structures, as it does in the conventional macroeconomic setting. Rather, it is a mathematical simplification for modeling sequences of frequent trading interactions without having to deal with the usual "hot potato" problem generated by a finite horizon. It shares this structure with repeated games and agency relationships.

In the KW model, agents meet randomly with other agents and can, depending on whom they meet, trade for a good they will consume, trade for a good they will store in hopes of trading for something better later, or not trade. Storing goods is costly, with different goods having different storage costs. Under the assumption that the goods are not divisible and that each agent can only produce one unit of their production good, consume one unit of their consumption good, and store at most one unit of any good, the main result of the paper is a demonstration that commodity money equilibria arise quite naturally as a Nash equilibrium to the trading game in the model. The intuition behind the result is simple: using the cheapest-to-store commodity as a medium of exchange cuts through the double-coincidence-of-wants inefficiency of barter. Kiyotake and Wright then introduce durable fiat money, which has no value in either production or consumption, and is cheaper to store than commodities. The model with fiat money then has an equilibrium in which fiat money is not valued, and a second one in which it is valued and plays the role of medium of exchange. In their discussion of this result, KW state that:

> This "tenuousness" of fiat currency is shared by the overlapping generations model, although not by the cash-in-advance model, and we think that it is a property that a good theory of money ought to have. The value of any medium of exchange, and especially fiat money, ultimately depends at least partially on faith. (Kiyotake & Wright, 1989, p. 943)

This observation points back to the debate at the Minnesota Fed conference of 1980, and forward to the ongoing development of more general and more realistic search-based models of money. Lagos and Wright (2005) extended the basic idea from Kiyotaki–Wright to a general framework for monetary policy analysis by introducing a dual market structure in which agents could trade specialized goods (as in Kiyotaki–Wright) on a decentralized search market, and standard (Walrasian) goods on a centralized market using money.

While a complete discussion of the evolution of the literature on search and money is beyond the scope of this project, we do want to comment briefly on recent work explicitly integrating search theoretic and OLG models of money. Before turning to this, though, we need to highlight the Corbae, Temzelides, and Wright (2003) paper (CTW henceforth) on matching markets, per a comment to us from Wright (personal communication, November 4, 2022):

> I have been pushing recently the line that simple search models and OLG models are both special cases of the general idea of a matching model. There is a set of agents and the agents interact over time in various ways. In Kiyotaki-Wright, e.g., each agent interacts each period (or at least in some periods) with a random draw from the population. In a standard simple OLG environment, let's say with one agent per generation for the sake of illustration, agent t interacts with agent t-1 at date t, and interacts with agent t+1 at date t+1, and that's it, although of course we can specify more than 2 period lived agents and make things more complicated. How the agents interact – bilaterally, in a large (Walrasian) market, etc. – is kind of a detail, which of course matters, but what is key is when and with whom they interact.

In the CTW model, agents have preferences over whom they are matched with, as in the famous Gale and Shapley (1962) matching paper, but the incentive to match depends on the economic state of the model: who wishes to produce, who to consume, and how to account for the trades that take place. The OLG aspect of this is clear once we recognize that saving for retirement creates resource slacks that in any efficient allocation must be used, which creates a need for the economy to match individuals who don't want to consume now (but do want to produce) with others who wish to consume but are not currently producing. This, of course, is just the intergenerational transfer process we associate with trade-in

OLG models. What the matching models show us is how closely tied the financial side of the economy is to this fundamental process.

On the subject of OLG and search, the first paper to formally integrate search and OLG was by Zhu (2008), which combined the standard two-period lived OLG model with the Lagos–Wright centralized and decentralized markets. Young agents in the model trade in two steps. In the first, they produce general goods and trade these with the co-existing old agents in exchange for money on the centralized Walrasian market. In the second step, they are randomly paired either as buyers or sellers with other young agents and can either produce or consume, depending on the matching, using money to facilitate these transactions. The surplus from these pairwise meetings is divided according to the Nash bargaining process. Since the pairing process is random, this introduces risk (as in Lagos–Wright), so that if old agents are risk-averse, changes in the money supply can induce real effects by altering the distribution of wealth. Zhu shows, for example, that if buyers in the matching markets have a large bargaining weight in the decentralized market, the optimal rate of inflation will be positive.

More recently, Altermatt (2019) integrated OLG and Lagos–Wright in a model with active fiscal policy – government spending financed by taxes and government debt – as well as assets with random payoffs in the aggregate, and showed (among other things) that there are significant general equilibrium effects in the determination of equilibrium portfolio holdings among money, assets, and bonds, which effectively tie together the real and financial sides of the economy in the model. Altermatt, in private communication with us, noted that (email November 7, 2022)

> [T]he OLG framework is particularly good at capturing the store of value role of money, while search is better at capturing the means of payment role of money. Thus, combining both allows to capture both roles of money, which is great in particular once one starts thinking about a world with multiple assets: Some might compete with money more as a means of payment, while others are inferior means of payments but better stores of value – and that may depend on policy, i.e., at the zero-lower bound, bonds and money serve equally well as a store of value.

Altermatt's model does include an infinite-lived agent (or a continuum of them under the perfect competition assumption), which formally makes the model a hybrid. In this model, though, the infinite-lived agent is not interpreted as a dynastic family, but rather as a firm, that is, an ongoing institution organized around production activities, managed by finite-lived individuals when they are young. The firm is useful in the model as it can profit from the purchase of bonds whenever bond prices get too low. The infinite-lived agent is also useful since it guarantees that real interest rates in the model will be non-negative.

8.5 COMPUTATION

The ability to simulate large-scale SOLG models has grown alongside the computing power needed to solve these models and with the development of algorithms for limiting the well-known problems that arise from the curse of dimensionality in all but the simplest simulations. The use of computers in economics goes back at least to the 1930s and attempts by Wassily Leontief to solve large systems of simultaneous equations, with a major boost from the work of John von Neumann in his forays into modeling economic growth and the development of game theory coupled with his role in the development of modern computing. (See Backhouse and Cherrier, 2017, for a detailed history of the use of computers in economics.)

For OLG models, one of the earliest methods for solving for the deterministic steady-state was introduced by Auerbach and Kotlikoff (1987) where they laid out the computational methods they used in their large-scale OLG simulation models. The solution techniques here involved solving for steady-state equilibria of the models under different policy regimes, and then computing the transition paths between the old and new regimes. Auerbach and Kotlikoff solve their model for the initial and (when possible) final steady-state equilibria using what they characterize as a Gauss–Seidel method. The approach involves guessing some plausible initial values for the aggregate variables – output, capital, labor supply, and any policy aggregates – and then using these to compute the individual household and firm decision variables generated by the assumed aggregates in the model. From these, new aggregates are obtained by adding up the results of the household and firm decisions, and these new aggregates are adopted as updated guesses for an iteration of the procedure. Auerbach–Kotlikoff says the procedure generally converges to the steady-state in 10–15 iterations. The same procedure can be used to compute the transition path between two steady-state equilibria, though the computation itself is more complicated and time-consuming.

Computation has also been an important analytic component for ILA models, going back to the work of Kydland and Prescott (1982) on real business cycle models. As these models have become more complex – with the introduction of imperfect competition in New Keynesian models, or the imposition of frictions like market incompleteness in Aiyagari–Bewley–Huggett models – computing power has also been a constraint. But unlike the work in SOLG models, the underlying computational algorithms for simulating ILA models haven't changed much since the pioneering work of Kydland and Prescott.

For ILA models, the recursive formulation we outlined in Chapter 4 is the key to solving models amenable to this specification. The fact that the recursive functional operator leading to the Bellman equation generates a contraction mapping is all one really needs to implement computational solutions for these models. Recall that the Banach contraction mapping theorem states that if an operator is a contraction, it has a unique fixed point, and this fixed point can be obtained by picking any starting value, and then applying the operator iteratively until it converges to the fixed point. In practice, since the contraction operator is typically applied to a function, the iterative result implies pointwise uniform convergence to the fixed point. For computational purposes, then, one only needs to discretize the underlying state space, pick an arbitrary starting value for the value function, and then iterate the operator on each point of the state space. For complicated applications, this procedure can be slow or computationally expensive, particularly for stochastic models. For these cases, various techniques have been developed to allow one to limit grid points to those most important for the computation. We can illustrate this with an example from Mitra, Montrucchio, and

Privileggi (2003), who show that for the standard log-linear/Cobb–Douglas stochastic one-sector growth model the support for the ergodic distribution for the model's equilibrium is a Cantor-like subset of the state space. Since Cantor-like sets are sparse, knowing that the equilibrium ergodic set has this property would allow one to restrict the grid in the state space for this model to an approximate guess about the likely realizations, and then dynamically adjust the grid as the model iterates toward a solution.

Coleman (1989) introduced a procedure known as policy function iteration which generalizes the value function approach and is applicable to models in which outcomes may not be Pareto optimal (such as in Aiyagari–Bewley–Huggett models). Both the value function and policy function iteration approaches take important advantage of the fact that the operator updating initial solution guesses is monotone, and in many of the early simple stochastic ILA models, this property was satisfied. For models with multiple sectors, heterogeneous agents, and real or financial frictions, though, a different approach was needed.

Working at roughly the same time as Coleman, Marcet (1988) introduced a distinctly different approach to computing stochastic general equilibrium models based on what he called the "parameterized expectations" approach (PEA). In this approach, one uses functional approximations of agents' forecasts of future endogenous variables (expectations) and then either mathematically or numerically computes the temporary equilibrium corresponding to the given forecast function. The temporary equilibrium as a function of the state variables is then used to update the forecast function, generally by using projection methods to approximate the temporary equilibrium using the same functional form as the initial forecast. Iterating this procedure to convergence then yields the rational expectations equilibrium.

The parametrized expectations approach was more suited to applications involving SOLG models because it didn't require that the first-order conditions or equilibrium conditions for the underlying model be a contraction. The approach was also logically grounded in the Stone–Weierstrass theorem's results on the density of various computable functions in the space of all continuous functions. However, as noted in Marcet and Den Haan (1990), the projection methods used to update forecasts were not guaranteed to converge, though, in applications, the process always did. Direct application of PEA has been supplanted over time by combining it with Coleman's policy function iteration approach, since the relevant policy and implied forecast functions are the same at the fixed point of the temporary equilibrium operators (i.e., at the rational expectations equilibrium).

An answer to the question of whether (and why, in most applications) the PEA approach worked was given by Feng et al. (2014) where the approach was extended to allow for correspondences (when there are multiple temporary equilibria), which then required adding continuation utility values as state variables. The authors then show that the resulting temporary equilibrium operator is monotone and contracting, making the Banach theorem applicable. Because Feng et al.'s procedure uses a generalization of the Duffie et al. approach, it also recursively generates the self-justifying sets (in Duffie et al.'s terminology), with the implication that if one discretizes the state space by using the temporary equilibrium values of endogenous variables generated by the exogenous and predetermined variables, this discretization will converge under iteration to the support of the equilibrium ergodic measure.

We note that there have also been fruitful applications of old techniques with new ones. Brumm and Kubler (2013), for example, adapt the Negishi approach used by Kehoe and Levine (1985) to provide an alternative way of finding the recursive equilibrium in SOLG models under assumptions on preferences and the structure of stochastic shocks that complement those typically used in simulations.

Contemporary work on computing economic models is embracing new discoveries in machine learning by leveraging the fact that neural networks are fundamentally functional learning machines. These can be used directly with the iterative techniques given by Feng et al. (2014) to let the neural network learn the rational expectations equilibria of a given model. The use of neural networks for this purpose in economics first appeared in Kelly and Shorish (2000) based on work they did in the mid-1990s on learning rational expectations equilibrium in two-period SOLG models. Other early contributors to the use of machine learning techniques in economics were Marimon, McGratten, and Sargent (1990) who used classifier systems to model the decision behavior of boundedly rational agents in simulations of a Kiyotaki–Wright model of money. Holland and Miller (1991) introduced genetic algorithms as a mode of boundedly rational adaptation in agent-based models, effectively launching a new field of study in economics, though this is somewhat far afield from our current focus on OLG models.

Given the overall focus of this book, our discussion of computation has necessarily been short and incomplete, so we refer the reader interested in learning more about this topic and the many additional contributions beyond what we have included here to consult Judd (1998) or Backhouse and Cherrier (2017) for details.

NOTES

1. Fast forwarding to the present, this would include Olivier Blanchard's 2019 Presidential address to the American Economics Association, published as Blanchard (2019).
2. Spear (1985) calls these equilibria strongly stationary and shows in the Appendix of the paper that the arguments used to establish non-existence for the i.i.d. shock case can be extended to apply to finitely-many lags of the shocks.
3. The fact that it could be difficult to draw sharp distinctions between sunspot and non-sunspot equilibria was also made in Spear, Srivastava, and Woodford (1990), though the paper doesn't elaborate on this.
4. This work was the basis for Diamond and Dybvig receiving the 2022 Nobel Prize in Economics.

CHAPTER 9

THE ASCENDANCE OF ILA AND THE FUTURE OF MACRO

9.1 WHY ILA?

Having now looked back at the development and applications of OLG models from their first appearance in the work of Allais and Samuelson through the recent past, we can now return to the question we initially raised in the Introduction: why isn't OLG the central workhorse model for modern macroeconomics?

We heard from a number of the protagonists in this story regarding their views as to why ILA became dominant. One reason cited was simply first-mover advantages: Ramsey's model was seen as the correct one for thinking about economic growth, and thus, much work in the early post-World War II era went into refining it, via the Solow–Meade–Swan neoclassical approach, and optimal growth approach of Koopmans–Malinvaud–Cass, as against the Keynesian-based Harrodian growth model (on this, see Young, 1989 and Spear & Young, 2014). OLG models were still not well understood when Kydland and Prescott introduced rational expectations based RBC models into macro, and *inertia* kept the basic RCK framework in place even as RBC models were abandoned – because they couldn't explain the data – in favor of the new neoclassical synthesis approach. Karl Shell put it this way (private email dated September 5, 2022):

> DSGE launched a generation of macro Ph.D.'s. There was room for some deep innovation, but there was also plenty of room for amending the basic DSGE to study the latest "puzzle" or the latest policy issue. Even the computer programs were ready to be used, originally written in Fortran. There is Thomas Kuhn history of science involved here. Young scholars and other scholars find safety in normal science. DSGE became normal science in macro.
>
> How do we define "macroeconomics"? The denotation definition is "economics based on the large macro variables defined in the national income accounts." The connotation includes much more including banking and finance. In this broader view, beliefs about beliefs of others play a very important role. Keynes, the Rheingold girl, animal spirits, bank runs, etc. In this way, macro

Overlapping Generations: Methods, Models and Morphology
International Symposia in Economic Theory and Econometrics, Volume 32, 183–198

Published under exclusive licence by Emerald Publishing Limited
ISSN: 1571-0386/doi:10.1108/S1571-038620230000032021

> is like game theory. Mostly DSGE has missed this. The typical DSGE exercise is to solve a representative agent optimization problem and take the dual prices as equilibrium prices, which they are for the single-agent economy. There are no bank runs in this economy; why would the single agent run on his own bank? There are exceptions: Roger Farmer, Jess Benhabib, and others have analyzed the role of interdependent beliefs within the superstructure of DSGE.

Shell hits on an important point here. The vicissitudes of getting promoted and tenured forced many junior scholars interested in OLG models to work in other, more promotable, areas. The difficulties associated with general OLG models likely also persuaded more senior OLG protagonists to pursue other interests.

We have noted previously that even OLG's English-language inventor, Paul Samuelson, did very little further with his own model for the remainder of his career. Manny Yaari's work with Cass on OLG models was all he wrote on the subject, with other topics in growth and general equilibrium theory occupying him for the rest of his career. Dave Cass moved away from OLG to do pioneering work on models of incomplete markets, most of which were based on simple models with only two periods. As we also noted earlier, Karl Shell and his student Jim Peck moved away from OLG toward game theory, initially as follow-up to the conjectures of the Philadelphia Pholk theorem involving imperfect competition, but later in exploring bank runs and other sunspot-like phenomena in a variety of different models. Jim Peck is now a highly respected applied game theorist. Jean Michel Grandmont embraced versions of the ILA model that admitted complex dynamics in his co-edited special issue of *JET*. Neil Wallace stopped pushing OLG as the definitive model of money in favor of search theoretic approaches, and while some of his later work continued to use the OLG model, much of it did not. Many of the search theoretic tools that Wallace used were developed by Peter Diamond and his collaborators. And finally, as we noted earlier, Bob Lucas never worked with OLG models after his initial foray with the Lucas (1972) paper. Alan Auerbach continued working with his coauthor, Larry Kotlikoff, on projects based around their numerical simulation model, but he also branched out with projects based on the stochastic RCK model, and with empirical macroeconometric analysis.

In the boomer generation, Tim Kehoe and David Levine continue to do some work using OLG models, but both have branched out to include work in more standard ILA-based DSGE models, game theory, and industrial organization. Rao Aiyagari turned away from OLG models to work with versions of the RCK model having incomplete markets. Spear and Srivastava are best known professionally for their work developing recursive techniques for analyzing infinitely repeated principal-agent problems. This research – together with that of Ed Green (see, e.g., Green, 1987) – became the basis for a large literature on dynamic public finance, virtually all of it based on the canonical ILA-based DSGE model. Mike Woodford wrote a well-known book, *Interest and Prices*, based on the combination of conventional ILA dynamics with monopolistically competitive intermediate goods and staggered wage/price adjustment. John Geanakoplos and Herakles Polemarchakis continued working in the general equilibrium paradigm, but moved away from OLG toward incomplete markets, game theory, and finance applications. Costas Azariadis continued working with models that could generate self-fulfilling prophecies, but followed Woodford in working with more conventional versions of the growth model or new Keynesian variations on it. And, while Victor Rios-Rull never abandoned the use of the modeling approach he pioneered, he too wrote a number of papers based on the dominant ILA paradigm as well as a number of important empirical papers.

Among all the main contributors to the history of OLG, only Larry Kotlikoff continued what we would characterize as a steady pursuit of results based on OLG economies. This included the ongoing work he did with coauthor Alan Auerback using their AK simulation model, but it also included new pioneering work with Jasmina Hasanhodzic using Rios-Rull's stochastic extension to study issues around the US Social Security system in a realistic SOLG setting. In light of Kotlikoff's dedication to OLG, it seems fitting that we quote him on the continuing problems he finds with the convention ILA paradigm (private email dated August 31, 2022):

> The ILA model has become the workhorse of macroeconomists despite its ludicrous assumptions and preposterous predictions - all of which are decisively rejected by the data. The explanation? Computational ease and analytical elegance. The result? Modern macroeconomics comprises beautiful models that are largely divorced from reality.

To put this in context, Kotlikoff is not referring here to the conventional DSGE model's ability to match moments or forecast financial crises or recessions. The data he refers to are the many theoretical and empirical studies of interfamily altruism and savings motives. As we've discussed previously, realistic models of family structure and non-paternalistic altruism yield too much neutrality. Empirical studies of interfamily gifts and bequests strongly reject the predictions of non-paternalistic altruism in dynastic families, and indicate instead that (as first noted by Arrow & Kurz, 1969) family altruism takes the form of investment in children's human capital or direct unrestricted gifts. Other studies, stimulated by Kotlikoff and Summers (1981) work on sources of wealth have shown that most households save for retirement and for precautionary purposes based on idiosyncratic health/mortality or income risk.

In light of this evidence against the assumption that the families that matter in a modern industrial economy are all organized as lineal dynasties, the only remaining plausible interpretation of the representative agent model is its original one: the optimizing agent is a central planner. And, in light of this, the only remaining option for any realistic model of how actual households in real economies interact is the overlapping generations model.

We share Kotlikoff's view on this and will detail why we share these views below. But before we undertake this analysis, we should point out that there have been other recent criticisms of the directions taken by contemporary macroeconomics, most notably those of Paul Romer in his 2015 American Economic Association panel discussion critique. In the discussion, Romer referred to the "mathiness"[1] of contemporary macro, meaning the use of sophisticated mathematics that contributed very little to the actual scientific understanding of the workings of the macroeconomy. In his working paper extension of this critique, Romer (2016) zeroes in first on the source of aggregate shocks in conventional

RBC models, calling these "phlogiston" and then on extensions of these shocks ("forcing variables").

While Romer doesn't mention OLG in this paper, the critique is clearly focused on the problems inherent in conventional RCK-based macro DSGE models. In an entry Romer (2015) on his blog entitled "What Went Wrong in Macro – Historical Details" Romer blames political differences between Keynesian macroeconomists – he singles out Robert Solow at MIT – and the new generation of macro theorists focused on rational expectations and microfoundations, based specifically on the policy questions of whether government intervention for business cycle stabilization was justified. Referring to the economists in the RE/microfoundations group as "the rebels," Romer states that because of the policy differences,

> [R]eal business cycle models, which were introduced by Prescott and Kydland in 1979, attracted support among the rebels, even though these models did an even worse job of matching the empirical evidence than the model that Lucas first proposed.
>
> In particular, they assumed away the possibility that monetary policy and inflation could have any interaction with output and employment. In a telling shift, the rebels also decided that econometrics was getting in the way. Word came down from the top that they were abandoning the cutting edge econometric work that Sargent had specialized in and using calibration in its place. (Romer, 2015)

Romer goes on to contend that there was a "window of opportunity" in 1978 when the policy/political disagreements could have been put aside in the interests of what Romer called "Feynman integrity" – a clear dedication to science – versus "Stigler conviction" – the belief in the correctness of one's own views, saying

> What's sad is that the rebels could simply have declared victory. They had won the battle for mindshare among the next generation of macroeconomists. They could have taken credit for killing off the large multi-equation models that had previously dominated macro policy analysis.
>
> From the MIT side, Lucas could have been embraced as a leading contributor to the larger intellectual program launched by Paul Samuelson, the founder of the department there. As Lucas solidified his position as the new intellectual leader at Chicago, he and Samuelson could then have healed the divide that had separated MIT and Chicago for decades. This divide had its roots in Stigler's political agenda, but it played out in economics at the more damaging methodological level of Samuelson versus Marshall. At least for the young Robert Lucas, it was clear which side to root for in this fight. (Romer, 2015)

The remainder of the blog post goes on to lay out a vision of how macro might have developed based on extending Lucas' pioneering 1972 work on stochastic OLG models, combined with Dixit and Stiglitz's (1977) model of monopolistic competition, which Romer had used so effectively in his endogenous growth models.

While we are sympathetic to this view, we don't believe it could ever have taken place given Paul Samuelson's attitude toward the microfoundations approach. As we have documented earlier, Samuelson held steadfast beliefs that macroeconomics should be based on observable relationships between aggregate variables, on the pressure the gas in a balloon exerts to keep it inflated, not on the trajectories of individual molecules inside. As Romer also notes in his working paper (and as we have noted earlier), Lucas himself abandoned his own pioneering model in favor of real business cycle models, endorsing the Kydland–Prescott approach in his 2003 Presidential address to the American Economic Association. Based on this, it seems highly unlikely that there could have been any reconciliation between what we now call the saltwater and freshwater approaches to macroeconomics.

The perspective outlined by Kotlikoff, that "computational ease and analytical elegance" were the main drivers of which macro models caught on, seem to us a more likely explanation of what went wrong with macro. We have referred several times to the seductive appeal of recursive dynamic programming which is at the heart of conventional DSGE macro models, so it is worth looking at how these techniques found their way into economics to begin with.

As we noted in our earlier discussion of the discounted dynamic programming framework, the mathematical techniques underpinning this were developed in the 1950s and 1960s by Richard Bellman and his student David Blackwell. The first applications of the forward DP algorithm in economics appear in Arrow (1957) and then in Radner (1967) and Radner (1973) in a stochastic context. The techniques were also introduced into Operations Research by Shapiro and Wagner (1967). As our examination of Lucas' introduction to the contraction mapping theorem showed, his discovery of Bellman's work was independent of either Arrow's or Radner's use of the technique. Lucas did, however, become aware of the discounted dynamic programming framework based on Blackwell's work during his time at Carnegie Mellon, since a typed set of lecture notes on the forward DP circulated among students at Carnegie Mellon and Chicago in the late 1970s and early 1980s. These lecture notes became the basis for the well-known text *Recursive Methods in Economics Dynamics* (referenced earlier) published in 1989. From an email from Nancy Stokey (dated May 20, 2022), she advised us that

> Indeed there was a set of notes that Bob wrote at GSIA, and they were the starting point for *Recursive Methods*. Chapter 2, much of the material in Chapter 3 and parts of Chapter 4 are direct descendants of those notes. There was also a treatment of systems with stochastic shocks, which (more loosely) was the starting point for Chapter 7.

The introduction and widespread use of this text cemented the dynamic programming technology into macroeconomic analysis, leading Sargent and Ljungqvist (2018) to title the first section of their book "Imperialism of Recursive Methods." Curiously, Stokey and Lucas do not cite Radner's 1967 or 1973 papers in their book, though they do cite Majumdar and Radner (1983) which references both of Radner's earlier papers.

The forward dynamic programming algorithm had a major impact on areas of economics other than macro. In applied micro, it gave researchers a tool with which to model partial equilibrium interactions over individual lifetimes, by using the fact that when modeling periods are short and agents discount the future, the difference between a finite horizon and an infinite one is very small. Similarly, in industrial organization, the repeated game results of Abreu, Pearce, and Stacchetti (1986) allowed researchers to work in well-defined dynamic partial equilibrium settings. In macro, recursion came in through two channels. One was the replacement of the Hamiltonian dynamic systems approach championed by Cass and Shell (and the need for transversality conditions) with Bellman's recursive optimization approach. As we've noted earlier, the Banach contraction mapping theorem made working with Bellman's functional equation easier (particularly for computational applications) than working directly with the state and costate variables in the Hamiltonian approach. The second channel was via the dynamic public finance applications that grew out of the work of Green, and Spear and Srivastava. Since the repeated agency results examined in these papers were based on a pair of infinitely lived agents, it was natural for macro applications of these results to be embedded in the conventional RCK framework, with the principal being the government and the agent being the private sector. But, at the end of the day, it was the ease with which the recursive methods could be applied that made working with models amenable to the forward dynamic programming approach so popular. Perhaps the most telling indicator of how popular the approach has become (and reflecting Shell's notion of the safety of normal science) was the development and publication of the Dynare software platform ("macroeconomic modeling for all") in 1996 by a group of computational economists affiliated with CEPREMAP. This software package allows macroeconomic practitioners to implement the various recursive computational techniques for simulating large-scale SILA models without having to write their own code. The platform will also solve some OLG problems, but these are limited to deterministic settings. To date, economists wanting to work with SOLG models must write their own code.

A second issue that separated OLG and ILA approaches to macro was one we've touched on repeatedly in the book: that of the correct specification of the state variables for macroeconomic models. Ljungqvist and Sargent, in the preface to their book, comment fairly extensively on the issue of the appropriate choice of state variables in macroeconomic applications, saying

> This book reflects progress economists have made in refining the notion of state so that more and more problems can be formulated recursively. The art in applying recursive methods is to find a convenient definition of the state. It is often not obvious what the state is, or even whether a finite-dimensional state exists (e.g., maybe the entire infinite history of the system is needed to characterize its current position). Extending the range of problems susceptible to recursive methods has been one of the major accomplishments of macroeconomic theory. (Ljungqvist & Sargent, 2018, p. xxxiv)

While it isn't clear that "convenience" should be an important characteristic in specifying the state variables for an economic model – the possibility that the underlying structure of the real world might determine this choice also suggests itself – it does seem to have been one of the guiding criteria in the development of macroeconomic models. As Ljungqvist and Sargent also note, it is possible for models to be history dependent – we've already seen how Woodford (1988) used the infinite history of shocks in a general SOLG model to demonstrate the existence of equilibrium – in most applications, there are relatively simple sufficient statistics for summarizing this history dependence. In the canonical deterministic RCK model, for example, iterating the policy function backward traces out the economy's dependence on the historical sequence of capital accumulations that lead to the current state of production. In Lucas (1972), the received convention of the two-period lived OLG model made it possible for Lucas to intuit that the exogenous shocks alone (given their i.i.d. specification) would be sufficient. In the early stochastic representative agent RBC models examined by Brock and Mirman, the aggregate capital stock is a sufficient statistic for the history of exogenous productivity shocks, since it together with the labor supply response of the representative agent completely determines the possible economic outcomes going forward. Hence, in these models, the capital stock and current exogenous shocks are the natural state variables. As one discovers on further reading in Ljungqvist and Sargent, various researchers have found clever ways of augmenting the states in more complex models to make seeming non-recursivities go away.

As we have seen, OLG models defy simple or convenient classification of the appropriate state variables, at least once one moves beyond the simplest specification of two-period lives. Even in these simple versions of the model, though, the development of the sunspot literature makes clear that intuitive choices for state variables may not encompass the full range of possibilities. Even the logical approach of McCallum's minimal state variable criterion breaks down when the model is history-dependent and requires the full infinite sequence of shocks to be understood. The discovery that general OLG models – two-period models with multiple goods in Spear's thesis result, or multi-period models with a single good in Aiyagari's lost working paper – were generically history-dependent made the question of appropriate state variables even more critical for general SOLG models. Following on from Woodford's 1988 results on using infinite histories of shocks as the state, the Spear and Srivastava, and Duffie et al.'s papers started the hunt for sufficient statistics for summarizing the history of shocks to provide a recursive Markovian mechanism for solving and simulating these models. As we have documented, this search culminated with the work of Citanna and Siconolfi on the generic applicability of Rios-Rull's intuition that the wealth distribution would be sufficient for summarizing the history of shocks.

Rios-Rull's simulation work showed that while the recursions based on carrying along the wealth distribution as a state variable were doable, they were also quite difficult. In general situations, the wealth distribution could itself be an infinite-dimensional object, and obviously, swapping one infinite-dimensional state variable for another was less than satisfactory. Krusell and Smith (1998) used the equivalence of probability distributions and their characteristic functions to use the first few moments of the wealth distribution as proxies for the full distribution, and in the stochastic growth model application of their paper, this approximation worked quite well. As we've seen, though, in SOLG applications such as Storesletten, Telmer, and Yaron (2007), the technique did not work.

There has been some progress in making SOLG simulations workable, however. The practice of working with a representative agent per generation can simplify the analysis somewhat, since each generation's asset holdings are the same. The fact that there is still heterogeneity across agents in different generations remains a complication, and as a result, to date, most of the simulation work limits the number of assets to one or two (typically, a bond or money plus an equity asset). One can speculate that to the extent the two-fund theorem associated with the standard capital asset pricing model holds, consideration of two assets might be sufficient. This possibility has been studied in static general equilibrium settings with incomplete markets by Geanakoplos and Shubik (1990), with some follow-on work done in the context of two-period lived OLG models, but none that we could find on more general SOLG models. But, even if this proves to be the case, the complexity of working with these simulations has been daunting enough that several academic generations of macroeconomists have either turned away from OLG in favor of ILA or worked in what amount to deterministic OLG settings by studying things like mortality or individual income risk which are plausibly idiosyncratic.

A third issue related both to the question of defining states and finding workable recursive formulations for solving a model is that of heterogeneity. In the SOLG setting, it is the heterogeneity of agents of different ages – the differences in their incomes, wealth and possibly preferences – that leads to the portfolio rebalancing activities and consequent external income effects in the model that force inclusion of the wealth distribution in the description of the state. The absence of heterogeneity in representative SILA models moots any need for tracking wealth, though, as Duffie et al. showed, when one introduces heterogeneity in these models, the need for augmenting the state space with lagged endogenous state variables also arises.

It is a great irony, though, that even as macroeconomics turned away from SOLG models in the 1990s and early 2000s, the limitations of the representative agent framework – in particular, the fact that in the absence of frictions the competitive equilibrium is always Pareto optimal, together with the lack of any role for money in the model – led cutting edge macro people to start looking at models with frictions that generated heterogeneities among agents or types of agents in the model. As we noted above, most of these models assumed that shocks were idiosyncratic rather than aggregate, but the results derived from this work were fruitful enough to motivate follow-on work that included aggregate shocks. While the Krusell–Smith approach did work fairly well in models where the heterogeneities were idiosyncratic, the need for computational methods for handling more general heterogeneities spawned a new literature on new techniques (see Hommes & LeBaron, 2018, for references). The irony, of course, is that if SOLG had become the dominant workhorse for macro, all of this work would have been started two decades ago and tailored to applications involving actual human life cycles and not the fantasy life of the upper 1% of the wealth distribution.

We close this section with a fitting quote from Larry Summers' paper "The Scientific Illusion in Empirical Macroeconomics" (Summers, 1991) where he notes in the conclusion "It is all too easy to confuse what is tractable with what is right." This sentiment was echoed by Robert Solow in his paper "Samuelsonian Economics in Twenty-first Century" (Solow, 2006), where he states:

> The power of the idea was established clearly with Peter Diamond's "National Debt in a Neoclassical Growth Model" (1965). The basic model was equipped with a stock of real capital, and with a paper asset to serve as an alternative way of holding wealth. The OLG set-up became established as one of the workhorse models for macroeconomics. It provided, among other things, a way to escape the temptation induced by use of the Ramsey model to formulate any long-run equilibrium process in a way that guarantees nice properties without further thought. (p. 39)

9.2 WHITHER MACROECONOMICS?

In October 2016, the University of Oxford hosted a conference organized by David Vines and Samuel Wills around the theme of "rebuilding macroeconomic theory." They invited several prominent economists, several of them Nobel prize winners, to present their thoughts on this topic. Vines and Wills viewed the financial crisis of 2007–2008 and the resulting recession as an economic event akin to the Great Depression or the stagflation of the 1970s in terms of presenting major challenges to the reigning economic orthodoxy of the time. Their charge to the conference invitees was to suggest ways that the standard New Keynesian DSGE model could be improved in light of the events of a decade prior. Specifically, they asked the conference group to address the following questions (taken from the published conference proceedings, Vines & Wills, 2018):

(i) Is the benchmark DSGE model fit for the purpose?
(ii) What additions to this model are necessary to help us understand growth from now on?
(iii) What are the important intertemporal complications?
(iv) What are the important intra-temporal complications?
(v) Should the above questions be discussed with big or small models?
(vi) How should our models relate to data?

The papers presented at this conference were:

1. The rebuilding macroeconomic theory project: an analytical assessment, *David Vines and Samuel Wills*
2. On the future of macroeconomic models, *Olivier Blanchard*
3. Ending the microfoundations hegemony, *Simon Wren-Lewis*
4. Where modern macroeconomics went wrong, *Joseph E. Stiglitz*
5. On the future of macroeconomics: a new monetarist perspective, *Randall Wright*
6. Is something really wrong with macroeconomics? *Ricardo Reis*
7. Good enough for government work? Macroeconomics since the crisis, *Paul Krugman*
8. Stagnant productivity and low unemployment: stuck in a Keynesian equilibrium, *Wendy Carlin and David Soskice*
9. Macro needs micro, *Fabio Ghironi*
10. An interdisciplinary model for macroeconomics, *A. G. Haldane and A. E. Turrell*
11. The financial system and the natural real interest rate: toward a "new benchmark theory model," *David Vines and Samuel Wills*
12. DSGE models: still useful in policy analysis? *Jesper Lindé*
13. The future of macroeconomics: macro theory and models at the Bank of England, *David F. Hendry and John N. J. Muellbauer*
14. Modeling a complex world: improving macro-models, *Warwick J. McKibbin and Andrew Stoeckel*

While all of these papers are interesting and offer important insights into why the conventional NK-DSGE model hasn't lived up to expectations, and while several of the authors – Vines and Wills, Blanchard, Stiglitz, and Reis – mention OLG models as being more realistic as foundational models, none of the papers here discuss the fundamental differences between the ILA and OLG structures, particularly in the context of stochastic modeling, that breaks the observationally equivalence claim about the two models. Indeed, none of the papers in this two-issue conference proceedings volume even cites Rios-Rull (1996).

The best summary of the recommendations coming out of this conference are actually contained in footnote 2 of a later issue of the *Oxford Review of Economic Policy* (Vines & Wills, 2020) entitled "The rebuilding of macroeconomic theory project part II: multiple equilibria, toy models, and policy models in a new macroeconomic paradigm." The summary of the previous project results states:

> We recommended four main changes to what we called the "core model": to emphasize financial frictions, to place a limit on the operation of rational expectations, to include heterogeneous agents, and to devise more appropriate microfoundations. Achieving this would, we said, require changing all of the behavioural equations in the model governing consumption, investment, and price setting, and inserting a wedge between the interest rate set by policy-makers and that facing consumers and investors. (Vines & Wills, 2020, p. 428)

Vines and Wills open the second volume with the question "Why do it all again?" They start to answer the question by stating:

> Last time we were much more conservative (see Vines & Wills, 2018). We accepted the NK-DSGE modelling paradigm, and were optimistic about how it might be developed – providing a list of frictions to be added to the model. We even believed that a perfect Platonic form might exist: the *ideal* NK-DSGE model. (Vines & Wills, 2020, p. 428)

They then state:

> We have changed our mind, basically because of the GFC and the COVID pandemic. Joe Stiglitz sets out the argument at the beginning of his article with Martin Guzman in this issue. (Vines & Wills, 2020, p. 429)

The quote from Guzman and Stiglitz (2020) states that:

> The central problem of macroeconomics is to explain the large, deep, and often persistent downturns, accompanied by high levels of unemployment, that episodically afflict capitalist economies. Macroeconomic crises are extreme examples of economic fluctuations. But they are the most relevant. They are the events that teach the most about the stability properties of the economic system, in a way that small inventory cycles do not. And they are the events that matter the most for the lives of millions of people. (Guzman & Stiglitz, 2020, p. 429)

Vines and Wills conclude their argument for the change of mind with two key points, stating that:

> First, thinking about large downturns requires models with good outcomes and bad outcomes. This means models with multiple equilibria. It is not good enough to say that bad shocks cause bad outcomes; the risk of a lurch to a permanently bad outcome is always present, even with a temporary shock. Macroeconomic policy should be designed to guard against this risk. But the NK-DSGE modelling tradition does not do lurches. ((Vines & Wills, 2020, p. 429)

Second, to think about large downturns requires a detailed empirical analysis of what can go wrong, and why. ((Vines & Wills, 2020, p. 430)

They then conclude by saying that:

Because of these two inadequacies we no longer think that the NK-DSGE model can be thought of as a "core model". Blanchard (2018) helpfully classifies macro models into five groups: foundational, toy, core, policy, and forecasting. In the first issue in this series we described the NK-DSGE model as a core model (Vines & Wills, 2018).

According to Blanchard, a core model should provide "a generally accepted theoretical framework for the profession." However, the inadequacies described above mean that the NK-DSGE does not satisfy this test. (Vines & Wills, 2018, p. 430)

The papers included in this volume were:

1. Mapping types of macromodel to types of macro user
   Simon Wren-Lewis
2. Implications of household-level evidence for policy models: the case of macro-financial linkages
   John Muellbauer
3. Some important macro points
   Ray C. Fair
4. Climate change and monetary policy: issues for policy design and modeling
   Warwick J. McKibbin, Adele C. Morris, Peter J. Wilcoxen, and Augustus J. Panton
5. Why some places are left behind: urban adjustment to trade and policy shocks
   Anthony J. Venables
6. Toward a dynamic disequilibrium theory with randomness
   Martin Guzman and Joseph E. Stiglitz
7. The importance of beliefs in shaping macroeconomic outcomes
   Roger E. A. Farmer
8. Clinical macroeconomics and differential diagnosis
   Jeffrey D. Sachs

None of these papers, with the exceptions of Wren-Lewis and Guzman and Stiglitz, mentions OLG *in any context*. While most of Wren-Lewis's paper focuses on the way different empirical needs shape the demand for different types of models, he does consider OLG a foundational model. Guzman and Stiglitz, in footnote 2 of their paper make the point that the indeterminacy of equilibrium in OLG models and the possibility of sunspot equilibria might be important for macroeconomics, stating that:

Hirano and Stiglitz (2019) show that in a rational expectations model with overlapping generations, there can be an infinity of trajectories. The large literature on sunspots (Benhabib &

> Farmer, 1999; Cass & Shell, 1983) focused on multiplicity of macroeconomic equilibria. Similarly, in debt markets there may be a low interest rate equilibrium, associated with and justified by low default rates; and another equilibrium with high interest rates, marked by high default, see Calvo (1988) and Greenwald and Stiglitz (2003a). For a general equilibrium discussion focusing on defaults in financial contracts, see Roukny et al. (2018). (Guzman & Stiglitz, 2020, p. 653)

The most surprising omission of any mention of OLG in the volume is Farmer's, since much of the development of the ideas he presents in the volume about the importance of beliefs for macroeconomics was developed using the OLG framework. For example, in Farmer (2017), he states directly that

> The representative household assumption is convenient because the mathematics of a model, populated by a representative household, is relatively simple. A single household facing a decision problem will always choose a unique action. But a household interacting with other households, most of whom have not yet been born, is a very different matter. Even if the physical world were unchanging, we would still face uncertainty as to the ways that our descendants will behave in the future. A model, populated by overlapping generations of finitely lived people, always has multiple equilibria.
>
> I will repeat that statement because it is so important and so misunderstood. *A model, populated by overlapping generations of finitely lived people, always has multiple equilibria.* (Farmer, 2017, p. 4)

A Google Scholar search with Farmer as author for the phrases "belief function" and "overlapping generations" returns 13 papers written since 1996. When we asked Farmer why he hadn't discussed the role of OLG in his *OxREP* paper, he said (email dated, September 23, 2022)

> The OxRep paper focuses on steady state indeterminacy and I wanted to use a familiar vehicle, the neoclassical RBC model, to showcase differences in labor market structures that I had originally modeled in my 2010 [*Economic Journal*] piece. The main idea is to generate demand-driven comovements in consumption and employment in a full blown DSGE model with capital. The resulting model has a lot in common with the old-style Keynesian cross, including a continuum of steady states, but with intertemporal asset markets. The multiplicities and dynamic indeterminacies that arise in OLG models cannot explain the consumption-employment comovements we see in data.

In Farmer's *OxREP* paper, indeterminacy of equilibrium arises because markets for the allocation of labor inputs to firms are incomplete. This statement bears some further unpacking. In the conventional general equilibrium view, wages on markets for labor are the signal to firms about the value of hiring an additional worker, and for workers the value of offering an additional hour of labor. The key insight to come out of the conventional search theoretic Diamond–Mortensen–Pissarides (DMP) model is that there can be commodities for which formal, organized markets don't exist, due typically to informational frictions. In labor markets, formal markets are hampered by the need for firms and workers to collect information by which to evaluate the quality of potential employment matches. The informational frictions at work here for the firm arise from the fact that worker productivity can be hidden *ex ante* and hence, must be learned over time. On the worker's side, the working environment and support provided by the firm for enhancing productivity are also unknown *ex ante*. Overcoming these moral hazard and adverse selection problems requires effort, and this effort is captured in search models by assuming there is a matching technology that evaluates the quality of otherwise randomly occurring matches and determines the number of workers available to the firm. In conventional DMP models of the labor market, wages are then determined by a bargaining process – typically, the Nash bargaining solution – and that closes the model, since workers are still assumed to be motivated to search by the level of wages available.

Farmer (2006) developed a model of what he called "Keynesian search theory," following the lead of Howitt and McAfee (1987), in which the standard search process determined employment matches, but firms hiring decisions were driven by the need to meet demand. In Farmer's model, firms and workers do not bargain to determine the wage. Rather, wages were determined competitively, in the sense that once the firm has determined how much labor to use in production, workers are paid their marginal product. This can be justified based solely on profit maximization or cost minimization principles.[2] On the worker side, workers do not view the wage as a measure of the marginal value of their time, since they understand the problems associated with finding appropriate employment matches and allocate some fraction of their own or their family's time to job search.

These two key assumptions – that firms meet demand and workers don't respond to wage signals – lead to the indeterminacy of steady-state equilibria in Farmer's model. To close his model, Farmer adds a belief function by which workers form expectations about their wealth or purchasing power, and this determines demand. One of the most interesting features of this kind of model is that as long as beliefs are changing in some way – Farmer uses an adaptive formation subject to random shocks – an initial belief condition will then pin down a unique trajectory for the economy. Because of the indeterminacy in the model, these *ad hoc* beliefs are self-fulfilling (just as they are in the conventional indeterminacy-based sunspot equilibria) and hence the equilibrium constitutes a rational expectations equilibrium. But, because of the indeterminacy of the steady-state equilibrium, the model itself is silent on what happens to the economy if the shocks to beliefs are shut down.

As Farmer noted in his email to us, this kind of search friction can be developed in both ILA and OLG environments. Some very recent and preliminary work by Kim, Sood and Spear (2023) shows that the indeterminacy generated by Farmer's labor market incompleteness and Keynesian search microfoundation generate different results in the OLG model. Specifically, in general, multiperiod SOLG settings, product market clearing endogenously determines the wealth distribution (which, we recall, must be carried along as a state variable in any recursive equilibrium). This, in turn, means that agents' expectations can't be arbitrary, as they can in the ILA setting, if they are to be rational. Nevertheless, the indeterminacy of the steady state remains, and different specifications for stochastic processes of output will generate different sets of REE expectations consistent with the given output process. As with other indeterminacies, it becomes possible to introduce extrinsic randomization – sunspots or sentiment – into the model. What kinds of dynamic stochastic behavior are possible in this framework is a matter of further research.

Viewed through the lens of our OLG project, one can't help but notice the similarity between Farmer's belief functions and Grandmont's earlier expectations function approach to temporary equilibrium. Both Grandmont and Farmer view beliefs/expectations as primarily psychological constructs, akin to consumer preferences. While Farmer's model uses indeterminacy to generate self-fulfilling rational expectations equilibria, his work in Farmer (1991), (2002), and (2013) critiquing the Lucas critique and the natural rate of unemployment suggests that, like Grandmont, he has a skeptical view of the rational expectations hypothesis.

Farmer's approach and the fact that the Keynesian search model generates path-dependent equilibrium trajectories have been controversial. One of the earlier criticisms of the temporary equilibrium approach was that one could explain just about anything in a temporary equilibrium model by positing an expectations function tailored to deliver the result. Indeed, this weakness and the *ad hoc* nature of adaptive expectations in the Keynesian models of the 1960s were an important motivating force in the development of the rational expectations paradigm. The fact that one can make the same criticism about the choice of driving processes for models that exploit indeterminacy – and indeed it was Grandmont himself who raised this issue with Woodford's 1986 *JET* paper (as we've documented above) – suggests that there is important interdisciplinary work to be done in understanding how human forward-looking psychology works. Some of this work is currently being done by economic theorists looking at learning (see, e.g., Evans & Honkapohja, 2012) and in the development of new theories of social learning. At the same time, empirical evidence strongly suggests that macroeconomic time-series are not stationary in the way most macroeconomic models assume, once the model is detrended to account for economic growth. The literature on learning in non-stationary environments goes counter to the kinds of results found by Evans and Honkapohja and suggests that rational expectations may not be the right way to model forward-looking behavior.

From a purely technical perspective, rational expectations – and its deterministic precursor, perfect foresight – serve to close dynamic economic models and make the equilibria they generate self-contained. These assumptions also serve (as we noted above) to discipline what results come out of a model by injecting a conservative bias that makes obtaining arbitrary results difficult. This is one of the key reasons why the findings of indeterminacy in OLG models, and the possibility of sunspot equilibria was so surprising to the economics profession. This is probably a likely reason why even economists like Farmer continue to present results based on indeterminacy and the existence of multiple equilibria as rational expectations equilibria. Until there is a compelling psychological theory of expectations formation, abandoning the rational expectations hypothesis in economics will be difficult. Indeed, this is akin to the way that economists continue to use expected utility formulations in their models despite the empirical evidence against it; until we know better how human beings process uncertainty, we stick with the theory that can explain key economic responses to uncertainty like insurance and portfolio balance.

While there are other issues – such as how to bring path-dependent models to data, or whether the apparent statistical regularities in economic data can be generated by path dependence – that suggest we still don't fully understand macroeconomics, the indeterminacy school of macroeconomics that Farmer has pushed so consistently clearly deserves to be taken seriously (as evidenced by the Vines and Wills *OxREP* volume advocating for this approach). From our perspective, the overlapping generations model, with its realistic treatment of the human lifecycle, needs to be front and center in this effort.

As with any change in fundamental paradigms, the indeterminacy program won't implement itself. Per the quote at the start of this chapter from Karl Shell, representative agent ILA-based DSGE models are now received science in macroeconomics. The economics profession has trained generations of practitioners to work with this model. It has directed the collection of data to support the analysis of the received model – per Einstein's dictum that "it is the theory which decides what we can discover." There is a deep computational infrastructure – Dynare – dedicated to the model.

The one major element in favor of the push for a new macroeconomics based on indeterminacy and multiple equilibria is the body of work that has gone into the development of general equilibrium theory and the overlapping generations model. Indeed, from our perspective, if OLG becomes the dominant workhorse model for macro (as it should have many years ago), the indeterminacy/multiple equilibria program of Vines and Wills will follow naturally. Unfortunately, much of the basic knowledge needed to understand this approach isn't taught in graduate economics programs anymore. An informal survey of the content of core economics Ph.D. programs at top universities should convince the reader that general equilibrium theory either isn't taught or has been relegated to a couple of weeks of coverage as part of the core first-semester micro course. What used to be a semester of general equilibrium theory has been replaced by game theory and related content like contract theory and information economics. We don't view this displacement as a bad thing – indeed, modern game theoretic tools are critical (even in general equilibrium contexts) for understanding how mass production technologies generate large firms with significant market power, and for understanding how such large players interact.

When Dave Cass died in 2007, one of us (Spear) and Alex Citanna went through the papers in his office and at his home to try and preserve what we thought might be important for the historical record. One of the things we found was a set of hand-written notes from 1995 on "The future of general equilibrium," which Cass had apparently jotted down in response to his negative reaction to the focus of a conference in honor of Gerard Debreu earlier that year. Among other things, Cass noted that conventional general equilibrium theory was foundational for both macroeconomics and finance, and that the natural "allies" for people doing general equilibrium theory were likely to be found in these subdisciplines. Our takeaway from this observation is that because general equilibrium theory is foundational for macroeconomics, advanced versions of it should be taught in graduate programs as part of the macro sequence. Today, in most programs, it is not, and the reason for this is that understanding the conventional ILA-based DSGE model doesn't require much more (beyond basic general equilibrium theory) than an understanding of forward dynamic programming.

What current graduate students don't see anymore is detailed modeling of the way income effects generate multiple equilibria in conventional GE models, and the need for carrying along the wealth distribution as state variables in SOLG and heterogeneous agent SILA models.

This is changing, though, even in macro programs that are still focused on the conventional DSGE model, since the basic failures of the model are forcing even very conventional macroeconomists to consider models with heterogeneous agents, models with market incompleteness, and models of macro-finance with things like money and bonds and equity assets actively traded. As these models come to the fore – and as macro practitioners begin to realize that all of these possibilities are captured in the stochastic overlapping generations model – the need for teaching deeper general equilibrium theory as the foundation for macroeconomics and finance will become apparent. Looking beyond this, however, a full accounting for the operations of modern industrial (even post-industrial) macroeconomies will require modeling the oligopolies that populate the modern world, their interaction with government regulatory agencies, the political economy that dictates the environment in which these strategic rivals operate, and the financial lubricants that keep the whole system running.

For this work, we will need all of the tools of game theory, contact theory, and finance. And the modeling architecture in which this overarching theory is developed should be that of Samuelson's overlapping generations model.

NOTES

1. A play on Stephen Colbert's use of the word "truthiness" to refer to made-up facts.
2. We note that the wage could equally well be determined in a model of monopsony or other forms of imperfect competition such as the Shapley-Shubik market game.

CHAPTER 10

MORPHOLOGY OF OLG MODELS AND METHODS IN COMPARATIVE PERSPECTIVE

In the chapters above, we have presented a wide ranging and detailed account of the origins, evolution, development, and dissemination of the OLG approach in economics. We have also dealt with the ILA approach in this context. This chapter attempts to bring together the diverse elements in our story by applying a general and systematic analytical method, that is to say, morphological analysis. Morphology deals with *both* structure and form and assists in determining evolutionary relationships (Zwicky, 1969). The main focus of morphological analysis has been in the physical and biological sciences. In these disciplines, it is applied with reference to the analysis of the form of, and structural relationships between, various elements in what is being studied, and their formative processes. Prior to Zwicky's work, the morphological approach – as applied to social and managerial sciences – was not systematized, as in the physical and biological sciences. From the late 1940s onwards, Zwicky generalized the "morphological approach" – as applied to the social and managerial sciences – so as to deal with possible solutions to multidimensional non-quantifiable problems. As he wrote (Zwicky, 1969, p. 34):

> Attention has been called to the fact that the term morphology has long been used in many fields of science to designate research and structural interrelations – for instance in anatomy, geology, botany and biology … I have proposed to *generalize* and *systematize* the concept of morphological research and include not only the study of the shapes of geometrical, geological, biological, and generally material structures, but also to study the more abstract structural interrelations among phenomenon, concepts, and ideas, whatever the character might be. [our italics]

This is "General Morphological Analysis" (GMA) (Álvarez & Ritchey, 2015).

Overlapping Generations: Methods, Models and Morphology
International Symposia in Economic Theory and Econometrics, Volume 32, 199–207

ISSN: 1571-0386/doi:10.1108/S1571-038620230000032023

In economics, early morphological approaches were applied to the business cycle in its various forms, from the seventeenth century onwards. Indeed, Mercantilists, Physiocrats, Smith and the English Classical School, and others concerned with economic affairs mused over the nature of economic crises in terms of causes and characteristics. And, over the nineteenth and early twentieth centuries, individuals using the tools of political economy, and later economic science, developed various morphological frameworks describing "credit," "trade," "industrial," and "business" cycles, respectively, analyzing their length, phases, and characteristics accordingly. Schumpeter (1939, pp. 169–183) noted the distinction between three classes of cycles short, medium, and long-term. He identified the short-term cycle proposed by Kitchin (3–5 years), as against the medium-term cycle (7–11 years) of Juglar, and the long-term cycle of Kondratieff (45–60 years). But he went even further, noticing that the distinction between these cycles – in terms of what we now call "impulse" and "propagation," was based mainly on economic factors and shocks. Regarding the Kitchin cycle, it was based on the inventory cycle; the Juglar cycle on fluctuations in fixed investment, while the Kondratieff cycle was the possible outcome of a number of factors, such as technological change, wars or revolutions, new countries being discovered, or fluctuations in gold production, the latter two mainly reflecting cycles from the seventeenth century onwards.

Moreover, besides Kitchin–Juglar–Kondratieff, there are a number of additional theories of cycles or "waves": infrastructure investments, Kuznets (1930); aggregate demand and aggregate investment fluctuations, Kaldor (1935) and Kalecki (1940); cyclical growth based on wage-share unemployment dynamics, Goodwin (1967); financial instability and propensity to boom-bust, Minsky (1964, 1986); and finally, that of Schumpeter (1934, 1939, 1942) himself, technological innovation and "creative destruction" processes.

The GMA approach provides us with a systematic way to analyze the structures and evolution of OLG as against ILA models. It provides us with the following tools: (i) tree diagrams; (ii) category grids; (iii) morphology boxes; and (iv) morphology fields (Zwicky, 1969, pp. 115–120).

Another phenomenon described in the book that can be analyzed further using morphology is that of *symbiosis and cross-fertilization* of ideas between various cohorts at the main institutions where work on OLG was going on. This is addressed by the use of a morphology tree as below. We can delineate three forms of cross-fertilization: generic ("in the air"), concurrent, and sequential. Cohort cross-fertilization would encompass faculty-faculty, faculty–student, and student–student cases. The main institutions involved, as noted in the book, are Stanford, Yale (Cowles), Penn, MIT, and Minnesota.

In the OLG morphology tree diagram below, we first identify four main branches of economic analysis which played dominant roles in shaping the OLG approach: General Equilibrium, Macroeconomics, Monetary Economics, and Dynamic Systems. These branches were extended – singularly or in combination – via the development of OLG approaches dealing with theoretical and applied issues. We can identify a group of *founding fathers* and three *successive cohorts* of economists who advanced the overlapping generations approach. These cohorts are identified via the geometric figures in which they appear: *founding fathers* (rectangular); *successive cohorts* (curved-sided rectangular, elliptical, and pentagonal, respectively). The contributions of these individuals are described in the book. We note that the connections in the diagram aren't meant to indicate direct influences (though in some cases they do), but rather the way the development and application of ideas about the OLG model played out in practice. Thus, for example, we link Auerbach, Kotlikoff, and Summers to Tobin because of Tobin's early pioneering work in using OLG models with long-lived agents for policy simulation experiments.

Among the founding fathers' group, Samuelson would have had a direct influence on his MIT colleagues like Diamond and Shell (prior to Shell's moving to Penn), as well as on the next generation of MIT students that we document in the tables below, including Blanchard, Burke, Muller, and Woodford. The influence of Stanford's faculty working on general equilibrium and growth – Arrow, Kurz, and Uzawa – clearly prepared the next generation of their students – Cass, Shell, and Yaari – for their later collaborations on the OLG model. In Spear and Young (2018), we documented the role that the University of Chicago, then home to the Cowles Foundation, played in bringing together faculty and graduate students with like-minded interests in macroeconomics and growth theory. Both Edmond Malinvaud and Tjalling Koopmans spent time at Cowles in the late 1950s and early 1960s. Hirofumi Uzawa also spent time there and organized several conferences that involved the younger generation of theorists, including Cass, Lucas, and Shell. Neil Wallace was a Ph.D. student at Chicago at the time and, as we've noted earlier, got interested in Lucas' 1972 paper in part because he and Lucas and been grad students together. Harvard and Yale also contributed to the mix of scholars who ended up working on OLG issues, including Jim Tobin (whose interest, as we've seen, came later in his career), Tim Kehoe, and Robert Barro.

On the faculty-faculty collaboration nexus, the Cass-Shell partnership is legendary, as is the Kehoe–Levine connection (Kehoe and Peter Diamond were Levine's thesis supervisors). Prior to Cass and Shell collocating at Penn, Cass, and Lucas traded ideas over lunches at Carnegie Mellon University's Graduate School of Industrial Administration, where Lucas did the work leading to his breakthrough 1972 paper. Karl Shell's French connections brought Yves Balasko into the OLG arena and saw Jean-Michel Grandmont as a frequent visitor at Penn. Cass and Shell hired Costas Azariadis and set the stage for the contentious sunspot collaboration.

Among the large group of students trained by the Silent Generation scholars, we have detailed their interactions in the book. But, by way of indicating the interconnections among these scholars and the institutions they trained at, we present two grids based upon purposive samples. In the first, we delineate – at three institutions – OLG-related doctoral dissertations along temporal, advisory and publication vectors, over the period 1981–2000. We observe that the decade of the 1980s reflects the accelerated OLG research program at these institutions accordingly, with the major publication outlet being *JET*.

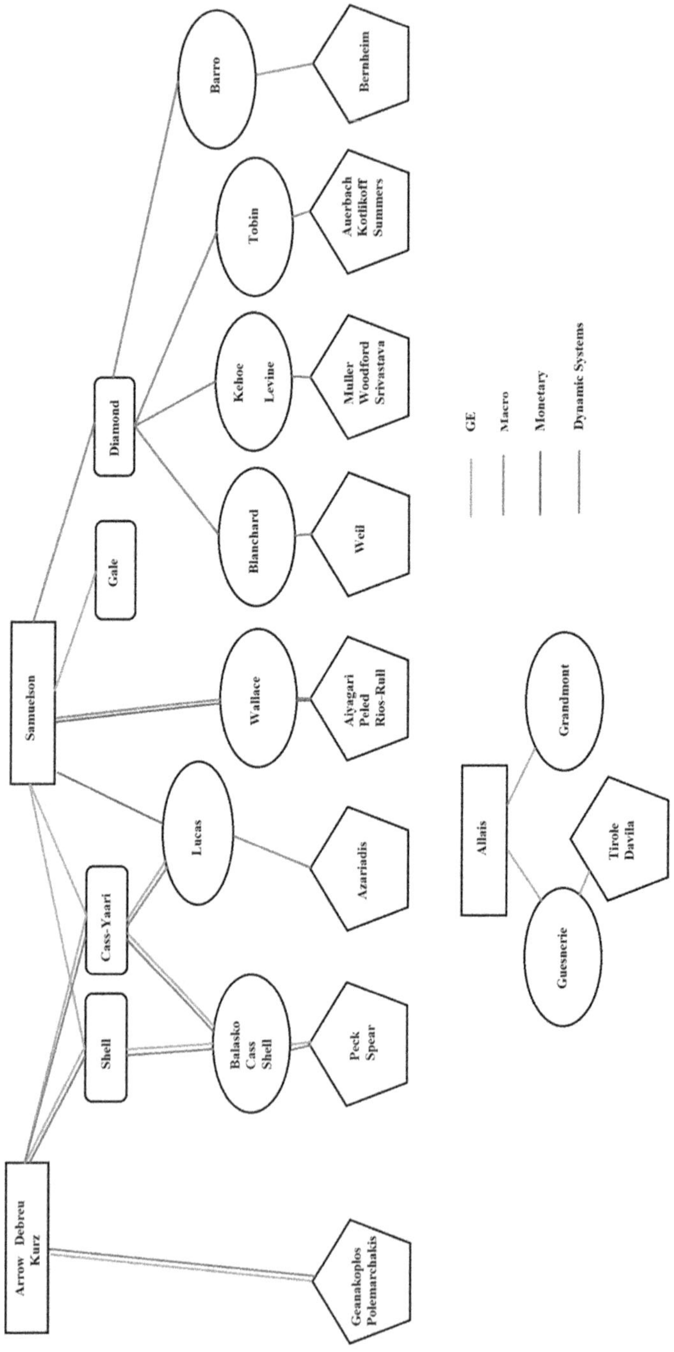

OLG Morphology.

OLG Dissertations, 1980–1990, University of Pennsylvania.

Institution	Student	Title of Thesis	Year	Advisor	Journal Outlet
Penn	Spear	Three essays on the role of expectations in dynamic economic models	1982	Cass	*JET* (1984, 1985)
	Chae	Three essays in economic theory	1985	Cass	*JET* (1987, 1988)
	Peck	Essays in intertemporal economic theory	1985	Shell	*JET* (1987, 1988)
	Puhakka	On the foundations of disequilibrium macroeconomics	1985	Azariadis	*Scan. Jnl. Econ.* (1988)
	Bertocchi	Essays on the financial structure of a dynamic economy	1988	Azariadis	*EdLet* (1991), *JEDC* (1995)
	Chang	International macroeconomic policy in optimizing models	1989	Azariadis	*JME* (1990)
	Heathcote	Frictions and incomplete markets: three essays in macroeconomics	1998	Atkeson	*WP U. Penn*
	Nishiyama	Altruism, uncertainty and intergenerational transfers	2000	Rios-Rull	*RED* (2002)

Source: Compiled by authors.

OLG Dissertations, 1980–1990, University of Minnesota.

Institution	Student	Title of Thesis	Year	Advisor	Journal Outlet
Minnesota	Aiyagari	Putty-clay durable capital in stochastic overlapping generation models	1981	Wallace	*JET* (1985)
	Arango	On the uniqueness of the equilibrium in overlapping generation models	1981	Wallace	*UCMadrid WP* (1983)
	Millan	On the existence of optimal competitive equilibria in the overlapping generations model	1981	Wallace	*UA Barcelona WP* (1982)
	Huffman	An overlapping generations model with asset pricing	1983	Wallace	*JnlFin* (1985), *CanJEc* (1986), *IER* (1986)
	Leone	Inflation and the relative price of durable and non-durable goods in overlapping generations models	1983	Brownlee	*Cen. Bank. Arg. WP* (1983)
	Batima	An overlapping generations model with endogenous fertility	1985	Rosenzweig	*Jnl. PubEc.* (1986, 1987)
	Loewy	An overlapping generations model with endogenous policy	1986	Wallace	*JME* (1988) *EcLet* (1988)
	Wright	Labor markets and labor contracts in an overlapping generation model with infinite-lived employers	1986	Wallace	*JOLE* (1988)
	Manuelli	Topics in intertemporal economics	1986	Prescott	*JET* (1990)
	Maeda	Pairwise trading in overlapping generation models	1990	Wallace	*JET* (1991)

Source: Compiled by authors.

OLG Dissertations, 1980–1990, Massachusetts Institute of Technology.

Institution	Student	Title of Thesis	Year	Advisor	Journal Outlet
MIT	Woodford	Essays in intertemporal economics	1983	Kehoe	*JET* (1988)
	Mueller	Stationary overlapping generations economies with production and infinitely lived consumers	1984	Kehoe	*JET* (1988)
	Burke	Essays on equilibria in dynamic economics	1985	Kehoe	*Jnl. Math Econ* (1987), *JET* (1988, 1989)

Source: Compiled by authors.

The second category grid shows a purposive sample of OLG-related NSF grants over the period 1974–2004, along temporal, institutional, and publication vectors. We observe that one institution, Penn, led the field in terms of grants, followed by Carnegie Mellon, where former Penn and Minnesota Ph.D. students now served on the faculty. Furthermore, almost half of the papers that emanated from these OLG-related NSF grants were published in one journal, again, *JET*.

OLG-related NSF Awards, Purposive Sample, 1974–2004.

Investigators	Institution	Title of Award	Period	Amount (US $)	Publications
Wallace (Aiyagari)	Minn	Theoretical Analysis of Alternative Exchange Rate Regimes (7722743)	1978–1980	69,300	*JET* (1985) Aiyagari
Cass, Shell	Penn	The Positive and Normative Roles of Fiat Money in Intertemporal Allocation (7806157)	1978–1980	175,171	*JET* (1980a, 1980b) with Balasko
Cass, Shell, Balasko	Penn	General Equilibrium Foundations of Intertemporal Decisions-The Overlapping-Generations Model (8007012)	1980–1983	377,398	*JPE* (1983)
Cass (Benveniste)	Penn	The Role of Financial Instruments in Facilitating Exchange (8309049)	1983–1986	101,400	*JPE* (1986)
Karni, Zilcha	Johns Hopkins	An Economic Analysis of Life Insurance, Annuities and Social Security in an Overlapping Generations Model with Uncertain Lifetime (8408670)	1984–1986	91,781	*JPubEc* (1986, 1989)
Srivastava, Spear	Carnegie-Mellon	Equilibrium in Stochastic Overlapping Generations Models (8420486)	1985–1986	73, 013	*RES* (1987) *JPubEc* (1988) *JET* (1988, 1990)
Smolensky, (Aiyagari)	Wisconsin	Overlapping Agents and the Representative Agent (8520440)	1986–1987	27,213	*JET* (1988, 1989) *QJE* (1989) Aiyagari

Investigators	Institution	Title of Award	Period	Amount (US $)	Publications
Woodford	Chicago	Sunspot Equilibria in Infinite Horizon Competitive Economics (8710219)	1987–1990	52,538	*JET* (1990)
Wright	Penn	Foundations of Monetary Theory: Money as a Medium of Exchange (8821225)	1989–1991	46,749	*EcTh* (1993) with Shell
Rios-Rull	Carnegie-Mellon	Heterogenous Agents Economies with Capital: Model Development and Applications (9110911)	1991–1994	63,195	*RES* (1996)
Krueger, Kubler	Penn/ Stanford	Social Security and the Wealth Distribution with Overlapping Generations and Aggregate Uncertainty (0004376)	2001–2004	265,338	*AER* (2002, 2006)
Brock and Scheinkman	Chicago	Optimal paths generated by optimal control problems (7419692	1974–1979	223,400	*In Models of Monetary Economies* (1980)

Source: Compiled by authors from NSF Awards 1974–2004.

The following table summarizes NFS grant activity from 1960 to 2020 in terms of grant support for research projects on the two types of models. As one can see, support for ILA-based research during what we might call the RBC/ new neo-classical synthesis decades of the 1980s and 1990s' outpaces support for OLG-based projects two-to-one. This evens out during the first two decades of the 2000s, though at markedly lower levels of overall support for both research programs.

NSF Grants by Period (Same Keywords as in Dissertations Table).

Years/Model	OLG	ILA
1960–1979	3	4
1980–1999	17	30
2000–2020	10	11
Total	**30**	**45**

Source: Compiled by authors from NSF awards 1960–2020.

In their paper "The Seven Properties of Good Models" Gabaix and Laibson (2008) delineate properties that can be applied in our morphological analysis of OLG as against ILA-based models. We have used three of the properties from their approach – parsimony, tractability, and prediction – and have added one, *teachability*. We can construct a morphology grid as below. There are various ways to fill in the cells and different readers may wish to fill the grid out differently. We have filled our grid is based on the arguments we have presented in the book.

Comparative Morphology.

		Models			
		OLG	SOLG	ILA	SILA
Properties	*Parsimony*	Yes	Somewhat	Yes	Yes
	Tractability	Yes	No	Yes	Yes
	Prediction	Open	Yes	Open	Open
	Teachability	Yes	Yes	Yes	Yes

Source: Compiled by authors.

On the parsimony dimension, both the OLG and ILA models abstract heavily from reality in the interest of providing workable analytic frameworks for models of dynamic economic equilibrium. The two stochastic extensions of these models are also parsimonious in terms of their abstraction, but they differ significantly in terms of the state variables needed for characterizing rational expectations equilibria. This difference is the basis for describing the SOLG model as "somewhat" parsimonious, since it requires an infinite dimensional state variable for the characterization of competitive (and imperfectly competitive – see Kim and Spear, 2021b) rational expectations equilibrium. The SILA model without heterogeneity needs only the aggregate stock of capital and exogenous shocks as state variables, giving it a particularly simple structure. Of course, once one begins looking at heterogeneous agent models, SOLG and SILA both require carrying along lagged endogenous state variables so that parsimony and tractability differences become negligible. Similar concerns with the state variables underlie our "No" designation for SOLG on the tractability dimension, and for our "Yes" indication on predictability, because the structure of the recursive stochastic equilibrium generates testable predictions on the fractal nature of equilibrium prices (see Brock et al., 1991; Kim & Spear, 2021c), and on the history dependence of rational expectations equilibrium. Finally, all versions of the two models are taught in the published graduate texts on general equilibrium theory and macroeconomics, as we document in the Appendix. We note, however, that the ILA model gets the most emphasis in these texts (with a few exceptions), and the treatment of solution methods for SOLG is sparse at best.

In the morphology grid below, we present the relative utilization of various OLG models based on the dimensions of *time* and *stochasticity*. The data are from EconLit, covering the period 1986–2022.

Comparative Morphology.

		Models	
		OLG	SOLG
Time treatment	*Discrete*	34	6
	Continuous	78	4

Source: Compiled by authors.

In the morphology table above, continuous time assumptions are due to *tractability;* differential equations are easier to solve than difference equations. The discrete-time assumption is based on realism: people don't spend every nanosecond optimizing. Rather, they make plans and then execute them over discrete periods of time. A fully realistic treatment would allow the length of time periods to be variable, contingent on unforeseen events. But these kinds of models (mixed differential/difference equations) are difficult to work with. On the stochastic dimension, continuous time stochastic differential equations are harder to work with than their discrete-time counterparts, though they are used extensively in finance. This could be a second reason the discrete-time growth model became prominent at the time that Brock and Mirman were working on stochastic extensions. At the same time, economic activity isn't constantly buffeted by random shocks the way rockets in flight are, so the discrete-time/discrete shocks assumption is also reality-based.

CHAPTER 11

SUMMARY AND CONCLUSION

As we have seen, the foundational OLG model (using the terminology of Blanchard, 2018, p. 52) of Allais, Samuelson, and Diamond has come a long way since its inception. While DSGE models now dominate macroeconomics, they are essentially based on a "common core, roughly an RBC structure with one main distortion, nominal rigidities" which, as Blanchard notes "seems too much at odds with reality" (Blanchard, 2018, p. 52).

OLG, for its part, has metamorphosized from the two- and three-generational approaches of Samuelson–Diamond vintage to multigenerational models such as those pioneered by Dolde and Tobin, and Auerbach and Kotlikoff. Moreover, it has been applied in widespread fields such as Public Finance and Taxation; Social Security; Labor and Demographic economics; Money and Monetary economics; International economics and trade; and Environmental and Natural Resource economics, among other areas of investigation over the years since its initial formalization. The table below provides some indication of the extent of its application in the areas listed above (based on *EconLit.,* including books, published articles, working papers, etc.).

As seen in the table, the most extensive application of OLG was in the area of labor and demographic economics, followed by public finance and taxation. Applications of OLG in the areas of Social Security and international economics and trade are of the same magnitude, followed by monetary economics. Regarding environmental and natural resource economics, the early applications of OLG did not focus on these areas, but with the increasing importance of environmental issues and the implications of climate change for future generations, OLG applications have bloomed.

This book has presented a wide-ranging and detailed survey of the origins, evolution, development, and dissemination of the OLG approach – one of the workhorse models of modern economics – in contrast to the ILA approach, with which it competes in terms of efficacy and application. And, since the book's focus has been on this relationship between the two approaches and their respective

Overlapping Generations: Methods, Models and Morphology
International Symposia in Economic Theory and Econometrics, Volume 32, 209–211

ISSN: 1571-0386/doi:10.1108/S1571-038620230000032026

OLG Applications.

Area	Number of Publications
Labor and Demographic economics	1,548
Public Finance and Taxation	853
Social Security	686
International economics and trade	638
Money and Monetary economics	581
Environmental and Natural Resource economics	437

Source: Compiled from *EconLit* database 1958–2020.

relative impact, the widespread application of the OLG approach noted above has not been dealt with in detail and remains a subject for further survey and exposition.

In order to present a coherent conclusion to the mass of material presented in the book, we utilized the morphological approach outlined in the previous chapter. We can identify two essential model types: foundational and augmented, in addition to four areas of model efficacy: theoretical, computational, policy, and pedagogical (see, e.g., Jordi, 2018, p. 87). Given this, we propose that the plasticity of the two respective approaches enabled their metamorphosis from foundational to augmented types.

Now, the formalized canonical foundational OLG model of Samuelson (1958) took almost a decade to have an impact, and this came via the contribution of Diamond (1965). In the same year as Diamond's classic AER paper, path-breaking works by Cass and Koopmans applying the Ramsey (1928) approach appeared; this constituted what can be termed the canonical foundational Ramsey-Cass-Koopmans (RCK) ILA approach (see Spear & Young, 2014). Both the OLG and ILA approaches took time to disseminate through the profession, although the planning version of the RCK model was used early on. By 1972, Lucas had produced a canonical foundational stochastic version of OLG. A decade later, Kydland and Prescott (1982) presented the canonical foundational stochastic ILA model, based on the Brock and Mirman (1972) stochastic extension of the RCK model, which was termed the Real Business Cycle (RBC) Model.

Canonical augmentations of the OLG approach were the outcome of the work of Auerbach and Kotlikoff from the mid-1980s onwards, and, for the ILA model, the parallel development of the macroeconomic DSGE approach, of both New Classical and New Keynesian vintage, with RBC at its core. This was further augmented to provide both Representative Agent and later Heterogenous Agent New Keynesian (RANK and HANK) models (Kaplan et al., 2018).

As we have documented, the ILA approach became dominant because of its relative advantages along the dimensions of tractability and teachability, particularly for stochastic variants of the two models. These advantages stemmed from the fact that dynamic programming allowed for tractable model solutions, if not on paper, then in simulations, something not available in the stochastic OLG case. However, the addition of heterogenous agents to the ILA and SILA frameworks

Approach and Application.

Canonical Model Type	OLG	SOLG	ILA	SILA
Foundational	Samuelson-Diamond	Lucas	Ramsey-Cass-Koopmans	Kydland-Prescott
Augmented	Auerbach-Kotlikoff	Rios-Rull	Ubiquitous	King-Goodfriend (NKDSGE)
Augmented Model Type				
Augmented Model	Auerback-Kotlikoff	Rios-Rull	RANK	HANK
Efficacy				
Theoretical	Yes	Yes	Yes	Yes
Computational	Yes	Limited	Yes	Limited
Policy	Yes	Yes	Yes	Yes
Pedagogical	Limited	Limited	Limited	Limited

Source: Authors compilation.

makes them as difficult to solve/simulate as the standard SOLG model (with a representative agent or multiple heterogenous agents, see Duffie et al., 1994).

The grid above gives us some illustration of the comparison between OLG and ILA approaches in the book.

From the mid-1990s onwards, critiques of the empirical foundations of ILA-based models were raised by (among others) Deaton (1992), Hansen and Heckman (1996), and Browning, Hansen, and Heckman (1999). The focus of their criticism ranged from issues of heterogeneity in terms of preferences, information, agents' skills and attitudes toward risk and discounting, and aggregation issues, in addition to problems relating to the accumulation of capital and the distribution of wealth. To sum up, as Deaton put it (Deaton, 1992, p. ix):

> Representative agents have two great failings; they know too much, and they live too long. An aggregate of individuals with finite lives and with heterogenous information is not likely to behave like the single individual of the textbook.

And indeed, this is the comparative advantage of the OLG approach in all its variants – it is simply more realistic.

APPENDIX 1: GRADUATE TEXTBOOK COVERAGE OF OLG

In this appendix, we survey the prominent graduate-level textbooks in macroeconomics and comment on their treatment of the OLG model and its role in macro. This survey should not be interpreted as a review or endorsement of any of the texts examined. Rather, our comments are meant to highlight the treatment of OLG models – deterministic and stochastic – in the pedagogy provided to graduate students in economics. Our intent here is to buttress our morphological claims about OLG along the teachability dimension. The textbooks are ordered chronologically by the date of the first publication of each book.

<table>
<tr><th>Year</th><th>Author(s)</th><th>Title</th><th>Publisher</th></tr>
<tr><td>1989</td><td>Blanchard and Fischer</td><td>Lectures on Macroeconomics</td><td>MIT Press</td></tr>
<tr><td colspan="4">This text provides a pretty good treatment of OLG. While it omits much of Balasko-Shell/BCS results, this is to be expected in a macr text. It includes a discussion of Grandmont's chaos work and Azariadis' work on sunspots, as well as Day's work on chaos, but not Benhabib-Day, and no Cass-Shell on sunspots. It covers RBC with aggregate shocks in detail and includes Lucas '72 as an example of OLG with shocks, but no mention of the problem of history dependence in more general models.</td></tr>
<tr><td>1989</td><td>Stokey and Lucas</td><td>Recursive Methods in Economic Dynamics</td><td>Harvard U. Press</td></tr>
<tr><td colspan="4">The only OLG consideration in the book is based on the Lucas '72 model presented in the context of the model itself, and then in the sections on various fixed point theorems. There is no consideration of history dependence, no discussion of Rios-Rull, and one brief mention of DGMM and Blume results. The material in the last chapter on equilibrium with distortions looks at examples where various people have figured out tricks for solving models with frictions when there are lagged endogenous state variables. However, aside from the brief historical mention of DGMM, there is nothing in the book that indicates for general SOLG models, the DGMM results must be used.</td></tr>
<tr><td>1991</td><td>McCandless and Wallace</td><td>Introduction to Dynamic Macroeconomic Theory</td><td>Harvard U. Press</td></tr>
<tr><td colspan="4">As one would expect of a book co-authored by Neil Wallace, this text is organized around the OLG model. The text is pitched as an advanced undergraduate text, but the overall development of the deterministic OLG model would be useful to any macrograduate student. No consideration of stochastic models, however.</td></tr>
<tr><td>1993</td><td>Azariadis</td><td>Intertemporal Macroeconomics</td><td>Wiley-Blackwell</td></tr>
<tr><td colspan="4">This text uses a dynamic systems approach to frame the study of the intertemporal macro. Much of the analysis in the book is based on the deterministic OLG model, and the penultimate chapter on market psychology introduces the concept of sunspot equilibrium in the context of the two-period SOLG model. Beyond this, however, this is no further discussion of stochastic economies.</td></tr>
</table>

(Continued)

(Continued)

<table>
<tr><td>2002</td><td>De la Croix and Michel</td><td>A Theory of Economic Growth: Dynamics and Policy in Overlapping Generations</td><td>Cambridge U. Press</td></tr>
<tr><td colspan="4">This text provides a very good treatment of deterministic OLG models. There is no stochastic analysis, but one mention of Rios-Rull extending the Auerbach-Kotlikoff simulation framework to allow for aggregate shocks.</td></tr>
<tr><td>2002</td><td>Heijdra and Ploeg</td><td>Foundations of Modern Macroeconomics</td><td>Oxford U. Press</td></tr>
<tr><td colspan="4">REQUESTED COPY FROM AUTHORS</td></tr>
<tr><td>2004</td><td>Ljungqvist and Sargent</td><td>Recursive Macroeconomic Theory</td><td>MIT Press</td></tr>
<tr><td colspan="4">The text provides a good comprehensive development of deterministic OLG with coverage of models with idiosyncratic shocks, and some mention of aggregate shocks – Rios-Rull's work and DGMM paper – but no discussion of the fact that general multiperiod SOLG models have history-dependent equilibria. Aiyagari's 1977 JET paper on observational equivalence is in the references, but not cited anywhere in the text.</td></tr>
<tr><td>2007</td><td>Bewley</td><td>General Equilibrium, Overlapping Generations Models, and Optimal Economic Growth Theory</td><td>Harvard U. Press</td></tr>
<tr><td colspan="4">There is mixed coverage of both ILA and OLG in the text, but the stochastic analysis is limited to ILA and permanent income applications.</td></tr>
<tr><td>2009</td><td>Acemoglu</td><td>Introduction to Modern Economic Growth</td><td>MIT Press</td></tr>
<tr><td colspan="4">The text provides a rudimentary treatment of deterministic OLG, and very basic stochastic OLG (two-period, one good). There is no discussion of history dependence issues in general OLG.</td></tr>
<tr><td>2009</td><td>Sargent</td><td>Dynamic Macroeconomic Theory</td><td>Harvard U. Press</td></tr>
<tr><td colspan="4">The book covers OLG as a model of money, plus stochastic OLG with two-period lives and one good (basic Lucas '72 model). There is no discussion of general stochastic OLG.</td></tr>
<tr><td>2010</td><td>Tvede</td><td>Overlapping Generations Economies</td><td>Palgrave-MacMillan</td></tr>
<tr><td colspan="4">This text obviously focuses on OLG, taking a good general equilibrium approach, following the Balasko-Shell formulation, with simplified analysis of the optimality criterion in the Balasko-Shell II paper. However, it provides no stochastic consideration.</td></tr>
<tr><td>2010</td><td>Benassy-Quere et al.</td><td>Economic Policy</td><td>Oxford U. Press</td></tr>
<tr><td colspan="4">This text takes a very different approach than the others in this list by focusing on policy applications of the two workhorse economic models. The focus is one that Blanchard, in his Forward to the book, states that he wishes he had taken in a follow-on to his own text. The book gives a reasonably complete treatment of deterministic OLG models in a variety of applications, including some from political economy. There is no treatment of SOLG models, however.</td></tr>
<tr><td>2012</td><td>Romer</td><td>Advanced Macroeconomics</td><td>McGraw-Hill</td></tr>
<tr><td colspan="4">The text provides a rudimentary treatment of the deterministic Diamond model, but no consideration of SOLG at all. DSGE is defined as the New Keynesian variation of the conventional RBC model.</td></tr>
</table>

APPENDIX 2: RIOS-RULL FOLLOW-ON CITATIONS

This appendix presents the citations to the papers that cited Rios-Rull's 1996 *ReStud* paper. The citations are organized according to the criterion we used to classify the work as genuine follow-on work ("relevant"); work that cited the paper as being similar to or different from the work presented in the paper ("in passing"); work using models similar to Rios-Rull's but without aggregate shocks ("tangential"); work that summarized Rios-Rull's work for pedagogical purposes ("summary"); and work that cited Rios-Rull for no discernable reason ("vacuous"). All of these tables were compiled by the authors using information from Google Scholar.

Relevant citations: Total = 32.

Citation	Published	Date	Top 5	Theory
Carvalho, Vasco, Alberto Martin, and Jaume Ventura. "Bubbly business cycles." (2011).	NA	2011		
Chun, Young Jun. "The redistributive effect of risky taxation." International Tax and Public Finance 8.4 (2001): 433–454. (Actually extends Muller-Woodford to aggregate shocks)	INTL.TAXFIN	2001		
Citanna, A., Siconol, P. "Recursive equilibrium in stochastic OLG economies: Incomplete markets." Journal of Mathematical Economics (2012)	J. MAT	2012		x
Citanna, Alessandro, and Paolo Siconolfi. "On the nonexistence of recursive equilibrium in stochastic OLG economies." Economic Theory 37.3 (2008): 417–437.	ET	2008		x
Citanna, Alessandro, and Paolo Siconolfi. "Recursive equilibrium in stochastic OLG economies: Incomplete markets." Journal of Mathematical Economics 48.5 (2012): 322–337.	J. MATH	2012		x
Citanna, Alessandro, and Paolo Siconolfi. "Recursive equilibrium in stochastic overlapping-generations economies." Econometrica 78.1 (2010): 309–347.	ETRICA	2010	x	x
Citanna, Alessandro, and Paolo Siconolfi. "Short-memory equilibrium in stochastic overlapping generations economies." Journal of Economic Theory 134.1 (2007): 448–469.	JET	2007		x
Ferraro, Domenico, and Giuseppe Fiori. "The aging of the baby boomers: Demographics and propagation of tax shocks." American Economic Journal: Macroeconomics 12.2 (2020): 167–93.	AEJ: Macro	2020		
Glover, Andrew, et al. "Intergenerational redistribution in the great recession." Journal of Political Economy 128.10 (2020): 3730–3778.	JPE	2020	x	
Gomme, Paul, et al. "The business cycle and the life cycle." NBER Macroeconomics Annual 19 (2004): 415–461.	NBER AN	2004		

(Continued)

(Continued)

Citation	Published	Date	Top 5	Theory
Gomme, Paul. Measuring the welfare costs of inflation in a life-cycle model. No. 08001. Concordia University, Department of Economics, 2008.	NA	2008		
Hansen, Gary D., and Selahattin İmrohoroğlu. "Business cycle fluctuations and the life cycle: How important is on-the-job skill accumulation?" Journal of Economic Theory 144.6 (2009): 2293–2309.	JET	2009		
Hasanhodzic, Jasmina, and Laurence J. Kotlikoff. Generational risk-is it a big deal?: Simulating an 80-period OLG model with aggregate shocks. No. w19179. National Bureau of Economic Research, 2013.	NBER WP	2013		
Heer, Burkhard, and Alfred Maussner. "Business cycle dynamics of a new Keynesian overlapping generations model with progressive income taxation." (2006). (Probably use Krusell-Smith for solution)	NA	2006		
Heer, Burkhard, and Alfred Maußner. "Distributional effects of monetary policies in a new neoclassical model with progressive income taxation." Computing in Economics and Finance. Vol. 12. 2005. (Believe they use Krusell-Smith)	COMP.ECFIN	2005		
Heer, Burkhard, and Alfred Maussner. "The burden of unanticipated inflation: Analysis of an overlapping generations model with progressive income taxation and staggered prices." Available at SSRN 977126 (2007). (Again, use Krusell-Smith approach)	NA	2007		
Heer, Burkhard, and Alfred Maußner. "The burden of unanticipated inflation: Analysis of an overlapping-generations model with progressive income taxation and staggered prices." Macroeconomic Dynamics 16.2 (2012): 278–308. (They use Krusell-Smith technique, per their book)	MD	2012		
Heer, Burkhard, Stefan Rohrbacher, and Christian Scharrer. "Aging, the great moderation, and business-cycle volatility in a life-cycle model." Macroeconomic Dynamics 21.2 (2017): 362–383. (Likely they use Krusell-Smith)	MD	2017		
Kim, Eungsik, and S. E. Spear. "Singular Invariant Markov Equilibrium in Stochastic Overlapping Generations Models." JEDC (2019).	JEDC	2019		x
Krebs, Tom. "Recursive equilibrium in endogenous growth models with incomplete markets." Economic Theory 29.3 (2006): 505–523. (First counter-example to recursive equilibrium paper)	ET	2006		
Krueger, Dirk, and Felix Kubler. "Computing equilibrium in OLG models with stochastic production." Journal of Economic Dynamics and Control 28.7 (2004): 1411–1436.	JEDC	2004		
Kubler, Felix, and Karl Schmedders. "Life-cycle portfolio choice, the wealth distribution and asset prices." Swiss Finance Institute Research Paper 10-21 (2015).	NA	2015		
Larin, Benjamin. "A quantitative model of bubble-driven business cycles." (2016).	NA	2016		
Larin, Benjamin. Bubble-driven business cycles. No. 143. Working Paper, 2016.	NA	2016		

(Continued)

Citation	Published	Date	Top 5	Theory
Matovu, John. "Composition of government expenditure, human capital accumulation, and welfare." (2000).	NA	2000		
Mennuni, Alessandro. "Labor force composition and aggregate fluctuations." (2013).	NA	2013		
Nakajima, Makoto. "Rising earnings instability, portfolio choice, and housing prices." Portfolio Choice, and Housing Prices (July 3, 2005) (2005).	PORT.CH	2005		
Pries, Michael J. "Social security reform and intertemporal smoothing." Journal of Economic Dynamics and Control 31.1 (2007): 25–54.	JEDC	2007		
Ríos-Rull, José-Víctor. "On the quantitative importance of market completeness." Journal of Monetary Economics 34.3 (1994): 463–496.	J.MONETARY	1994		
Ríos-Rull, José-Víctor. "Population changes and capital accumulation: The aging of the baby boom." The BE Journal of Macroeconomics 1.1 (2001).	BELL Macro	2001		
Silos, Pedro. "Housing, portfolio choice and the macroeconomy." Journal of Economic Dynamics and Control 31.8 (2007): 2774–2801.	JEDC	2007		
Wong, Arlene. "Refinancing and the transmission of monetary policy to consumption." Unpublished manuscript 20 (2019).	NA	2019		

In passing citations: Total = 63

Note: We don't summarize publication outlets and top 5 or theory status here since these aren't relevant to our analysis. We provide the citations by way of documenting the extent of our analysis.

Alvarez-Albelo, Carmen D. "Endogenous versus exogenous efficiency units of labour for the quantitative study of Social Security: two examples." Applied Economics Letters 11.11 (2004): 693–697. (Deterministic model; RR parameterizations)

Angeletos, George-Marios, and Laurent-Emmanuel Calvet. "Idiosyncratic production risk, growth and the business cycle." Journal of Monetary Economics 53.6 (2006): 1095–1115. (ILA)

Bagchi, Shantanu. "Can overconfidence explain the consumption hump?" Journal of Economics and Finance 35.1 (2011): 41–70. (Continuous time; RR parameterizations)

Basso, Henrique S., and Omar Rachedi. "The young, the old, and the government: Demographics and fiscal multipliers." American Economic Journal: Macroeconomics 13.4 (2021): 110–141. (Econometrics)

Benzoni, Luca, and Olena Chyruk. "Human capital and long-run labor income risk." Available at SSRN 2361497 (2013). (Continuous time)

Böhm, Volker, Tomoo Kikuchi, and George Vachadze. "Asset pricing and productivity growth: the role of consumption scenarios." Computational Economics 32.1 (2008): 163–181. (Two period model)

Bohn, Henning. "Risk sharing in a stochastic overlapping generations economy." (1998). (Two-period OLG)

Bonneuil, Noël, and Patrick Saint-Pierre. "Beyond optimality: Managing children, assets, and consumption over the life cycle." Journal of Mathematical Economics 44.3–4 (2008): 227–241. (Continuous time, deterministic)

Bowlus, Audra, Haoming Liu, and Chris Robinson. "Business cycle models, aggregation, and real wage cyclicality." Journal of Labor Economics 20.2 (2002): 308–335. (Econometrics, RR parameterization)

Budría, Santiago, and Javier Díaz-Giménez. "Economic inequality in Spain: the European community household panel dataset." Spanish Economic Review 9.1 (2007): 1–38. (Econometrics)

Budría, Santiago, and Javier Díaz-Giménez. "Economic inequality in Spain: the European Union Household panel dataset." (2004). (Econometrics)

(Continued)

(Continued)

Budrıa, Santiago, et al. "New facts on the distributions of earnings, income and wealth in the US." Federal Reserve Bank of Minneapolis Quarterly Review 26 (2002): 2–35. (Econometrics)

Bullard, James, and John Duffy. "Learning and excess volatility." Macroeconomic Dynamics 5.02 (2001): 272–302. (Deterministic model)

Bütler, Monika. "The political feasibility of pension reform options: the case of Switzerland." Journal of Public Economics 75.3 (2000): 389–416. (Deterministic model)

Castaneda, Ana, Javier Dıaz-Giménez, and José-Victor Rıos-Rull. "Exploring the income distribution business cycle dynamics." Journal of Monetary Economics 42.1 (1998): 93–130. (Aiyagari-Bewley model)

Cazzavillan, Guido, and Patrick A. Pintus. "Capital externalities in OLG economies." Journal of Economic Dynamics and Control 30.7 (2006): 1215–1231. (Two period model)

Chalk, Nigel A. "The sustainability of bond-financed deficits: an overlapping generations approach." Journal of Monetary Economics 45.2 (2000): 293–328. (Tw-period OLG)

Chatterjee, Satyajit, et al. "A quantitative theory of unsecured consumer credit with risk of default." Econometrica 75.6 (2007): 1525–1589. (Perpetual youth)

Choi, Sekyu, Alexandre Janiak, and Benjamín Villena-Roldán. "Unemployment, participation and worker flows over the life-cycle." (2013). (Econometric; builds on results from RR model on labor hours, but no formal model presented)

Cournède, Boris, et al. "Enhancing economic flexibility: what is in it for workers?" (2016). (Econometrics; RR paramerizations)

d'ALBIS, Hippolyte, and Emmanuelle Augeraud-Véron. "Continuous-time overlapping generations models." Optimal Control of Age-structured Populations in Economy, Demography, and the Environment. Routledge, 2013: 63–87. (Continuous time)

d'Albis, Hippolyte, and Emmanuelle Augeraud-véron. "Competitive growth in a life-cycle model: existence and dynamics." International Economic Review 50.2 (2009): 459–484. (Continuous time, RR paramerization)

Den Haan, Wouter J. "Solving Dynamic Models With Aggregate Shocks And Heterogeneous Agents." Macroeconomic Dynamics 1.2 (1997): 355–386. (Aiyagari-Bewley Solution Technique)

Denk, Oliver, and Jean-Baptiste Michau. "Optimal social security with imperfect tagging." (2013). (Continuous time)

Denk, Oliver. "How do product market regulations affect workers?: Evidence from the network industries." (2016). (Econometrics)

Dubovyk, Tetyana, and CeRP-Collegio Carlo Alberto. "Macroeconomic aspects of Italian Pension Reforms of 1990s." Center for Research on Pensions and Welfare Policies Working Paper 101 (2010): 40. (Deterministic OLG)

Farmer[1], Roger EA, and Pawel Zabczyk. "The fiscal theory of the price level in overlapping generations models." (2019).

Feigenbaum, James. "Can mortality risk explain the consumption hump?." Journal of Macroeconomics 30.3 (2008): 844–872. (Perpetual youth model)

Ferraro, Domenico, and Giuseppe Fiori. "The aging of the baby boomers: Demographics and propagation of tax shocks." American Economic Journal: Macroeconomics 12.2 (2020): 167–193. (Econometrics)

Ferraro, Domenico, and Giuseppe Fiori. "The aging of the baby boomers: demographics and propagation of tax shocks." Available at SSRN 2848156 (2016). (Econometrics)

Gervais, Martin, et al. "What should I be when I grow up? Occupations and employment over the life cycle and business cycle." NBER Working Paper S 20628 (2014). (Matching model)

Gornemann, Nils, Keith Kuester, and Makoto Nakajima. "Doves for the rich, hawks for the poor? Distributional consequences of monetary policy." Distributional Consequences of Monetary Policy (April 2016) (2016). (ILA)

Gornemann, Nils, Keith Kuester, and Makoto Nakajima. "Monetary policy with heterogeneous agents." (2012). (ILA)

Hairault, Jean-Olivier, François Langot, and Thepthida Sopraseuth. "Quantifying the Laffer curve on the continued activity tax in a dynastic framework." International Economic Review 49.3 (2008): 755–797. (ILA, RR parameterizations)

(Continued)

Hairault, Jean-Olivier, François Langot, and Thepthida Sopraseuth. "The pre-retirement job search: a basic explanation of the older worker employment." Journal of European Economic Association 8.5 (2010): 1034–1076. (Econometrics)

Heathcote, Jonathan, Kjetil Storesletten, and Giovanni L. Violante. "The macroeconomic implications of rising wage inequality in the United States." Journal of Political Economy 118.4 (2010): 681–722. (Perpetual youth)

Heer, Burkhard, and Stefan Franz Schubert. "Unemployment and debt dynamics in a highly indebted small open economy." Journal of International Money and Finance 31.6 (2012): 1392–1413. (Continuous time)

Heijdra, Ben J., and Jenny E. Ligthart. "Fiscal policy, monopolistic competition, and finite lives." Journal of Economic Dynamics and Control 31.1 (2007): 325–359. (Continuous time)

Heijdra, Ben J., and Jochen O. Mierau. "The individual life cycle and economic growth: an essay on demographic macroeconomics." De Economist 159.1 (2011): 63–87. (Continuous time; RR paramerizations)

Heijdra, Ben J., and Jochen O. Mierau. "The individual life-cycle, annuity market imperfections and economic growth." Journal of Economic Dynamics and Control 36.6 (2012): 876–890. (Continuous time, RR parameterization)

Huggett, Mark, and Gustavo Ventura. "On the distributional effects of social security reform." Review of Economic Dynamics 2.3 (1999): 498–531. (Idiosyncratic risk)

İmrohoroglu, Ayşe, Selahattin Imrohoroglu, and Douglas H. Joines. "A life cycle analysis of social security." Economic theory 6.1 (1995): 83–114. (Idiosyncratic risk)

Jaimovich, Nir, Seth Pruitt, and Henry E. Siu. "The demand for youth: Explaining age differences in the volatility of hours." American Economic Review 103.7 (2013): 3022–3044. (ILA, RR parameterizations)

Jedwab, Remi Camille, Daniel Pereira, and Mark Roberts. "Cities of Workers, Children, or Seniors? Age Structure and Economic Growth in a Global Cross-Section of Cities." Age Structure and Economic Growth in a Global Cross-Section of Cities (October 15, 2019). World Bank Policy Research Working Paper 9040 (2019). (Econometrics)

Kawaguchi, Daiji, and Tetsushi Murao. "Who bears the cost of the business cycle? Labor-market institutions and volatility of the youth unemployment rate." IZA Journal of Labor Policy 1.1 (2012): 1–22. (Econometric)

Krebs, Tom, Pravin Krishna, and William Maloney. "Trade policy, income risk, and welfare." The Review of Economics and Statistics 92.3 (2010): 467–481. (ILA idiosyncratic risk; primarily econometric)

Krusell, Per, and Anthony A. Smith, Jr. "Income and wealth heterogeneity in the macroeconomy." Journal of political Economy 106.5 (1998): 867–896. (ILA)

Leung, Charles Ka Yui, and Guang-Jia Zhang. "Inflation and capital gains taxes in a small open economy." International Review of Economics & Finance 9.3 (2000): 195–208. (Deterministic)

Ljungqvist, Lars, and Thomas J. Sargent. "Indivisible Labor, Human Capital, Lotteries, and Personal Savings: Do Taxes Explain European Employment?." NBER Macroeconomics Annual 21 (2006): 181–246. (ILA, RR parameterizations)

Lugauer, Steven. "Demographic change and the great moderation in an overlapping generations model with matching frictions." Macroeconomic Dynamics 16.5 (2012): 706–731. (Matching model)

Lugauer, Steven. "Estimating the effect of the age distribution on cyclical output volatility across the United States." Review of Economics and Statistics 94.4 (2012): 896–902. (Econometrics)

Maliar, Lilia, and Serguei Maliar. "Heterogeneity in capital and skills in a neoclassical stochastic growth model." Journal of Economic Dynamics and Control 25.9 (2001): 1367–1397. (ILA model contrasted with other OLG in the literature)

Mennuni, Alessandro. "The aggregate implications of changes in the labour force composition." European Economic Review 116 (2019): 83–106. (ILA)

Mitra, Indrajit, and Yu Xu. "Youth unemployment and jobless recoveries: a risk-based explanation." Available at SSRN 3036185 (2017). (ILA Search model)

Ohtaki, Eisei. "Tractable graphical device for analyzing stationary stochastic OLG economies." Journal of Macroeconomics 40 (2014): 16–26. (Two-period SOLG)

(Continued)

(Continued)

Pica, Giovanni. "Capital Markets Integration and Labor Market Institutions." CSEF WP 144 (2005). (Two-period OLG)
Pries, Michael J. "Social security reform and intertemporal smoothing." Journal of Economic Dynamics and Control 31.1 (2007): 25–54. (Two period, RR paramerizations)
Ragot, Xavier. "A theory of low inflation in a non Ricardian economy with credit constraints." (2005). (Two-period OLG)
Rioja, Felix K. "Roads versus schooling: growth effects of government choices." Topics in Macroeconomics 5.1 (2005). (Two-period model)
Rios-Rull, Jose-Victor. "Theory of Stagnation." The Review of Economic Studies 63.2 (1996): 301–329. (Political economy model; RR parameterizations)
Silva, André C. "Taxes and labor supply: Portugal, Europe, and the United States." Portuguese Economic Journal 7.2 (2008): 101–124. (Determininstic)
Smith Jr, Anthony A., and Cheng Wang. "Dynamic credit relationships in general equilibrium." Journal of Monetary Economics 53.4 (2006): 847–877. (Perpetual youth)
Storesletten, Kjetil. "Sustaining fiscal policy through immigration." Journal of political Economy 108.2 (2000): 300–323. (Idiosyncratic risk)
Verani, Stéphane. "Aggregate Consequences of Firm-Level Financing Constraints." University of California, Santa Barbara (2010). (Perpetual youth)

Summary citations: Total = 42

Athreya, Kartik, et al. "Student Loan Borrowing and Repayment Decisions: Risks and Contingencies 1." The Routledge Handbook of the Economics of Education. Routledge, 2022: 458–511.
Azariadis, Costas, James Bullard, and Lee Ohanian. "Trend-reverting fluctuations in the life-cycle model." Journal of Economic Theory 119.2 (2004): 334–356.
Bryant, Ralph C., and Warwick J. McKibbin. Incorporating demographic change in multi-country macroeconomic models: some preliminary results. na, 2001.
Bryant, Ralph C., and Warwick J. McKibbin. Issues in modeling the global dimensions of demographic change. Brookings Institution, 1998.
Brzoza-Brzezina, Michał, et al. "Monetary policy in a non-representative agent economy: a survey." Journal of Economic Surveys 27.4 (2013): 641–669.
Carbonari, Lorenzo, Vincenzo Atella, and Paola Samà. "Hours worked in selected OECD countries: an empirical assessment." International Review of Applied Economics 32.4 (2018): 525–545. (Econometrics)
Chari, V. V., and Patrick J. Kehoe. "Response from VV Chari and Patrick J. Kehoe." The Journal of Economic Perspectives 22.1 (2008): 247–250.
Chari, Varadarajan V., and Patrick J. Kehoe. Reply to Solow. Federal Reserve Bank of Minneapolis, Research Department, 2007.
Cooley, Thomas F., and Edward C. Prescott. Frontiers of Business Cycle Research. Vol. 3. Princeton, NJ: Princeton University Press, 1995.
Cubeddu, Luis, and José-Víctor Ríos-Rull. Marital Risk and Capital Accumulation. Vol. 235. Federal Reserve Bank of Minneapolis, Research Department, 1997.
Cui, Wei, Randall Wright, and Yu Zhu. "Endogenous liquidity and capital reallocation." Available at SSRN 3881116 (2021). (ILA search)
Doepke, Matthias, and Michèle Tertilt. "Families in macroeconomics." Handbook of macroeconomics. Vol. 2. Elsevier, 2016: 1789–1891. (Sociological discuss of families in macro)
dos Santos, Marcelo Rodrigues, and Pedro Cavalcanti Ferreira. The Effect of Social Security, Demography and Technology on Retirement. Escola de Pós-Graduação em Economia, 2008.
Farmer, Mr Roger, and Pawel Zabczyk. A requiem for the Fiscal Theory of the Price Level. International Monetary Fund, 2019.
Guvenen, Fatih. "Macroeconomics with heterogeneity: A practical guide." (2011).
Hansen, Gary D., and Edward C. Prescott. "2. Recursive Methods for Computing Equilibria of Business Cycle Models." Frontiers of business cycle research. Princeton University Press, 2021: 39–64.

(Continued)

Heijdra, Ben J., and Jenny E. Ligthart. "The transitional dynamics of fiscal policy in small open economies." (2006). (Perpetual youth)
Homburg, Stefan. A study in monetary macroeconomics. Oxford University Press, 2017.
İmrohoroğlu, Selahattin. "The risk-sharing implications of alternative social security arrangements: a comment." Carnegie-Rochester Conference Series on Public Policy. Vol. 50. North-Holland, 1999.
İmrohoroğlu, Selahattin. Social Security, benefit claiming, and labor force participation: a quantitative general equilibrium approach. Vol. 436. DIANE Publishing, 2011.
Joines, Douglas H., Imrohoroglu A., and Imrohoroglu S. "Computing models of social security." Computational Methods for the Study of Dynamic Economies. Oxford University Press, London (1999).
Kotlikoff, Laurence J. "Pension System Solvency—From Linguistics to Economics." Swiss Journal of Economics and Statistics 152.2 (2016): 83–102.
Krueger, Dirk. Risk Sharing with Incomplete Markets: Macroeconomic and Fiscal Policy Implications. University of Minnesota, 1999.
Kubler, Felix, and Herakles Polemarchakis. "Stationary Markov equilibria for overlapping generations." Economic Theory 24.3 (2004): 623–643.
Kubler, Felix. "Verifying competitive equilibria in dynamic economies." The Review of Economic Studies 78.4 (2011): 1379–1399.
Kuncl, Martin, and Alexander Ueberfeldt. Monetary policy and the persistent aggregate effects of wealth redistribution. No. 2021-38. Bank of Canada Staff Working Paper, 2021. (Perpetual youth)
Kydland, Finn E. "Inflation, Personal Taxes, and Real Output: A Dynamic Analysis: Comment." Journal of Money, Credit and Banking 23.3 (1991): 575–579.
Kydland, Finn E. "Quantitative aggregate economics." American Economic Review 96.5 (2006): 1373–1383.
Kydland, Finn E. "Quantitative aggregate theory." Nobel Prize Lecture (2004).
Kydland, Finn E., and D. M. Peterson. "Does being different matter?." Economic Review-Federal Reserve Bank of Dallas (1997): 2–11.
Ljungqvist, Lars, and Thomas J. Sargent. "Recursive Macroeconomic Theory Second edition." (2004).
Marcet, Albert. "Simulation analysis of dynamic stochastic models: Applications to theory and estimation." Advances in Econometrics. Sixth World Congress. 1994.
Michaelides, Alexander, and Michael Haliassos. "Calibration and computation of household portfolio models." University of Cyprus Department of Economics Working Paper No. 00-04 (2000).
Nagypál, Éva. "[The Business Cycle and the Life Cycle]: Comment." NBER Macroeconomics Annual 19 (2004): 462–477.
Nagypál, Éva. "Discussion of "Business Cycle and the Life Cycle" by Paul Gomme, Richard Rogerson, Peter Rupert, and Randall Wright." NBER Macroeconomics Annual (2004).
Novales, Alfonso. "The role of simulation methods in Macroeconomics." Spanish Economic Review 2.3 (2000): 155–181.
Ohanian, Lee E. "The economic crisis from a neoclassical perspective." Journal of Economic Perspectives 24.4 (2010): 45–66.
Quadrini, V., and José-Víctor Ríos-Rull. "Dimensions of inequality: facts on the US distribution of earnings, income and wealth." Federal Reserve Bank of Minneapolis Quarterly Review 21.2 (1997): 3–21.
Quadrini, Vincenzo, and José-Víctor Ríos-Rull. "Inequality in macroeconomics." Handbook of income distribution. Vol. 2. Elsevier, 2015: 1229–1302.
Rodriguez, Santiago Budria, et al. "Updated facts on the US distributions of earnings, income, and wealth." Federal Reserve Bank of Minneapolis Quarterly Review 26.3 (2002).
Sargent, Thomas J. "Adaptation of macro theory to rational expectations." manuscript. Hoover Institution and (1995).
Scott, Bernard. Computational methods for the study of dynamic economies. Oxford University Press, 1999.
Stachurski, John. Economic Dynamics: Theory and Computation. MIT Press, 2009.

Tangential citations: Total = 51
Note: Since these are relevant to our analysis, we include the publication, top 5 and theory classifications.

Citation	Published	Date	Top 5	Idiosyncratic
Altig, David, and Charles T. Carlstrom. "Inflation, personal taxes, and real output: a dynamic analysis." Journal of Money, Credit and Banking 23.3 (1991): 547–571. (Idiosyncratic risk)	JMCB	1991		x
Attanasio, Orazio, Sagiri Kitao, and Giovanni L. Violante. "Financing Medicare: A general equilibrium analysis." Demography and the Economy. University of Chicago Press, 2010. 333–366. (Idiosyncratic risk)	DEMOG. EC.	2010		x
Bonneuil, Noël. "Viability, optimality and sustainability in vintage models." Optimal Control of Age-structured Populations in Economy, Demography, and the Environment. Routledge, 2013. 126–143. (Idiosyncratic shocks)	OPT.CONT.	2013		x
Börsch-Supan, Axel, Alexander Ludwig, and Joachim Winter. "Aging, pension reform, and capital flows: a multi-country simulation model." MEA Discussion Papers 64 (2004). (Idiosyncratic risk)	NA	2004		x
Bucciol, Alessandro. "Social security, self-control problems and unknown preference parameters." (2009): 001. (Behavioral, idiosyncratic risk)	NA	2009		x
Bullard, James, and James Feigenbaum. "A leisurely reading of the life-cycle consumption data." Journal of Monetary Economics 54.8 (2007): 2305–2320. (Idiosyncratic risk)	J.MON.EC	2007		x
Bütler, Monika. "Anticipation effects of looming public-pension reforms." Carnegie-Rochester Conference Series on Public Policy. Vol. 50. North-Holland, 1999. (Idiosyncratic risk)	CARN.ROCH	1999		x
Castaneda, Ana, Javier Diaz-Gimenez, and Jose-Victor Rios-Rull. "Accounting for the US earnings and wealth inequality." Journal of Political Economy 111.4 (2003): 818–857. (Idiosyncratic risk)	JPE	2003	x	x
Chambers, Matthew S., Carlos Garriga, and Don Schlagenhauf. "Mortgage innovation, mortgage choice, and housing decisions." Federal Reserve Bank of St. Louis Review 90.6 (2008): 585–608. (Idiosyncratic risk)	FED. ST.L	2008		x
Chambers, Matthew, and Don E. Schlagenhauf. Household Portfolio Allocations, Life Cycle Effects and Anticipated Ination. Mimeo, 2003. (Idiosyncratic risk)	NA	2003		x
Chambers, Matthew, Carlos Garriga, and Don E. Schlagenhauf. "Housing tenure and investment decisions." manuscript, Florida State University (2005). (Idiosyncratic shocks)	NA	2005		x

(Continued)

Citation	Published	Date	Top 5	Idiosyncratic
Chambers, Matthew, Carlos Garriga, and Donald Schlagenhauf. "Mortgage contracts and housing tenureduration decision." Federal Reserve Bank of Atlanta conference "Housing, Mortgage Finance, and the Macroeconomy," May 2005. (Idiosyncratic shocks)	FED. ATL.	2005		x
Conesa, Juan C., and Dirk Krueger. "Social security reform with heterogeneous agents." Review of Economic Dynamics 2.4 (1999): 757–795. (Idiosyncratic risk)	RED	1999		x
Cubeddu, Luis, and José-Víctor Ríos-Rull. "Families as shocks." Journal of the European Economic Association 1.2–3 (2003): 671–682. (Idiosyncratic risk)	JEEA	2003		x
De la Croix, David, Olivier Pierrard, and Henri R. Sneessens. "Aging and pensions in general equilibrium: labor market imperfections matter." Journal of Economic Dynamics and Control 37.1 (2013): 104–124. (Idiosyncratic risk)	JEDC	2013		x
Den Haan, Wouter J. "The importance of the number of different agents in a heterogeneous asset-pricing model." Journal of Economic Dynamics and Control 25.5 (2001): 721–746. (Idiosyncratic shocks) (Econometric analysis, no formal model)	JEDC	2001		
Dyrda, Sebastian, Greg Kaplan, and José-Víctor Ríos-Rull. Business cycles and household formation: the micro vs the macro labor elasticity. No. w17880. National Bureau of Economic Research, 2012. (Perpetual youth)	NA	2012		
Edmond, Chris, and Laura Veldkamp. "Income dispersion and counter-cyclical markups." Journal of Monetary Economics 56.6 (2009): 791–804. (Idiosyncratic risk)	J. MON. EC.	2009		x
Feigenbaum, James, and Geng Li. "A semiparametric characterization of income uncertainty over the lifecycle." Available at SSRN 1247451 (2010). (Idiosyncratic risk)	NA	2010		x
Feigenbaum, James. The Contributions of Borrowing Constraints and Uncertainty to Aggregate Saving. Working Paper, 2006. (Idiosyncratic risk)	NA	2006		x
Galasso, Vincenzo. "The US social security system: what does political sustainability imply?" Review of Economic Dynamics 2.3 (1999): 698–730. (Idiosyncratic risk)	RED	1999		x
Golosov, Mikhail, and Aleh Tsyvinski. "Designing optimal disability insurance: a case for asset testing." Journal of Political Economy 114.2 (2006): 257–279. (Parameter specification taken from RR; model is essentially ILA)	JPE	2006	x	

(Continued)

(Continued)

Citation	Published	Date	Top 5	Idiosyncratic
Hairault, Jean-Olivier, Thepthida Sopraseuth, and François Langot. "Distance to retirement and older workers 'employment: the case for delaying the retirement age." Journal of the European Economic Association 8.5 (2010): 1034–1076. (Non-stochastic model, uses RR parameterizations)	JEEA	2010		
Haliassos, Michael, and Alexander Michaelides. "Calibration and computation of household portfolio models." L. Guiso and M. Haliassos and T. Jappelli (2002): 55–101. (Idiosyncratic risk)	NA	2002		x
Hansen, Gary D., and Selahattin İmrohoroğlu. "Consumption over the life cycle: the role of annuities." Review of Economic Dynamics 11.3 (2008): 566–583. (Idiosyncratic risk)	RED	2008		x
Heathcote, Jonathan, Kjetil Storesletten, and Giovanni L. Violante. "The Cross-sectional implications of rising wage inequality in the united states." Available at SSRN 527645 (2004). (Idiosyncratic risk)	NA	2004		x
Huang, He, Selahattin Imrohoroglu, and Thomas J. Sargent. "Two computations to fund social security." Macroeconomic Dynamics 1.1 (1997): 7–44. (Idiosyncratic risk)	MD	1997		x
Huggett, Mark, and Gustavo Ventura. "Understanding why high income households save more than low income households." Journal of Monetary Economics 45.2 (2000): 361–397. (Idiosyncratic risk, use RR paramerizations)	J.MON.EC	2000		x
İmrohoroğlu, Ayşe, Selahattin İmrohoroğlu, and Douglas H. Joines. "Social security in an overlapping generations economy with land." Review of Economic Dynamics 2.3 (1999): 638–665. (Idiosyncratic risk; use RR parameterizations)	RED	1999		x
İmrohoroğlu, Ayşe, Selahattin İmrohoroğlu, and Douglas H. Joines. "Time-inconsistent preferences and social security." The Quarterly Journal of Economics 118.2 (2003): 745–784. (Perpetual youth)	QJE	2003	x	
İmrohoroğlu, Selahattin. "A quantitative analysis of capital income taxation." International Economic Review (1998): 307–328. (Idiosyncratic risk; uses RR parameterizations)	IER	1998		x
Jaimovich, Nir, and Henry E. Siu. "The young, the old, and the restless: demographics and business cycle volatility." American Economic Review 99.3 (2009): 804–826. (No formal model)	AER	2009	x	
Kaplan, Greg. "Moving back home: insurance against labor market risk." Journal of Political Economy 120.3 (2012): 446–512. (Repeated game, finite horizon)	JPE	2012	x	
Kawaguchi, Daiji, and Tetsushi Murao. "Labor–market institutions and long-term effects of youth unemployment." Journal of Money, Credit and Banking 46.S2 (2014): 95–116.	JMCB	2014		

(Continued)

Citation	Published	Date	Top 5	Idiosyncratic
Kopecky, Joseph. "An aging dynamo: demographic change and the decline of entrepreneurial activity in the United States." Available at SSRN 2907198 (2017). (Idiosyncratic risk)	NA	2017		x
Krusell, Per, and Jose-Victor Rios-Rull. "On the size of US government: political economy in the neoclassical growth model." American Economic Review 89.5 (1999): 1156–1181. (Pol. Econ.)	AER	1999	x	
Krusell, Per, and Jose-Victor Rios-Rull. "Vested interests in a positive theory of stagnation and growth." The Review of Economic Studies 63.2 (1996): 301–329. (Political economy)	RESTUD	1996	x	
Kubler, Felix, and Karl Schmedders. "Approximate versus exact equilibria in dynamic economies." Econometrica 73.4 (2005): 1205–1235. (Approximation theory)	ETRICA	2005	x	
Meghir, Costas, and Luigi Pistaferri. "Earnings, consumption and life cycle choices." Handbook of labor economics. Vol. 4. Elsevier, 2011: 773–854. (Empirical, no formal model)	HBLABOR	2011		
Miles, David, and Aleš Černý. "Risk return and portfolio allocation under alternative pension systems with imperfect financial markets." Available at SSRN 268281 (2001). (Idiosyncratic risk; no actual citation in text)	NA	2001		x
Miles, David, and Aleš Černý. "Risk, return and portfolio allocation under alternative pension arrangements with imperfect financial markets." (2001). (Idiosyncratic shocks)	NA	2001		x
Obrizan, Maksym, Martin Karlsson, and Mykhailo Matvieiev. "The Macroeconomic Impact of the 1918–19 Influenza Pandemic in Sweden." (2020). (Idiosyncratic shocks)	NA	2020		x
Park, Hyeon, and James Feigenbaum. "Bounded rationality, lifecycle consumption, and social security." Journal of Economic Behavior & Organization 146 (2018): 65–105. (Adaptive expectations – not sure how to classify)	JEBO	2018		
Pugsley, Benjamin Wild, and Ayşegül Şahin. "Grown-up business cycles." The Review of Financial Studies 32.3 (2019): 1102–1147. (Partial equilibrium finance model)	RFS	2019	x	
Pytka, Krzysztof. "Shopping effort in self-insurance economies." Work (2018). (Idiosyncratic risk)	WORK	2018		x
Rios-Rull, Jose-Victor. "Working in the market, working at home, and the acquisition of skills: a general-equilibrium approach." The American Economic Review (1993): 893–907. (Two-period OLG)	AER	1993	x	

(Continued)

(Continued)

Citation	Published	Date	Top 5	Idiosyncratic
Santos, Marcelo Rodrigues dos, and Thiago Neves Pereira. "Moving to a consumption-based tax system: a quantitative assessment for Brazil." Revista Brasileira de Economia 64 (2010): 209–228. (Idiosyncratic risk)	BRAZIL	2010		x
Serrano-Puente, Darío. "Optimal progressivity of personal income tax: a general equilibrium evaluation for Spain." SERIEs 11.4 (2020): 407–455. (Idiosyncratic shocks)	SERIES	2020		x
Simon, Laure. "Fiscal Stimulus and Skill Accumulation over the Life Cycle." European University Institute, Mimeo (2019). (Idiosyncratic shocks)	NA	2019		x
Straub, Ludwig. "Consumption, savings, and the distribution of permanent income." Unpublished manuscript, Harvard University (2019). (Idiosyncratic risk)	NA	2019		x
Ventura, Gustavo. "Flat tax reform: a quantitative exploration." Journal of Economic Dynamics and Control 23.9–10 (1999): 1425–1458. (Idiosyncratic risk)	JEDC	1999		x
Xu, Xin. "The business cycle and health behaviors." Social Science & Medicine 77 (2013): 126–136. (Static econometric model)	SOCSCIMED	2013		

Vacuous citations: Total = 31

Angeletos, George-Marios. "Idiosyncratic investment risk in a neoclassical growth economy." Unpublished manuscript, Massachusetts Institute of Technology (2003).

Basso, Henrique S., and Omar Rachedi. "The young, the old, and the government: demographics and fiscal multipliers." (2018).

Benzoni, Luca, and Olena Chyruk. "The value and risk of human capital." (2015).

Bohn, Henning. "Intergenerational risk sharing and fiscal policy." UCSB Department of Economics Working Paper. Available at http://econ.ucsb.edu/%7Ebohn/papers/igrisk.pdf (2003).

Börsch-Supan, Axel, Alexander Ludwig, and Joachim Winter. "Ageing, pension reform and capital flows: a multi-country simulation model." Economica 73.292 (2006): 625–658. (Deterministic model)

Börsch-Supan, Axel, and Alexander Ludwig. "Old Europe Ages. Can it still prosper?." (2009).

Brumm, Johannes, and Felix Kuebler. "Applying Negishi's method to stochastic models with overlapping generations." NCCR FINRISK Working Paper Series 851 (2013).

Chambers, Matthew, Carlos Garriga, and Don E. Schlagenhauf. "Accounting for changes in the homeownership rate." International Economic Review 50.3 (2009): 677–726. (Perpetual youth model)

Chambers, Matthew, Carlos Garriga, and Don Schlagenhauf. "Equilibrium mortgage choice and housing tenure decisions with refinancing." Available at SSRN 1028118 (2007). (Idiosyncratic risk)

Chambers, Matthew, Carlos Garriga, and Don Schlagenhauf. "Mortgage contracts and housing tenure decisions." Available at SSRN 1014448 (2007).

Chari, Varadarajan V., and Patrick J. Kehoe. "Modern macroeconomics in practice: how theory is shaping policy." Journal of Economic Perspectives 20.4 (2006): 3–28.

Chari, Varadarajan V., Lawrence J. Christiano, and Patrick J. Kehoe. "Policy analysis in business cycle models." Frontiers of Business Cycle Research 12 (1995).

DE TRABAJO, D. O. C. U. M. E. N. T. O. S. "Serie Economía." (2007).

(Continued)

Díaz Giménez, Javier, and Josep Pijoan-Mas. "Flat tax reforms in the US: a boon for the income poor." Available at SSRN 936973 (2006).
Elder, Erick. "Dynamic fiscal policy with regime-duration uncertainty: The Tax-Cut Case." Journal of Macroeconomics 21.1 (1999): 29–55. (Idiosyncratic risk)
Emenogu, Ugochi, and Brian Peterson. Unregulated Lending, Mortgage Regulations and Monetary Policy. No. 2022-28. Bank of Canada, 2022.
Fitzgerald, Terry J. "Work schedules, wages, and employment in a general equilibrium model with team production." Review of Economic Dynamics 1.4 (1998): 809–834.
Fonseca, Raquel, and Thepthida Sopraseuth. "Distributional effects of social security reforms: the case of France." Canadian Journal of Economics/Revue Canadienne D'économique 52.3 (2019): 1289–1320. (Idiosyncratic shocks)
Gong, Jing, Brad N. Greenwood, and Yiping Amy Song. "Uber might buy me a Mercedes Benz: an empirical investigation of the sharing economy and durable goods purchase." Available at SSRN 2971072 (2017).
Grafenhofer, Dominik, et al. "Probabilistic aging." (2006).
He, Hui. "Skill premium, schooling decisions, skill-biased technological and demographic change: a macroeconomic analysis." Manuscript, University of Minnesota (2006).
Heathcote, Jonathan, Kjetil Storesletten, and Giovanni L. Violante. "Quantitative macroeconomics with heterogeneous households." (2009).
Iacoviello, Matteo, and Marina Pavan. "Housing and debt over the life cycle and over the business cycle." Journal of Monetary Economics 60.2 (2013): 221–238. (Use Krusell-Smith approach)
Ji, Yan. "Job search under debt: Aggregate implications of student loans." Journal of Monetary Economics 117 (2021): 741–759.
Jones, Callum. "Aging, secular stagnation and the business cycle." The Review of Economics and Statistics (2016): 1–46.
Kocherlakota, Narayana R. "The effects of moral hazard on asset prices when financial markets are complete." Journal of Monetary Economics 41.1 (1998): 39–56.
Krebs, Tom, Pravin Krishna, and William Maloney. "Human capital, trade liberalization and income risk." Trade, Globalization and Poverty 10 (2007): 84.
Mehrotra, Neil R., and Dmitriy Sergeyev. "Debt sustainability in a low interest rate world." Journal of Monetary Economics 124 (2021): S1–S18.
Miles, David, and Aleš Černý. "Risk, return and portfolio allocation under alternative pension systems with incomplete and imperfect financial markets." The Economic Journal 116.511 (2006): 529–557.
Miles, David. "Modelling the impact of demographic change upon the economy." The Economic Journal 109.452 (1999): 1–36. (Deterministic model)
Ragot, Xavier. "Monetary policy with heterogenous agents and credit constraints." (2005).
Singh, Aarti. "Human capital risk in life-cycle economies." Journal of Monetary Economics 57.6 (2010): 729–738.

REFERENCES

Abel, A., Mankiw, G., Summers, L., & Zeckhauser, R. (1989). Assessing dynamic efficiency: Theory and evidence. *Review of Economic Studies*, *56*(1), 1–19.

Abreu, D., Pearce, D., & Stacchetti, E. (1986). Optimal cartel equilibria with imperfect monitoring. *Journal of Economic Theory*, *39*(1), 251–269.

Aiyagari, S. R. (1981). *Putty-clay durable capital in stochastic overlapping generations models*. Ph.D. thesis, University of Minnesota, Minneapolis, MN.

Aiyagari, S. R. (1985). Observational equivalence of the overlapping generations and the discounted dynamic programming frameworks for one-sector growth. *Journal of Economic Theory*, *35*(2), 201–221.

Aiyagari, S. R. (1987). Optimality & monetary equilibria in stationary overlapping generations models with long-lived agents: Growth versus discounting. *Journal of Economic Theory*, *43*(2), 292–313.

Aiyagari, S. R. (1988). Nonmonetary steady states in stationary overlapping generations models with long lived agents and discounting: Multiplicity, optimality, and consumption smoothing. *Journal of Economic Theory*, *45*(1), 102–127.

Aiyagari, S. R. (1994). Uninsured idiosyncratic risk and aggregate saving. *Quarterly Journal of Economics*, *109*(3), 659–684.

Aiyagari, S. R., & Peled, D. (1991). Dominant root characterization of pareto optimality and the existence of optimal equilibria in stochastic overlapping generations models. *Journal of Economic Theory*, *54*(1), 69–83.

Aliprantis, C., & Border, K. (2006). *Infinite dimensional analysis: A Hitchhiker's guide*. New York, NY: Springer.

Allais, M. (1947). *Économie et intérêt*. Paris: Imprimerie National.

Altermatt, L. (2019). Savings, asset scarcity, and monetary policy. *Journal of Economic Theory*, *182*(C), 329–359.

Altig, D., & Nosal, E. (2017). An interview with Neil Wallace. *Macroeconomic Dynamics*, *21*(7), 1790–1810.

Álvarez, A., & Ritchey, T. (2015). Applications of general morphological analysis. *Acta Morphologica Generalis*, *4*(1), 1–40.

Ameriks, J., Caplin, A., Laufer, S., & Van Nieuwerburgh, S. (2011). The joy of giving or assisted living? Using strategic surveys to separate public care aversion from bequest motives. *Journal of Finance*, *66*(2), 519–561.

Anderson, R. (1991). Non-standard analysis with applications to economics. In W. Hildenbrand & H. Sonnenschein (Eds.) *Handbook of mathematical economics* (1st ed., Vol. 4, Chap. 39, pp. 2145–2208). Amsterdam: Elsevier.

Angeletos, G., & La'O, J. (2013). Sentiments. *Econometrica*, *81*(2), 739–779.

Araujo, A. (1991). The once but not twice differentiability of the policy function. *Econometrica*, *59*(5), 1383–1393.

Arrow, K. (1957). Statistics and economic policy. *Econometrica*, *25*(4), 523–531.

Arrow, K., & Kurz, M. (1969). Optimal consumer allocation over an infinite horizon. *Journal of Economic Theory*, *1*(1), 68–91.

Aubin, D., & Dalmedico, A. (2002). Writing the history of dynamical systems and chaos. *Historia Mathematica*, *29*(3), 273–339.

Auerbach, A. (1979). The optimal taxation of heterogeneous capital. *Quarterly Journal of Economics*, *93*(4), 589–612.

Auerbach, A., & Kotlikoff, L. (1983a). National savings, economic welfare, and the structure of taxation. In M. Feldstein (Ed.), *Behavioral simulation methods in tax policy analysis* (pp. 459–498). Chicago, IL: University of Chicago Press.

Auerbach, A., & Kotlikoff, L. (1983b). Investment versus savings incentives: The size of the bang for the buck and the potential for self-financing business tax cuts. In L. H. Meyer (Ed.), *The economic consequences of government deficits* (pp. 121–149). Dordrecht: Springer.

Auerbach, A., & Kotlikoff, L. (1985). *The efficiency gains from social security benefit-tax linkage*. NBER Working Paper No. 1645. National Bureau of Economic Research, Inc, Cambridge, MA.

Auerbach, A., & Kotlikoff, L. (1987a). *Dynamic fiscal policy*. Cambridge: Cambridge University Press.

Auerbach, A., & Kotlikoff, L. (1987b). Evaluating fiscal policy with a dynamic simulation model. *American Economic Review*, *77*(2), 49–55.

Azariadis, C. (1981). Self-fulfilling prophecies. *Journal of Economic Theory*, *25*(3), 380–396.

Azariadis, C., & Guesnerie, R. (1986). Sunspots and cycles. *Review of Economic Studies*, *53*(5), 725–737.

Backhouse, R., & Cherrier, B. (2017). "It's computers, stupid!" The spread of computers and the changing roles of theoretical and applied economics. *History of Political Economy*, *49*(Suppl.), 103–126.

Balasko, Y. (2009). *The equilibrium manifold: Postmodern developments in the theory of general economic equilibrium*. Cambridge, MA: MIT Press.

Balasko, Y. (2016). *Foundations of the theory of general equilibrium* (2nd ed.). Singapore: World Scientific.

Balasko, Y., Cass, D., & Shell, K. (1980). Existence of competitive equilibrium in a general overlapping-generations model. *Journal of Economic Theory*, *23*(3), 307–322.

Balasko, Y., & Shell, K. (1980). The overlapping-generations model, I: The case of pure exchange without money. *Journal of Economic Theory*, *23*(3), 281–306.

Balasko, Y., & Shell, K. (1981a). The overlapping-generations model, II: The case of pure exchange with money. *Journal of Economic Theory*, *24*(1), 112–142.

Balasko, Y., & Shell, K. (1981b). The overlapping-generations model, III: The case of log-linear utility functions. *Journal of Economic Theory*, *24*(1), 143–152.

Barnett, W., & Chen, G. (2015). Bifurcation of macroeconometric models and robustness of dynamical inferences. *Foundations and Trends in Econometrics*, *8*(1–2), 1–144.

Barnett, W., & Eryilmaz, U. (2022). *Monetary policy & determinacy: An inquiry in open economy new keynesian framework*. Working Paper. Department of Economics, University of Kansas, Lawrence, KS.

Barro, R. (1974). Are government bonds net wealth?. *Journal of Political Economy*, *82*(6), 1095–1117.

Barro, R. (1989). The neoclassical approach to fiscal policy In R. Barro (Ed.), *Modern business cycle theory* (pp. 178–235). Cambridge, MA: Harvard University Press.

Barro, R., & Becker, G. (1986). Altruism and the economic theory of fertility. *Population and Development Review*, *12*(Suppl.), 69–76.

Barro, R., & Becker, G. (1988). A reformulation of the economic theory of fertility. *Quarterly Journal of Economics*, *103*(1), 1–25.

Barro, R., & Becker, G. (1989). Fertility choice in a model of economic growth. *Econometrica*, *57*(2), 481–501.

Beel, J., & Gipp, B. (2009). Google scholar's ranking algorithm: An introductory overview. In B. Larsen & J. Leta (Eds.), *Proceedings of the 12th international conference on scientometrics and informetrics*, Rio de Janeiro, Brazil (Vol. 1, pp. 230–241).

Bénassy-Quéré, A. (2010). *Economic policy: Theory and practice*. New York, NY: Oxford University Press.

Benhabib, J. (2021). *Cycles and chaos in economic equilibrium*. Princeton, NJ: Princeton University Press.

Benhabib, J., & Bisin, A. (2018). Skewed wealth distributions: Theory and empirics. *Journal of Economic Literature*, *56*(4), 1261–1291.

Benhabib, J., & Day, R. (1982). A characterization of erratic dynamics in the overlapping generations model. *Journal of Economic Dynamics and Control*, *4*(1) 37–55.

Benhabib, J., & Farmer, R. (1999). Indeterminacy and sunspots in macroeconomics. In J. Taylor & M. Woodford (Eds.), *Handbook of macroeconomics* (Vol. 1A, pp. 387–448). Amsterdam: North-Holland.

Benhabib, J., Miao, J., & Wang, P. (2016). Chaotic banking crises and regulations. *Economic Theory*, *61*(2), 393–422.

Benhabib, J., Wang, P., & Wen, Y. (2015). Sentiments and aggregate demand fluctuations. *Econometrica, 83*(2), 549–585.

Benveniste, L., & Cass, D. (1986). On the existence of optimal stationary equilibria with a fixed supply of fiat money: I. The case of a single consumer. *Journal of Political Economy, 94*(2), 402–417.

Bernheim, B. (1989). Intergenerational altruism, dynastic equilibria & social welfare. *Review of Economic Studies, 56*(1), 119–128.

Bernheim, B. (1991). How strong are bequest motives? Evidence based on estimates of the demand for life insurance and annuities. *Journal of Political Economy, 99*(5), 899–927.

Bernheim, B., & Bagwell, K. (1988). Is everything neutral? *Journal of Political Economy, 96*(2), 308–338.

Bernheim, B., Schleifer, A., & Summers, L. (1986). The strategic bequest motive. *Journal of Labor Economics, 4*(3, Part 2), S151–S182.

Bewley, T. (1977). The permanent income hypothesis: A theoretical formulation. *Journal of Economic Theory, 16*(2), 252–292.

Bewley, T. (1986). Stationary monetary equilibrium with a continuum of independently fluctuating consumers. In W. Hildenbrand & A. Mas-Colell (Eds.), *Contributions to mathematical economics in honor of Gerard Debreu* (pp. 27–102). Amsterdam: North Holland.

Bhattacharya, J., & Russell, S. (2003). Two-period cycles in a three-period overlapping generations model. *Journal of Economic Theory, 109*(2), 378–401.

Bierwag, G., Grove, M., & Khang, C. (1969). National debt in a neo-classical growth model: Comment. *American Economic Review, 59*(1), 205–210.

Blackorby, C., & Russell, R. (1992). *On the observational equivalence of models with infinitely lived agents and models with overlapping generations*. Working Paper No. 92–15. Anderson Graduate School of Management, University of California, Riverside, CA.

Blanchard, O. (1985). Debt, deficits, and finite horizons. *Journal of Political Economy, 93*(2), 223–247.

Blanchard, O. (2018). On the future of macroeconomic models. *Oxford Review of Economic Policy, 34*(1–2), 43–54.

Blanchard, O. (2019). *Public debt: Fiscal and welfare costs in a time of low interest rates*. Policy Briefs No. PB19-2. Washington, DC: Petersen Institute for International Economics.

Blanchard, O., & Kahn, C. (1980). The solution of linear difference models under rational expectations. *Econometrica, 48*(5), 1305–1311.

Bloise, G. (2001). A geometric approach to sunspot equilibria. *Journal of Economic Theory, 101*(2), 519–539.

Bloise, G. (2004). A note on sunspot equilibrium in sequential economies. *Research in Economics, 58*(1), 59–74.

Bloise, G., & Calciano, F. (2008). A characterization of inefficiency in stochastic overlapping generations economies. *Journal of Economic Theory, 143*(1), 442–468.

Blume, L. (1982). New techniques for the study of stochastic equilibrium processes. *Journal of Mathematical Economics, 9*(1–2), 61–70.

Bosi, S., & Seegmuller, T. (2005). *Animal spirits in Woodford & Reichlin economies: The representative agent does matter*. Working Paper No. 05-01, EPEE, University of Evry.

Brock, W., & Gale, D. Optimal growth under factor augmenting progress. *Journal of Economic Theory, 1*(3), 229–243.

Brock, W., Hsieh, D., & Le Baron, B. (1991). *Nonlinear dynamics, chaos, and instability: Statistical theory and economic evidence*. Cambridge, MA: MIT Press.

Brock, W., & Mirman, L. (1972). Optimal economic growth & uncertainty: The discounted case. *Journal of Economic Theory, 4*(3), 479–513.

Browning, M., Hansen, L., & Heckman, J. (1999). Micro data & general equilibrium models. In J. Taylor & M. Woodford (Eds.), *Handbook of macroeconomics* (Vol. 1A, pp. 543–633). Amsterdam: North-Holland.

Brumm, J., & Kubler, F. (2013). *Applying Negishi's method to stochastic models with overlapping generations*. NCCR FINRISK Working Paper Series 851. FINRISK.

Brunner, K., & Meltzer, A. (1971). The uses of money: Money in the theory of an exchange economy. *American Economic Review, 61*(5), 784–805.

Bruss, F. (1984). A note on extinction criteria for bisexual Galton–Watson processes. *Journal of Applied Probability, 21*(4), 915–919.

Buchanan, J. (1976). Barro on the Ricardian equivalence theorem. *Journal of Political Economy*, *84*(2), 337–342.

Burke, J. L. (1999). The robustness of optimal equilibrium among overlapping generations. *Economic Theory*, *14*(2), 311–329.

Cass, D. (1965). Optimum growth in an aggregative model of capital accumulation. *Review of Economic Studies*, *32*(3), 233–240.

Cass, D. (1982). On the existence of an optimal stationary equilibrium with a fixed supply of fiat money II: The case of many consumers with arbitrary lifetimes. Retrieved from https://econ.tepper.cmu.edu/spear/cass92.pdf.

Cass, D. (1989). Sunspots and incomplete financial markets: The leading example. In G. Feiwel (Ed.). *The economics of imperfect competition and employment* (pp. 677–693). London: Palgrave Macmillan.

Cass, D., & Shell, K. (1983). Do sunspots matter? *Journal of Political Economy*, *91*(2), 193–227.

Cass, D., & Yaari, M. (1965). *Individual saving, aggregate capital accumulation, and efficient growth*. Cowles Foundation Discussion Paper 198, November.

Cass, D., & Yaari, M. (1966a). A re-examination of the pure consumption loans model. *Journal of Political Economy*, *74*(4), 353–367.

Cass, D., & Yaari, M. (1966b). *A note on the role of money in providing sufficient intermediation*. Cowles Foundation Discussion Paper 215, September.

Castaneda, A., Diaz-Gimenez, J., & Rios-Rull, J-V. (2003). Accounting for the US earnings and wealth inequality. *Journal of Political Economy*, *111*(4), 818–857.

Chatelain, J.-B., & Ralf, K. (2018). Publish & perish: Creative destruction & macroeconomic theory. *History of Economic Ideas*, *26*(2), 65–101.

Chattopadhyay, S., & Gottardi, P. (1999). Stochastic OLG models, market structure, and optimality. *Journal of Economic Theory*, *89*(1), 21–67.

Cherrier, B., & Saidi, A. (2018). The indeterminate fate of sunspots in economics. *History of Political Economy*, *50*(3), 425–481.

Citanna, A., & Siconolfi, P. (2007). Short-memory equilibrium in stochastic overlapping generations economies. *Journal of Economic Theory*, *134*(1), 448–469.

Citanna, A., & Siconolfi, P. (2008). On the nonexistence of recursive equilibrium in stochastic OLG economies. *Economic Theory*, *37*(3), 417–437.

Citanna, A., & Siconolfi, P. (2010). Recursive equilibrium in stochastic overlapping-generations economies. *Econometrica*, *78*(1), 309–347.

Clower, R. (1967). A reconsideration of the microfoundations of monetary theory. *Economic Inquiry*, *6*(1), 1–8.

Coleman, W. (1989). *An algorithm to solve dynamic models*. International Finance Division Discussion Paper 351. Washington, DC: Federal Reserve Board of Governors.

Conesa, J., & Krueger, D. (1999). Social security reform with heterogeneous agents. *Review of Economic Dynamics*, *2*(4), 757–795.

Corbae, D., Temzelides, T., & Wright, R. (2003). Directed matching & monetary exchange. *Econometrica*, *71*(3), 731–756.

Cutler, D. (1993). Review of L. Kotlikoff. *Generational Accounting, National Tax Journal*, *46*(1), 61–67.

De Nardi, M., Imrohoro⊠lu, S., & Sargent, T. (1999). Projected US demographics and social security. *Review of Economic Dynamics*, *2*(3), 575–615.

De Nardi, M., Imrohoroglu, S., & Sargent, T. (2001). Saving and pension reform in general equilibrium models. *Oxford Review of Economic Policy*, *17*(1), 20–39.

Deardorff, A. (1976). The optimum growth rate for population: Comment. *International Economic Review*, *17*(2), 510–515.

Deaton, A. (1992). *Understanding consumption*. New York, NY: Oxford University Press.

Debreu, G. (1951). The coefficient of resource utilization. *Econometrica*, *19*(3), 273–292.

Debreu, G. (1954). Valuation equilibrium and Pareto optimum. *Proceedings of the National Academy of Sciences*, *40*(7), 588.

Debreu, G. (1970). Economies with a finite set of equilibria. *Econometrica*, *38*(3), 387–392.

Debreu, G. (1974). Excess demand functions. *Journal of Mathematical Economics*, *1*(1), 15–21.

Demange, G. (2002). On optimality in intergenerational risk sharing. *Economic Theory*, *20*(1), 1–27.

Den Haan, W., & Marcet, A. (1990). Solving the stochastic growth model by parameterizing expectations. *Journal of Business and Economic Statistics*, *8*(1), 31–34.

Diamond, P. (1963, May). *Essays in optimal economic growth*. Ph.D. thesis, MIT, Cambridge, MA.

Diamond, P. (1965). National debt in a neoclassical growth model. *American Economic Review*, *55*(5), 1126–1150.

Diamond, P. (1967, 1970). *Incidence of an interest income tax*. MIT Working Paper (1967), subsequently published in *Journal of Economic Theory*, *2*(3), 211–224.

Diamond, P. (1973). Taxation and public production in a growth setting. In N. Stern & J. Mirrlees (Eds.), *Models of economic growth* (pp. 215–240). London: Palgrave Macmillan.

Diamond, P. (2014). My research strategy. In M. Szenberg & L. Ramrattan (Eds.), *Eminent economists II: Their work and life philosophies* (pp. 111–117). New York, NY: Cambridge University Press.

Diamond, P., Koopmans, T., & Williamson, R. (1962). Stationary utility and time perspective. Cowles Foundation Discussion Paper 371, August.

Dimand, R. (2022). *James tobin on life cycle-OLG, general equilibrium and macroeconomics in perspective*. Working Paper, Brock University.

Dixit, A., & Stiglitz, J. (1977). Monopolistic competition and optimum product diversity. *American Economic Review*, *67*(3), 297–308.

Dolde, W., & Tobin, J. (1981, May). *Mandatory retirement saving & capital formation*. Cowles Foundation Discussion Paper No. 830. Cowles Foundation, Yale University, New Haven, CT.

Duffie, D., Geanakoplos, J., Mas-Colell, A., & McLennan, A. (1994). Stationary Markov equilibria. *Econometrica*, *62*(4), 745–781.

Duq, F., & Ghiglino, C. (1998). Optimality of barter steady states. *Journal of Economic Dynamics and Control*, *22*(7), 1053–1067.

Durlauf, S. (2007). An interview with costas azariadis. *Macroeconomic Dynamics*, *11*(2), 249–271.

Engineer, M., & Welling, L. (2004). Overlapping generations models and graded age-set societies. *Journal of Institutional and Theoretical Economics*, *160*(3), 454–476.

Erdos, P., & Renyi, A. (1959). On random graphs I. *Publications Mathematicae*, *6*, 290–297.

Evans, G., & Honkapohja, S. (2012). *Learning and expectations in macroeconomics*. Princeton, NJ: Princeton University Press.

Farmer, R. (1984). A new theory of aggregate supply. *American Economic Review*, *74*(5), 920–930.

Farmer, R. (1986). Deficits and cycles. *Journal of Economic Theory*, *40*(1), 77–88.

Farmer, R. (1991). The Lucas Critique, policy invariance and multiple equilibria. *Review of Economic Studies*, *58*(2), 321–332.

Farmer, R. (2002). Why does data reject the Lucas Critique? *Annales d'économie et de Statistique*, *67/68*, 111–129.

Farmer, R. (2008). Old Keynesian economics. Paper originally presented at a conference in honor of Axel Leijonhufvud, UCLA, August 30, 2006. In R. Farmer (Ed.). (2009). *Macroeconomics in the small and large* (pp. 23–43). Cheltenham: Elgar.

Farmer, R. (2010, November). *Animal spirits, persistent unemployment and the belief function*. National Bureau of Economic Research Working Paper No. 16522. NBER, New York.

Farmer, R. (2013). The natural rate hypothesis: An idea past its sell-by date. *Bank of England Quarterly Bulletin*, Quarter 3, *September*, 244–256.

Farmer, R. (2017). Post-Keynesian dynamic stochastic general equilibrium theory. *European Journal of Economics and Economic Policies*, *14*(2), 173–185.

Farmer, R. (2020). The importance of beliefs in shaping macroeconomic outcomes. *Oxford Review of Economic Policy*, *36*(3), 675–711.

Farmer, R., & Woodford, M. (1984, 1997). Self-fulfilling prophecies and the business cycle. [Legacy paper]. *Macroeconomic Dynamics*, *1*(4), 740–769.

Favero, C., & Hendry, D. (1992). Testing the Lucas critique: A review. *Econometric Reviews*, *11*(3), 265–306.

Fehr, H., & Kotlikoff, L. (1995, April). *Generational accounting in general equilibrium*. NBER Working Paper 5090.

Feng, Z., Miao, J., Peralta-Alva, A., & Santos, M. (2014). Numerical simulation of non-optimal dynamic equilibrium models. *International Economic Review*, *55*(1), 83–110.

Fisher, I. (1907). *The rate of interest*. New York, NY: Macmillan.

Fisher, I. (1930). *The theory of interest*. New York, NY: Macmillan.

Gabaix, X., & Laibson, D. (2008). The seven properties of good models. In A. Caplin & A. Shotter (Eds.), *The methodologies of modern economics: Foundations of positive and normative economics* (pp. 292–319). New York, NY: Oxford University Press.

Gale, D. (1969). *Price equilibrium for infinite horizon economic models*. Working Paper No. ORC 69-23. Operations Research Center, College of Engineering, University of California, Berkeley, CA.

Gale, D. (1973). Pure exchange equilibrium of dynamic economic models. *Journal of Economic Theory*, *6*(1), 12–36.

Gale, D., & Shapley, L. (1962). College admissions & the stability of marriage. *American Mathematical Monthly*, *69*(1), 9–15.

Gale, W., & Scholz, J. (1994). Intergenerational transfers and the accumulation of wealth. *Journal of Economic Perspectives*, *8*(4), 145–160.

Galor, O., & Weil, D. (2000). Population, technology, and growth: From Malthusian stagnation to the demographic transition and beyond. *American Economic Review*, *90*(4), 806–828.

Geanakoplos, J. (1989). Overlapping generations model of general equilibrium. In J. Eatwell, M. Milgate, & P. Newman (Eds.), *General equilibrium* (pp. 205–233). London: Palgrave Macmillan.

Geanakoplos, J., & Brown, D. (1982). *Understanding overlapping generations economies as lack of market clearing at infinity*. Yale University, Mimeo. Presented at NBER conference on General Equilibrium, Northwestern University, March 1982 (revised 1985, 1986).

Geanakoplos, J., Magill, M., & Quinzii, M. (2004). Demography and the long-run predictability of the stock market. *Brookings Papers on Economic Activity*, *1*, 241–325.

Geanakoplos, J., & Shubik, M. (1990). The capital asset pricing model as a general equilibrium with incomplete markets. *Geneva Papers on Risk and Insurance Theory*, *15*(1), 55–71.

Gilman, M. (Ed.) (2012). *Robert Lucas's collected papers on Monetary Theory*. Cambridge, MA: Harvard University Press.

Glover, A., Heathcote, J., Krueger, D, & Rios-Rull, V. (2020). Intergenerational redistribution in the great recession. *Journal of Political Economy*, *128*(10), 3730–3778.

Goenka, A. (2003, October). *Non-fungibility and mental accounting: A model of bounded rationality with sunspot equilibria*. Working Paper, Department of Economics, University of Essex and National University of Singapore, Singapore.

Goenka, A. (2017). *Mental accounting & sunspot equilibria*. University of Birmingham WP August, Birmingham.

Gokhale, J., Kotlikoff, L., Sefton, J., & Weale, M. (2001). Simulating the transmission of wealth inequality via bequests. *Journal of Public Economics*, *79*(1), 93–128.

Gomme, P. (2015). Measuring the welfare costs of inflation in a life-cycle model. *Journal of Economic Dynamics and Control*, *57*(C), 132–144.

Gomme, P., Rogerson, R., Rupert, P., & Wright, R. (2004). The business cycle and the life cycle. *NBER Macroeconomics Annual*, *19*, 415–461.

Grandmont, J. M. (1970). *On the temporary competitive equilibrium*. Ph.D. thesis, University of California at Berkeley, Berkeley.

Grandmont, J. M. (1973). On the short-run equilibrium in a monetary economy. In J. Dreze (Ed.), *Allocation under uncertainty: Equilibrium and optimality* (pp. 213–228). London: Macmillan.

Grandmont, J. M. (1983). *On endogenous competitive business cycles*. CEPREMAP Discussion Paper No. 8316. Center for Economic Research and Applications, Paris.

Grandmont, J. M. (1984, January). *On endogenous competitive business cycles*. Technical Report Number 438, Center for Research on Organizational Efficiency, IMSSS, Stanford University, Stanford, CA.

Grandmont, J. M. (1985). On endogenous competitive business cycles. *Econometrica*, *53*(5), 995–1045.

Grandmont, J. M. (1989). Report on Maurice Allais' scientific work. *Scandinavian Journal of Economics*, *9*(1), 17–28.

Grandmont, J. M., & Malgrange, P. (1986). Introduction to the symposium volume on nonlinear dynamics. *Journal of Economic Theory*, *40*(1), 3–12.

Green, E. (1987). Lending and the smoothing of uninsurable income. In E. Prescott & N. Wallace (Eds.), *Contractual arrangements for intertemporal trade* (pp. 3–25). Minneapolis, MN: University of Minnesota Press.

Guzman, M., & Stiglitz, J. (2020). Towards a dynamic disequilibrium theory with randomness. *Oxford Review of Economic Policy*, *36*(3), 621–674.

Hansen, G., & Prescott, E. (2002). Malthus to solow. *American Economic Review*, *92*(4), 1205–1217.

Hansen, L., & Heckman, J. (1996). The empirical foundations of calibration. *Journal of Economic Perspectives*, *10*(1), 87–104.

Harenberg, D., & Alexander, L. (2015). Social security in an analytically tractable overlapping generations model with aggregate and idiosyncratic risks. *International Tax and Public Finance*, *22*(4), 579–603.

Hasanhodzic, J., & Kotlikoff, L. (2013, June). *Generational risk-is it a big deal?: Simulating an 80-period OLG model with aggregate shocks*. Working Paper No. W191979, National Bureau of Economic Research, Cambridge, MA.

He, H., Imrohoroglu, S., & Sargent, T. (1997). Two computations to fund social security. *Macroeconomic Dynamics*, *1*(1), 7–44.

Heer, B., & Maussner, A. (2009). *Dynamic general equilibrium modeling: Computational methods and applications*. Heidelberg: Springer.

Heer, B., & Maussner, A. (2012). The burden of unanticipated inflation: Analysis of an overlapping generations model with progressive income taxation & staggered prices. *Macroeoconomic Dynamics*, *16*(2), 278–308.

Helwig, M. (1980). Stochastic processes of temporary equilibria: A note. *Journal of Mathematical Economics*, *7*(3), 287–299.

Hendricks, K., Judd, K., & Kovenock, D. (1980). A note on the core of the overlapping generations model. *Economics Letters*, *6*(2), 95–97.

Henriksen, E., & Spear, S. (2012). Endogenous market incompleteness without market frictions: dynamic suboptimality of competitive equilibrium in multiperiod overlapping generations economies. *Journal of Economic Theory*, *147*(2), 426–449.

Holland, J., & Miller, J. (1991). Artificial adaptive agents in economic theory. *American Economic Review*, *81*(2), 365–370.

Hommes, C., & LeBaron, B. (Eds.). (2018). *Computational economics: Heterogeneous agent modeling*. Amsterdam: Elsevier.

Howitt, P., & McAfee, R. (1987). Costly search and recruiting. *International Economic Review*, *28*(1), 89–107.

Huffman, G. (1986). The representative agent, overlapping generations, and asset pricing. *Canadian Journal of Economics*, *19*(3), 511–521.

Huggett, M. (1993). The risk-free rate in heterogenous-agent incomplete-insurance economies. *Journal of Economic Dynamics and Control*, *17*(5–6), 953–969.

Jones, L., & Manuelli, R. (1992). Finite lifetimes & growth. *Journal of Economic Theory*, *58*(2), 171–197.

Judd, K. (1998). *Numerical methods in economics*. Cambridge, MA: MIT Press.

Kaldor, N. (1940). A model of the trade cycle. *Economic Journal*, *50*(197), 78–92.

Kalecki, M. (1935). A macro dynamic theory of business cycles. *Econometrica*, *3*(3), 327–344.

Kareken, J., & Wallace, N. (1977). Portfolio autarky: A welfare analysis. *Journal of International Economics*, *7*(1), 19–43.

Kareken, J., & Wallace, N. (Eds.). (1980). *Models of monetary economics*. Minneapolios, MN: Federal Reserve Bank of Minneapolis.

Kareken, J., & Wallace, N. (1981). On the indeterminacy of equilibrium exchange rates. *Quarterly Journal of Economics*, *96*(2), 207–222.

Kehoe, T., & Levine, D. (1984). Regularity in overlapping generations exchange economies. *Journal of Mathematical Economics*, *13*(1), 69–93.

Kehoe, T., & Levine. D. (1985). Comparative statics and perfect foresight in infinite horizon economies. *Econometrica*, *53*(2), 433–453.

Kehoe, T., Levine, D., & Romer, P. (1992). On characterizing equilibria of economies with externalities and taxes as solutions to optimization problems. *Economic Theory*, *2*(1), 43–68.

Kelly, D., & Shorish, J. (2000). Stability of functional rational expectations equilibria. *Journal of Economic Theory*, *95*(2), 215–250.

Keynes, J. M. (1936). *The general theory of employment, interest and money*. London: Macmillan.

Kim, E. (2019, May). Preference heterogeneity, aggregate risk & the welfare effects of social security. *Three essays in the stochastic overlapping generations models* (pp. 1–53, chapter 1). Unpublished Ph.D. thesis, Tepper School of Business, Carnegie Mellon University, Pittsburg, PA.

Kim, E., & Li, J. (2020). *Endogenous fluctuations in overlapping generations models with time inconsistency*. Working Paper, Department of Economics, University of Kansas, Lawrence, KS.

Kim, E., & Spear, S. (2021a). Determinate perfect foresight forecasting in overlapping generations models. *Economic Theory*, *71*(2), 505–531.

Kim, E., & Spear, S. (2021b). *The rich are not like you and me: Income, price dispersion and risk sharing*. Working Paper, Tepper School of Business, Carnegie Mellon University, Pittsburg, PA.

Kim, E., & Spear, S. (2021c). A characterization of Markov equilibrium in stochastic overlapping generations models. *Journal of Economic Dynamics and Control*, *124*, 104023.

Kim, E. H., Morse, A., & Zingales, L. (2006). What has mattered to economics since 1970. *Journal of Economic Perspectives*, *20*(4), 189–202.

Kiyotaki, N., & Wright, R. (1989). On money as a medium of exchange. *Journal of Political Economy*, *97*(4), 927–954.

Kocherlakota, N. (2010, May). *Modern macroeconomic models as tools for economic policy*. Annual Report (2009) Essay. Federal Reserve Bank of Minneapolis, Minneapolis, MN.

Kollmann, R. (2020, March). *A tractable overlapping generations structure for quantitative DSGE models*. Working Paper ECARES 2022-07. Universite Libre de Bruxelles, Bruxelles.

Koopmans, T., Diamond, P., & Williamson, R. (1964). Stationary utility and time perspective. *Econometrica*, *32*(1–2), 82–100.

Kotlikoff, L. (1983, June). *Theoretical & empirical analysis of altruistic linkages within the extended family*. Mimeo.

Kotlikoff, L. (1988). Intergenerational transfers and savings. *Journal of Economic Perspectives*, *2*(2), 41–58.

Kotlikoff, L. (1993). *Generational accounting: Knowing who pays, and when, for what we spend*. New York, NY: Free Press.

Kotlikoff, L., & Summers, L. (1979). Tax incidence in a life cycle model with variable labor supply. *Quarterly Journal of Economics*, *93*(4), 705–718.

Kotlikoff, L., & Summers, L. (1981). The role of intergenerational transfers in aggregate capital accumulation. *Journal of Political Economy*, *89*(4), 706–732.

Krebs, T. (2004). Non-existence of recursive equilibria on compact state spaces when markets are incomplete. *Journal of Economic Theory*, *115*(1), 134–150.

Krueger, D., & Kubler, F. (2002). Intergenerational risk-sharing via social security when financial markets are incomplete. *American Economic Review*, *92*(2), 407–410.

Krueger, D., & Kubler, F. (2004). Computing equilibrium in OLG models with stochastic production. *Journal of Economic Dynamics and Control*, *28*(7), 1411–1436.

Krueger, D., & Kubler, F. (2006). Pareto-improving social security reform when financial markets are incomplete!? *American Economic Review*, *96*(3), 737–755.

Krusell, P., & Smith, A. (1998). Income and wealth heterogeneity in the macroeconomy. *Journal of Political Economy*, *106*(5), 867–896.

Kubler, F., & Polemarchakis, H. (2004). Stationary Markov equilibria for overlapping generations. *Economic Theory*, *24*, 623–643.

Kubler, F., & Schmedders, K. (2005). Approximate versus exact equilibria in dynamic economies. *Econometrica*, *73*(4), 1205–1235.

Kurz, M. (1984). Capital accumulation & the characteristics of private inter-generational transfers. *Economica*, *51*(201), 1–22.

Kuznets, S. (1930). *Secular movements in production and prices*. New York, NY: Houghton Mifflin.

Kydland, F., & Prescott, E. (1982). Time to build & aggregate fluctuations. *Econometrica*, *50*(6), 1345–1370.

Labadie, P. (1986). Comparative dynamics & risk premia in an overlapping generations model. *Review of Economic Studies*, *53*(1), 139–152.

Lagos, R., & Wright, R. (2005). A unified framework for monetary theory and policy analysis. *Journal of Political Economy*, *113*(3), 463–484.

Lee, R. (2019). Samuelson's contributions to population theory & overlapping generations in economics. In R. Cord (Ed.). *Paul Samuelson, master of modern economics* (pp. 471–495). London: Palgrave Macmillan

Lerner, A. (1959). Consumption-loan interest and money. *Journal of Political Economy*, *67*(5), 512–518.

Ljungqvist, L., & Sargent, T. (2018). *Recursive macroeconomic theory*. Cambridge, MA: MIT Press.

Lucas, R. (1972). Expectations and the neutrality of money. *Journal of Economic Theory*, *4*(2), 103–124.

Lucas, R. (1978). Asset prices in an exchange economy. *Econometrica*, *46*(6), 1429–1445.

Lucas, R. (1984). Money in a theory of finance. *Carnegie-Rochester Conference Series on Public Policy*, *21*, 9–46.

Lucas, R. (1986). Adaptive behavior and economic theory. *Journal of Business*, *59*(4), S401–S426.

Lucas, R. (1996). Monetary neutrality. *Journal of Political Economy*, *104*(4), 661–682.

Lucas, R. (2001). *Professional memoir*. Lecture given in the Nobel Economists Lecture Series at Trinity University, San Antonio, TX, April 5. Reprinted in W. Breit & B. Hirsch (Eds.). (2009). *Lives of the Laureates* (5th ed.). Cambridge, MA: MIT Press [page references to original].

Lucas, R., & Rapping, L. (1969). Real wages, employment, and inflation. *Journal of Political Economy*, *77*(5), 721–754.

Lucas, R., & Stokey, N. (1987). Money and interest in a cash-in-advance economy. *Econometrica*, *55*(3), 491–513.

Majumdar, M., & Radner, R. (1983). Stationary optimal policies with discounting in a stochastic activity analysis model. *Econometrica*, *51*(6), 1821–1837.

Malinvaud, E. (1953). Capital accumulation and efficient allocation of resources. *Econometrica*, *21*(2), 233–268.

Malinvaud, E. (1972). *Lectures on microeconomic theory*. Amsterdam: North-Holland.

Malinvaud, E. (1987). The overlapping generations model in 1947. *Journal of Economic Literature*, *25*(1), 103–105.

Malinvaud, E. (1985). In A. Silvey (Trans.) *Lecons de theorie microeconomique* (Vol. 2). *Lectures on Microeconomic Theory*. Amsterdam: North-Holland.

Mankiw, N. G., & Weil, D. (1989). The baby boom, the baby bust, and the housing market. *Regional Science and Urban Economics*, *19*(2), 235–258.

Manuelli, R. (1990). Existence and optimality of currency equilibrium in stochastic overlapping generations models: The pure endowment case. *Journal of Economic Theory*, *51*(2), 268–294.

Manuelli, R., & Peck, J. (1992). Sunspot-like effects of random endowments. *Journal of Economic Dynamics and Control*, *16*(2), 193–206.

Marcet, A. (1988). *Solving non-linear models by parameterized expectations*. Working Paper. Carnegie-Mellon University, Graduate School of Industrial Administration, Pittsburg, PA.

Marimon, R., McGrattan, E., & Sargent, T. (1990). Money as a medium of exchange in an economy with artificially intelligent agents. *Journal of Economic Dynamics and Control*, *14*(2), 329–373.

Mather, J. (1970). Stability of C∞ mappings: V, transversality. *Advances in Mathematics*, *4*(3), 301–336.

McCallum, B. (1983). The role of overlapping generations models in monetary economics. *Carnegie-Rochester Conference Series on Public Policy*, *18*(1), 9–44.

McCallum, B. (1999). Role of the minimal state variable criterion in rational expectations models. *International Tax and Public Finance*, *6*(4), 621–639.

McCandless, G., & Weber, W. (1995). Some monetary facts. *Federal Reserve Bank of Minneapolis Quarterly Review*, *19*(Summer), 2–11.

McFadden, D., Mas-Colell, A., Mantel, R., & Richter, M. (1974). A characterization of community excess demand functions. *Journal of Economic Theory*, *9*(4), 361–374.

Meckling, W. (1960). An exact consumption-loan model of interest: A comment. *Journal of Political Economy*, *68*(1), 72–76.

Mirrlees, J. (1971). An exploration in the theory of optimum income taxation. *Review of Economic Studies*, *38*(2), 175–208.

Mirrlees, J., & Stern, N. (Eds.). (1973). *Models of economic growth*. London: Palgrave Macmillan.

Mitra, T., Montrucchio, L., & Privileggi, F. (2003). The nature of the steady state in models of optimal growth under uncertainty. *Economic Theory*, *23*(1), 39–71.

Modigliani, F. (1988). The role of intergenerational transfers and life cycle saving in the accumulation of wealth. *Journal of Economic Perspectives*, *2*(2), 15–40.

Muench, T. (1977). Optimality, the interaction of spot and futures markets, and the non-neutrality of money in the Lucas model. *Journal of Economic Theory*, *15*(2), 325–344.

Muller, W., & Woodford, M. (1988). Determinacy of equilibrium in stationary economies with both finite and infinite lived consumers. *Journal of Economic Theory*, *46*(2), 255–290.

Negishi, T. (1960). Welfare economics and existence of an equilibrium for a competitive economy. *Metroeconomica*, *12*(2–3), 92–97.
Okuno, M., & Zilcha, I. (1980). On the efficiency of a competitive equilibrium in infinite horizon monetary economies. *Review of Economic Studies*, *47*(4), 797–807.
Ordover, J., & Phelps, E. (1975). Linear taxation of wealth & wages for intragenerational lifetime justice: Some steady-state cases. *American Economic Review*, *65*(4), 660–673.
Peck, J. (1988). On the existence of sunspot equilibria in an overlapping generations model. *Journal of Economic Theory*, *44*(1), 19–42.
Peck, J., & Shell, K. (1991). Market uncertainty: Correlated and sunspot equilibria in imperfectly competitive economies. *Review of Economic Studies*, *58*(5), 1011–1029.
Peck, J., & Shell, K. (2003). Equilibrium bank runs. *Journal of Political Economy*, *111*(1), 103–123.
Peled, D. (1984). Stationary pareto optimality of stochastic asset equilibria with overlapping generations. *Journal of Economic Theory*, *34*(2), 396–403.
Phelps, E. (1965). Second essay on the golden rule of accumulation. *American Economic Review*, *55*(4), 793–814.
Phelps, E., & Riley, J. (1978). Rawlsian growth: Dynamic programming of capital and wealth for intergeneration maximin justice. *Review of Economic Studies*, *45*(1), 103–120.
Phelps, E., & Shell, K. (1969). Public debt, taxation, and capital intensiveness. *Journal of Economic Theory*, *1*(3), 330–346.
Pissarides, C. (1992). Loss of skill during unemployment and the persistence of employment shocks. *Quarterly Journal of Economics*, *107*(4), 1371–1391.
Pontryagin, L., Boltyanskii, V., & Revaz, V. (1960). *The theory of optimal processes. I. The maximum principle*. DTIC, AD0264147, 10-01. TRW Labs, Los Angeles, CA.
Poterba, J. (2004). The impact of population aging on financial markets. NBER *Working Paper* 10851, October. NBER, New York.
Poterba, J., Weil, D., & Shiller, R. (1991). House price dynamics: The role of tax policy and demography. *Brookings Papers on Economic Activity*, *22*(2), 143–203. Comments and discussion by Weil and Shiller, 184–203.
Radner, R. (1967). Dynamic programming of economic growth. In E. Malinvaud & M. Bacharach (Eds.), *Activity analysis in the theory of growth and planning* (pp. 111–141). London: Macmillan.
Radner, R. (1973). Optimal stationary consumption with stochastic production and resources. *Journal of Economic Theory*, *6*(1), 68–90.
Ramsey, F. (1928). A mathematical theory of saving. *Economic Journal*, *38*(152), 543–559.
Reichlin, P. (1986). Equilibrium cycles in an overlapping generations economy with production. *Journal of Economic Theory*, *40*(1), 89–102.
Ríos-Rull, J. V. (1994). On the quantitative importance of market completeness. *Journal of Monetary Economics*, *34*(3), 463–496.
Rios-Rull, J. V. (1996). Life-cycle economies and aggregate fluctuation. *Review of Economic Studies*, *63*(3), 465–489.
Roberts, R. (1984). A positive model of private charity and public transfers. *Journal of Political Economy*, *92*(1), 136–148.
Robinson, A. (2016). *Non-standard analysis*. Princeton, NJ: Princeton University Press.
Romer, P. (1990). Endogenous technological change. *Journal of Political Economy*, *98*(5, Part 2), S71–S102.
Romer, P. (2015). What went wrong in macro-historical details. Retrieved from https://paulromer.net/what-went-wrong-in-macro-history/
Romer, P. (2016). *The trouble with macroeconomics*. Available at Google Scholar.
Rosen, S. (1985). Implicit contracts: A survey. *Journal of Economic Literature*, *23*(3), 1144–1175.
Salter, W. (1960). *Productivity and technical change*. Cambridge: Cambridge University Press.
Samuelson, P. (1943). Dynamics, statics, and the stationary state. *Review of Economic Statistics*, *25*(1), 58–68.
Samuelson, P. (1947). *Foundations of economic analysis*. Cambridge, MA: Harvard University Press.
Samuelson, P. (1958). An exact consumption-loan model of interest with or without the social contrivance of money. *Journal of Political Economy*, *66*(6), 467–482.

Samuelson, P. (1959). Consumption-loan interest and money: Reply. *Journal of Political Economy, 67*(5), 518–522.
Samuelson, P. (1960). Infinity, unanimity, and singularity: Reply. *Journal of Political Economy, 68*(1), 76–83.
Samuelson, P. (1968). The two-part golden rule deduced as the asymptotic turnpike of catenary motions. *Economic Inquiry [Western Economic Journal]*, *6*(2), 85.
Samuelson, P. (1975a). The optimum growth rate for population. *International Economic Review, 16*(3), 531–538.
Samuelson, P. (1975b). Optimum social security in a life-cycle growth model. *International Economic Review, 16*(3), 539–544.
Samuelson, P. (1976). The optimum growth rate for population: Agreement and evaluations. *International Economic Review, 17*(2), 516–525.
Samuelson, P., & Solow, R. (1956). A complete capital model involving heterogeneous capital goods. *Quarterly Journal of Economics, 70*(4), 537–556.
Santos, M. (1991). Smoothness of the policy function in discrete time economic models. *Econometrica, 59*(5), 1365–1382.
Sargent, T. (1996). Expectations and the non-neutrality of Lucas. *Journal of Monetary Economics, 37*(3), 535–548.
Scarf, H. (1960). Some examples of global instability of the competitive equilibrium. *International Economic Review, 1*(3), 157–172.
Schumpeter, J. (1939). *Business cycles* (Vol. 1). New York, NY: McGraw-Hill.
Shapiro, J., & Wagner, H. (1967). A finite renewal algorithm for the knapsack and turnpike models. *Operations Research, 15*(2), 319–341.
Shell, K. (1966). Toward a theory of inventive activity and capital accumulation. *American Economic Review, 56*(1/2), 62–68.
Shell, K. (1971). Notes on the economics of infinity. *Journal of Political Economy, 79*(5), 1002–1011.
Shell, K. (1977, November). Monnaie et Allocation Intertemporelle. *Séminaire d'économétrie de M. Edmond Malinvaud.*
Shell, K., & Wright, R. (1993). Indivisibilities, lotteries, and sunspot equilibria. *Economic Theory, 3*(1), 1–17.
Shiller, R. (1978). Rational expectations and the dynamic structure of macroeconomic models: A critical review. *Journal of Monetary Economics, 4*(1), 1–44.
Solow, R. (2006). Overlapping generations. In M. Szenberg, L. Ramrattan, & A. Gottesman (Eds.) *Samuelsonian economics in twenty-first century* (pp. 35–41). Oxford: Oxford University Press.
Spear, S. (1984). Sufficient conditions for the existence of sunspot equilibria. *Journal of Economic Theory, 34*(2), 360–370.
Spear, S. (1985). Rational expectations in the overlapping generations model. *Journal of Economic Theory, 35*(2), 251–275.
Spear, S. (1988). Existence and local uniqueness of functional rational expectations equilibria in dynamic economic models. *Journal of Economic Theory, 44*(1), 124–155.
Spear, S. (1989). Are sunspots necessary? *Journal of Political Economy, 97*(4), 965–973.
Spear, S. (1991). Growth, externalities, and sunspots. *Journal of Economic Theory, 54*(1), 215–223.
Spear, S., & Srivastava, S. (1986). Markov rational expectations equilibria in an overlapping generations model. *Journal of Economic Theory, 38*(1), 35–62.
Spear, S., Srivastava, S., & Woodford, M. (1990). Indeterminacy of stationary equilibrium in stochastic overlapping generations models. *Journal of Economic Theory, 50*(2), 265–284.
Spear, S., & Wright, R. (1998). Interview with David Cass. *Macroeconomic Dynamics, 2*(4), 533–558.
Spear, S., & Wright, R. (2001). An interview with Karl Shell. *Macroeconomic Dynamics, 5*(5), 701–741.
Spear, S., & Young, W. (2014). Optimum savings & optimal growth: The Cass–Malinvaud–Koopmans Nexus. *Macroeconomic Dynamics, 18*(1), 215–243.
Spear, S., & Young, W. (2018). Endogenous growth theory & models: The "First Wave," 1952–1973. *Macroeconomic Dynamics, 22*(6), 1695–1720.
Starrett, D. (1972). On golden rules, the 'biological theory of interest,' and competitive inefficiency. *Journal of Political Economy, 80*(2), 276–291.
Stewart, F. (1977). *Fundamentals of age-group systems*. New York, NY: Academic Press.

Stockman, A. (1996). *Introduction to economics*. Fort Worth, TX: Dryden Press.

Stokey, N., Lucas, R., & Prescott, E. (1989). *Recursive methods in economic dynamics*. Cambridge, MA: Harvard University Press.

Storesletten, K., Telmer, C., & Yaron, A. (2007). Asset pricing with idiosyncratic risk & overlapping generations, *Review of Economic Dynamics*, *10*(4), 519–548.

Summers, L. (1991). The scientific illusion in empirical macroeconomics. *Scandinavian Journal of Economics*, *93*(2), 129–148.

Thaler, R. (1999). Mental accounting matters. *Journal of Behavioral Decision Making*, *12*(3), 183–206.

Vines, D., & Wills, S. (2018). The rebuilding macroeconomic theory project: An analytical assessment. *Oxford Review of Economic Policy*, *34*(1–2), 1–42.

Vines, D., & Wills, S. (2020). The rebuilding macroeconomic theory project part II: Multiple equilibria, toy models, and policy models in a new macroeconomic paradigm. *Oxford Review of Economic Policy*, *36*(3), 427–497.

Von Neumann, J. (1937). Über ein ökonomisches Gleichungssystem und eine Verallgemeinerung des Brouwerschen Fixpunktsatzes. In K. Menger (Ed.), *Ergebnisse eines mathematischen Kolloquiums*, 1935–36. [English translation (1945). A model of general economic equilibrium. *Review of Economic Studies*, *13*(1), 1–9].

Wahl, J. (2003). From riches to riches: Intergenerational transfers and the evidence from estate tax returns. *Social Science Quarterly*, *84*(2), 278–296.

Wallace, N. (1977a, June). *On simplifying the theory of fiat money*. Working Paper No. 22. Federal Reserve Bank of Minneapolis.

Wallace, N. (1977b, September). Samuelson's pure consumption loans model with constant returns-to-scale storage. Staff Report No. 23. Federal Reserve Bank of Minneapolis, Minneapolis, MN.

Weil, P. (1989). Overlapping families of infinitely-lived agents. *Journal of Public Economics*, *38*(2), 183–198.

Weil, P. (2008). Overlapping generations: The first jubilee. *Journal of Economic Perspectives*, *22*(4), 115–134.

Woodford, M. (1986a). Stationary sunspot equilibria in a finance constrained economy. *Journal of Economic Theory*, *40*(1), 128–137.

Woodford, M. (1986b, September). *Stationary sunspot equilibria – The case of small fluctuations around a deterministic steady state*. Working Paper. University of Chicago and New York University. Retrieved from http://blogs.cuit.columbia.edu/mw2230/files/2017/08/Sunspot.pdf0.

Woodford, M. (1990). Learning to believe in sunspots. *Econometrica*, *58*(2), 277–307.

Wright, R. D. (1988). The observational implications of labor contracts in a dynamic general equilibrium model. *Journal of Labor Economics*, *6*(4), 530–551.

Wright, R. (2005). Models of monetary economies II: The next generation. *International Economic Review*, *46*(2), 305–316.

Yaari, M. (1964). On the consumer's lifetime allocation process. *International Economic Review*, *5*(3), 304–317.

Yaari, M. (1965). Uncertain lifetime, life insurance, and the theory of the consumer. *Review of Economic Studies*, *32*(2), 137–150.

Yoo, J. (2013, May). *The role of inter vivos giving in general equilibrium*. Working Paper. Ajou University, Yeongtong-gu.

Young, W. (1987). *Interpreting Mr Keynes: The IS-LM Enigma*. Cambridge: Polity-Blackwell.

Young, W. (1989). *Harrod and his trade cycle group*. London: Macmillan.

Young, W. (2010). The IS-LM diagram. In M. Blaug & P. Lloyd (Eds.). *Famous figures and diagrams in economics* (pp. 262–267). Cheltenham: Edward Elgar

Young, W. (2014). *Real business cycle models in economics*. London: Routledge.

Zhu, T. (2008). An overlapping-generations model with search. *Journal of Economic Theory*, *142*(1), 318–331.

Zwicky, F. (1969). *Discovery, invention, research through the morphological approach*. Toronto, ON: Macmillan.

INDEX

Experiential Marketing

Rose Leahy, Pio Fenton & Holly Barry

Experiential Marketing

Integrated Theory & Strategic Application

SAGE

Los Angeles | London | New Delhi
Singapore | Washington DC | Melbourne

SAGE

Los Angeles | London | New Delhi
Singapore | Washington DC | Melbourne

SAGE Publications Ltd
1 Oliver's Yard
55 City Road
London EC1Y 1SP

SAGE Publications Inc.
2455 Teller Road
Thousand Oaks, California 91320

SAGE Publications India Pvt Ltd
B 1/I 1 Mohan Cooperative Industrial Area
Mathura Road
New Delhi 110 044

SAGE Publications Asia-Pacific Pte Ltd
3 Church Street
#10-04 Samsung Hub
Singapore 049483

Editor: Matthew Waters
Assistant editor: Cassandra Seibel
Production editor: Manmeet Kaur Tura
Copyeditor: Sarah Bury
Proofreader: Christine Bitten
Indexer: Cathryn Pritchard
Marketing manager: Lucia Sweet
Cover design: Francis Kenney
Typeset by: C&M Digitals (P) Ltd, Chennai, India
Printed in the UK

Library of Congress Control Number: 2021943736

British Library Cataloguing in Publication data

A catalogue record for this book is available from the British Library

ISBN 978-1-5297-4219-0
ISBN 978-1-5297-4218-3 (pbk)

CONTENTS

LIST OF FIGURES AND TABLES

LIST OF FIGURES

LIST OF TABLES

ABOUT THE AUTHORS

Rose Leahy is a Senior Lecturer and research supervisor in the area of marketing in Munster Technological University (MTU). Rose is an experienced academic, who has presented at conferences both nationally and internationally, and who also has published papers in international journals. Rose has over 20 years of teaching experience at third level to both undergraduate and postgraduate students and has also supervised many students successfully at both masters and doctorate level. She has extensive experience of working with companies and carrying out research for companies in the marketing discipline.

Pio Fenton is Head of the Department of Marketing and International Business at Munster Technological University (MTU) where he has overseen the development of MTU's extensive suite of Marketing, Digital Marketing, Sales and International Business programmes. Graduating in 2001 with a Bachelor of Science in Computer Applications, Dr Fenton went on to complete a PhD specialising in Artificial Intelligence applications for Production Scheduling problems. Subsequently, Dr Fenton pursued research interests in topics as diverse as data-mining, mass-spectrometry interfaces and Project Management before participating in IESE's renowned Faculty Development Programme in Barcelona. In parallel to this, Dr Fenton assumed a national leadership position within a suicide prevention organisation operating in Ireland and the UK. The Department of Marketing and International Business recently won a prestigious national Education award for its emphasis on Business Collaboration. The department is home to 950 students.

Holly Barry is the Brand Strategist in Barry Group, a leading wholesale distribution company in Cork, Ireland. Holly has vast experience in both academia, having spent time lecturing in Munster Technological University, and marketing practice, working with leading national and international brands. It is Holly's ability to merge her experience from both realms that has led to her success to date, presenting at conferences throughout Europe and consulting with businesses on marketing effectiveness, brand development and marketing strategy.

ONLINE RESOURCES

Experiential Marketing is accompanied by PowerPoint slides for instructors to help support teaching. These resources are available at: **https://study.sagepub.com/leahy**

FOR INSTRUCTORS

- Easily **integrate the chapters** into your weekly chapters with the **PowerPoint slides** created by the author.

ACKNOWLEDGEMENTS

We have thoroughly enjoyed writing this book. We began the process before the Covid-19 pandemic and finished at a time where the world is truly a different place. This book has been an anchor for us through what has been a turbulent time, both professionally and personally. The completion of this book owes much to academic colleagues and industry partners, of whom there are too many to mention individually. However, we would specifically like to thank all those company representatives who so willingly gave their time to be interviewed for this book. Their insights and expertise have formed the basis for much of the contributions that we offer in this book. In MTU, we would like to give special mention to the School of Business, the Research Office and all our colleagues who in different ways helped and supported us along the way. Special thanks also to the Barry Group for their constant support and expertise on all things marketing and particularly experiential marketing-related. Every effort has been made to trace and acknowledge ownership of copyright, and we would like to acknowledge all those whose work has informed our thinking and practice.

1 THE EXPERIENTIAL MARKETING ENVIRONMENT

CHAPTER OVERVIEW

In the storied history of marketing there has never been a time like the present. The sudden and unprecedented changes in consumption, the unparalleled disruption to supply chains that provided unending change and challenge to businesses, and the fevered changes in consumer behaviour are simply without historical comparison.

It was against this backdrop that this book was written. Focusing on experiential marketing as an area that was neglected by academia, the authors wanted to shine a light on the practice of experiential marketing and relate that to existing theory while addressing gaps in the accepted knowledge of how experiential marketing can be planned and assessed. The research carried out in the book was executed in a time period that straddled the onset of the Covid-19 pandemic and, as such, the book's contents reflect an intended philosophy of ensuring that the attempt to rebuild experiential marketing practices is set on a firm footing for the times we live in.

Regardless of Covid-19, however, there was a real need to take stock of experiential marketing as a sub-discipline of Marketing. Its history is complicated with varied theoretical roots. Its practice has been driven by multiple sectors, all of which have brought a different set of mechanisms for its planning, implementation and evaluation. It has become a neglected child in academic circles with very little focus on it in recent major marketing journals.

This book therefore sets out to offer a reset to those who are interested in experiential marketing. We seek to reflect a new era of experiential marketing – one that combines a cautious, less tactile customer base with the need to ensure greater and more transparent returns on experiential activities. Our intention is to ensure that experiential marketing is seen properly as something that can be strategised. Moving from an *ad-hoc*, experimentative and hopeful approach to one that is based on frameworks, metrics and purpose represents a considerable shift for experiential marketing.

Throughout the book, the reader will be presented with insight drawn from a range of practitioners that will help to illuminate the choices made by effective experiential marketers. By establishing the somewhat confusing and multi-faceted theoretical foundations, the book will equip academics with the means to better prepare learners and others for careers such as experiential marketers and will equip practitioners with the tools they need to be successful in their experiential endeavours. The next section presents an outline of the context that has shaped the development of this book and within it we set out the key objectives of this work.

CONTEXT: WHERE ARE WE?

Marketing has become much more difficult in recent years. It was never easy, but the proliferation of new technologies, platforms and channels has really helped move it much closer to being a science than being an art (although it is definitely both an art and a science nonetheless). The ability to measure the impact of marketing activity – particularly that which occurs online – has lent itself to an increased credibility for marketing among top-level executives. There is now an established expectation around knowing what marketing tactics are most directly related to successful marketing strategy and, in turn, how that supports corporate strategy. While the main support for this shift has occurred because of the more trackable properties of the digital marketing platforms, it has helped position marketing as a whole in a more favourable light. This has been good for the profession and the discipline of marketing. There has never been a more exciting time to be a marketer. However, one could also say there has never been a more challenging time to be a marketer. Due to expectations around transparency and tracking, there is a greater need for marketers to convey the effectiveness and efficacy of all their marketing activities. So, non-digital focused activities are the subject of greater scrutiny. For example, traditional advertising budgets are not seen merely through the lens of 'We must be on TV', but rather from the perspective of 'Does TV or online offer us better bang for our buck?'. As an established area of activity, traditional advertising has various mechanisms that allow us to assess that question. Ratings systems, monitoring of online interactions and surveys of customers[1] can all give us insight into what is driving uptake on a brand's product or service. There is work to be done perhaps on translating that insight into corporate strategy objectives – particularly when those 'translations' are co-positioned with digital analytics that have a capability and granularity of previously unimagined proportions. In short, the data we can garner from traditional advertising are still quite paltry compared to what is available for digital marketing activities. This is despite traditional advertising being the main focus of the marketing industry for most of its existence, apart perhaps then for the past 15 years or so.

The emergence of a 'digital first' mentality within the marketing profession has created a hostile environment for all traditional marketing activities. While we have looked at the example of TV advertising, there is no doubt that other areas of

traditional marketing have the same problem. In some cases that challenge is much worse. Experiential marketing is one such area.

Experiential marketing, as we will show in this book, has confused roots – it has emerged from various different areas of practice and theory – and its present standing is very uncertain. Much of this arises from the Covid-19 pandemic but, even in advance of that occurring, experiential marketing had obstacles to overcome that were particular to this type of marketing and not shared by other, more established areas. It has been unfairly categorised as an expensive marketing tactic with low levels of impact. Senior practitioners without experience of it, and non-marketing executives hold at least a disregard or suspicion about it.

By examining various industry reports we can see that experiential marketing is not a focal point for discussion. The 2021 edition of the Salesforce *State of Marketing Report* doesn't make explicit reference at any point to experiential marketing (Blitzer, 2020). However, it has a strong focus throughout on customer experience, identifying that this is a critical issue for consumers and an important platform for innovation. The explicit link that experiential marketing – as distinct from the concept of customer experience – plays in developing more intimate relationships with customers is not presented. An emerging theme in the report is the 'bridging of online and offline experiences'. The potential for amplified experiential activations in 'greying' the digital divide receives no attention.

A report by HubSpot (2020) has a similar approach with, again, no emphasis on experiential marketing but with many references to experience. This may not be surprising given the online first tendency of the market for HubSpot (similar to Salesforce) but it is nonetheless glaring that in a report constituted with the input of many thousands of marketing professionals that experiential marketing does not emerge as a matter of consequence. Yet, it is extremely likely that experiential marketing is part of their marketing armoury. Reports from GlobalWebIndex (GWI) (2021) and others also underline this disparity.

The American Marketing Association (2021) has some industry-focused material that makes reference to experiential activations and activities, but this is nearly always contextualised by a focus on customer experience and/or some other pure psychological dimension, for example hedonism. The UK-based Chartered Institute of Marketing (2021) presents just one search result for 'Experiential' on its website compared to 102 results for the string 'Customer Experience'. Again, this is despite the fact that most major consumer brands and many major business-to business (B2B) brands practise experiential marketing on an ongoing basis and have built an entire marketing strategy around it in some cases.

This disregard of experiential as a discussion topic is not limited to the practitioner world. A review of major academic journals between 2015 and 2021 shows that it rarely features in any meaningful way. Major advances in our understanding of its theory, the view from practitioners and the integration of these two perspectives has not been given any significant attention. It has received scant regard resulting in a theoretical ambiguity and lack of definition clarity. This tallies with our review in composing this book – simply, the practitioner view and academic

perspective are poorly aligned in all respects other than, perhaps, there may be a collective opinion that experiential marketing is just something that you have to 'get on with'. A mindset of trial and error underpinned by a limited evidence base for efficacy helps to create an aura of ostracisation for this sub-discipline. This book will focus on codifying the theory of experiential marketing so that it can better aid practitioners and executives in realising its potential. While we will focus on concepts like amplification, integrated planning and return on experience as a means to assist practitioners in better undertaking activations, we will also place those outputs on a much firmer theoretical footing.

In so doing, we will show how, with proper planning, experiential marketing can have that traceability that is pervasive in marketing nowadays and become more trusted by marketing and business executives.

Key challenges for experiential marketing

- It has unclear theoretical roots which gives the discipline an air of confusion.
- Experiential marketing tends not to be taken seriously by senior executives, particularly those without marketing experience.
- It has been found to be an expensive mechanism to deploy.
- Often the objectives of the organisation's marketing strategy are poorly aligned to the experiential campaign's objectives (if they even exist).
- It has received poor levels of attention from top-tier academic journals, leading to its general neglect as a sub-discipline.
- Experiential marketing has been poorly integrated into the marketing mix even by organisations which are relatively successful at implementing it.

COVID-19 AND ITS IMPLICATIONS

Acknowledging that marketing is difficult – and is getting more difficult – while knowing that experiential marketing is even harder is the stance we adopted for this book. This was even before the pandemic. What has occurred in the meantime, however, has stretched not just the credibility of experiential marketing but has also shattered many of the preconceived, tried-and-tested beliefs marketers have had about this tactic. While once there was an undoubted coterie of *aficionados* in the marketing profession who knew that it was an excellent way to get the brand 'on the ground' and to get some close-up interaction with segments of the customer base, we now dwell (at the time of writing) in a world that has changed profoundly, and the notion of 'experience' has been delimited massively. This, of course, has come about as a result of the Covid-19 pandemic.

The pandemic has had a major impact on how people experience one another. It has changed the most mundane of activities – such as shopping, entertainment

and dining – in ways that were simply unimaginable previously. Such activities were at the heart of many experiential activities before 2020. The world became less tactile, more distanced and very trepidatious in a very short period of time. Equally, the willingness of people to engage in experiential activations required a form of intimacy, closeness and adventure from the participants – all of these things the polar opposite of the guidelines and public health messaging pervasive during the Covid-19 pandemic.

Thus, almost entirely, experiential marketing stopped. The range of activations that normally took place in shopping centres, bars, sports grounds, concerts, festivals, and many other areas all became hostages to an environment where, if such things were allowed at all, they were under the most rigid of circumstances. The wearing of masks, adoption of social distancing and a heightened sense of hygiene became obstacles to running any kind of effective and safe activation. Brands pivoted with respect to all their messaging. Out went adventure, carefreeness and having it your own way, and in came safety, a need for reassurance and the requirement to be seen to be doing the right thing. The tone that emerged was very much a variation of 'We can get through this together, even though we are apart'. Various brands that would previously have been pioneers in experiential activations had to find new ways of offering that new message to customers. Campaigns by Nike, Guinness, Ikea and Coca-Cola are all great examples of how this was achieved.

The question could justifiably be asked, then: is this the end for experiential marketing? Thankfully, evidence is emerging that brands are beginning to find new ways of activating experience and as the world starts to recover from the pandemic there is a sense that at some stage experiential marketing can emerge fully from the ashes. Even in advance of emerging from the pandemic, some brands are outlining their commitment to experiential marketing – because of the faith they have in its effectiveness – albeit that the nature of the activation has to reflect the times we live in.

Adapting at Heineken®

In January 2020, Mark Noble, Heineken® Marketing Manager in Ireland, spoke at an annual company conference in Cork to outline the brand's plans for what was shaping up to be an eventful year.

Having led the way over the previous decade in terms of experiential marketing, Heineken® was setting out upon a year of experiential innovation. Events around music festivals and rugby matches were to be joined for the first time by sponsorship of UEFA Euro 2020, allowing the brand to implement some of their most adventurous experiential activations to date, while also ensuring that in-store and in-bar experiential activities continued to bring little moments of 'joy' to Irish consumers.

(Continued)

By March 2020, those best laid plans had to be abandoned as it became clear that the impact of Covid-19 was going to be felt immediately on brands that centre on a sense of sociability. The mere fact that social settings were prohibited gave rise to immediate challenges for any brand that built its experiential activations around people coming together to enjoy themselves. Everything 'changed overnight'. The focus for the brand, from an experiential perspective, was reset. It was clear that experiential marketing would need to pivot to in-store and digital settings where the customers' need for reassurance and safety could be met.

In-store experiential marketing was stripped back to ensure that 'ease of shop' was emphasised. As the pandemic endured, thoughts turned to how to reconnect with consumers through experiential marketing activations and to bring back those 'little moments of joy'. Plans to create 'in-home' experiences were developed and the notion of a 'staycation summer' was the subject of creative attention led by Category & Shopper Marketing Controller, Ruth Hankin.

For any marketing team, the implications of the Covid-19 pandemic were to be significant, but they were particularly notable for a brand that values connecting with customers in settings where people are relaxed and at ease. Noble attests that their response to the pandemic has showcased the 'sheer resilience of people' – consumers, customers and colleagues. His philosophy as regards the former is 'to engage with consumers as people – you need a consumer first mindset – that sense of understanding of what motivates and appeals to people is at the heart of everything'. Engaging with consumers on that level – particularly by focusing on the hope that a fresh beginning brings for us all – is the name of the game for their planned activities as we emerge from the pandemic.

EXPERIENTIAL MARKETING IN A POST-PANDEMIC WORLD

Given that changes to how brands think and how consumers engage is part of a 'new normal', there are questions about how brands will use experiential marketing as consumption reignites in the years ahead. While it is accepted that some things may change in a post-Covid world, there is at least a substantial belief that some things will return to a version of normality. The need for interaction, enjoyment and connection has not died. Experiential marketing, which centres strongly on these needs, will use old and new ways to allow people to become 'part' of a brand. There are already some trends emerging that we may see becoming part of how experiential marketing finds itself in the coming years.

Later in this book we will show how theories around consumer experience, relationship marketing, consumer collectives, brand management, word-of-mouth marketing and digital amplification all have had a bearing on the shape of experiential marketing to date. In a post-Covid world, the same holds. In order to

be effective as experiential marketers in the future, marketing teams will need to reflect on each of these factors. Being excellent at experiential marketing and making customers feel safe and involved will require brands to consider how, for example, consumer collectives play a role in generating brand salience in a post-Covid world. These, you will find, are considerations that we have built into the Experiential Marketing Implementation Model and, as such, all of these factors will be considered in the design of an activation. There are significant numbers of organisations whose mere existence is centred on the viability of an 'events' industry – something which is significantly curtailed at the moment. Organisations such as Freemans[2] operate as events companies and have substantial insight into many of the logistical and strategic decisions that can shape experiential activations. Reviewing their advice for 2021, it is clear that the essence of their approach is in ensuring that events are safe but meaningful. For practitioners, this means questioning, at each stage of planning and implementation, in a much more structured way. The stakes are raised. Being guided by a multi-context implementation framework makes it more likely that the overall strategy for an activation will reflect the customers' need for reassurance.

In summary, while much of the context for experiential marketing has changed, the planning and design process that we outline in this book actually enables experiential activations to be framed by decision-making that reflects the context of the day. Brands will understand that it will always be important for experiential marketing to reflect their customer and their customers' values. The Experiential Marketing Implementation Model that we develop in this book allows those customer values to be ingrained in experiential activations regardless of the prevailing context at the time.

OBJECTIVES OF THE BOOK

Whether you are an academic studying experiential marketing or a practitioner whose role involves planning and the deployment of experiential activations, you are likely already aware of what such activations 'look like'. Even as consumers, we will all have had experience at a concert or in a store, for example, of what it feels like to participate in an experiential event. The link with emotion and a sense of intimacy with a brand is definite (especially when done properly). Setting aside that familiarity, however, there is much 'under the hood' that has not really received the appropriate attention it deserves. There has never been a clear framework integrating experiential activations into marketing communications. The role of digital amplification in ensuring an audience and participation for activations has never been properly explored. There is a substantial gap in our knowledge of how to evaluate experiential campaigns holistically. The role of various underpinning theories has been lost over the years. This book therefore sets about the following objectives as a means to enhance the practice and study of experiential marketing.

Objective 1 – To explore the theoretical underpinnings of experiential marketing as a sub-discipline with specific emphasis on areas like relationship marketing, brand management and customer experience as they relate to what is now practised as experiential marketing.

Objective 2 – To integrate the implantation activities of experiential marketing into an amplification framework that leverages digital capabilities while also reflecting the power of consumer collectives in unleashing the full potential of activations.

Objective 3 – To position experiential marketing as a tool of marketing strategy that affords brands the opportunity to build closer bonds with consumers as part of an integrated process of marketing communications.

Objective 4 – To evaluate and assess the impact of experiential campaigns by use of a mechanism that gives a holistic measure of campaign effectiveness that can be interpreted as required by various internal audiences.

In summary, this book helps to develop a theoretical and practical structure around experiential marketing that positions it more fully as a means of connecting with customers that is purposeful, integrated and measurable. The next section outlines how this book achieves that.

BOOK STRUCTURE

This book includes 12 chapters which detail a narrative on experiential marketing that extends from its historical roots to an expected future that is hallmarked by technological adoption. We structure each chapter so that the academic and practical aspects of experiential marketing are given prominence. We endeavour to include significant examples of experiential marketing practices drawn from various industries. Each chapter also concludes with a sample of questions to help expand the reader's thinking and some resources to inform that thinking. Permeating the entire book is an attention on the strategic positioning of experiential marketing as we elevate it from a tactical approach to marketing.

- Chapter 1 gives contextual background to the need for this book as well as establishing the key things that this book will contribute to the knowledge of the reader.
- Chapter 2 provides the reader with a historical overview of the development of experiential marketing as it emerged, messily, from concepts such as customer experience. The chapter will outline the key milestones in that development with a view to having a clearer understanding of the influences which now shape its practice.
- Chapter 3 provides some definitional clarity and explores the link with emotion that is central to the effectiveness of experiential marketing as a practice. Examples supporting the chapter include insights from the practices of major brands, such

as McDonalds, Disney and WeightWatchers, among others. This is perhaps the most theoretically dense chapter of the book but it is key to understanding why experiential marketing is successful.

- Chapter 4 brings related areas, such as Relationship Marketing, into focus. The chapter stresses how important interactions and engagements are for building brand–customer relationships and the bonds that support them. Experiential marketing is sometimes seen as a standalone activity - this perspective is misplaced. We outline how, among other things, consumer collectives underpin the success of experiential activations.
- Chapter 5 presents the key topic of Brand Management and how it and experiential marketing interrelate. With an intention of understanding how experiential marketing can help build brand equity, we focus on Kotler's 6-Step Branding Conceptual Model as a means to better understand how to deploy experiential marketing more meaningfully. We use evidence from a range of large brands to show how experiential marketing can really strengthen brand health.
- Chapter 6 presents important concepts such as viral marketing and word-of-mouth marketing as overlooked components of experiential marketing. Simply, these are the engines that drive successful experiential activations and which can lend themselves to ensuring that experiential marketing fits into the broader marketing landscape of the organisation. We introduce the concept of 'Digitally Enabled Closeness' and highlight the importance of taking a time-phased approach to amplification.
- Chapter 7 presents the Experiential Marketing Implementation Model and outlines the various steps involved in planning the strategic use of experiential activations. Working through segmentation approaches, campaign objectives, key performance indicators (KPIs) and budgeting, the chapter places experiential marketing on a more structured footing.
- Chapter 8 positions the Experiential Marketing Implementation Model firmly in the Integrated Marketing Communications Model. Ultimately, the success of experiential marketing is determined by its integration into an overall marketing campaign, and in this chapter we outline how to do this. It is an important chapter in positioning experiential marketing firmly in the communications toolkit of the modern marketer.
- Chapter 9 focuses on budgeting for experiential marketing, with an overview on how to set campaign budgets in the context of an overall marketing budget and how marketing spend on experiential activities can be justified.
- Chapter 10 outlines how holistic measures of success can be designed and reviewed with respect to specific experiential activations. Return on integrated experience (ROIE) is established as a means to do this, based on research with a significant number of brands.
- Chapter 11 charts a case study of the 'Race and Taste Festival' that illustrates the critical success factors in planning experiential events. Building on Chapter 8, this chapter emphasises the strong link between experiential marketing and other marketing communications tools.

- Chapter 12 explores how best to compose marketing teams and how to structure communication strategically amongst those teams before casting an eye on the likely trajectory of experiential marketing in the years ahead.

Each chapter concludes by highlighting the main takeaways from that chapter's topic as well as some questions that can support learning. The book will give readers a strong insight into the current theoretical position of experiential marketing and how it has and can be used to further marketing objectives.

NOTES

1. https://smallbusiness.chron.com/evaluate-tv-advertising-results-22135.html
2. www.freeman.com/emea/about/

REFERENCES

American Marketing Association (2021). Website. [Online]. Available at: www.ama.org [accessed 3 June 2021].

Blitzer, A. (2020). *State of Marketing Report.* Available at: www.salesforce.com/blog/top-marketing-trends-navigate-change/

Chartered Institute of Marketing (2021). *CIM Search.* [Online]. Available at: www.cim.co.uk [accessed 3 June 2021].

GlobalWebIndex (2021). *Consumer Trends in 2021.* London: GWI.

HubSpot (2020). *Not Another State of Marketing Report.* Cambridge, MA: Hubspot.com.

2 ORIGINS OF EXPERIENTIAL MARKETING

CHAPTER OVERVIEW

The emergence of experiential marketing as a tool of marketing communications and, increasingly, as a part of the strategic armoury of marketing units has been gradual. As an academic topic it has roots in consumer behaviour and aspects of psychology while from a practical perspective it has been shaped by the shifting nature of the economy – from a product-centred focus, through a service-oriented economy to what is considered by some to have succeeded that – the experience economy. This chapter will provide an overview of how experiential marketing has developed as an important aspect of modern marketing by tracing its academic and practical origins.

Specifically, the chapter will present the following:

- The key phases of the development of experiential marketing since the 1960s.
- An overview of the changes in the consumption experience and how that mirrors changes in marketers' attitudes to their marketing tasks.
- A look at the various studies which added depth and refinement to the experience concept, and which paved the way for the emergence and establishment of experiential marketing as a core marketing approach.
- An introduction to the necessity of creating customer engagement and memorable interactions.

Upon completion of the chapter, the reader should have a strong understanding of the forces that have shaped experiential marketing and be able to chart the chronology of the key theoretical and applied milestones over the years.

EVOLUTION OF EXPERIENTIAL MARKETING

This section presents a high-level overview of the key influences on the development of experiential marketing as well as the key theories that found credence.

An overview is presented in Figure 2.1 before we delve further into the detailed evolution of the practice and theory of experiential marketing.

In effect, there are four key phases to the development of experiential marketing. These phases relate respectively to the following questions:

1. What comes after 'services' as part of the continuum of economic offerings to serve changes in consumer behaviour?
2. What then is 'Experience' and why is it a topic of economic value such that there is an emergence of an Experience Economy?
3. What are the components of experiential marketing that make it an important aspect of what a marketer might decide to do as part of the communications mix?
4. How can experiential marketing become an enabler of strategic competitive advantage?

This chapter begins the process of addressing these questions. Throughout this book, we will look at how an effective understanding of the theoretical aspects of experiential marketing might be applied in a commercial context in a manner that allows strategic management of the experiential marketing activities. But let's begin by looking at the evolution of experiential marketing from the 1960s to the present day, as presented in Figure 2.1.

1960S TO THE PRESENT DAY

The 1960s saw a shift in consumption patterns. Buoyed by increasing wealth and casting off the post-Second World War economic gloom and paucity, consumers became increasingly focused on broadening their consumer choices. Economic offerings that had much earlier focused entirely on products had shifted to a focus on services – and more often a mix of product and service – that reflected increasing technological advances. The first waves of globalisation can also be seen at this time.

The McDonald's experience

In the early 1960s, McDonald's used market research to find out what customers identified with, and they came up with the option of offering their customers an instore experience. For this, Ronald McDonald was introduced to the McDonald's brand. Moreover, the first McDonald's restaurant with seating was opened in Denver, Colorado. This initiative was a big change for the brand. Customers were able to start living a different experience, being able to taste the food in the restaurant itself, and with the introduction of Ronald McDonald, the company marked the beginning of instilling brand loyalty in customers at a young age.

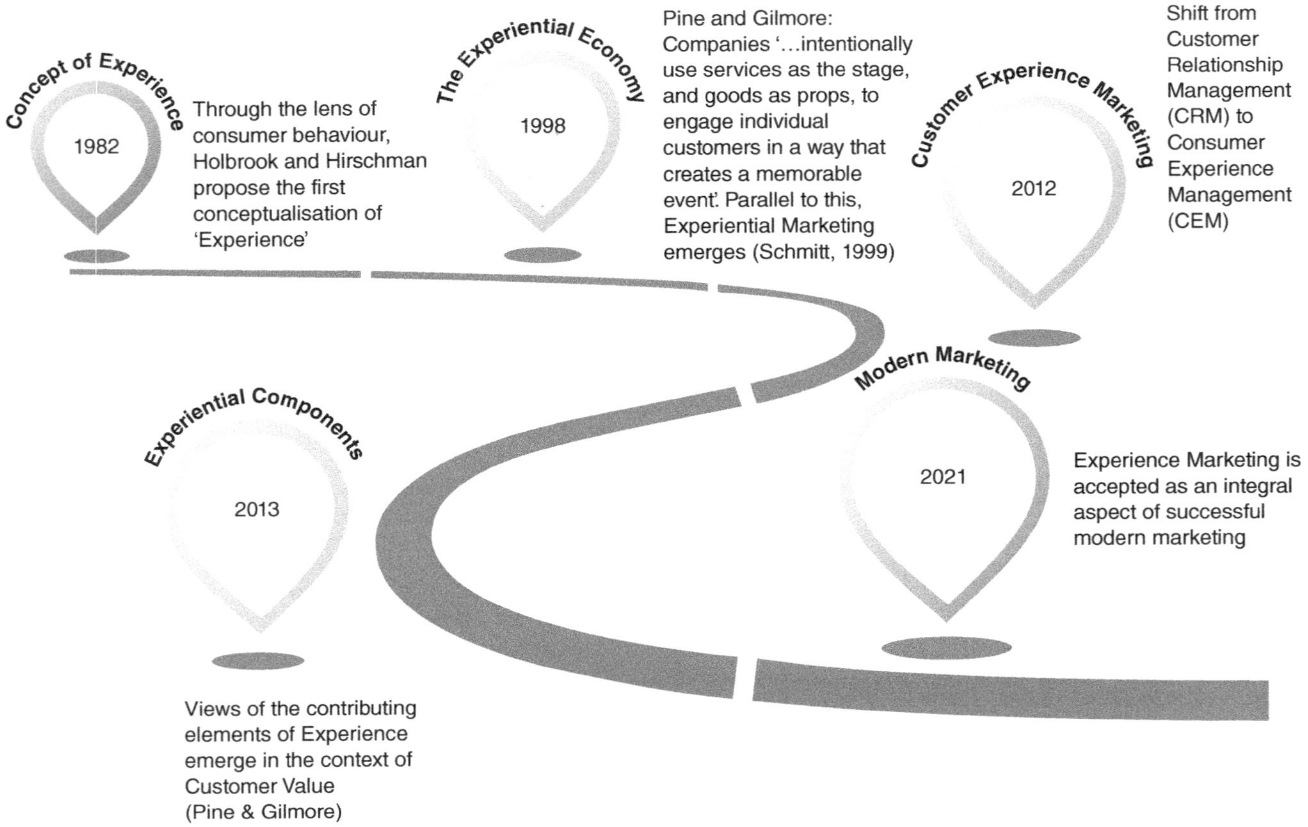

Concept of Experience
1982
Through the lens of consumer behaviour, Holbrook and Hirschman propose the first conceptualisation of 'Experience'
The Experiential Economy
1998
Pine and Gilmore: Companies '...intentionally use services as the stage, and goods as props, to engage individual customers in a way that creates a memorable event'. Parallel to this, Experiential Marketing emerges (Schmitt, 1999)
Customer Experience Marketing
2012
Shift from Customer Relationship Management (CRM) to Consumer Experience Management (CEM)
Experiential Components
2013
Views of the contributing elements of Experience emerge in the context of Customer Value (Pine & Gilmore)
Modern Marketing
2021
Experience Marketing is accepted as an integral aspect of successful modern marketing

Figure 2.1 Chronological evolution of experiential marketing

Moving beyond services in the 1970s, Toffler, in his book *Future Shock* (1970: 221), asked 'Where does the economy go next? After the services, what?'. There was increased interest in how consumers could be more engaged in their spending activities. The focus moved to the idea of 'Experience' and the simple concept that consumers wanted to be satisfied in new ways as they consume.

Feelings for Toyota

During the 1970s, Toyota launched some of its most memorable marketing campaigns, using tag lines that included 'You Asked For It / You Got It!' and the hit campaign with the slogan 'Oh What A Feeling!'. This campaign included the popular 'Toyota Jump', and was a first attempt at incorporating customer involvement in its advertising and marketing activities.

From this focus, and through the 1980s, there was a deep exploration of what an experience economy might feature. Building on the contributions by Holbrook and Hirschman (1982), Pine and Gilmore (1998) explored the experiential view of consumer behaviour and concluded that the growing popularity of experiential benefits among customers led to a new stage of economic development called 'the experiential economy'. By 1985, Ogilvy, the co-founder of the Global Business Network, had identified the need for vivid experiences which he believed were contributing to the growth of the US economy during that period (Ogilvy, 1985). During this time, there was a realisation that experiences could find application in marketing.

Experiencing the extreme with Red Bull

Red Bull was founded by Dietrich Mateschitz in 1987 and is now often seen as the birth of a totally new product category and a unique marketing concept. One year later, in 1988, they began using extreme events as a feature of their marketing activity. They worked with World Cup skier Werner Grissmann, to develop the 'Dolomitenmann' – which has been considered the 'toughest team race under the sun'. Today, this contest has earned a reputation of being an unofficial World Cup of extreme sports and is inextricably linked with Red Bull.

As we moved into the 1990s, other researchers and practitioners were becoming more interested in the components of experience that made it so potentially fruitful for marketing. Although there had been discussions in the literature on the concept

of experience in the consumption situation, there was no defined, agreed terminology until the 1990s when Pine and Gilmore (1999) further explored it and defined it as 'customer experience'. This led to the emergence of the concept of experiential marketing as a means to better link commercial activities with the consumption needs and desires of consumers. Essentially, experiential marketing emerged as the need to entertain, stimulate and emotionally affect customers.

Experiences in the 1990s

In 1996, Coca-Cola presented a total experiential approach in the Olympic Village in Atlanta erecting 5,000 vending machines and spray coolers throughout the city. Additionally, the brand also built a theme park in Atlanta called Olympic City which was blasted with the brand's iconic colour, red.

Nike created a 'Just Do It' poster in braille, introducing the world to a concept that they relaunched many years later with basketball star Kobe Bryant.

Coca-Cola Christmas packaging became available in the USA, the UK, Australia, Hong Kong, South Africa, Singapore and the Philippines, where 'Santa packs' made the drink into a pre-wrapped Christmas gift.

In 1997, YSL (Yves Saint Laurent) sponsored the Christmas lights on Regents Street, London. The lights had the YSL logo on them and it was the first effort by that company to be part of a communal experience.

As the millennium approached, consumption was now viewed as a holistic experience. Coinciding with the dominance of relationship marketing during the 2000s, experiences and the use of experiential marketing became centrally important in adding value to customer–brand relationships. Building on the popularity of Customer Relationship Management, Berry, Carbone and Haeckel (2002) proposed the move to Customer Experience Management, where experiences assumed centrality in the quest to build and strengthen relationships.

Yoo-hoo Chocolate Milk's 'Big Stinkin' Summer Tour'

In the early 2000s, the primary modes of experiential execution were pop-up shops, street promotions and national tours. In 2002, Yoo-hoo, a leading American chocolate milk brand, facilitated an experiential marketing roadshow in the form of a 32-foot truck that visited popular concert venues and sporting

(Continued)

events around the USA. Considering that Yoo-hoo had a cult-like following, this activation afforded the brand the opportunity to generate a lot of buzz by seeking out these passionate brand evangelists and building those important relationships. At each stop of this branded roadshow, Yoo-hoo milk and branded merchandise was given away and the promotional team facilitated brand-led games and interaction with the audience.

Since 2010, the use of technology and customer participation in marketing activities enabled experiences to be the connecting force between brands and customers. Concepts such as 'social currency' and 'amplification strategies' became the buzzwords of the modern marketer.

Experiences in the Sky

Virgin Atlantic teamed up with Universal Orlando and Virgin Holidays to promote 'The Wizarding World of Harry Potter'. A huge Harry Potter decal[1] was applied to the plane. In 2013, to mark the 25th anniversary of Where's Wally, the airline hid Wally in the livery on Barbarella, one of their Boeing 747 planes, for a year. This was a period when Virgin Atlantic was using popular children's characters to create a more playful, family-oriented brand.

In summary, the landscape of modern marketing now entails a reasonably refined but very broad conceptualisation of experiential marketing. The next sections provide details on how this became more seriously accepted by marketing practitioners.

THE CONSUMER: MORPHING FROM RATIONAL TO EMOTIONAL AND THE NEED FOR 'MORE'

A number of key strands map the development of the concept of experience over the last seven decades. In some contexts, the strands emerged from concepts relating to entertainment. Other strands were based on the idea of a deeper economic offering that extended beyond product and service and that perhaps placed the consumer more firmly in the consumption process as emotional beings rather than as functional consumers. While the origins of experience in the marketing context are rooted in the work of Holbrook and Hirschman (who, as we will see, make an enormous contribution to this field), it is interesting to note that elements of experience had previously been discussed by multiple authors in previous decades.

- Abbott (1955) emphasised the importance of the role of services performed by products to provide consumption experiences as a core basis for customer value.
- In a similar timeframe, Alderson (1957) highlighted the significance of the consumption experience.
- Following on from these contributions, Goffman (1959) adapted the core principles of theatre to social situations and work. In this context, he referred to theatre not as a metaphor, but as a business model.

Despite these innovative insights, mainstream literature on consumer behaviour at the time portrayed customers as rational decision makers. The conventional wisdom was that consumers moved through a rational decision-making process when purchasing products, and consequently traditional marketing strategies focused on satisfying customers' needs and wants. Marketers therefore emphasised the features and benefits of their products, categorised along narrow product definitions, in order to increase sales to those consumers.

In the 1980s, however, Holbrook and Hirschman were instrumental in changing this dominant perspective by offering a new experiential approach which revolutionised the common rationale of customer behaviour. The duo's innovative work addressed 'those facets of behaviour that relate to the multi-sensory, fantasy, and emotive aspects of product use' (Holbrook & Hirschman, 1982: 99) and gave a glimpse of a revolutionary movement which signified the transition from the traditional information-processing approach of consumer behaviour to one focused on emotions and consumer experiences. These were the critical perspectives that unlocked the potential of experience.

Much of the approach of Holbrook and Hirschman had the aim of contrasting the differences between the informational-processing (rational) and the experiential-view (emotional) elements of consumer behaviour. Moving beyond the rational, the experiential frame of reference considers consumption as 'a primary subjective state of consciousness with a variety of symbolic meanings, hedonic responses and aesthetic criteria' (Same, 2012: 4). Holbrook and Hirschman's experiential view of consumption states that consumers continuously seek what became known as the Three Fs: fantasy, feelings and fun (Figure 2.2).

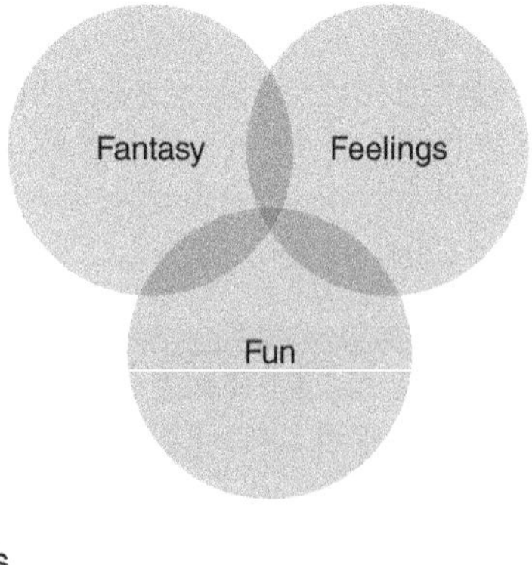

Figure 2.2 The Three Fs

Source: Holbrook, M.B., Hirschman, E.C., The Experiential Aspects of Consumption: Consumer Fantasies, Feelings and Fun. Journal of Consumer Research, 1982, 9(2), pp. 132–140, by permission of Oxford University Press.

Contrary to the dominant idea of information processing as rational – with a focus on product attributes, utilitarian functions and conscious and verbal thought processes – this new experiential view encompasses consumption as a subjective state of consciousness, which stresses the symbolic meaning, subconscious process and non-verbal cues which arise from consumption. Importantly, how the customer is affected plays a primary role, not just in behavioural and attitude influences, but in terms of the full scale of consumer emotions (i.e. love, pride, anger, joy, etc.) (Schmitt, 2010). Schmitt, another key player in the development of experiential marketing, chronicled experiential marketing as a communications method which allows customers to sense, feel, think, act and relate with companies and brands.

In summary, it can be said that the contributions by Holbrook and Hirschman led to the rise that we see today in the popularity of experiential marketing. With the benefit of hindsight, various authors have identified many significant points which have acted as a strong foundation to the development of experiential marketing.

- First, they highlighted the need to investigate the consumption experience in its totality from pre-purchase through to disposal.
- Second, emotion as a critical aspect of consumption came to the fore as an issue which had attracted the interest of many academics, including Richins (1997), Bagozzi, Gopinath and Nyer (1999) and Winsted (2000).
- Third, they posit that individuals do not simply take part in experiences in a multi-sensory mode, but they also react and respond to the stimulus, therefore placing interaction at the core of the experience.
- Finally, they proposed that customers can not only recall memories in response to an experience, but they can also respond by imagining events which they have never experienced. Therefore, imagination and nostalgia contribute to an individual's experience (Tynan & McKechnie, 2009).

The research at the time highlighted the need to entertain, stimulate and emotionally affect customers throughout the consumption experience in its totality. Consumers were no longer viewed as solely rational purchasers, but rather were now regarded as emotional at the core, with a significant need for 'more' in their purchase behaviour. The advances in thinking on consumer behaviour at this time helped shape the concept of *experience* as being of value in an economic context and therefore resulted in it being the subject of scrutiny in business models and marketing circles. There were merging commercial activities that showed that experience could not be ignored and had merit in application. The next section explores the economic offering that centred on experience.

EXPERIENTIAL VS ENTERTAINMENT ECONOMY: UNLEASHING MORE VALUE WITHIN CONSUMPTION BEHAVIOUR

As identified, throughout the 1980s, the broad concept of experience was garnering much academic attention, which in turn resulted in its growing application in

business practice. Indeed, the need for vivid experiences, which it was believed were contributing to the growth of the US economy at that time, was increasingly under the microscope.

Building on the work of the 1980s, which viewed consumer behaviour through an experiential lens, Pine and Gilmore's (1998) work was significant in proposing that the growing popularity of experiential benefits among customers had resulted in a new stage of economic development called '**the experiential economy**'. Essentially, the development of value from commodities to products, services and experiences, by depicting experience as a new economic offering, specifically differentiating it from goods and services, was increasingly discussed. The 'experience economy' encapsulates an era where companies 'intentionally use services as the stage, and goods as props, to engage individual customers in a way that creates a memorable event' (Pine & Gilmore, 1998: 98). However, in addition to entertaining customers, these staged experiences were a communication tool used to engage with customers in a personal and memorable manner.

While the experience economy as a new stage of economic development generated both interest and criticism alike, one of the more interesting iterations came from Wolf (1999), who also identified a change in economic offering. However, instead of referring to it in terms of experience, Wolf described it as the 'entertainment economy'. Essentially, this proposition reflected some of the roots of the experience concept in the entertainment domain. Both the experience economy and the entertainment economy acknowledge customer inclusion and the staging of entertaining experiences as the next step in marketing development. Specifically, however, in the entertainment economy, there is a clear fusion of the entertainment element with the media, with the dominant characteristics being emotion and escapism.

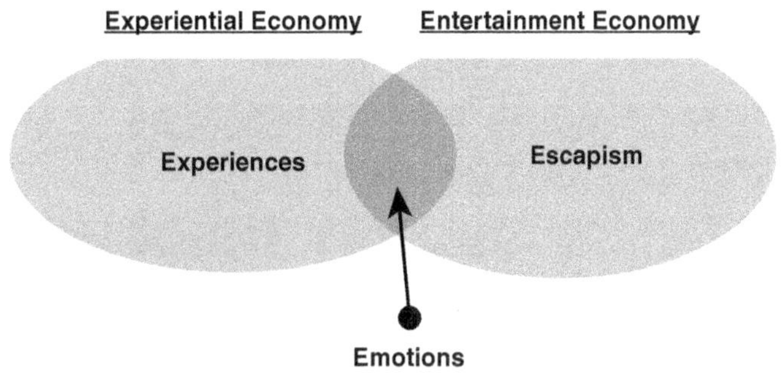

Figure 2.3 Experiential economy vs entertainment economy

There is a clear progression of thought in the business sense here, as, traditionally, businesses had not considered entertainment as a marketing strategy. However, by infusing entertainment into the core economic offering, the consumers' purchasing choice was radically influenced. Through the use of entertainment, marketers were now communicating through the medium of emotion and escapism, making the product or brand relatable to the consumer. Essentially, 'It's about stories that move us; characters we can root for, ideas that transform the cultural

landscape, special effects that take us to a world we've never seen before, situations and lines that make us laugh, and ideas that are universal, they forever change the way we live' (Wolf, 1999: 295). In this case, entertainment represents telling a story and allowing customers to relate to the brand.

Netflix entertaining fans

For Netflix, the entertainment factor of experiential marketing activations is imperative as in-home entertainment is the nature of their business. To cultivate and drive consumer awareness for its *Gilmore Girls* sequel, the streaming service provider constructed 200 pop-up cafés around the USA that emulated the set-up of 'Luke's Diner', an iconic set from the show. At these pop-ups, fans had the opportunity to immerse themselves in the Luke's Diner share-worthy experience while drinking free coffee. This experiential launch generated online buzz and engagement, while cultivating interest in the premiere of the sequel.

The increasing acceptance that experience was a key aspect of the economy during the late 20th century and into the new millennium offered businesses the potential to exploit commercial opportunity in an innovative and exciting way. Experiences were viewed as a new economic offering, often in the context of entertainment, with a focus on delivering experiential benefits to customers. The next section presents some key research into both experiences and the development of the experiential marketing concept as it came to the fore at the turn of the century.

EXPERIENCE AND EXPERIENTIAL MARKETING: INTRODUCING COMPONENTS AND KEY THEORIES

In this section, we will begin by exploring what is meant by customer experiences, which are a key component of the experiential approach to marketing. It is a concept that differs substantially from the long-standing traditional marketing approach.

Customer Experience

As previously outlined, there had been an increased focus through the 1980s and 1990s on the concept of experience in the consumption situation. Pine and Gilmore (1999) provided a pivotal focus to these discussions, moving 'customer experience' into the realm of a new paradigm, where a firm's primary marketing

objective is to continually stage unique and memorable experiences which appeal to their customers' physical and emotional connection to their brand. In this view, customers are regarded as willing to pay a premium price for personalised experiences which are exclusive, non-transferable and memorable.

This time period is fundamental to the development of the experience concept, where depth and refinement of the concept paved the way for the emergence and establishment of experiential marketing as a core marketing approach.

Deep-dive into Customer Experiences

According to Schmitt (1999), customers can have five different types of experiences. These are termed **strategic experiential modules (SEMs)**, and include:

1. **Sense (sensory experiences)**: Sense experiences are sensual and tangible elements of a product or service that appeal to the five senses of sight, sound, scent, taste and touch. The overall purpose of this marketing activity is to provide aesthetic pleasure, excitement, beauty and satisfaction through sensory stimulation.
2. **Feel (affective experiences)**: Feel experiences focus on the creation of moods and emotions and have the objective of influencing consumers' attitude towards a more positive outlook of the brand or product.
3. **Think (creative cognitive experiences)**: The objective of the think experience is to encourage consumers to engage in elaborative and innovative thinking that may solve problems. This marketing activity initiates customers' ideas and creates emotions of surprise, joy and anger.
4. **Act (physical experiences and entire lifestyles)**: The act experience focuses on the physical experience and the way in which it affects people's lives. The act experience enhances customers' lives by enriching their physiological experiences, portraying different methods of doing things, alternative lifestyle choices and interactions. These changes in behaviour and lifestyle often motivate, inspire and generate an emotional response.
5. **Relate (social identity experiences)**: Relate experiences contain elements of sense, feel, think and act, but expand beyond an individual's personal, private feelings and emotions. Campaigns of this nature appeal to an individual's need for self-improvement. They appeal to the desire to be perceived positively by others and so relate the person to a broader social system, therefore establishing strong brand relations and active brand communities.

These five types of experiences present the first successful effort at codifying, in a person-centric way, the aspects of experience that can be best linked to marketing activity. Similar to these types of experiences are Pleasure Dimensions, as defined by Dubé and Le Bel (2003). These include Emotional, Intellectual, Physical and Social pleasures.

Further work in this area by Gentile, Spiller and Noci (2007) distinguished the following **Experiential Components**:

1. **Sensorial**: This relates to the senses and how aesthetic pleasure and satisfaction provoke them.
2. **Emotional**: This involves moods, feelings and emotional experiences which provoke an affective relationship with a company, its brands and its products.
3. **Cognitive**: This component relates to the thinking or conscious mental processes that encourage customers to exercise their creativity or problem-solving mechanisms so they revise their assumptions about a product.
4. **Pragmatic**: This relates to experiences derived from the act of doing something and its usability.
5. **Lifestyle**: This encompasses experiences derived from the assertion of values and personal beliefs.
6. **Relationships**: This involves experiences which emerge from relationships and the social context that happen during consumption as part of a real or imagined community or that assert social identity.

Volkswagen embracing the fun

Volkswagen created a concept called 'the fun theory'. They tried to change people's behaviour by adding an element of fun. In one campaign, they created a set of 'piano' stairs, right next to the escalator, in a subway stop in Germany. This was an attempt to pivot people to choose the stairs rather than the escalator. As an additional bit of fun, as people ascended and descended the stairs, musical notes would play. With this initiative, a lot more people used the stairs. It may seem odd for a car company to do this, because this had nothing to do with their product, but they tried to be associated with an emotion of fun. In the end, the strategy worked because people essentially had fun and this was an important aspect for the brand image.

As a more rounded understanding of the experience concept began to take hold, Pine and Gilmore (2013) furthered their earlier work and identified that **Participation** and **Connection** are central to customers' personalised experiences. When looking at these in more detail, the following questions need to be asked:

1. **Guest participation**: How immersed is the individual in the experience? Are they passive or active participants?
2. **Connection**: What connects the individual to the experience? Are they engaged with the experience from a distance (absorption) or are they physically or virtually partaking in the experience itself (immersion)?

By engaging an individual through participation and connection, a positive experience can result. Through the amalgamation of these two elements, there emerged four

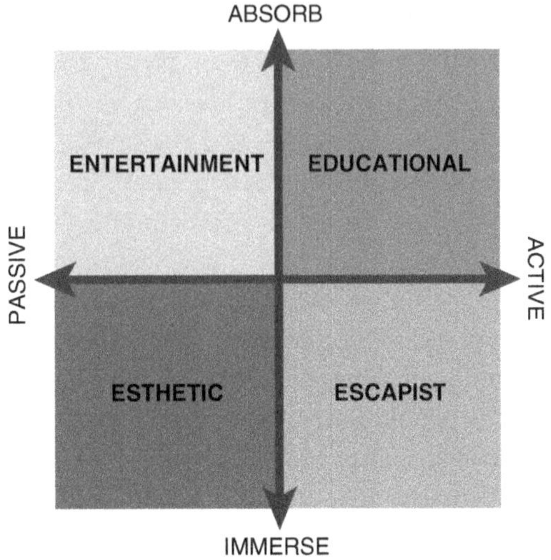

Figure 2.4 Four realms of experience

Source: Pine and Gilmore (2013) Copyright Harvard Business Press (2011), printed with permission.

realms of an experience. These include Entertainment, Education, Escapist and Esthetic (Figure 2.4).

- **Entertainment**: These are everyday experiences that we passively absorb, for example, watching television or attending a concert.
- **Education**: The individual is actively engaged in the experience but is still watching from a distance rather than being immersed in the action. The key objective is to increase their knowledge of the brand or functionalities of the product. In educational experiences, the individual is an interactive learner.
- **Escapist**: These experiences can teach just as well as educational events, or amuse participants just as well as entertaining experiences, but they involve greater customer immersion.
- **Esthetic**: The individual is fully immersed in the experience but they themselves have little or no effect on it.

In the centre of this is what is termed the '**sweet spot**', which is essentially any compelling experience that incorporates all four realms of an experience. By activating an experience of this kind, it is envisaged that consumers create and recall memories that are significantly distinct from the mundane world of goods and services.

It is clear now that there is a substantive, broad consensus that experience is not a nebulous concept but rather is framed by quite relatable components. Armed, therefore, with an understanding of the experience concept, the next section explores the experiential marketing concept as it emerged from the focus on experiences.

EXPERIENTIAL MARKETING

The concept of customer experience paved the way for the development of the experiential marketing concept. Srinivasan and Srivastava (2010) encapsulated the essence of the concept well by defining experiential marketing as an activity in which the involvement of the consumer is mandatory in the form of participation and which aims to exceed the customer's identified needs and wants. Fundamentally, experiential marketing not only addresses the customer's needs and wants, but also an individual's self-image, values, dormant emotions and desires. Experiential marketing seeks to offer a unique, memorable and personal experience to the customer and, as outlined earlier, is a communication method that allows customers to sense, feel, think, act and relate with companies and brands. By identifying these variables, finding a correlation between them and the brand, and communicating them through experiential activities, it is possible to build a relationship between the customer and the brand. (This will be explored in detail in Chapter 4.) In differentiating experiential marketing from traditional marketing, it can be seen that a focus on products is found in traditional marketing, while experiential marketing attaches greater importance to the experience and the involvement of the customer. The core concept of experiential marketing, then, is not only to provide customers with goods and services which satisfy them, but also to offer them unique, memorable and personalised experiences. Indeed, it can be said that experiential marketing offers a broader view of the consumption situation, taking a holistic approach which views the consumer as emotional as well as rational decision makers (Schmitt, 2000). The view from the traditional marketing perspective is that the consumer, being a rational decision maker necessitates an analytical quantitative, verbal marketing approach. In contrast, experiential marketing adopts a diverse, visual and multi-faceted approach to marketing (Schmitt, 2000).

Somewhat parallel to the establishment of experiential marketing in mainstream marketing literature, and as mentioned earlier in this chapter, we see the emergence of the concept of **Consumer Experience Management (CEM)**, which was conceptualised by Berry et al. (2002). As has been outlined, customer experiences derive from interactions which occur between a customer and a product or company. Experiences are personal, existing only in the mind of an individual who has been engaged with, on an emotional, physical, intellectual or even spiritual level. Therefore, no two people can have the same experience given that each experience is a result of a staged event and the individual's state of mind. The success of customer experience depends on the comparison between the customer's expectations and how satisfied they are with staff interaction at different moments of contact or touchpoints. As such, CEM embodies the process used to manage a customer's cross-channel exposure and transactions with a company, brand or service. Through modern marketing management, there has been a shift from customer relationship management (CRM) to the new concept of CEM, further elevating the position of experiential marketing in the repertoire of the modern-day marketing.

CONCLUSION AND SUMMARY

This chapter has described a timeline of the key developments which have resulted in what we view as modern-day experiential marketing. Table 2.1 provides an overview of this development while also highlighting the key theoretical emergences.

Fundamentally, this chapter asserts that customer requirements have evolved, and the influential modern-day consumer has needs and wants that are no longer satisfied by traditional marketing practices. Rather, they want brands to be responsive to their individual needs and to build brand experiences that are memorable and immersive. This assertion forms an essential component of the current practice of experiential marketing. The next chapter looks at the fundamentals of experiential marketing and the different types of experiential marketing activations.

Table 2.1 Summary of the development and theory of experiential marketing

View of consumer	Key emergence	Key theory & considerations
Nascent		
Rational decision makers with vague awareness of emotive aspect of consumption	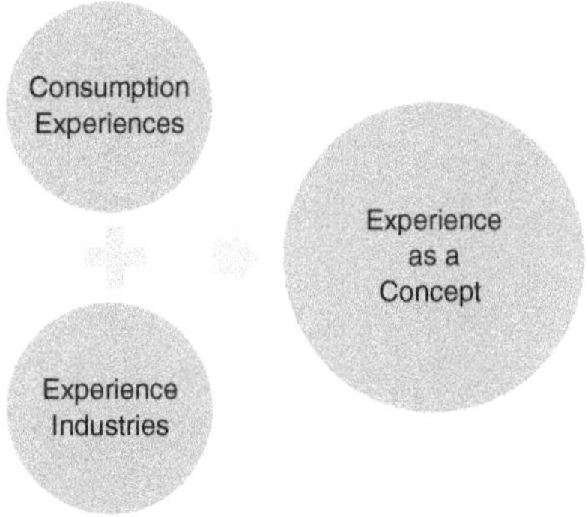	**What comes after services?** Experience as a concept – Holbrook and Hirschman Experience industries – Toffler Consumption experience from pre-purchase to disposal Emotion as an aspect React and interact Imagine
Formation		
Creating value for customers through experiences	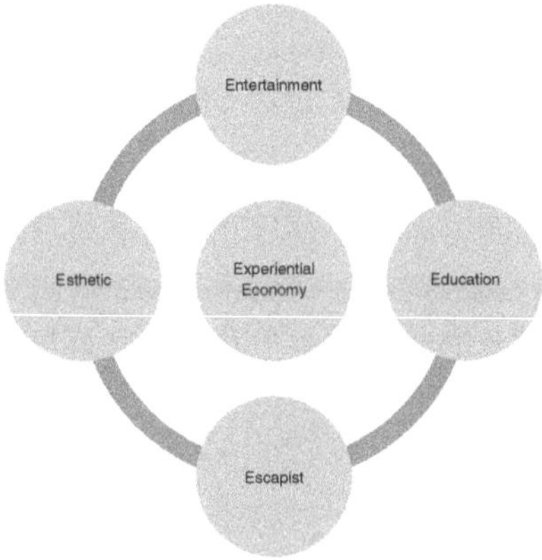	**What is the nature of experience?** Experience as an economic offering – Pine and Gilmore Is the value in the experience or in the marketing of experience? – Schmitt The four realms of experience Emergence of Customer Experience Co-creation of experience

(Continued)

Table 2.1 (Continued)

View of consumer	Key emergence	Key theory & considerations
Focus		
Orienting to provide more than value but memorable experience	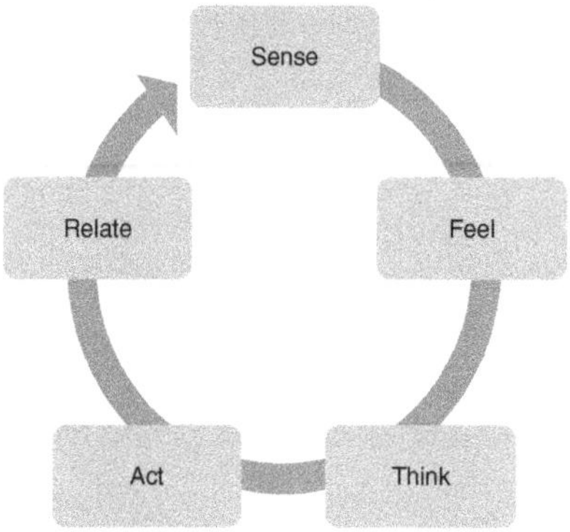	**What are the components of an Experiential Marketing experience?** Increased emphasis on customer Strategic experience modules Pleasure dimensions Experiential components
Strategic exploitation		
Holistic Customer Experience	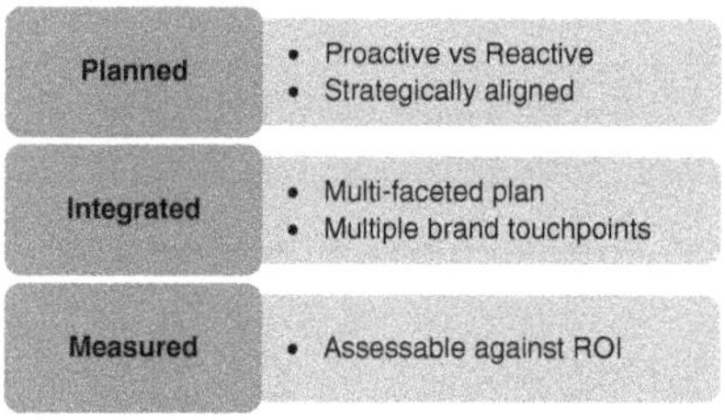	**How can Experiential Marketing be leveraged strategically?** An economic offering and an integral element of modern marketing strategy (Pine & Gilmore, 1998; Smith & Hanover, 2016)

MAIN TAKEAWAYS FROM CHAPTER 2

- Experiential marketing has its origins in the 1960s and has evolved and changed over the decades as companies turned their attention to the creation of experiences for customers.
- The emergence of experiential marketing coincided with a shift from thinking about consumers as largely rational purchasers to one which realised that emotions play a substantial part in the consumer purchasing process.
- Experiential marketing focuses on many concepts, including fun, escapism, personalisation and relationships.
- Marketers are cognisant of the fact that there are different types of experiences and different components to the experiences.

CONCLUDING QUESTIONS

1. Is the modern economy increasingly experience-oriented?
2. How has digitalisation impacted the experience economy? Does it limit or expand the potential?
3. Give examples of companies that place a stronger emphasis on traditional rather than experiential marketing and explain why they might do this.
4. Why might some marketing units overlook the value of experiential marketing?
5. Although experiential marketing has been around for nearly 70 years, it is still regarded as a relatively new concept. Why do you think this is?
6. Are there any situations where experiential marketing might not be appropriate?
7. Should all companies have a customer experience manager? Why?
8. Provide examples of marketing in practice that fit into each of Schmitt's identified types of experience?

NOTE

1. A decorative, sometimes temporary covering used in marketing to change the look of a structure or object.

REFERENCES AND FURTHER READING

Abbott, L. (1955). *Quality and Competition*. New York: Columbia University Press.

Alderson, W. (1957). *Marketing Behavior and Executive Action*. Homewood, IL: Richard D. Irwin.

Bagozzi, R.P., Gopinath, M., & Nyer, P.U. (1999). The Role of Emotions in Marketing. *Journal of the Academy of Marketing Science*, 27(2), 184–206.

Berry, L.L., Carbone, L.P., & Haeckel, S.H. (2002). Managing the Total Customer Experience. *MIT Sloan Management Review*, 43(3), 85–89.

Dubé, L., & Le Bel, J. (2003). The Content and Structure of Laypeople's Concept of Pleasure. *Cognition and Emotion*, 17(2), 263–295.

Engel, J. F., Kollat, D. T., & Blackwell, R. D. (1968). *Consumer Behavior*. New York: Holt Rinehart and Winston.

Gentile, C., Spiller, N., & Noci, G. (2007). How to Sustain the Customer Experience: An Overview of Experience Components that Co-create Value with the Customer. *European Management Journal*, 25(5), 395–410.

Goffman, E. (1959). *The Presentation of Self in Everyday Life*. New York: Anchor.

Hirschman, E.C., & Holbrook, M.B. (1982). Hedonic Consumption: Emerging Concepts, Methods and Propositions. *Journal of Marketing*, 46(3), 92–101.

Holbrook, M.B., & Hirschman, E.C. (1982). The Experiential Aspects of Consumption: Consumer Fantasies, Feelings and Fun. *Journal of Consumer Research*, 9(2), 132–140.

Ogilvy, J. (1985). *The Experience Industry: A Leading-edge Report from the Values and Lifestyles Program* (No. 724). Menlo Park, CA: SRI International Business Intelligence.

Pine, B. Joseph, & Gilmore, J.H. (1998). Welcome to the Experience Economy. *Harvard Business Review*, 76(4), 97–105.

Pine, B. Joseph, & Gilmore, J.H. (1999). *The Experience Economy: Work is Theatre & Every Business a Stage*. Boston, MA: Harvard Business Press.

Pine, B. Joseph, & Gilmore, J.H. (2013). *The Experience Economy* (Updated Edition). Boston, MA: Harvard Business Press.

Richins, M.L. (1997). Measuring Emotions in the Consumption Experience. *Journal of Consumer Research*, 24(September), 127–146.

Same, S. (2012). *Understanding Experience Marketing: Conceptual Insights and Differences from Experiential Marketing*. In Jean-Claude Andreani and Umberto Collesei (Eds.), *International Marketing Trends Conference* (1–23). Venice: Marketing Trends Association (Paris-Venice Association), ESCP Europe.

Schmitt, B.H. (1999). *Experiential Marketing*. New York: The Free Press.

Schmitt, B.H. (2000). *Experiential Marketing: How to Get Customers to Sense, Feel, Think, Act, Relate to your Company and Brands*. New York: The Free Press.

Schmitt, B.H. (2010). *Customer Experience Management: A Revolutionary Approach to Connecting with Your Customers* (2nd ed.). New York: John Wiley & Sons.

Smith, K. & Hanover, D. (2016). *Experiential Marketing: Secrets, Strategies, and Success Stories from the World's Greatest Brands*. Hoboken, NJ: John Wiley & Sons.

Srinivasan, S.R., & Srivastava, R.K. (2010). Creating a Futuristic Retail Experience through Experiential Marketing: Is it Possible? An Explorative Study. *Journal of Retail and Leisure Property*, 9(3), 193–199.

Toffler, A. (1970). *Future Shock*. New York: Bantam Books.

Tynan, C., & McKechnie, S. (2009). Experience Marketing: A Review and Reassessment. *Journal of Marketing Management*, 25(5/6), 501–517.

Winsted, K.F. (2000). Service Behaviours that Lead to Satisfied Customers. *European Journal of Marketing*, 34(3/4), 399–417.

Wolf, M.J. (1999). *The Entertainment Economy: How Mega-media Forces are Transforming Our Lives*. London: Times Books.

Yaffe, J., Moose, A., & Marquardt, D. (2019). *The experience economy is booming, but it must benefit everyone*, World Economic Forum Annual Meeting, Available at: https://www.weforum.org/agenda/2019/01/the-experience-economy-is-booming-but-it-must-benefit-everyone/

3
THE EXPERIENTIAL CONCEPT

CHAPTER OVERVIEW

Experiential marketing has found its place as a key aspect of modern marketing and is accepted as an effective means to reach new customers, strengthen bonds with these customers and make them more likely to consume a company's products or services. Despite this success and acceptance, there are ongoing challenges around defining precisely what experiential marketing is and how it relates to areas like event marketing and similar, while also posing a question about how it can be effectively measured and managed operationally and strategically. This chapter explores the nature of experiential marketing, presenting a range of examples across various sectors. The matter of measurement and strategic effectiveness is taken up in Chapter 10.

In modern marketing practice, immersive and interactive marketing methods have grown in popularity over their traditional counterparts. This has predominately been influenced by the surge in both brands and customers favouring brand experiences as a form of communication in both business-to-business (B2B) and business-to-customer (B2C) markets. By staging brand experiences, brands are actively trying to differentiate themselves from both direct and indirect competing brands by partially eschewing conventional marketing methods and favouring methods of communication that allow them to focus and nurture relationships between brands and their audiences by bringing the brand's unique attributes to life. Essentially, experiential marketing is an immersive marketing tool, and while there are merits to the implementation of traditional marketing methods[1] in isolation, traditional marketing practices do not typically fulfil brand requirements of building immersive and authentic connections with a brand audience. The reason why this topic is so important is precisely because experiential marketing is so impactful when it comes to connection and relationship development.

In this chapter, we will discuss the following topics:

1. Experience: We will see that there are differing perspectives on its nature and focus.
2. Experiential marketing: In presenting definitions of experiential marketing, we will work towards a definition that is reflected throughout this book.
3. The interplay between experiential and traditional marketing: This will more clearly position experiential marketing as part of a spectrum of marketing activities.
4. Experiential value: Setting the tone for further chapters, we will commence the discussion about the value of experiential marketing.

WHAT DO WE MEAN BY EXPERIENCE?

Experience is at the heart of experiential marketing. Knowing what is meant by experience is key to fully utilising the best possible experiential marketing tactics and strategies. Creating a memorable experience for a customer (be they business or consumer) can have the impact of exciting that customer. Exciting the customer creates memory and memory, in turn, creates connection. Multiple authors and practitioners have considered the boundaries and nature of experience over the years, and a general belief now exists that it is intrinsically linked to the human senses – delight consumers through whatever means, tap into their emotions (positively) and give them reason to reflect. In Chapter 2 we provided an initial deep-dive into the theoretical foundations of the concept of experience. Here we continue that deep-dive by exploring the concept in greater detail.

Some argue that the reason there remains a lack of clarity regarding a universal definition of experiential marketing lies in the fact that there are multiple ways in which the term *experience* can be applied. In a review of experiential marketing practice, Tynan and McKechnie (2009: 502) conclude that experience is both a noun and a verb, and

> is used to variously convey the process itself, participating in the activity, the affect or way in which an object, thought or emotion is felt through the senses or the mind, and even the outcome of an experience by way of a skill or learning for example. Therefore, it is not evident whether experience is active or passive for the customer involved, whether it is expected to influence certain results including customer loyalty or skill development or finally if customer interaction is essential for the experience to be deemed successful.

Various people offer a take on this. Each seems hard to argue with, but each nonetheless positions experience slightly differently. For example, Poulsson and Kale (2004) assert that an experience refers to the mental state that materialises in any given individual, at any given conscious moment. However, Carbone and Haeckel (1994: 8) believe that an experience is the 'takeaway impression formed by people's encounters with products, services, and businesses – a perception produced when

humans consolidate sensory information'. Razi and Iajevardi (2016) acknowledge that organisations utilise experience as a platform to facilitate immersive and immersive service delivery. Companies use their products as tools in order to centre the service offering around the customer's experience, with the aim of creating an experience that will be unforgettable to participants who are immersed in the servicescape. These unforgettable experiences are such because they are internal. They exist in each individual customer's heart, and they are an outcome of personal physique, emotion and knowledge. Others argue that every experience is a collective of multiple micro experiences and each of these smaller experiences are what offers a brand a competitive advantage (Conway, 2016). Brakus, Schmitt and Zarantonello (2009) assert that brand experiences are not static, but vary in both intensity and strength; that is, some brand experiences are stronger and can have a more profound impact than others. Therefore, it is important to tailor the brand experience to the intended audience in order for it to create the desired brand effect and campaign outcome. One aspect of this that needs further attention is the difference between direct and indirect experiences.

The Nature of Experiences

Experiences can arise through either direct or indirect methods. Indirect experience occurs when customers are exposed to, or immersed in, intangible aspects of marketing communications, whereas direct experiences take place when a customer either purchases or consumes a product or service. To offer context to this, an example of an indirect experience would be if an individual was walking in their local park and an experiential activation was taking place for Cadbury chocolate and they engaged with it. For example, perhaps Cadbury are hosting a flash-mob. An example of a direct experience, on the other hand, would involve the individual buying a bar of Cadbury chocolate from a retail outlet. Both of these categories of experiences are useful for brands which aim to gain competitive advantage as they offer multiple rich touchpoints to the brand which we know to be important.

We know that an experience is not merely of itself but part of a brand landscape (metaphorically) that will include multiple points of interest, vary depending on vantage point, and will ultimately satisfy or dissatisfy based on the customer's ability to engage with that landscape to an extent that fulfils their needs. This positions experience as being possible online or offline, as a once-off or ongoing encounter and as having an impact that might be anything from negligible, through transient to persistent and altering.

- Platform: There is increasing emphasis on digital/online experiences and of interlocking such experiences with offline/traditional experiences with either human-activated bridges between both or technological enablers (e.g. virtual and augmented reality), creating a more holistically connected experience. Platform is important also in terms of the impact of word-of-mouth marketing (WOMM), which will be explored in Chapter 6.

- Nature of persistence of experience: The experience, by design, might be fleeting or it might be part of a planned series that reconnects the consumer with the brand on an ongoing basis. Often, for example, radio stations will deploy experiential events at a series of music festivals over a summer period. This contrasts with a one-off tasting for a food product in a supermarket.
- The extent of impact of experience: A designer of an experience will most likely want the positive impact of the experience to linger. However, effectiveness may be found in other ways. For example, an experience with a Cola brand that leads to an impulse purchase in a store is a success. On the other hand, the pleasure derived from perusing an Apple Store™ (an experience) might linger to affect multiple subsequent purchases.

Caru and Cova (2003) have also identified that there is a difference between the mere satisfaction derived from an ordinary or mundane experience and the enjoyment achieved through an extraordinary or flow experience. Ordinary experiences are simply everyday occurences that are routine and result in passive stimulation (Schmitt, 2010). However, extraordinary experiences are unique, not commonly experienced and transcend the realm of everyday life (Bhattacharjee & Mogilner, 2014). Extraordinary experiences have been the subject of many academic articles and have been referred to as 'flow' (Csikszentmihalyi, 1990: 4) or 'epiphanies' (Denzin, 1992: 26), and are believed to 'transcend customer experiences' (Schouten et al., 2007: 358). These definitons are further reiterated by Sussman and Alter's (2012) discussion of the concept. They state that purchases can be categorised along a continuum from ordinary (a common occurence) to exceptional (sporadic and unusual).

Despite the term *experience* being frequently discussed by academics and practioners alike, the premise of each of the definitions by leading academics in this field focus on different elements of the concept. From a theoretical perspective, therefore, we can capture the leading thought on the nature of experience, which will help us to define it (see Table 3.1).

Table 3.1 Lexicon of experience

Author	Experience focus
Holbrook and Hirschman (1982)	Experiential aspects
Csikszentmihalyi (1990)	Flow experiences
Arnould and Price (1993)	Extraordinary experience
Carbone and Haeckel (1994)	Customer experience engineering
Pine and Gilmore (1998)	Distinct economic offering, memorable, experience economy
Schmitt (1999b)	Experiential marketing
Poulsson and Kale (2004)	Commercial experience
Boswijk, Thijssen and Peelen (2005)	Meaning experience
Tarssanen and Kylänen (2007)	Experience pyramid, personal change

Source: Same and Larimo (2012)

Hence, the term experience is broad and open to interpretation. Experiences, by nature, can take form in a multitude of ways and at different stages of the consumption experience. The next section progresses the evaluation of this topic and offers insight on each stage of the consumption experience. Rather than looking at experience as a whole concept, we now look more closely at it as we deconstruct its linkage with consumption.

The Stages of the Consumption Experience

In the experiential perspective, the consumption experience is not merely limited to 'pre-purchase activity (the stimulation of a need, the search for information, assessment etc.), nor to some post-purchase activity, e.g. the assessment of satisfaction, but includes a series of other activities which influence consumers' decisions and future actions' (Vézina, 1999: 62). Therefore, the consumption experience is prolonged over a period of time, which can be divided into four stages (Arnould, Price, & Zinkhan, 2002; see Figure 3.1). It helps to consider these in the context of the idea of 'immersion' – the depth to which you participate in an experience.

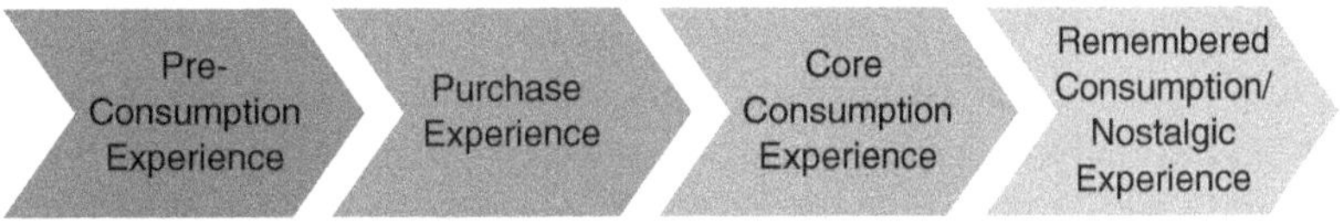

Figure 3.1 The stages of the consumption experience

Source: Copyright McGraw-Hill (2002), printed with permission

- The *pre-consumption experience*, which derives from the seeking of, planning for, daydreaming about, or imagining of the experience. This may be, for example, the desire to visit the Volkswagen car dealership.
- The *purchase experience*, comprised of the choice, payment or transaction, and the packaging. It is the overall encounter with the service and the environment. Perhaps taking the car for a test-drive, the haggle over price, the coffee while the paperwork is finalised.
- The *core consumption experience*, which includes the impression, the satiety, the levels of satisfaction/dissatisfaction, the irritation/flow and the transformation. This is the physical experience of driving the car, the pride in being seen in the car and the happiness of possessing it on an ongoing basis.
- The *remembered consumption experience* and the *nostalgic experience* evokes a reaction through the medium of photographs and videos to relive a past experience. This stage is established through recalling stories and arguments with friends about the past, all of which can be accounted for through the classification of memories (Arnould et al., 2002). Continuing our example, this might be the feeling of pride that an individual experiences when they see an old TV advertisement for their Volkswagen, the one they loved and associated with a particular time in their lives.

Therefore, the consumption experience cannot simply involve the service encounter, but must consider the experience in totality, from pre-consumption to the remembered consumption and nostalgic experience.

The next prospect is the creation of experiences that inherently help us to reach new customers as we integrate marketing and experiences as a holistic, coherent offering.

EXPERIENTIAL MARKETING... WHAT DOES IT REALLY MEAN?

Given the relative newness of experiential marketing it is not a surprise that there is a lack of agreement on a usable definition – we recall this from Chapter 2. This can often be the case as the theoretical aspects of a discipline catch up with the practical application of a given topic. Therefore, there is a substantial set of definitions that fall, broadly, into two categories. In this section we will briefly point to the existing muddled perspectives before exploring the two categories into which most definitions fall. We will outline the key practical developments – captured in the experiential event marketing paradigm – that represent the most tangible identifier of that practice that is often contracted to, simply, experiential marketing. This section will lead to an exploration of the contrast between experiential marketing and 'traditional' marketing, while also pitching experiential marketing now as a clear aspect of marketing practice.

Theoretical Overview of Experiential Marketing

> Experiential marketing is essentially concerned with the six senses: smell, sight, taste, hearing, touch and balance. Experiential marketing has grown in importance because traditional marketing has largely ignored the notion of experiences. (McCole, 2004: 535)

Meier (2010) refers to a comment made by Hauser in 2007, in which the latter stated that the 'definition of experiential marketing is fluid – as is the methodology itself. It was once little talked about and is now being embraced as a silver bullet.' In fact, Hauser had previously posted on the Experiential Marketing Forum, asking for the definition of experiential marketing. He received over 200 definitions from more than 150 countries (Meier, 2010).

The most basic definitions point to experiential marketing as a *tactic* which is utilised by a business to combine an experience with elements of entertainment to turn it into the offering, with the intention of reinforcing the product or service in the consumer's mind (Atwal & Williams, 2009; Lee, Hsiao, & Yang, 2011; Pine & Gilmore, 1999; Yuan & Wu, 2008). Lenderman (2005: 19) states 'experiential marketing uses credible voices, sensory experiences, and respect for the consumer

in its tactics and strategies, and it is employed to create direct and meaningful connections between companies and their customers'. Companies that practise experiential marketing take a brand's essence and implement it in the form of an event, experience or interaction. This in turn will allow consumers to understand the brand at an intimate level by being active, rather than passive, participants (Gautier, 2003).

The core functionality of the experiential approach is that the live brand experience is centred on two-way communication occurring in real time, thereby establishing a profound consumer bonding process (Kailani & Ciobotar, 2015). Considering that experiential marketing can occur as an isolated personal experience, there is a clear relationship and dependency on digital marketing and word-of-mouth marketing (WOMM) (Barry, Leahy, & Fenton, 2019; Prahalad & Ramaswamy, 2004) when we consider its effectiveness. Due to social media's innate ability to reach the mass market, WOMM has acquired a new dimension as it is now being used by brands to amplify their brand marketing message and to expand the reach of an experiential activation (Kozinets et al., 2014). We will explore this further later in Chapter 6.

With Gautier's (2003) implementation in mind, we can see that experiential methods including an event, an experience or an interaction can take place through a multitude of mechanisms, including:

- Brandscaping (Kailani & Ciobotar, 2015; Mikunda, 2004; Mitchell & Orwig, 2002). As part of McDonald's 'Day of Joy' Campaign, the brand collaborated with Jessie J, a popular singer and entertainer, and a mutually beneficial partnership developed which was expressed through the content generated. A group of competition winners were led to believe that they were going to a secret concert venue, when Jessie J joined them on the bus for an hour-long performance which was livestreamed across McDonald's social platforms. Prior to the experiential event, both McDonald's and Jessie J posted cryptic tweets on their social media channels relating to the event, which created anticipation and a sense of exclusivity for the selected attendees.
- Promotions (Bruzzese, 1992; Lichtenstein, et al., 1993). Doc McStuffin is a popular Disney Jr television show which narrates the story of a six-year-old girl named Doc who heals toys from a backyard clinic. The experiential event involved a re-creation of a typical show scenario and offered fans of the show the opportunity to heal their own toys. These experiential activations consisted of a UK roadshow of Doc McStuffin check-up clinics in 20 cities in Tesco's, Smyths and Toys R Us retail outlets, where children were invited to conduct check-ups on life-size teddy bears who required a diagnosis. After the live activation, children were awarded a Doc McStuffin certificate and gifted a 'Doc is in the House' door hanger.
- Instore experiences (Park, 2003; Smilansky, 2018). When IKEA discovered there was a Facebook group with over 100,000 members, titled 'I wanna sleepover in IKEA', they hosted a competition for 100 of the group's members to sleepover in their furniture warehouse in Essex, UK. During this time, the selected winners

were given goodie bags, massages and manicures. Movies were played on large screens and a bedtime story was read by a reality TV star. Lastly, sleep experts were on site for this activation to advise each customer on the best mattress for their needs.

- Guerrilla marketing (Lenderman, 2005). Tinder users were surprised to see their favourite Marvel character Deadpool appear in their potential matches ahead of the movie's Valentine's Day release. If the Tinder user "swiped right" and were lucky enough to match with the character, they were directed to a link where they could purchase tickets to the movie.
- Live brand experiences, also referred to as experiential event marketing (Kailani & Ciobotar, 2015; Smilansky, 2009). WeightWatchers acknowledged that the primary reason people opt for drive-thru meal solutions was the factor of convenience. With this in mind, the brand created a healthy pop-up drive thru to launch its new Flex meal plan, so that customers did not have to choose between a healthy meal and convenience. Their promotion afforded customers the opportunity to build relevant memory structures as it showcased the range of meals available on the plan and how easy they were to create.
- Online (Constantinides, 2004; Mathwick, et al., 2001; Rose, et al., 2011). In a partnership with Google, Burberry facilitated an online experiential marketing campaign to showcase a new range of Burberry lipsticks. Entitled 'Burberry Kisses', this campaign employed a digital first technology where participants took a picture of their lips to capture a kiss that could then be shared (through email and across social networks) with a personalised message and the option to further customise their kiss using a lipstick from the range.
- Digital technologies as a conduit (Bonetti, et al., 2018; Bulearca & Tamarjan, 2010; Eyüboğlu, 2011; Yaoyuneyong et al., 2016). To launch its new caramel flavoured chocolate, M&M's transformed Times Square into an interactive 'ARcade' which was activated by participants using the augmented reality app Blippar on their smartphone. Using the Blippar app, customers could scan billboards and prominent advertisements in the location to access vintage arcade games. Once the augmented reality activated, Times Square appeared to be fully branded by M&M's as the games came to the fore.

Although there are a multitude of activation possibilities, the area of events-based experiential marketing is deserving of prominence. In recent years, experiential event marketing has become the experiential marketing method of choice for brands and marketers. A key rationale is because this form of experiential marketing can create both consumer and consumption experiences and tends to be more effective in achieving communications goals and objectives (Adeosun & Ganiyu, 2012). In academic literature, experiential event marketing is viewed as a form of experiential marketing and has been defined in many ways. Although Kotler's (2003: 94) definition – 'occurrences designed to communicate particular messages to target audiences' – may be viewed as not specific enough, it does epitomise the communications potential for such an event. Offering a more specific viewpoint of the practice, Wood (2009) offers three other definitions:

1. An event that is created with the core purpose of marketing a product/service, place, person or idea.
2. Any events that simply communicate with a target audience.
3. Any event where there is a probable chance that brand representatives will communicate with customers.

To summarise, Jack Morton Worldwide (2006), an experiential marketing agency, defines experiential event marketing as live events where audience members or customers have the opportunity to interact with a product or a brand in a face-to-face manner. Table 3.2 lists some examples of experiential marketing events which fall into this categorisation.

Table 3.2 Examples of experiential event marketing

Incentive/ Reward Events	Product Launches	Open Days
Conferences	Product Sampling	Publicity Events
Brand Created Events	Road Shows	Press Conferences
Charity Fundraisers	Exhibitions	Product Visitor Attractions

Source: Wood (2009)

THE PERFORMANCE PERSPECTIVE OF EXPERIENTIAL MARKETING

As outlined in the previous discussions of the types of experiential marketing, it is clear that experiential marketing occurs on a smaller scale and that it typically carries a higher cost per person ratio when compared to traditional mass media efforts (Heitzler et al., 2008; Nigam, 2012). This is an implicit consequence of the marketing technique as it does not merely broadcast one-way messages, but provides two-way dialogue, hands-on experience and develops a more intimate relationship between the brand and the consumers (Nigam, 2012). Kerwin (2004: 94) concurs with this view, stating that 'the beauty of a well-designed experience is that while it doesn't reach nearly as many people as a TV spot, it can attract the very customers who are most likely to buy'. Therefore, experiential marketing can be considered a 'customer-focused discipline' (Lenderman, 2005: 27). Research conducted by SRI International, an international market research organisation, stated that experiential marketing resulted in more immediate results than traditional methods, with consumers communicating that it impacted on the speed of their purchase decision. The same research also asserted that experiential marketing made consumers readily responsive to other forms of associated advertising (Allen, 2005). Therefore, it results in high-quality consumer engagement, but with a lower number of impressions compared to the reach achievable through mass media utilisation (Lenderman, 2005). This perspective of experiential marketing places a premium on the functional impact of the experience. Table 3.3 summarises the main contributory definitions of the performance perspective of experiential marketing.

Table 3.3 Experiential marketing definitions: Performance perspective

Author	Definition
Lee et al. (2011: 37)	'Experiential marketing is one of the marketing approaches that gives a great framework to combine experience and entertainment elements into a product or service.'
Yuan and Wu (2008: 389)	'Experiential marketing can be seen as a marketing tactic designed by a business to stage the entire physical environment and the operational processes for its customers to experience.'
Williams (2006: 485)	'Experiential marketing is about taking the essence of a product and amplifying it into a set of tangible, physical, interactive experiences which reinforce the offer. Rather than seeing the offer in a traditional manner, through advertising media such as commercials, print or electronic messaging, consumers feel it by being part of it.'
Pine and Gilmore (1999: 2)	'When one buys an experience, one buys a series of memorable events that a company stages – as in a theatrical play – to engage him in a personal way.'
Smilansky (2018: 12)	'Experiential marketing is the process of identifying and satisfying customer needs and aspirations profitably, engaging them through authentic two-way communications that bring brand personalities to life and add value to the Target Audience.'

THE EMOTIONS/SENSES PERSPECTIVE OF EXPERIENTIAL MARKETING

While the various definitions examined so far focus on the experience at hand, they fail to acknowledge the emotions and feelings associated with the consumer's experience. Although a core element of experiential marketing is about taking the essence of a brand and amplifying it through an engaging experience, marketers must also ensure that it offers an engaging, personalised and memorable experience to consumers as a result (Li & Yang, 2010). Nigam (2012) concludes that experiential marketing is primarily focused on extracting the core traits of a brand and creating intangible, physical and interactive experiences which enhance the value of a brand. The practice enables customers to be immersed in the brand experience, generating an unforgettable feeling and satisfying their needs in order to win and retain customer trust and loyalty in the long term (Liu, 2006).

Considering the consumer impact of experiential marketing, Srinivasan and Srivastava (2010) believe that the practice involves consumer participation and transcends their perceived needs. The practice does not merely address perceived needs and wants, but the self-image, social goals, emotional response, values and desires of the consumer (Srivastava, 2008). The methods of segmentation, the resultant segments, and the analysis of same can be more significantly personalised. By addressing all of these requirements, the brand will achieve consumers' individual engagement and empowerment, memorable feelings and maximum levels of

satisfaction, while ultimately winning their loyalty and trust (Li & Yang, 2010). As a consequence, not only has a relationship been generated with new customers, but it also maintains the relationship with existing customers. These loyal customers are vital for organisational success as they will not only generate profit, but will also promote the brand through word of mouth both offline and online (Zena & Hadisumarto, 2012). Therefore, the primary aim of experiential marketing is to create a relationship with consumers.

Table 3.4 highlights the main contributors to this interpretation of experiential marketing.

Table 3.4 Experiential marketing definitions: Emotions, feelings, and senses perspective

Author	Definition
Adeosun and Ganiyu (2012: 21)	'Experiential Marketing is the process of engaging customers with in-depth experiences of the product or a brand. Its purpose is to appeal to the emotional senses of the customers and to influence their choice decision.'
Nigam (2012: 70)	'It is a private event that happens to people in response to some kind of internal or external stimulus resulting in an experiential aspect about products and services. The aim of experiential marketing is to make the customer delighted in exultant jubilation.'
Li and Yang (2010: 1)	'Experiential marketing not only attaches importance to goods and services, but also pays much attention to practical experiences, which gives consumers individual engagement and empowerment, unforgettable feelings and maximum mental satisfaction, thus winning their loyalty and trust.'
Srinivasan and Srivastava (2010: 194)	'Experiential marketing creates memorable experiences. The customer fondly remembers them, and even shares them with peers and family, generating increasing sales through the power of word of mouth and customer loyalty. The experience deepens with each successive interaction.'
Heitzler et al. (2008: 188)	'The goal of experiential marketing is to tie a product or campaign to an experience that is relevant to the target audience, the premise being that letting people discover the characteristics of a product or service on their own is more effective than having them see or hear about it through a passive medium such as television or radio.'
Srivastava (2008: 70)	'Experiential marketing is said to be practiced when marketers go beyond meeting basic needs to excite the consumer, to build consumer enthusiasm by becoming part of the everyday life experiences of the shopper.'

With the definitions presented in Table 3.4 in mind, it is worth noting that in order for these emotional and sensory reactions to be cultivated, brands must ensure that experiential marketing activations should not intrude. The optimal approach is for the activation to enhance an individual's experience with the brand or campaign message (Lenderman, 2005). It is recommended that a positive emotional component to experiences is added, as this ensures that participants link their sensory and emotional systems, which gives rise to the unconscious fantasies, equipping them to romanticise on their memories and connecting them to positive emotions over time (Smilansky, 2018). By combining the sensory benefits of experiential marketing with traditional marketing practices, there is a clear benefit, which we will explore in the next section.

THE EXPERIENTIAL 'ADD' TO MARKETING

It can be argued that modern consumers take marketing elements of a product or service, including its promised benefits, its aesthetics and features, as a given. Therefore, marketers have had to develop their strategic activities to ensure that they significantly feature customer experience touchpoints. It is therefore essential to outline the added value that experiential marketing brings to the marketing mix. Understanding the practical limitations of 'traditional' marketing activities gives a better sense of the opportunities that experiential marketing presents to a marketing team. As such, we begin by outlining a critique of non-experiential marketing activities.

According to Schmitt, one of the key authors in this area, the practice of traditional marketing considers the following:

1. Consumers evaluate products or services by first looking at their functional features.
2. They then evaluate products and services in terms of the importance of those features and any trade-offs by comparing them to a similar offering.
3. Finally, they select their desired product or service by deciding which has the 'highest overall utility' (Schmitt, 1999a: 56).

Traditional marketing emphasises mass production and consumption, growth of the consumer base, and the recruitment of new customers (Srinivasan & Srivastava, 2010). In their research on the foundations of marketing, Fahy and Jobber (2012) depict traditional marketing as a method of satisfying consumer needs while under-cutting competitors, through methods which are required in order to successfully fulfil organisational goals. In line with this method, products and services would suffer price reductions, therefore resulting in unsustainable price wars (Razi & Iajevardi, 2016). Although these definitions of traditional marketing all highlight different components of the practice, collectively, an analysis of these perspectives offers an in-depth understanding of the facets of the practice. However, research conducted by Riordan (2020) suggests that for brands that solely rely on the use of digital and traditional marketing methods, it can be difficult to capture and hold

customers' attention. This is predominately due to the accelerated frequency of media cycles and the sheer volume of content that is presently being circulated. In short, marketing is confronted with message overload and as a consequence customers need a stronger link with the brand in order for it to stand out from the crowd. One possible solution is to give customers an experience that focuses on the brand. While traditional marketing's core objective is based on delivering a large volume of target audience impressions through brand exposure, experiential marketing evolves this approach. By employing experiential marketing techniques, a brand interacts and engages with a smaller audience, creating authentic and bespoke customer experiences, which influence customer perception and brand affinities (Lawler, 2013).

Therefore, experiential marketing is a divergence from the practices of traditional marketing that reiterates the importance of brand–consumer relationships through an explicit emphasis on the customer–brand interaction. The crux of experiential marketing is that the primary concern of a brand should not be customer satisfaction, as seen in traditional marketing, but rather the creation of an emotional consumer attachment with the brand (Lenderman, 2005; Wohlfiel & Whelan, 2004). In practical terms, marketers need to ideate and develop immersive methods of connecting with their customers with the aim of creating an ongoing emotional attachment.

Experiential marketing creates an opportunity for marketers to create such memorable experiences through offering a series of experiential benefits which are strategically tailored to the target market (Mathwick et al., 2001; Pine & Gilmore, 1998; Schmitt, 2000). While customers are seeking these memorable and captivating experiences, authors, including Ritzer (2004) and Goulding (2000), offer an additional perspective on this, stating that companies must allow customers to escape their ordinary life by immersing them in a pre-conceptualised, pre-established and themed brand world. Upon successfully achieving this, the consumption experience and the relationship it generates with the consumer is the ultimate point of brand differentiation in an overcrowded marketplace (Chaney et al., 2018; Holbrook, 1999; Pine & Gilmore, 1999; Schmitt, 2000; Sherry, 1998). This again underpins the value of experiential marketing in the current consumption landscape.

What, then, sets experiential marketing apart from traditional marketing? Experiential marketing has key inherent attributes that differentiate it:

- Its primary emphasis is on the consumer's experience, the consumption situation and an awareness of both the logical and emotional aspects of the customer decision-making process (Chou, 2009). A well-constructed experience garners the attention of the consumer, emotionally engages with them, and becomes a memory dependent on individual interpretation (Hoch, 2002). In comparison to traditional marketing, which has a primary focus on gaining customer satisfaction, experiential marketing appeals to a customer's emotions, cultivating an emotional bond between the customer and the brand, product or service (McCole, 2004). We can see examples of this with Apple™ products, Coca-Cola and Red Bull.

- Instead of viewing customers as inactive message receivers, experiential marketing considers customers to be actively engaged in the creation of marketing plans (Jain & Lohia, 2014). The sensory, emotional and nostalgic elements of an experience hold a greater possibility of impacting consumer preferences than the product or service attributes (Zaltman, 2003). Evidently, customers desire experiences and for businesses to capitalise on this, they must create memorable experiences that capture customers' attention and ultimately build customer loyalty (Adeosun & Ganiyu, 2012). As a result of this evolution in marketing, marketers who engage in experiential activities are witnessing a deeper, more genuine connection with customers (Lawler, 2013). Often, the focus is humour. For example, PaddyPower.com is famed for its controversial approach to marketing, but they often employ experiential marketing activities that are intended to be more than fun.

In Chapter 2, we presented an initial overview of the differences between traditional and experiential marketing. In the context of this more evolved analysis, Table 3.5 presents a more detailed perspective on these differences.

Table 3.5 The contrasting focus of traditional marketing vs experiential marketing

	Traditional marketing	Experiential marketing
Customers	Inactive message receivers	Actively engaged in the creation of marketing plans
Targeting	Mass market	Tailored to a target market
Relationship	Transactional relationship	Two-way brand consumer relationship
Primary emphasis	Mass production consumption, growth on customer base and recruitment of new customers	Consumer's experience, the consumption situation, awareness of logical and emotional aspects of the consumer decision-making process
Engagement	Satisfying consumer needs while undercutting competitors	Engages emotionally and becomes memory dependent on individual interpretation
Appeal	Primary focus on gaining customer satisfaction	Appeals to a customer's emotions, cultivating emotional bonds between the customer and the brand, product or service

EXPERIENTIAL VALUE

Building on the theoretical development of experiential marketing, it is essential to note that one of the most fundamental concepts of this communications tool is that value does not merely exist in the object of consumption, but in searching for and processing information about products or services. It also resides in the experience of consumption (Kim et al., 2018; Schmitt, 2011; Zarantonello, 2013).

Lee and Overby (2004) believe that value is subjective and is generated based on the exchange of experience that is created in the process of a transaction or during the development of individual perceptions. Therefore, value is not confined to utilitarian value (functional value), but also involves hedonic value (experiential value) (Addis & Holbrook, 2001). Gentile, Spiller and Noci (2007) conclude that experiential value can be achieved through a unique, memorable and relatable consumption experience.

Developing from the consumption viewpoint of experiential value, Ritzer (2009) presents an alternative view. According to Ritzer (2009), there has been a shift from the concept of consumption to prosumption. Prosumption is the amalgamation of both the production and consumption of products or services, rather than focusing on one element of this duo exclusively (Ritzer & Jurgenson, 2010). In *The McDonaldization of Society,* written by Ritzer (2008 [1993]), he discusses how consumers have, over time, developed into the workers of the fast-food industry. This is due to the fact that co-creation is a key factor in this value chain as consumers to a certain extent serve themselves, i.e. they choose their table, bring their food to it, select their own condiments and clean up afterwards. A series of social and technological changes, related to the internet and Web 2.0, have given this concept greater relevance (Ritzer & Jurgenson, 2010). Web 2.0 is characterised by users' ability to produce content collaboratively, in comparison to Web 1.0 where content was provider-generated (Ritzer & Jurgenson, 2010). While discussing consumption and the emergence of prosumption in services, it is important to note that experiential value can take form in many dimensions, which will be further discussed in the following section.

Experiential Value Dimensions

Experiential value has received vast academic attention over the past 25 years. Holbrook (1994) conducted research on the values that consumers acquire from an experiential offer and categorised them according to the dimensions of **intrinsic vs extrinsic** and **active vs reactive**. In this framework, extrinsic value relates to the utilitarian benefits of shopping, while intrinsic value refers to the 'appreciation of an experience for its own sake, apart from any other consequence that may result' (Holbrook, 1994: 40). Holbrook (1999) later stated that the concept of value is built on a three-pronged approach. First, value is comparative, as it can be compared to other products or services. Second, value is personal, as it develops from subjective personal experiences. Lastly, value is situational, as it is dependent on the context of the experience at hand. Moreover, Holbrook (2000) later expanded his original research, and argued that consumption experiences using methods including fantasies, feelings and fun will have a positive impact on the customer decision-making process. Therefore, Holbrook (2000) incorporated three new elements into the traditional concept of experiential value: extrinsic value/intrinsic value, active value/reactive value, self-oriented value/other-oriented value. Influenced by the seminal work conducted by Holbrook (1994), multiple

sources of experiential value have been established (Gentile et al., 2007; Schmitt & Zarantonello, 2013; Tynan & McKechnie, 2009; Varshneya et al., 2017). Table 3.6 presents an overview of experiential value dimensions and their key related authors.

Table 3.6 Experiential value dimensions

Experiential value dimensions	Authors
Sensory	Agapito et al. (2014), Schmitt (1999a, 1999b)
Emotional	Mathwick et al. (2001), Richins (1997), Sánchez et al. (2006), Schmitt (1999a), Sweeney and Soutar (2001)
Functional/utilitarian	Arnould et al. (2004), Mathwick et al. (2001), Sánchez et al. (2006), Sweeney and Soutar (2001)
Hedonic	Babin et al. (1994), Varshneya et al. (2017)
Relational	Fournier (1998), Gainer (1995), Lusch et al. (2007), Schmitt (1999a), Tynan and McKechnie (2008), Vargo and Lusch (2008)
Social	Andrews et al. (2007), Sánchez et al. (2006), Sweeney and Soutar (2001), Trevinal and Stenger (2014), Varshneya and Das (2017)
Cognitive/informational	Poulsson and Kale (2004), Schmitt (1999a), Varshneya and Das (2017)
Novelty	Poulsson and Kale (2004)
Utopian	Maclaren and Brown (2005)
Ethical	Varshneya and Das (2017)

Sources: Österle et al. (2018); Tynan & McKechnie (2009); Varshneya et al. (2017)

Consequently, when generating brand experiences, it is valuable for marketing practitioners to consider the multitude of experiential value dimensions which may apply. It is fundamental to appreciate the role that value dimensions play in the successful implementation of experiential marketing, and also to understand that value is a subjective topic and may vary from customer to customer. Thus, it must be examined from multiple perspectives.

Typology of Experiential Value

Further to this, and also based on the foundations paved by Holbrook (1994, 1999, 2000), Mathwick et al. (2001) developed the experiential value scale (EVS), which incorporates four values – playfulness, aesthetics, customer return on investment (CROI) and service excellence – to evaluate virtual shopping experiences, although they can also be adapted for real-world experiences (see Figure 3.2).

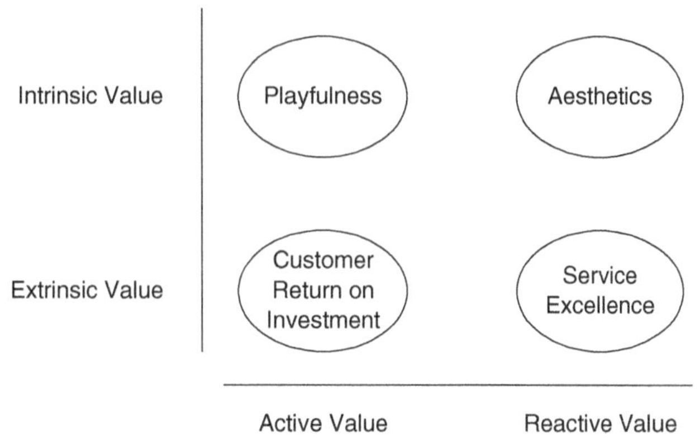

Figure 3.2 Typology of experiential value

Source: Mathwick et al. (2001) Copyright Elsevier (2001). Used with permission

As seen in Figure 3.2, the intrinsic (hedonic) value dimension includes playfulness and aesthetics.

- Playfulness relates to feelings of escapism from everyday activities, as well as intrinsic enjoyment due to the high levels of engagement in absorbing activities (Shobeiri et al., 2014). To launch their new 4G internet, Vodafone placed a branded slide in a shopping centre next to the escalators to show that their 4G internet was faster than solutions from alternative providers. Customers were invited to use the slide rather than the escalator, which resulted in those customers arriving at their destination in a faster and more memorable way.
- Aesthetics is composed of the two elements: visual appeal and entertainment (Harris & Goode, 2010). While aesthetics refers to the physical attractiveness of the experiential environment, playfulness relates to the dramatic aspects of the experience in which the customers are immersed, therefore lifting their spirits (Shobeiri et al., 2014) . Fabric conditioner brand Comfort created an immersive garden in London's Covent Garden to launch their new Comfort Intense range. The garden comprised flowers, trees and fountains that were created out of clothing from the charity Oxfam. Each garment was freshly washed in products from the Comfort Intense range, which included the following fragrances – Fuschia Passion, Fresh Sky, Ocean Pearl and Sunburst. Customers were invited into the garden to effectively sample the product and take part in a memorable and immersive experience.

The extrinsic (utilitarian) value dimension includes the customer return on investment and service excellence.

- Customer return on investment (CROI) includes the 'active investment of financial, temporal, behavioural and psychological resources that potentially yield a return' (Mathwick et al., 2001: 41). This type of experiential value consists of economic

and efficiency utilities, which emulate affordable quality and efficiency of the exchange encounter (Shobeiri et al., 2014).

- Service excellence is a measure of the ideal standard of quality to which a brand or an organisation delivers, as well as their ability to deliver on its promises by portraying expertise (Shobeiri et al., 2014). Mathwick et al. (2001) state that perceptions of service excellence are created on the level to which customers believe that a brand or organisation delivers on its brand promise and performed tasks.

In line with the research presented by Mathwick et al. (2001), Chou (2009) believes that experiential value will be determined by consumers as they evaluate the aesthetic, playfulness, service excellence, and CROI attached to the brand or organisation. However, Wu and Liang (2009) portray an opposing view, arguing that the experiential value is evaluated according to the levels of the service efficiency, service excellence, aesthetic and playfulness experienced in the service encounter. Wang and Lin (2010) concluded that there is a positive correlation between experiential marketing and experiential value, and, as a result, an effective experiential marketing campaign has the ability to generate positive experiential value in return.

CONCLUSION AND SUMMARY

In seeking to define experiential marketing, we have examined the phenomenon from the perspective of our understanding of experience in the first instance, positing a performance perspective and an emotions/senses perspective. Contrasting experiential activity with traditional marketing, we developed a clear line of argument that experiential marketing is centred on tightening the relationship with the consumer. We further argued that a possible multi-faceted emotional response is the key to the success or failure of the relationship. We then presented some work on classifying experience from the perspective of value. In so doing, we propose the following definition of experiential marketing:

> Experiential marketing is a customer-focused marketing approach that inherently incorporates identifiable brand–consumer interaction across the stages of consumption with a view to increasing emotional attachment as part of a relationship with the brand while eliciting a measurable impact to both the consumer and the brand.

While we have explored aspects of this in the book to date, we will use the next chapters to examine the relationship aspect in more depth before contextualising this in practical terms in an era where much of the consumption process has a strong digital component. Measurability – strategically, tactically and financially – will also receive attention.

MAIN TAKEAWAYS FROM CHAPTER 3

- The term *experience* has been at the heart of much debate. In the context of experiential marketing, it is essential to understand both the nature and focus of 'experience', and then to relate that to the staging of experiences for consumers with the specific intention of immersing those consumers in an engaging and memorable branded experience.
- The consumer experience consists of a series of stages through which the consumer moves. When designing experiences for the consumer, it is essential to consider the experience in its totality from pre-consumption through to the nostalgic experience.
- Experiential marketing can be viewed from a performance perspective and/or an emotional perspective, activated using a possible multitude of mechanisms, all of which have the purpose of adding value for the consumer.
- Experiential marketing should be viewed as adding value to the traditional marketing mix by adding multiple touchpoints for the consumer in their brand–customer interactions and relationships.

CONCLUDING QUESTIONS

1. Discuss your understanding of the term 'experience'.
2. Using your own example, detail the stages of the consumption experience.
3. What are the differences between the performance perspective of experience marketing and the emotions perspective. Which perspective are you most drawn to and why?
4. In your opinion, should experiential marketing be viewed as separate from traditional marketing or as an inherent part of any marketing-mix toolkit?
5. Using your own example, illustrate how experiential marketing can build authentic two way communication in line with the practice of traditional marketing methods.
6. Critique the definition of experiential marketing that we have presented at the end of this chapter.

NOTE

1. When we refer to 'traditional marketing' we are focusing on marketing methods that do not employ experiential marketing techniques as a specific aspect.

REFERENCES AND FURTHER READING

Addis, M., & Holbrook, M.B. (2001). On the Conceptual Link between Mass Customisation and Experiential Consumption: An Explosion of Subjectivity. *Journal of Consumer Behaviour*, 1(1), 50–66.

Adeosun, L.P.K., & Ganiyu, R.A. (2012). Experiential Marketing: An Insight into the Mind of the Consumer. *Asian Journal of Business Management Sciences*, 2(7), 21–26.

Agapito, D., Valle, P., & Mendes, J. (2014). The Sensory Dimension of Tourist Experiences: Capturing Meaningful Sensory-informed Themes in Southwest Portugal. *Tourism Management*, 42, 224–237.

Allen, W. (2005). *Successful Meetings*, 54(4), 26–39.

Andrews, L., Kiel, G., Drennan, J., Boyle, M.V., & Weerawardena, J. (2007). Gendered Perceptions of Experiential Value in Using Web-based Retail Channels. *European Journal of Marketing*, 41(5/6), 640–658.

Arnould, E.J., & Price, L.L. (1993). River Magic: Extraordinary Experience and the Extended Service Encounter. *Journal of Consumer Research*, 20(1), 24–45.

Arnould, E., Price, L.L., & Zinkhan, G. (2002). *Consumers*. New York: McGraw-Hill.

Arnould, E., Price, L.L., & Zinkhan, G. (2004). *Consumers* (2nd ed.). Boston, MA: McGraw-Hill/Irwin.

Atwal, G., & Williams, A. (2009). Luxury Brand Marketing: The Experience is Everything! *Journal of Brand Management*, 16(5/6), 338–346.

Babin, B.J., Darden, W.R., & Griffin, M. (1994). Work and/or Fun: Measuring Hedonic and Utilitarian Shopping Value. *Journal of Consumer Research*, 20(4), 644.

Barry, H., Leahy, R., & Fenton, P. (2019). A Strategic Approach to Amplifying an Experiential Event using Social Currency to Reach a Mass Audience. Paper presented at the Academy of Marketing Annual Conference, London, July 3.

Bhattacharjee, A., & Mogilner, C. (2014). Happiness from Ordinary and Extraordinary Experiences. *Journal of Consumer Research*, 41(June), 1–17.

Bonetti, F., Warnaby, G., & Quinn, L. (2018). Augmented Reality and Virtual Reality in Physical and Online Retailing: A Review, Synthesis and Research Agenda. In *Augmented Reality and Virtual Reality* (pp. 119–132). Cham, Switzerland: Springer.

Boswijk, A., Thijssen, J.P.T., & Peelen, E. (2005). *A New Perspective on the Experience Economy: Meaningful Experience*. Amsterdam, Netherlands: Pearson Education.

Brakus, J.J., Schmitt, B.H., & Zarantonello, L. (2009). Brand Experience: What is it? How is it Measured? Does it Affect Loyalty? *Journal of Marketing*, 73, 52–68.

Bruzzese, A. (1992). Hedging their bets. *Incentive*, 166(September), 36–43.

Bulearca, M., & Tamarjan, D. (2010). Augmented Reality: A Sustainable Marketing Tool. *Global Business and Management Research: An International Journal*, 2(2), 237–252.

Carbone, L.P., & Haeckel, S.H. (1994). Engineering Customer Experiences. *Marketing Management*, 3(3), 8–19.

Caru, A., & Cova, B. (2003). Revisiting Consumption Experience: A More Humble but Complete View of the Concept. *Marketing Theory*, 3(2), 267–286.

Chaney, D., Lunardo, R., & Mencarelli, R. (2018). Consumption Experience: Past, Present and Future. *Qualitative Market Research: An International Journal*, 21(4), 402–420.

Chou, H.-J. (2009). The Effect of Experiential and Relationship Marketing on Customer Value: A Case Study of International American Casual Dining Chains in Taiwan. *Society for Personal Research*, 37(7), 993–1008.

Constantinides, E. (2004). Influencing the Online Consumer's Behaviour: The Web Experience. *Internet Research*, 14(2), 111–126.

Conway, D. (2016). *Harnessing the Power of Many*. London: KPMG Nunwood Consulting Limited.

Csikszentmihalyi, M. (1990). *Flow: The Psychology of Optimal Experience*. New York: Harper and Row.

Denzin, N.K. (1992). *Symbolic Interactionism and Cultural Studies: The Politics of Interpretation*. Cambridge, MA: Blackwell Publishers.

Eyüboğlu, E. (2011). Augmented Reality as an Exciting Online Experience: Is it Really Beneficial for Brands? *International Journal of Social Sciences and Humanity Studies*, 3(1), 113–123.

Fahy, J., & Jobber, D. (2012). *Foundations of Marketing*. New York: McGraw-Hill Education.

Fournier, S. (1998). Consumers and Their Brands: Developing Relationship Theory in Consumer Research. *Journal of Consumer Research*, 24(4), 343–374.

Gainer, B. (1995). Ritual and Relationships: Interpersonal Influencers on Shared Consumption. *Journal of Business Research*, 32(3), 253–260.

Gautier, A. (2003). Think Again: Why Experiential Marketing is the Next Big Thing. *New Zealand Marketing Magazine*, 22(8), 8–14.

Gentile, C., Spiller, N., & Noci, G. (2007). How to Sustain the Customer Experience: An Overview of Experience Components that Co-create Value with the Customer. *European Management Journal*, 25(5), 395–410.

Goulding, C. (2000). The Commodification of the Past, Postmodern Pastiche, and the Search for Authentic Experiences at Contemporary Heritage Attractions. *European Journal of Marketing*, 34(7), 835–853.

Harris, L.C., & Goode, M.M.H. (2010). Online Servicescapes, Trust and Purchase Intention. *Journal of Services Marketing*, 24(3), 230–243.

Heitzler, C.D., Asbury, L.D., & Kusner, S.L. (2008). Bringing 'Play' to Life. *American Journal of Preventative Medicine*, 34(6), 188–193.

Hoch, S.J. (2002). Product Experience is Seductive. *Journal of Consumer Research*, 29(3), 448.

Holbrook, M.B. (1994). The Nature of Customer Value: An Axiology of Services in the Consumption Experience. In R.T. Rust & R.L. Oliver (Eds.), *Service Quality: New Directions in Theory and Practice* (pp. 21–71). Newbury Park, CA: Sage.

Holbrook, M.B. (1999). *Consumer Value: A Framework for Analysis and Research*. London: Routledge.

Holbrook, M.B. (2000). The Millennial Consumer in the Texts of Our Times: Experience and Entertainment. *Journal of Micromarketing*, 20(2), 178–191.

Holbrook, M.B., & Hirschman, E.C. (1982). The Experiential Aspects of Consumption: Consumer Fantasies, Feelings and Fun. *Journal of Consumer Research*, 9(2), 132–140.

Jack Morton Worldwide (2006). *Global Experiential Marketing Study: 2006 Survey Reveals Insights, Benefits*. Jack Morton Worldwide. [Online]. Available at: http://360.jackmorton.com/articles/article0621062.php [accessed 30 June 2016].

Jain, S., & Lohia, S. (2014). Experiential Marketing: Emerging Issues and Suggestions. *International Journal of Advances in Management and Economics*, 3(2), 197–203.

Kailani, C., & Ciobotar, N. (2015). Experiential Marketing: An Efficient Tool to Leverage Marketing Communication Impact on Consumer Behaviour. *International Conference on Marketing and Business Development Journal*, 1(1), 1–7.

Kerwin, K. (2004). *When the Factory is a Theme Park*. New York: Bloomberg. [Online]. Available at: www.bloomberg.com/news/articles/2004-05-02/when-the-factory-is-a-theme-park [accessed 12 July 2018].

Kim, C., Takashima, K., & Newell, S. (2018). How do Retailers Increase the Benefits of Buyer Innovationess? An Intra- and Inter-Organisation Perspective. *Asia Pacific Journal of Marketing and Logistics*, 30(3), 571–586.

Kotler, P. (2003). *Marketing Management* (11th ed.). Englewood Cliffs, NJ: Prentice-Hall.

Kozinets, R.V., de Valck, K., Wojnicki, A., & Wilner, S.J.S. (2014). Lost in Translation: The Social Shaping of Marketing Messaging. *GfK-Marketing Intelligence Review*, 6(2), 22–27. https://doi.org/10.2478/gfkmir-2014-0094

Lawler, E. (2013). *The Rise of Experiential Marketing*. Ad Age. [Online]. Available at: http://brandedcontent.adage.com/pdf/experientialmarketing.pdf [accessed 12 December 2017].

Lee, E.J., & Overby, J.W. (2004). Creating Value for Online Shoppers: Implications for Satisfaction and Loyalty. *Journal of Consumer Satisfaction, Dissatisfaction and Complaining Behaviour*, 17, 54–67.

Lee, M.S., Hsiao, H.D., & Yang, M.F. (2011). The Study of Relationships among Experiential Marketing, Service Quality, Customer Satisfaction and Customer Loyalty. *International Journal of Organizational Innovation*, 3(2), 353–379.

Lenderman, M. (2005). *Experience the Message: How Experiential Marketing is Changing the Brand World*. New York, NY: Carroll & Graf Publishers.

Li, A., & Yang, D. (2010). Business Advertising Strategy in Experiential Marketing. Paper presented at The 2010 International Conference on Management and Service Science, Wuhan, China, 24-26 August.

Lichtenstein, D.R., Ridgway, N.M., & Netemeyer, R.G. (1993). Price Perceptions and Consumer Shopping Behaviour: A Field Study. *Journal of Marketing Research*, 30(May), 234–245.

Liu, Y. (2006). Word of Mouth for Movies: Its Dynamics and Impact on Box Office Revenue. *Journal of Marketing*, 70(3), 74–89.

Lusch, R.F., Vargo, S.L., & O' Brien, M. (2007). Competing through Service: Insights from Service-Dominant Logic. *Journal of Retailing*, 83(1), 5–18.

Maclaren, P., & Brown, S. (2005). The Centre Cannot Hold: Consuming the Utopian Marketplace. *Journal of Consumer Research*, 32(2), 311–323.

Mathwick, C., Malhotra, N., & Rigdon, E. (2001). Experiential Value: Conceptualization, Measurement, and Application in the Catalog and Internet Shopping Environment. *Journal of Retailing*, 77(1), 39–56.

McCole, P. (2004). Refocusing Marketing to Reflect Practice: The Changing Role of Marketing for Business. *Marketing Intelligence Planning*, 22(5), 531–539.

Meier, D. (2010). *Reading List Challenge: 19 Experiential Marketing Books*. Hampshire, UK: Javelin. [Online]. Available at: http://javelinexperiential.com/experiential-marketing/reading-list-challenge-19-experiential-marketing-books/ [accessed 7 April 2017].

Mikunda, C. (2004). *Brands Lands, Hot Spots & Cool Spaces: Welcome to the Third Place and the Total Marketing Experience*. London & Sterling, VA: Kogan Page.

Mitchell, M.A., & Orwig, R.A. (2002). Consumer Experience Tourism and Brand Bonding. *Journal of Product and Brand Management*, 11(1), 30–41.

Nigam, A. (2012). Modeling Relationships between Experiential Marketing, Experiential Value and Purchase Intensions in Organized Quick Service Chain Restaurants Shoppers using Structural Equation Modelling Approach. *Paradigm*, 16(1), 70–79.

Österle, B., Kuhn, M.M., Hensler, J. (2018). Brand Worlds: Introduing Experiential Marketing to B2B Branding. *Industrial Marketing Management*, 72, 71–98.

Park, C. (2003). Hedonic-Experiential Values in Online Shopping Antecedents and Consequences. *Asia Pacific Journal of Informative Systems*, 13(4), 73–96.

Pine, B. Joseph, & Gilmore, J.H. (1998). Welcome to the Experience Economy. *Harvard Business Review*, 76(4), 97–105.

Pine, B. Joseph, & Gilmore, J.H. (1999). *The Experience Economy: Work is Theatre & Every Business a Stage*. Boston, MA: Harvard Business Press.

Poulsson, S., & Kale, S. (2004). The Experience Economy and Commercial Experiences. *The Marketing Review*, 4(3), 267–277.

Prahalad, C.K., & Ramaswamy, V. (2004). Co-creation Experiences: The Next Practice in Value Creation. *Journal of Interactive Marketing*, 18(3), 5–14.

Razi, F.F., & Iajevardi, M. (2016). Sense Marketing, Experiential Marketing, Customer Satisfaction and Repurchase Intention. *Journal of Marketing and Consumer Research*, 21.

Richins, M.L. (1997). Measuring Emotions in the Consumption Experience. *Journal of Consumer Research*, 24(September), 127–146.

Riordan, R. (2020). *Experiential Marketing Industry Report: Leveraging the Power of Immersive Experience to Create Deep Connections, Extend Reach and Generate Measurable ROI*. Bookmark.

Ritzer, G. (1993) *The McDonaldization of Society: The Changing Character of Comtemporary Social Life*. Newbury Park, CA: Pine Forge.

Ritzer, G. (2004). An Introduction to McDonaldization. In G. Ritzer, *The McDonaldization Society*. Thousand Oaks, CA: Sage.

Ritzer, G. (2009). *Correcting a Historical Error*. Keynote Address at the Conference on Prosumption, Frankfurt, Germany.

Ritzer, G., & Jurgenson, N. (2010). Production, Consumption and Prosumption: The Nature of Capitalism in the Age of the Digital 'Prosumer'. *Journal of Consumer Culture*, 10(1), 13–36.

Rose, S., Hair, N., & Clark, M. (2011). Online Customer Experience: A Review of the Business-to-Customer Online Purchase Context. *International Journal of Management Reviews*, 13(1), 24–39.

Same, S., & Larimo, J. (2012). *Marketing Theory: Experience Marketing and Experiential Marketing*. Presented at 7th International Scientific Conference, Business and Management 2012, Vilnius Gediminas Technical University, Vilnius, Lithuania.

Sánchez, J., Callarisa, L., Rodríguez, R.M., & Moliner, M.A. (2006). Perceived Value of the Purchase of a Tourism Product. *Tourism Management*, 27(3), 394–409.

Schmitt, B.H. (1999a). Experiential Marketing. *Journal of Marketing Management*, 15(1–3), 53–67.

Schmitt, B.H. (1999b). *Experiential Marketing*. New York: The Free Press.

Schmitt, B.H. (2000). *Experiential Marketing: How to Get Customers to Sense, Feel, Think, Act, Relate to your Company and Brands*. New York: The Free Press.

Schmitt, B.H. (2010). *Customer Experience Management: A Revolutionary Approach to Connecting with Your Customers* (2nd ed.). New York: John Wiley & Sons.

Schmitt, B.H. (2011). Experience Marketing: Concepts, Frameworks and Consumer Insights. *Foundations and Trends in Marketing*, 5(2), 55–112.

Schmitt, B.H., & Zarantonello, L. (2013). Consumer Experience and Experiential Marketing: A Critical Review. In N.K. Malhotra (Ed.), *Review of Marketing Research* (pp. 25–61). Bingley, UK: Emerald Group Publishing.

Schouten, J., McAlexander, J., & Koening, H. (2007). Transcendent Customer Experience and Brand Community. *Journal of the Academy of Marketing*, 35(2), 357–368.

Sherry, J. (1998). The Soul of the Company Store: Nike Town Chicago and the Emplaced Brandscape. In J. Sherry (Ed.), *Servicescapes: The Concept of Place in Contemporary Markets*. Lincolnwood, IL: NTC Business Books.

Shobeiri, S., Mazaheri, E., & Laroche, M. (2014). Improving Customer Website Involvement through Experiential Narketing. *Service Industry Journal*, 34(11), 885–900.

Smilansky, S. (2009). *Experiential Marketing: A Practical Guide to Interactive Brand Experiences*. London: Kogan Page.

Smilansky, S. (2018). *Experiential Marketing: A Practical Guide to Interactive Brand Experiences* (2nd ed.). London: Kogan Page.

Srinivasan, S.R., & Srivastava, R.K. (2010). Creating a Futuristic Retail Experience through Experiential Marketing: Is it Possible? An Explorative Study. *Journal of Retail and Leisure Property*, 9(3), 193–199.

Srivastava, R.K. (2008). How Experiential Marketing Can Be Used to Build Brands: A Case Study of Two Speciality Stores. *Innovative Marketing*, 4(2).

Sussman, A., & Alter, A. (2012). The Exception is the Rule: Underestimating and Overspending on Exceptional Expenses. *Journal of Consumer Research*, 39(December), 800–814.

Sweeney, J.C., & Soutar, G.N. (2001). Consumer Perceived Value: The Development of a Multiple Item Scale. *Journal of Retailing*, 77(2), 203–220.

Tarssanen, S., & Kylänen, M. (2007). A Theoretical Model for Producing Experiences: A Touristic Perspective. In M. Kylänen (Ed.), *Articles on Experiences* 2 (pp. 134–154). Rovaniemei, Finland: Lapland University Press.

Trevinal, A.M., & Stenger, T. (2014). Toward a Conceptualization of the Online Shopping Experience. *Journal of Retailing and Consumer Services*, 21(3), 314–326.

Tynan, C., & McKechnie, S. (2008). Co-creating Value through Experience Marketing. Paper presented at the Academy of Marketing Conference, The Robert Gordon University, Aberdeen.

Tynan, C., & McKechnie, S. (2009). Experience Marketing: A Review and Reassessment. *Journal of Marketing Management*, 25(5/6), 501–517.

Vargo, S., & Lusch, R.F. (2008). Service-dominant Logic: Continuing the Evolution. *Journal of the Academy of Marketing Science*, 36(1), 1–10.

Varshneya, G., & Das, G. (2017). Experiential Value: Multi-item Scale Development and Validation. *Journal of Retailing and Consumer Services*, 34, 48–57.

Varshneya, G., Das, G., & Khare, A. (2017). Experiential Value: A Review and Future Research Directions. *Marketing Intelligence and Planning*, 35(3), 339–357.

Vézina, R. (1999). Pour comprendre et analyser l'expérience du consommateur. *Gestion*, 24(2), 59–65.

Wang, C.Y., & Lin, C.H. (2010). A Study of the Effect of TV Drama on Relationships among Tourists' Experiential Marketing, Experiential Value and Satisfaction. *International Journal of Organisational Innovation*, 2(3), 107–123.

Williams, A. (2006). Tourism and Hospitality Marketing: Fantasy, Feeling and Fun. *International Journal of Contemporary Hospitality Management*, 18(6), 482–495.

Wohlfiel, M., & Whelan, S. (2004). Investigating Consumer's Motivations to Participate in Marketing Events. In *Proceedings of the Irish Academy of Management*. Dublin: Trinity College.

Wood, E.H. (2009). Evaluating Event Marketing: Experience or Outcome? *Journal of Promotion Management*, 15, 247–268.

Wu, C.H.J., & Liang, R.D. (2009). Effects of Experiential Value on Customer Satisfaction with Service Encounters in Luxury-Hotel Restaurants. *International Journal of Hospitality Management*, 28(4), 588.

Yaoyuneyong, G., Foster, J., Johnson, E., & Johnson, D. (2016). Augmented Reality Marketing: Consumer Preferences and Attitudes toward Hypermedia Print Ads. *Journal of Interactive Advertising*, 16(1), 16–30.

Yuan, Y.H., & Wu, C. (2008). Relationship among Experiential Marketing, Experiential Value and Customer Satisfaction. *Journal of Hospitality and Tourism Research*, 32(3), 387–410.

Zaltman, G. (2003). *How Consumers Think: Essential Insights into the Mind of the Market*. Boston, MA: Harvard Business School Press.

Zarantonello, L. (2013). The Impact of Event Marketing on Brand Equity: The Mediating Roles of Brand Experiences and Brand Attitude. *International Journal of Advertising*, 32(2), 255–280.

Zena, P.A., & Hadisumarto, A.D. (2012). The Study of Relationship among Experiential Marketing, Service Quality, Customer Satisfaction, and Customer Loyalty. *Asean Marketing Journal*, 4(1), 37–56.

4
EXPERIENCES AND RELATIONSHIP MARKETING

CHAPTER OVERVIEW

The role of experiences in the development of consumer–brand relationships is considered by many to be one of the most significant characteristics of experiential marketing. For many decades, academics and practitioners have explored ways that marketing could be used to build relationships with customers. These relationships are centrally important in driving loyalty to the brand. This chapter will review the relationship marketing concept and the importance of interactions and engagements in the development of relationships so that we can later examine how these link to the design of good experiences. Effective experiential marketing requires a proper understanding of relationships between businesses and consumers, as well as between businesses and other businesses.

Experiences are now regarded as the focus of relationship interactions and engagements. We therefore present the role of experiential marketing in the quest for stronger relationships. Relationships that are socially based are seen as having many advantages, and so this chapter will examine marketplace cultures (consumer tribes, brand communities) with a view to understanding how consumers ultimately experience 'togetherness' within market-mediated environments. Specifically, this chapter will discuss:

- The relationship marketing concept: we will provide a brief theoretical overview supported by practical examples.
- Business-to-business (B2B) relationships and examples of these that highlight the link with experiential marketing.
- The importance of interactions and engagements for relationship development.
- The nature of consumer–brand relationships, specifically considering the various types of these relationships.
- The role of marketplace cultures in consumer experiences.
- The role of experiential marketing in building and nurturing consumer–brand relationships.

This chapter will also highlight some of the interesting practical implementations of consumer–brand relationships across a variety of sectors.

THE RELATIONSHIP MARKETING CONCEPT

Imagine the scene: the year is 1342 AD in a market town in England on a summer Saturday. Traders populate their spots, establishing their space to sell their own goods, be they animals, crops, food, building materials or household goods. The local townspeople mingle to gather the things they need, with many different and competing offerings available. The street is loud with noise as customers haggle and barter to gain the best price from the trader that they believe can provide them with the best value. Meanwhile, the traders ply their wares with a view to gaining as much custom as possible. Perhaps special offers for new customers to help build trust, discounts to old customers as a reward for loyalty, or maybe just a jocular story to keep customers entertained.

Building relationships with customers has been a cornerstone of business for centuries and it continues to be so to this day. The old-style market traders lived or died on the relationships they developed and this business fundamental has remained central right through to the modern era. It wasn't until the mid-to-late 20th century, however, that literature started to emerge exploring this core objective of attracting and keeping customers in the long term. This literature primarily focused on Industrial and Services Marketing, and it wasn't until the start of the 21st century that the concept was examined in the context of mass consumer markets. By now, various industries, including hospitality, transportation, banking, manufacturing, healthcare, utilities, etc. have all focused on converting buyer behaviour from a fleeting casual encounter to a committed relationship. This is underpinned by a generally accepted belief that it is a more productive way of retaining business and applies in both the business-to-business (B2B) world as well as the business-to-consumer (B2C) marketplace.

Relationship marketing in action examples

British Airways' (BA) Executive Club was established to recognise the loyalty of its 'members' and to promote long-term relationships. Members receive benefits for frequently flying with BA that include real-time special offers, speedy communications and an excellent level of customer service. Through the collection and analysis of customer information, and more targeted products and

(Continued)

services to maintain existing customer relations, British Airways worked to differentiate itself in the full-service carrier segment of the airline market.

The Ritz-Carlton Hotel group have long been regarded as pioneers in applying relationship marketing in efforts to build relationships with customers. Returning guests are greeted by name, their room preferences are remembered and offered at check in, they are given priority offers, etc. This approach is further reinforced through the 'Ritz Carlton Incentive Awards', where guests receive points that can be redeemed for a free-of-charge night's stay. These relationship-building efforts encourage customers to continue to return and stay at a Ritz-Carlton hotel.

Because of the success of companies like these, the relationship marketing concept gained a firm foothold in the marketing domain, with its advocates arguing that it was almost a revolution of marketing thinking. As such, marketing practice shifted from one focused on developing, selling and delivering products, to one where the focus was progressively more concerned with the development and maintenance of mutually satisfying relationships with customers.

Essentially, this relationship philosophy relies on cooperation and a trusting relationship with customers, who should not be treated as interchangeable, unknown persons but as individuals with specific needs and wants. The relationship needs to be a mutually rewarding connection between the company or brand and the customer – there must be a reward, or extra value, for both the customer *and* the company. In such a situation, both parties establish an effective, efficient, enjoyable, enthusiastic and ethical relationship, one that is mutually rewarding. Various definitions have found acceptance but most centre on the stages of development (initial, ongoing) and the concept of value. Table 4.1 outlines the main definitions of relationship marketing found in the literature.

Table 4.1 Definitions of relationship marketing

Author	Definition
Berry (1983: 25)	'Relationship marketing is attracting, maintaining and, in multi-service organisations, enhancing customer relationships.'
Jackson (1985: 128)	'Relationship marketing is marketing to win, build and maintain strong, lasting relationships with industrial customers.'
Shani and Chalasani (1992: 44)	'Relationship marketing is an integrated effort to identify, maintain and build up a network with individual consumers and to continuously strengthen the network for the mutual benefit of both sides, through interactive, individualised and value-added contacts over a long period of time.'
Evans and Laskin (1994)	'Relationship marketing is a customer-centred approach by which firms seek long-term business relationships with prospective and existing customers.'
Parvatiyar and Sheth (2000: 9)	'Relationship marketing is the ongoing process of engaging in cooperative and collaborative activities and programmes with end-user customers to create or enhance mutual economic value at reduced cost.'

Over a number of decades marketing practitioners began to design more creative ways to develop relationships with their customers – be they consumers or other businesses – and began to explore the elements of relationship marketing where they could best solidify that connection. This pushed marketers towards the types of features that we now associate with experiential marketing, as will be explained a little later in this chapter. First, however, we will explore the role of relationships in B2B marketing, before turning our attention to relationships in B2C markets. How these relationships then link with the experiences that consumers have, and ultimately inform the design of experiential marketing strategies, will be a core theme which we will continue to develop as you read this book.

BUSINESS-TO-BUSINESS MARKETING RELATIONSHIPS

It is a common pitfall of the novice marketer to fail to see that marketing is about much more than reaching consumers. Our frame of reference as consumers means it is often easy to feel that consumers equal customers and customers equal consumers. The reality is that the vast majority of purchase transactions are entirely corporate, with businesses at either end of the transaction. This fact poses a challenge to all marketers to better understand the business relationships that precede consumption. Within this, there is a need to recognise business relationships and marketing activity that might support these relationships. Consider the scenario below.

Businesses are Customers too

You decide to spend a weekend break at your favourite destination booking into one of the many local hotels. Your choice of hotel may be based on many factors: price, size, quality, customer service, the experiences of friends who may have stayed there, the location, its facilities or maybe its family-friendliness. These are normal parts of our consumption decisions in such a scenario and are well understood. Regardless, the hotel must provide you, the consumer, with the experience that you want and are willing to pay for. For example, they will want to ensure that the best food and drink is available to you at the hotel, that the rooms are comfortable and warm, that the swimming pool is clean, that the common areas look bright and inviting, that the towels are clean and fresh, and that the bed linen lends itself to a good night's sleep.

Do we think, as marketers, about the decisions and relationships that underpin these experiences? Do we think about the choice of energy supplier that might afford the hotel the best service at the cheapest prices? Do we think

(Continued)

about the relationships with local food suppliers and the motivations that might be at play there? Do we think, in turn, about whether they outsource their laundry to reduce costs? Think further, then, on how an outsourced industrial laundry might gain and retain the custom of that hotel as part of its customer portfolio. Think about how that industrial laundry might expend effort on maintaining a good relationship with that hotel. Prompt service at a good price will be an aspect of it. Equally, having a responsive customer service will help to maintain a good relationship, which will in turn result in better experiences for the consumer. The strength of such a relationship might simply depend on good interpersonal relationships between the marketing team of the laundry and the purchasing team of the hotel.

For that laundry, reaching new customers – new hotels or hospitals, for example – will involve developing those new relationships from scratch. Intuitively, as marketers, we should be thinking about how trust can be developed, how commitment can be demonstrated and how buy-in can be achieved. We might start to think about how experiences in a B2B context might play their part in such relationships being successful, and how those successful relationships will subsequently be of benefit to the relationships the business can develop with its end use consumers.

More specifically, the following should be borne in mind:

- B2B relationship marketing is big business and is a critical area of the marketing discipline.
- Businesses use all sorts of tools and mechanisms to build relationships with other businesses. The digital proliferation of recent years builds upon a strong and ongoing suite of activities, such as trade shows, roadshows and traditional lead-generation activities.
- Experiential marketing is a part of B2B relationship marketing.

We will explore throughout this book this aspect of marketing and will encourage you to consider it with prompts and cases.

ENGAGEMENTS AND INTERACTIONS FOR RELATIONSHIP DEVELOPMENT

When we accept that a relationship is not a unidirectional concept, we begin to focus on constructs that ensure the bidirectionality of a relationship. The central aspects of this are interaction and exchange. Social psychology has been instrumental in providing insight for marketers in their relationship development strategies, with the main characteristics of relationships (interactions and exchanges) outlined as:

Figure 4.1 Characteristics of relationships

These characteristics show that business relationships do not just happen, they must be made to start, to work, to develop and be kept in good working order. They require active instigation, continued attention and ongoing effort. In this way, fundamentals such as trust, liking, empathy and commitment can deepen over time – just as they would in human relationships. A deep-dive into the meaning of relationships shows us that it takes two to tango. One-sided attractions are not evidence of a relationship; both parties must acknowledge the existence of a relationship and work to build interactions and engagement. As outlined earlier, building relationships has long been central to business success. However, the changing market environment of the 1980s and 1990s compelled businesses to renew the strategic focus of their relationships with customers. The main changes in the environment at this time included:

- **Globalisation**: the changing emphasis from convenience in customer relationships to one emphasising value, regardless of location, meant that marketers and others in business had to slow down their response times in customer interactions.
- **Maturity and lower growth rates**: business growth in advance of more identifiable waves of technology was sluggish and businesses needed to retain customers as a priority.
- **Changing business environment**: ethical and responsible behaviour was becoming more valuable, and this resulted in businesses looking towards meaningful relationships that were characterised by commitment.
- **Technology and communication**: the means for interaction with customers had broadened as a result of technological advances and businesses were feeling the need to use these technologies in order to demonstrate responsiveness.
- **Intangible resources**: the service aspect to the purchase situation grew in importance. No longer were consumers purchasing only a product, they were purchasing a collection of intangible benefits. (Palmer, 1999: 1–2)

We can see from this that the drivers of a strategic relationship marketing approach were mature markets and intense competition, along with technology and database marketing. These drivers resulted in customer relationship management (CRM) featuring highly in the approach of most marketers. The CRM approach used technology-enhanced customer interaction to shape appropriate marketing offers, which were designed to nurture ongoing company interactions with individual customers. At the time, the approach dominated the marketing landscape. It was a means to help the marketing team understand the customer better and, in turn, to demonstrate to that customer that the brand understood them.

Using CRM to build relationships with consumers of Guinness Draught in a can

Through the 2000s, the key at-home product that Guinness was offering was cans of Guinness Draught. With an objective of converting pub/bar drinkers to also consume Guinness at home, Guinness launched an extensive relationship-building programme with their customers. The intention was to leverage the relationship between the brand and the customer and to build further brand loyalty by offering incentives, competitions and prizes to those customers who signed up. In addition to encouraging customers to consume Guinness at home, the incentives also had the objective of encouraging customers to consume Guinness more frequently in the bar/pub, when they might have the tendency to consume competitor's products on occasion. Guinness knew for example that customers often preferred more refreshing lagers in the summer months and thus switched to alternative products. Having signed up for the programme in the bar, the customer received an initial *Welcome Pack* (containing some vouchers, Guiness merchandise, etc.) in the post within six weeks and then continued to receive maintenance communications on a frequent basis thereafter. The intention was that when the black envelopes from Guinness came through the door, customers would begin to anticipate a great night out, or in, depending on the offer in the envelope, with the subtle reassurance of a pint waiting for them. Competition incentives in each mailing ranged from sports tickets to holiday prize draws. Focusing on the at-home draught in a can product, the initial communication also invited the consumer to sign up three friends, who would then receive invitations to the host's house the week before a big soccer match. All parties received reminder SMS communications on the week and day before the match, reminding them to go to the host's house for the match on Saturday. A kit-box was delivered the week before the match and included vouchers for the Guinness Draught product, glasses and a welcome mat which hosts were invited to put outside the door to prompt the guys to 'let

themselves in, the match is on'. To encourage the consumer to remain loyal to Guiness when on a night out, vouchers to be exchanged in the bar for a pint of Guiness were also included in the envelope. In this way, Guiness not only focused on encouraging loyalty off trade, but also on trade, with the hope that one would continue to reinforce the other.

Building relationships with business consumers to attract tourists to Croke Park

Croke Park is the national stadium in Ireland where the indigenous games of football and hurling are played. The Gaelic Athletic Association (GAA) run these games and own Croke Park. For an amateur organisation, the GAA has been enormously successful in promoting their games and as part of that promotional strategy decided to target the tourist market on the basis that a Championship Sunday is an experience no tourist should miss. The top 850 international tour operators that sell Ireland as part of their portfolio were targeted in a B2B focused campaign to help sell unsold Championship tickets. The concept was based on 'Sell our Sights, then Sell Our Soul'. A direct mail campaign was sent to tour operators to elevate the thrill of GAA football and hurling, where tour operators were pointed to the e-commerce site to purchase tickets. Sales came in from inbound tour operators all over the world resulting in a series of international group bookings. The end result was a very exciting new sales channel for Croke Park and the beginning of direct relationships with the tour operators, who could now be directly interacted and communicated with.

Essentially, at this time (and as evidenced in these examples) companies used personalised communication, usually delivered via mail or email, in their attempts at building relationships with customers. However, despite the success of this approach, in some industries (typically B2B and services, where a person-to-person interaction also existed) it was argued by some that the limited interpersonal interaction and the anonymity of customers in mass consumer markets made relationship development difficult. In reality, consumers were receiving direct mail/emails from a company, which didn't quite develop the kinds of relationships that existed in B2B and services where personal contact dominated. Consider the difference between the tens of thousands of consumers receiving personalised, one-way communications from Guinness, with the less than 1,000 tour operators who could personally interact and communicate with officials in Croke Park to organise group tours and bookings. This anonymity in

B2C markets, coupled with the difficulties associated with potentially intrusive communication via phone, mail, SMS or email, resulted in an interesting shift in marketing thinking through the 2000s.

Reluctant to dispense with the concept of building relationships with customers, but conscious of the shortcomings of a relationship marketing strategy across all industries, attention turned to how relationships between a brand and a customer could be built that were personal to each individual consumer and that didn't rely on direct marketing types of communication. Building consumer engagements and interactions with trust and commitment are characteristics inherently attractive to any marketer. However, it was recognised that the CRM approach to building relationships didn't create those characteristics where there was an absence of person-to-person interaction. Instead, focusing on the brand and how the brand can be used to engage the consumer and how experiences and the use of experiential marketing can add value to customer–brand relationships received a lot of attention at this time. Indeed, building on the popularity of customer relationship management, Berry et al. (2002) proposed the move to customer experience management (CEM), where experiences assumed centrality in the quest to build and strengthen relationships. This, as explored in Chapter 2, was the first seriously received conflation of the idea of experience and relationships. The following section will examine this shift to consumer–brand relationships, highlighting the new emphasis on experience.

CONSUMER–BRAND RELATIONSHIPS

The roots of our current knowledge on consumer–brand relationships can be found in the brand loyalty literature. Brand loyalty – a long-standing objective of any marketer – is a measure of the attachment that a customer has to a brand. Essentially, brand loyalty refers to a consumer's consistent repurchase of a favoured brand. Considerable discussion exists among researchers and practitioners over what exactly constitutes brand loyalty. Typically, there are two main perspectives on brand loyalty:

- The first perspective focuses on loyalty expressed in terms of revealed behaviour and cognitive thought processes.
- The second perspective focuses on attitudes and the meaning and hedonic-emotive aspects of brand loyalty.

When we discuss revealed behaviour in the context of brand loyalty we focus on a haphazard process of trial and error. Essentially, through trial and error, the brand, which provides a satisfactory experience, is chosen. Rational thought processes dominate where loyalty to the brand is the result of repeated satisfaction with the brand.

This perspective on loyalty is in line with the rational consumer decision-making process outlined in Chapter 2, which dominated thinking for some time. Despite significant amounts of research examining brand loyalty in this way, many argued that traditional measures of loyalty from a behavioural perspective failed to capture its nuances (e.g., Fournier, 1998), with a growing body of literature over the last two decades analysing brand loyalty at an emotional or attitudinal level. This stood in contrast to the behavioural approach that impacted so much of the earlier thought-formation.

The approach to assessing brand loyalty at an emotional level was based on the consumers' attitude towards the product as well as on their purchase behaviour, and has at its core a psychological commitment to the brand. The importance of attitudinal and emotional aspects of brand loyalty means that there must be a strong attitudinal commitment to a brand for true loyalty to exist. Evidently, studying brand loyalty in this way focuses on the attitudes that consumers hold towards brands. These attitudes take the form of a consistently favourable set of stated beliefs towards the brand purchased. Therefore, with brand loyalty comes commitment (one of the characteristics of relationships). Experiential marketing has the unique ability to aid the development and maintenance of relationships between brands and consumers as the primary ambition of the communications tool is to create an ongoing emotional attachment through the enactment of memorable experiences. This *psychological commitment* results not only in the consistent repurchase of the same brand over time, but in a deep and abiding connection to that brand.

The ultimate display of affection: The tattoo

Tattoos represent an intricate web of experiences, feelings and memories. People are willing to tattoo the names of their loved ones on their bodies, but to be willing to also tattoo a brand onto your body, and to experience the associated pain and thrill, is the ultimate display of loyalty, devotion and affection for the brand. Harley Davidson and Nike are two brands that are frequently demanded of tattoo artists. Indeed, there was a time when the Nike Swoosh was the most popular tattoo to be requested in tattoo parlours across the USA.

Time and time again we see that brand awareness, perceived quality and an effective, clear brand identity can contribute to the goal of generating strong brand loyalty. The brand identity needs to provide a value proposition to the customer. This value proposition is a statement of the functional, emotional and self-expressive benefits delivered by the brand, which provide value to the customer, in the hope that the value proposition will lead to a brand–customer relationship and,

consequently, long-term loyalty. The importance of emotions here cannot be over-emphasised. As Kalbfell (2000: 8) suggests, "consumers are looking for fun and entertainment, not just the rational side of life". The creation of experiences for consumers is crucial, as the experiences that consumers have lead to those positive emotions, which ultimately lead to brand–customer relationships.

Experiencing 'Hey Jude'

What better example of a brand offering fun and entertainment can you get beyond T-Mobile's project of getting 13,000 people into Trafalgar Square to sing 'Hey Jude' together. Having the American singer-songwriter Pink in the crowd for a 'surprise appearance' during the singalong brought out all the emotions... and the teary eyes.

With the promise of loyalty and strong brand–customer relationships at stake, many brands move beyond a brand identity to a brand personality. This allows the brand to adopt the personality of a person, thereby encouraging the development of a relationship. It is often the case that customers interact with brands as if they were people, and there is evidence that some people often refer to brands as if they were human. The role that brands play in the lives of consumers, coupled with the personification of brands to enliven them as relationship partners, is significant in the study of experiential marketing. A noteworthy brand provides meaning and is important to a person because it connects with their life, and they have behavioural, attitudinal and emotional involvement which results in many experiences. It is argued that there exists a need to maintain the brand–customer relationship when we intertwine such a strong anthropomorphic identity into the relationship.

Sports fans and their emotional involvement

Ask someone about the football team they follow and you might very quickly gain an insight into the importance of the team in that person's life. True fans (consumers) are committed to their team (brand) from the cradle to the grave, and express the importance of that team in their lives through a high degree of consumer commitment and emotional involvement. This makes the opportunity to build brands and strong relationships with consumers of sport possible, where the experiences that the consumer has with the brand deepen the emotional involvement.

What we find particularly interesting is how the literature on bonds and bonding further adds to this discussion. Bonds join two parties together, and when present can lead to the development of brand loyalty. Examples of bonds that can develop between customers and brands include:

- Trust
- Commitment
- Empathy
- Satisfaction

Bonds can develop between customers and brands either as a result of repeated satisfaction with a brand or as a result of holding strong favourable attitudes towards a brand. If we compare bonds to characteristics of relationships, as outlined earlier, we can see that they are essentially the same. So, where bonds develop and result in brand loyalty, it can also be seen that those same bonds work to develop and maintain the desired brand–customer relationship. Where bonds grow in intensity, the attachment that the customer has for the brand deepens. Connections such as these demonstrate the powerful emotional attachments that can form when brands connect with customers in deep and significant ways. Fournier's (1998) work was instrumental in broadening an understanding of the role of bonds in brand–customer relationships. Her work proposed that bonds can range in intensity, from what might be considered superficial to liking, friendly affection and passionate love, culminating in addictive obsession. Where these bonds exist,

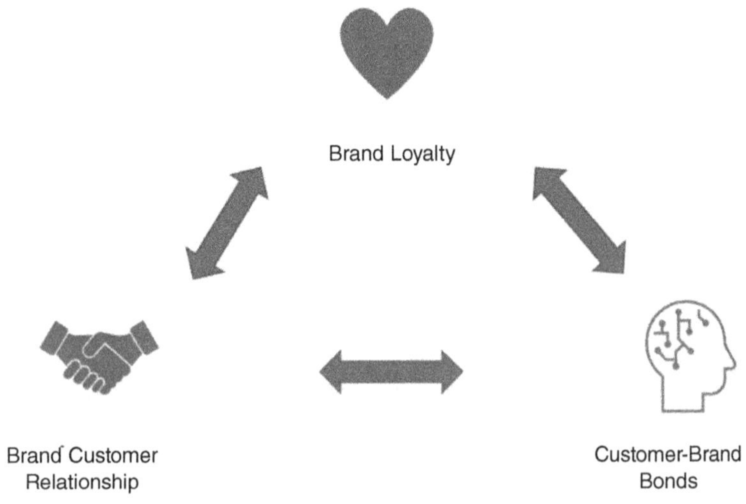

Figure 4.2 Bonds, loyalty and relationships

the brand contributes to the customers' life in significant ways. Figure 4.2 shows how bonds can result in brand loyalty which can then work to develop and maintain brand–customer relationships.

As marketers, the goal must be to understand why bonds exist and to attempt to nurture them to enhance the strength of the consumers' attitudes towards a brand and, in turn, strengthen the loyalty and the relationship that exists.

Bonds and babies

Mothers, in particular first-time mothers, or what we call novice consumers, develop dependencies on products that suit their babies and appear to keep their babies' needs well satisfied. Mothers develop deep and abiding bonds with brands that keep babies happy, resulting in the development of strong brand loyalty. Baby care and cleansing products, infant formula, etc. all benefit from deep emotional customer loyalty as a result of the bond that develops between Mom and the brand. These brands can become so important to the mother that very often, Mom won't look beyond those brands in the purchase situation, and indeed can become an advocate for that brand.

The brand loyalty literature brings the importance of brand–customer relationships to the fore. In this context, the creation of experiences that build bonds between the customer and the brand and enhance brand loyalty came to prominence. As mentioned earlier in the chapter, this work led to the proposal that CEM should replace CRM, with the focus on experiences rather than technology to build and strengthen relationships. Before we explore more deeply the role of experiences and experiential marketing in building consumer–brand relationships, the next section looks at the relationships that exist in marketplace cultures and the resulting opportunity for the creation of experiences therein.

BRAND RELATIONSHIPS AND MARKETPLACE CULTURES

When exploring the literature on brand–customer relationships, the importance of social relationships that are formed around brands emerges as significant to the study of experiential marketing. Brand communities and brand tribes are two examples of such social relationships that are often seen to be key aspects of the success of experiential marketing. Here, we delve into these a little further.

Brand Communities

A brand community is a collective of social relationships that are created around a specific brand. The community is not geographically bound and is based upon a mutual interest and love for the brand that has been formed through brand experience. Brand communications can occur anywhere, and this lack of geographical restraints means that brand communities can take place in:

- Online and offline realms
- Small groups
- A large format through a virtual medium
- Brandfests

Within this 'consumer collective construct', members co-create value for one another generally through their knowledge, skills and abilities, along with their emotional connection to the brand, which is expressed through their actions. As the formation of brand communities is independent of the prescribed marketing plan, the brands themselves must abdicate their control of brand meanings and permit the community to format their own brand meaning based on personal experience and expression. In turn, this form of customer empowerment strengthens the brand through rites and rituals. For example, the success of brands like Apple are considered benchmarks for this type of marketing activity.

The relationships built in brand communities have been regarded as a key driver for the intense brand loyalty that derives from community members towards the brands. When consumers have relationships with a brand, they are often provoked to interact and identify with networks of others who share their passion, enthusiasm and infatuation for the brand. Sequentially, members of these communities motivate each other and boost levels of self-esteem, therefore cultivating community-centric behaviours. Developing from these community-centric behaviours, brand communities share:

- Rituals and methods of play
- Unique ways of rationalising experiences
- Thoughts and traditions
- A deep connection and sense of moral responsibility with other community members
- A quasi-religious adoration towards the focal brand.

Brand communities: The Harley Owner's Group

In 1983, Harley Davidson launched their first brand community called the Harley Owner's Group. The community was focused on connecting customers with

(Continued)

one another. Those customers were identified as having shared interests with the focus on a lifestyle experience of fulfilling dreams. The community centred on feelings of pride, exclusivity, camaraderie and customer experiences. Symbols, such as T-shirts and tattoos, and rituals, such as the Posse Ride Oath, bonded the members of the group together, not to forget the commotion the riders made on entering a town or village.

The co-creation of value by brands and customers is essential in maintaining brand values, increasing community members' love and commitment to the brand and offering brands a channel to communicate with their most loyal customers and advocates. Brand communities can emerge organically, but they can also be planned, strategic initiatives. In the latter case, brands maintain some ownership as the community develops. Brand communities are more likely to be successful where a clear vision is established, supported by an authentic brand proposition, where consumers only need a prompt to show their willingness to participate in the brand community. In short, it must make sense – the brand community must feel valuable to the consumer.

Consumer Tribes

Other forms of consumption collectives are also present where the members do not form around one particular brand. Less concerned with the brand and the attributes of the brand, which are seen in brand communities, many consumption collectives develop weaker connections with a consortium of brands, services and products. This observation has led to the development of another form of consumption collective – the consumer tribe. Cova's (1997) and Cova and Cova's (2002) research is particularly interesting on this topic. They characterise tribal consumption as the development of social links with others through the 'linking value' that has been created during an experience or through the common use of brands, products or services. Essentially, a consumer tribe is a group of individuals who are connected through a shared brand affinity which in turn creates a community of brand advocates. It is essential to note that tribal brands do not have customers, but rather, followers, and therefore require a common means of identifying each other. For tribes to be successful, their followers must feel unique as opposed to mainstream; they unite through a shared experience, a story, a myth or a narrative that affords them the opportunity to easily connect with others. Consumer tribes are often a feature of the LGBT+ community, for example, with brands that act as allies often finding more favour within the community.

Wellness tribes and athleisure brands: Who is Sweaty Betty?

The growth in both athletic wear and wellness over the past few years has given rise to the opportunity for brands to differentiate themselves by connecting with consumers in ways that enable them to carve out clear and unique brand identities. With a goal to make the consumer feel 'powerful and amazing', Sweaty Betty empowers women to feel beautiful. In doing so, the brand has created a solid tribe of followers. Bonding on the basis that they want to work out but definitely like cake, the tribe of followers feel connected through their love of the brand and the brand values of happiness, personal experiences, going green and family, while always embracing their rebellious side.

In general, consumer tribes are distinct in comparison to brand communities in multiple ways. These differences can be summed up in four key characteristics: multiplicity, playfulness, transience and entrepreneurialism.

1. **Consumer tribes are multiple**: Unlike brand communities, tribes rarely govern consumers' everyday lives. Rather, they represent an interim escape from the pressures and stresses that derive from the working week. Therefore, followers are not subjected to following only one form of tribe or community. On the contrary, tribal theory emphasises the occurrence of flows between altering identities under diverse circumstances.
2. **Consumer tribes are playful**: Tied to the variety of membership and fluidity of identity, tribal consumption is typically devoid of the long-term moral responsibility or 'religious' adoration that is often felt by members of a brand community. Instead, the consumer tribe places value on active play with marketplace resources. These include:

    - Emotions
    - Material culture
    - Aesthetics
    - Institutions
    - Brands
    - Places
    - Media
    - Fashion
    - Music

In the process of active play, tribal followers pillage these resources, that is, they deconstruct and reassemble them, introducing fast-moving, intertextual performances in forms that are personally relevant to members of the tribe.

3. **Consumer tribes are transient**: Connected to these characteristics of multiple identities and play, tribes emerge, morph and disappear again as the combinations of people and resources modify. This generates situations that are unpredictable and uncontrollable, leading Cova Pace and Park et al., (2007: 8) to characterise tribes as 'double agents', a form of consumer collective that is content 'to be misled, to remember and forget, and then mislead, and then manipulate these manipulations in ways that enliven their daily lives'.
4. **Consumer tribes are entrepreneurial**: Rather than waiting for and relying on ready-made consumption resources, tribes typically produce or customise market offerings as entrepreneurial ventures. This can result in an altering of the power balance between brands and the tribal followers, as the consumer tribes take the lead in dictating procedures of co-production.

A tribe that maintains the characteristics of multiplicity, playfulness, transience and entrepreneurialism will remain engaged, passionate and desired. Fundamentally, a consumer tribe will remain in a state of co-creation with all brand experiences.

The ultimate tribe: The Lego creators

Lego, it could be argued, is one of the great examples of a brand with a strong tribe. Enabling the creation of experiences through the purchase of a product is exactly what Lego does. The consumer has to be a co-creator – this is the core attribute of the product. Social media has been instrumental in facilitating the growth of the tribe, as groups and clubs devoted to Lego building can share images of their creations with other members of the tribe.

Although consumption connectives can have a profound impact on a brand, it is essential to note that these communities typically account for a small percentage of a brand's customer base. As stated by Sharp (2010: 111):

> Within every brand's customer base there are a few people who feel much more attitudinally committed to the brand. It may be part of their self-image, used to signal what sort of person they are to themselves and to others. But the marketing consequences of these brand fan(atic)s turn out to be very limited. Most of a brand's customers think and care little about the brand, but the brand manager should care

about these people because they represent most of the brand's sales; the brand needs these people if it is to increase its sales.

Therefore, although it is essential to consider the influence of consumption communities when creating brand experiences, it is also important to remember the impact that other segments of the customer base can make. The following section draws together what we have learned so far in this chapter in the context of experiences and experiential marketing.

EXPERIENTIAL MARKETING IN BUILDING CONSUMER–BRAND RELATIONSHIPS

The importance of building consumer–brand relationships has been well established so far in this chapter, and it is here that experiential marketing comes to the fore. The crux of experiential marketing is that the primary concern of a brand should not be customer satisfaction as seen in traditional marketing, but the creation of an emotional consumer attachment with the brand. Using experiential marketing, marketers create immersive methods of connecting with their audience. Relevant and relatable experiences that a consumer has with a brand cements the brand–customer relationship over the long term.

Experiential marketing is aligned to how brands want to connect with their consumers. This has been driven by the reality that traditional marketing communications do not have the same participative allure, given, in general, the passive nature of such communications and the lack of experiential activities. Instead, brands seek to create unique events to connect with their consumers. The experiences that the consumer has improves the customer's trust and commitment to the brand, resulting in a longer-term relationship. *Think back to the experience of getting a tattoo, attending a football match, singing with Pink and thousands of people in Trafalgar Square, bonding with a baby, and so on.* Experiential dimensions such as sensory perceptions, emotions, thinking, etc. are highly correlated with trust and commitment, and thus with relationship quality. In essence, consumers tend to trust brands more when they are able to 'feel' connected to them.

Vita Coco and the sensory experience: Initiating relationships

Vita Coco implemented an experiential marketing campaign in 2016 with the objective of creating a sampling experience which immersed consumers in the brand by actively getting them to work up a thirst as part of their '#JustGetThirsty' campaign.

(Continued)

Embodying the vibrant brand personality, they created an immersive, beach-inspired pop-up event where consumers could listen to live music played by a DJ, challenge a friend to climb up a 30-foot coconut tree, while trying to beat the scores of fellow attendees as well as some celebrity participants, or take a gif (an animated image) with their 'surfer dudes' activation staff. Attendees also sampled the Vita Coco coconut water range from an on-site beach shack, ate street food from the street vendor, Kerb, cooked with Vita Coco coconut oil and other coconut-inspired dishes from street chef Oli Baba. The multiple touchpoints encouraged exploration of the different elements of the event and supported a sense of curiosity, surprise and fun. Attendees were entered into a prize draw to win one of two adventure trips. Throughout the two-day event, which occurred in London, Manchester and Birmingham, 50,000 consumers interacted with the brand, over 750 people participated in the Coconut Tree Climb, and 844 gifs were shared across social media platforms with a reach of 176,000 (Benjamin, 2016; Creative Brief, 2016).

Enhancing customer involvement in the brand is as much an objective of relationship building as it is of experiential marketing. Effective experience management requires brands to continuously design cues to conjure joy and interest in customers, thereby enhancing their involvement with the brand. The consumption experience and the relationship it generates between the brand and the consumer is the ultimate point of brand differentiation as it affords brands the opportunity to create memorable experiences through offering a series of experiential benefits which are strategically tailored to the target market. Thus, the consumption experience, and the relationship it cultivates with customers, acts as a point of difference for brands in overcrowded and competitive marketplaces.

CONCLUSION AND SUMMARY

This chapter has explored the development of the relationship concept and how brand–customer relationships can be built and nurtured through an experiential marketing approach. Brand–customer relationships can be supported where social relationships develop in brand communities and brand tribes. Experiences that can happen either organically or through strategic intervention by the brand are fundamental in nurturing the bonds that connect the consumer with the brand. These bonds can over time result in consumer involvement and psychological commitment to the brand. We refer you to the case study below of Queen B Athletics, which illustrates many of the points made in this chapter.

MAIN TAKEAWAYS FROM CHAPTER 4

- The relationship marketing concept that garnered much success in the B2B and service industries ultimately led to the focus on building brand–customer relationships.
- Brand–customer relationships can develop as a result of bonds that connect a consumer to a brand, and can lead to long-term customer loyalty. Indeed, the bonds that lead to loyalty can also work to develop and maintain the brand–customer relationship.
- The social relationships that develop among members of brand communities and brand tribes can also enhance and maintain brand–customer relationships.
- The experiences that consumers have when they connect with and interact with brands are fundamental in building bonds, loyalty and, ultimately, relationships.
- Experiential marketing is a strategic marketing tool used to build these experiences that can connect the consumer to the brand.

CASE STUDY: QUEEN B ATHLETICS[1]

Queen B Athletics is an Irish, Cork-based company that designs and manufacturers sportswear for women. Founded by Brid Ryan and her sister Áedín, Queen B Athletics started its life as a rowing brand. Having been a rower for many years, Brid believed that high-quality kit designed specifically for women should be at the forefront of the sportswear market.

Since its launch in 2013, athletes at all levels, including many international high-profile athletes, proudly wear Queen B. Collaborating with events such as the Henley Women's Regatta (the second biggest women's regatta in the world) and with teams such as the Irish Women's Hockey team[2] has elevated Queen B firmly onto the world stage. Keeping it real, however, Brid is quick to point out that Queen B's local customers are what keeps the business going, particularly through the Covid-19 pandemic. 'The big moments are amazing, but it is being part of a community that also inspires us. Partnering with the Carrigaline Ladies Football Club, walking into the chemist shop in Carrigaline and seeing the staff who wear our kit doing local deliveries, these are the things that keep our heads up during the bad times.'

And it is truly that sense of community, brand loyalty and solid customer relationships that have been central to the Queen B brand since its inception. Building a sportswear brand on a limited budget was a challenge, but recognising that the experience of actually trying on the clothes and being part of a growing tribe of followers was key, Brid and Aedin choose sporting events

to grow the brand. Pop-up shops at events such as rowing regattas, hockey matches and crossfit championships proved instrumental in growing brand awareness and increasing sales. Engaging with potential customers at these events was something that Brid excelled at. She knew that sending women off to the local toilets, or into their pop-up changing tent, with armfuls of clothes would result in sales. Once the women had experienced the feel and texture of the clothes and had fun with their friends trying them on, the sales naturally followed. The interaction and engagement that happened both with Brid and Aedin and between the customers themselves at these events were critical to the fun element of the experience. Taking photos with customers and putting them on Instagram, engaging with the athletes at the events and tagging them on social media quickly resulted in a growing community of followers. The fun element of this digital amplification also proved critical for engaging with customers and potential customers who were not at the event.

The digital engagement and interaction has kept the business going through the Covid-19 pandemic. 2020 has been a tough year for small businesses, but Queen B have kept spirits up through Instagram stories, with their 'Lockdown Launches' scoring as a particular highlight. 'We were in a bit of a quandary', says Brid, 'like so many other businesses we had big plans for 2020, including launching new products. We found ourselves in lockdown with boxes of new stock and new products arriving for events that had been cancelled. Rather than focus on what we couldn't control, we took to social media and started to launch our products online. Instead of using models, we had to wear the kit ourselves and instead of fancy backgrounds and settings it was me alone in the office. It was a lot of fun and our followers seemed to enjoy it as much as we did!'.

Queen B have gone from strength to strength over the years. Interactions and engagements with customers, both physically and online, have resulted in strong brand–customer relationships, and experiences with the brand at sporting events have grown the Queen B community. The resulting customer trust in the brand is mirrored in the personal attention and communication that customers receive from Brid and Aedin. The bonds that are nurtured in these interactions are the firm foundation for long-term customer loyalty and commitment. After the challenges of Covid-19, Queen B are optimistic about the future. 'Our website has exploded, our phones are inundated with messages and calls, and it is beyond all our expectations to be ending this year, of all years, on a high.'

CONCLUDING QUESTIONS

1. Explain how the original relationship marketing concept evolved into the modern approach to building relationships between consumers and brands.

2. Using the social psychology literature, discuss the characteristics of relationships.
3. Discuss the connections between bonds, loyalty and relationships using a diagram to illustrate your answer.
4. Explain how experiences are fundamental in building the connections that exist between bonds, loyalty and relationships.
5. Using your own personal experiences, (a) identify examples where consumers have relationships with brands across a number of different industries, and (b) describe the types of bonds that might exist in these brand–consumer relationships?
6. Provide examples of experiences that you as a consumer have had that positively impacted on your relationship with a brand?
7. Is it possible that consumers do not or cannot have relationships with brands? Explain your answer.
8. Identify a brand community and examine how social relationships in that brand community can positively impact on the consumer–brand relationship.
9. Identify a brand tribe and analyse how social relationships in that brand tribe can positively impact on the consumer–brand relationship.
10. Explain the role of experiential marketing in B2B marketing and in doing so discuss its applicability in a B2B context.

NOTES

1. Queen B Athletics, Unit 5 Innovation Business Park, Carrigaline Industrial Estate, Crosshaven Road, Co. Cork, www.queenbathletics.com; www.instagram.com/queenbathletics/;
2. In 2018 Queen B became the official sportsbra partner to the Irish Women's Hockey team, the first partnership of its kind in Ireland. The team qualified for the Olympics in 2019 and Queen B Athletics could not be happier for their success. 'To partner with a national team is a huge honour for a small business, but to see that team go on and make history by qualifying for the Olympics is really a dream come true', says Brid. When the initial one-year partnership agreement came to an end with Hockey Ireland, Queen B were thrilled when they were asked to renew the partnership for another four years.

REFERENCES AND FURTHER READING

Benjamin, K. (2016). Vita Coco to Host London Beach Experience. *Event Magazine* [Online]. Available at: www.eventmagazine.co.uk/vita-coco-host-london beach-experience/brands/article/1400345 [accessed 12 July 2017].

Berry, L. (1983). Relationship Marketing. In L. Berry, L. Shostack, & G. Upah (Eds.), *Emerging Perspectives of Services Marketing* (pp. 25–28). Chicago, IL: American Marketing Association.

Berry, L., Carbone, L.P., & Haeckel, S.H. (2002). Managing the Total Customer Experience. *MIT Sloan Management Review*, 43(3), 85–89.

Cova, B. (1997). Community and Consumption: Towards a Definition of the 'Linking Value' of Product of Services. *European Journal of Marketing*, 31(3/4), 297–316.

Cova, B., & Cova, V. (2002). Tribal Marketing: The Tribalism of Society and its Impact on the Conduct of Marketing. *European Journal of Marketing*, 36(5/6), 595–620.

Cova, B., Pace, S., & Park, D.J. (2007). Global Brand Communities across Borders: The Warhammer Case. *International Marketing Review*, 24(3), 313–329.

Creative Brief (2016). *Vita Coco Case Study*. Creative Brief. [Online]. Available at: www.creativebrief.com/agency/work/24503/11610/vita-coco-by-seen-presents?search=1 [accessed 7 December 2017].

Evans, J., & Laskin, R. (1994). The Relationship Marketing Process: A Conceptualization and Application. *Industrial Marketing Management*, 23(5), 439–454.

Fournier, S. (1998). Consumers and Their Brands: Developing Relationship Theory in Consumer Research. *Journal of Consumer Research*, 24(4), 343–374.

Jackson, B. (1985). Build Customer Relationships that Last. *Harvard Business Review*, 63(November/December), 120–128.

Kalbfell, K.-H. (2000). In R. Clifton & E. Maughan (Eds.), *The Future of Brands: Twenty-Five Visions*. Basingstoke: Macmillan.

Palmer, R. (1999). So Precisely What is Relationship Marketing? In D. McLoughlin & C. Horan (Eds.), *Proceedings of the 15th Annual Industrial Marketing and Purchasing Conference* (pp. 1–15). Dublin: UCD.

Parvatiyar, A., & Sheth, J. (2000). The Domain of Conceptual Foundations of Relationship Marketing. In J. Sheth & A. Parvatiyar (Eds.), *Handbook of Relationship Marketing* (pp. 3–38). Thousand Oaks, CA: Sage.

Shani, D., & Chalasani, S. (1992). Exploiting Niches Using Relationship Marketing. *Journal of Business Strategy*, 6(4), 43–52.

Sharp, B. (2010). *How Brands Grow: What Marketers Don't Know*. New York: Oxford University Press.

5
BRAND MANAGEMENT AND EXPERIENTIAL MARKETING

CHAPTER OVERVIEW

Brand management is a process which focuses on the development of a brand – and its various characteristics – such that its overall perceived value increases. Brands that are not well managed are less likely to succeed, so we find that successful marketing teams place a premium on this part of the marketing function. We have also seen in previous chapters that experiential marketing has extended the means by which marketers can impress new and existing customers. In managing a brand, the creation of experiences for consumers of that brand is now considered essential, particularly in the context of brand communities and tribes, as we described in the previous chapter. We can say with certainty that brands that deploy experiential marketing should do so while being fully aware of its potential impact on brand management, and vice versa. A key aspect of this book is about focusing on the integration of experiential marketing more solidly into the broader marketing strategy. Thus, in this chapter we will link experiential marketing to traditional theories on brand management and illustrate how, when, and why experiential marketing should be used.

Specifically, this chapter will explore the following important topics and link them to some of the exciting industry practices that use experiential marketing:

- The role of experiential marketing in helping to manage a brand and the impact of brand management on the experience.
- How to design experiences that connect with more traditional brand management and communication strategies.
- The importance of brand infrastructures and memory recall when implementing experiential marketing.
- How to build brand equity through experiential marketing.

THE ROLE OF EXPERIENTIAL MARKETING IN MANAGING A BRAND

Up to this point, this book has presented a comprehensive immersion into experiences from a marketing perspective. We have seen how they have emerged as a significant tool in the armoury of professional marketers. The last chapter explored the role of experiences in building relationships between brands and consumers. This chapter continues that theme, by looking in more detail at the overall management of a brand when experiences and experiential marketing are at the core of that brand's management. We have seen that experiential marketing has the unique ability to develop and maintain relationships between brands and consumers as its primary ambition is to create ongoing emotional attachment (McCole, 2004). We also know, in turn, that strong relationships are an important aspect of building a brand. This is achieved through the enactment of memorable experiences that are strategically tailored to a specific target market (Mathwick et al., 2001). Research has shown that the vast majority of marketing professionals perceive superior, relatable and memorable customer experiences as the next arena of competition among brands competing for market share. Experiential marketing provides an opportunity for marketers to create these memorable experiences where the consumption experience and the relationship it generates with the consumer is the ultimate point of brand differentiation in an overcrowded marketplace (Holbrook, 1999; Pine & Gilmore, 1999; Schmitt, 2000; Sherry, 1998). In the last two decades we have seen an even stronger emphasis on the use of experiential marketing to improve brands. However, quite a bit of the work on experiential marketing has failed to integrate it into brand management. The consequence of this is that brands are not leveraging the experiential activity fully and, conversely, there may be aspects of a brand's management that are impeding the full potential activation of a meaningful experience. In this chapter you will read about examples of organisations that are beginning to combine these activities well.

Meanwhile, we are faced with an initial challenge. While building and managing relationships is central to brand management, if for a moment we turn our attention to broader brand management theories, we realise that we can quite quickly be overwhelmed by the plethora of branding theories and models in the academic and practitioner literature. It is a complicated and extensive area as can be seen in Figure 5.1 which depicts some of the areas of focus for brand management theories.

We can find ourselves sinking in a sea of brand management theories. These theories invariably have a wide range of properties that lend themselves to a discussion of the synergies with experiential marketing. We have decided to frame our integration of experiential marketing around the work of marketing guru Philip Kotler. He brings much of this together in his 6-Step Branding Conceptual Model (see Figure 5.2), which proposes that brands need to start with articulating their purpose before moving to positioning, differentiation, identity, trust and beneficence.

Figure 5.1 Focus of brand management theories

Figure 5.2 Kotler's 6-Step Branding Conceptual Model

Source: Copyright The Marketing Journal (2016), printed with permission

In this section, we use Kotler's model to illustrate the role that experiential marketing can play in each step of the process.

Brand Purpose

Brand purpose is the essence of what the brand promises to accomplish for the buyer. Essentially, marketers articulate how the brand is going to change the lives of consumers and meet their expectations. What is its *raison d'être*? Only by knowing this can marketers measure their success. Brand purpose also provides the scaffolding on which to make decisions. By acting as a more granular version of a mission statement, brand purpose can inform other decisions about how to manage the brand. According to Coco Chanel, 'In order to be irreplaceable one must always be different'. This ethos guides not only the brand's contribution to the bottom line, but also their impact on the world by placing a premium on innovation and desirability. Brands that do not know their purpose – that cannot articulate it succinctly – lack the power to truly succeed. Accounting software company Sage understood the fact that their customers were often overstretched HR or Payroll Managers. Their award-winning Big HR & Payroll Quiz allowed

them to gain a better understanding of their customers' needs, which they have integrated into their brand purpose, thus indicating that their business offer is not just about technology, but also about helping their customers and addressing their needs.

On a journey with Fulfil

Fulfil bars are high in protein, low in sugar and fill the gap in the market for a great tasting bar that is good for you. The brand's purpose is to help people to live and snack more healthily. The brand recognises that consumers are trying to stay healthy and therefore positions itself as fundamental in helping the consumer to stay on that journey. The Fulfil bar feels like a treat, albeit a healthy one. So, if the consumer has a Fulfil bar, they won't 'fall off the wagon' and it might keep them going until the weekend when they can let go a little. In this way the consumer can have a liveable diet and healthy lifestyle.

The brand uses experiential marketing to amplify the message that they are trying to help the consumer on a journey. The experiential marketing deployment centres on a truck which is branded Fulfil. The truck goes to sporting, fitness, healthy food and wellness events and is used for mass sampling or selling the product. To amplify the message further, the company invested in a branded agility ring, which is used by all the professional soccer teams in the world as a training tool. Football teams use it to build agility and speed, so the ring represents a very attractive and engaging experiential marketing piece. When the customer enters into the ring, they can see a leader board listing some of the best players in the world. The aim is to hit the ball on the flashing red, green and orange lights as they move around the ring. If the player hits a red light, they lose a point, if they hit a green light, they gain a point. People enter into the ring, play the game and win either a case of Fulfil bars or a couple of bars.

Experiential strategies such as these reinforce the brand purpose and connect with consumers in an engaging and fun way, while ensuring that the consumer tries and experiences a great-tasting product.

Lush Cosmetics' dedication to brand purpose

Lush Cosmetics is a cruelty-free cosmetic brand whose brand purpose is built on the cornerstone of ethical commitments. The brand has advocated for many causes, including Fair Trade, the Black Lives Matter campaign, government malpractice and animal cruelty. An experiential activation which was produced

on a global scale by the brand was their 'Fighting Animal Testing' campaign in 2012. This campaign's core purpose is to bring animal testing back into the public eye. For one component of this global initiative, Lush utilised the window of their store in Regent Street, London, to stage animal testing experiments on a human test subject to depict the inhumane nature of this practice. The test subject for this activation was a 24-year-old female actor, who was dragged by a rope by actors dressed as laboratory scientists and placed on a bench inside the store window, where the testing that is standard procedure in animal testing laboratories was enacted. Shoppers witnessed the test subject having eye drops put in her eyes, being injected, having some of her hair shaved off and being force-fed while her mouth was held open with separators. This activity was repeated over a 10-hour period and was livestreamed across the world. Outside the store, staff were on hand to share the purpose of this demonstration with shoppers and to offer spectators the opportunity to sign a petition to ban the sale of animal-tested products in the European Union. This activation clearly depicted Lush Cosmetics' ethical commitments, while also trying to raise awareness for causes that the brand advocates for.

Brand Positioning

Brand positioning is the act of designing a brand in such a way that it occupies the mind of the target buyers in a manner that makes it feel different from other brands. By positioning the brand in a particular way, the aim is to guide the target audience to think about that brand in the same way. This is generally accepted as being a prerequisite to a successful interplay between messaging, communication and increased market share. Brands with good 'top-of-mind' success, such as Coca-Cola, Nestlé, BMW, Apple, Microsoft, etc., will be known to you and will typically represent adherence to principles and processes that allow for the creation of strong and effective brand positioning.

Quick and tasty with Flahavans Quick Oats

Flahavans Progress Oats is the well-established oat brand on the Irish market, with Quick Oats being a sub-brand of that brand family. Quick Oats is positioned for a consumer who wants the benefits of oats but in a more convenient way in terms of preparation. Therefore they are oats that you can prepare within two minutes in the microwave. They are ideal for people who are on the go and who

(Continued)

eat their breakfast at their desk, which reflects the time-poverty of many modern consumers. To position Quick Oats in this way in the marketplace, the brand partnered with a company which rents out 'cool' office spaces in the heart of Dublin city. A pop-up was created for the experiential activation, where hot porridge was served with an array of toppings. The experiential activation ran for four days, it was promoted on social media and leaflets were dropped in offices around the area. The numbers participating in the activation doubled day-on-day. The consumers loved the idea of getting free healthy porridge, and they loved the theatrical element in terms of all the toppings, colour and options.

Brand Differentiation

Differentiating your brand is ultimately about setting it apart from the competition. This might be achieved through superior performance, affordability, quality, etc. Ultimately, the brand should offer what the competitors do not, or at least do something better than the competitors. Effective brand differentiation is about placing one or more of its appealing characteristics as the prominent edifice of the overall brand. The same approach can be applied for B2C- and B2B-focused brands. DHL, the logistics provider, differentiates its brand with an emphasis on customer service and develops its business operations to support this.

Tinder achieving brand differentiation through digital experiential marketing methods

During the Covid-19 pandemic, brands were faced with a challenge of trying to create authentic and immersive interactions with their audience without staging live physical experiential events. Instead, they focused solely on digital experiential marketing methods. The popular dating app Tinder launched their interactive Swipe Night event in Brazil, Germany, Spain, France, Italy, Indonesia, India, Korea, Australia and the UK. The aim of this event was to help its users find love while living in apocalyptic-like times. This move acted as a differentiation mechanism within the competitive dating app market by affording app users the opportunity to meet new people and entertain themselves – two things that were difficult as the world was in lockdown. The digital experiential marketing activation employed a story-telling approach, asking users to decide the direction in which the narrative developed, effectively crowdsourcing. Tinder users were asked to log onto their app for this live event, where they could direct a story about a group of

friends in their last hours before an asteroid hits Earth by swiping at key moments to determine their next move. The activation participants played the main character in the storyline and as the plot developed, the user had to make key decisions which influenced the outcome. However, swiping towards their preferred outcome not only decided how the story ended, but also correlated who each user matched with and what they ended up talking about.

Brand Identity

The identity of a brand is simply described as the unique set of brand associations that represent what the brand stands for and promises to customers. The company needs to use *positioning* and *differentiation* to communicate the brand's purpose and ultimately enrich the brand's identity. Brand identity is the tangible and visible elements that are connected to a brand and that are used to give it life. Having a strong brand identity is dependent on understanding the brand purpose. A recognisable brand identity is inherently linked to good design of those physical and tangible artefacts. Identity also relates to personality and emotion. And yet, it is more than that. Thinking of the Apple brand identity and contrasting it with that of the B2B company Salesforce (the customer management software company), it is easy to see that the scope of these brand aspects is much more nebulous. It is the aspects of brand identity that relate to personality and emotion, and these in turn lend themselves to experiential marketing.

Identifying with Propercorn's pattern project

Propercorn is a brand that has been created with a clear visual identity. Rather than taking inspiration from its competitors in the fast-moving consumer goods (FMCG) sector, it turned to fashion and lifestyle brands to form its visual assets. Boasting bright colours and bold illustrations, Propercorn's packaging follows this narrative, along with its marketing communications. An experiential campaign enacted by the brand aimed to bring this eye-catching nature to the streets of London, where they commissioned emerging designer Rachel Thomas, who has worked on brands including Anya Hindmarch, Mulberry and Vogue, to create brand patterns. These brand patterns focused on popcorn over the Propercorn brand, but injected the brand's distinctive visual identity. The patterns were then used to turn mundane spaces into colourful hubs, donning Propercorn's iconic popcorn pattern, as created by Rachel Thomas. Routemaster buses, phone boxes, footpaths and buildings were covered with the brand's popcorn pattern, becoming visual representations for the brand. Brand representatives were also on hand to give away samples of the product.

Creating the Breyers identity

Breyers Delights is a relatively *new to market* ice-cream that was launched into the Irish market in 2017 by Unilever. It is a low-sugar, low-calorie, high in protein ice-cream, which really connects with its target audience of young people who want to be fit, look after their bodies, stay in shape, are watching their diet or at least what they eat, and who are body conscious. More specifically, the target market ranges from the extreme gym-goer to the more casual gym user who likes to get fit for the summer. Soon after the brand launched, the company had the objective of building a strong brand identity with unique brand associations. Recognising the benefits of an experiential approach to do so, they ran an experiential event to which they invited a number of influencers, two macro influencers – Vogue Williams and Rob Lipsett – and a number of media and micro influencers. Vogue and Rob ran two workout sessions, one in the morning and one in the early afternoon, after which they hosted brunch for the attendees where Breyers Delights featured in a number of different recipes, from shakes to smoothies to pancakes, etc. A lot of fruit and non-alcoholic cocktails were also included. Running a social media campaign in parallel ensured that as many people as possible experienced the event, which made a positive impact in terms of the brand and the brand identity. Key to this was running the event alongside a traditional advertising campaign where important brand associations could be built.

Brand Trust

Every marketer should want their brand to be trustworthy. A fundamental part of any brand strategy is that the customer will believe that the brand will deliver what it claims. Brands must instill confidence. Brands with high trust levels impact directly on buying decisions. In the US, retail company Whole Foods is recognised by the high levels of positive sentiment that consumers have for it. There must also be a belief that the brand does what it says it will do. Experiences can be used to deliver this message.

Trusting the Taste

Denny Fire & Smoke is an emerging brand of seven pre-packed lines of ham, chicken and turkey, as well as two deli-counter lines. Fire & Smoke's recipes are inspired by the 'pitmaster craft of the American Deep South', using fire and smoke cooking methods to create a great-tasting product range. The meat is cooked at a low temperature for a long time, first over flames and then smoked with oak wood chips. The target market for this product is sophisticated in terms of product flavours and the brand aims to deliver excitement in the cooked meats category. To

deliver on this brand promise and to generate trust that the brand will indeed deliver great flavour, an experiential campaign was created. Occupying an area in Smithfield Square in Dublin, a pop-up rustic, Deep South, American-style barbecue barn was created. There was a fire pit, a few smokers and barbecues and DJ BBQ, a YouTube star with a large following who specialises in barbecue cooking. The event centred on providing barbecue cooking classes to those people who were lucky enough to attend, and to teach them the barbecue basics like smoking meat, fire grilling, and low and slow cooking. After the cooking class, attendees could eat the food, and both PR and social media communications were used to amplify the event. The event firmly established Fire & Smoke on the market and enhanced the credibility and trustworthiness of the brand, proving it to be a product with 'cracking flavour' in a food category that was lacking in excitement.

Brand Beneficence

Brand beneficence is concerned with examining whether or not the brand serves the customer and society in a positive way. A brand with high levels of beneficence needs to shape its offering to minimise the personal or societal ill-effects of their brand and to maximise its positive contributions. The Covid-19 pandemic has brought this concept closer to the consumer's mind in recent times. For example, a study by marketing firm Edelman (2019) has found that consumers are disinclined to support a brand if there is a sense that the brand values profit over people. Lack of compassion – entailed in a marketing message or through other actions – has acted as a prompt for some consumers to speak negatively of that brand. The examples below typify the concept of brand beneficence and its value.

Making a minute for positivity

Dairygold butter is a truly international brand, exporting from Ireland to over 50 countries. Keen to emphasise the beneficence of a brand that has been on the market for 30 years, an experiential roadtrip was designed where good deeds and micro volunteering were encouraged and promoted. A Citroen van was branded up as a 'Roller Toaster' and travelled around giving people tasty treats featuring the Dairygold butter product. In addition, the 'Make A Minute for the Good Stuff' campaign was promoted. The idea behind the campaign was that because Dairygold butter spreads straight from the fridge, the consumer gains an extra minute to do something else. So the brand encourages

(Continued)

people to use that minute to do something good and positive, such as phoning your mom or giving your husband a hug before you go out to work. Essentially, the consumer is encouraged to give that minute to someone who needs it, because research tells us that when you do good for someone, you feel good. Building on this theme, the brand also wanted to reward people who were giving their extra minutes to help someone else. Lots of different charitable organisations were visited, the people in them were treated to some tasty food bites, and the work of the charities was promoted and amplified online. The brand used the experiential roadtrip to elevate awareness of the 'Make A Minute' campaign, to bring it to life, making it mean something and, in addition, giving something back through the treats given to attendees of the road trip pitstops.

Remember, one goal of this book is to ensure that practitioners can better implement experiential strategies as integrated aspects of their activities. The approaches taken by various organisations have been presented and outlined above. The next section will explore how marketers can design experiences that connect with more traditional brand management approaches, and will use a new construct – the Timeline of Campaign – to structure this discussion.

HOW TO DESIGN EXPERIENCES THAT CONNECT WITH MORE TRADITIONAL BRAND MANAGEMENT AND COMMUNICATION STRATEGIES[1]

The use of experiential marketing should be strategically managed and timed in the development of a brand plan, so that its rewards can be maximised. Importantly, and as stated by Smilansky (2009), experiential marketing should not be used in isolation, but rather should be a fully integrated part of a brand management plan. Experiential marketing should not be used without the support of traditional marketing activities. This is primarily due to the fact that experiential marketing alone does not have the ability to communicate key messages in a controlled manner; it is the job of more traditional brand communication strategies to do this. Figure 5.3 presents a timeline for the use of experiential marketing in the context of traditional brand approaches that allows for the confluence of experiential and traditional mechanisms to be better planned and integrated.

Step 1: Targeted Traditional Marketing

Based on extensive research with some major international brands, it is our contention that before an experiential marketing campaign is launched, it is essential to first

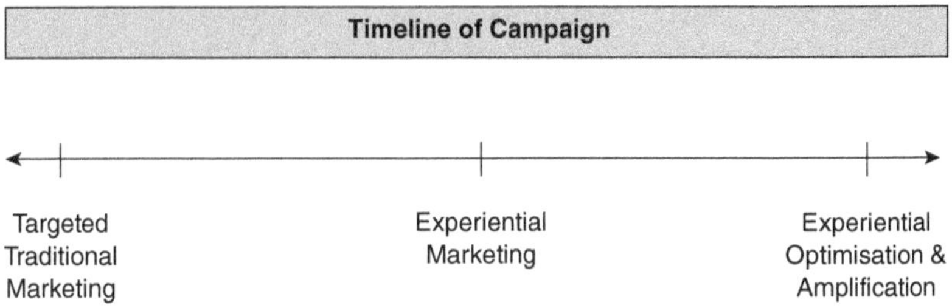

Figure 5.3 Timeline of Campaign

conduct a targeted, more traditional marketing activity in order to build brand awareness and identity. Traditional marketing, by nature, offers marketers mass reach due to its widespread scale (Peppers & Rogers, 1995). When building brand awareness and identity, the following communications tools are long regarded as pivotal:

- Print media
- Out of home advertising
- Radio and television broadcast
- Digital marketing
- Email marketing
- Direct mail
- Sponsorship

Endorsing the utilisation of traditional mass marketing activities when managing a brand, Sharp (2010: 39) states that 'smart marketers know they need to reach all buyers (i.e. buyers of the category, and everyone from light to heavy buyers of a brand) in order to reinforce buying propensities, and to win new sales'. The intent of traditional marketing being positioned first in this triad of activities, as presented in Figure 5.3, lies with the premise that (a) it is controllable by the brand, (b) it can ensure campaign amplification, and (c) it builds relevant memory structures for the mass audience. The advantage of using traditional marketing methods lies in the fact that the content can always be *polished*, and be designed to be *100% on brand throughout*, and should explain the brand's values and what the brand stands for. Essentially, it is in a brand's best interest to build a clear foundation through traditional brand building methods so that when experiential marketing is employed, the target market is already aware of the brand. We argue in this book that experiential marketing should not be utilised unless a brand has a healthy level of brand penetration and consumers are aware of the brand they are interacting with. In this way, consumers develop a deeper understanding of the brand due to their immersion in the brand's values and the Brand Manager is less likely to misuse an opportunity. It is our contention that experiential marketing will only be successful if the brand infrastructure and key messaging have already been established and disseminated through traditional wide reaching brand messaging approaches. Once the initial stage of brand messaging has been completed,

brands then have the ability, through the use of experiential marketing, to give the campaign a new dimension through two-way communication. Some quotations from our research illustrate this really well:

> So, I think in terms of a new brand campaign, I would probably take the direction still of traditional marketing tools, but I see opportunity in the next stage of execution of that campaign being experiential. I suppose experiential gives you the opportunity to flesh out and engage with your audience at a closer proximity than TV or outdoor ever do. But, for a new campaign, I still think that you need TV or outdoor for everyone to see it and that is important for awareness. To further get your key messages out there, what you can do from an experiential point of view is really engage with people and have fun with it to get more cut through. I think what experiential marketing does is it gets cut through and that is so important in the FMCG market when there is so much going on and it is really competitive.
>
> But then how do you drive that to get the maximum benefit around the subtle messages that are difficult to communicate and elaborate on with above-the-line media like TV, radio, or outdoor or any of those traditional media, that is where the experience comes in similar to digital. You can expand on these subtle messages. So, for example, we use our "simply made" messaging in the ad but that is not enough to explain it. So, the experiential side of it, along with social and digital gives us the opportunity to expand on that messaging and really help consumers to understand and make it compelling for them.
>
> (Marketing Manager in an FMCG company)

Step 2: Experiential Marketing[2]

Experiential marketing affords a brand the opportunity to expand on a core message to help consumers understand what the brand's essence is. It also aids the product being seen as more relevant to customers on a personal level as they build their own relationship with it through staged activations. In this stage, authentic two-way interactions are created through experiential marketing initiatives that bring the brand's memory structures, narratives and cues to life, offering the consumer the opportunity to make them personally relevant in their lives. This cannot be achieved in the first stage of this process as there is no authentic and personalised interaction with the customer base; that is why it is essential to always use mass marketing and experiential marketing sequentially and to use each of these communications tools to their strengths.

Step 3: Experiential Optimisation and Amplification[3]

After the experiential marketing activation has occurred, brands must ensure that the marketing activation transcends the physical barriers of the experience, and allow it to live on a greater platform, be that online or offline, to ensure an efficient

and effective return on the investment. This can be achieved through two mechanisms: experiential amplification and experiential optimisation. Experiential amplification requires capturing content created during the experience and sharing it on social media platforms so that people do not have to be physically at the experience to immerse themselves in the activation. It typically comes in the form of videos, pictures or user-generated content and leverages the potential of social media and word-of-mouth publicity. Experiential optimisation requires capturing this content and repurposing it, using it for further marketing intentions. For example, brands taking a long-form video and creating a series of shorter videos or using user-generated content to create content for their own social media platforms. Two prevalent mechanisms for amplification of experiential activities are:

1. An experiential activation for a small number of people that is amplified extensively.
2. A mass marketing experiential activation where a brand interacts with as many consumers as possible.

In summary, in this section we have proposed that for experiential marketing to be successful, the brand infrastructure and key messaging must already have been established and disseminated. It is advised to only use experiential marketing when the brand has a healthy level of brand penetration and when consumers have a clear understanding of the brand's values. Following this, brand management must ensure that the experience is optimised and amplified to maximise the benefits to the brand.

Optimising Coca-Cola

Coca-Cola's iconic 'Share A Coke' campaign benefited from applying this approach. One of the most recognised components of this campaign was that Coca-Cola changed the artwork on their bottle from simply saying 'Coca Cola' to saying 'Share a Coke with' and replaced the traditionally recognisable 'Coca-Cola' script with popular names. But if your name was not available, they also held experiential activations in the form of pop-up events globally where you could customise your own personal bottle of Coca-Cola. However, in order to build awareness and generate demand for these pop-up events, the brand utilised traditional advertising by displaying pre-emptive messaging on out of home advertising, print media and through a targeted digital campaign. Additionally, besides alerting customers to attend their 'Share A Coke' pop-ups, they carried out top-line brand-building marketing campaigns that were activated prior to and during the experiential mechanism as consumers could conveniently pick up a bottle of Coca Cola in retail outlets which had popular names on them in the Coca Cola trademark font. At each of the 'Share A Coke' pop-ups, content was captured by their team and shared across the brand's social media channels, not only to build hype around the concept, but also to further build brand sentiment, brand recall and excitement among their customer base.

THE IMPORTANCE OF MEMORY STRUCTURES AND RECALL WHEN IMPLEMENTING EXPERIENTIAL MARKETING

Bryon Sharp (2010) tells us that 'memory structures' are the collection of mental associations we have in our minds about a brand name, which are developed and refreshed over time through experiences such as buying and using the brand, being exposed to its marketing and hearing about it from other people. The more extensive, fresh, coherent and emotionally positive a brand's 'memory structures' are, the more likely it is to get noticed or thought about in buying situations. Therefore, it is imperative for marketers to understand that each customer must be interacted with strategically at an individual level. It is here that experiential marketing is invaluable.

As brands treat customer interactions as a bespoke and individual encounter, it is also important to note that the development of each brand memory structure in the brain happens in a way that is not only unique to that experience, but also to that person's perception of the encounter (Greenfield, 2000). Over time, these experiences are stored in a customer's memory and should form a lasting impact on their customer satisfaction and brand loyalty (Oliver, 1997; Reicheld, 1997). This, as we explored in Chapter 4, is important in developing brand–customer relationships. The stronger the relationship, the greater the brand loyalty and the easier the brand memory structures are to recall (Beardi, 2000; Romaniuk & Sharp, 2016; Sharp, 2010).

Effective experiential marketing management requires brands to continuously design cues to conjure joy and interest in customers (Haeckel et al., 2003). The challenge lies in cultivating strong emotional connections and cues, which in turn leads to the development of positive brand memory structures (Romaniuk & Sharp, 2016; Sharp, 2010), positive word of mouth both online and offline (Batat, 2019) and, in turn, consumer collectives (Kozinets, Hemetsberger, & Schau, 2008; Närvänen et al., 2013). For a brand to successfully generate brand meaning through experiences, it is vital that brands stimulate memories and stories in customers' minds, instil a longing for community and communicate a message that resonates with customers (Brown et al., 2003). For a brand to be successful when activating a campaign, it is imperative that they earnestly co-create brand meaning through experiential marketing activations with their customers by establishing customer-centric brand strategies (Berthon et al., 2009). For commodities to evolve to brands, and brands to be relevant in consumers' lives, it is essential for active engagement and interaction to be present. The staging of experiential marketing activations affords brands the opportunity to build authentic interactions with customers, thus enriching the customers' relationship with the brand.

Structuring the Lego memory

Lego is an iconic brand that has captured the attention of children and adults alike. Although one could argue that the brand is already established with memory structures instilled in the minds of their customer base, there are certain occasions where these memory structures need to be refreshed and strengthened, for example at Christmas. Christmas is a cluttered time of the year for advertisers looking to build brand awareness as brands compete to ensure that their creative and brand narratives are unique enough to grasp the attention of the consumer. A key concern that Lego identified was that parents often get overwhelmed and anxious looking for activities to entertain their children over the festivities, while they complete their Christmas shopping. Lego's 'Build Your Own Adventure' experiential marketing activation was devised in order to engage shoppers and their children in the East Gate Shopping Mall in Johannesburg and the Gateway centre in Durban, South Africa. Lego created a play zone that included a mini Lego theatre, Lego pits and Lego Duplo areas for younger fans of the brand. They also created a Lego maze that shoppers could go through. Each component of this activation was accompanied with educational activities, competitions and prizes. The memory structures that derived from this activation were twofold:

1. Parents were delighted that Lego eased their anxiety around entertaining their children while they shopped.
2. The children built strong memory structures with the brand, leading to an uplift in sales as children added the brand's products to their Christmas lists.

As is evident from the Lego example, using experiential marketing to build positive memory structures is an essential part of brand management. Building on these positive memories to develop memory recall, or indeed brand salience, is the next step. The concept of salience is typically associated with the ability of a brand, product, service or item to stand out from its environment, its category and competitors (Guido, 1998). Brand salience is referred to as 'the propensity of the brand to be thought of in buying situations. This is reflected in the quantity (how many) and the quality (how fresh and relevant) of the network of brand information in memory, or the brand's "share of mind"' (Romaniuk & Sharp, 2004: 334). Having multiple cues to which a brand is linked increases the likelihood that the customer will interact with the brand in a buying situation. Thus, the brand will have a greater propensity to come to mind and be a purchase option (Romaniuk & Sharp, 2004). In this way, experiential activation aids the development of brand salience, which in turn will contribute to the development of brand loyalty. In essence, experiential marketing:

- Allows the consumer to reduce the risk of purchase.
- Allows the brand to conduct market research.
- Allows consumers to build memory structures and develop brand recall.

Captain Birdseye

Captain Birdseye is the mascot for the frozen Birds Eye food brand. Using the Captain Birdseye image in its communication strategies is a key part of building brand memory structures and recall. For decades, Captain Birdseye has delighted and charmed customers in the target market. From an experiential marketing perspective, when Captain Birdseye hosts an experiential activation, then immediately all those memory structures that customers have in terms of the recognisability of the brand and the distinctiveness of the brand are tapped into and reinforced. In this way, the experiential campaign has close affinities to the memory structures that have previously been built through past strategy, marketing campaigns and brand activations. As stated by Sharp (2010: 132), 'It is only when there is discipline in this consistency that distinctive brand assets build'.

In the modern marketplace, experiential marketing has emerged as a way of creating authentic interactions with target markets that affords two-way communication and enables brand–consumer relationships to be cultivated.

Maxing the challenge for brand recall

Pepsi Max has run its 'Taste Challenge' over the lifespan of the brand. The Taste Challenge asks consumers to taste the product alongside competing cola brands and to choose their favourite. When running this campaign, the marketing team will endeavour to tap into existing brand memory structures, established through traditional mass marketing, through the use of imagery on digital screens, point-of-sale materials, etc. Making the connection with consumers by evoking positive memory structures is fundamental. Activations of this nature allow the customers who experience them to have unique interactions with a brand and to develop their own brand meaning. This increases the possibility of enhanced message penetration and the creation of consumer tribes.

As you read through this chapter, it should start to become evident that the use of experiential marketing in managing a brand should positively impact on the brand equity. The last section of this chapter takes up this point.

BUILDING BRAND EQUITY THROUGH EXPERIENTIAL MARKETING

'Brand equity' is a marketing term that describes a brand's value. That value is determined by consumers' perception of, and experiences with, the brand. When people think highly of a brand, it has positive brand equity, and of course the reverse is also the case. Brand equity relates strongly to tangible and intangible value: tangibles include profit or revenue increase/decrease; intangibles are brand awareness and goodwill. Clearly, then, generating positive brand equity is important to a company, if for no other reason than it is a valuation on a company's balance sheet, and thus will impact on a company's valuation and stock market price (if applicable).

A cursory glance at any branding book or article will tell you that building strong brand equity is a marketing task that begins with building brand awareness and continues with communicating brand values, building positive perceptions, trust and loyalty. Indeed, if we return to the start of this chapter, all of the steps in Kotler's Branding Conceptual Model should positively impact on brand equity. When we relate this to experiential marketing, we see that as customers encounter and interact with brands, thoughts and feelings are generated about the experience at hand. When this happens, brand memory structures develop and enrich a brand's equity (Romaniuk & Sharp, 2016; Sharp, 2010).

Weighing in on positive brand associations

In a bid to reposition the brand from a diet brand to a healthy lifestyle company, Lean Cuisine turned to experiential marketing and co-creation to aid the development of new consumer memory structures. In the campaign entitled '#WeighThis', the brand encouraged women to weigh what really mattered to them, such as their accomplishments, rather than valuing themselves by the number that was displayed on a weighing scale. To complement this narrative, an installation was erected in Grand Central Station's Vanderbilt Hall, New York, as part of the experiential component of this campaign. Here, women were asked to 'weigh what matters' and write it on the weighing scale. These scales were then hung up on a large display wall where an alternative narrative emerged, which in turn built new memory structures for not only the participants, but also for passers-by and people who watched the campaign video online. Through the development of authentic memory structures, Lean Cuisine effectively altered the brand perception and messaging.

The Lean Cuisine example illustrates how experiential marketing can be used to build brand equity through positive brand positioning and differentiation in the consumer's mind. Chapters 9 and 10 will examine more specifically how experiential marketing can result in an increase in revenue and profit for a brand.

Before concluding this chapter, we need to look at how an experiential marketing campaign can be integrated within the overall brand management plan (see Figure 5.4).

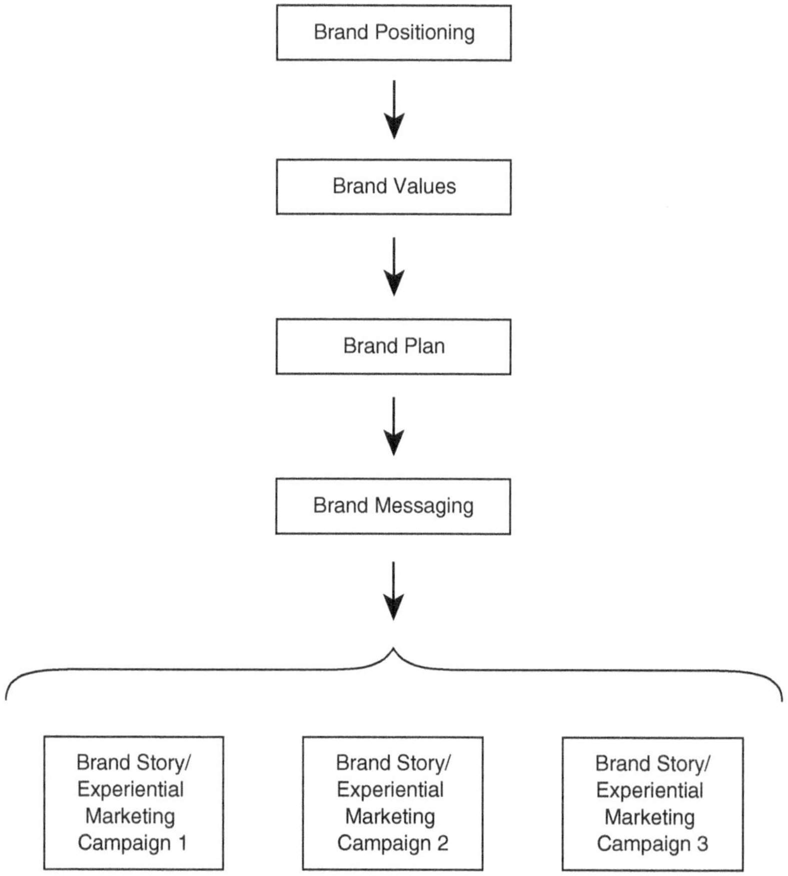

Figure 5.4 Brand planning and consistency

As depicted in Figure 5.4, a brand must have a brand positioning statement, brand values, a brand plan and documented strategic brand messaging in order to successfully activate their brand. The brand positioning statement should clearly state the desired consumer perception of the brand. The brand values refer to the beliefs of the brand or, in Kotler's (2016) terms, the brand beneficence. The brand plan and strategic messaging statement should document what needs to happen for the brand position and values to be attained. Once these marketing structures are in place, a brand can then work on generating experiential marketing campaign

narratives that tie in with the brand positioning, values, brand plan and the brand messaging. This ensures a consistent brand message and tone, therefore allowing customers to buy into the brand. It is essential that through any experiential marketing initiative, marketing professionals ensure that branding and key messaging is consistent with the core values of the brand. In this way, strong brand resonance will be built.

CONCLUSION AND SUMMARY

This chapter set out to link more closely the practice of experiential marketing with existing theories around brand management. This was our goal because experiential marketing can't be successful in isolation. It lives or dies based on how it is successfully integrated into broader marketing activities and equities. We demonstrated how a range of brands have used experiential marketing to strengthen key aspects of their brand management. For the practitioner, we have highlighted how it is clear that they must consider all aspects of brand management when designing and executing brand activities. More particularly, we have outlined a framework for experiential activities that better reflects a more nuanced approach to exploiting the impact of experiential marketing. Crucially, it links traditional marketing into the framework. We consider it important to treat experiential activities as the 'meat in the sandwich' that allows the promotion of the activity on the one side and the promotion and exploitation of its impact on the other. The next chapter looks at how we can best do that.

MAIN TAKEAWAYS FROM CHAPTER 5

- Experiential marketing creates an opportunity for marketers to create memorable experiences for consumers with the goal of differentiating the brand in an overcrowded marketplace. In this context, experiential marketing is essential in effectively managing a brand.
- Experiential marketing can be used at each and every step of the brand management process.
- In effectively managing a brand, experiential marketing needs to be integrated with more traditional brand management approaches to ensure overall consistency in brand messaging.
- Using experiential marketing to build brand infrastructures and to aid brand memory recall is an essential aspect of brand management.
- Experiential marketing, when used strategically in conjunction with traditional brand management approaches, can substantially improve the equity of the brand.

CONCLUDING QUESTIONS

1. Using examples, explain how experiential marketing can be used at each step of Kotler's conceptual model of branding.
2. Why is it important to integrate experiential marketing with traditional branding approaches when managing a brand?
3. Present and discuss a timeline for the use of experiential marketing in the context of traditional brand approaches, which can work to maximise the positive impact of any experiential marketing strategy.
4. Explain what is meant by memory structures and memory recall, and discuss their importance in the context of experiential marketing.
5. In your opinion, is experiential marketing important in the building of brand equity? Explain your answer using examples.

NOTES

1. Chapter 8 will provide a detailed framework for integrating experiential marketing with an overall communications campaign. The purpose of this section is to provide some introductory context for this.
2. This concept is explored fully throughout the book. The purpose here is to situate it in a communications timeline.
3. Chapter 6 will provide more detail on experiential optimisation and amplification. The purpose of this section is to provide some introductory context.

REFERENCES AND FURTHER READING

Batat, W. (2019). *Experiential Marketing: Consumer Behaviour, Customer Experience and the 7Es*. London: Routledge.

Beardi, C. (2000, 6 November). Revved up to Relate: FCB Finds Brand Loyalty Mirrors Interpersonal Relationships. *Advertising Age*, 71, 86.

Berthon, P.R., Pitt, L.F., & Campbell, C. (2009). Does Brand Meaning Exist in Similarity or Singularity? *Advances in Brand Management*, 62(3), 256–361.

Brown, S., Kozinets, R.V., & Sherry, J.F. (2003). Teaching Old Brands New Tricks: Retro Branding and the Revival of Brand Meaning. *Journal of Marketing*, 67(3), 19–33.

Edelman (2019). *Edelman Trust Barometer Special Report: In Brands We Trust.* [Online]. Available at: www.edelman.com/research/trust-barometer-special-report-in-brands-we-trust [accessed 16 April 2021].

Greenfield, S. (2000). *The Private Life of the Brain*. London: Allen Lane.

Guido, G. (1998). The Dichotic Theory of Salience: A Framework for Assessing Attention and Memory. *European Advances in Consumer Research*, 3(3), 114–119.

Haeckel, S.H., Carbone, L.P., & Berry, L.L. (2003). How to Lead the Customer Experience. *Journal of Marketing Management*, 12(1), 18–23.

Holbrook, M.B. (1999). *Consumer Value: A Framework for Analysis and Research*. London: Routledge.

Kotler, P. (2016). Branding: From Purpose to Beneficence. *The Marketing Journal*, 22 March. [Online]. Available at: www.marketingjournal.org/brand-purpose-to-beneficence-philip-kotler/ [accessed 27 November 2017].

Kozinets, R.V., Hemetsberger, A., & Schau, H.J. (2008). The Wisdom of Consumer Crowds Collective Innovation in the Age of Networked Marketing. *Journal of Micromarketing*, 28(4), 339–354.

McCole, P. (2004). Refocusing Marketing to Reflect Practice: The Changing Role of Marketing for Business. *Marketing Intelligence Planning*, 22(5), 531–539.

Mathwick, C., Malhotra, N., & Rigdon, E. (2001). Experiential Value: Conceptualization, Measurement, and Application in the Catalog and Internet Shopping Environment. *Journal of Retailing*, 77(1), 39–56.

Närvänen, E., Kartastenpää, E., & Kuusela, H. (2013). Online Lifestyle Consumption Community Dynamics: A Practice-based Analysis. *Journal of Consumer Behaviour*, 12(5), 358–369.

Oliver, R.L. (1997). A Cognitive Model of Antecedents and Consequences of Satisfaction Decisions. *Journal of Marketing Research*, 17(4), 460–469.

Peppers, D., & Rogers, M. (1995). A New Marketing Paradigm: Share of Customer, Not Market Share. *Managing Service Quality*, 5(3), 48–51.

Pine, B. Joseph, & Gilmore, J.H. (1999). *The Experience Economy: Work is Theatre & Every Business a Stage*. Boston, MA: Harvard Business Press.

Reicheld, F. (1997). *The Loyalty Effect: The Hidden Force behind Growth, Profits and Lasting Value*. Boston, MA: Harvard Business School Press.

Romaniuk, J., & Sharp, B. (2004). Conceptualizing and Measuring Brand Salience. *Marketing Theory*, 4(4), 327–342.

Romaniuk, J., & Sharp, B. (2016). *How Brands Grow: Part 2*. Sydney, NSW: Oxford University Press.

Schmitt, B.H. (2000). *Experiential Marketing: How to Get Customers to Sense, Feel, Think, Act, Relate to your Company and Brands*. New York: The Free Press.

Sharp, B. (2010). *How Brands Grow: What Marketers Don't Know*. New York & Oxford: Oxford University Press.

Sherry, J. (1998). The Soul of the Company Store: Nike Town Chicago and the Emplaced Brandscape. In J. Sherry (Ed.), *Servicescapes: The Concept of Place in Contemporary Markets*. Lincolnwood, IL: NTC Business Books.

Smilansky, S. (2009). *Experiential Marketing: A Practical Guide to Interactive Brand Experiences*. London: Kogan Page.

6

EXPERIENTIAL MARKETING AND DIGITAL MARKETING

CHAPTER OVERVIEW

In the previous chapter, we saw that effective management of a brand requires that the marketing activation of an experiential event must transcend the physical barriers of the experience and live on a greater platform, usually but not exclusively in an online environment. The value of the experience in and of itself has been established. We know that those who participate benefit from their exposure to the brand and that the brand, in turn, develops that elusive closer relationship with the customer. However, in a world that is increasingly digital-first, and where participation in an event is an increasingly nebulous concept, we must examine the potential that digital and social amplification allows in designing effective experiential activations. Through the unrelentingly challenge of the Covid-19 crisis, 2020 has demonstrated, in a very new way, that digital participation is an acceptable conduit – in some circumstances – for engagement in experiences. We know also that the role of digital marketing is essential in optimising and amplifying an experiential activation. More broadly, however, we will explore in this chapter the use of word-of-mouth marketing and social media to support experiential activities through the lifetime of a campaign. We will also look at some digitally-oriented experiential activations that have taken place largely as a result of the Covid-19 pandemic.

Specifically, this chapter will explore the following:

- Viral marketing and word-of-mouth marketing to support experiential activations in the context of social currency.
- Technological developments, such as virtual reality (VR) and augmented reality (AR), and the growth in popularity of the social media environment and its central role in experiential marketing.
- How to amplify an experiential marketing campaign through digital and other tools.
- The use of digital experience as a means of developing closeness with customers.

Social currency is strongly related to concepts such as word-of-mouth marketing (WOMM) and amplification. Remember, we are seeking to demonstrate how experiential marketing can be best deployed to be impactful and how we can best assess that impact. Understanding WOMM is critical to this. Social Currency is a concept that is hard to describe; it has been likened to gravity in that we feel its effects daily, but it is unclear what that looks like and is maybe difficult to put in concrete terms. It can be seen as the tendency to share (online or offline) the things that reflect well on us, either intrinsically or by association e.g. being connected with an exciting brand or funny meme might offer some element of 'coolness'.

While companies are, of course, aware of the conversation happening between the brand and consumers, they also need to consider the value generated by consumers communicating with each other through consumption collectives and exchanging brand relevant information, which falls beyond the company's control (Lobschat et al., 2013). The role of social currency in driving those conversations, in shaping behaviour and in forming attitudes is clear. For brands to successfully implement an experiential marketing activation then, it is recommended that they co-create brand meanings by actively communicating with brand communities and consumer tribes who are effectively key influencers in the success or failure of a marketing campaign's online and offline activity (Berthon et al., 2009). Understanding social currency is useful in this regard.

We also introduce the topic of digitally enabled closeness. This concept is increasingly relevant in the context of the Covid-19 pandemic and the general acceptance – for now at least – that 'experience' for marketing purposes will need to reflect stronger digital entry and access points, while also recognising the impact of how much closer brands are to consumers by virtue of their digital proximity and the nature of that proximity. Connecting the pervasiveness of digital platforms and the challenges currently faced by experiential marketing practitioners brings to the fore the potential for quite seismic change in this domain.

VIRAL MARKETING AND WORD-OF-MOUTH MARKETING

There are two driving factors behind the exponential growth of experiential marketing. First, in today's social media-oriented environment, individuals like to tell people about an occurrence in their life, and second, they have the ability to do this and to amplify their experience on various digital platforms (Perrett, 2016). These mechanisms, as they relate to experiential marketing, are not dissimilar to the general tendency for people to share the many aspects of their lives, from the mundane (what I had for breakfast) to the more exciting (a new six pack of beer). The blurring of the online world and offline world is well and truly underway. The boundaries

are highly permeable and our activities as marketers, and specifically as experiential marketers, need to reflect that. What's more, we can also take advantage of that. Combining the power of both online and offline experiences results in consumers being 'informed, networked, empowered and active' (Prahalad & Ramaswamy, 2004: 5). This can be achieved through word-of-mouth marketing (WOMM) (Kozinets et al., 2010). The potential for involvement in the event, and the consequent feelings of connection to a brand, increase through WOMM.

WOMM is the 'influence of consumer-to-consumer communications by professional marketing techniques' (Kozinets et al., 2010: 71). Trusov, Bucklin and Pauwels (2009) state that it comprises the placement of products or services to a targeted group of consumers with the aim of encouraging them to disseminate a positive message about the brand, which in turn escalates brand awareness and sales. Also referred to as 'amplified word of mouth'(Sernovitz, 2012; Kozinets et al., 2010; Liabai et al., 2010), 'viral marketing' (Hinz et al., 2011) or 'buzz marketing' (Kelly, 2007; Rosen, 2009; Hinz et al., 2011; Jaffe, 2007; Kelly, 2007; Kozinets et al., 2010; Liabai et al., 2010; Rosen, 2009; Sernovitz, 2006, 2012; Trusov et al., 2009), organisations globally are revisiting 'WOMM as a powerful marketing tool' (Sweeney et al., 2012: 237). The utilisation of WOMM in integrated marketing communication plans is becoming noted as an "influential" and "credible" marketing conduit (Lopez & Sicilia, 2014). Its utilisation has now transcended beyond its traditional use and is being employed as a communication and promotional medium.

WOMM is a naturally-arising phenomenon that has always held a role in the consumer purchasing decision process – even in the most remedial and primitive of technological eras. However, academics and scholars have recently begun to investigate the importance of consumer-generated content in online environments and its connection to the word-of-mouth process. Due to the internet's reach and ease of accessibility, WOMM has acquired a new dimension which is being utilised by marketers to amplify their brand message to larger audiences (Kozinets et al., 2014). For example, an investigation conducted by Liu (2006) identified that the measure of online WOMM interactions, positive or negative, best forecasts the success of box office movies. A multitude of other studies have examined the effects of online recommendation behaviours from customers on Amazon.com (Chevalier & Mayzlin, 2006), social networking outlets (Trusov et al., 2009), and online communities (Mathwick et al., 2008; Zhu & Zhang, 2010). Of these, only Trusov et al. (2009) explored the effects of messaging dissemination in the realm of social networks. It is accepted that being able to generate WOMM buzz around a product or service is indisputably impactful on the brand.

Viral marketing, as a strongly related concept, is considered a defining marketing trend of the decade. It plays a vital part in the success of an experiential event and its transition online through the aid of social currency (Ferguson, 2008). Social currency refers to the ways in which consumers share a brand with others, and consequently derive social benefit from those interactions (see below for more information on this concept). Bonchi et al. (2011) define viral marketing as a

process of targeting influential users, referred to as *seeds*, of a social network to induce a chain-reaction of influence to disperse a message in a timely manner. It has been demonstrated to be an effective marketing tool in social networks (Leskovec et al., 2007) and has attracted much attention in more recent research (Wang & Street, 2018). Compared to targeted traditional marketing tasks, viral marketing avoids the outlay of contacting all members of a target group. Only a small, concentrated amount of influential 'seeds' need to be triggered in order for a message to be dispersed to a vast network.

Viral marketing and WOMM have transformed the practice of marketing as marketers no longer have to rely solely on creating customer relationships through loyalty and database marketing; they now have the ability to generate interest in a brand through unique experiential marketing campaigns, videos and interactive advert-games (Serra-Cantallops et al., 2018). The defining difference between viral marketing and WOMM is one of cause and effect. Viral marketing, an activity used through the premise of experiential marketing to build awareness and buzz, is the cause. Positive WOMM, which leads to trial and acquisition, is the effect (Ferguson, 2008). Consider this in practical terms: influential or connected consumers experience a product or service and – for whatever reason – decide to highlight their consumption to others in their network. The reasons may be that they enjoyed the product or service, that its benefits were beyond that of comparable products, that they feel good being associated with the brand, or that they may have enjoyed an experience relating to the consumption. This latter reason is obviously an area of focus for marketers, but all of these reasons, and many others, relate to the merging of online and offline worlds in experiential marketing.

Fiat – Quenching Consumers' Thirst

In June 2016, Fiat implemented an experiential marketing campaign in London to utilise social currency to reach the mass market with their message. The brand aimed to communicate modern-day Italy at the launch of the new Fiat 500, which featured a fresh and bold colour palette (Benjamin, 2016). Fiat created a pop-up granita bar with the intent of quenching commuters' thirst and communicating the car's new image. The bar was situated in Old Street underground station and offered commuters ice-cold drinks in six flavours that were inspired by the new Fiat 500 model: cranberry, sour apple, pomegranate, juicy lemon, blackberry and blueberry (Deighton, 2016). To receive a granita, commuters had to participate by using their social currency. They had to take a picture of their chosen flavour and share it on Twitter, Facebook or Instagram with the hashtag #FreshNew500, and show their post at the bar to redeem and

(Continued)

collect their granita (Deighton, 2016). With 70,000 individuals passing through Old Street tube station daily, Fiat were able to amplify the message through social currency, encouraging participants to share the message online. Through social media and the hyper-reach of WOMM and viral marketing, the campaign was dispersed to a much larger audience (Benjamin, 2016).

The accessibility, reach and transparency of the modern-day internet has garnered the attention of marketers and marketing researchers. They aim to influence and monitor WOMM through a global online platform, as social media enables companies to communicate with their customers while also allowing those customers to talk to one another (Kozinets et al., 2010; Mangold & Faulds, 2009). By employing WOMM tactics when implementing an experiential activation, it allows the marketing effort to transcend beyond a planned experiential event itself to increase the potential reach on social media platforms, therefore, supercharging the experience (Agency EA, 2019; Perrett, 2016). By one participant sharing a message, image or video from the event, the experiential campaign has the potential to reach more people than those directly involved. Where those not directly involved likewise act to share, we see the concept of virality at play. Through social media, brands have the ability to multiply an experience that was directed at hundreds of people to millions of others through online platforms (Smith & Hanover, 2016). These interactions are referred to as a brand's social or experiential currency.

Virality and social currency are strongly related to tightly bonded brand communities. We have explained the importance of brand communities in Chapter 4. Here we see how the use of experiential marketing and WOMM further enables the establishment of brand communities. The bonds that develop among the community further strengthens the consumer–brand relationship and are essential in creating value for all involved.

Walkers tweet to eat

When implementing their iconic 'Do Us A Flavour' campaign, the Walkers marketing team noticed that in campaign analysis they were under performing (under indexing) on the 16–34-year-old demographic. This was due to the fact that their campaign relied heavily on television adverts and this cohort were light TV viewers, while being heavy users of social media. Typically, they were technology *aficionados* and enjoyed being engaged by new experiences. Tasked with creating an engaging out of home campaign that appealed to this audience, their agency partner transformed three London bus shelter panels into digital, tweet-activated interactive vending machines. People viewing the digital

screens would see vignettes of Gary Lineker, the TV celebrity associated with the Walkers brand, who appeared to be sitting inside the panel. Consumers could interrupt 'Gary' from his everyday tasks and interact with him via a tweet by using a uniquely generated hashtag. On doing this, 'Gary' dispensed a packet of crisps from the panel to the participant in real time. During the campaign, 500 packets of crisps were dispensed and 5.7 million Twitter impressions were generated, up 200% on the previous two weeks. As a result, Walkers saw a 22% increase in positive brand sentiment.

The velocity of consumer-to-consumer interactions has increased over recent years due to the prevalence of digital communications and the popularity of social media platforms (Bugshan, 2014; Franklin et al., 2014; Miller et al., 2009). As a result, consumers readily have the ability to gather and disseminate information about brands openly and instantly within their social network (Trudeau & Shobeiri, 2016). Interactions in online social networks provide consumers with the opportunity to share brand-related information and aid them in gaining an in-depth understanding of the brand's value. Multiple studies have shown online brand-related forums, which are typically formed by consumer collectives, positively affect consumers' impressions of brands (Adjei, Noble, & Noble, 2010; Marzocchi, Morandin, & Bergami, 2013; Scarpi, 2010). It is here that the link between experiential marketing and WOMM becomes clearer. The WOMM generated among and outside the brand community enables the original experiential event to continue to live on an online platform, enabling amplification at a level that marketers could only have dreamt about in the past (Howe, 2008; Lehdonvirta, 2013; Mercurio, 2016).

It should now be apparent that for an experiential event to reach the mass market, elements of its strategy must be executed through the medium of social, exploiting social currency and WOMM, and thus expanding the brand effect and reach of an experiential event. By designing for these elements, marketers are well placed to produce events that reach beyond those that directly participate.

DIGITAL EXPERIENCE: BRINGING CONSUMERS TO EXPERIENCES IN NEW WAYS

The Covid-19 pandemic has forced experiential marketing practitioners to review their actions and activities as never before. Experiential marketing has always been a mainly 'out of home' activity. Those working in the area could comfortably fall into despair at the prospect of this particular marketing practice becoming defunct or unusable during the pandemic. On the other hand, perhaps the

current tumult presents marketers with the opportunity to reflect on how to innovate their field. We suggest that there are a range of factors that can be considered in the design of experiential events that until now have been sidelined because of lack of urgency:

- Good marketers know more about their customers than ever before. Marketers in many areas have exploited this knowledge. However, experiential marketers could be considered to be lagging in this respect. How can they bring their customers into experiential events with their digital knowledge of them? Can they use their knowledge to lead them to experiences that occur 'at home'?
- The willingness of consumers to participate in various types of online events has increased because of the pandemic. Experiential marketers no longer need to hesitate in instigating online experiential activities. Work needs to be done to design meaningful experiences that replicate (or exceed) the expectations of consumers who are now more open to digital activation and participation. People have sung, danced, learned, shared meals, comforted loved ones and carried out all manner of work activities online. Is it still reasonable to argue that online experiences remain elusive?
- The technological conduits are extremely pervasive. Smartphones and tablets present a key to opening doors into online and hybrid experiences that can be rich and entertaining. What can marketers do to more fully embrace the technological developments that are now in the hands (literally) of consumers?

We offer the term '**digitally enabled closeness**' as a concept for framing a new way of thinking about the consumers that marketers seek to target for experiential events. Technology has brought us closer to them, has allowed us to know more about them and, at the same time, allows us to connect with them in a meaningful way.

The popularity of social media, the ubiquity of connected devices and the sense of adventure of marketers has led to an increase in the use of experiential marketing. This phenomenon is also aided by other technological advances. According to the *Brand Experience Report 2016* (Arrigo et al., 2016), virtual reality (VR) will be a popular method of hosting digitally led experiential marketing activations. With the increased availability of 360-degree video cameras, the ability to create engaging content for a wider audience is a growing opportunity (Arrigo et al., 2016). Another avenue of opportunity highlighted in the report is augmented reality (AR). Augmented reality has the ability to add an incremental layer onto the real-word experience via an AR device (which may be a phone, tablet or through some other projection device) and allows the user to decide how involved they want to be in the activity (Event Marketing Institute, 2015; Zaveri & Amin, 2019). Smartphone adoption is at an all-time high, and this alone allows access to consumers with unprecedented simplicity. As marketers, when we consider digitally enabled closeness, we open up significant opportunities for marketing experiences.

Boursin and virtual reality

Boursin, a soft cheese brand, provides us with an example of how to integrate experiential marketing and technology. They utilised virtual reality and a custom-made 360° CGI film in a bid to fully immerse consumers in a contemporary brand experience. Despite having relatively high levels of brand awareness in the UK, Boursin discovered that awareness of its flavours and formats was not at satisfactory levels. The brand embarked on a journey to engage a new generation of fans, and therefore increase Boursin's importance in consumers' everyday lives, while maintaining its luxury status.

They created 'The Boursin Sensorium', which used Oculus Rift VR headsets and CGI animation, combined with a soundtrack, moving chairs, cool air, scented fans and product samples. It was launched at Westfield Shopping Centre in London, and was followed by a roadshow to county shows and regional food festivals, with a team of brand ambassadors dressed as French waiters. The reaction of all those who participated in the VR experience was filmed in a six-second clip that the participant could share across social media platforms using the hashtag #BoursinSensorium. The live experience was publicised by lifestyle influencers and food bloggers and targeted digital activity. To further utilise the impact of social currency, Boursin erected a photo-booth to capture photos of participants inside a fridge surrounded by Boursin products.

In the six Boursin Sensorium roadshow events, 5,097 consumers participated in the immersive activity, 86,298 samples were consumed by consumers and footage of the event was viewed on Facebook over 450,000 times. Prior to the event, 19% of consumers bought from the brand on a regular basis. Two months later, this figure had increased to 36%. As a result of this experiential campaign, brand awareness grew from 93% to 98%.

In writing this book, we have undertaken in-depth, extensive research with some highly significant international brands. A specific theme that was explored was the use of technology in experiential activations. From our research, we see a surprising perspective among practitioners regarding the utilisation of technology in experiential marketing activity. The use of augmented reality (AR) was predicted to increase in utilisation levels as it adds an incremental layer onto real-world experiences and allows a participant to decide how involved they want to be in an experiential activation (Arrigo et al., 2016; Event Marketing Institute, 2015; Zaveri & Amin, 2019). This observation was not prevalent in the interviews that we conducted with the industry professionals. In fact, there are two predominant barriers which impede the utilisation of AR.

First, a key barrier to utilisation of AR is the cost to implement it. For augmented reality to be employed as a component of an experiential activation, substantial investment is required. This investment is twofold: there is the initial investment

in the AR technology and also in the additional cost of amplification when it is not a shared experience but an individual experience.

Another key barrier, which is pertinent to FMCG food and beverage brands, is that by creating the experience virtually it removes the taste element of the experience. For food and beverage brands, this proves to be a key obstacle when the core premise of them employing experiential marketing is to appeal to the senses.

SOCIAL MEDIA AND STRATEGIC AMPLIFICATION

The core functionality of the experiential marketing approach is that the live brand experience is centred on two-way communication occurring in real time, therefore establishing a profound consumer bonding process (Kailani & Ciobotar, 2015). Considering that experiential marketing results in a personal experience, there is a clear relationship and dependency on digital marketing and WOMM (Barry et al., 2019; Prahalad & Ramaswamy, 2004) in order for a larger potential to be realised. Due to social media's innate ability to reach the mass market, WOMM is now supported by new platforms and channels and we have quickly seen it being used purposefully by brands to amplify their brand marketing message and expand the reach of an experiential activation (Kozinets et al., 2014).

As we discussed in Chapter 5, the experience must be followed by an optimisation and amplification strategy using digital marketing to reach a mass audience. Here we outline how this amplifcation process must occur over three distinct time periods, as identified by O'Dell (2001): before, during and after the experience. We propose that each of these time periods must have its own specific objectives. By strategically adopting a time-phased approach, marketers have the opportunity to ensure that the message is effectively amplified to the mass market.

Planning for the *before* phase is essential as the volume of attendance at the experiential event is closely linked to how it is activated during this *before* phase. Marketers call this *pre-seeding*. Utilising social media in the *before* phase allows a brand to communicate with their target market, ensuring that there is no wasted media spend on individuals who do not identify with the brand or do not fall into the target market. It is also important that the *before* phase is utilised to generate interest and conversation.

In the second phase of experiential amplification, brands are required to use social media platforms to ensure that the experience does not merely exist in the moment, but can be experienced remotely or even after the event, for example by making a video of it to be amplified later. However, this is the phase that brands typically find the most challenging due to the fact that they cannot actively control it – with event management and logistical challenges at play. In this *during* phase, brands will have to rely on event participants to amplify the event. In order to encourage this participation, a *hook* needs to be created, something on the day that encourages event participants to amplify the event.

Not all brands are necessarily actively promoting their event while it is live, so in order for content to be created, it is important to ensure that the activation is still being captured as video/pictures for social media. The content created and disseminated in this phase can effectively be employed in the *after* phase. Although the event itself is where the content is created, it is after the event where the content is most useful and where it tends to have the most impact on the reach of the event. During the *after* phase, the content showcasing the experiential event can be amplified, typically in the form of a video. When shared on social media, this allows the activation to transcend the physical barriers of the offline event and it can be shared with the mass audience. During this phase it is also important for brands to interact with the event participants who engaged with the brand on social media, particularly through social currency mechanisms. Table 6.1 summarises the objectives of the time-phased approach, as presented here.

Table 6.1 Objectives of a time-phased approach when amplifying an experiential marketing activation

Before	During	After
• Pre-seed content	• Transcend the physical barriers of experiential event marketing	• Sum up the event
• Advertise the upcoming event to a targeted audience	• Crowdsource content	• Promote future events
	• Adopt social currency	• Interact with individuals who participated

To summarise, for a brand to capitalise on an experiential marketing event it is best to apply the three-pronged time-phased approach (see Table 6.1). This ensures that the activation transcends the physical barriers of the event and reaches a mass audience. In this way, marketers acknowledge that implementing an experiential marketing activation does not simply occur in the moment, but will require effective marketing practitioners to manage the experience long after it has concluded as a physical entity. The strategic implementation of experiential marketing must be considered, and brands must capitalise on every opportunity in the *during* phase by creating content to fuel the *after* phase, ensuring its success. Also, investing time in the *during* phase to amplify the *after* phase optimises the return on investment (ROI) of the experiential marketing activity. The following section further expands on the time-phased approach, discussing the critical success factors of this amplification strategy.

CRITICAL SUCCESS FACTORS OF THE AMPLIFICATION STRATEGY

Smilansky (2009) identified that brands should utilise digital media, public relations (PR), advertising and live broadcasts in order to amplify an activation to reach

the mass audience. Although advertising and live broadcasts are still relevant to modern marketing practice, they can be costly amplification tools and, as a result, are not often used by brands. In this book, we propose that Smilansky's (2009) offering should be updated to include four critical success factors (CSFs), which are necessary for the amplification process. These CSFs are:

- Digital
- PR
- Media partnerships
- Influencer marketing

In order for a brand to effectively amplify an experiential event to the mass audience, multiple media streams must be utilised. Although this can prove costly, the combined potential reach of these media streams allows the activation to reach the mass audience, which in turn contributes positively to the overall financial return. Digital and PR are two factors which have the potential to amplify the experiential event in this way.

Although digital and PR can be viewed as mass marketing amplification tools that have traditionally been used to amplify marketing messages, the second two critical success factors – media partnerships and influencer marketing – allow brands to specifically target certain audiences. Media partnerships offer brands another opportunity to partner with media platforms to leverage their audiences and further expand their reach into specific demographics (i.e. more of their targeted demographic), extend their range of demographics (i.e. reach people not previously considered worthy of targeting) and psychographics (reach people based on their common activities, interests and opinions). Influencer marketing has been developed as an extension of WOMM, where brands interact with consumers through the medium of influencers who have a large number of followers on social media platforms (Khamis et al., 2017). Although the concept of influencers may not be unfamiliar because brands have worked with celebrities to advertise and/or endorse products for many years, influencers differ because they are regular social media users who have amassed a large social media following by posting content that is deemed to be credible, authentic and of interest to a specific audience. Through their large social following, influencers have the ability to amplify marketing messages and experiential events to their audience, contributing to interactions with the mass audience. The authenticity and perceived 'realness' of influencers cultivates a deeper bond with audiences, which can lead to a higher intention to purchase the endorsed products than happens with traditional advertising with celebrities, as consumers feel that they identify with influencers on a more intimate level (Tran & Strutton, 2014).

Drawing together what we have learned so far in this chapter, Figure 6.1 presents what we call the time-phased amplification approach. Here we combine the critical success factors for amplification with the time-phased approach and in this way present a structure for successful and strategic amplification.

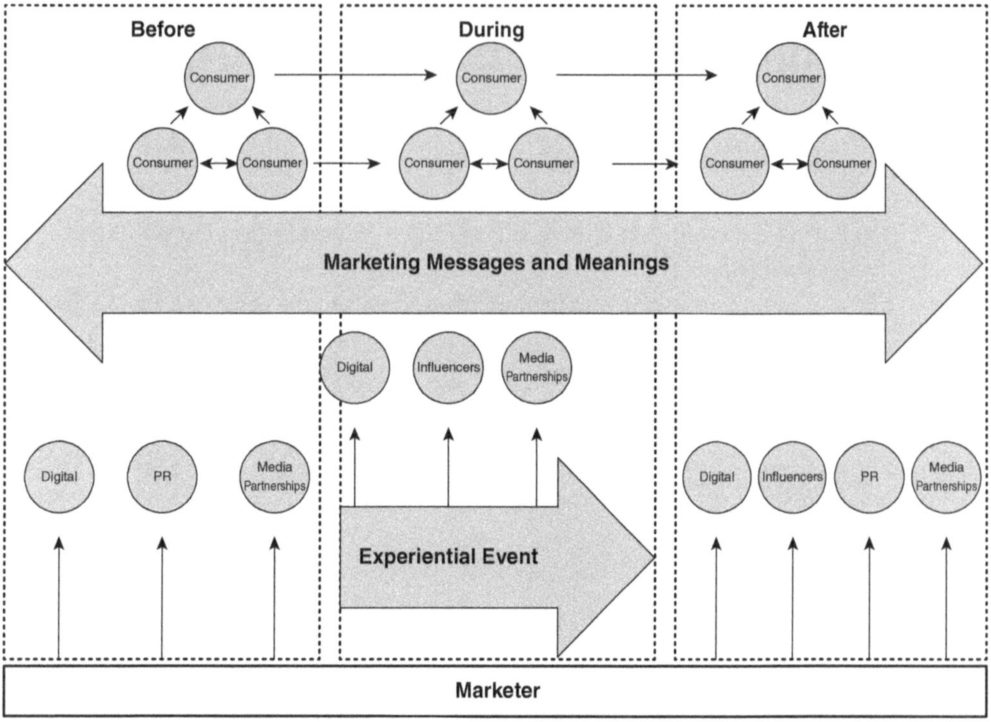

Figure 6.1 Time-phased amplification approach

CONCLUSION AND SUMMARY

Experiential marketing and digital technologies are inextricably linked. We have shown that technology is not only a conduit to the promotion of and participation in experiential activations, but also a means to amplify the messaging and impacts of these activations to targeted and mass audiences. The promotion of experiential activities is a key part of their intended success and it is clear that web-based marketing underpins that strongly. Participation in experiences can be assisted and enriched by technologies such as augmented and virtual reality. Equally, there are business and technological impediments to these technologies being fully utilised and deployed. The amplification of experiences requires a considered, time-phased approach to maximise the potential reach of the activation. There are various critical success factors which assist in this.

The key conclusion is that the amplification of experiential activations needs to be planned for and subsequently, assessed against that plan. The time-phased amplification approach provides a structured mechanism to better plan and assess activations and their impact.

MAIN TAKEAWAYS FROM CHAPTER 6

- Experiential marketing is more effective when there is a conscious effort to ensure that amplification through digital and WOMM is factored into its design.
- Amplification strategies require forethought and planning and a time-phased approach allows for increased success.
- The time-phased amplification approach can be used to ensure that various marketing tools, techniques and strategies can be designed and implemented to support the experiential activation.

CONCLUDING QUESTIONS

1. What are the current impediments to technological adoption in supporting experiential events?
2. Explain the potential impact of the Covid-19 pandemic on increasing the use of AR and VR in experiential activations.
3. Evaluate the impact of a time-phased approach to messaging and amplification of experiential events in a business-to-business context.
4. Discuss the role of PR as a mechanism in the amplification of experiential activations.
5. Compare and contrast the relevance of digitally enabled closeness during the Covid-19 pandemic and in a post-pandemic world.
6. In your opinion, is the concept of WOMM in danger of losing relevance and impact due to digital fatigue?

REFERENCES AND FURTHER READING

Adjei, M.T., Noble, S.M., & Noble, C.H. (2010). The Influence of C2C Communications in Online Brand Communities on Customer Purchase Behaviours. *Journal of Academy of Marketing Science*, 38(5), 634–653.

Agency EA (2019). *The State of Experiential: A Research Study 2020*. London: Agency EA.

Algesheimer, R., Dholakia, U.M., & Herrmann, A. (2005). The Social Influence of Brand Community: Evidence from European Car Clubs. *Journal of Marketing*, 69(3), 19–34.

Arrigo, Y., Gyton, G., Benjamin, K., & Carter, B. (2016). *Brand Experience Report 2016*. London: Haymarket Media Group.

Barry, H., Leahy, R., & Fenton, P. (2019). *A Strategic Approach to Amplifying an Experiential Event Using Social Currency to Reach a Mass Audience*. Paper presented at the Academy of Marketing Annual Conference, London.

Benjamin, K. (2016). Fiat Hosts Granita Bar to Mark Launch a New Fiat 500 Model. *Event Magazine*. [Online]. Available at: www.eventmagazine.co.uk/fiat-hosts-granita-bar-mark-launch-new-fiat-500-model/brands/article/1397338 [accessed 12 July 2017].

Berthon, P.R., Pitt, L.F., & Campbell, C. (2009). Does Brand Meaning Exist in Similarity or Singularity? *Advances in Brand Management*, 62(3), 256–361.

Bonchi, F., Castillo, C., Gionis, A., & Jaimes, A. (2011). Social Network Analysis and Mining for Business Applications. *ACM Transactions on Intelligent Systems and Technology (TIST)*, 2(3), 1–37.

Bugshan, H. (2014). Co-innovation: The Role of Online Communities. *Journal of Strategic Marketing*, 23(2), 1–12.

Burmann, C. (2010). A Call for 'User-Generated Branding'. *Journal of Brand Management*, 18, 1–4.

Chevalier, J., & Mayzlin, D. (2006). The Effect of Word of Mouth on Sales: Online Book Reviews. *Journal of Marketing Research*, 43(3), 345–354.

Davis, J.A. (1970). Clustering and Hierarchy in Interpersonal Relations: Testing Two Graph Theoretical Models on 742 Sociomatrices. *American Sociological Review*, 35(5), 843–851.

Deighton, K. (2016). Fiat Looks to Find the Right 'Balance of Italian' in its Marketing with Pop-up Underground Granita Bar. *The Drum* [Online]. Available at: www.thedrum.com/news/2016/06/10/fiat-looks-find-right-balance-italian-its-marketing-pop-underground-granita-bar [accessed 12 July 2017].

Emerson, R. (1976). Social Exchange Theory. *Annual Review of Sociology*, 2(1), 335–362.

Event Marketing Institute (2015). *Event Track 2015* (No. 4). Norwolk, CT: Event Marketing Institute.

Ferguson, R. (2008). Word of Mouth and Viral Marketing: Taking the Temperature of the Hottest Trends in Marketing. *Journal of Consumer Marketing*, 25(3), 179–182.

Franklin, J., Mainelli, M., & Pay, R. (2014). Measuring the Value of Online Communities. *Journal of Business Strategy*, 35(1), 29–42.

Godes, D., & Mayzlin, D. (2004). Using Online Conversations to Study Word-of-mouth Communication. *Marketing Science*, 23(4), 545–560.

Groeger, L., & Buttle, F. (2014). Word-of-Mouth Marketing Influence on Offline and Online Communications: Evidence from Case Study Research. *Journal of Marketing Communications*, 20(1/2), 21–41. https://doi.org/10.1080/13527266.2013.797736

Hardey, M. (2011). To Spin Straw into Gold? New Lessons from Consumer-generated Content. *International Journal of Research in Marketing*, 53(1), 13–15.

Hinz, O., Skiera, B., Barrot, C., & Becker, J.U. (2011). Seeding Strategies for Viral Marketing: An Empirical Comparison. *Journal of Marketing*, 75(6), 55–71.

Holland, P.W., & Leinhardt, S. (1971). Transitivity in Structural Models of Small Groups. *Comparative Group Studies*, 2(2), 107–124.

Howe, J. (2008). *Crowdsourcing: Why the Power of the Crowd is Driving the Future of Business*. New York: Crown.

Jaffe, J. (2007). *Join the Conversation: How to Engage Marketing-weary Consumers with the Power of Community, Dialogue and Partnership*. New York: John Wiley & Sons.

Kailani, C., & Ciobotar, N. (2015). Experiential Marketing: An Efficient Tool to Leverage Marketing Communication Impact on Consumer Behaviour. *International Conference on Marketing and Business Development Journal*, 1(1), 1–7.

Kasriel, D.A. (2015). Top 10 Global Consumer Trends of 2015. *Euromonitor International*. Brussels: Euromonitor.

Kelly, L. (2007). *Beyond Buzz: The Next Generation of Word-of-Mouth Marketing*. New York: AMACOM.

Khamis, S., Ang, L., & Welling, R. (2017). Self Branding, 'Micro-Celebrity' and the Rise of Social Media Influencers. *Celebrity Studies*, 88(2), 191–208.

Kozinets, R.V., de Valck, K., Wojnicki, A.C., & Wilner, S.J.S. (2010). Networked Narratives: Understanding Word-of-Mouth Marketing in Online Communities. *Journal of Marketing*, 74(March), 71–89.

Kozinets, R.V., de Valck, K., Wojnicki, A.C., & Wilner, S.J.S. (2014). Lost in Translation: The Social Shaping of Marketing Messaging. *GfK-Marketing Intelligence Review*, 6(2), 22–27. https://doi.org/10.2478/gfkmir-2014-0094

Lehdonvirta, V. (2013). A History of the Digitalization of Consumer Culture. In J. DenegriKnott and M. Molesworth (Eds.), *Digital Virtual Consumption* (pp. 18–35). New York: Routledge.

Leskovec, J., Adamic, L.A., & Huberman, B.A. (2007). The Dynamics of Viral Marketing. *ACM Transactions on Web*, 1(1).

Liabai, B., Bolton, R., Bügel, M.S., De Ruyter, K., Götz, O., Risselada, H., & Stephen, A.T. (2010). Customer-to-Customer Interactions: Broadening the Scope of Word of Mouth Research. *Journal of Service Research*, 13(3), 267–282.

Liu, Y. (2006). Word of Mouth for Movies: Its Dynamics and Impact on Box Office Revenue. *Journal of Marketing*, 70(3), 74–89.

Lobschat, L., Zinnbauer, M.A., Florian, P., & Joachimsthaler, E. (2013). Why Social Currency Becomes a Key Driver of a Firm's Brand Equity: Insights from the Automotive Industry. *Long Range Planning*, 46, 125–148.

López, M., & Sicilia, M. (2014). How to Develop WOM Marketing. In F. Liebana-Cabanillas, F. Munoz-Leiva, J. Sanchez-Fernandez, & M. Martinez-Fiestas (Eds.), *Electronic Payment Systems for Competitive Advantage in E-Commerce*. IGI Global.

Mangold, W.G., & Faulds, D.J. (2009). Social Media: The New Hybrid Element of the Promotional Mix. *Business Horizons*, 52, 357–365.

Marzocchi, G., Morandin, G., & Bergami, M. (2013). Brand Communities: Loyal to the Community or the Brand? *European Journal of Marketing*, 27(1/2), 93–114.

Mathwick, C., Wiertz, C., & De Ruyter, K. (2008). Social Capital Production in a Virtual p3 Community. *Journal of Consumer Research*, 34(6), 832–849.

Mercurio, R. (2016). *Organizational Networks for Innovations*. Barcelona: EGEA.

Miller, K.D., Fabian, F., & Lin, S.J. (2009). Strategies for Online Communities. *Strategic Management Journal*, 30(3), 305–322.

O'Dell, T. (2001). Are you Experienced? *Kulturella Perspecktiv*, 3, 27–33.

Perrett, M. (2016). Why Brands like Heineken and Innocent are Putting More Budget Behind Experiential. *Campaign Live*. [Online]. Available at: www.campaignlive.co.uk/article/why-brands-heineken-innocent-putting-budget-behind-experiential/1386987 [accessed 11 December 2016].

Prahalad, C.K., & Ramaswamy, V. (2004). Co-creation Experiences: The Next Practice in Value Creation. *Journal of Interactive Marketing*, 18(3), 5–14.

Rapoport, A. (1953). Spread of Information through a Population with Socio-Structural Bias: II. Various Models with Partial Transitivity. *Bulletin of Mathematical Biology*, 15(4), 535–546.

Rosen, E. (2009). *The Anatomy of Buzz Revisited*. New York: Doubleday Business.

Sawhney, M., Verona, G., & Prandelli, E. (2005). Collaborating to Create: The Internet as a Platform for Customer Engagement in Product Innovation. *Journal of Interactive Marketing*, 19(4), 4–17.

Scarpi, D. (2010). Does Size Matter? An Examination of Small and Large Web-based Brand Communities. *Journal of Interactive Marketing*, 24(1), 14–21.

Sernovitz, A. (2006). *Word of Mouth Marketing: How Smart Companies Get People Talking*. Chicago, IL: Kaplan Business Publishing.

Sernovitz, A. (2012). *Word of Mouth Marketing: How Smart Companies Get People Talking*. Austin, TX: Greenleaf Book Group Press.

Serra-Cantallops, A., Ramon-Cardona, J., & Salvi, F. (2018). The Impact of Positive Emotional Experiences on eWOM Generation and Loyalty. *Spanish Journal of Marketing*, 22(2), 142–162.

Simmel, G., & Wolff, K.H. (1950). *The Sociology of Georg Simmel*. New York: Simon & Schuster.

Smilansky, S. (2009). *Experiential Marketing: A Practical Guide to Interactive Brand Experiences*. London: Kogan Page.

Smith, K., & Hanover, D. (2016). *Experiential Marketing: Secrets, Strategies, and Success Stories from the World's Greatest Brands*. Hoboken, NJ: John Wiley & Sons.

Statista (2017). Number of Internet Users Worldwide from 2005 to 2017 (in millions). Statista. [Online]. Available at: www.statista.com/statistics/273018/number-of-internet-users-worldwide/ [accessed 12 April 2018].

Sweeney, J.C., Soutar, G.N., & Mazzarol, T. (2012). Word of Mouth: Measuring the Power of Individual Messages. *European Journal of Marketing*, 46(1/2), 237–257.

Tran, G.A., & Strutton, D. (2014). Has Reality Television Come of Age as a Promotional Platform? Modeling the Endorsement Effectiveness of Celebreality and Reality Stars. *Psychology & Marketing*, 31(4), 294–305.

Trudeau, S., & Shobeiri, S. (2016). Does Social Currency Matter in Creation of Enhanced Brand Experience? *Journal of Product and Brand Management*, 25(1), 98–114.

Trusov, M., Bucklin, R.E., & Pauwels, K. (2009). Effects of Word-of-Mouth versus Traditional Marketing: Findings from an Internet Social Networking Site. *Journal of Marketing*, 73(5), 90–102.

Wang, W., & Street, N.W. (2018). Modeling and Maximizing Influence Diffusion in Social Networks for Viral Marketing. *Applied Network Science*, 3(6).

Weimann, G. (1983). The Strength of Weak Conversational Ties in the Flow of Information and Influence. *Social Networks*, 5(3), 245–267.

Zaveri, B., & Amin, P. (2019). Augmented and Virtual Reality: Future of Marketing Trends. *Journal of Commerce and Management*, 6(1), 16–25.

Zhu, F., & Zhang, X. (2010). Impact of Online Consumer Reviews on Sales: The Moderating Role of Product and Consumer Characteristics. *Journal of Marketing*, 74(2), 133–148.

7 EXPERIENTIAL MARKETING IMPLEMENTATION MODEL

CHAPTER OVERVIEW

Perhaps the greatest challenge for marketers in the past two decades has been the integration of new and exciting tools and techniques into an existing repertoire of marketing activities. The impact of the digital revolution on how marketers could – and should – be more effective has been well documented. Nevertheless, it has taken many organisations a long time to understand how to structure and mould their marketing teams to reflect the power that digital platforms offer. Operationally, the challenges of upskilling, training and recruitment left marketing managers floundering. Tactically, marketers found themselves perplexed and overwhelmed by the broad range of choices they could now make to execute marketing campaigns. While the situation overall has improved, it was chaotic at times. On the one hand, there was significant divergence as marketers failed to recognise that many of their existing practices were to be cast aside and replaced, and, on the other hand, that other practices needed to be maintained and built upon.

We sometimes act as though this should be surprising – that the failure to respond to digital integration was as a result of a profession that was, for the first time, facing new conduits for reaching customers. However, it is our belief that marketers and the marketing profession have previously been poor at developing and integrating newer practices into how they managed marketing activities and executed marketing campaigns. The best example of this has been in the area of experiential marketing. The earlier chapters of this book have focused on outlining what experiential marketing is, how some organisations have used it and how it can positively support brand management. But the usage of experiential marketing has been *ad hoc*. There has been no framework or roadmap for managing an experiential campaign or, indeed, for integrating experiential campaigns into marketing activities. It has relied, as much as anything, on trial-and-error implementations – just like the early days of digital marketing.

This chapter will show how this can be rectified. We will propose a framework for the successful execution of an experiential marketing campaign building upon existing best practice. In the current literature on experiential marketing, there is a significant gap in terms of 'how to do' experiential marketing correctly. Many practitioners essentially 'learn on the job'. This has some merit, but we want to move beyond that and provide a framework to guide marketers in the development of an experiential campaign. We will show how experiential marketing can be incorporated into existing, tried-and-tested marketing models. Our model will help marketing practitioners to design their marketing communications in a manner that reflects the best of modern marketing practice – structure, strategy and measurability. By integrating experiential marketing into our long-standing, accepted mechanism for executing marketing campaigns, we are providing a better platform for success.

Specifically, this chapter will present information on:

- The steps required to develop an experiential marketing campaign that reflects the key opportunities afforded by experiential marketing while not neglecting the well-established features of marketing activity planning and design.
- Timing an experiential campaign for optimum success. This is a feature of experiential marketing that has not received attention. By giving prominence to timing, marketers will be better equipped to resource their experiential activity elements in a more nuanced way.
- A framework for amplifying experiential marketing. It is not enough to 'run' experiential events. The digital environment offers a much greater potential to amplify both the content of experiential marketing campaigns and the outcomes.

THE EXPERIENTIAL MARKETING IMPLEMENTATION MODEL

Recent years have seen the development of the academic literature on experiential marketing with significant contributions by Smilansky (2009, 2018), Kailani and Ciobotar (2015), Pine and Gilmore (1999, 2013), Schmitt (2000, 2011), Yuan and Wu (2008) and Lenderman (2005). However, there is no agreed perspective on experiential marketing, and a multitude of opinions on its theoretical foundations and the application of practice. Although the outcome of experiential marketing is clear in terms of consumer engagement and brand–customer relationships, the mechanics of delivering experiential campaigns lack meaningful, cogent and accepted academic research. There has been limited effort at understanding what works and does not work, and how that may be related to non-experiential activities, but little thought has been given to the application and activation of experiential marketing. Indeed, we can conclude that guidance on the following components of experiential marketing is lacking:

- How to effectively target market segments when implementing an experiential marketing activation for a brand.
- The use and optimisation of timelines for activating experiential marketing.
- How to approach budget allocations for experiential marketing activity in a manner that allows for better accountability.
- How to then measure the outcome of an experiential marketing activation while incorporating all the relevant metrics.

To address these shortcomings in the existing literature on experiential marketing, this chapter will present 'The Experiential Marketing Implementation Model'. This model has been developed following an exhaustive research process that involved engagement with representatives of some major brands, all of which have had extensive experience with experiential marketing activities. The research sought to identify the various elements of experiential marketing that these practitioners viewed as leading to success, and thereby to develop a model to enhance the

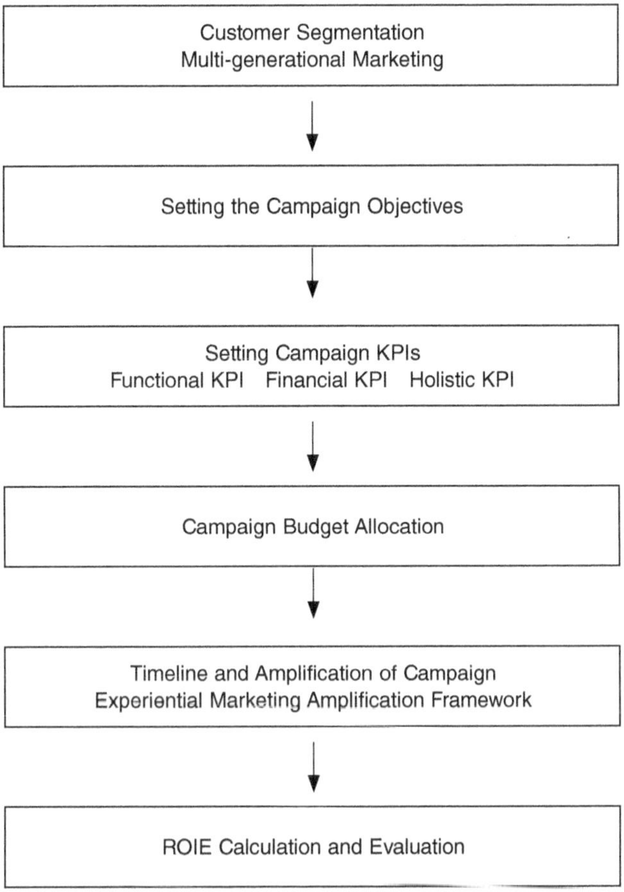

Figure 7.1 The Experiential Marketing Implementation Model

integrated marketing communication concept. The research provided many opportunities to understand how the execution of experiential activities can be bettered. The implementation model presented in this chapter has been tested in a number of settings and has proved itself to be impactful. The sections that follow outline, in detail, each of the steps of the implementation model, as depicted in Figure 7.1.

STEP 1: CUSTOMER SEGMENTATION

The logical first step of any marketing campaign is to be clear about the target audience. The campaign needs to know the target audience and make decisions on pursuing them, by assessing the value of the segment that best serves the purpose of their campaign. It is apparent, from our research, that some brands conclude that experiential marketing is most relevant for younger generations, including Generation Z and Millennials, and so engage in a generational segmentation approach. The predominant reason for the selection of these generations is due to their perceived receptiveness towards digital technologies and social media (Duffett, 2017; James & Levin, 2015; McCrindle & Wolfinger, 2009; McKenzie et al., 2012). Other brands however, engage in a multi-generational approach, where demographics of the target audience are not the predominant concern. Simms (2008) defines this as an *ageless society*, where people are not defined by age but by the activities they are involved in. In order for experiential marketing to generate a positive return on investment, we argue that although experiential marketing is certainly applicable to Generation Z and Millennials, it should not be isolated to these generational cohorts. Rather, a brand will have a greater return on its experiential marketing investment if it engages in a multi-generational segmentation approach. Numerous brands in our research indicated this. As long as an audience's preferences are considered and the campaign is tailored to meet these, along with the campaign objectives, experiential marketing is relevant to all generational cohorts. The benefit of this approach is explicitly stated by Binet and Field (2013: 26): 'the efficiency of broad-reaching campaigns aimed at both existing and potential customers is dramatically greater (by a factor of 10) than those targeting either type of customers alone'.

The appropriate approach is not to segregate generational cohorts, but to identify the desired characteristics, interests, needs or wants that are relevant to the product or the marketing campaign and to ensure that they are shared among many cohorts. As long as an experiential activation is authentic and relevant to a customer base, any audience, regardless of generational cohort, will react positively to the marketing tool. However, the design of the experiential activation needs to be crafted to reflect this. Essentially, we propose that the personality characteristics of the target audience are perceived as being more important than demographic segregation. This approach harnesses relevant interests, hobbies, opinions, personality traits and values to ensure that the experiential marketing will activate relevant

memory structures. Each of these segmentation tools can account for multiple demographical cohorts and offer a broad but still relevant target market. Thus, by employing a multi-generational approach, experiential marketing can positively enhance the consumer–brand relationship more broadly.

The multi-generational approach: House of Vans

In a bid to promote their new shoe line, which honoured the career and legacy of David Bowie, Vans hosted 'House of Vans' pop-ups in skateparks in cities in the USA, including New York and Chicago. While the core premise of these events was the launch of their new product line, Vans also grasped the opportunity to bring their brand pillars to life, including action sport, art, music and street culture. At these events, participants could skate in a David Bowie branded skatepark, listen to live music, participate in games and workshops, check out art installations and buy the shoes.

Vans identified with the fact that their brand attracts a lifestyle, not a demographic. Therefore, they did not market to a generational cohort, but opened these free events to all. This event rewarded their loyal customers while also intriguing the interest of other skateboarders, in their shared place of interest – the skatepark. In their approach to their experiential marketing activations, Vans were able to maximise potential interest in the event and attract a multitude of brand users.

Once the brand has accurately identified their desired customer segments, it is essential to set campaign/experiential objectives. The next section discusses this step in the Experiential Marketing Implementation Model.

STEP 2: SETTING THE CAMPAIGN OBJECTIVES

The importance of setting objectives for marketing campaigns has been widely researched and recognised (for example, Doyle, 2004; Hammer & Champy, 1994; Keegan & Rowley, 2017; Keung & Kawalek, 1997; Young, 1966). Fifield (2012: 176) defines marketing objectives as 'the aim or goal to which all marketing activities in the organization must be directed over the planning period'. They are generated as a benchmark to aid the measurement of the performance of a firm's campaign while taking into consideration the business and marketing objectives. By nature, objectives used for marketing communications are hierarchically related with

strategic corporate objectives that are relevant to all levels of the organisation (Leppäniemi & Karjaluoto, 2008). Additionally, it is essential to emphasise that the objectives and strategies pertaining to individual campaigns are linked and contribute to the overarching marketing communications objectives and the corporate marketing communications (Pickton & Broderick, 2005). Objectives of this nature are typically related to building and generating brand and product or service awareness, disseminating information and the development of attitudinal components or affecting consumer behaviour (Delozier, 1976). Customarily, objectives are created in the pre-campaign planning process and offer direction for the key performance indicators (KPIs) and collated metrics post campaign (Keegan & Rowley, 2017). They are an often-overlooked step in experiential marketing as less experienced practitioners focus on the experience itself as the objective rather than what the experiential activation can achieve.

It is worth noting that objectives pertaining to a marketing campaign should be SMARRTT: Specific, Measurable, Achievable, Realistic, Relevant, Targeted and Timed. It is no different for experiential campaigns. By designing objectives that are SMARRTT, it ensures that from the outset there are clear and precise goals to build a successful strategy to effectively evaluate its outcome (Pickton & Broderick, 2005). Marketers implementing experiential activities should be cognisant of the following:

- Specific: When designing objectives for experiential campaigns, marketers should ensure that those objectives are clear and give precise direction.
- Measurable: Experiential objectives should have a quantified outcome.
- Achievable: The objectives set must be achievable given the timelines.
- Realistic: In line with the above, the objectives must also be realistic given the timelines.
- Relevant: The objectives must be appropriate to the overall campaign and marketing objectives.
- Targeted: The objectives must be appropriate given the target audience (See Step 1)
- Timed: The objectives must relate to a clearly defined timeframe (See Step 5 & 6).

Our model confirms that the setting of campaign objectives is the logical next step when creating an experiential marketing campaign. Indeed, the direction a campaign takes, whether it is an instore or external marketing activation working in isolation or as a component of a larger marketing campaign, depends heavily on the campaign objective and what the brand wants to achieve in that particular point in time. Accordingly, campaign objectives form a key part of experiential marketing as all activity should relate back to the core objective. The following are examples of typical experiential marketing campaign objectives:

- Brand in hand (The potential for a sample of a product to be delivered into consumers' hands.)
- Increase customer lifetime value
- Improve brand saliency and demand for new products
- Increase brand awareness
- Increase brand relevance in consumers' lives

- Enhance brand and customer affinities
- Produce authentic interactions, assisting the customers to understand the brand.

When we talk to practitioners who have had various levels of success with experiential marketing, brands such as Nestlé, Birds Eye, Propercorn and Pepsi Max all emphasise the importance of having defined campaign objectives in order to assess the suitability of experiential marketing as a communication tool and the method in which it will be delivered. Furthermore, the setting of campaign objectives is essential to the measurement of the success or otherwise of an experiential marketing campaign, as we will see later.

Experiential marketing: Guided by the objectives

Guided by the campaign objective to encourage its customers to utilise their Inter-European travel offering, SNCF, France's national railway system, implemented an experiential marketing initiative that captured the hearts of their nation and spurred the travel bug in many.

SNCF installed colourful doors in high-traffic areas around Paris. Digital interactive flatscreens, which were connected via satellite to a multitude of European cities, were placed inside each door. Upon opening a door, people came face to face with a variety of experiences, including dancing with a hip-hop dance tribe in Berlin, having their portrait drawn in Brussels, participating in mimes with mime artists in Milan or joining a group of friends on a bike ride in Stuttgart, thus affording participants to become immersed in other European cities.

By sharing these cultural experiences, SNCF encouraged participants to then travel to these destinations via the easiest route, their railway system. The campaign resulted in an uplift of customers availing of this service.

Having set the campaign objective(s), additional planning is then required through the formation of campaign key performance indicators (KPIs), which will be discussed in the following section.

STEP 3: SETTING THE CAMPAIGN KPIS

Having highlighted the importance of establishing campaign objectives, the identification of key performance indicators is the next critical aspect in guiding and effectively evaluating a marketing campaign (Keegan & Rowley, 2017). Bauer (2004: 63) defines KPIs as 'quantifiable metrics which reflect the performance of an organisation in achieving its goals and objectives'. We can use this definition in measuring a campaign's performance. KPIs facilitate the measurement of performance of the

marketing campaigns and initiate a benchmarking process. Essentially, they indicate the effectiveness and efficiency of the performance of a marketing campaign (Vucomanovic, Radujkovic, & Nahod et al, 2010). For KPIs to be an effective measurement system, the following characteristics must be apparent (Maskel, 1991; Parmenterg, 2007; University of Warwick, 2006):

1. They must be connected to the overall business strategy to ensure operational success.
2. They must encompass both financial and non-financial measures.
3. They must be frequently measured and adapted to reflect changes in strategy.
4. They must be understood by all key stakeholders to ensure the optimal outcome.
5. They tie responsibility to an individual or a team.

Built on this theoretical foundation, it is the contention of this book that there are three main categories of KPIs which offer structure to marketing practitioners when setting these business metrics for experiential marketing. These are the outputs of the research undertaken for this book.

1. **Functional KPIs** relate to the implementation of experiential marketing and the measurement of its many components to ensure all elements are accounted for in assessing the success or failure of a given campaign. This category of KPI can be divided into three central components: digital marketing, experiential event marketing and public relations.
2. **Financial KPIs** reflect the financial aspirations of implementing an experiential marketing campaign. It is essential to account for KPIs of this nature as they remove the ambiguities that are usually associated with the return of experiential marketing. As marketers, we must ensure that marketing activities are accountable and contribute to brand and financial growth. Experiential marketing cannot be held to a lower standard. Although we generalise the categorisation of KPI as ROI measurement, financial KPIs can come to the fore in many ways. Typically, a KPI of this nature can be achieved when projected sales or market share targets are met.
3. **Holistic KPIs**, which involve brand health metrics, correlate with the long-term effect of the experiential marketing campaign. Brand health refers to a collective of measures, including brand awareness, brand usership status, brand sentiment, brand recall, brand image and brand relationships. This category of KPI brings the true essence of experiential marketing to life through its ability to aid brand health, the development of emotional ties and two-way communication with customers.

Table 7.1 Categories of key performance indicators (KPIs)

Functional KPI	Financial KPI	Holistic KPI
Digital marketing	Return on investment	Brand health
Event metrics	Sales targets	Consumer–brand relationships
Public relations	Market share metrics	

Dividing KPIs into these three categories is about providing structure so that practitioners can better incorporate the diverse methods of measurement. In Table 7.1 we see what elements typically fall into each category of KPI, although it is also important to note that in each of the three categories, brands may attribute more than one KPI. In line with Locke and Latham's (1990) view of goal-setting theory, we suggest that by utilising these categories of KPIs, this structured nature of campaign planning should enhance the marketing activity.

The following section will discuss the fourth step in this process, campaign budget allocation – a very challenging area for experiential marketing practitioners.

STEP 4: ALLOCATING THE CAMPAIGN BUDGET

Once the campaign objectives and the three categories of KPIs have been established appropriately for the campaign, the next step in the Experiential Marketing Implementation Model is allocating the campaign budget. Chapter 9 will deal exclusively with setting budgets for experiential marketing campaigns, so for now, we provide an overview of this step.

We see that, in practice, most companies will first prioritise traditional and mass market communications in budget allocations before they assign a budget to an experiential marketing campaign. The former area is better understood. The tangibility of such activities lend themselves to budget-setting and the consequent accountability required. By contrast, it is more difficult to convince budget-setters of the value of experiential and – crucially – to justify the spend through outcomes (see Chapter 9). As a result, in general, experiential marketing does not receive the majority of the marketing budget of most brands which engage in experiential activations.

The research conducted for this book suggests that 10–40% of marketing spend is a typical amount allocated to experiential marketing, with the degree of variance depending on the scope to which experiential marketing is required to meet the campaign objective and prescribed KPIs. This is the practice of those brands that have ongoing success with experiential marketing.

Once the campaign budget has been allocated, the campaign timeline needs to be planned and the most appropriate marketing tools need to be chosen. This will be discussed in the following section.

STEP 5: SETTING THE TIMELINE AND AMPLIFICATION STRATEGY

The strategic timing of experiential marketing in the lifespan of a marketing campaign was discussed in Chapter 5. However, ambiguity still exists around the timing of an experiential campaign at a tactical level. For a campaign using experiential

marketing to be deemed a success, precise timing and the optimisation and amplification of each component is required. As we outlined in Chapter 5, experiential marketing is best preceded by traditional marketing activities (including digital activities), whose focus is on brand awareness and core brand messaging (see Figure 5.3). The most effective brands in our research have demonstrated that planning and timing are the best bedrock for effective execution. Once this has been achieved, the brand can move into the experiential marketing stage of the timeline.

As we have seen with the previous steps in the model, experiential marketing implementation is not prescriptive and no one approach will be applicable to all brands, as the type of activation is derived from the campaign objectives and KPIs. Keeping that in mind, it becomes apparent that the decision to activate experiential marketing activity after traditional marketing can be influenced by many factors, including: (1) budget allocation, (2) the brand's preference towards internal or external activations, (3) the responsiveness of the relevant target market(s), and (4) the brand's stage in the product life cycle.

1. **Budget allocation**: As outlined earlier, we recommend that brands should spend between 10% and 40% of their marketing budget on experiential marketing. Each brand must decide on the appropriate budget for their brand, and this will largely depend on the size of the business, their turnover, the money allocated to the overall marketing budget, the campaign objectives and KPIs. Knowing how much is to be spent on experiential marketing relative to more traditional marketing methods indicates its overall prominence and role in the integrated marketing campaign.
2. **The selection of internal or external activations**: As discussed in Chapter 3, experiential marketing activations can be implemented through many different mechanisms which can be loosely considered as internal or external experiential activations. Internal experiential activations refer to experiential activity that is confined within a retail outlet, for example, and its external counterparts refer to experiential activity that happens in alternative typically outdoor environments, including car parks, festivals, events and public places, as an isolated event or as part of a roadshow. A brand's preference towards either of these types of brand activations, along with the chosen campaign objectives and KPIs, can heavily influence the implementation of experiential marketing in the timeline of the campaign. There are benefits to each of these activation methods, including the fact that partnering with other brands results in transferrable memory structures. Research conducted by Rao et al., (1999) suggests that when a lesser-known brand is partnered with an established one, shoppers extend their associations of the known brand to the lesser-known brand. Featuring a brand in an associated retail outlet through an experiential activation increases the shoppers' familiarity with the brand and reduces the perceptual threshold, making the brands easier to process and recall (Guerreiro et al., 2015; Pechmann & Stewart, 1990), therefore building memory structures. However, research conducted for this book suggests that internal activations tend to under-deliver on brand health and awareness metrics. This is due to the fact that unless the brand owns the retail outlet in which an activation in planned, they do not have complete control. For example, some

supermarket chains have specific sampling agencies and display specifications to which brands have to adhere. This may inhibit the potential success of an activation, as displays and set-ups may have to be scaled down, and if agency staff have to be utilised, they may not have the same understanding of the product as someone employed by a brand. For brands that implement external experiential activations, it is essential that they develop a clear call to action which directs a participant to their nearest store to purchase the product. Without this, experiential marketing is merely an overpriced entertainment endeavour. A campaign may also require both internal and external activations. This strategy would evidentially prolong the experiential marketing implementation stage of the timeline as it requires multiple components of experiential marketing to effectively engage with the target market while also fulfilling the campaign requirements.

3. **The responsiveness of the relevant target market(s)**: As we have outlined earlier, we advocate for an approach to experiential marketing that uses multi-generational segmentation. As such, it is important that the same approach is adopted by brands when formulating their more traditional marketing strategies to ensure an overall integrated, strategic approach. While many brands focus on demographic characteristics when segmenting the market, it is our contention that if experiential marketing is to follow more traditional marketing approaches, then the same multi-generational segmentation approach needs to be followed. Understanding the segments, knowing the segments' responsiveness and the overall ability to assess that responsiveness lead to a more nuanced timeline.
4. **The brand's stage in the product life cycle (PLC)**: When deciding on an experiential marketing strategy, it is essential to consider the PLC stage of the brand. Experiential marketing can satisfy different objectives at different stages of the PLC, for example, building brand awareness in the Introduction and Growth stages, and aiding in brand memory recall in the Mature and Decline stages. However, irrespective of the stage of the PLC, the timeline of the campaign has to be considered, with brands adjusting their experiential approach to ensure an optimal outcome of the marketing activity, where experiential marketing follows more traditional marketing approaches. Hence, brands must track growth and development from a PLC perspective in order to effectively activate experiential marketing activity.

Asics' product launch during the Covid-19 pandemic

Brands which had scheduled product launches during the Covid-19 pandemic were faced with the challenge of either cancelling their brand launches or harnessing virtual methods of experiential marketing to ensure that the product

(Continued)

being launched gained sufficient publicity to fuel demand. An example of a brand that was faced with these challenges was Asics, a sporting apparel brand. With three new products scheduled to launch in spring 2020, the brand had to revisit their global media launch strategy which was hosted in their Japanese HQ (titled the Innovation Summit) and where key influencers and journalists were invited to attend. With this event cancelled, the brand revisited their experiential launch strategy and instead employed virtual reality to ensure that participants still had a memorable and immersive experience. Virtual reality headsets were sent to each of the attendees of the Innovation Summit. The headsets took them on a virtual tour of the Asics Innovation Labs where the Asics team could showcase the technology that was used to create each of the new products and the attendees had the opportunity to interact with the Asics team.

Although the products could not be launched through traditional experiential methods, the brand was still able to grasp the attention of the journalists and key influencers who would influence the success of the launch and disseminate the message to their audiences.

After the experiential marketing activation has occurred, optimisation and amplification assume centrality. As we have previously discussed, the objective here is to ensure that the marketing activation transcends the physical barriers of the experience, allowing it to live on a greater platform (online) to maximise an efficient and effective return on the investment. This is achieved through two mechanisms: experiential amplification and experiential optimisation (see Chapter 5). You will have read in Chapter 6 about the importance of using a time-phased approach when amplifying an experiential marketing activation online. Using that learning and combining it with what we know from this chapter, Figure 7.2 provides a visual illustration of the development of strategic timing and the implementation of a marketing campaign utilising experiential marketing.

As discussed by Dunn (2009), the completion of any marketing campaign must be followed by an evaluation of its success. The following stage of the Experiential Marketing Implementation Model is the calculation and evaluation of the return on integrated experience (ROIE) formula.

STEP 6: CALCULATING AND EVALUATING RETURN ON INTEGRATED EXPERIENCE

The concluding stage of this framework requires the evaluation of the campaign. There are several methods of evaluating experiential marketing in the literature, including MROI (marketing return on investment), ROE^2 (return on experience × engagement) and ROX (return on experience), which are examined in Chapter 10.

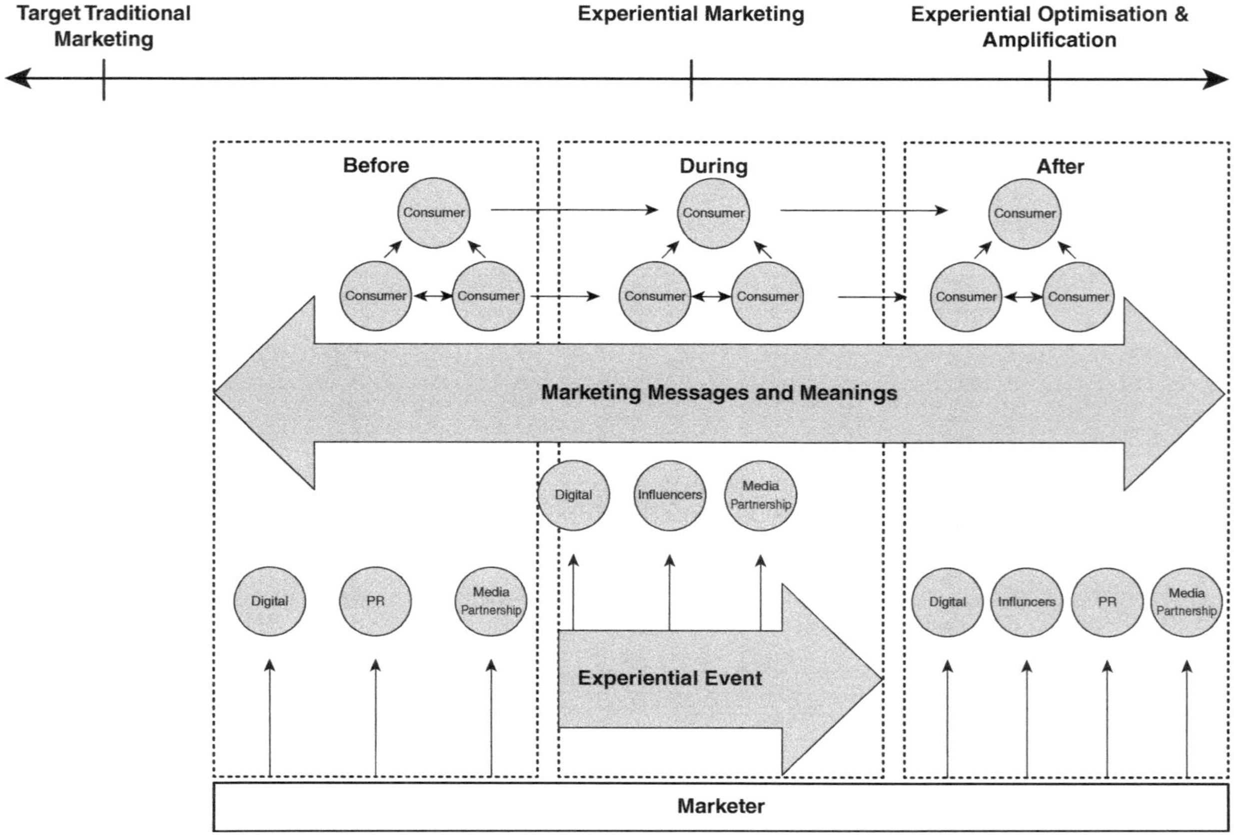

Figure 7.2 Experiential Marketing Amplification Framework

However, a critical analysis of what happens in practice shows us that many marketing professionals do not use these measures, as they do not evaluate all the essential key metrics which are critical to the success of an experiential marketing campaign. To address this issue, we present a formula for measuring the success of experiential marketing termed the **return on integrated experience (ROIE)** formula. ROIE offers marketers the ability, first, to account for all key metrics in the evaluation of an experiential marketing activation and, second, to uncover the contribution that an experiential marketing activation makes towards the overall success of an integrated marketing campaign. Chapter 10 provides a detailed account of this formula.

CONCLUSION AND SUMMARY

Experiential marketing is very effective. However, its effectiveness at a campaign level depends on the approach the practitioner takes to its implementation, while being bounded by their own organisational settings and concerns. For many practitioners, success in experiential marketing has resulted from trial and error and many cycles of refinement. This chapter has taken account of that trial and error, codified the insight gained by the practitioners and brands involved, and proposed a testable implementation model for experiential activations. Critically, this model untangles experiential marketing from the predisposition to set it entirely apart from other marketing activities and objectives. Instead, it positions experiential marketing as an integrated practice that requires adherence to a timeline of actions and functions while orienting towards a measurable and useful impact. Following this model will allow practitioners to better underline the impact of experiential marketing to others in the organisation.

MAIN TAKEAWAYS FROM CHAPTER 7

- The Experiential Marketing Implementation Model is an important contribution to the marketing practitioner's toolbox as it provides a step-by-step approach that practitioners can follow when implementing experiential marketing.
- Experiential marketing should adopt a multi-generational segmentation approach, have clear campaign objectives and KPIs, allocate an appropriate campaign budget, have a well-developed timeline for execution of the campaign and, ultimately, have a clear method of measuring the campaign outcomes.
- The Experiential Marketing Amplification Framework illustrates how brands can effectively amplify experiential events using a carefully considered strategic approach.

CONCLUDING QUESTIONS

1. Describe the steps in the Experiential Marketing Implementation Model.
2. How comprehensive do you consider the Experiential Marketing Implementation Model to be?
3. Using examples, discuss when a generational segmentation approach is appropriate and when a multi-generational approach applies.
4. Using examples, analyse the differences between campaign objectives and key performance indicators.
5. Using the Experiential Marketing Amplification Framework, explain the importance of effective timing in an experiential marketing campaign.

REFERENCES AND FURTHER READING

Bauer, K. (2004). KPIs: The Metrics that Drive Performance Management. *Information Management*, 14(9), 63.

Binet, L., & Field, P. (2013). *The Long and the Short of It: Balancing Short and Long-term Marketing Strategies*. London: Institute of Practitioners in Advertising.

Delozier, M.W. (1976). *The Marketing Communications Process*. London: McGraw-Hill.

Doyle, J.K. (2004). Introduction to Interviewing Techniques. In D.W. Wood (Ed.), *Handbook for IQP Advisors and Students*. Worchester, MA: Worchester Polytechnic Institute.

Duffett, R.G. (2017). Influence of Social Media Marketing Communications on Young Consumers' Attitudes. *Young Consumer*, 18(1), 19–39.

Dunn, M. (2009). *The Marketing Accountability Imperative: Driving Superior Returns on Marketing Investments*. Chichester: John Wiley and Sons.

Fifield, P. (2012). *Marketing Strategy*. Abingdon, UK: Routledge.

Guerreiro, J., Rita, P., & Trigueiros, D. (2015). Attention, Emotions and Cause-related Marketing Effectiveness. *European Journal of Marketing*, 49(11/12), 1728–1750.

Hammer, M., & Champy, J. (1994). *Reengineering the Corporation: A Manifesto for Business*. London: Nicholas Brealey.

James, A., & Levin, J. (2015). Digital Natives: A Portrait of Tech and Urban Youth. *Sunday Times Generation Next*, 16.

Kailani, C., & Ciobotar, N. (2015). Experiential Marketing: An Efficient Tool to Leverage Marketing Communication Impact on Consumer Behaviour. *International Conference on Marketing and Business Development Journal*, 1(1), 1–7.

Keegan, B.J., & Rowley, J. (2017). Evaluation and Decision Making in Social Media Marketing. *Management Decision*, 55(1), 15–31.

Keung, P., & Kawalek, P. (1997). Goal-based Business Process Models: Creation and Business Process. *Management Journal*, 3(1), 17–38.

Lenderman, M. (2005). *Experience the Message: How Experiential Marketing is Changing the Brand World*. New York: Carroll & Graf Publishers.

Leppäniemi, M., & Karjaluoto, H. (2008). Mobile Marketing: From Marketing Strategy to Mobile Marketing Campaign Implementation. *International Journal of Mobile Marketing*, 3(1), 50–61.

Locke, E., & Latham, G. (1990). *A Theory of Goal Setting and Task Performance*. Englewood Cliffs, NJ: Prentice-Hall.

Maskel, B. (1991). *Performance Management for World Class Manufacturing*. Cambridge, MA: Productivity Press.

McCrindle, M., & Wolfinger, E. (2009). *The ABC of XYZ: Understanding the Global Generations*. Sydney, NSW: University of New South Wales Press.

McKenzie, S.B., McGuire, R., & Hartwel, S. (2012). *The First Generation of the Twenty-First Century*. Minneapolis, MN: Frank N. Magid Associates. [Online]. Available at: https://static1.squarespace.com/static/56d7388222482e1e2c87c683/t/56e0cdc2cf80a14684670194/1457573327672/MagidPluralistGenerationWhitepaper.pdf [accessed 3 July 2019].

Parmenterg, D. (2007). *Key Performance Indicators: Developing, Implementing and Using Winning KPIs*. Hoboken, NJ: Wiley.

Pechmann, C., & Stewart, D.W. (1990). The Effects of Comparative Advertising on Attention, Memory and Purchase Intentions. *Journal of Consumer Research*, 17(2), 317–329.

Pickton, D., & Broderick, A. (2005). *Integrated Marketing Communications*. London: Prentice Hall.

Pine, B. Joseph, Gilmore, J.H. (1999). *The Experience Economy: Work is Theatre & Every Business a Stage*. Boston, MA: Harvard Business Press.

Pine, B. Joseph, & Gilmore, J.H. (2013). *The Experience Economy: Work is Theatre & Every Business a Stage* (Updated edition). Boston, MA: Harvard Business Press.

Rao, A.R., Qu, L., & Ruekert, R.W. (1999). Signaling Unobservable Product Quality Through a Brand Alley. *Journal of Marketing Research*, 36(2), 258–268.

Schmitt, B.H. (2000). *Experiential Marketing: How to Get Customers to Sense, Feel, Think, Act, Relate to your Company and Brands*. New York: The Free Press.

Schmitt, B.H. (2011). Experience Marketing: Concepts, Frameworks and Consumer Insights. *Foundations and Trends in Marketing*, 5(2), 55–112.

Simms, J. (2008). Shades of Grey. *Marketing*, 30 April, 14.

Smilansky, S. (2009). *Experiential Marketing: A Practical Guide to Interactive Brand Experiences*. London: Kogan Page.

Smilansky, S. (2018). *Experiential Marketing: A Practical Guide to Interactive Brand Experiences* (2nd ed.). London: Kogan Page.

University of Warwick (2006). *Performance Measuring and Costing: Logistics and Operations Management*. Warwick, UK: University of Warwick.

Vucomanovic, M., Radujkovic, M., & Nahod, M. (2010). Leading, Lagging and Performance Measures in the Construction Industry. *International Journal of Organizational Technology and Management in Construction*, 2(1), 103–111.

Young, R.C. (1966). Goals and Goal-Setting. *Journal of the American Institute of Planners*, 32(2), 76–85. https://doi.org/10.1080/01944366608979361.

Yuan, Y.H., & Wu, C. (2008). Relationship among Experiential Marketing, Experiential Value and Customer Satisfaction. *Journal of Hospitality and Tourism Research*, 32(3), 387–410.

8

INTEGRATING EXPERIENTIAL MARKETING WITH THE COMMUNICATIONS STRATEGY

CHAPTER OVERVIEW

Our review of experiential marketing to date emphasises that it is a communications tool valued by both brands and consumers. Its increasing pervasiveness in the industry as well as its established academic credibility are evidence of this. The main reasons for its success are as follows:

- It allows brands to be nimbler – a feature that can distinguish it from other methods of communications.
- It drives behavioural change among consumers by generating brand love and awareness.
- It affords brands the opportunity to stage authentic and meaningful interactions with their target market, which inevitably immerses them into the brand's culture, essence and ethos.
- It builds emotional connections and bonds between brands and their customers.
- It creates memorable experiences which, in turn, build memory structures and brand recall – an explicit goal of most marketing activity.

These are significant and important advantages, and you will have learned in Chapter 7 how to design an experiential marketing campaign that can deliver on these. Given the importance of experiential marketing in overall brand management, its role in building consumer–brand relationships and its strong connections

with digital marketing, it should be clear that experiential marketing should not be used as a stand-alone tactic, but rather as an integrated component of an overall marketing strategy. As Smilansky (2009) suggests, experiential marketing should always be activated as a component of an integrated marketing campaign (IMC), and never in isolation.

The success of an experiential campaign is largely determined by its integration in a complete marketing campaign, and here we will present the building blocks of such a campaign and how it interfaces with the experiential aspect of the campaign. Specifically, this chapter will present information on the following:

- The importance of integrating an experiential marketing campaign with other traditional communication approaches.
- The importance of strategic brand messaging to ensure that the experiential element is effective.
- How to design an experiential marketing campaign as part of an integrated communications approach.
- Measuring experiential marketing in the context of an IMC approach.

In essence, we will show how to ensure that experiential activities are more successful by being consistent, timely and creative, and how to more easily evaluate such activities.

INTEGRATING EXPERIENTIAL MARKETING WITH TRADITIONAL MARKETING

A successful experiential activation requires integrating an experiential activation with an overarching marketing campaign. In line with the findings of Smilansky (2009), we propose that in order for experiential marketing to offer the optimal return for a brand, it must be integrated into the larger marketing strategy. Tactically, operationally and strategically, experiential marketing activities need to be aligned with the tactics, operations and strategy of a general marketing approach.

By employing multiple communications tools and strategically combining them, brands have the ability to amplify a brand message through the application of multiple touchpoints (Keller, 2016). Put simply, a brand will not get the reach to impact enough people to improve on a brand's performance without using traditional media channels. To be efficient and effective, experiential marketing has to be fully integrated into a communications plan to drive scale. Indeed, as you will have learned in Chapter 7, not only should experiential marketing not be used in isolation, it should not be used without the support of traditional marketing activities throughout the lifespan of the campaign. This is primarily due to the fact that it is difficult to communicate key messages in a controlled manner through experiences alone. As discussed, experiential marketing must not be used at the beginning of the life cycle of the marketing campaign, but preferably after the utilisation of traditional marketing activities. This suggests that it is in a brand's best interest to build a clear foundation through traditional brand-building methods so that when

experiential marketing is employed, the target market is already aware of the brand and/or campaign. This increases the possibility of enhanced message penetration with the target market and consumer tribes. However, although traditional marketing should be utilised in advance of experiential marketing, once the basic brand message has been disseminated, experiential marketing can bring the brand to life in an invigorated way.

For example:

> For a new campaign I still think that you need TV or outdoor for everyone to see it and that is important for awareness. To further get your key messages out there, what you can do from an experiential point of view is really engage with people and have fun with it to get more cut through (Brand Manager)
>
> It is important to get the fundamentals of your brand right on big channels like TV and radio, all of your signed off one-way content and then once people know your brand, experiential can have a great role in building it and adding in a little bit of a personality (Brand Manager).

It is interesting to look in a little more detail at how the reach of experiential marketing can be categorised once the groundwork has been laid through more traditional forms of marketing. Essentially, we propose two reach mechanisms:

1. An experiential activation for a small number of people that is amplified extensively (see the Chase and Southwest example below).
2. A mass marketing experiential activation where a brand interacts with as many consumers as possible (see the WWF example below).

Chase and Southwest Airlines delivering honeymoons without the airmiles

As the world shut down during the Covid-19 global pandemic, many milestone events were put on hold, including weddings and honeymoons. With this in mind, Chase, an online banking company and Southwest Airlines teamed up with Brides.com to create backyard/garden pop-up honeymoon experiences for five essential worker couples whose weddings and honeymoons had to be cancelled in the US. They devised a competition in which couples had to share their love stories and choice of honeymoon destination to enter. The winners were picked and their pop-up experience was inspired by their love story and honeymoon destination. Each of the backyard honeymoons was documented by a professional photographer and videographer to capture the special moment for the lucky couples and shared on the brand's social media channels. Each couple also received 200,000 Southwest Rapid Reward points to go on their dream honeymoon as they wish.

WWF #EndWildlifeCrime

The World Wide Fund for Nature (WWF) created an experiential activation in London during a conference that was taking place on the illegal ivory trade, with the objective of highlighting the plight of elephants. Aiming to build awareness on wildlife crime while also delivering an immersive experience, the WWF displayed a hologram of a five-foot elephant, along with other endangered species, including turtles and leopards, on the streets of London. Deriving from this activation, the WWF compiled 124,600 signatures on their petition to stop wildlife crime and trafficking.

We propose that for experiential marketing to be successful, the brand infrastructure and key messaging must already have been established and disseminated. Experiential marketing should not be utilised unless a brand has a healthy level of brand penetration and consumers are aware of the brand they are interacting with. Through the staged interaction, consumers then build a deeper understanding of the brand as a result of their immersion into the brand values. So, not only does experiential marketing rely on traditional marketing to first develop the core brand identity, it is clear that, depending on the aims of the experiential marketing campaign, marketers also rely on other channels, including advertising, sales promotion, sponsorship, public relations, social media marketing etc., where every channel has specific goals and objectives. Furthermore, and as you will have learned in Chapter 6, although the use of word-of-mouth marketing (WOMM) and social currency is required when disseminating an experiential event, brands should also utilise digital, public relations (PR), media partnerships and influencer marketing in order to amplify the activation to reach the mass audience. Essentially, the integration of experiential marketing with more traditional marketing methods is required throughout.

Lidl surprises

In 2014, Lidl, a European discounter chain, departed from their use of traditional marketing methods only and began their journey in multi-channel marketing with the campaign #LidlSurprises. With the aim of discreetly showcasing their local produce, Lidl created an exclusive farmers market in East London, where their private label product was on offer, but shoppers were only told that the produce was from Lidl after they had tasted it. In order to build awareness prior to this experiential activation, the farmers market was advertised on promotional flyers at store level, through media partnerships and advertising on social media and food blogs. Post event, a television advert went live which captured a snapshot of participants' reactions to tasting the produce and finding out that it was all available at Lidl under their private label offering.

UTILISING EXPERIENTIAL MARKETING OUTSIDE THE PLAN

In an ideal world, and as outlined so far in this chapter, experiential marketing would be a planned, integrated activity from the outset. On occasion, however, and for different reasons, brands may need to utilise experiential marketing that had not been planned for. For example, as a marketing campaign develops it may be necessary to effectively immerse consumers in the brand in a way that was not previously anticipated. It is also possible, and indeed likely, that changes in the marketscape might call for the use of sampling, for example, to rejuvenate sales. Indeed, it is true to say that although experiential marketing works best when used as a central component of an integrated marketing plan, it also has the ability to be used purely as an engagement tool to maintain or regain mind or market share. However, it is important to note that experiential marketing should always be used in a controlled and structured manner where there is a consistent brand message in line with the brand plan. Thus, while the activity might not have been planned for in an integrated way, it is essential that the messaging is completely on point with the broader brand messaging.

One prime example of the utilisation of experiential marketing outside an integrated marketing campaign is industry events. These are not typically hosted by the showcasing brand but by an event organiser. Experiential activations used in this scenario pose difficulties as the brand is not hosting the event and thus does not have control over the event. However, it is still critical that the experiential activation is in sync with the central brand communications message. If the branding and key messaging is consistent with the core values of the brand, strong brand resonance will be built.

INTEGRATED MARKETING COMMUNICATIONS FRAMEWORK

So far in this chapter we have discussed the importance of integrating experiential marketing with other more traditional marketing methods, and in particular with ensuring that the experiential marketing messaging is in line with the overall brand messaging. Practitioners will need to know how to integrate experiential marketing into the overall marketing mix. To explore this in more detail we will use Belch et al., (2001) Integrated Communications Planning Model. It is apparent from the literature that this model is the most cited and best-known framework for guiding the development of an integrated marketing communications strategy. However, it does not include experiential marketing (most likely given the timeline of its development) and it is now our contention that this needs to be rectified, as shown in Figure 8.1.

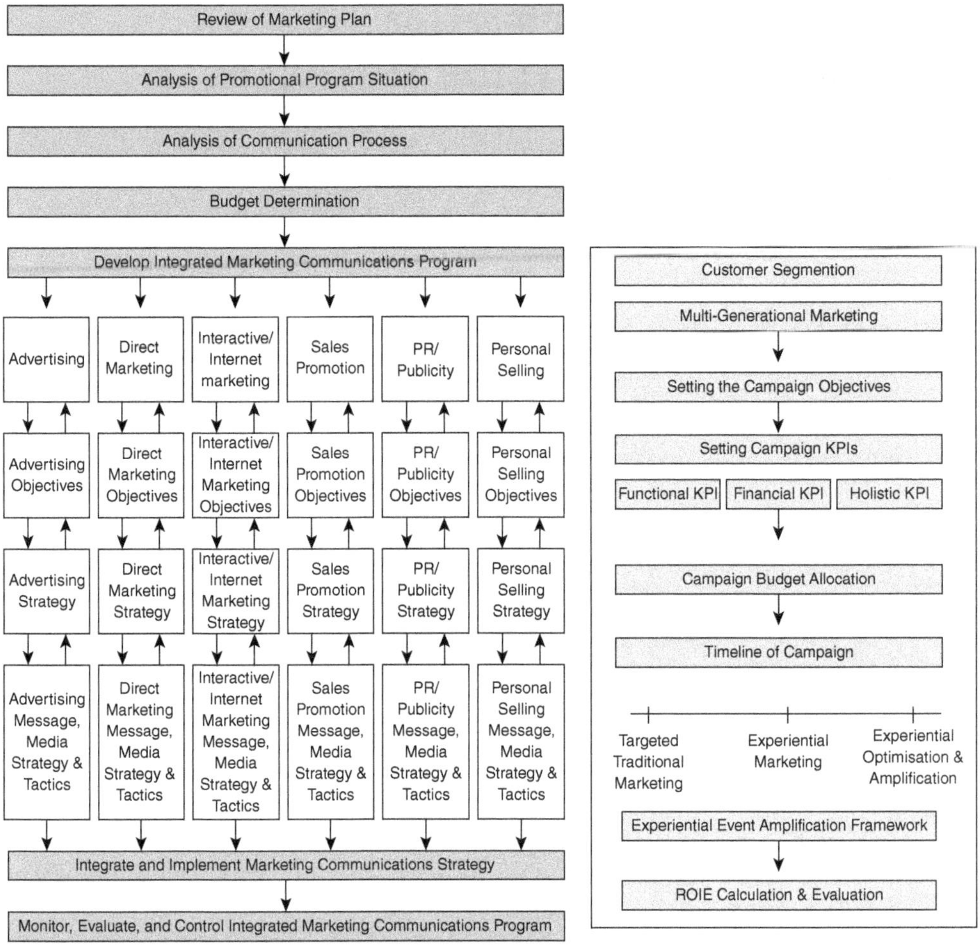

Figure 8.1 Framework for integrating marketing communications

Source: Adapted from Belch et al.'s (2001) model

Chapter 7 presented the Experiential Marketing Implementation Model, a newly developed framework to guide the development of experiential marketing based on research with major brands. Given that we now know that it is essential for experiential marketing to be integrated with the overall brand message, Figure 8.1 illustrates how the Experiential Marketing Implementation Model should congruently work in line with step five in Belch et al.'s (2001) model. In this way, we can see that experiential marketing is a key communications tool that needs to be recognised as such in the communications planning process. When experiential marketing forms part of an overall integrated marketing communications approach it has the following results:

- It optimises the return on investment (ROI) of experiential marketing when it is combined with mass marketing activities.

- Alone, experiential marketing cannot deliver on reach metrics, and therefore requires supporting mass-marketing activities in order to inform customers about the product.
- As traditional marketing does not facilitate authentic interactions and two-way communication with customers (Schmitt, 1999, 2000), experiential marketing complements the reach mechanisms of traditional mass marketing by creating opportunities for these interactions to take place (Kailani & Ciobotar, 2015; LaSalle & Britton, 2003; Lenderman, 2005; Li & Yang, 2010).

As seen in Figure 8.1, Belch et al.'s (2001) Integrated Communications Planning Model retains all the fundamental steps required in the implementation of an integrated marketing campaign (IMC). However, through the introduction of experiential marketing and the Experiential Marketing Implementation Model, additional steps happen in this process that require consistency. Considering that the steps in the Integrated Communications Planning Model are deemed important in the planning of an integrated campaign, the Experiential Marketing Implementation Model compliments it by additionally including experiential marketing. The utilisation of the Experiential Marketing Implementation Model commences at the fifth step of the Integrated Communications Planning Model, where the development of the IMC plan happens by selecting the appropriate communications methods. In this way experiential marketing becomes a critical component of an integrated marketing campaign.

Step 1: Review of the Marketing Plan

It is helpful at this point to review the overall IMC process to illustrate how experiential marketing fits into this process. The first step of the IMC process is to review the marketing plan and objectives. It is known that before a promotional plan is developed the marketer must understand how the brand is positioned in the market and what the plans are for its future. Without this understanding, any promotional plan will fall short. As illustrated throughout this book, experiential campaigns are best planned with a deep understanding of the brand and the brand messaging. The importance of this is reinforced at this first step of the IMC process. The marketer will know the role which all of the promotional-mix elements will play in the overall marketing programme and, furthermore, they will focus on the information in the marketing plan that is most relevant to the development of the promotional strategy. This information will prove highly useful when planning the timeline of an experiential campaign, and when seeking to amplify the experience.

Step 2: Analysis of the Promotional Situation

The second step in the IMC process involves conducting the situation analysis. The situation analysis focuses on the factors that might influence the development of

the promotional strategy. These factors tend to be broken into internal and external factors. Examples of internal factors include the product offering, the company, the brand image, any unique selling points. Examples of the external factors include customers, market segments, competitors, the environment. This information is necessary if relevant and effective promotional strategies are to be developed. Throughout this process, the marketer must constantly assess how each element of the promotional mix will be impacted by the situational analysis and how it can be designed to achieve the fullest effect in the context of the analysis.

Step 3: Analysis of the Communications Process

The third step in the process involves an analysis of the communications process. This stage of the process examines how the company can effectively communicate with consumers in the target market. The marketer must think about the process that the customer will go through when responding to the promotional communication. Here, the marketer must consider, for example:

- The nature of the product (high or low involvement, for example)
- The existence or otherwise of a brand–customer relationship
- The source, message and channel through which the promotional message will be delivered.

This step is extremely important in the context of experiential marketing, given the nature of experiences, the involvement of the consumer and the need for amplification and optimisation following the experience. Indeed, considerations such as the use of influencers or media partnerships need to be carefully considered given the overlap and multiple roles these can play across different promotional mix elements. Consider, for example, the use of an influencer at an experiential event, the role of that influencer across PR and digital channels, as well as the role of that influencer acting as an endorser of a brand on more traditional channels, such as TV or radio. All of these considerations will influence the design of the overall promotional strategy, where media mix considerations and costs are at play.

At this stage of the communications process, it is also important to establish clear communication goals and objectives. Communication objectives refer to what the firm seeks to accomplish with its promotional programme. These are often stated in terms of what communication effects are to be achieved, such as, for example, creating awareness, creating a brand image or influencing purchase intentions. Emphasised thus far in the book has been the role that experiential marketing can play in building relationships with consumers, generating online activity and encouraging sampling and interaction with the brand, whereas if the objective of the communications is to build awareness, for example, greater emphasis would be given to more traditional promotional elements, such as TV, radio and print media. The communication objectives that are decided at this point should be the guiding force for the development of the overall marketing communication strategy as well

as for the development of objectives for each element of the promotions mix to be used. In the context of experiential marketing activities, this means that these activities must align well with the communications objectives and reflect the strengths of experiential marketing as a communications tool.

Step 4: Budget Determination

The fourth stage of the IMC process is budget determination. Typically, two questions will be asked at this point: What will the promotional programme cost and how will the money be allocated? All of the stages conducted to this point should aid in this determination. Chapter 9 provides further information on budget allocations.

Steps 5 and 6: Integrated Marketing Communications Programme and Implementation Strategy

Developing the IMC programme is the most detailed step of the promotional planning process. Given the promotional mix elements typically available (advertising, direct marketing, digital marketing, sales promotions, PR, personal selling and experiential marketing), each must be assessed in terms of their advantages and limitations, the role and significance of each in the overall mix, and how they can be coordinated together with best effect. As can be seen in Figure 8.1, each element of the promotional mix has its own set of objectives, budget and strategy. Decisions must be made with regard to the specific activities that each mix element must perform, and procedures must be designed for evaluating performance.

In summary, this is where the detail of the planning, integration and implemention of each communications approach happens. The most important consideration is to ensure that each element of the communications mix is planned in a coordinated way.

Step 7: Monitoring, Evaluating and Controlling the Promotional Programme

The final stage of the IMC process is monitoring, evaluating and controlling the promotional programme. It is important to determine how well the promotional programme meets communications objectives and helps the firm accomplish its overall marketing goals and objectives. The next section explores this in more detail.

MEASURING AN INTEGRATED APPROACH

As has been pointed out previously in this book, measuring the impact of experiential marketing has always been problematic. Many of the methods of measuring

traditional marketing strategies are simply not fit for purpose when it comes to experiential marketing, and many of the methods proposed for measuring experiential marketing fail to take account of all the possible outcomes. Equally, its many measurement methods fail to understand the true nature of experiential activations. These problems, however, are compounded when aiming to measure experiential marketing as part of an overall IMC campaign. What has tended to happen is that practitioners isolate the experiential element from the rest of the campaign to measure its return. Metrics including ROE^2 and ROX are used to measure the impact of experiential marketing in isolation, which is not the recommended approach, according to Smilansky (2009), nor the reality.

In order for a campaign to optimally amplify a message and generate two-way communication, the marketing message should not be isolated to specific elements of the marketing mix, but rather consistently shared for maximum brand penetration (Smilansky, 2009). Therefore, it is essential that a method of calculation for evaluating the success of a marketing campaign, including experiential marketing, is conceptualised. There are many data sources that can actively contribute to this, for example, in the FMCG sector Kantar Millward Brown, Nielsen and Dunhumby, are information, data and market measurement companies where commercial data and consumer data can be bought. However, it can be hard to distinguish the effect that different activations have in isolation on a brand when analysing this data. The providers of data will typically tell you trial and awareness scores, affinity scores, etc., but it can be difficult to assess specific activations and how they have performed.

We propose solutions to all these issues in Chapter 10.

CONCLUSION AND SUMMARY

Having included experiential marketing into the IMC model, it is our contention that the applicability of the IMC model has significantly improved as it now has relevance in modern marketing communications. In particular, this is true when we consider that experiential marketing plays an essential role in marketing due to its innate ability to cultivate authentic two-way communication during staged brand activations. Given the embedded Experiential Marketing Application Framework, along with the proposed Timeline of the Campaign, the link with digital marketing is now clearer also. Indeed, if we reflect on other concepts discussed thus far in this book, we can see that Figure 8.1 also harnesses the links with concepts such as relationship marketing and consumer collectives. By integrating experiential marketing with more established marketing and communication strategies, experiential marketing can be deemed an accountable method of marketing communications, providing the opportunity to cultivate significant brand growth and development while at the same time creating unique and invaluable interactions with customers, which ultimately result in brand development, brand relationships and consumer tribes.

As we have shown throughout this book, it is essential to develop consistent brand messaging and the right mechanics to effectively implement experiential

marketing and to realise its benefits. This chapter takes that core concept and builds on it by situating the Experiential Marketing Implementation Model firmly in the Integrated Marketing Communications Process. It is essential that experiential marketing is used in tandem with the other promotional mix methods and to recognise that each of these communications tools interact with customers in a different way. By recognising the synergies between them, experiential marketing can work with the other communications mix elements to cultivate both reach and interaction. It is crucial to note that experiential marketing must not be undertaken without preparatory and foundation work building upon traditional marketing activities. Traditional marketing is a controlled marketing communications tool which communicates with the masses, building brand saliency by portraying a consistent message in a creative way. However, experiential marketing affords customers the opportunity to build on the memory structures that have been previously formed through traditional marketing campaigns, and allows the customers who interact with the experiential activation to have unique interactions with a brand while developing their own brand meaning. This increases the possibility of enhanced message penetration with consumer tribes. Cognisance of the different roles that communication mix elements can play is essential for the modern marketer who wants to communicate effectively with their consumers.

MAIN TAKEAWAYS FROM CHAPTER 8

- Experiential marketing should not be used as a stand-alone tactic, but rather as an integrated component of an overall marketing strategy.
- The success of an experiential campaign is largely determined by its integration into an overall marketing campaign.
- Experiential marketing should always be used in a controlled and structured manner where there is a consistent brand message in line with the brand plan.
- Inserting experiential marketing into the integrated marketing communications programme improves the applicability of the IMC model as it now has relevance in modern marketing communications where experiential marketing plays an essential role due to its innate ability to cultivate authentic two-way communication during staged brand activations.

CONCLUDING QUESTIONS

1. Why should experiential marketing not be used as a stand-alone activity, but rather as one that integrates with other communication mix elements?

2. What are the primary advantages of utilising experiential marketing after the use of more traditional marketing communication elements?
3. Outline how the Experiential Marketing Implementation Model fits into Belch et al.'s (2001) Integrated Marketing Communications Model.
4. Using examples, provide an overview of how you would design an experiential marketing campaign that fits into an IMC approach.

REFERENCES AND FURTHER READING

Belch, G.W., Belch, G.E., & Belch, M.A. (2001). *Advertising and Promotion: An Integrated Marketing Communications Perspective*. New York: McGraw-Hill.

Kailani, C., & Ciobotar, N. (2015). Experiential Marketing: An Efficient Tool to Leverage Marketing Communication Impact on Consumer Behaviour. *International Conference on Marketing and Business Development Journal*, 1(1), 1–7.

Keller, K.L. (2016). Unlocking the Power of Integrated Marketing Communications: How Integrated is Your IMC Program? *Journal of Advertising*, 45(3), 286–301. https://doi.org/10.1080/00913367.2016.1204967

LaSalle, D., & Britton, T.A. (2003). *Priceless: Turning Ordinary Products into Extraordinary Experiences*. Boston, MA: Harvard Business School Press.

Lenderman, M. (2005). *Experience the Message: How Experiential Marketing is Changing the Brand World*. New York: Carroll & Graf Publishers.

Li, A., & Yang, D. (2010). *Business Advertising Strategy in Experiential Marketing*. Paper presented at the 2010 International Conference on Management and Service Science, Wuhan, China, 24-26 August.

Schmitt, B.H. (1999). Experiential Marketing. *Journal of Marketing Management*, 15(1–3), 53–67.

Schmitt, B.H. (2000). *Experiential Marketing: How to Get Customers to Sense, Feel, Think, Act, Relate to your Company and Brands*. New York: The Free Press.

Smilansky, S. (2009). *Experiential Marketing: A Practical Guide to Interactive Brand Experiences*. London: Kogan Page.

9

BUDGETING FOR EXPERIENTIAL MARKETING

CHAPTER OVERVIEW

So far in this book, you have been equipped with the tools and knowledge that are required to successfully plan and execute an experiential marketing activation. Through the introduction of the Experiential Marketing Implementation Model and the Experiential Marketing Amplification Framework, which have been conceptualised based on observations on how world leading brands utilise this marketing tool, there is a clear and unified approach. However, we have yet to examine in detail one major component: how to set and justify a budget for an experiential marketing campaign. Experiential marketing is widely regarded as an expensive activity, and thus, it is critical that marketers know how to effectively set an appropriate budget. Before we can discuss allocating money to experiential marketing, we need to begin with a broader discussion on how funds are allocated to marketing in general, to different marketing activities and then to different elements of the communications mix.

Specifically, in this chapter we will discuss:

- How funds are allocated to and among marketing activities.
- How to successfully allocate appropriate funds to the different elements of communications in an integrated marketing campaign to optimise the campaign outcome.
- How to effectively allocate budgetary funds to experiential marketing.
- How to justify the experiential marketing budgetary allocation.

METHODS OF ALLOCATING BUDGETARY FUNDS TO MARKETING

A topic that has garnered much academic attention in recent years is the optimal allocation of financial resources to marketing budgets. A primary responsibility of

marketing managers is to evaluate and identify the optimal levels and allocation of marketing resources (Sridhar et al., 2011). To effectively do this, it is essential that decisions are fact-based rather than intuitive (Fischer et al., 2011). Marketing budgets can come to fruition in many ways, typically, commencing at a top management level. Each department then decides the specific allocation of the funds (top-down distribution). Alternatively, the budget may commence in the marketing department where a proposal is collated and presented to top management (floor-up distribution), or it may be created through a combination of top-down and floor-up methods (Alon et al., 2012). The most common types of budget allocation methods that derive from top-down and floor-up approaches are outlined in Table 9.1.

Table 9.1 Methods for determining the marketing budget

Objective and Task Budget Method	Budgets are formed based on the costs of tactics that are compiled in order to fulfil the specified marketing plan objectives. This is a suitable floor-up method for large organisations that (1) have invested time in brand planning prior to budgeting, (2) can identify specific tactics for specific objectives, and (3) can invest in campaign reporting which ensures accountability and transparency. When using this form of budgeting, it is important not to allocate too high a budget that surpasses the organisation's resources.
Econometric Modelling Method	Using formulas that take into account identified areas of interest, including budget restraints, anticipated customer sentiment, forecasted profitability and excess share of voice (ESOV) forecasts, this floor-up algorithmic approach calculates a suggested budget that takes into account key economic factors.
Affordability Budget Method	Employing a top-down approach, management set the marketing budget based on what the organisation can afford. Then the marketing manager creates the marketing plan based on this figure. This method does not take into account competitive forces, economic conditions, potential profits or other variable factors.
Percentage Budget Method	The marketing budget is formulated based on a percentage of the previous year's annual turnover and next year's expected turnover, while also taking into account product profit margins. This method solely focuses on internal factors and does not consider the economic environment or market conditions.
Competitive Parity Budget Method	Management sets the marketing budget based on industry average budgets and competitors' average marketing spend. In this case, a marketing budget would be set at a minimum, equal to that of a competitor, if not exceeding it. However, this method comes with risk as no two organisations are the same, have the same processes or the other's financial information. Therefore, this approach may be disadvantageous and work against the optimal and efficient management of brands.

Source: Armstrong (2009)

In essence, although top-down methods of budget setting are relatively easy to apply, they fail to recognise the importance of the investment that is required to fulfil marketing plan objectives. Similar observations can be made for floor-up methods as they typically focus on the marketing activity and disregard the economic and competitive environment. In practice, it is recommended to apply a combination of top-down and floor-up methods, guided by business planning, strategic marketing planning, observations based on the economic and competitive environment, and budgetary confinements based on affordability.

Once the overall marketing budget has been established, it is the responsibility of the marketing manager to divide it up between specific activations, while also balancing long-term brand building with short-term sales activations. According to Binet and Field (2013), the correct allocation is 60/40: 60% of your marketing activity should be brand building and 40% should be sales-focused activations. Brand building campaigns tend to be emotive by nature, are highly creative and tend to cultivate brand fame. As a result, they tend to have more long-term business effects, fuelling the long-term viability of the brand. The Dove examples below illustrate how a brand would allocate funds to brand building and to sales activations. The first example shows how Dove used the Selfie Self-Esteem Project to build the brand's image and vision, and the second example demonstrates how Dove built on this campaign to drive sales of its bath products for children.

Dove's Selfie Self-Esteem Project

A recent example of a successful brand building campaign implemented by Dove skincare is their 'Selfie Self-Esteem Project'. As the brand's vision states, Dove believes that beauty should be a source of confidence for women, not anxiety. Dove aims to help women globally to develop a positive relationship with their appearance, building their self-esteem and fulfilling their personal potential. Linked to this vision, Dove launched their emotive Selfie Self-Esteem campaign based on research which shows that, by the age of 13, 85% of girls are using retouching apps and filters on pictures of themselves due to low levels of self-esteem. These photo-editing tools enable users to alter their appearance, making their skin look smoother, and lighter and altering the shape of both their face and physique. In research conducted by the Dove Selfie Self-Esteem Project, the brand uncovered that the longer girls spent editing their photos, the lower they reported their levels of self-esteem. As part of their project, and to address this growing issue in the younger generation, Dove released a campaign video titled 'Reverse Selfie'. The video shows a young girl doing her makeup, taking a photograph of herself and heavily editing it before uploading the selfie, but in a reverse sequence. It presents the 'perfect woman' at the beginning of the video and ends with a young, natural girl sitting in her

(Continued)

bedroom. Aiming to aid the delivery of Dove's brands vision, this campaign aims to overcome the modern-day presence of retouched and edited images online and aid young girls to be more self-confident. To further help tackle this problem, the Dove Self-Esteem Project have devised free 'Confidence Kits' which can be downloaded from the brand's website. These kits contained information on bullying, socal media, effective communication and body functionality for parents and children to ensure they have the tools to build body confidence.

Dove launches new bath products for kids

Building on what they learned from the Dove Selfie Self-Esteem Project, Dove launched a new bath collection for kids where the product packaging featured positive affirmations tailored to the target audience. They used a QR code on the packaging to give consumers access to interactive body confidence resources, including the previously mentioned 'Confidence Kits'. The range of tear-free products, made with 100% skin natural ingredients and 100% post-consumer recyclable plastics, was launched through a multi-channel campaign where the primary objective was to drive sales for this new product range.

While emotional campaigns directly correlate with brand building initiatives, rational campaigns produce a short-term sales effect and deliver on short-term results. Emotional campaigns can produce a strong sales return, and they can have an impact on long-term success. It is therefore necessary to ensure that there is an effective distribution of budgetary funds between brand building and sales-focused activations in order to have an efficient return on marketing spend.

Marketing managers also account for the fixed overheads that may occur during brand activations. Depending on the scale of the business, budget allocations may also have to be shared between products, regions, activities, segments, business units, brands or product categories.

If we were to imagine an experiential activation being used in the case of Dove, for example, an activation focused on brand building would run alongside the Selfie Self-Esteem Project, while an activation focused on sales would run alongside the Bath Products campaign, with the funds coming from the appropriate budgets.

BUDGETING FOR AN INTEGRATED MARKETING CAMPAIGN

Once the marketing budget has been decided and, furthermore, once it is clear what funds are available for a communications programme, the next step is to allocate funds to the different elements of an integrated marketing communications strategy. As a general rule of thumb, the 70/20/10 rule should be applied: 70% of the budget should be allocated towards media that has been tried and tested by the organisation; 20% of the budget should be used on testing and learning; and 10% of the budget should be completely exploratory. Here, it is recommended to test new creatives, messages or platforms that essentially are a safe bet. For example, a new creative on an Out of Home (OOH) campaign. The exploratory budget can be spent on tools or platforms that are new to the business and are deemed to be a complete gamble that may not deliver on the KPIs but are worth taking a chance on as they show promise. Another potential use of the exploratory budget is to garner media or competitive attention.

When breaking down an annual marketing budget, campaigns and activations will typically take form in an integrated approach. This is to ensure campaign effectiveness by increasing the campaign touchpoints and utilising marketing communications tools that work in harmony to ensure the most effective outcome. Depending on the budget allocated to an integrated marketing campaign, different communications tools may be employed. In modern marketing, there are communications methods that are typically employed to increase reach, improve effectiveness and facilitate authentic interactions. However, the order in which they are used and the investment that is allocated to them can vary depending on the campaign and the budget. In research conducted by the authors of this book, it was identified that traditional and mass marketing communications are prioritised, and the remaining funds are typically allocated towards experiential activations.

> We look at point of sale, how much point of sale is going to be, and if we can afford an experiential at that end of it, that is how it would go, and we just see what happens. But, what tends to happen is that the budgets tend to be cannibalised because we do place a lot of importance on just activating the campaigns, but you do need your standard point of sale kit, FSDUs,[1] posters, wobblers the list goes on. (Experiential Execution Excellence Manager)

> There is a lot that would come before experiential in budget allocation. If we have enough budget, we will do experiential. Instore point of sale, secondary siting, FSDUs and online tend to come first, then experiential would be done if we have the budget. (Shopper Activation Manager)

> There would not be a distinct experiential allocation. It comes out of the overall brand budget and would be funded from within that. The experiential supports the brand campaign rather than trying to find ways to execute experiential. (Marketing Manager)

> We would look at what assets are available to us from a media point of view, we would then identify the spend that we need in order for us to hit the metric that is set for us in terms of awareness. Then we would look at the spend in the budgets for the activation and look at what is left over that can be set aside for experiential, social, PR and all of that. It is not a case of where we have a possible budget that we will have specific allocations. It is more around an objective where we need to hit a certain coverage from a media perspective and then we revisit the budget after that and see what is available to us in terms of experiential and all of that. (Marketing Manager)

Evidently, in IMCs there is a clear reliance on traditional marketing tools in order to ensure campaign reach and awareness KPIs are achieved. Thus, traditional marketing methods are allocated a significant proportion of the campaign budget due to their innate ability to deliver rich consumer touchpoints instore and in high footfall areas. Although the reach mechanism has been clearly identified as a valuable attribute of traditional marketing methods, it is also recognised that marketing tools of this nature do not possess the ability to facilitate authentic and immersive customer interactions that are essential to develop the relationship between the consumer and the brand.

The Field Museum's integrated marketing campaign #StopAWarrior

In a bid to drive attendance and awareness for their special exhibition on China's ancient terracotta warriors, The Field Museum in Chicago decided to bring the attractions to a mass audience through a strategic integrated marketing campaign (IMC) called #StopAWarrior. The core component of the campaign was focused on showcasing replicas of the Chinese terracotta warriors at surprise locations in Chicago including Maggie Daley Park, the Chicago Cubs Baseball Stadium and Queens Landing at Monroe Harbour. To maximise exposure and interaction, they opted for traditional marketing methods first to build buzz and brand awareness. OOH advertising methods were used, including lamp post banners and billboard advertisements, to alert potential attendees to this experiential activation. Paid media campaigns were also launched prior to the activation. These displayed interactive ad units, offering customers another touchpoint to interact with the immersive campaign. Clues to the possible locations of the statues were announced on the museum's social media platforms hours before the monuments were due to appear, generating true viral engagement. Influencers with a special interest in activation locations were appointed 'Cultural Ambassador' status to attend and further amplify the #StopAWarrior campaign. After the event, 360° videos were launched on social media to help the campaign transcend the physical barriers of the event in Chicago and allow it to live on a global platform.

The #StopAWarrior campaign is an exemplar case because it shows that while the experiential activation required a proportion of the campaign budget to ensure its effectiveness, the majority of the budget was invested in traditional marketing methods to generate the buzz and awareness needed to achieve campaign success. Nevertheless, experiential marketing has an important role to play in modern integrated marketing communications, facilitating authentic and memorable interactions between brands and consumers.

So, let's recap where we are now before moving on. Once the marketing budget has been decided, a marketing team will typically spend 60% of the budget on brand building activities and 40% of the budget on sales focused activities. When choosing the media channels for these activities, marketers are guided by the 70/20/10 rule. Therefore, when we combine the tendency to spend most of the budget on tried-and-trusted media with the necessity of using traditional media prior to an experiential activation, we see that experiential marketing is likely to receive a much smaller proportion of the budget than other marketing communications tools. The next section outlines the typical proportion that experiential marketing receives, based on the research conducted for this book.

BREAKDOWN OF THE BUDGET ALLOCATION TO EXPERIENTIAL MARKETING

Through research conducted by the authors, the optimal budget allocation on experiential marketing was identified. Depending on the size of the campaign and the given campaign objectives, the allocation of funds to experiential in an integrated marketing campaign lies between 10% and 40% of the overall campaign budget. While there is an identified range of how much to allocate towards experiential marketing, brands do not have a structured approach as to how they exactly decide how much exactly the allocate to experiential marketing, but rather base their decisions solely on the campaign objective. Depending on the role that experiential marketing plays in successfully meeting the campaign objective and key performance indicators (KPIs), experiential marketing can be used in a multitude of ways. It means different amounts of the budget are allocated to the communications tool. For example, if the objective of a campaign is to build brand saliency, experiential marketing will form a large component of an IMC, possibly garnering a high percentage of the 10-40% budget allocation. In order to fulfil the 'brand in hand' objective where brands want consumers to taste of interact with the brand, experiential marketing would play a fundamental role. However, if the campaign objective was to increase brand recall, traditional forms of outdoor advertising and digital marketing with a high reach frequency will be favoured over experiential marketing. In this case, the experiential marketing budget allocation will fall cover to 10% of the campaign budget allocation.

Of course, budget allocation can also be influenced by the innovation and inventiveness of the marketing team, and their willingness to move away from tried-and-tested media and to experiment with newer channels. If a company has already had success with experiential marketing activations, they may begin to consider experiential marketing as 'tried and trusted', and budget accordingly. Whereas a company using experiential marketing for the first time is likely to be much more cautious in its approach and allocate a much smaller budget to the experiential marketing component.

JUSTIFYING THE EXPERIENTIAL MARKETING BUDGET ALLOCATION

Equipped with the knowledge on how to allocate a budget to experiential marketing, the next challenge that may arise is justifying this spend. As previously stated in this book, experiential marketing has falsely been perceived as being expensive and with a low return on investment. Marketing managers therefore need to be able to justify their decision-making when utilising experiential marketing as part of an integrated marketing campaign. The following reasons explain why experiential marketing is an integral part of a marketing campaign:

- Emotions drive our decision-making and experiential marketing is all about creating emotional bonds between a customer and a brand, which it achieves through facilitating authentic interactions. Research conducted by Zaltman (2003) found that 95% of purchasing decisions are made by someone's subconscious mind. Thus, if marketers want customers to favour and buy a brand, it is essential to facilitate an authentic, intimate and personal interaction through an experiential marketing activation.
- Experiential marketing affords marketers the opportunity to collate rich data in the moment. Consumers enjoy the two-way communication that is facilitated through branded activations and are happy to interact with brand representatives. Thus, it is a great opportunity to test new product variants, ask consumers for feedback and conduct sentiment studies. All of these data collection opportunities cannot be facilitated through traditional marketing to the same extent.
- At experiential marketing events, consumers have the opportunity to sample the product, thus reducing the future risk of purchase in their mind while building deeper connections with the brand, which in turn enriches memory structures.
- As an experiential marketing activation is conducted in a controlled, branded environment, it creates positive associations with the brand that are authentic and individual. If consumers feel ambiguous about a product, experiential marketing helps them to understand the product, brand or service, which

cannot be developed to the same level through other advertising methods. The brand becomes more relevant to customers as they build their own relationship with the brand, which further enhances brand relevancy. This type of active participation generates a higher recall rate, which results in greater levels of brand advocacy and loyalty. When experiential marketing is consistent with the core branding values and key messaging, strong brand resonance will be built.

- Experiential marketing has a higher rate of shareability as it cultivates social currency and consumers share their experiences online. This allows experiential marketing to transcend the physical barriers of a marketing event and to reach a much larger audience. Consumers' participation in the marketing activity further enhances their understanding of the brand in a virtuous circle of benefits.

CONCLUSION AND SUMMARY

Budgeting for marketing can often be a difficult and complex business, and is made even more so if the C-suite (Corporate executive) doesn't appreciate the role that marketing can play in company success. This difficulty is often compounded when allocating funds to experiential marketing, given the relative newness of the concept and the lack of guidelines for its implementation and, indeed, its evaluation. In this chapter we have outlined the ways in which funds can be allocated to marketing, and subsequently to experiential marketing. We have recommended the typical percentages of a budget that ideally should be allocated to an experiential marketing campaign, in the context of the market and the overall objectives of the campaign.

MAIN TAKEAWAYS FOR CHAPTER 9

- Companies typically use one of five methods to allocate funds to marketing: the objective and task budget method; the econometric modelling method; the affordability budget method; the percentage budget method; and the competitive parity budget method (Armstrong, 2009).
- Most marketing campaigns will direct 60% of the funds towards brand building activities and the remaining 40% of the funds for driving sales.
- When funds are allocated to the different elements of a marketing communication programme, experiential campaigns can expect to receive between 10% and 40% of the overall budget. The variation in amount is

(Continued)

driven by the objectives of the campaign, the experience and innovation of the marketing team, the necessity to spend on traditional media before undertaking the experiential activation, the target market and the types of KPIs in use.

- Marketers should feel confident in their use of experiential marketing and in requesting sufficient funds to develop spectacular campaigns, given the potentially significant outcomes that can be achieved.

CONCLUDING QUESTIONS

1. Outline the ways in which companies can choose to allocate funds to marketing.
2. Explain why you think the 60/40 breakdown in a typical marketing budget between brand building and sales activation is a good or a bad idea.
3. If you were a marketing manager for a vintage clothing company, would you be inclined to spend more than the recommended 20% and 10% on new and novel marketing content and channels? Explain your answer.
4. Discuss the reasons behind the variation in the typical 10–40% of the budget that is allocated to experiential marketing.
5. In your opinion, what component of an experiential marketing campaign consumes most of the budget?

NOTE

1. FSDU: Free Standing Display Unit. These are stand-alone display units that would be used instore to display product with key messaging on the unit relating to a specific campaign or promotion.

REFERENCES AND FURTHER READING

Alon, N., Gamzu, I., & Tennenholtz, M. (2012). Optimizing Budget Allocation among Channels and Influencers. *Proceedings of the 21st International Conference on World Wide Web*, April, 381–388. https://doi.org/10.1145/2187836.2187888

Armstrong, G. (2009). *Marketing: An Introduction*. Harlow: Pearson.

Binet, L., & Field, P. (2013). *The Long and the Short of It: Balancing Short and Long-term Marketing Strategies*. London: Institute of Practitioners in Advertising.

Fischer, M., Albers, S., Wagner, N., & Frie, M. (2011). Practice Prize Winner: Dynamic Marketing Budget Allocation across Countries, Products, and Marketing Activities. *Marketing Science*, *30*(4), 568–585.

Sridhar, S., Mantrala, M., Naik, P., & Thornson, E. (2011). Dynamic Marketing Budgeting for Platform Firms: Theory, Evidence and Application. *Journal of Marketing Research*, Online first, 1 December. https://doi.org/10.1509/jmr.10.0035

Zaltman, G. (2003). *How Consumers Think: Essential Insights into the Mind of the Market*. Boston, MA: Harvard Business School Press.

10 MEASURING THE RETURN OF EXPERIENTIAL MARKETING

CHAPTER OVERVIEW

This book has laid out the endless possibilities that experiential marketing offers as a marketing tactic and strategy. The creative use of this strategic communications tool has potentially impactful consequences on brand health, customer engagement and many other factors. The question remains, however, how best to measure these impacts in a way that makes sense not only for the marketing team, but also for those to whom the marketing team is accountable, whether that is a board of directors or a finance team. Being able to measure the impact of experiential marketing activities in a manner that reflects its strategic intention, while also translating that impact into measures that are meaningful to a non-marketing audience, is the key challenge. In essence, successful experiential marketing activity must be predicated on transparency and accountability in the same way as other marketing activities are. But this is not a challenge that has been well met. There is extensive practice-based confusion about the best approach to measurability. Equally, the academic literature – while being interesting – is not being deployed consistently by practitioners. This chapter will show that much of this relates to a tension between concepts such as reward and return as they relate to experiential marketing. Specifically, this chapter will present information on the following:

- The key difficulties in establishing a principle of measurability for experiential marketing.
- The differences in perspectives between an emphasis on 'return on investment' and 'return on experience' based on input from practitioners.
- A justification for the use of 'return on integrated experience' (ROIE) as a mechanism to provide a holistic and functional measure of return.

- An implementation plan for deploying ROIE to measure an integrated marketing campaign.

This chapter concludes with a worked example of ROIE.

BACKGROUND AND CONTEXT

In this section we will present the primary methods of evaluating the success of experiential marketing. We will later explore the practitioner perspective that will then aid the development of the ROIE approach which was developed as part of our research with major international brands.

Today, in the marketing sector, accountability for the actual or potential success of a campaign is an integral element of marketing strategy. Simply, marketing is now much more focused on measurability. This is partly as a result of marketing casting off the shackles of its poor reputation in this discipline and partly as a result of the increased potential for measurability that has emanated from its positioning in a digital world. For firms to successfully measure the return on marketing, they need to treat the allocation of marketing expenditure as an investment (Hughes et al., 2019). Traditionally, marketing has been myopically viewed as a short-term expense (Rust et al., 2004), only to be indulged in when finances allow and being the first for belt-tightening when times are leaner. The issues with this approach are well established (Binet & Field, 2018). For marketing expenditure to be considered as an investment, comparable to other tangible and intangible company assets, the marketing function has to play a role in the organisational strategy (Schultz & Gronstedt, 1997). Marketers are now expected to provide quantifiable evidence that marketing investments are contributing to real, preferably tangible, results (Kehrer, 2015). In an effort to aid marketers in the presentation of this tangible data, marketing metrics used to quantify this have been created. Binet and Field (2013) state that marketing metrics can be divided into two categories: short-term metrics and long-term metrics. Both metrics have different brand effects. Short-term metrics measure brand promotional activity offering short-term growth, and long-term metrics measure brand building tactics that offer long-term growth. Both categories of metrics are essential as they each relate to different components of success.

Traditionally, the return on marketing activities has been calculated through a marketing return on investment (MROI), also commonly referred to as return on marketing investment formula (ROMI) (Kehrer, 2015). MROI creates positive value for a firm by demonstrating the marketing activity or campaign costs versus its payback (Young & Aitken, 2007). There are fundamental differences between the traditional return on investment (ROI) used in the financial sector and MROI, which is specifically used in marketing. To calculate ROI, the benefit (or return) of an investment is divided by the cost of the investment. The result is expressed as a percentage or a ratio. MROI is an estimate of the incremental financial value of marketing activity or campaign, generated by identifiable marketing expenditures, minus the cost of the specified expenditures as a percentage of the expenditures (Farris et al., 2015):

$$\text{MROI} = \frac{\text{Incremental financial value generated by marketing} - \text{Cost of marketing}}{\text{Cost of marketing}}$$

MROI is viewed as a *predictive* formula, utilised by a business or brand to demonstrate cost versus payback (Harden & Heyman, 2011; Young & Aitken, 2007). However, it is not merely a reflection of the past success or failure of a marketing campaign, but also a valuable tool in forecasting.

There are three distinct differences between ROI and MROI (summarised by Farris et al., 2015):

1. ROI metrics tend to be calculated in the form of annual returns; in contrast, MROI is typically allocated to the current period.
2. ROI is linked to a specified time period, but in MROI, marketing investments typically generate profit over an extended time period (i.e. multiple years), building cumulative impact and generating assets with a potential future value.
3. Unlike other types of investments, marketing funds tend to be liquid and not investments tied to inventories, fixed assets, or receivables.

In an attempt to quantify the return on experiential marketing, alternative methods to MROI have been developed, typically referred to as 'return on experience' (ROX) in marketing practice or 'return on engagement' (ROE) in academic literature. These are explored in the following section.

MEASURING THE RETURN ON EXPERIENCE

Experiential marketing is a complicated strategy. As we have shown in this book, it is most successful when close attention is paid to various aspects, ranging from design of experience through to amplification. Furthermore, it is accepted that without the emphasis on amplification, the numbers of those impacted by an experiential activation can be quite small and, as such, it can be an expensive way to reach customers. With each participatory interaction, the cost of experiential marketing rises due to the growing scale of the event:

> One of the challenges with experiential marketing is that it is really expensive because you can only afford to net a certain number of people to have that experience. So, the cost per contact or the conversion per contact is quite high and expensive. (European Marketing Director)

Cost per interaction can certainly act as a barrier to implementation. The lack of availability of long-term brand effect data and consumer tracking acts as another barrier when calculating the return of experiential marketing, which must also be considered.

> You just don't ultimately know if you are sampling an on-the-go product, we have no way of knowing if they came back. You can spend the money; it can be a great experience and they can go away feeling brilliantly but they may not have come back to your brand. In that case, the only thing you can use is your share, your volume of sales or your value of sales. But you don't know that's how they came back. It definitely is a challenge but that does not mean you don't do it because of the challenge, you just need to be mindful that it is not a perfect science. (Marketing Manager)

In short, from a measurability perspective, there is a lot to be considered in developing an appropriate measure of success/impact. Given the emphasis on customer experience in modern marketing, it is increasingly difficult not to include ROE as an aspect of the metrics and measurability landscape. Although return on investment (ROI) can be deemed a reliable method of calculation, it does not currently deliver on the principle of inclusivity with respect to measuring the impact of experiential activities, nor does it capture the development of relationships as a result of experiential marketing activity (Frawley, 2015). Harris (2016) considers the concept of MROI to be losing relevance due to the ever-changing nature of marketing. Despite these limitations and the increasing acceptance of the need to measure ROE, there currently exists no defined method for its measurement.

Lenderman (2005) tells us that return on experience represents a long-term measurement of consumer satisfaction, comprising consumer experiences, interactions and reactions. Smith and Hanover (2016) state that the metrics utilised to quantify ROE are subjective, and depend on the brand and the campaign at play. They suggest a selection of the following metrics: attendee demographics, satisfaction, mindshare, journey, sales leads, acquisition costs, lifetime value, revenue and sales growth, event body language, digital body language, press impact, advocacy, sales impact, sales velocity, speed to action, net promoter score and message retention. As a customer learns about a brand through an authentic engagement interaction, they are more likely to develop favourable attitudes towards the brand or business, which will produce favourable economic outcomes. Any increase in perceived value cultivates loyalty and trust, which also influence purchase frequency (Reinartz & Ulaga, 2008). These aspects must be measured if the experiential activation is to be properly evaluated. Evidently, then, challenges arise when trying to create a universal measurement for these parameters and in determining their effectiveness (Srinivasan & Srivastava, 2010).

Although ROE has attracted the attention of marketing practitioners, this has not been widely shared in the academic world, possibly because of the difficulties that arise in its measurement and its less than solid theoretical base. Academics prefer to stick with the more traditional, tried-and-tested methods of measurement and evaluation. However, according to Gill et al., (2017), engagement initiatives have quintessential differences from traditional marketing methods, and these differences must be reflected in methods of evaluation. First, unlike traditional marketing activities, engagement initiatives' primary goal is not generating a sale but to cultivate

strong, long-term relationships with customers. Second, unlike conventional marketing methods that tend to be formed by one-way communication, engagement initiatives tend to be interactive and elicit conversation and authentic experiences. In fact, Van Doorn et al. (2010) found that customers who have participated in brand experiences have a higher perceived connectedness to a brand, even when they do not purchase the brand. It is essential that these interactions are measured and managed in order to build stronger relationships, which can potentially lead to profitable value extraction (Gill et al., 2017). Thus, for many brands trying to quantify the benefits of their experiential spend, ROE, despite the lack of defined measurement methods and less than enthusiastic academic support, offers a more compelling and relevant metric than what has gone before, as it enables brands to gauge the effectiveness of live customer experiences. As experiential marketing utilises personalisation to segment and target markets, or to differentiate experiences between target markets, measuring the ROE allows businesses to individually measure and improve the experience according to each target market segment (Harris, 2016).

In addition to the ROE method, the concept of ROE^2 (return on experience × engagement), conceptualised by Frawley (2014), has also been created to determine the return on experiential marketing. In comparison to MROI, which calculates the short-term measurement of specific, individual campaigns, ROE^2 correlates a long-term, holistic measurement of consumers' brand experience in its totality and their level of engagement (Frawley, 2015). In essence, it measures the emotional connection with a brand and customers' actions as a result, such as referring the brand to friends and family, becoming a loyal customer or downloading a brand's app (Frawley, 2014). Fundamentally, 'ROE^2 starts with an actionable brand idea that triggers a positive consumer experience and engagement, leading to a higher return on brand and business equity' (Frawley, 2014: 54). In comparison to ROE, ROE^2 is mathematically correlated through multiple regression analysis. Regression analysis is used to determine how a set of variables predict or explain an outcome variable of interest. It creates an algorithm that quantifies the correlation between the explanatory variables and the outcome variable (von Eye & Schuster, 1998). In mathematical terms, the equation is:

$$ROE^2 = f\,(EX_i + EN_i + O_i)$$

where:

ROE^2 = measures of brand business equity (the outcome variable)
EX_i = measures of customer experience
EN_i = measures of customer engagement
O_i = other variables that influence ROE^2

Source: Frawley (2014) Copyright John Wiley & Sons Limited (2014), printed with permission

Poulsson and Kale (2004) believe that for brand experiences to be successfully implemented, they should be personally relevant to the customer, be novel, offer an element of surprise, be authentic, and engage with the customer. However, live brand experiences are rarely implemented as an isolated marketing tactic, but rather are integrated with a multitude of marketing tactics using a broad array of channels (Ruchi et al., 2017), and herein lies a problem with the utilisation of ROE^2. This method of calculation requires brands to use experiential marketing in isolation and for no other marketing activity to take place in a similar time duration. This is problematic for us, as you will know by now that we strongly advocate for an integrated approach to the use of experiential marketing, which ultimately demands an integrated approach to its measurement, something that is not accounted for by either ROE or ROE^2.

Most recently, PricewaterhouseCoopers (PWC) published a new measurement for calculating return on experience (or as they refer to it, ROX). According to the PWC report on the metric (PWC, 2019: 12): 'An ROX framework zeroes in on customer touchpoints that need shoring up. It can also help identify the things your company does exceptionally well, and then make sure your IT systems, data infrastructure, business processes and performance metrics are aligned with those capabilities.' PWC refer to their ROX measurement as a virtuous cycle that strengthens the value of:

1. The emotional commitment to and pride in brand strategy and brand purpose.
2. The involvement of internal and external brand ambassadors or influencers and sources of emotional energy.
3. The behaviours that typically define a brand's culture and values, which are typically assessed in performance management.
4. The value drivers not only from the consumers' perspective but also from the perspective of the employees.
5. The financial outcomes that are produced by a higher ROX.

(Cornwell, 2020; PWC, 2019)

While not providing a precise calculation, we summarise that ROX is a repetitious measurement formed on the foundation of both customer touchpoints and employees as essential contributors to the culture of an experience. It is set apart from the previous experiential marketing evaluation frameworks by its focus on the employees as well as customers and recognises feedback loops (Cornwell, 2020; PWC, 2019). Although this model sets a strong foundation for the implementation of successful experience events, the outcome of the return of experience from this perspective has not been examined. However, a key limitation of this calculation is that it does not account for ROI metrics, and thus, potentially, lacks academic veracity.

With the growth in experiential marketing comes a growing requirement for brands to employ appropriate measurement tactics, and while we have outlined

some measurement methods that can be employed, there is no one method employed by practitioners that is deemed complete and appropriate, nor does one exist in the academic literature. Indeed, our research has shown that brands use different methods, or a combination of methods, as they deem appropriate. Nevertheless, all our research participants articulated that they were not completely happy with any measurement tactic.

Having established that ROE^2, MROI or ROX are not the best approaches to evaluating the return of an experiential marketing campaign, in the next section we present what we believe to be a complete method of measuring experiential marketing, which we call 'return on integrated experience' (ROIE).

RETURN ON INTEGRATED EXPERIENCE

To recap, there are several methods available to marketers to aid them in evaluating the outcome of an experiential marketing campaign. These include the concept of return on marketing investment (MROI, also referred to as ROMI), as discussed by Lenskold (2003) and Powell (2002), return on experience (ROE), as discussed by Lenderman (2005), Frawley's (2014) ROE^2 and PWC's (2019) ROX, which evaluates the accumulative effect of the customer experience and the employee experience. These methods are not wonderfully suited to evaluating experiential marketing activations in a way that is both operationally and strategically valuable. We believe that the primary reason for this is that these calculations do not account for all the relevant metrics that brands are measuring, and therefore do not offer a view of the campaign result in totality. The lack of focus on 'integration' – as an established point of importance in the successful implementation of experiential marketing – severely limits a holistic view of return and reward. Essentially, the previously discussed metrics either primarily focus on the return of investment or the return on experience in isolation. We know that practitioners have compelling reasons for using both of these forms of metrics. Therefore, there is significant need to develop a method of calculation that comprises all the relevant metrics.

This book presents a method of calculating the return on experiential marketing that is comprised of all the required metrics to successfully appraise the outcome of an experiential marketing campaign. It is essential that this approach is constituted of both ROI and ROE measurements to ensure a comprehensive evaluation of the marketing practice – as an integrated element of an overall campaign or strategy. Return on integrated experience (ROIE) offers academics and marketing practitioners a formula which accounts for all the fundamental categories of metrics which have not been considered in the previously published ROE measurements. ROIE lies in the middle of the continuum of ROI and ROE (Figure 10.1), and allows analysis of both of these critical factors to occur in one convenient calculation.

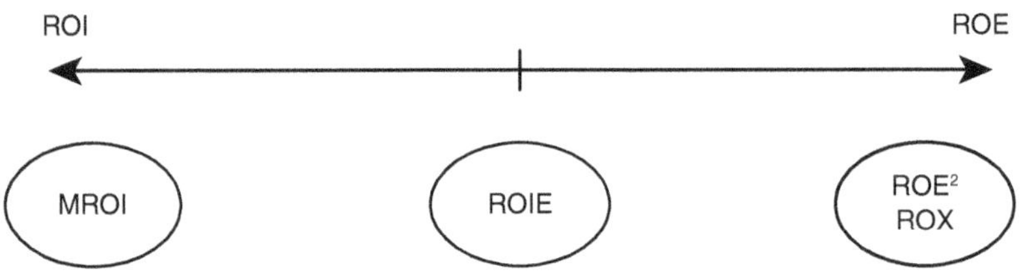

Figure 10.1 The continuum of experiential return calculations

Return on Integrated Experience: An Overview

Because there are quintessential differences between engagement initiatives and traditional marketing methods (Gill et al., 2017), the former must be reflected in the methods of evaluation. There are a multitude of metrics that brands can measure through key performance indictors (KPIs), including social media metrics, event metrics, PR metrics, brand health metrics and financial measurements of data from retailer EPOS (electronic point of sale) and category sales uplift. We have reviewed the metrics that are employed by brands and have compartmentalised them into three categories:

1. Functional metrics
2. Financial metrics
3. Holistic metrics

The categorisational structure of these metrics takes inspiration from Kaplan and Norton's (1992) paper outlining the Balanced Scorecard Approach, where operational effectiveness is reviewed from a variety of perspectives. Similarly, with ROIE we can appraise the outcome of an experiential marketing activation from more than one approach. Through these three categories, we can measure the campaign metrics, the financial performance of the campaign and the effect that the marketing campaign has had on the brand. Table 10.1 lists all the metrics that industry practitioners use when evaluating the practice of experiential marketing (gathered from our research), which we have sorted into these three categories. Using the three categories of metrics, we detail below how they collectively offer the foundation of the return of integrated experience (ROIE) formula.

As well as the Balanced Scorecard approach (Kaplan & Norton, 1992), the ROIE calculation also takes inspiration from Marshall's (1890) cost–benefit analysis, based on the principles of evaluation outlined by Dupuit in an article written in 1848. Building on the core premise of Marshall's Cost-Benefit theory, which measures the costs and benefits pertaining to a specific action, our research suggests that the key metrics in the ROIE equation should be divided into two categories, *return* and *reward*.

In Table 10.1, *return* comprises two categories of metrics – functional metrics and financial metrics – and *reward* constitutes the holistic metrics. Both the functional and financial return components can be classified as a campaign outputs they are measurable and constitute an action on the brand's behalf. The *return* component of the campaign directly correlates to the campaign strategy, which is developed from the campaign objective and KPIs. Through the correct targeting, positioning and selection of communication tools, the *return* should theoretically portray a positive outcome correlating to the prescribed action. Analysis of the metrics listed in these categories will help the marketer to make an informed decision as to whether or not a return has been yielded from the campaign. Where there is no return, there is no profit.

The remaining category, holistic reward, measures the outcome of the marketing activation using brand health metrics. The success of the metrics that are being measured in this category will be directly correlated to the success of the outcome of the functional and financial return. The *reward* component of this formula assesses the strength and validity of the marketing strategy, targeting and positioning, and tests whether it successfully appealed to the target market and not only generated a positive campaign outcome, but also contributed to the development of brand health and brand equity. Since the holistic reward category of measurement has the ability to increase brand value over time, rather than result in immediate impact, it can result in additional profit. Therefore, it is an enabler of brand performance. However, because the holistic reward can be measured over the long term, it is essential to establish the period of time during which the category is measured. Most marketing activities affect customers who won't buy a brand on a frequent basis, and therefore the sale effects can be spread out into the future (Sharp, 2010). Brands must decipher the period during which they are willing to assess the brand health metrics, as it is unsustainable to continue the campaign indefinitely. This is because the effect of the campaign will only be relevant to a certain timeframe.

Essentially, the *functional* and *financial return* measures the short-term effect and the *holistic reward* measures the long-term success. This approach is in line with that adopted by Binet and Field in their report *The Long and the Short of It*, where they state that 'emotional metrics are more likely to predict long-term success, whilst rational metrics are more likely to predict short term success' (Binet & Field, 2013: 9).

Similar to the theoretical framework behind Marshall's (1890) cost–benefit analysis, for the experiential campaign to be deemed a success the *reward* must exceed the value of the *return*. The reason lies in the premise that the *return* component is the direct output of the experiential campaign. The *reward* accounts for a longer-term effect where brands measure growth as a result of the campaign. Therefore, if the long-term effect outweighs the immediate effect, then the campaign has been successful and has positively impacted the brand.

Table 10.1 Return on integrated investment metrics

Methods						
Functional Metrics		Financial Metrics		Holistic Metrics		
					Customer	Commercial
Digital Marketing Metrics	Social Reach	ROI	Figures Coming In	Brand Health Metrics	Brand Usership Status	Brand Penetration
	Digital Amplification		Benchmarking		Brand Sentiment	Brand Growth
	Link Clicks		Working/ Non-Working Spend		Brand Recall	Brand Uplift
	Hashtags Utilisation		Projected ROI versus Real ROI		Brand Image	ESOV
	Social Engagement		Category Sale Uplift		Brand Relationships	
	Positive Earned Mentions		Investment Vs The Period		Brand Relevancy	
	Consumer Tracking		Conversion		Emotional Engagement	
	Digital Impressions		Value Set		Brand Saliency	
	Competition Entries		Market Share		Brand Love	
	Page Views				Affinity Score	
	Bounce Rate				Trial Awareness Score	
	Conversation Rate				Net Promoter Score (NPS)	
	Email Open Rate					
	Click Through Rate (CPR)					
	Influencers Outreach Coverage					
	Social Impressions					
	Google Hits and Spikes					
	Average Session Duration					
	Website Traffic					
	Cost Per Click (CPC)					
	Ranking of Specified Keywords					

Event Metrics	People Interacted with the Brand	
	Footfall	
	Freebie Dissemination	
	Samples Distributed	
	Consumer Feedback	
	Volume Targets	
	Cost per Sample	
	Revenue Generated on the Day	
	Leads Captured	
	Event Check Ins	
	Completed Attendee Satisfaction Surveys	
	Live Polling Response Rate	
	Total Registrations	
	GDPR Approved Emails Gathered for Mailing List	
	Attendance versus Activation Footfall	
Public Relations	Publicity Reach	
	General Sentiment	
	Media Impressions	
	Media Value	
	Readership of Articles	
	PR Mentions	
	Share of voice	
	Media Outreach	
	Key Message Penetration	
	Publicity Engagement	

Return on Integrated Experience: Operationalising

Operationalising the ROIE calculation is best performed by those who have access to relevant data and have a proper understanding of the strategic goals of the experiential marketing campaign and also how this translates into detail. This is not to suggest that it is difficult to use this calculation, merely that it requires informed input. From the outset, it is important to state that the purpose of ROIE is to evaluate the experiential contribution of an overall marketing campaign. The measurement works in tandem with the Experiential Marketing Implementation Model, presented in previous chapters, and therefore has two shared steps at the beginning of the process: setting the campaign objects and the key performance indicators (KPIs) (see Table 10.2). The inclusion of these steps in both the Experiential Marketing Implementation Model and ROIE highlight the importance of campaign planning and structure. Without this crucial information at the outset of both the Experiential Marketing Implementation Model and the ROIE formula, there is no basis for the successful implementation or evaluation of a marketing campaign. Major brands, such as Pepsi Max, underline the importance of being clear about campaign objectives before attempting to measure the output of a marketing campaign, as this informs the campaign measurements.

Table 10.2 ROIE Formulation Part 1

<table>
<tr><th colspan="6">ROIE Formulation</th></tr>
<tr><td colspan="6">Campaign Objective:</td></tr>
<tr><th colspan="6">Campaign KPIs</th></tr>
<tr><td colspan="2">KPI 1: Functional KPI</td><td colspan="2">KPI 2: Financial KPI</td><td colspan="2">KPI 3: Holistic KPI</td></tr>
<tr><td colspan="2"></td><td colspan="2"></td><td colspan="2"></td></tr>
<tr><td colspan="2">Functional Return</td><td colspan="2">Financial Return</td><td colspan="2">Holistic Reward</td></tr>
<tr><td>Target Metric</td><td>Actual Metric</td><td>Target Metric</td><td>Actual Metric</td><td>Target Metric</td><td>Actual Metric</td></tr>
</table>

Step 1: Metric selection: Once the campaign objectives and KPIs have been established, the brand must select the relevant metrics for the campaign. It is essential that the metrics are in line with the applicable category of KPI to accurately evaluate the success of the marketing campaign. For this to be achieved, the marketer must select five metrics from each category in Table 10.1 and establish a target for each one of them. The selection of five metrics in each of the

three categories is to ensure an element of focus. For example, in the category of digital marketing metrics, which resides in *functional reward,* the interview participants in our research identified 21 metrics that they have used to date. However, experiential marketing is prescriptive by nature and, depending on the campaign objectives, only certain metrics will be relevant. Thus, although 21 digital marketing metrics are mentioned in this category, not all of them will be relevant to a given experiential marketing campaign under review. Clear selection and forethought of metrics will allow for a malleable framework that can be adapted as required. This mirrors the approach established in the Balanced Scorecard (Kaplan & Norton, 1992).

Step 2: Capture metrics data: Once the campaign is completed, the brand must return to the ROIE framework and record the attained metrics of the experiential activation.

Step 3: Apply multiplier: Once the documentation of these metrics has been completed, in order to make the metrics in each category comparable, the ROIE evaluation approach applies a multiplier effect to each category in the form of a point system. As previously stated, it is essential to measure each category of metrics, but a key issue lies in the fact that without a multiplier effect, one cannot compare or contrast the metrics as they are presented in different forms. For example, in the Digital Marketing Metrics category in *functional return,* impressions may be measured. However, when trying to compare impressions to the outcome of retailer EPOS data in the *financial return* category or brand sentiment in the *holistic reward* category, there is no way of reading the data that offers insight into the accumulative effect of the experiential marketing activation. In essence, by utilising a multiplier effect, it allows brands to successfully assess the experiential marketing activation in totality and to clearly see its contribution towards the overall integrated marketing campaign.

Step 4: Assign points: Specific points are allocated upon successfully meeting the set metric targets (see Table 10.3). These points are divided according to the two key categories *return* and *reward,* each being assigned an equal weighting of 100 points. For the *return* segment, the two primary metrics are functional and financial reward. The functional reward is an essential component considering that ROIE was established with the core purpose of evaluating marketing campaigns that utilise an experiential component as a communications tool. In this case, there will always be a live action (be that virtual, in person, or hybrid) element, thus event metrics will always be relevant. The types of data that can be used include footfall, samples distributed and attendee satisfaction surveys. Following on from the experiential activation, digital marketing and public relations are key factors in amplifying the core campaign messaging, and therefore act as a central component and a critical metric to include and evaluate. Such metrics include impressions, click-through, press coverage and mentions. The financial return has one category of metric: ROI. It is essential to consider the investment in the campaign and the sales it is

generating. Other metrics may include sales and market share. Each of these four categories will have an allocation of 25 points, 5 points per metric, which will be awarded if the metrics target is met or exceeded.

Step 4: Understanding reward: In the *reward* segment, there is one category: holistic reward. It has one component, brand health metrics. Such metrics will vary from industry to industry. For example, in the FMCG sector this information is predominately informed by bespoke consumer studies or from research bodies, including Nielsen, Kantar MillwardBrown, and Dunhumby. As previously discussed, this metric is measured over a longer period of time, traditionally as a continuous practice, as it will not have an immediate effect from a marketing campaign, unlike its *return* counterpart. Although brands should consistently be monitoring brand health metrics, for the purpose of ROIE they must identify a time period to evaluate the success of the experiential contribution to the overall marketing campaign. This section has an allocation of 100 points, 20 points per metric, which will be awarded if the metrics target is met or exceeded. At this point, it is important to acknowledge the fact that holistic metrics are awarded 20 points each, while functional and financial metrics are awarded 5 points each upon successful completion. The rationale for this allocation of points lies in the premise that there are more metrics to be accounted for in the functional and financial metrics. The holistic return directly relates to brand health, which accounts for the long-term brand effect. Brands do not employ as many metrics for brand health as they would when measuring the return from digital marketing, PR or event metrics.

Where the ROIE approach differs is that it is not measuring the campaign results, but rather the campaign effect of the brand. Therefore, once the campaign is completed, the actual metrics have been accounted for and the points applied to each metric, if the experiential component was successfully implemented and tied in correctly with the overall brand campaign, the value of the points allocated to the *reward* should exceed the value of the points allocated to the *return*. In this case, the campaign can be deemed a success, positively contributing to brand growth and profitability. However, if the value of the points allocated to the *return* exceed the value of the points allocated to the *reward*, then the experiential component of the campaign has not positively contributed to the success of the campaign or the development of brand health. This may be due to a flaw in the strategy plan, a poor allocation of the budget to the campaign, failure to successfully integrate the experiential marketing activity with the overall campaign or the effect of the experiential activation being isolated to the activity rather than contributing to the overall integrated campaign and, as a result, brand health.

Using the sample dataset in Table 10.4 as a working example, all fields have been filled with the target metrics, actual metrics and the point allocations. In this dataset, the *return* figure is 50 and the *reward* figure is 80. In this case, the experiential activation can be deemed to have made a positive contribution to the overall marketing campaign. However, considering that this research set out to create a

Table 10.3 ROIE Formulation Part 2

ROIE Formulation														
Campaign Objective:														
Campaign KPIs														
KPI 1: Functional Return					**KPI 2: Financial Return**					**KPI 3: Holistic Reward**				
Functional Return					**Financial Return**					**Holistic Reward**				
		Target Metric	**Actual Metric**	**Points Allocated**			**Target Metric**	**Actual Metric**	**Points Allocated**			**Target Metric**	**Actual Metric**	**Points Allocated**
25 points	**Digital Marketing Metrics**	1			25 points	**ROI**	1			100 points	**Brand Health Metrics**	1		
		2					2					2		
		3					3					3		
		4					4					4		
		5					5					5		
25 points	**Event Metrics**	1												
		2												
		3												
		4												
		5												
25 points	**Public Relations**	1												
		2												
		3												
		4												
		5												

Table 10.4 ROIE sample dataset

<table>
<tr><th colspan="15">ROIE Formulation</th></tr>
<tr><td colspan="15">Campaign Objective: To build brand awareness and encourage brand in hand for our NPD line</td></tr>
<tr><th colspan="15">Campaign KPI's</th></tr>
<tr><td colspan="5">KPI 1: Functional KPI</td><td colspan="5">KPI 2: Financial KPI</td><td colspan="5">KPI 3: Holistic KPI</td></tr>
<tr><td colspan="5">Successful implementation of a sampling initiative with online amplification</td><td colspan="5">Uplift in retail and category sales</td><td colspan="5">Post 6-week uplift</td></tr>
<tr><th colspan="5">Functional Return</th><th colspan="5">Financial Return</th><th colspan="5">Holistic Reward</th></tr>
<tr><th></th><th></th><th>Target Metric</th><th>Actual Metric</th><th>Points Allocated</th><th></th><th></th><th>Target Metric</th><th>Actual Metric</th><th>Points Allocated</th><th></th><th></th><th>Target Metric</th><th>Actual Metric</th><th>Points Allocated</th></tr>
<tr><td rowspan="5">25 points
Digital Marketing Metrics</td><td>1: Social Reach</td><td>500,000</td><td>520,000</td><td>5</td><td rowspan="5">25 points
ROI</td><td>1: Retailer EPOS: SV (Period: 00/00/00-00/00/00)</td><td>8,000
60/40</td><td>6
60/40</td><td>0
5</td><td rowspan="5">100 points
Brand Health Metrics</td><td>1: Brand Saliency</td><td>65%</td><td>72%</td><td>20</td></tr>
<tr><td>2: Competition Entries</td><td>500</td><td>420</td><td>0</td><td>2: Working/Non-Working Spend</td><td>30%
4%</td><td>32.10%
5.2%</td><td>5
5</td><td>2: Brand Growth</td><td>4% increase</td><td>4.3% increase</td><td>20</td></tr>
<tr><td>3: Digital Impressions</td><td>300,000</td><td>200,000</td><td>0</td><td>3: Projected Vs Real ROI</td><td>3.2% increase</td><td>3% increase</td><td>0</td><td>3. Brand Usership Status</td><td>5% increase</td><td>11% increase</td><td>20</td></tr>
<tr><td>4: Website Traffic</td><td>400,000</td><td>410,000</td><td>5</td><td>4: Category Sale Uplift</td><td></td><td></td><td></td><td>4: Brand Recall</td><td>72%</td><td>57%</td><td>20</td></tr>
<tr><td>5: Influencer Outreach Coverage</td><td>40 Influencers</td><td>26 Influencers</td><td>0</td><td>5: Market Share</td><td></td><td></td><td></td><td>5: ESOV</td><td>3% increase</td><td>2.6% increase</td><td>0</td></tr>
</table>

Event Metrics 25 points	1: Sales on the Day	€4,000	€5,430	5		
	2: Event Check-Ins	15,000	14,304	0		
	3: Footfall	2,000	3,250	5		
	4: Samples Distributed	2,000	2,000	5		
	5: Completed Attendee Satisfaction Surveys	500	350	0		
Public Relations 25 points	1: PR Mentions	40	45	5		
	2: Share of Voice	10%	5%	0		
	3: Publicity Reach	400,000	367,526	0		
	4: Publicity Engagement	350,000	351,748	5		
	5: Key Message Penetration	12	8	0		

100 points are allocated to the Return metrics

35 | 15

Total Return **50**

100 points are allocated to the Reward metrics

80

Total Reward **80**

Table 10.5 ROIE margins of success

Return \ Reward	5	10	15	20	25	30	35	40	45	50	55	60	65	70	75	80	85	90	95	100
5	0	5	10	15	20	25	30	35	40	45	50	55	60	65	70	75	80	85	90	95
10	-5	0	5	10	15	20	25	30	35	40	45	50	55	60	65	70	75	80	85	90
15	-10	-5	0	5	10	15	20	25	30	35	40	45	50	55	60	65	70	75	80	85
20	-15	-10	-5	0	5	10	15	20	25	30	35	40	45	50	55	60	65	70	75	80
25	-20	-15	-10	-5	0	5	10	15	20	25	30	35	40	45	50	55	60	65	70	75
30	-25	-20	-15	-10	-5	0	5	10	15	20	25	30	35	40	45	50	55	60	65	70
35	-30	-25	-20	-15	-10	-5	0	5	10	15	20	25	30	35	40	45	50	55	60	65
40	-35	-30	-25	-20	-15	-10	-5	0	5	10	15	20	25	30	35	40	45	50	55	60
45	-40	-35	-30	-25	-20	-15	-10	-5	0	5	10	15	20	25	30	35	40	45	50	55
50	-45	-40	-35	-30	-25	-20	-15	-10	-5	0	5	10	15	20	25	30	35	40	45	50
55	-50	-45	-40	-35	-30	-25	-20	-15	-10	-5	0	5	10	15	20	25	30	35	40	45
60	-55	-50	-45	-40	-35	-30	-25	-20	-15	-10	-5	0	5	10	15	20	25	30	35	40
65	-60	-55	-50	-45	-40	-35	-30	-25	-20	-15	-10	-5	0	5	10	15	20	25	30	35
70	-65	-60	-55	-50	-45	-40	-35	-30	-25	-20	-15	-10	-5	0	5	10	15	20	25	30
75	-70	-65	-60	-55	-50	-45	-40	-35	-30	-25	-20	-15	-10	-5	0	5	10	15	20	25
80	-75	-70	-65	-60	-55	-50	-45	-40	-35	-30	-25	-20	-15	-10	-5	0	5	10	15	20
85	-80	-75	-70	-65	-60	-55	-50	-45	-40	-35	-30	-25	-20	-15	-10	-5	0	5	10	15
90	-85	-80	-75	-70	-65	-60	-55	-50	-45	-40	-35	-30	-25	-20	-15	-10	-5	0	5	10
95	-90	-85	-80	-75	-70	-65	-60	-55	-50	-45	-40	-35	-30	-25	-20	-15	-10	-5	0	5
100	-95	-90	-85	-80	-75	-70	-65	-60	-55	-50	-45	-40	-35	-30	-25	-20	-15	-10	-5	0

Black = red
Grey = orange
White = green

financial calculation that provides an output that is valuable not only to academics and marketing practitioners, but also to a senior management team, how the outcome of ROIE is presented is critical. Therefore, by merely saying that the *reward* has exceeded the *return* is not sufficient. The contribution to the brand can be extrapolated from the difference between the *return* and the *reward*. For example, in the dataset in Table 10.4, the *return* figure is 50 and the *reward* figure 80, leaving a differential value of 30. The success or failure of the campaign lies in this figure. Table 10.5 provides a framework to contextualise this numeric value through a traffic light system.

As previously discussed, when the return exceeds the reward, this does not constitute campaign success as the experiential component did not contribute to the development of brand health, that is the experiential activation was deemed more successful than the campaign outcome on brand health. The success of the experiential activation is isolated to the activity itself and did not positively aid brand development, resulting in campaign failure. To date, campaign success has been categorised as a result when the reward exceeds the return. However, this is not always the case. Experiential success occurs when the differential value falls between 20 and 45 points (the green area in Table 10.5). This signifies that, in isolation, the experiential activation was a success. Building on this, it was conceptualised through a strong campaign strategy, was successfully integrated into the overall campaign and therefore, positively contributed towards brand growth. If the differential value falls into the orange zone comprising two categories falling between 5–15 points and 50–70 points, then the campaign can be deemed a success, but there are factors which must be investigated in more detail. In the case of the differential value falling below the optimal range (5–15 points), it may signify that the success was marginal and could have been further optimised through a stronger contribution towards brand health. Where the differential figure falls in the 50–70 points range, which is slightly above the optimal value, the experiential activation can also be deemed a success, but with the same caveats. However, if the differential value falls between 75 and 100 or 0 and –95 points (the red zone), this is a concerning outcome. Here, the reward exceeds the return and therefore, although there was strong growth in brand metrics, the experiential activation did not contribute to this development.

CONCLUSION AND SUMMARY

Experiential marketing is a marketing tool valued by academic and marketing practitioners alike due to its innate ability to create an authentic two-way interaction between a brand and a consumer. Where experiential marketing lacks credibility is in the fact that it is difficult to calculate the return on the practice as the current available measurement mechanisms, ROI, MROI and ROE^2, do not account for all the components that are deemed essential to measure. We propose a new approach, ROIE, which offers an alternative method of evaluating the contribution of experiential

marketing to the overall marketing campaign, while taking into consideration all the fundamental campaign metrics.

Through the development of ROIE, academics and marketing practitioners can evaluate all the key metrics in the newly introduced categories: *functional return, financial return* and *holistic reward.* Not only does ROIE provide a formula that is inclusive of the key metrics, but it also allows marketing practitioners to prove the commercial relevance of experiential marketing by demonstrating that the holistic reward enhances brand value over time, therefore generating profit. This formula clearly depicts the success or failure of a marketing campaign utilising experiential marketing and offers insight into how this outcome was formed as marketers can reflect on the individual components, resulting in learnings for future marketing activations.

MAIN TAKEAWAYS FROM CHAPTER 10

- Measuring the return of an experiential marketing campaign is complex and involves many factors and metrics.
- Traditional methods of evaluating a marketing campaign, such as ROI and MROI, are not appropriate measures for gauging the success of experiential campaigns.
- ROE and ROE^2 measure the success of an experiential campaign in isolation and not as part of an integrated marketing approach.
- The return on integrated experience (ROIE) measurement tool enables the marketer to measure the experiential contribution of the total marketing campaign.

CONCLUDING QUESTIONS

1. Which method of measurement would you recommend a marketing team to use to measure the success of an experiential campaign, and why?
2. Explain the difference between ROI, MROI and ROE.
3. How could a small marketing team use the ROIE mechanism to strengthen its strategic positioning within its own organisation?
4. Give an example of the type of situation that may lead to a low return and high reward outcome (and vice versa) when evaluated through ROIE.
5. What are the elements of ROIE that are most problematic in terms of how it can be applied to assess the impact of an experiential activation in a business-to-business setting?

REFERENCES AND FURTHER READING

Binet, L., & Field, P. (2013). *The Long and the Short of It: Balancing Short and Long-term Marketing Strategies*. London: Institute of Practitioners in Advertising.

Binet, L., & Field, P. (2018). *Effectiveness in Context*. London: Institute of Practitioners in Advertising.

Cornwell, T.B. (2020). *Sponsorship in Marketing: Effective Partnerships in Sports, Arts and Events*. London: Routledge.

Farris, P.W., Hanssens, D.M., Lanskold, J.D., & Reibstein, D.J. (2015). Marketing Return on Investment: Seeking Clarity for Concept and Measurement. *Applied Marketing Analytics: The Peer-Reviewed Journal*, 1(3), 267–282.

Frawley, A. (2014). *Igniting Customer Connections: Fire Up your Company's Growth by Multiplying Customer Experience X Engagement*. New York: John Wiley & Sons.

Frawley, A. (2015). ROI is Dead: A New Metric is Needed for Customer Relationships. *Ad Age*, 4 March. [Online]. Available at: http://adage.com/article/digitalnext/brands-measureexperience-engagement/297426/ [accessed 14 June 2017].

Gill, M., Sridhar, S., & Grewal, R. (2017). Return on Engagement Initiatives: A Study of a Business-to-Business Mobile App. *Journal of Marketing*, 81(July), 45–66.

Harden, L., & Heyman, B. (2011). *Marketing by the Numbers: How to Measure and Improve the ROI of Any Campaign*. London: AMACOM.

Harris, M. (2016). Return on Experience is the new ROI. *Digital Marketing Magazine*, 27 April. [Online]. Available at: http://digitalmarketingmagazine.co.uk/customer-experience/return-on-experience-is-the-new-roi/3315 [accessed 12 December 2017].

Hughes, M., Hughes, P., Yan, J., & Sousa, C.M. (2019). Marketing as an Investment in Shareholder Value. *British Journal of Management*, 30(4), 943–965.

Kaplan, R.S., & Norton D.P. (1992). The Balanced Scorecard – Measures that Drive Performance. *Harvard Business Review*, January–February, 71–79.

Kehrer, D. (2015). The Right Way to Calculate Marketing ROI. *Forbes*. [Online]. Available at: www.forbes.com/sites/forbesinsights/2015/07/29/the-right-way-to-calculate-marketing-roi/#39b36a7470d3 [accessed 12 December 2017].

Lenderman, M. (2005). *Experience the Message: How Experiential Marketing is Changing the Brand World*. New York: Carroll & Graf Publishers.

Lenskold, J. (2003). *Marketing ROI: The Path to Campaign, Customer, and Corporate Profitability*. New York: McGraw-Hill Professional.

Marshall, A. (1890). *Principles of Economics*. London: Macmillan.

Poulsson, S., & Kale, S. (2004). The Experience Economy and Commercial Experiences. *The Marketing Review*, 4(3), 267–277.

Powell, G.R. (2002). *Return on Marketing Investment: Demand More from Your Marketing and Sales Investments*. Brighton, UK: Guy Powell.

PWC. (2019). *It's Time for a Consumer-Centred Metric: Introducing 'Return on Experience' Global Consumer Insights Survey 2019*. London: Price Water Cooper.

Reinartz, W., & Ulaga, W. (2008). How to Sell Services More Profitably. *Harvard Business Review*, 86(5), 90–96.

Ruchi, G., Ritu, C., Tapan Kumar, P., & Aarti, K. (2017). *Driving Customer Appeal Through the Use of Emotional Branding*. Hershey, PA: IGI Global.

Rust, R.T., Zeitaml, V.A., & Lemon, K.N. (2004). Customer-Centred Brand Management. *Harvard Business Review*, 82(9), 110–118.

Schultz, D.E., & Gronstedt, A. (1997). Making Marcom an Investment. *Marketing Management*, 6(3), 40–48.

Sharp, B. (2010). *How Brands Grow: What Marketers Don't Know*. New York: Oxford University Press.

Smith, K., & Hanover, D. (2016). *Experiential Marketing: Secrets, Strategies, and Success Stories from the World's Greatest Brands*. Hoboken, NJ: John Wiley & Sons.

Srinivasan, S.R., & Srivastava, R.K. (2010). Creating a Futuristic Retail Experience Through Experiential Marketing: Is it Possible? An Explorative Study. *Journal of Retail and Leisure Property*, 9(3), 193–199.

Van Doom, J., Lemon, K.N., Mittal, V., Naas, S., Pick, D., Pirner, P., & Verhorf, P.C. (2010). Customer Engagement Behaviour: Theoretical Foundations and Research Directions. *Journal of Service Research*, 12(3), 253–266.

von Eye, A., & Schuster, C. (1998). *Regression Analysis for Social Sciences*. London: Academic Press.

Young, A., & Aitken, L. (2007). *Profitable Marketing Communications: A Guide to Marketing Return on Investment*. London: Kogan Page.

11

CRITICAL SUCCESS FACTORS FOR EXPERIENTIAL MARKETING

CHAPTER OVERVIEW

Critical success factors (CSFs) are generally understood to be the elements that are necessary for a company/project/strategy to achieve its goals. In the context of experiential marketing, we discuss CSFs as those elements that are central to the success of an experiential campaign. Many of these elements have already been identified throughout the previous ten chapters. However, in this chapter, we use a real-life case study to illustrate the factors that were central to the success of an experiential campaign. The chapter should help the reader to understand more generally the factors that are critical to the success of experiential marketing.

Specifically, therefore, this chapter will present information on:

- The factors critical to the success of the Barry Group 'Race and Taste' experiential event.
- The importance of setting key performance indicators when planning experiential campaigns.
- Following the Experiential Marketing Implementation Model when designing an experiential event.

CASE STUDY: RACE AND TASTE FESTIVAL

In May 2019, Barry Group, in collaboration with Cork Racecourse Mallow in the Republic of Ireland, held the Race and Taste Festival. This event was a unique, weekend-long opportunity to showcase and celebrate Cork's fantastic food, arts and culture. Essentially, the Race and Taste Festival combined thrilling horseracing with live music and entertainment for all. Highlights over the weekend included interactive

food demonstrations, wine and spirits masterclasses, garden games and most stylish ladies' event, while the vast array of food stalls from leading producers ensured there was something for every visitor.

Barry Group is Ireland's leading family-run wholesale distribution company, servicing over 1,500 customers nationwide through its franchise and wholesale business divisions. Barry Group has the symbol brands: Costcutter Ireland, Carry Out Off Licence and Quik Pick. This offering is supported by a portfolio of concept brands, including Urban Sips Coffee, Freezi Licks Ice Cream and Market St. Deli, which enhance their retail offering, acting as revenue and footfall drivers. While Barry Group is an extremely successful and competitive organisation, the marketing department realised that there was a lack of connection in the minds of the consumer between Barry Group and its symbol brands. With a keen awareness of the benefit of experiential marketing, the decision was made to join forces with Cork Racecourse, Mallow, and to use the Race and Taste Festival as a conduit to building the connections that they felt were missing. As official sponsor of the event, the marketing team recognised that by following the Experiential Marketing Implementation Model as set out in Chapter 7 (Figure 7.1), they could design an experiential campaign that was unique, and which would ultimately result in the attainment of the identified objectives. As a quick reminder, the steps in the Experiential Marketing Implementation Model are as follows:

1. Customer segmentation
2. Setting the campaign objectives
3. Setting the campaign KPIs
4. Allocating the campaign budget
5. Setting the timeline and amplification strategy
6. Calculating and evaluating the return on integrated experience (ROIE).

Step 1: Customer Segmentation

The benefit of employing multi-generational target marketing methods comes to light in this case study. Considering the nature of this event, the market could have been segmented according to each of the brands through a traditional target market segmentation method that would include the following:

- The Race and Taste Festival
- Cork Racecourse
- Barry Group
- Costcutter
- Carry Out

If this had been the adopted approach, it is likely that the market would have mirrored that of a traditional generational segmentation strategy, where, for example, racegoers for Cork Racecourse could have been defined as mature males with an

interest in horse racing, patrons at the Race and Taste Festival might have been identified as family-oriented females, while Carry Out customers could have been identified as male and female Generation X and Millenials. However, this would have resulted in a convoluted target market strategy trying to account for each brand and their traditional market segments. Instead, the audience of these brands was considered collectively through a multi-generational target market strategy, where an audience is identified by personal values, interests, hobbies, opinions and personal traits that enact specific memory structures. These included:

- Supporters of Irish food producers.
- People interested in Irish horse racing.
- Avid fans of the celebrity chefs hosting sessions at the event, who have an appreciation for food.
- People who appreciate premium whiskey and fine wines.
- People with busy lifestyles who are looking for a weekend event where they can relax and enjoy some time with friends and family.
- People who enjoy gourmet Irish food and drink produce.

Once the multi-generational marketing strategy was decided, the groundwork commenced to develop the campaign objective, which was to cultivate a connection and create brand recall between Barry Group and its symbol brands. Connecting closely with the racecourse and the Race and Taste Festival, commonalities across all target markets were identified, paving the way for the creation of experiences that would be relevant to consumers who had shared values, opinions and personality traits, irrespective of demographic variables.

Step 2: Setting the Campaign Objectives

Having identified the marketing problem as a lack of connection in the minds of the consumer between Barry Group and its symbol brands, the team set the following objectives for the experiential campaign:

- Build memory structures in the mind of the consumer between Barry Group and its symbol brands.
- Build brand awareness of the symbol brands, their concept brands and product range.
- Offer a platform to have the nation to taste their new coffee brand Urban Sips.

The achievement of these objectives would collectively address the marketing problem faced by the marketing team. The importance of specifying objectives that are SMARRTT (specific, measurable, achievable, realistic, relevant, targeted and timed) has been outlined in Chapter 7. The objectives outlined for this event were essential in driving the design of the experiential campaign, and the team were cognizant of ensuring that all the experiential activity related back to these core objectives.

Step 3: Setting the Campaign KPIs

To recap from Chapter 7, Bauer (2004: 63) defines key performance indicators as 'quantifiable metrics which reflect the performance of an organisation in achieving its goals and objectives'. KPIs facilitate the measurement of performance of marketing campaigns and initiate benchmarking. KPIs can take many forms, however. In this book we propose that there are three main categories of KPIs which offer structure to marketing practitioners when setting these business metrics for experiential marketing. These categories are functional KPIs, financial KPIs and holistic KPIs. Dividing KPIs into these three categories provides structure so that the diverse measurement metrics can be better incorporated by practitioners, and in so doing enhance the marketing activity. Keeping this in mind, and focusing on the campaign objectives, the KPIs for the campaign are set out in Table 11.1.

Table 11.1 The Barry Group's campaign KPIs for the Race and Taste Festival event

KPI	Description
Functional	To build buzz online, at the event and in the media in order to generate interest and ultimately footfall.
Financial	To generate strong ROI in the six weeks after the event and to increase sales of Urban Sips by 4%.
Holistic	Increase brand salience of Barry Group and its symbol brands. Increase memory recall through the building of brand memory structures.

Step 4: Allocating the Campaign Budget

In many situations, we see that the budget set for experiential marketing is often what is 'left' after more traditional marketing methods are accounted for. In this case, however, the marketing team recognised the importance of this experiential event and the potential for it to address the core problem of a lack of connection between the Barry Group and its core brands. The decision was therefore made to allocate 80% of the sponsorship fee for the event to the experiential activation. This was a significant amount of money and a statement of the confidence that the marketing team had in this experiential event. The budget was spent on:

- Branding and signage for the event.
- Ticket giveaways on social media.
- Videographer and photographer.
- Promotional staff at the event.
- A branded pop-up bar at the event.
- Giveaways of products at the event.
- Setting up pop-up units for Freezi Licks and Urban Sips.
- Influencer promotional packs and tickets to attend the event.

The budget gave the marketing team scope in the design of the event. There was optimism among the team that this experiential marketing campaign would meet the campaign objective and prescribed KPIs. Managing the suite of brands at play required a budget that would showcase the ability of experiential marketing to aid in the development and maintenance of relationships between the brands and consumers. The enactment of memorable experiences at the event was strategically tailored to the identified market segments. Recognising that superior, relatable and memorable customer experiences are essential to effectively managing a brand, the marketing team were satisfied that the budget would enable them to create experiences that would solve the marketing problem.

Step 5: Setting the Timeline and Amplification Strategy

For a campaign using experiential marketing to be deemed a success, precise timing and the optimisation and amplification of each component are required. As we have shown so far in this book, experiential marketing is best preceded by traditional marketing activities (including digital marketing), whose focus is on brand awareness and core brand messaging. Once this has been achieved, the brand can move into the experiential marketing stage of the timeline. Figure 5.3 presents the ideal timeline for launching an experiential campaign. The marketing team began with what are considered traditional marketing activities. Chapter 7 outlines factors that can influence the specific timing of any campaign. Of course, all the traditional marketing activities enacted by the brand team (through their integrated marketing campaign (IMC) programme) can be considered as influencing factors. The 'before' traditional marketing activities specific to this experiential campaign, which happened approximately one month prior to the experiential campaign, are outlined in Table 11.2.

Table 11.2 Targeted 'before' traditional marketing activities

- Broadcast Advertising: Adverts and giveaways of tickets on radio shows
- Out of Home: Billboards and bus stop shelters
- Broadsheet: Adverts and competitions for tickets in national newspapers
- TV Advertising: Slot on a TV show on a primary TV network in Ireland with an additional competition for tickets
- Media partnerships with broadsheet and online media platforms
- Influencer drops with product and tickets to the event
- Online competitions for tickets to the event
- Broadcast Advertising: Adverts and giveaways of tickets on both national and local radio shows
- Programmatic campaign
- Announcement of event sponsors on social media platforms, in the trade press and broadsheets

Because the objectives for this campaign largely centred on memory structures and brand awareness, the running of these activities in the month prior to the actual event was considered critical to meeting those objectives. The experiential activities that then took place during the two-day Race & Taste Festival are outlined in Table 11.3.

Table 11.3 Experiential marketing activities of the Race & Taste Festival

- The participation of influencers at the event and coverage of the event on the influencers' social media channels
- Live social media coverage
- Competitions to generate social currency for attendees
- The presence of media partners at the event and their inclusion in the coverage of the event
- Live broadcasting from the event by national radio stations
- Sampling and tasting of products
- Staged interactions between staff and attendees at the event

During the experiential marketing event, the live brand experience was centred on two-way communication occurring in real time between the attendees and the brands. This creates a bonding experience for the consumer that is personal and is therefore dependent on digital marketing and word-of-mouth marketing (WOMM) for a larger audience to be reached. Thus, we see that in line with the time-phased approach to experiential marketing (see Table 6.1), the amplification process began prior to the event, with the pre-seeding of content and advertising of the event to the target audience. This continued during the event, with crowdsourcing of content and the generation of social currency, and, importantly, was optimised after the event with the activities as outlined in Table 11.4.

Table 11.4 Experiential optimisation and amplification of the Race & Taste Festival event

- Professional videography and photography used as content for all brand channels
- Influencers amplifying the activation and sharing the event with followers
- Coverage of the event in local and national broadsheet papers
- Coverage of the event in popular online media platforms
- Inclusion in the 'social pages' of prominent Irish magazines
- Campaigns generated from the videography taken at the event (e.g. the Urban Sip #WorthAShot Campaign)

The importance of digital marketing and WOMM in optimising and amplifying the event for a larger audience is clearly illustrated here.

A summary video of these activities can be viewed by scanning the following QR code:

The video demonstrates how the campaign was planned over a well-considered timeline, and how the amplifcation process had to occur over three distinct time periods – before, during and after the experience – as identified by O'Dell (2001). The marketing team had set specific objectives for each time period that were in line with the overall campaign objectives. This approach maximised the potential for the team to effectively amplify the message to the mass market.

Step 6: Calculating and Evaluating the Return on Integrated Experience

The final step of the campaign is to calculate and evaluate the return on integrated experience (ROIE). In Chapter 10, we explained ROIE and, with the aid of an example, illustrated how to calculate the return of an experiential campaign. You can refer to Appendix 1 and 2 at the end of this chapter to see how the return was calculated for the Race & Taste Festival. For now, it is sufficient to say that once the ROIE was calculated, the effectiveness of the campaign was confirmed, and the objectives of the campaign were met.

So why was this experiential campaign a success and what were the critical factors in that success? The next section will address that very question.

CRITICAL FACTORS TO THE SUCCESS OF BARRY GROUP AND RACE AND TASTE COLLABORATION

Integration of Experiential Marketing with the Overall Integrated Marketing Communications Programme

It should now be clear that experiential marketing should not be used as a stand-alone tactic, but rather as an integrated component of an overall marketing strategy. Our recommendation is that experiential marketing must be used in tandem with traditional marketing activity as each of these communications tools interact with customers in a different way and it is essential to employ them together to cultivate both reach and interaction. Furthermore, experiential marketing must not be undertaken without preparatory and foundation work building on traditional marketing activities. Traditional marketing is a controlled marketing communications tool which communicates with the masses, building brand saliency by portraying a consistent message in a creative way. Experiential marketing then affords customers the opportunity to build on the memory structures that have been previously created during the traditional marketing campaign, and allows the customers who interact with the experiential activation

to have unique interactions with a brand while developing their own brand meaning.

Integrated marketing communication plays a vital role in the successful implementation of experiential marketing. This is primarily due to three main reasons:

1. It optimises the ROI of experiential marketing when it is combined with mass marketing activities.
2. Alone, experiential marketing cannot deliver on reach metrics which depict how many people have seen the campaign creative or perhaps clicked a link to a landing page.
3. As traditional marketing does not facilitate authentic interactions and two-way communication with customers (Schmitt, 1999, 2000), experiential marketing complements the reach mechanisms of traditional mass marketing by creating opportunities for these interactions to take place (Kailani & Ciobotar, 2015; LaSalle & Britton, 2003; Lenderman, 2005; Li & Yang, 2010).

The success of an experiential campaign, then, is largely determined by its integration into an overall marketing campaign, which is apparent in the Race and Taste Festival example. The overarching marketing campaign goal for Barry Group was defined as 'maximising mental availability'. The strategic initiative was further defined as 'enhancing brand saliency of Barry Group and its symbol brands'. The Race & Taste Festival was the experiential marketing tactic that worked in tandem with other communication methods (including sales promotions, out of home (OOH) advertising, personal selling and public relations) to achieve the overall marketing goal.

Multi-Generational Segmentation

When choosing a segmentation strategy for an experiential marketing campaign, many options are available. For example, one can choose a more traditional segmentation approach based on geographic or demographic specifications. However, providing an audience's preferences are considered and the campaign is tailored to meet these preferences, a multi-generational segmentation strategy is particularly relevant to experiential marketing. Although experiential marketing is typically synonymous with interactions with small target audiences, by amplifying the practice through online resources and digital platforms, the experiential activation lives beyond the physical event and can reach the masses. This ensures that the experiential activation has maximum penetration and a higher return on investment. Importantly, therefore, brands should not assume that experiential marketing is only relevant for younger generations, including Generation Z and Millennials (due to their perceived receptiveness towards digital technologies and social media). Rather, brands should first ask themselves 'how relevant is this product and marketing activation to our target market?', and second, they should ensure that the activation is applicable to all the relevant groups, without alienating some or labeling others. This is achieved by identifying the consistent characteristics across generations that are

relevant to the key campaign message, a process called psychographic customer segmentation.

This thinking is in line with what Simms (2008) defined as an *ageless society*, where people are not defined by age but by the activities they pursue. Although experiential marketing is certainly applicable to Generation Z and Millennials, it is not isolated to these generational cohorts. Usually, when a brand's market share grows, the more diverse their customer base becomes. As long as an experiential activation is authentic and relevant to the customer base, any audience, regardless of the generational cohort, will react positively to the marketing tool.

Therefore, market segmentation for an experiential activation should be conducted using multi-generational psychographic customer segmentation, where customers' interests, hobbies, opinions, personality traits and values are the critical factors to ensuring that the experiential marketing activity is relevant to them, and thus will elicit strong memory structures. Through the consideration of each of these critical factors, one can account for multiple demographical cohorts and offer a broad but still relevant target market. In the Barry Group case study, the target audience was identified according to values and interests. This approach guided the development of the experiential activities, which were focused on building brand awareness and memory structures that tapped into commonalities across all target markets. The tasting platforms for the products being showcased were focused on increasing the brand awareness of the Barry Group and its portfolio of brands.

Setting Key Performance Indicators

Setting KPIs are essential to the planning of experiential activity and its subsequent measurement. For KPIs to be an effective measurement system, the following characteristics must be apparent (Maskel, 1991; Parmenterg, 2007; University of Warwick, 2006):

1. They must be connected to the overall business strategy to ensure operational success.
2. They must encompass both financial and non-financial measures.
3. They must be frequently measured and adapted to reflect changes in strategy.
4. They must be understood by all key stakeholders to ensure the optimal outcome.
5. They tie responsibility to an individual or a team.

As shown in Table 11.1, KPIs were created for the three categories – functional, financial and holistic – to ensure that all critical components of an experiential activation were considered and measurable. Ensuring that the KPIs are clear leaves little room for ambiguity when designing the experiential activity. The Barry Group's KPIs were central to the success of the campaign, as they provided clear direction to successfully evaluate the success of the Race & Taste Festival. The three categories of KPIs also comprise of key metrics by which the successful implementation

of an experiential activation is measured. In line with Locke and Latham's (1990) view of goal-setting theory (see Chapter 7), utilising these three categories of KPIs ensured the structured nature of campaign planning and thus enhanced the marketing activity. The assignment of a KPI to each of these key categories therefore ensured that all three pillars were considered and that all core components are accounted for.

Timeline of the Campaign

The strategic timing of experiential marketing in the lifespan of a marketing campaign is critical to the ultimate success or otherwise of a campaign. For a campaign using experiential marketing to be deemed a success, it requires precise timing and the optimisation and amplification of each component.

Tables 11.2, 11.3 and 11.4 detail the very defined timeline of activities designed for the Barry Group's experiential campaign. The amplification and optimisation strategy was designed to happen over the pre, during and post stages of the event, thus ensuring that the potential effectiveness of the campaign was optimised. The 'before' stage of the event (Table 11.2) utilised a number of marketing communication techniques that were specifically enacted in the month prior to the experiential event. They not only laid the foundation for the success of the experiential marketing activities at the Race and Taste event (Table 11.3), but also built on years of brand building by the Barry Group through an overall integrated approach to marketing communications. Table 11.4 illustrates the 'after' activities which ensured that the outcome of the event was amplified and optimised, which in turn continued to reinforce brand messaging.

Bringing the Brand's Narratives and Cues to Life

It is essential that, through any experiential marketing initiative, marketing professionals ensure that branding and key messaging is consistent with the core values of the brand, in order for strong brand resonance to be built. Experiential marketing affords a brand the opportunity to expand on a core message to help consumers understand what the brand's essence is. It also allows customers to engage on a personal level as they build their own relationship with the products and the brand through staged activations. In this way, authentic two-way interactions are created that bring the brand's narratives and cues to life, offering the consumer the opportunity to make them personally relevant in their lives, and thus cementing memory structures and associations between consumers and brands that can potentially be lifelong. The Barry Group created these links by ensuring that the Barry Group, Costcutter and Carry Out Off Licence logos were visible on all the activation touchpoints and collateral (Point of Sale, Digital Assets, etc.), building brand saliency and recall. At the event, there were Freezi Licks, Urban Sips and Carry Out Off Licence pop-up shops where attendees could purchase products and interact with

promotional staff members to get to know the brands and products and learn of their availability.

An additional campaign called '#WorthAShot' was executed for Urban Sips during this event. The purpose of this campaign was twofold: to encourage attendees to try Urban Sips and decide for themselves if it was 'worth a shot', and to cement the brand in people's minds by linking the brand with a feeling, sensation or memory, through the action of asking them to reflect on the moment in their own lives that were 'worth a shot'. Not only did this campaign build strong memory structures and brand recall at the live event, it then formed the basis of a social media video campaign, allowing it to transcend the physical borders of the event and resonate with a wider audience.

The campaign video can be viewed by scanning this QR code:

CONCLUSION AND SUMMARY

The Barry Group case study should assist you in understanding the factors that are critical to the success of an experiential marketing campaign. Through the detail given on the Race and Taste Festival, you can see how the planning, integration and implementation of the event resulted in the success of the campaign.

MAIN TAKEAWAYS FOR CHAPTER 11

- For experiential marketing to be successful, it must be a component of an integrated marketing communication strategy. It should always be preceded by traditional marketing in order to effectively achieve campaign reach.
- Multi-generational psychographic methods of customer segmentation should be employed when implementing an experiential marketing activation. It is essential not to make assumptions about receptive target markets through generalisations, but rather to adopt a multi-generational mindset where the personality characteristics of the target audience are perceived as more important than age, demographic or geographical segmentation that are typically employed in traditional methods of generational segmentation.
- To ensure the success of, and to justify the investment in, experiential marketing, marketers should identify campaign objectives and key performance indicators (functional, financial and holistic) in order to track all the critical components of the campaign and to identify the key learning points during the analysis phase.

CONCLUDING QUESTIONS

1. Outline the importance of setting KPIs for an experiential marketing activation.
2. Explain the importance of employing multi-generational segmentation methods when planning an experiential marketing activation.
3. Why is it important to integrate experiential marketing within the overall integrated marketing communication programme?
4. Discuss the strategic importance of employing traditional marketing methods before executing an experiential marketing activation.
5. In your opinion, what role do brand memory structures, narratives and cues play in an experiential marketing activation?

REFERENCES AND FURTHER READING

Bauer, K. (2004). KPIs: The Metrics that Drive Performance Management. *Information Management*, 14(9), 63.

Kailani, C., & Ciobotar, N. (2015). Experiential Marketing: An Efficient Tool to Leverage Marketing Communication Impact on Consumer Behaviour. *International Conference on Marketing and Business Development Journal*, 1(1), 1–7.

LaSalle, D., & Britton, T.A. (2003). *Priceless: Turning Ordinary Products into Extraordinary Experiences*. Boston, MA: Harvard Business School Press.

Lenderman, M. (2005). *Experience the Message: How Experiential Marketing is Changing the Brand World*. New York: Carroll & Graf Publishers.

Li, A., & Yang, D. (2010). Business Advertising Strategy in Experiential Marketing. Paper presented at the 2010 International Conference on Management and Service Science, Wuhan, China, 24-26 August.

Locke, E., & Latham, G. (1990). *A Theory of Goal Setting and Task Performance*. Englewood Cliffs, NJ: Prentice-Hall.

Maskel, B. (1991). *Performance Management for World Class Manufacturing*. Cambridge, MA: Productivity Press.

O'Dell, T. (2001). Are you Experienced? *Kulturella Perspecktiv*, 3, 27–33.

Parmenterg, D. (2007). *Key Performance Indicators: Developing, Implementing and Using Winning KPIs*. Hoboken, NJ: Wiley.

Schmitt, B.H. (1999). Experiential Marketing. *Journal of Marketing Management*, 15(1–3), 53–67.

Schmitt, B.H. (2000). *Experiential Marketing: How to Get Customers to Sense, Feel, Think, Act, Relate to your Company and Brands*. New York: The Free Press.

Sharp, B. (2010). *How Brands Grow: What Marketers Don't Know*. New York: Oxford University Press.

Simms, J. (2008). Shades of Grey. *Marketing*, 30 April, 14.

University of Warwick (2006). *Performance Measuring and Costing: Logistics and Operations Management*. Warwick, UK: University of Warwick.

Functional Return										Financial Return				Holistic Reward			
			Target Metric	Actual Metric	Points Allocated				Target Metric	Actual Metric	Points Allocated				Target Metric	Actual Metric	Points Allocated
25 points	**Digital Marketing Metrics**	1: Social Reach	625,000	734,637	5	25 points		1: Category Sales Uplift	5%	6.8%	5	100 points	**Brand Health Metrics**	1: Brand Saliency	6% increase	7.2% increase	20
		2: Competition Enteries	9,500	10,436	5		**ROI**	2: Working/ Non Working Spend	60/40	55/45	0						
		3: Link Clicks	25,000	21,537	0			3: Retailer EPOS for a specified period of time	28460	33,638	5			2: Brand Recall	6% increase	6.3% increase	20
		4: Website Traffic	80,000	91,000	5			4: Category Growth	2%	3.6%	5			3. Brand Penetra-tion	4% increase	4.7% increase	20
		5: Influencer Outreach Coverage	10 Influencers	7 Influencers	0			5: Market Share	2.0% increase	1.6% increase	0			4: NPS Score	10 point increase	15 point increase	20
25 points	**Event Metrics**	1: Footfall	15,000	21,426	5									5: ESOV	3.6% increase	4.8% increase	0
		2: Samples Distributed	15,000	14,304	5												
		3: Emails gathered for mailing list	5,000	4,215	0												
		4: Wine Tasting Event Attendance	500	628	5												
		5: Completed Attendee Satisfaction Surveys	400	375	0												
25 points	**Public Relations**	1: Media Value	500,000	750,000	5												
		2: Share of Voice	7%	6%	0												
		3: Publicity Reach	750,000	914,628	5												
		4: Publicity Engagement	500,000	420,005	0												
		5: Key Message Penetration	9	6	0												
100 points are allocated to the Return metrics												100 points are allocated to the Reward metrics					
40											15				80		
Total Return 55													Total Return 80				

Appendix 1 Barry Group ROIE calculation

Return \ Reward	5	10	15	20	25	30	35	40	45	50	55	60	65	70	75	80	85	90	95	100
5	0	5	10	15	20	25	30	35	40	45	50	55	60	65	70	75	80	85	90	95
10	–5	0	5	10	15	20	25	30	35	40	45	50	55	60	65	70	75	80	85	90
15	–10	–5	0	5	10	15	20	25	30	35	40	45	50	55	60	65	70	75	80	85
20	–15	–10	–5	0	5	10	15	20	25	30	35	40	45	50	55	60	65	70	75	80
25	–20	–15	–10	–5	0	5	10	15	20	25	30	35	40	45	50	55	60	65	70	75
30	–25	–20	–15	–10	–5	0	5	10	15	20	25	30	35	40	45	50	55	60	65	70
35	–30	–25	–20	–15	–10	–5	0	5	10	15	20	25	30	35	40	45	50	55	60	65
40	–35	–30	–25	–20	–15	–10	–5	0	5	10	15	20	25	30	35	40	45	50	55	60
45	–40	–35	–30	–25	–20	–15	–10	–5	0	5	10	15	20	25	30	35	40	45	50	55
50	–45	–40	–35	–30	–25	–20	–15	–10	–5	0	5	10	15	20	25	30	35	40	45	50
55	–50	–45	–40	–35	–30	–25	–20	–15	–10	–5	0	5	10	15	20	25	30	35	40	45
60	–55	–50	–45	–40	–35	–30	–25	–20	–15	–10	–5	0	5	10	15	20	25	30	35	40
65	–60	–55	–50	–45	–40	–35	–30	–25	–20	–15	–10	–5	0	5	10	15	20	25	30	35
70	–65	–60	–55	–50	–45	–40	–35	–30	–25	–20	–15	–10	–5	0	5	10	15	20	25	30
75	–70	–65	–60	–55	–50	–45	–40	–35	–30	–25	–20	–15	–10	–5	0	5	10	15	20	25
80	–75	–70	–65	–60	–55	–50	–45	–40	–35	–30	–25	–20	–15	–10	–5	0	5	10	15	20
85	–80	–75	–70	–65	–60	–55	–50	–45	–40	–35	–30	–25	–20	–15	–10	–5	0	5	10	15
90	–85	–80	–75	–70	–65	–60	–55	–50	–45	–40	–35	–30	–25	–20	–15	–10	–5	0	5	10
95	–90	–85	–80	–75	–70	–65	–60	–55	–50	–45	–40	–35	–30	–25	–20	–15	–10	–5	0	5
100	–95	–90	–85	–80	–75	–70	–65	–60	–55	–50	–45	–40	–35	–30	–25	–20	–15	–10	–5	0

Appendix 2 Barry Group ROIE evaluation

Black = red
Grey = orange
White = green

12

EXPERIENTIAL MARKETING FOR THE 21ST CENTURY

CHAPTER OVERVIEW

The aim of the final chapter is to bring together the concepts, ideas and frameworks presented in this book, and to do so in a manner that addresses the realities of business in a post-Covid world. Armed with this knowledge, the 21st-century marketer will be positioned to use experiential marketing as part of an overall marketing strategy, and to confidently create experiences for consumers that result in strong customer – brand bonds. This chapter offers a holistic view of the key learning points from this book and provides the reader with additional guidelines on how to implement an experiential marketing campaign from conceptualisation to evaluation. Moreover, we look at the emerging trends that relate to experiential marketing – from both an academic and practitioner perspective – and outline the challenges that currently exist in ensuring that this sub-discipline remains a useful aspect of marketing in the years ahead.

On completion of this chapter, the reader will understand:

- The key questions to be answered in planning for an experiential marketing activity.
- What to consider in implementing an experiential activation, with a focus on team composition and leadership.
- How to communicate with the C-suite on matters relating to experiential marketing.
- The emerging trends in experiential marketing, both academical and practical.

THE CHANGING GLOBAL LANDSCAPE

The world has changed. In 2020, with the onset of a pandemic that has radically impacted consumers, businesses and society in almost every conceivable way, we became a more distanced (literally), less tactile, more guarded species. There were

good reasons for this, with the encroachment of a virus – that we poorly understood – in a world that was hyper-connected. Nevertheless, the impact of this massive change on the use of experiential marketing has been extensive. Experiential marketing is at its best when it can elicit a positive emotional response while actively engaging customers. Both aspects were tested by the prevailing circumstances that emerged in response to the pandemic. However, at the time of writing, as the success of the vaccine rollout provides optimism that the world will return to some version of normality, experiential marketing will remain part of the marketing landscape. There may be increased pressures on marketing budgets, accelerated implementation of marketing campaigns, and a renewed focus on connecting with consumers and customers. All of this places a greater onus on marketers to ensure that they are working more effectively, that their campaigns and tactics are strategically aligned, and that their activities are yielding positive returns and rewards for their brands. The use of a framework that supports the implementation of experiential activations and thereby a broader marketing strategy, is critical to the ongoing success of experiential marketing. That such a framework is holitistic in how it supports planning and measuring, and is then supported by a digital amplification approach, is also essential to that success. This book has set out the key areas on which to focus in establishing effective experiential marketing activities. In this chapter, we set out an approach for the overall planning and deployment of experiential activations in a way that ensures they contribute most strongly to strategic success. We also discuss the emerging trends and challenges that may need to be considered by marketing teams in the coming years. We explore the technological and social factors that will need to be borne in mind – including digital experiential activities. Finally, we outline the move from customer experience to business experience.

PLANNING FOR EXPERIENTIAL MARKETING: AN OVERVIEW OF KEY CONCEPTS

The importance of planning in all areas of business is so accepted that it has descended firmly into cliché. 'Fail to plan; plan to fail' is perhaps the most prominent of such clichés. However, we need to remind ourselves that they represent a common truth – success, when not by luck or caprice, is built on careful forethought, consideration and planning. This holds for experiential marketing no less than any other area of marketing. As we have demonstrated in this book, too often experiential marketing tends to be *ad hoc*, unstructured and centred 'on itself' rather than being placed in an ecosystem of marketing strategy. Here, we set out how to avoid this scenario by ensuring that the planning of experiential activations reflects the best intentions of strategic and integrated marketing. Although it may seem like we are sometimes stating the obvious, we do so deliberately and with the intention of making experiential marketing a more structured process. We pitch our discussion as a series of key questions.

Key Question 1 – Why Experiential Marketing and Why Now?

Much of the time, when you review available guides to planning experiential marketing activities, you will not see this question being asked. It may be the case that with a limited budget, and perhaps even more limited attention from the board of directors or C-suite, there may be no advantage to undertaking an experiential activation. Equally, its allure for marketers is undoubted, so with an enthusiastic marketing team pushing the proposal, it may become an irresistible activity. Using experiential marketing, and getting the best from the implementation model for experiential marketing, can only happen successfully when we get satisfactory answers to the following questions:

- What do we want to accomplish?
- Does our plan help us achieve our marketing objectives and, in turn, assist with our corporate objectives? If so, in what way?
- Are there other ways to achieve or exceed those same goals without using experiential marketing?
- Does investing time and resources in experiential marketing represent the best potential return at this time?
- Could there be other impacts to the brand (beyond the costs of time and resources) if the objectives of the campaign are not met?
- Do we have the means to assess and measure the impact and success of the campaign?
- Will the experiential marketing campaign improve our competitive advantage?

The process for answering these questions may vary from organisation to organisation. It should involve a marketing team working in close association with supporting departments within the organization so that marketing activity is integrated into the fabric of the organisation while also being holistically integrated as a strategy itself. It requires the ability to undertake honest appraisals of the competitive landscape. It needs marketing teams to understand their customers. Effective experiential marketing will be built upon the ability to ask and answer questions without rushing to implement. Knowing 'why' and 'why now' is as critical as putting in place the most creative and impactful of events/activations.

Key Question 2 – With Whom Do We Want to Connect?

The beauty of experiential marketing is its ability to bring your brand closer to your customer in a way that is more intimate than other marketing tactics. In planning an experiential event, we need to consider our target market – with whom do we want to connect more closely? This assumes, of course, that we have actively

decided that experiential marketing makes sense now (although we commit to keeping that question under scrutiny as we continue to plan in more detail). Any good marketing strategy will reflect the positioning, segmentation and messaging of a brand as being essential to its success. There should be a clear sense of who is being targeted for the organisation's products or services. In planning experiential marketing, because of the high costs involved, there is a greater need to understand the segment of the target audience you wish to reach. Remember, a central element of experiential marketing is relationship management. With your limited time and funds, with whom do you want to create that closer relationship? You might consider the following questions to find your answer:

- Is there a micro segment of our customer base that we want to develop a stronger relationship with through our experiential activation?
- What do we want these customers to feel? How will this feeling add value to our relationship?
- Are those we connect with representative of the brand's customers overall? How can we better understand all of our customers through the segment we encounter in our experiential activities?
- What types of experience work for this group of customers?

These are overarching questions that may prompt some more detailed thinking. Of most importance is squaring the audience, the marketing strategy and the use of an experiential activation in developing a closer, more intimate relationship with customers. Connecting these features puts the planning of the experience itself on a firmer footing.

Key Question 3 – How Do We Keep Our Plan Relevant?

While we prescribe a framework of considerations for the planning and implementation of experiential activations, it is important to maintain a holistic view throughout the planning process. Flexibility will be needed as considerations shift, information is gathered and interpreted, and feasibility issues arise. You will need to keep the total plan in mind and review decisions on a regular and iterative basis.

Key Question 4 – How Does Our Experiential Marketing Campaign Sit in the Overall Marketing Plan?

With the emphasis on integration, we need to ensure that our use of experiential marketing is reflective of an overall marketing plan that may also include elements such as advertising, direct marketing, digital marketing, sales/promotion, PR and

maybe even personal selling. Each of these approaches needs to be considered in parallel to the plan for the experiential activation. Timelines and budgets for each approach may be different. We always need to ask what helps us to achieve our objectives more easily. While running different marketing activities at the same time, we will better understand our experiential marketing success if we monitor for the potential of non-experiential marketing tools in case of cross-contamination. This will require an expert marketing approach to be able to assess this. The resultant integrated marketing communications programme becomes a bible for planning experiential activations in more detail.

Key Question 5 – How Do We Segment for Experiential Marketing?

This builds on Key Question 2 and grounds strategic questions about target audiences in questions that are more specific to our actual activation. In experiential marketing there is a tendency to use generational segmentation, with an emphasis on Generation Z and Millennial audiences. The question should be actively explored, however, as there may be more suitable mechanisms for segmentation and indeed combinations of mechanisms. We strongly suggest that marketers keep an open mind here, while not trying to be overly narrow. As we have shown in this book, there are plenty of examples where carefully designed activations resonate with more than the intended audience. The activation must be authentic and relevant to the audience, but we must remember that we are trying to harness customers' interests, hobbies, personality traits and values to build a closer bond with our brand. Thus, we must actively engage with those interests and values in order to provide a meaningful context for the activation. Segmentation should not be superficial.

Key Question 6 – What Are Our Campaign Objectives?

The campaign objectives will be partly bound by the resources available to the brand, the intended timeline for results, and the segments involved. However, the objectives must be fully underpinned by the business objectives. The planning and implementation of our experiential activation must align with our overall goals. Within that context, the following questions can guide the development of a plan:

- What are our objectives? Do we seek to affect behaviour, raise brand and/or product awareness, disseminate information?
- How SMARTT are our objectives?
- How do the campaign objectives link to the business objectives?
- How do the objectives link to the integrated marketing strategy plans?
- What can we learn from other brands that we can apply in this campaign?

Key Question 7 – Can We Link Our Objectives to Our KPIs?

The campaign objectives should be translated into key performance indicators. The science of choosing and evaluating KPIs is complex and poses challenges for many different disciplines. We suggest identifying the types of KPI that relate to financial, functional and holistic measures (see Chapter 7 to 10). Remember, truly successful experiential marketing must be evaluated. Using ROIE to assess activations, there is a range of means by which practitioners can ensure a breadth of measures that link closely to campaign, marketing and business objectives.

Key Question 8 – How Do We Budget and Schedule Our Campaign?

Experiential activations can be expensive. The 'production values' attendant with these events can be a significant upfront cost. Often, experiential marketing is labour-intensive. Planning for such occasions requires careful consideration of budgets with respect to personnel, materials, props, location-related expenses and supporting marketing activities. An effective experiential marketing budget will use experience and insight on how to best distribute resources. Equally, it will be designed so that it can subsequently be assessed for performance. Promotion of the event will require a budget as well as amplification before, during and after the experiential activation. The schedule for the activation must reflect the target audience and the campaign objectives primarily. However, evaluation of impact must also be filtered into this timeline so that the overall contribution of the event is captured in a reasonable timeframe and thereafter communicated appropriately.

Key Question 9 – How Can We Shape the Experiential Activation?

This is often the sole focus of the experiential marketer. However, as we know, we can only create valuable experiences for consumers and brands when we design and implement events in the context of the overall business objectives. An interesting activation that targets the wrong customers, or that does not get amplified, may appear successful but in fact it may just be a fancy looking failure. However, even a well-planned experiential marketing campaign needs a *pièce de résistance*. This will often be the amplification itself. Through creativity, technology, enthusiasm and a true authenticity to the brand, marketers can create the types of memorable events that are so critical to brand salience and relationship development with customers. The tendency to be adventurous should be encouraged, provided it fits in with the campaign objectives. Plan for fun. Use technology. Aim for immersion. Decide on

how your product/service fits into the event. To plan such events often requires inspiration from many quarters and works best in a marketing team that is able to hear new ideas.

Key Question 10 – How Will People Know about the Experiential Marketing Event?

We must plan to amplify. We have proposed the Experiential Marketing Amplification Framework (see Figure 7.2), which acts as a prompt for maximising the potential of what might otherwise be limited events. It requires marketing activities to be planned before, during and after the event. This can be quite detailed but must reflect the campaign message. In advance, there is generally a need to create awareness of the event in order to ensure participation and to create anticipation. During the event, the brand will want to leverage participants' enthusiasm and any buzz that centres on the event through social media. And afterwards, the brand may want to distribute the outputs of the event as a means to further the event's effects. In each case, the marketing team will have specific timelines, goals and budgets to support the various activities. These should be reviewed on a rolling basis.

Key Question 11 – Did Our Plan Work?

We must plan to evaluate. The brand must include time to assess the campaign overall. Depending on the stage of maturity of the brand, this may be a formal or informal process. It must always happen, however. We suggest recording lessons learned, in particular as the marketing strategy develops.

In conclusion, while experiential marketing is an inherently creative process, this does not preclude the use of planning. In fact, it makes planning even more important. Creativity can flourish in a planned environment. Successful planning can increase the opportunity for more creativity to be baked into the process.

DEPLOYMENT AND MANAGEMENT OF EXPERIENTIAL MARKETING

Deploying well-planned experiential events still requires a masterful hand. Nothing has been achieved until you 'go live'. For many brands, the deployment of the experiential activation will be in-house. Often this will be because the team has the requisite skills and know-how to take what was planned and implement it. For other organisations, the implementation of the planned activities may be led by a specialist experiential marketing company. The outsourcing approach may appeal to organisations that do not have the full range of in-house skills that are required

to effectively realise the experience. In either case, the following considerations need to be actively considered when implementing experiences:

- Experiential activations need the appropriate number of staff members to ensure they run with the intended precision and according to the plan. Equally, those staff members need a mixture of skills to reflect the nature of the planned activity. A creatively designed activation will likely include active participation by members of the public, some technological element, a means of amplification, an aura of 'buzz', an energy that requires logistical nous and adherence to some timing restrictions, product distribution, giveaways, etc., and perhaps the challenges of operating in unfamiliar physical territory. From this list, we can see that such a skillset may not be present in just one individual. Equally, to get the best from the activation, the diversity of skillsets required will range from, say, a people-oriented team member who can generate audience participation to someone who can manage the timing, space allocation and safety requirements of the event. Team members knowing their role, committing to working together, and being adaptable in the moment are the hallmarks of success.
- The detailed plan for the event needs to be followed. Good experiential marketing teams will not only have a detailed plan, but will also abide by it. Identifying a lead for each event and empowering them to direct is critical to good outcomes. The more experience such a person has, the stronger the event is likely to be. While brands experiment with activations, there is an accepted need that those driving the events understand the unique challenges of experiential marketing.
- Audience participation generates the energy that drives the emotive aspect of experiential marketing. Without this, very few activations succeed. However, the emotive aspect also introduces the greatest risks. We want our participants to feel like the activation has been a good use of their time. We need them to feel like they have had a good time. We want them to feel safe. Ultimately, we want them to commit to our brand and encourage others to do so. A meaningless interaction, or one which is bland or misdirected, is likely to have the opposite impact in one or more of those areas. The execution of a planned event that reflects the intended energy of the event requires particular types of personality. Lively, bubbly and energetic staff will aid the event enormously.
- The method of amplification for the event requires specific expertise. As we know, the time-phased approach to amplification involves before, during and after elements. In executing the plan for the lead up to the activation, there is more time to get it right. It is less likely to be frenzied. Executing the plan during the activation can be more challenging. Amplification and recording the event as it happens will benefit from having a dedicated individual or team working on it (depending on the scale of the event and/or organisation). The requirement to focus on 'production values', including capture and editing, the appropriate tagging and messaging around social media for immediate dissemination, and the parallel focus on capturing the event for subsequent marketing activities, is a challenging balance to make. It cannot be achieved effectively if the event's staff members are immersed in running the logistical or 'theatrical' aspects of the experiential event.

In summary, the reason why we plan experiential events before implementing them is centred on ensuring success. Following the plan at implementation stage is a management responsibility that itself requires know-how and expertise. The energy, excitement and verve of an active experience might appear fresh, casual and spontaneous, but this appearance requires a marketing manager's expertise. Organisations that use experience for marketing purposes to a great extent need to reflect the unique challenges of this channel in the composition of their marketing team. The type of marketer who is good at experiential marketing may not be as suited to other types of marketing, and indeed vice versa. Where experiential marketing becomes a substantial aspect of a marketing department's activities, then organisations should consider specifically recruiting for the required skillsets. The lack of resources to do so is often why some organisations fully or partially outsource their activations.

EVALUATION OF EXPERIENTIAL MARKETING

Marketing has always struggled to convey its value to an organisation at board level. This is highlighted by the noted absence of marketers on executive boards, the tendency for senior marketers to not progress to CEO positions, and the general lack of respect for marketing that was often a feature of senior-level leadership. It is reflective, perhaps, of the lack of accountability that sometimes accompanies the marketing profession, with the old adage about '50% of Marketing works really well – we just don't know which 50%' being a shibboleth for those that do not see its value. That historic position has undoubtedly evolved with the advent of digital marketing and the increased transparency regarding its effectiveness. Online activity, in the B2B and B2C sectors, can be more easily related to the marketing activities that lead to sales, for example. That traceability has a positive impact on being able to outline the cause and effect of marketing that CEOs and boards crave. However, even with these developments, it remains much harder for marketing practitioners to convey the value of experiential activations. In Chapters 10 and 11, we have shown how this can be overcome and how marketing teams can provide data to support the effectiveness of experiential campaigns. The main point is that marketing managers do need to convince the board that experiential marketing works, and they need data to do it.

Let's adopt the perspective of the board momentarily. The mindset is often focused on results, with an emphasis on value for money. Experiential marketing, even by the most ardent of exponents, is an activity that is challenged by being able to demonstrate outcomes linked to the events and, equally, is a costly undertaking that can superficially appear to impact on a limited number of customers. These are the obstacles that need to be overcome when communicating its value to the organisation. The solution, as this book argues throughout, is in translating experiential activations into the language of strategic marketing (and, indeed, strategy in general).

- Experiential marketing should not be presented, in terms of its outcomes, as a stand-alone activity. Its integration with other activities of marketing strategy has to be the context. Experiential marketing does not exist in a vacuum, and communicating its success is as much about linking its outcomes to overall marketing goals and activities as it is about talking about 'footfall', etc. The board is interested in sales and revenue. Experiential marketing supports the goals and objectives that lead to increased revenue. If marketing managers want to talk the language of the boardroom, they need to be able to show how experiential marketing can accomplish company objectives.
- The time-phased amplification approach to experiential marketing creates a broader range of metrics that can be used at board level to support arguments for its success. A competent marketing manager should be able to link the narrative of the event to social media reach, positive sentiment and, even on a grounded level, the creation of meaningful and usable marketing collateral.
- While the focus of a board or CEO may be on revenue, they will also be interested in brand sentiment and its components. Depending on the size and resources of the brand, there may be an opportunity to measure such sentiment before and after a period of experiential marketing. Even the most cynical CEO will appreciate that positive brand sentiment has commercial value. Being able to show that experiential marketing contributes to this value will certainly find favour.

Smaller organisations will have different dynamics at play. The need to link the impact of an activation to increased sales is much stronger in those settings. This approach may be more relevant where an owner/founder acts as managing director and is inclined towards the micro-management of marketing spend. The antidote, again, is sound strategy. Elevating experiential marketing beyond a tactic to a channel that allows the brand to reach and excite new customers in a measurable way offers a clearer sense of value to such an MD than simply knowing that 100 people attended an event.

THE FUTURE OF EXPERIENTIAL MARKETING

This book set out to place experiential marketing on a firmer footing theoretically and practically. It is hoped that the many examples we have provided and the focus on developing implementation and evaluation models support a firmer encapsulation of the theory related to the discipline. We have acknowledged that the onset of the Covid-19 pandemic in 2020 has had a particularly virulent impact on experiential marketing activities, the consequences of which will likely persist into the future, even if we don't yet know how they will play out. Nevertheless, it is still possible to highlight some emerging trends and factors which will need academic attention as well as being at the forefront of practitioners' minds.

Technology

Throughout this book we have provided examples of experiential activations that have utilised various technologies. The internet is now a regular and integral part of the experiential landscape, but technologies such as virtual reality (VR) and augmented reality (AR) are also beginning to play a role. The latter trend is likely to continue as the sharp increase in digital participation since March 2020, when Covid-19 generally moved life online, has expedited a growing digital readiness among consumers to take part in online experiential activities. While the technologies are not new, and their adoption has been gradual, it is our view that they will emerge from a somewhat inchoate status as potential technologies in the minds of marketers to become a much more prevalent and accepted means of engaging with customers. It is likely that a 'killer application' of the technologies will lead to this change, and as yet that change might not be fully envisioned. Much like the smartphone changed the web, the use of AR and VR will move from being a niche, 'nice-to-play-with' novelty into something that will become indispensable in creating customer experiences. For marketers, that means being open about the use of such technologies. It means being willing to experiment and, where budgets allow, to accept that not everything in this regard will work. Even for smaller brands, the increasingly low cost of such technologies may make their adoption much easier and more common than people expect. Any use of VR or AR, however, needs to remain true to the brand and must be used after a genuine assessment of the benefits is made.

Business Experience

Our book has taken the reader on a journey through the theoretical background of experiential marketing as it has emerged from the Customer Experience (Cx) and various other business sub-disciplines. We have codified in previous chapters where that has taken us and we have, through our models, furthered the knowledge required to better understand and implement experiential marketing. However, an emerging trend that needs to be reflected in our thinking is the concept of Business Experience (Bx). An Accenture report from late 2020 heralds the concept of experience as being so essential to organisations that it now needs to occupy space in all aspects of business (Accenture, 2020). They say 'Today, experience is still paramount. Not in terms of creating a branded veneer to company-centric processes and systems, but as something much more expansive' (Accenture, 2020: 3). The emerging emphasis on Bx will see a move from 'optimising customer touchpoints' to a requirement to 'solve ... human needs around a purpose'. Its positioning as a holistic, rounded approach to growth has moved the concept of experience from being a marketing concern to one where it is now a board priority, as it becomes an overarching way of doing things. Furthermore, the evolution of customer demands is such that expectations of experience are not bounded by those offered in similar categories of product/service, but rather from a baseline of expectation that centres

on their best experiences, from wherever they have emerged. For example, consumers will expect high levels of experience in marketing because they have received high levels in other areas of business e.g. customer service. A final conclusion of the Accenture report is that the variety of exposure that typical customers have to digital services sets a new bar for what they expect from each brand they interact with.

The challenge for marketers as the Bx revolution takes hold is to ensure that they position their discipline as being able to inform the adoption of the Bx mindset, by virtue of their experience with Cx. It means recognising that the emphasis in Bx is entirely on the customer's wants, and building all types of experience to support and satisfy those wants. This moves Bx beyond the realm of an interaction with a product or service at some emotive level to 'prioritising purpose' as a driver of innovation and business success. Marketers, particularly senior marketers, are best placed to drive that change, particularly if they can engineer a shift of mindset in their own behaviours and attitudes.

ACADEMIC CONSIDERATIONS

As noted earlier in this book, there are some academic challenges around experiential marketing. A review of the major marketing journals shows little or no evidence of experiential marketing being given serious consideration with a view to establishing a solid theoretical base.

The experiential marketing concept has become bound in some ways by Customer Experience Management (CEM) research. A seminal piece by Lemon and Verhoef (2016) expounds in detail the current state of play in the CEM literature. As a result of CEM and Experiential Marketing having a similar theoretical ancestry, there can be a mistaken view that experiential marketing is shaped largely by the same literature. There is a correlation between CEM and experiential marketing (Lemon & Verhoef, 2016; Schmitt & Zarantonello, 2013). Evidence of the use of CEM is found in a range of practices, including improving and strengthening the quality and length of a consumer's lifetime value (Das & Hota, 2014) and in the creation of loyalty-driven programmes (Smilansky, 2009) where the primary differentiator is through immersive experiences at every consumer touchpoint.

However, it is also important to acknowledge the different factors between these two related practices. Yuan and Wu (2008) find that experiential marketing is a *tactic* employed by a brand to create a meaningful physical environment as fully as possible in order for its customers to have an immersive experience. When discussing the concept of CEM, Schmitt (2003) states that it represents the methodology that it utilised to manage a customer's cross-channel exposure, personal interaction and transaction with a brand, product, company or service. Cantone and Risitano (2011) share this sentiment, stating that CEM is not a tactic, but rather a programme or schedule.

In fact, research to date on CEM is fragmented across a multitude of contexts and is differentiated from other marketing management concepts. It does not integrate

the key components of CEM, elaborate on its underpinning in marketing management theory or evaluate the feasibility of its utilisation as a stand-alone concept (Homberg et al., 2017). Alternatively, the few studies available have a primary focus on the service context, in particular the creation of methods of service experience design from a service-dominant perspective. The essence of this composite overview of CEM is that there is a distinction between work on pure CEM on the one hand, and the customer experience itself on the other hand. These are overlapping but separate concepts.

There is a challenge for marketing academics to take the practice of experiential marketing as it currently exists and to build it into the extant theoretical landscape.

CONCLUSION AND SUMMARY

This book has presented an overview of the theory of experiential marketing with an interwoven emphasis on what is happening in practice. With an increased emphasis on planning an integrated strategy, the practice of experiential marketing can be directed to a more measurable, transparent methodology that will ultimately serve to further its potential. While much is likely to change as the world emerges from the Covid-19 pandemic, there is plenty to build on as experiential marketing (re)gains a place as a tried-and-tested aspect of marketing strategy.

MAIN TAKEAWAYS FROM CHAPTER 12

- When deciding on an experiential marketing campaign, marketing managers need to take stock and ask themselves a number of key questions to ensure the optimum success of the campaign.
- A team composition of innovative thinkers with complementary and varied skillsets is essential when activating an experiential campaign.
- Communicating with the executive board in a language that they understand is important in garnering support for experiential marketing.
- The global business landscape is altering at a fast pace, and experiential marketing is primed to take advantage of these changes and to do so very successfully.

CONCLUDING QUESTIONS

1. Discuss some of the key questions that a marketing manager should address before deciding on an experiential marketing campaign.
2. In your opinion, what are the critical components of a successful experiential activation?

3. Address some of the main factors that will have an impact on the development of experiential marketing over the next few years.
4. Develop a strategy for persuading the executive board of the merits of an experiential marketing campaign.

REFERENCES AND FURTHER READING

Accenture (2020). *Growth, It Comes Down to Experience*. [Online]. Available at: www.accenture.com/us-en/insights/interactive/business-of-experience [accessed 21 February 2021].

Cantone, L., & Risitano, M. (2011). Building Consumer Brand Relationships for the Customer Experience Management. *Proceedings of the 10th International Marketing Trend Conference*, Paris, 20–22 January.

Das, N., & Hota, K. (2014). A Conceptual Study on Customer Experience Management. *International Journal of Management and Business Studies*, 4(3), 30–33.

Homberg, C., Jozic, D., & Kuehni, C. (2017). Customer Experience Management: Toward Implementing and Evolving Marketing Concept. *Journal of the Academy of Marketing Science*, 45, 377–401.

Lemon, K.N., & Verhoef, P.C. (2016). Understanding Customer Experience throughout the Customer Journey. *Journal of Marketing*, 80(6), 69–96.

Schmitt, B.H. (2003). *Customer Experience Management: A Revolutionary Approach to Connecting with Your Customers*. New York: John Wiley & Sons.

Schmitt, B.H., & Zarantonello, L. (2013). Consumer Experience and Experiential Marketing: A Critical Review. In N.K. Malhotra (Ed.), *Review of Marketing Research* (pp. 25–61). Bingley, UK: Emerald.

Smilansky, S. (2009). *Experiential Marketing: A Practical Guide to Interactive Brand Experiences*. London: Kogan Page.

Yuan, Y.H., & Wu, C. (2008). Relationship among Experiential Marketing, Experiential Value and Customer Satisfaction. *Journal of Hospitality and Tourism Research*, 32(3), 387–410.

INDEX

Page numbers in *italic* indicate figures and in **bold** indicate tables.

Printed in the USA
CPSIA information can be obtained
at www.ICGtesting.com
JSHW050004170524
63287JS00004B/35

9 781837 530533